Honda
CR Motocross
Bikes
Owners
Workshop
Manual

by Alan Ahlstrand
and John H Haynes
Member of the Guild of Motoring Writers

Models covered:

CR80R, 1986 through 2002
CR80RB Expert, 1996 through 2002
CR85R, 2003 through 2007
CR85RB Expert, 2003 through 2007
CR125R, 1986 through 2007
CR250R, 1986 through 2007
CR500R, 1986 through 2001

 (2222 - 10N3) ABCDE FG

Haynes Publishing
Sparkford Nr Yeovil
Somerset BA22 7JJ England

Haynes North America, Inc
859 Lawrence Drive
Newbury Park
California 91320 USA
www.haynes.com

Acknowledgments

Our thanks to Honda of Milpitas, Milpitas, California, and Grand Prix Sports, Santa Clara, California, for providing the motorcycles used in these photographs. Special thanks to Nikki Frolich for lending us her CR125R and to Bill Hunt for lending us his CR250R. Thanks also to Pete Sirett, service manager at Honda of Milpitas, and Anthony Morter, service manager at Grand Prix Sports, for arranging the facilities and fitting the mechanical work into their shops' busy schedules.

Bruce Farley and Steve Van Horn at Honda of Milpitas and Craig Wardner at Grand Prix Sports, the technicians who did the mechanical work, deserve special mention both for their extensive knowledge and for their ability to explain things.

A book in the Haynes Owners Workshop Manual Series

Printed in Malaysia

ISBN-13: 978-1-56392-892-5
ISBN-10: 1-56392-892-2

Library of Congress Control Number: 2010939148

Contents

Honda CR500R

About this manual

Its purpose

The purpose of this manual is to help you get the best value from your motorcycle. It can do so in several ways. It can help you decide what work must be done, even if you choose to have it done by a dealer service department or a repair shop; it provides information and procedures for routine maintenance and servicing; and it offers diagnostic and repair procedures to follow when trouble occurs.

We hope you use the manual to tackle the work yourself. For many simpler jobs, doing it yourself may be quicker than arranging an appointment to get the vehicle into a shop and making the trips to leave it and pick it up. More importantly, a lot of money can be saved by avoiding the expense the shop must pass on to you to cover its labor and overhead costs. An added benefit is the sense of satisfaction and accomplishment that you feel after doing the job yourself.

Using the manual

The manual is divided into Chapters. Each Chapter is divided into numbered Sections, which are headed in bold type between horizontal lines. Each Section consists of consecutively numbered paragraphs or steps.

At the beginning of each numbered Section you will be referred to any illustrations which apply to the procedures in that Section. The reference numbers used in illustration captions pinpoint the pertinent Section and the Step within that Section. That is, illustration 3.2 means the illustration refers to Section 3 and Step (or paragraph) 2 within that Section.

Procedures, once described in the text, are not normally repeated. When it's necessary to refer to another Chapter, the reference will be given as Chapter and Section number. Cross references given without use of the word 'Chapter' apply to Sections and/or paragraphs in the same Chapter. For example, 'see Section 8' means in the same Chapter.

References to the left or right side of the vehicle assume you are sitting on the seat, facing forward.

Motorcycle manufacturers continually make changes to specifications and recommendations, and these, when notified, are incorporated into our manuals at the earliest opportunity.

Even though we have prepared this manual with extreme care, neither the publisher nor the authors can accept responsibility for any errors in, or omissions from, the information given.

NOTE

A **Note** provides information necessary to properly complete a procedure or information which will make the procedure easier to understand.

CAUTION

A **Caution** provides a special procedure or special steps which must be taken while completing the procedure where the Caution is found. Not heeding a Caution can result in damage to the assembly being worked on.

WARNING

A **Warning** provides a special procedure or special steps which must be taken while completing the procedure where the Warning is found. Not heeding a Warning can result in personal injury.

Introduction to the Honda CR Motocross bikes

The Honda CR series are highly popular and successful motocross bikes. The CR80R/85R and its taller-wheeled version, the CR80RB/85RB Expert, are well suited to beginning motocross riders. The CR125R and CR250R, with their technically advanced suspensions and engine power valve systems, have been consistently successful in the two most competitive motocross classes. The CR500R, with its light weight and powerful engine, offers high performance to skilled riders.

The engine on all models is a liquid-cooled two-stroke single. CR125R and CR250R models are equipped with the Honda Power Port (HPP), Radical Combustion (RC) system or Composite Racing Valve (CRV), which regulate exhaust gas flow for efficient performance throughout the engine's rpm range. Power is transmitted through a five-speed or six-speed transmission, depending on model. All models use a wet multi-plate clutch and chain final drive.

Fuel is delivered to the cylinder by a slide-type carburetor.

The front suspension consists of telescopic forks mounted in upper and lower triple clamps. The rear suspension uses a single shock absorber/ coil spring unit and Honda's Pro-Link progressive rising rate suspension linkage. A disc brake is used at the front on all models. Early models used a drum brake at the rear; later models use a disc brake.

Identification numbers

The frame serial number is stamped into the front of the frame and printed on a label affixed to the frame. The engine number is stamped into the right side of the crankcase. Both of these numbers should be recorded and kept in a safe place so they can be furnished to law enforcement officials in the event of a theft.

The frame serial number, engine serial number and carburetor identification number should also be kept in a handy place (such as with your driver's license) so they are always available when purchasing or ordering parts for your machine.

The models covered by this manual are as follows:
CR80R, 1986 through 2002
CR80RB Expert, 1996 through 2002
CR85R, 2003 through 2007
CR85RB Expert, 2003 through 2007
CR125R, 1986 through 2007
CR250R, 1986 through 2007
CR500R, 1986 through 2001

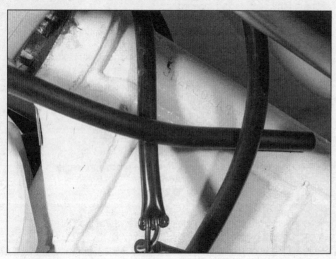

The frame serial number is located at the front of the frame

The engine serial number is located on the left side of the crankcase

Identifying models and years

CR80R

Engine code	HE04E

Engine number range

1986	5300051-5306864
1987	5400011-5404982
1988	5500005-5502709
1989	5600001 on
1990	5700001-5701602
1991	5800001-5801465
1992	5900001-5900947
1993	6000001-6002776
1994	6100001 on
1995	6004943 on
1996	6100001-6104186
1997	6105077 on
1998	6109918 on
1999	6200001 on
2000 through 2002	6200001 on

Frame code

1999 and earlier	HE040
2000 and later	HE04C

Frame number range

1986	GK300048-306849
1987	HK400008-404964
1988	JK500005-502703
1989	KK600001 on
1990	LK700001-701582
1991	MK800001-801513
1992	NK900001-900719
1993	PK000001-002411
1994	RK100001 on
1995	SK200001 on
1996	TK300001-302613
1997	VK400004 on
1998	WK500001 on
1999	XK600001 on
2000	YK700001 on
2001	1K800001 on
2002	2K900001 on

CR80RB Expert

Engine code HE04E
Engine number range
  1996 6100001-6104186
  1997 .... 6105078 on
  1998 .... 6109915 on
  1999 .... 6200001 on
  2000 .... 6200001 on
  2001 .... Not available
Frame code
  1999 and earlier HE040
  2000 and later HE04C
Frame number range
  1996 .... TK300001-302613
  1997 .... VK100003 on
  1998 .... WK200001 on
  1999 .... XK300001 on
  2000 .... YK700001 on
  2001 .... 1K500001 on
  2002 .... Not available

CR85R

Engine code HE07E
Engine number range
  2003, 2004 .... 500001 to 599999
  2005 ....510001 to 519999
  2006 .... 510001-on
  2007 .... Not available
Frame code JH2HE07C
Frame number range
  2003 .... 3K000001 to 3K099999
  2004 .... 4K100001 to 4K199999
  2005 .... 5K200001 to 5K299999
  2006 .... 6K300001-on
  2007 .... 7K400001 to 7K499999

CR85RB Expert

Engine code HE07E
Engine number range
  2003, 2004 .... 500001 to 599999
  2005 .... 510001 to 519999
  2006 .... 510001-on
  2007 .... Not available
Frame code JH2HE073
Frame number range
  2003 .... 3K000001 to 3K099999
  2004 .... 4K100001 to 4K199999
  2005 .... 5K200001 to 5K299999
  2006 .... 6K300001-on
  2007 .... 7K400001 to 7K499999

CR125R

Engine code JE01E
Engine number range
  1986 2700032-2711245
  1987 5800025-5807715
  1988 5900000-5008885
  1989 .... 5000015 on
  1990 5100025-5107602
  1991 5200012-5207714
  1992 5300009-5305629
  1993 5400015-5406462
  1994 5500012-5507316
  1995 .... 5600001 on
  1996 .... 5700001 on

  1997 .... 5800001 on
  1998 .... 5900001 on
  1999 .... 6000001 on
  2000 .... 6100001 on
  2001 .... 6200001 on
  2002 .... 6300001 to 6399999
  2003 .... 6400001 to 6499999
  2004 .... 6500001 to 6599999
  2005 .... 6600001 to 6659999
  2006 .... 6700001 to 6859999
  2007 .... Not available
Frame code
  1999 and earlier JE010
  2000 and later (and 1998 California and all 1999 models)...... JE013
Frame number range
  1986 .... GC700018-708180
  1987 .... HC800020-806942
  1988 .... JM900005-904170
  1989 .... KM00006 on
  1990 .... LM100013-103521
  1991 .... MM200008-202551
  1992 .... NM300006-302172
  1993 .... PM400010-403033
  1994 .... RM500008-503009
  1995 .... SM600001 on
  1996 .... TM700001 on
  1997 .... VM800001 on
  1998 except California .... WM900001 on
  1998 California .... WM000001 on
  1999 .... XM1000001 on
  2000 .... YM100001 on
  2001 .... 1M300001 on
  2002 .... 2M400001 on
  2003 .... 3M400001 on
  2004 .... 4M600001 on
  2005 .... 5M700001 on
  2006 .... 6M800001 on
  2007 .... 7M900001 on

CR250R

Engine code ME03E
Engine number range
  1986 2800040-2809499
  1987 5900101-5906845
  1988 5000001-5009970
  1989 .... 5100001-on
  1990 5200023-5208362
  1991 5300007-5308483
  1992 5400013-5408442
  1993 5500021-5507773
  1994 5600013-5608582
  1995 .... 5700009-on
  1996 .... 5800009-on
  1997 .... 5900001-on
  1998 .... 6000001 on
  1999 .... 6100001 on
  2000 .... 6200001 on
  2001 .... 6300001 on
  2002 .... 6400001 to 6499999
  2003 .... 6500001 to 6599999
  2004 .... 6600001 to 6699999
  2005 .... 6700001 to 6899999
  2006 .... 6800001 to 6899999
  2007 .... Not available
Frame code ME030

CR250R (continued)

Frame number range

1986	GC800021-808068
1987	HC900016-905384
1988	JM000001-004826
1989	KM100001 on
1990	LM200013-203598
1991	MM300005-302994
1992	NM400009-403206
1993	PM500015-504128
1994	RM600010-604081
1995	SM700007 on
1996	TM800001 on
1997	VM900001 on
1998	WM000001 on
1999	XM100001 on
2000	YM200001 on
2001	1M300001 on
2002	2M400001 to 2M499999
2003	3M500001 to 3M599999
2004	4M600001 to 4M699999
2005	5M700001 to 5M799999
2006	6M800001 to 6M899999
2007	Not available

CR500R

Engine code PE02E
Engine number range

1986	5500036-5505153
1987	5600101-5604112
1988	5700008 on
1989	5800001 on

1990	5900001-5904044
1991	5000010-5003006
1992	5100009-5102184
1993	5200006-5201031
1994	5300005-5301886
1995	5400008 on
1996	5500001 on
1997	5600001 on
1998	5700001 on
1999	6000001 on
2000	6100001 on
2001	Not available

Frame code PE020*
Frame number range

1986	GC500018-505028
1987	HC60014-604005
1988	JM700005 on
1989	KM800001 on
1990	LM900001 on
1991	MM000006-001974
1992	NM100006-101487
1993	PM20005-201026
1994	RM300005-301029
1995	SM400001 on
1996	TM500001 on
1997	VM600001 on
1998	WM700001 on
1999	XM800001 on
2000	YM900001 on
2001	Not available

PE023 for 1998 California models.

Buying parts

Once you have found all the identification numbers, record them for reference when buying parts. Since the manufacturers change specifications, parts and vendors (companies that manufacture various components on the machine), providing the ID numbers is the only way to be reasonably sure that you are buying the correct parts.

Whenever possible, take the worn part to the dealer so direct comparison with the new component can be made. Along the trail from the manufacturer to the parts shelf, there are numerous places that the part can end up with the wrong number or be listed incorrectly.

New motorcycle parts - original equipment or aftermarket - are available from franchised dealers and phone or mail order outlets that advertise in motorcycle magazines. Original equipment parts (also called genuine parts) are sold by the same company that built the motorcycle. Aftermarket parts are produced by independent manufac-

turers. All franchised dealers, and some phone or mail order outlets, offer a complete range of original equipment parts. Franchised dealers usually also carry aftermarket high wear items such as chains, cables and brake pads, as well as accessories such as helmets and leathers. Dealers offer the advantage of face-to-face contact, so you can bring the used part in for comparison. Phone and mail order outlets may provide substantial discounts from original equipment prices, but it's a good idea to shop around before you order.

Used parts can be obtained for roughly half the price of new ones, but you can't always be sure of what you're getting. Once again, take your worn part to the salvage yard for direct comparison.

Whether buying new, used or rebuilt parts, the best course is to deal directly with someone who specializes in parts for your particular make.

General specifications

CR80R and CR80RB

Bore	47.0 mm (1.85 inch)
Stroke...	47.8 mm (1.88 inch)
Compression ratio	
1986..	8.7 to 1
1987 on...	8.4 to 1
Wheelbase	
CR80R	
1986	1250 mm (49.2 inches)
1987 through 1995..	1255 mm (49.4 inches)
1997 and 1998	1266 mm (49.8 inches)
1999 on	1246 mm (49.1 inches)
CR80RB Expert	1311 mm (51.6 inches)
Overall length	
CR80R	
1986	1810 mm (71.3 inches)
1987 through 1995..	1815 mm (71.5 inches)
1996 on	1831 mm (72.1 inches)
CR80RB Expert	1926 mm (75.8 inches)
Overall width	
CR80R	
1986 through 1995..	745 mm (29.3 inches)
1996 on	743 mm (29.25 inches)
CR80RB Expert	743 mm (29.25 inches)
Overall height	
CR80R	
1986	1070 mm (42.1 inches)
1987 through 1995..	1080 mm (42.5 inches)
1996 on	1132 mm (44.6 inches)
CR80RB Expert	1166 mm (45.9 inches)

CR80R and CR80RB (continued)

Seat height
CR80R
  1986 .... 800 mm (31.5 inches)
  1987 through 1995 .... 810 mm (31.9 inches)
  1996 on .... 842 mm (33.1 inches)
CR80RB Expert .... 869 mm (34.2 inches)
Ground clearance
CR80R
  1986 .... 305 mm (12.0 inches)
  1987 through 1995 .... 310 mm (12.2 inches)
  1996 on .... 3340 mm (13.0 inches)
CR80RB Expert .... 358 mm (14.1 inches)
Dry weight
CR80R
  1986 .... 62.5 kg (137.8 lbs)
  1987 through 1991 .... 62.7 kg (138.2 lbs)
  1992 through 1995 .... 63.0 kg (138.9 lbs)
  1996 on .... 65.0 kg (143.3 lbs)
CR80RB Expert .... 67.0 kg (147.7 lbs)

CR85R

Bore .... 47.5 mm (1.87 inches)
Stroke .... 47.8 mm (1.88 inches)
Compression ratio
  2003 and 2004 .... 8.4 to 1
  2005 and later .... 8.45 to 1
Wheelbase
  2003 and 2004 .... 1249 mm (49.2 inches)
  2005 and later .... 1248 mm (49.1 inches)
Overall length
  2003 and 2004 .... 1812 mm (71.3 inches)
  2005 and later .... 1803 mm (71.0 inches)
Overall width
  2003 and 2004 .... 772 mm (30.4 inches)
  2005 and later .... 769 mm (30.3 inches)
Overall height
  2003 and 2004 .... 1125 mm (44.3 inches)
  2005 and later .... 1126 mm (44.3 inches)
Seat height
  2003 and 2004 .... 827 mm (32.6 inches)
  2005 and later .... 824 mm (32.4 inches)
Ground clearance
  2003 and 2004 .... 315 mm (12.4 inches)
  2005 and later .... 311 mm (12.2 inches)
Dry weight
  2003 and 2004 .... 68.8 kg (151.7 lbs)
  2005 and later .... 69.9 kg (154.1 lbs)

CR85RB

Bore .... 47.5 mm (1.87 inches)
Stroke .... 47.8 mm (1.88 inches)
Compression ratio
  2003 and 2004 .... 8.4 to 1
  2005 and later .... 8.45 to 1
Wheelbase
  2003 and 2004 .... 1285 mm (50.6 inches)
  2005 and later .... 1289 mm (50.7 inches)
Overall length
  2003 and 2004 .... 1899 mm (74.8 inches)
  2005 and later .... 1881 mm (74.1 inches)
Overall width
  2003 and 2004 .... 772 mm (30.4 inches)
  2005 and later .... 769 mm (30.3 inches)
Overall height
  2003 and 2004 .... 1167 mm (45.9 inches)
  2005 and later .... 1170 mm (46.1 inches)
Seat height
  2003 and 2004 .... 868 mm (34.2 inches)
  2005 and later .... 864 mm (34.0 inches)

Ground clearance
  2003 and 2004 .... 356 mm (14.0 inches)
  2005 and later .... 353 mm (13.9 inches)
Dry weight
  2003 and 2004 .... 70.2 kg (154.8 lbs)
  2005 and later .... 71.5 kg (157.6 lbs)

CR125R

Bore .... 54.0 mm (2.1 inches)
Stroke
  1986 .... 54.0 mm (2.1 inches)
  1987 on .... 54.5 mm (2.15 inches)
Compression ratio
  1986 .... 8.4 to 1
  1987 and 1988 .... 8.8 to 1
  1989 though 1991 .... 8.9 to 1
  1992 .... 9.1 to 1
  1993 through 1999 .... 8.8 to 1
  2000 and 2001 .... 8.75 to 1
  2002 .... 8.7 to 1
  2003 .... 7.1 to 1
  2004 .... 9.1 to 1
  2005 and later .... 8.6 to 1
Wheelbase
  1986 .... 1460 mm (57.5 inches)
  1987 and 1988 .... 1450 mm (57.1 inches)
  1989 and 1990 .... 1455 mm (57.3 inches)
  1991 .... 1445 mm (56.9 inches)
  1992 .... 1442 mm (56.8 inches)
  1993 .... 1448 mm (57.0 inches)
  1994 .... 1444 mm (56.9 inches)
  1995 and 1996 .... 1450 mm (57.1 inches)
  1997 .... 1442 mm (56.8 inches)
  1998 .... 1460 mm (57.5 inches)
  1999 .... 1465 mm (57.7 inches)
  2000 .... 1467 mm (57.8 inches)
  2001 .... 1471 mm (57.9 inches)
  2002 .... 1458 mm (57.4 inches)
  2003 .... 1470 mm (57.9 inches)
  2004 .... 1466 mm (57.7 inches)
  2005 and later .... 1470 mm (57.9 inches)
Overall length
  1986 .... 2140 mm (84.3 inches)
  1987 and 1988 .... 2135 mm (84.1 inches)
  1989 and 1990 .... 2140 mm (84.3 inches)
  1991 and 1992 .... 2130 mm (83.9 inches)
  1993 .... 2134 mm (84.0 inches)
  1994 .... 2130 mm (83.9 inches)
  1995 .... 2139 mm (84.2 inches)
  1996 .... 2138 mm (84.2 inches)
  1997 .... 2131 mm (83.9 inches)
  1998 .... 2154 mm (84.8 inches)
  1999 .... 2157 mm (84.9 inches)
  2000 .... 2169 mm (85.3 inches)
  2001 .... 2173 mm (85.6 inches)
  2002 .... 2173 mm (85.6 inches)
  2003 .... 2162 mm (85.1 inches)
  2004 .... 2157 mm (84.9 inches)
  2005 and later .... 2163 mm (85.2 inches)
Overall width
  1986 through 1988 .... 825 mm (32.5 inches)
  1989 through 1991 .... 835 mm (32.9 inches)
  1992 and 1993 .... 825 mm (32.5 inches)
  1994 and 1995 .... 835 mm (32.9 inches)
  1996 .... 830 mm (32.7 inches)
  1997 and 1998 .... 827 mm (32.6 inches)
  1999 .... 828 mm (32.6 inches)
  2000 on .... 823 mm (32.4 inches)

CR125R (continued)
Overall height
1986 through 1988	1230 mm (48.4 inches)
1989 and 1990	1250 mm (49.2 inches)
1991	1255 mm (49.4 inches)
1992	1257 mm (49.5 inches)
1993	1261 mm (49.6 inches)
1994	1275 mm (50.2 inches)
1995 and 1996	1265 mm (49.8 inches)
1997	1267 mm (49.9 inches)
1998	1264 mm (49.8 inches)
1999	1269 mm (50.0 inches)
2000	1283 mm (50.5 inches)
2001	1271 mm (50.03 inches)
2002	1278 mm (50.3 inches)
2003	1279 mm (50.4 inches)
2004	1280 mm (50.4 inches)
2005 and later	1282 mm (50.5 inches)

Seat height
1986 and 1987	930 mm (86.6 inches)
1988	925 mm (36.4 inches)
1989	945 mm (37.2 inches)
1990	970 mm (38.2 inches)
1991	975 mm (38.4 inches)
1992	980 mm (38.6 inches)
1993 and 1994	978 mm (38.5 inches)
1995	950 mm (37.4 inches)
1996 and 1997	949 mm (37.36 inches)
1998	932 mm (36.7 inches)
1999	943 mm (37.1 inches)
2000	942 mm (37.08 inches)
2001	936 mm (36.9 inches)
2002	947 mm (37.3 inches)
2003	949 mm (37.4 inches)
2004	952 mm (37.5 inches)
2005 and later	954 mm (37.6 inches)

Ground clearance
1986 through 1990	355 mm (14.0 inches)
1991	360 mm (14.2 inches)
1992	368 mm (14.5 inches)
1993	365 mm (14.4 inches)
1994	362 mm (14.3 inches)
1995	354 mm (13.94 inches)
1996 and 1997	353 mm (13.89 inches)
1998	331 mm (113.0 inches)
1999	338 mm (13.3 inches)
2000	340 mm (13.4 inches)
2001	332 mm (13.1 inches)
2002	345 mm (13.6 inches)
2003	347 mm (13.7 inches)
2004	349 mm (13.74 inches)
2005 and later	352 mm (13.8 inches)

Dry weight
1986 through 1991	87.5 kg (192.9 lbs)
1992 and 1993	87.0 kg (191.8 lbs)
1994 on	87.5 kg (192.9 lbs)

CR250R
Bore	66.4 mm (2.61 inches)
Stroke	72.0 mm (2.83 inches)
Displacement	249.3 cc (15.2 cubic inches)

Compression ratio
1986	9.0 to 1
1987	9.1 to 1
1988	9.0 to 1
1989	8.8 to 1
1990 and 1991	8.5 to 1
1992 through 2001	8.7 to 1
2002 and 2003	8.5 to 1

2004	8.6 to 1
2005 and later	9.0 to 1

Wheelbase

1986 through 1988	1480 mm (58.3 inches)
1989	1495 mm (58.9 inches)
1990 and 1991	1488 mm (58.6 inches)
1992	1467 mm (57.8 inches)
1993	1471 mm (57.9 inches)
1994 through 1996	1483 mm (58.4 inches)
1997	1483 mm (58.4 inches)
1998 and 1999	Not available
2000 and 2001	1487 mm (58.5 inches)
2002 and 2003	1491 mm (58.7 inches)
2004	1482 mm (58.3 inches)
2005 and later	1487 mm (58.5 inches)

Overall length

1986 through 1988	2180 mm (85.8 inches)
1989	2195 mm (86.4 inches)
1990 and 1991	2188 mm (86.1 inches)
1992	2161 mm (85.1 inches)
1993	2165 mm (85.2 inches)
1994	2177 mm (85.7 inches)
1995 and 1996	2182 mm (85.9 inches)
1997	2185 mm (86.0 inches)
1998 and 1999	Not available
2000 and 2001	2189 mm (86.2 inches)
2002 and 2003	2190 mm (86.2 inches)
2004	2173 mm (85.5 inches)
2005 and later	2185 mm (86.0 inches)

Overall width

1986 through 1988	825 mm (32.5 inches)
1989 through 1991	835 mm (32.9 inches)
1992 and 1993	825 mm (32.5 inches)
1994 through 1996	835 mm (32.9 inches)
1997	827 mm (32.6 inches)
1998 and 1999	Not available
2000 through 2004	823 mm (32.4 inches)
2005 and later	821 mm (32.3 inches)

Overall height

1986 through 1988	1215 mm (47.8 inches)
1989	1253 mm (49.3 inches)
1990 and 1991	1255 mm (49.4 inches)
1992	1262 mm (49.7 inches)
1993	1243 mm (48.9 inches)
1994	1242 mm (48.9 inches)
1995 and 1996	1244 mm (40.0 inches)
1997	1249 mm (49.1 inches)
1998 and 1999	Not available
2000 and 2001	1263 m (49.7 inches)
2002 and 2003	1269 mm (50.0 inches)
2004	1263 mm (49.7 inches)
2005 and later	1275 mm (50.2 inches)

Seat height

1986	960 mm (37.8 inches)
1987 and 1988	950 mm (37.4 inches)
1989 through 1992	970 mm (38.2 inches)
1993 and 1994	958 mm (37.7 inches)
1995 and 1996	937 mm (36.9 inches)
1997	933 mm (36.1 inches)
1998 and 1999	Not available
2000 and 2001	933 mm (30.7 inches)
2002 and 2003	950 mm (37.4 inches)
2004	952 mm (37.5 inches)
2005 and later	950 mm (37.4 inches)

Ground clearance

1986 through 1988	340 mm (13.4 inches)
1989 through 1992	350 mm (13.8 inches)
1993	343 mm (13.5 inches)
1994	345 mm (13.6 inches)

CR250R (continued)

Ground clearance (continued)
1995 and 1996	333 mm (13.1 inches)
1997	326 mm (12.8 inches)
1998 and 1999	Not available
2000-on	331 mm (13.0 inches)
2002 and 2003	346 mm (13.6 inches)
2004	339 mm (13.3 inches)
2005 and later	347 mm (13.7 inches)

Dry weight
1986 and 1987	97.5 kg (214.9 lbs)
1988 through 1991	97.0 kg (213.8 lbs)
1992 and 1993	96.5 kg (212.7 lbs)
1994 through 2001	97.0 kg (213.8 lbs)
2002 and 2003	96.5 kg (212.3 lbs)
2004	96.6 kg (212.5 lbs)
2005 and later	96.4 kg (212 lbs)

CR500R

Bore	89.0 mm (3.5 inches)
Stroke	79.0 mm (3.1 inches)
Displacement	491.4 cc (29.9 cubic inches)

Compression ratio
1986	7.0 to 1
1987-on	6.8 to 1

Wheelbase
1986 through 1990	1500 mm (59.1 inches)
1991	1495 mm (58.9 inches)
1992 and 1993	1489 mm (58.6 inches)
1994	1491 mm (58.7 inches)
1995-on	1485 mm (58.5 inches)

Overall length
1986 through 1990	2200 mm (86.6 inches)
1991	2195 mm (86.4 inches)
1992 and 1993	2183 mm (85.9 inches)
1994	2185 mm (86.0 inches)
1995-on	2179 mm (85.8 inches)

Overall width
1986 through 1988	825 mm (32.5 inches)
1989 and 1991	835 mm (32.9 inches)
1992 through 1994	825 mm (32.5 inches)
1995-on	835 mm (32.9 inches)

Overall height
1986 through 1988	1200 mm (48.0 inches)
1989	1260 mm (49.6 inches)
1990 and 1991	1255 mm (49.4 inches)
1992 through 1994	1240 mm (48.8 inches)
1995-on	1237 mm (48.7 inches)

Seat height
1986 through 1988	950 mm (37.4 inches)
1989 and 1991	970 mm (38.2 inches)
1992 and 1993	964 mm (38.0 inches)
1994	961 mm (37.8 inches)
1995-on	937 mm (36.9 inches)

Ground clearance
1986 through 1988	330 mm (13.0 inches)
1989 through 1991	350 mm (13.8 inches)
1992 and 1993	343 mm (13.5 inches)
1994	341 mm (13.4 inches)
1995-on	328 mm (12.9 inches)

Dry weight
1986 through 1991 (without muffler)	101.5 kg (223.7 lbs)
1992-on	101.0 kg (222.7 lbs)

Maintenance techniques, tools and working facilities

Basic maintenance techniques

There are a number of techniques involved in maintenance and repair that will be referred to throughout this manual. Application of these techniques will enable the amateur mechanic to be more efficient, better organized and capable of performing the various tasks properly, which will ensure that the repair job is thorough and complete.

Fastening systems

Fasteners, basically, are nuts, bolts and screws used to hold two or more parts together. There are a few things to keep in mind when working with fasteners. Almost all of them use a locking device of some type (either a lock washer, locknut, locking tab or thread adhesive). All threaded fasteners should be clean, straight, have undamaged threads and undamaged corners on the hex head where the wrench fits. Develop the habit of replacing all damaged nuts and bolts with new ones.

Rusted nuts and bolts should be treated with a penetrating oil to ease removal and prevent breakage. Some mechanics use turpentine in a spout type oil can, which works quite well. After applying the rust penetrant, let it -work for a few minutes before trying to loosen the nut or bolt. Badly rusted fasteners may have to be chiseled off or removed with a special nut breaker, available at tool stores.

If a bolt or stud breaks off in an assembly, it can be drilled out and removed with a special tool called an E-Z out (or screw extractor). Most dealer service departments and motorcycle repair shops can perform this task, as well as others (such as the repair of threaded holes that have been stripped out).

Flat washers and lock washers, when removed from an assembly, should always be replaced exactly as removed. Replace any damaged washers with new ones. Always use a flat washer between a lock washer and any soft metal surface (such as aluminum), thin sheet metal or plastic. Special locknuts can only be used once or twice before they lose their locking ability and must be replaced.

Tightening sequences and procedures

When threaded fasteners are tightened, they are often tightened to a specific torque value (torque is basically a twisting force). Over-tightening the fastener can weaken it and cause it to break, while under-tightening can cause it to eventually come loose. Each bolt, depending on the material it's made of, the diameter of its shank and the material it is threaded into, has a specific torque value, which is noted in the Specifications. Be sure to follow the torque recommendations closely.

Spark plug gap adjusting tool

Feeler gauge set

Control cable pressure luber

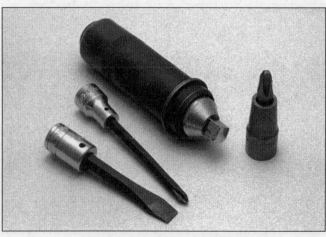

Hand impact screwdriver and bits

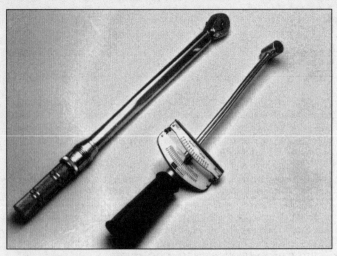

Torque wrenches (left - click; right - beam type)

Snap-ring pliers (top - external; bottom - internal)

Allen wrenches (left), and Allen head sockets (right)

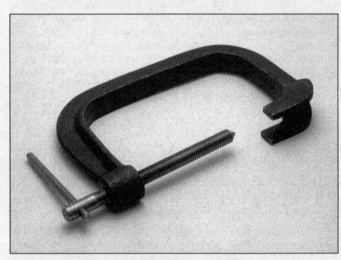

Valve spring compressor

Fasteners laid out in a pattern (i.e. cylinder head bolts, engine case bolts, etc.) must be loosened or tightened in a sequence to avoid warping the component. Initially, the bolts/nuts should go on finger tight only. Next, they should be tightened one full turn each, in a criss-cross or diagonal pattern. After each one has been tightened one full turn, return to the first one tightened and tighten them all one half turn, fol-

Piston ring removal/installation tool

lowing the same pattern. Finally, tighten each of them one quarter turn at a time until each fastener has been tightened to the proper torque. To loosen and remove the fasteners the procedure would be reversed.

Disassembly sequence

Component disassembly should be done with care and purpose to help ensure that the parts go back together properly during reassembly. Always keep track of the sequence in which parts are removed. Take note of special characteristics or marks on parts that can be installed more than one way (such as a grooved thrust washer on a shaft). It's a good idea to lay the disassembled parts out on a clean surface in the order that they were removed. It may also be helpful to make sketches or take instant photos of components before removal.

When removing fasteners from a component, keep track of their locations. Sometimes threading a bolt back in a part, or putting the washers and nut back on a stud, can prevent mix-ups later. If nuts and bolts can't be returned to their original locations, they should be kept in a compartmented box or a series of small boxes. A cupcake or muffin tin is ideal for this purpose, since each cavity can hold the bolts and nuts from a particular area (i.e. engine case bolts, valve cover bolts, engine mount bolts, etc.). A pan of this type is especially helpful when working on assemblies with very small parts (such as the carburetors and the valve train). The cavities can be marked with paint or tape to identify the contents.

Whenever wiring looms, harnesses or connectors are separated, it's a good idea to identify the two halves with numbered pieces of masking tape so they can be easily reconnected.

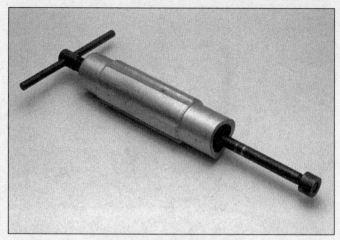

Piston pin puller

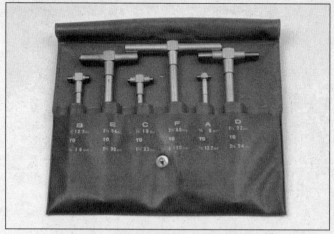

Telescoping gauges

0-to-1 inch micrometer

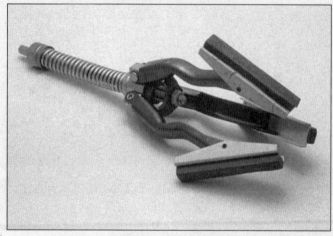

Cylinder surfacing hone

Gasket sealing surfaces

Throughout any motorcycle, gaskets are used to seal the mating surfaces between components and keep lubricants, fluids, vacuum or pressure contained in an assembly.

Many times these gaskets are coated with a liquid or paste type gasket sealing compound before assembly. Age, heat and pressure can sometimes cause the two parts to stick together so tightly that they are very difficult to separate. In most cases, the part can be loosened by striking it with a soft-faced hammer near the mating surfaces. A regular hammer can be used if a block of wood is placed between the hammer and the part. Do not hammer on cast parts or parts that could be easily damaged. With any particularly stubborn part, always recheck to make sure that every fastener has been removed.

Avoid using a screwdriver or bar to pry apart components, as they can easily mar the gasket sealing surfaces of the parts (which must remain smooth). If prying is absolutely necessary, use a piece of wood, but keep in mind that extra clean-up will be necessary if the wood splinters.

After the parts are separated, the old gasket must be carefully scraped off and the gasket surfaces cleaned. Stubborn gasket material can be soaked with a gasket remover (available in aerosol cans) to soften it so it can be easily scraped off. A scraper can be fashioned from a piece of copper tubing by flattening and sharpening one end. Copper is recommended because it is usually softer than the surfaces to be scraped, which reduces the chance of gouging the part. Some gaskets can be removed with a wire brush, but regardless of the method used, the mating surfaces must be left clean and smooth. If for some reason the gasket surface is gouged, then a gasket sealer thick enough to fill scratches will have to be used during reassembly of the components. For most applications, a non-drying (or semi-drying) gasket sealer is best.

Hose removal tips

Hose removal precautions closely parallel gasket removal precautions. Avoid scratching or gouging the surface that the hose mates against or the connection may leak. Because of various chemical reac-

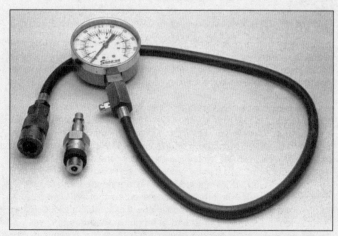

Cylinder compression gauge

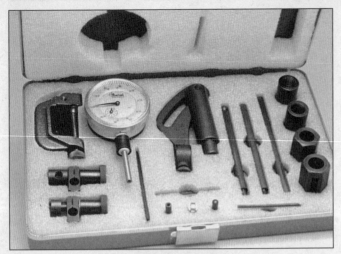

Dial indicator set

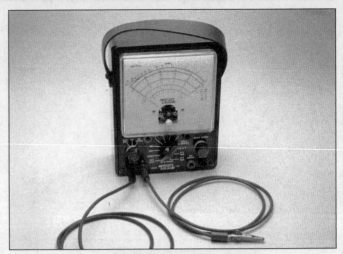

Multimeter (volt/ohm/ammeter)

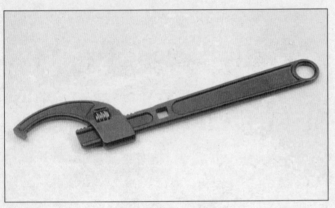

Adjustable spanner

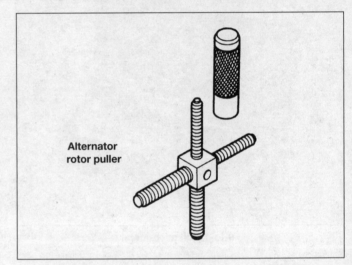

Alternator rotor puller

tions, the rubber in hoses can bond itself to the metal spigot that the hose fits over. To remove a hose, first loosen the hose clamps that secure it to the spigot. Then, with slip joint pliers, grab the hose at the clamp and rotate it around the spigot. Work it back and forth until it is completely free, then pull it off (silicone or other lubricants will ease removal if they can be applied between the hose and the outside of the spigot). Apply the same lubricant to the inside of the hose and the outside of the spigot to simplify installation.

If a hose clamp is broken or damaged, do not reuse it. Also, do not reuse hoses that are cracked, split or torn.

Tools

A selection of good tools is a basic requirement for anyone who plans to maintain and repair a motorcycle. For the owner who has few tools, if any, the initial investment might seem high, but when compared to the spiraling costs of routine maintenance and repair, it is a wise one.

To help the owner decide which tools are needed to perform the tasks detailed in this manual, the following tool lists are offered: *Maintenance and minor repair, Repair and overhaul* and *Special*. The newcomer to practical mechanics should start off with the *Maintenance and minor repair* tool kit, which is adequate for the simpler jobs. Then, as confidence and experience grow, the owner can tackle more difficult tasks, buying additional tools as they are needed. Eventually the basic kit will be built into the *Repair and overhaul* tool set. Over a period of time, the experienced do-it-yourselfer will assemble a tool set complete enough for most repair and overhaul procedures and will add tools from the *Special* category when it is felt that the expense is justified by the frequency of use.

Maintenance and minor repair tool kit

The tools in this list should be considered the minimum required for performance of routine maintenance, servicing and minor repair work. We recommend the purchase of combination wrenches (box end and open end combined in one wrench); while more expensive than open-ended ones, they offer the advantages of both types of wrench.

Combination wrench set (6 mm to 22 mm)
Adjustable wrench - 8 in
Spark plug socket (with rubber insert)
Spark plug gap adjusting tool
Feeler gauge set
Standard screwdriver (5/16 in x 6 in)
Phillips screwdriver (No. 2 x 6 in)
Allen (hex) wrench set (4 mm to 12 mm)
Combination (slip-joint) pliers - 6 in
Hacksaw and assortment of blades
Tire pressure gauge
Control cable pressure luber
Grease gun
Oil can
Fine emery cloth
Wire brush
Hand impact screwdriver and bits
Funnel (medium size)
Safety goggles
Drain pan
Work light with extension cord

Repair and overhaul tool set

These tools are essential for anyone who plans to perform major repairs and are intended to supplement those in the Maintenance and minor repair tool kit. Included is a comprehensive set of sockets which, though expensive, are invaluable because of their versatility (especially when various extensions and drives are available). We recommend the 3/8 inch drive over the 1/2 inch drive for general motorcycle maintenance and repair (ideally, the mechanic would have a 3/8 inch drive set and a 1/2 inch drive set).

Alternator rotor removal tool
Socket set(s)
Reversible ratchet
Extension - 6 in
Universal joint
Torque wrench (same size drive as sockets)
Ball pein hammer - 8 oz
Soft-faced hammer (plastic/rubber)
Standard screwdriver (1/4 in x 6 in)
Standard screwdriver (stubby - 5/16 in)
Phillips screwdriver (No. 3 x 8 in)
Phillips screwdriver (stubby - No. 2)
Pliers - locking
Pliers - lineman's
Pliers - needle nose
Pliers - snap-ring (internal and external)
Cold chisel - 1/2 in
Scriber
Scraper (made from flattened copper tubing)
Center punch
Pin punches (1/16, 1/8, 3/16 in)
Steel rule/straightedge - 12 in
Pin-type spanner wrench
A selection of files
Wire brush (large)

Note: *Another tool which is often useful is an electric drill with a chuck capacity of 3/8 inch (and a set of good quality drill bits).*

Special tools

The tools in this list include those which are not used regularly, are expensive to buy, or which need to be used in accordance with their manufacturer's instructions. Unless these tools will be used frequently, it is not very economical to purchase many of them. A consideration would be to split the cost and use between yourself and a friend or friends (i.e. members of a motorcycle club).

This list primarily contains tools and instruments widely available to the public, as well as some special tools produced by the vehicle manufacturer for distribution to dealer service departments. As a result, references to the manufacturer's special tools are occasionally included in the text of this manual. Generally, an alternative method of doing the job without the special tool is offered. However, sometimes there is no alternative to their use. Where this is the case, and the tool can't be purchased or borrowed, the work should be turned over to the dealer service department or a motorcycle repair shop.

Paddock stand (for models not fitted with a centerstand)
Valve spring compressor
Piston ring removal and installation tool
Piston pin puller
Telescoping gauges
Micrometer(s) and/or dial/Vernier calipers
Cylinder surfacing hone
Cylinder compression gauge
Dial indicator set
Multimeter
Adjustable spanner
Manometer or vacuum gauge set
Small air compressor with blow gun and tire chuck

Buying tools

For the do-it-yourselfer who is just starting to get involved in motorcycle maintenance and repair, there are a number of options available when purchasing tools. If maintenance and minor repair is the extent of the work to be done, the purchase of individual tools is satisfactory. If, on the other hand, extensive work is planned, it would be a good idea to purchase a modest tool set from one of the large retail chain stores. A set can usually be bought at a substantial savings over the individual tool prices (and they often come with a tool box). As additional tools are needed, add-on sets, individual tools and a larger tool box can be purchased to expand the tool selection. Building a tool set gradually allows the cost of the tools to be spread over a longer period of time and gives the mechanic the freedom to choose only those tools that will actually be used.

Tool stores and motorcycle dealers will often be the only source of some of the special tools that are needed, but regardless of where tools are bought, try to avoid cheap ones (especially when buying screwdrivers and sockets) because they won't last very long. There are plenty of tools around at reasonable prices, but always aim to purchase items which meet the relevant national safety standards. The expense involved in replacing cheap tools will eventually be greater than the initial cost of quality tools.

It is obviously not possible to cover the subject of tools fully here. For those who wish to learn more about tools and their use, there is a book entitled *Motorcycle Workshop Practice Manual* (Book no. 1454) available from the publishers of this manual. It also provides an introduction to basic workshop practice which will be of interest to a home mechanic working on any type of motorcycle.

Care and maintenance of tools

Good tools are expensive, so it makes sense to treat them with respect. Keep them clean and in usable condition and store them properly when not in use. Always wipe off any dirt, grease or metal chips before putting them away. Never leave tools lying around in the work area.

Some tools, such as screwdrivers, pliers, wrenches and sockets, can be hung on a panel mounted on the garage or workshop wall, while others should be kept in a tool box or tray. Measuring instruments, gauges, meters, etc. must be carefully stored where they can't be damaged by weather or impact from other tools.

When tools are used with care and stored properly, they will last a very long time. Even with the best of care, tools will wear out if used frequently. When a tool is damaged or worn out, replace it; subsequent jobs will be safer and more enjoyable if you do.

Working facilities

Not to be overlooked when discussing tools is the workshop. If anything more than routine maintenance is to be carried out, some sort of suitable work area is essential.

It is understood, and appreciated, that many home mechanics do not have a good workshop or garage available and end up removing an engine or doing major repairs outside (it is recommended, however, that the overhaul or repair be completed under the cover of a roof).

A clean, flat workbench or table of comfortable working height is an absolute necessity. The workbench should be equipped with a vise that has a jaw opening of at least four inches.

As mentioned previously, some clean, dry storage space is also required for tools, as well as the lubricants, fluids, cleaning solvents, etc. which soon become necessary.

Sometimes waste oil and fluids, drained from the engine or cooling system during normal maintenance or repairs, present a disposal problem. To avoid pouring them on the ground or into a sewage system, simply pour the used fluids into large containers, seal them with caps and take them to an authorized disposal site or service station. Plastic jugs (such as old antifreeze containers) are ideal for this purpose.

Always keep a supply of old newspapers and clean rags available. Old towels are excellent for mopping up spills. Many mechanics use rolls of paper towels for most work because they are readily available and disposable. To help keep the area under the motorcycle clean, a large cardboard box can be cut open and flattened to protect the garage or shop floor.

Whenever working over a painted surface (such as the fuel tank) cover it with an old blanket or bedspread to protect the finish.

Safety first!

Regardless of how enthusiastic you may be about getting on with the job at hand, take the time to ensure that your safety is not jeopardized. A moment's lack of attention can result in an accident, as can failure to observe certain simple safety precautions. The possibility of an accident will always exist, and the following points should not be considered a comprehensive list of all dangers. Rather, they are intended to make you aware of the risks and to encourage a safety conscious approach to all work you carry out on your vehicle.

Essential DOs and DON'Ts

DON'T rely on a jack when working under the motorcycle. Always use a workstand to support the weight of the motorcycle and place it under the recommended lift or support points.

DON'T attempt to loosen extremely tight fasteners while the motorcycle is on a jack or stand - it may fall.

DON'T start the engine without first making sure that the transmission is in Neutral.

DON'T remove the radiator cap from a hot cooling system - let it cool or cover it with a cloth and release the pressure gradually.

DON'T attempt to drain the engine oil until you are sure it has cooled to the point that it will not burn you.

DON'T touch any part of the engine or exhaust system until it has cooled sufficiently to avoid burns.

DON'T siphon toxic liquids such as gasoline, antifreeze and brake fluid by mouth, or allow them to remain on your skin.

DON'T inhale brake lining dust - it is potentially hazardous (see *Asbestos* below).

DON'T allow spilled oil or grease to remain on the floor - wipe it up before someone slips on it.

DON'T use loose fitting wrenches or other tools which may slip and cause injury.

DON'T push on wrenches when loosening or tightening nuts or bolts. Always try to pull the wrench toward you. If the situation calls for pushing the wrench away, push with an open hand to avoid scraped knuckles if the wrench should slip.

DON'T attempt to lift a heavy component alone - get someone to help you.

DON'T rush or take unsafe shortcuts to finish a job.

DON'T allow children or animals in the work area while you are working on the motorcycle.

DO wear eye protection when using power tools such as a drill, sander, bench grinder, etc.

DO keep loose clothing and long hair well out of the way of moving parts.

DO make sure that any jack, lift or stand used has a safe working load rating adequate for the job.

DO get someone to check on you periodically when working alone on a vehicle.

DO carry out work in a logical sequence and make sure that everything is correctly assembled and tightened.

DO keep chemicals and fluids tightly capped and out of the reach of children and pets.

DO remember that your vehicle's safety affects that of yourself and others. If in doubt on any point, get professional advice.

Asbestos

Certain friction, insulating, sealing, and other products - such as brake linings, brake bands, clutch linings, torque converters, gaskets, etc. - may contain asbestos or other hazardous friction material. Extreme care must be taken to avoid inhalation of dust from such products, since it is hazardous to health. If in doubt, assume that they do contain asbestos.

Fire

Remember at all times that gasoline is highly flammable. Never smoke or have any kind of open flame around when working on a vehi-cle. But the risk does not end there. A spark caused by an electrical short circuit, by two metal surfaces contacting each other, or even by static electricity built up in your body under certain conditions, can ignite gasoline vapors, which in a confined space are highly explosive. Do not, under any circumstances, use gasoline for cleaning parts. Use an approved safety solvent.

On models so equipped, always disconnect the battery ground (-) cable at the battery before working on any part of the fuel system or electrical system. Never risk spilling fuel on a hot engine or exhaust component. It is strongly recommended that a fire extinguisher suitable for use on fuel and electrical fires be kept handy in the garage or work-shop at all times. Never try to extinguish a fuel or electrical fire with water.

Fumes

Certain fumes are highly toxic and can quickly cause unconsciousness and even death if inhaled to any extent. Gasoline vapor falls into this category, as do the vapors from some cleaning solvents. Any draining or pouring of such volatile fluids should be done in a well ventilated area.

When using cleaning fluids and solvents, read the instructions on the container carefully. Never use materials from unmarked containers.

Never run the engine in an enclosed space, such as a garage. Exhaust fumes contain carbon monoxide, which is extremely poisonous. If you need to run the engine, always do so in the open air, or at least have the rear of the vehicle outside the work area.

The battery

Never create a spark or allow a bare light bulb near a battery. They normally give off a certain amount of hydrogen gas, which is highly explosive.

Always disconnect the battery ground (-) cable at the battery before working on the fuel or electrical systems.

If possible, loosen the filler caps or cover when charging the battery from an external source (this does not apply to sealed or maintenance-free batteries). Do not charge at an excessive rate or the battery may burst.

Take care when adding water to a non maintenance-free battery and when carrying a battery. The electrolyte, even when diluted, is very corrosive and should not be allowed to contact clothing or skin.

Always wear eye protection when cleaning the battery to prevent the caustic deposits from entering your eyes.

Household current

When using an electric power tool, inspection light, etc., which operates on household current, always make sure that the tool is correctly connected to its plug and that, where necessary, it is properly grounded. Do not use such items in damp conditions and, again, do not create a spark or apply excessive heat in the vicinity of fuel or fuel vapor.

Secondary ignition system voltage

A severe electric shock can result from touching certain parts of the ignition system (such as the spark plug wires) when the engine is running or being cranked, particularly if components are damp or the insulation is defective. In the case of an electronic ignition system, the secondary system voltage is much higher and could prove fatal.

Hydrofluoric acid

This extremely corrosive acid is formed when certain types of synthetic rubber, found in some O-rings, oil seals, fuel hoses, etc. are exposed to temperatures above 750-degrees F (400-degrees C). The rubber changes into a charred or sticky substance containing the acid. Once formed, the acid remains dangerous for years. If it gets onto the skin, it may be necessary to amputate the limb concerned.

When dealing with a vehicle which has suffered a fire, or with components salvaged from such a vehicle, wear protective gloves and discard them after use.

Motorcycle chemicals and lubricants

A number of chemicals and lubricants are available for use in motorcycle maintenance and repair. They include a wide variety of products ranging from cleaning solvents and degreasers to lubricants and protective sprays for rubber, plastic and vinyl.

Contact point/spark plug cleaner is a solvent used to clean oily film and dirt from points, grim from electrical connectors and oil deposits from spark plugs. It is oil free and leaves no residue. It can also be used to remove gum and varnish from carburetor jets and other orifices.

Carburetor cleaner is similar to contact point/spark plug cleaner but it usually has a stronger solvent and may leave a slight oily residue. It is not recommended for cleaning electrical components or connections.

Brake system cleaner is used to remove brake dust, grease and brake fluid from the brake system, where clean surfaces are absolutely necessary. It leaves no residue and often eliminates brake squeal caused by contaminants.

Silicone-based lubricants are used to protect rubber parts such as hoses and grommets, and are used as lubricants for hinges and locks.

Multi-purpose grease is an all purpose lubricant used wherever grease is more practical than a liquid lubricant such as oil. Some multi-purpose grease is colored white and specially formulated to be more resistant to water than ordinary grease.

Gear oil (sometimes called gear lube) is a specially designed oil used in transmissions and final drive units, as well as other areas where high friction, high temperature lubrication is required. It is available in a number of viscosities (weights) for various applications.

Motor oil is the lubricant formulated for use in engines. It normally contains a wide variety of additives to prevent corrosion and reduce foaming and wear. Motor oil comes in various weights (viscosity ratings) from 0 to 50. The recommended weight of the oil depends on the season, temperature and the demands on the engine. Light oil is used in cold climates and under light load conditions. Heavy oil is used in hot climates and where high loads are encountered. Multi-viscosity oils are designed to have characteristics of both light and heavy oils and are available in a number of weights from 0W-20 to 20W-50.

Gasoline additives perform several functions, depending on their chemical makeup. They usually contain solvents that help dissolve gum and varnish that build up on carburetor and inlet parts. They also serve to break down carbon deposits that form on the inside surfaces of the combustion chambers. Some additives contain upper cylinder lubricants for valves and piston rings.

Brake and clutch fluid is a specially formulated hydraulic fluid that can withstand the heat and pressure encountered in break/clutch systems. Care must be taken that this fluid does not come in contact with painted surfaces or plastics. An opened container should always be resealed to prevent contamination by water or dirt.

Chain lubricants are formulated especially for use on motorcycle final drive chains. A good chain lube should adhere well and have good penetrating qualities to be effective as a lubricant inside the chain and on the side plates, pins and rollers. Most chain lubes are either the foaming type or quick drying type and are usually marketed as sprays. Take care to use a lubricant marked as being suitable for O-ring chains.

Degreasers are heavy duty solvents used to remove grease and grime that may accumulate on the engine and frame components. They can be sprayed or brushed on and, depending on the type, are rinsed with either water or solvent.

Solvents are used alone or in combination with degreasers to clean parts and assemblies during repair and overhaul. The home mechanic should use only solvents that are non-flammable and that do not produce irritating fumes.

Gasket sealing compounds may be used in conjunction with gaskets, to improve their sealing capabilities, or alone, to seal metal-to-metal joints. Many gasket sealers can withstand extreme heat, some are impervious to gasoline and lubricants, while others are capable of filling and sealing large cavities. Depending on the intended use, gasket sealers either dry hard or stay relatively soft and pliable. They are usually applied by hand, with a brush or are sprayed on the gasket sealing surfaces.

Thread locking compound is an adhesive locking compound that prevents threaded fasteners from loosening because of vibration. It is available in a variety of types for different applications.

Moisture dispersants are usually sprays that can be used to dry out electrical components such as the fuse block and wiring connectors. Some types an also be used as treatment for rubber and as a lubricant for hinges, cables and locks.

Waxes and polishes are used to help protect painted and plated surfaces from the weather. Different types of paint may require the use of different types of wax polish. Some polishes utilize a chemical or abrasive cleaner to help remove the top layer of oxidized (dull) paint on older vehicles. In recent years, many non-wax polishes (that contain a wide variety of chemicals such as polymers and silicones) have been introduced. These non-wax polishes are usually easier to apply and last longer than conventional waxes and polishes.

Troubleshooting

Contents

Engine doesn't start or is difficult to start

1 Kickstarter moves but engine won't start

1   Engine kill switch Off.
2   Wiring open or shorted. Check all wiring connections and harnesses to make sure that they are dry, tight and not corroded. Also check for broken or frayed wires that can cause a short to ground (see wiring diagrams, end of book).
3   Engine kill switch defective. Check for wet, dirty or corroded contacts. Clean or replace the switch as necessary (Chapter 5).

2 Kickstarter moves but engine does not turn over

1   Kickstarter mechanism damaged. Inspect and repair or replace (Chapter 2).
2   Damaged kickstarter pinion gears. Inspect and replace the damaged parts (Chapter 2).

3 Kickstarter won't engine turn over (seized)

Seized engine caused by one or more internally damaged components. Failure due to wear, abuse or lack of lubrication. Damage can include seized piston, crankshaft, connecting rod bearings, or transmission gears or bearings. Refer to Chapter 2 for engine disassembly.

4 No fuel flow

1   No fuel in tank.
2   Tank cap air vent obstructed. Usually caused by dirt or water. Remove it and clean the cap vent hole.
3   Clogged strainer in fuel tap. Remove and clean the strainer (Chapter 1).
4   Fuel line clogged. Pull the fuel line loose and carefully blow through it.
5   Inlet needle valve clogged. A very bad batch of fuel with an unusual additive may have been used, or some other foreign material has entered the tank. Many times after a machine has been stored for many months without running, the fuel turns to a varnish-like liquid and forms deposits on the inlet needle valve and jets. The carburetor should be removed and overhauled if draining the float chamber doesn't solve the problem.

5 Engine flooded

1   Float level too high. Check as described in Chapter 4 and replace the float if necessary.
2   Inlet needle valve worn or stuck open. A piece of dirt, rust or other debris can cause the inlet needle to seat improperly, causing excess fuel to be admitted to the float bowl. In this case, the float chamber should be cleaned and the needle and seat inspected. If the needle and seat are worn, then the leaking will persist and the parts should be replaced with new ones (Chapter 4).
3   Starting technique incorrect. Under normal circumstances (i.e., if all the carburetor functions are sound) the machine should start with little or no throttle. When the engine is cold, the choke should be operated and the engine started without opening the throttle. When the engine is at operating temperature, only a very slight amount of throttle should be necessary. If the engine is flooded, turn the fuel tap off and hold the throttle open while cranking the engine. This will allow additional air to reach the cylinder. Remember to turn the fuel tap back on after the engine starts.

6 No spark or weak spark

1   Spark plug dirty, defective or worn out. Locate reason for fouled plug using spark plug condition chart and follow the plug maintenance procedures in Chapter 1.
2   Spark plug cap or secondary wiring faulty. Check condition. Replace either or both components if cracks or deterioration are evident (Chapter 5).
3   Spark plug cap not making good contact. Make sure that the plug cap fits snugly over the plug end.
4   Defective alternator (see Chapter 5).
5   Defective CDI unit (see Chapter 5).
6   Ignition coil defective. Check the coil, referring to Chapter 5.
7   Kill switch shorted. This is usually caused by water, corrosion, damage or excessive wear. The kill switch can be disassembled and cleaned with electrical contact cleaner. If cleaning does not help, replace the switch (Chapter 5).
8   Wiring shorted or broken between:

   a) *CDI unit and engine kill switch*
   b) *CDI unit and ignition coil*
   c) *CDI unit and alternator*
   d) *Ignition coil and plug*

Make sure that all wiring connections are clean, dry and tight. Look for chafed and broken wires (Chapter 4).

7 Compression low

1   Spark plug loose. Remove the plug and inspect the threads. Reinstall and tighten to the specified torque (Chapter 1).
2   Cylinder head not sufficiently tightened down. If the cylinder head is suspected of being loose, then there's a chance that the gasket or head is damaged if the problem has persisted for any length of time. The head nuts and bolts should be tightened to the proper torque in the correct sequence (Chapter 2).
3   Faulty reed valve. Check and replace if necessary (Chapter 4).
4   Cylinder and/or piston worn. Excessive wear will cause compression pressure to leak past the ring(s). This is usually accompanied by a worn ring as well. A top end overhaul is necessary (Chapter 2).
5   Piston ring worn, weak, broken, or sticking. Broken or sticking piston rings usually indicate a lubrication or carburetion problem that causes excess carbon deposits or seizures to form on the piston and ring. Top end overhaul is necessary (Chapter 2).
6   Piston ring-to-groove clearance excessive. This is caused by excessive wear of the piston ring lands. Piston replacement is necessary (Chapter 2).
7   Cylinder head gasket damaged. If the head is allowed to become loose, or if excessive carbon build-up on a piston crown and combustion chamber causes extremely high compression, the head gasket may leak. Retorquing the head is not always sufficient to restore the seal, so gasket replacement is necessary (Chapter 2).
8   Cylinder head warped. This is caused by overheating or improperly tightened head nuts and bolts. Machine shop resurfacing or head replacement is necessary (Chapter 2).

8 Stalls after starting

1   Improper choke action. Make sure the choke knob is getting a full stroke and staying in the out position.
2   Ignition malfunction. See Chapter 5.
3   Carburetor malfunction. See Chapter 4.
4   Fuel contaminated. The fuel can be contaminated with either dirt or water, or can change chemically if the machine is allowed to sit for more than 24 hours. Drain the tank and float bowl and refill with fresh fuel (Chapter 4).
5   Intake air leak. Check for loose carburetor-to-intake joint connec-

tions or loose carburetor top (Chapter 3).
6   Engine idle speed incorrect. Turn throttle stop screw until the engine idles at the specified rpm (Chapter 1).
7   Crankcase air leak. Refer to Chapter 2 for testing procedure.

9   Rough idle

1   Ignition malfunction. See Chapter 5.
2   Idle speed incorrect. See Chapter 1.
3   Carburetor malfunction. See Chapter 4.
4   Idle fuel/air mixture incorrect. See Chapter 4.
5   Fuel contaminated. The fuel can be contaminated with either dirt or water, or can change chemically if the machine is allowed to sit for more than 24 hours. Drain the tank and float bowl and refill with fresh fuel (Chapter 4).
6   Intake air leak. Check for loose carburetor-to-intake joint connections or loose carburetor top (Chapter 4). Check for loose reed valve (Chapter 2).
7   Air cleaner clogged. Service or replace air cleaner element (Chapter 1).

Poor running at low speed

10   Spark weak

1   Spark plug fouled, defective or worn out. Refer to Chapter 1 for spark plug maintenance.
2   Spark plug cap or secondary wiring defective. Refer to Chapters 1 and 5 for details on the ignition system.
3   Spark plug cap not making contact.
4   Incorrect spark plug. Wrong type, heat range or cap configuration. Check and install correct plug listed in Chapter 1. A cold plug or one with a recessed firing electrode will not operate at low speeds without fouling.
5   CDI unit defective. See Chapter 5.
6   Alternator defective. See Chapter 5.
7   Ignition coil defective. See Chapter 5.

11   Fuel/air mixture incorrect

1   Air screw out of adjustment (Chapter 4).
2   Carburetor jetting or needle clip position incorrect for weather, temperature and track conditions (Chapter 4).
3   Jet or air passage clogged. Remove and overhaul the carburetor (Chapter 4).
4   Air bleed holes clogged. Remove carburetor and blow out all passages (Chapter 4).
5   Air filter element clogged, poorly sealed or missing (Chapter 1).
6   Air cleaner-to-carburetor boot poorly sealed. Look for cracks, holes or loose clamps and replace or repair defective parts.
7   Float level too high or too low. Check and replace the float if necessary (Chapter 4).
8   Fuel tank air vent obstructed. Make sure that the air vent passage in the filler cap is open.
9   Carburetor intake joint loose. Check for cracks, breaks, tears or loose clamps or bolts. Repair or replace the rubber boot and its O-ring.

12   Compression low

1   Spark plug loose. Remove the plug and inspect the threads. Reinstall and tighten to the specified torque (Chapter 1).
2   Cylinder head not sufficiently tightened down. If the cylinder head is suspected of being loose, then there's a chance that the gasket and

head are damaged if the problem has persisted for any length of time. The head nuts should be tightened to the proper torque in the correct sequence (Chapter 2).
3   Faulty reed valve. Check and replace if necessary (Chapter 2).
4   Cylinder and/or piston worn. Excessive wear will cause compression pressure to leak past the rings. This is usually accompanied by a worn ring as well. A top end overhaul is necessary (Chapter 2).
5   Piston ring worn, weak, broken, or sticking. Broken or sticking piston rings usually indicate a lubrication or carburetion problem that causes excess carbon deposits or seizures to form on the piston and ring. Top end overhaul is necessary (Chapter 2).
6   Piston ring-to-groove clearance excessive. This is caused by excessive wear of the piston ring lands. Piston replacement is necessary (Chapter 2).
7   Cylinder head gasket damaged. If the head is allowed to become loose, or if excessive carbon build-up on the piston crown and combustion chamber causes extremely high compression, the head gasket may leak. Retorquing the head is not always sufficient to restore the seal, so gasket replacement is necessary (Chapter 2).
8   Cylinder head warped. This is caused by overheating or improperly tightened head nuts and bolts. Machine shop resurfacing or head replacement is necessary (Chapter 2).

13   Poor acceleration

1   Carburetor leaking or dirty. Overhaul the carburetor (Chapter 4).
2   Timing not advancing. The CDI unit may be defective. If so, it must be replaced with a new one, as it can't be repaired.
3   Transmission oil viscosity too high. Using a heavier oil than that recommended in Chapter 1 can cause drag on the engine.
4   Brakes dragging. Usually caused by a sticking caliper piston (disc brakes) or brake cam (drum brakes), by a warped disc or drum or by a bent axle. Repair as necessary (Chapter 7).

Poor running or no power at high speed

14   Firing incorrect

1   Timing not advancing.
2   Air cleaner restricted. Clean or replace element (Chapter 1).
3   Spark plug fouled, defective or worn out. See Chapter 1 for spark plug maintenance.
4   Spark plug cap or secondary wiring defective. See Chapters 1 and 5 for details of the ignition system.
5   Spark plug cap not in good contact. See Chapter 5.
6   Incorrect spark plug. Wrong type, heat range or cap configuration. Check and install correct plugs listed in Chapter 1. A cold plug or one with a recessed firing electrode will not operate at low speeds without fouling.
7   CDI unit defective. See Chapter 5.
8   Ignition coil defective. See Chapter 5.

15   Fuel/air mixture incorrect

1   Air screw out of adjustment. See Chapter 4 for adjustment procedures.
2   Main jet clogged. Dirt, water or other contaminants can clog the main jet. Clean the fuel tap strainer, the float bowl area, and the jets and carburetor orifices (Chapter 4).
3   Carburetor jetting or needle clip position incorrect for temperature, weather or track conditions. See Chapter 4 for jetting details.
4   Throttle shaft-to-carburetor body clearance excessive. Refer to Chapter 4 for inspection and part replacement procedures.
5   Air bleed holes clogged. Remove and overhaul carburetor (Chapter 4).

6 Air cleaner clogged, poorly sealed, or missing.

7 Air cleaner-to-carburetor boot poorly sealed. Look for cracks, holes or loose clamps, and replace or repair defective parts.

8 Float level too high or too low. Check float level and replace the float if necessary (Chapter 4).

9 Fuel tank air vent or vent hose obstructed. Make sure the air vent passage in the filler cap is open and that the vent hose is not plugged or pinched.

10 Carburetor intake manifold loose. Check for cracks, breaks, tears or loose clamps or bolts. Repair or replace the rubber boots (Chapter 4).

11 Fuel tap clogged. Remove the tap and clean it (Chapter 1).

12 Fuel line clogged. Pull the fuel line loose and carefully blow through it.

13 Crankcase air leak. Refer to Chapter 2 for testing procedures.

16 Compression low

1 Spark plug loose. Remove the plug and inspect the threads. Reinstall and tighten to the specified torque (Chapter 1).

2 Cylinder head not sufficiently tightened down. If the cylinder head is suspected of being loose, then there's a chance that the gasket and head are damaged if the problem has persisted for any length of time. The head nuts and bolts should be tightened to the proper torque in the correct sequence (Chapter 2).

3 Reed valve faulty. Check and replace if necessary (Chapter 2).

4 Cylinder and/or piston worn. Excessive wear will cause compression pressure to leak past the ring(s). This is usually accompanied by a worn ring(s) as well. A top end overhaul is necessary (Chapter 2).

5 Piston ring(s) worn, weak, broken, or sticking. Broken or sticking piston rings usually indicate a lubrication or carburetion problem that causes excess carbon deposits or seizures to form on the piston and ring. Top end overhaul is necessary (Chapter 2).

6 Piston ring-to-groove clearance excessive. This is caused by excessive wear of the piston ring lands. Piston replacement is necessary (Chapter 2).

7 Cylinder head gasket damaged. If a head is allowed to become loose, or if excessive carbon build-up on the piston crown and combustion chamber causes extremely high compression, the head gasket may leak. Retorquing the head is not always sufficient to restore the seal, so gasket replacement is necessary (Chapter 2).

8 Cylinder head warped. This is caused by overheating or improperly tightened head nuts and bolts. Machine shop resurfacing or head replacement is necessary (Chapter 2).

17 Knocking or pinging

1 Carbon build-up in combustion chamber. Remove and decarbonize the cylinder head (Chapter 2).

2 Incorrect or poor quality fuel. Old or improper grades of fuel can cause detonation. This causes the piston to rattle, thus the knocking or pinging sound. Drain old fuel and always use the recommended fuel grade.

3 Spark plug heat range incorrect. Uncontrolled detonation indicates the plug heat range is too hot. The plug in effect becomes a glow plug, raising cylinder temperatures. Install the proper heat range plug (Chapter 1).

4 Improper air/fuel mixture. This will cause the cylinder to run hot, which leads to detonation. Clogged jets or an air leak can cause this imbalance. See Chapter 3.

18 Miscellaneous causes

1 Throttle valve doesn't open fully. Adjust the cable slack (Chapter 1).

2 Clutch slipping. May be caused by improper adjustment or loose or worn clutch components. Refer to Chapter 1 for adjustment or Chapter 2 for cable replacement and clutch overhaul procedures.

3 Timing not advancing.

4 Brakes dragging. Usually caused by debris which has entered the brake piston sealing boot, or from a warped disc or bent axle. Repair as necessary.

5 If the bike has an HPP, RC or CRV system (Chapter 4) inspect and clean the components. Make sure the exhaust valves open fully at full throttle.

Overheating

19 Engine overheats

1 Coolant level low. Check and add coolant (Chapter 1), then look for leaks (Chapter 3).

2 Air leak at carburetor intake manifold. Check and tighten or replace as necessary (Chapter 3).

3 Incorrect fuel-oil ratio (see Chapter 1). Discard fuel and start with a fresh batch of premix.

4 Carbon build-up in combustion chambers. Remove and decarbonize the cylinder head (Chapter 2).

5 Operation in high ambient temperatures.

20 Firing incorrect

1 Spark plug fouled, defective or worn out. See Chapter 1 for spark plug maintenance.

2 Incorrect spark plug (see Chapter 1).

3 Faulty ignition coil (Chapter 5).

21 Fuel/air mixture incorrect

1 Pilot screw out of adjustment (Chapter 4).

2 Main jet clogged. Dirt, water and other contaminants can clog the main jet. Clean the fuel tap strainer, the float bowl area and the jets and carburetor orifices (Chapter 4).

3 Carburetor jetting or needle clip position incorrect for temperature, weather or track conditions. See Chapter 4 for jetting details.

4 Air cleaner poorly sealed or missing.

5 Air cleaner-to-carburetor boot poorly sealed. Look for cracks, holes or loose clamps and replace or repair.

6 Fuel level too low. Check float level and replace the float if necessary (Chapter 4).

7 Fuel tank air vent or hose obstructed. Make sure that the air vent passage in the filler cap is open and the hose is not plugged or kinked.

8 Carburetor intake manifold loose. Check for cracks or loose clamps or bolts. Inspect the gasket and O-ring (Chapter 4).

22 Compression too high

1 Carbon build-up in combustion chamber. Remove and decarbonize the cylinder head (Chapter 2).

2 Improperly machined head surface or installation of incorrect gasket during engine assembly.

23 Engine load excessive

1 Clutch slipping. Can be caused by damaged, loose or worn clutch components. Refer to Chapter 2 for overhaul procedures.

2   Transmission oil viscosity too high. Using a heavier oil than the one recommended in Chapter 1 can cause drag on the engine.
3   Brakes dragging. Usually caused by a sticking caliper piston (disc brakes), brake cam (drum brakes), by a warped disc or drum or by a bent axle. Repair as necessary (Chapter 7).

24 Lubrication inadequate

1   Transmission oil level too low. Friction caused by intermittent lack of lubrication or from oil that is overworked can cause overheating. The oil provides a definite cooling function in the transmission. Check the oil level (Chapter 1).
2   Poor quality or incorrect oil type. Check the Chapter 1 Specifications and change to the correct oil.
3   Incorrect fuel-oil ratio (see Chapter 1). Discard fuel and start with a fresh batch of premix.

25 Miscellaneous causes

Modification to exhaust system. Most aftermarket exhaust systems cause the engine to run leaner, which makes it run hotter. When installing an accessory exhaust system, always rejet the carburetor.

Clutch problems

26 Clutch slipping

1   No clutch lever freeplay. Adjust freeplay (Chapter 1).
2   Friction plates worn or warped. Overhaul the clutch (Chapter 2).
3   Metal plates worn or warped (Chapter 2).
4   Clutch spring(s) broken or weak. Old or heat-damaged spring(s) (from slipping clutch) should be replaced with new ones (Chapter 2).
5   Clutch release mechanism defective. Replace any defective parts (Chapter 2).
6   Clutch center or housing unevenly worn. This causes improper engagement of the plates. Replace the damaged or worn parts (Chapter 2).
7   Clutch inner cable sticking. Caused by a frayed inner cable or kinked outer cable. Replace the clutch cable; repair of a damaged cable is not advised.

27 Clutch not disengaging completely

1   Clutch improperly adjusted (see Chapter 1).
2   Clutch plates warped or damaged. This will cause clutch drag, which in turn will cause the machine to creep. Overhaul the clutch assembly (Chapter 2).
3   Sagged or broken clutch spring(s). Check and replace the spring(s) (Chapter 2).
4   Transmission oil deteriorated. Old, thin, worn out oil will not provide proper lubrication for the discs, causing the clutch to drag. Replace the oil and filter (Chapter 1).
5   Clutch housing seized on shaft. Lack of lubrication, severe wear or damage can cause the housing to seize on the shaft. Overhaul of the clutch, and perhaps transmission, may be necessary to repair the damage (Chapter 2).
6   Clutch release mechanism defective. Worn or damaged release mechanism parts can stick and fail to apply force to the pressure plate. Overhaul the release mechanism (Chapter 2).
7   Loose clutch center bolt or nut. Causes housing and center misalignment putting a drag on the engine. Engagement adjustment continually varies. Overhaul the clutch assembly (Chapter 2).

Gear shifting problems

28 Doesn't go into gear or pedal doesn't return

1   Clutch not disengaging. See Section 27.
2   Shift fork(s) bent or seized. May be caused by lack of lubrication. Overhaul the transmission (Chapter 2).
3   Gear(s) stuck on shaft. Most often caused by a lack of lubrication or excessive wear in transmission bearings and bushings. Overhaul the transmission (Chapter 2).
4   Shift drum binding. Caused by lubrication failure or excessive wear. Replace the drum and bearing (Chapter 2).
5   Shift pedal return spring weak or broken (Chapter 2).
6   Shift pedal broken. Splines stripped out of pedal or shaft, caused by allowing the pedal to get loose. Replace necessary parts (Chapter 2).
7   Shift mechanism pawls broken or worn. Full engagement and rotary movement of shift drum results. Replace shaft assembly (Chapter 2).
8   Pawl spring broken. Allows pawl to float, causing sporadic shift operation. Replace spring (Chapter 2).

29 Jumps out of gear

1   Shift fork(s) worn. Overhaul the transmission (Chapter 2).
2   Gear groove(s) worn. Overhaul the transmission (Chapter 2).
3   Gear dogs or dog slots worn or damaged. The gears should be inspected and replaced. No attempt should be made to service the worn parts.

30 Overshifts

1   Pawl spring weak or broken (Chapter 2).
2   Shift drum stopper lever not functioning (Chapter 2).

Abnormal engine noise

31 Knocking or pinging

1   Carbon build-up in combustion chamber. Remove and decarbonize the cylinder head (Chapter 2).
2   Incorrect fuel-oil ratio. Drain the old fuel (Chapter 4) and always use the recommended grade fuel (Chapter 1).
3   Spark plug heat range incorrect. Uncontrolled detonation indicates that the plug heat range is too hot. The plug in effect becomes a glow plug, raising cylinder temperatures. Install the proper heat range plug (Chapter 1).
4   Improper air/fuel mixture. This will cause the cylinder to run hot and lead to detonation. Clogged jets or an air leak can cause this imbalance. See Chapter 4.
5   Crankcase air leak. See Chapter 2 for testing procedure.
6   Wrong grade of gasoline (octane too low).

32 Piston slap or rattling

1   Cylinder-to-piston clearance excessive. Caused by improper assembly. Inspect and overhaul top end parts (Chapter 2).
2   Connecting rod bent. Caused by over-revving, trying to start a badly flooded engine or from ingesting a foreign object into the combustion chamber. Replace the damaged parts (Chapter 2).
3   Piston pin or piston pin bore worn or seized from wear or lack of lubrication. Replace damaged parts (Chapter 2).

4 Piston ring worn, broken or sticking. Overhaul the top end (Chapter 2).
5 Piston seizure damage. Usually from lack of lubrication or overheating. Replace the pistons and bore the cylinder, as necessary (Chapter 2).
6 Connecting rod upper or lower end clearance excessive. Caused by excessive wear or lack of lubrication. Replace worn parts.

33 Other noise

1 Cylinder head gasket leaking.
2 Exhaust pipe leaking at cylinder head connection. Caused by improper fit of pipe, damaged gasket or loose exhaust flange. All exhaust fasteners should be tightened evenly and carefully. Failure to do this will lead to a leak.
3 Crankshaft runout excessive. Caused by a bent crankshaft (from over-revving) or damage from an upper cylinder component failure.
4 Engine mounting bolts or nuts loose. Tighten all engine mounting bolts and nuts to the specified torque (Chapter 2).
5 Crankshaft bearings worn (Chapter 2).
6 Loose alternator rotor. Tighten the mounting nut to the specified torque (Chapter 5).

Abnormal driveline noise

34 Clutch noise

1 Clutch housing/friction plate clearance excessive (Chapter 2).
2 Loose or damaged pressure plate and/or bolts (Chapter 2).
3 Broken clutch springs (Chapter 2).

35 Transmission noise

1 Bearings worn. Also includes the possibility that the shafts are worn. Overhaul the transmission (Chapter 2).
2 Gears worn or chipped (Chapter 2).
3 Metal chips jammed in gear teeth. Probably pieces from a broken clutch, gear or shift mechanism that were picked up by the gears. This will cause early bearing failure (Chapter 2).
4 Transmission oil level too low. Causes a howl from transmission. Also affects engine power and clutch operation (Chapter 1).

36 Final drive noise

1 Dry or dirty chain. Inspect, clean and lubricate (see Chapter 1).
2 Chain out of adjustment. Adjust chain slack (see Chapter 1).
3 Chain and sprockets damaged or worn. Inspect the chain and sprockets and replace them as necessary (see Chapter 4).
4 Sprockets loose (see Chapter 5).

Abnormal chassis noise

37 Suspension noise

1 Spring weak or broken. Makes a clicking or scraping sound.
2 Steering head bearings worn or damaged. Clicks when braking. Check and replace as necessary (Chapter 5).
3 Front fork oil level incorrect. Check and correct oil level (see Chapter 5).
4 Front fork(s) assembled incorrectly. Disassemble the fork(s) and check for correct assembly (see Chapter 5).
5 Rear shock absorber fluid level incorrect. Indicates a leak caused

by defective seal. Shock will be covered with oil. It may be possible to overhaul the shock and repair the damage; take the shock to a Honda dealer or motorcycle repair shop for inspection.
6 Defective shock absorber with internal damage. This is in the body of the shock. It may be possible to overhaul the shock and repair the damage; take the shock to a Honda dealer or motorcycle repair shop for inspection.
7 Bent or damaged shock body. Replace the shock with a new one (Chapter 6).

38 Brake noise

1 Squeal caused by pad shim not installed or positioned correctly (Chapter 7).
2 Squeal caused by dust on brake pads. Usually found in combination with glazed pads. Clean using brake cleaning solvent (see Chapter 7). If the pads are glazed, replace them.
3 Contamination of brake pads. Oil, brake fluid or dirt causing pads to chatter or squeal. Clean or replace pads (see Chapter 6).
4 Pads glazed. Caused by excessive heat from prolonged use or from contamination. Do not use sandpaper, emery cloth or carborundum cloth or any other abrasives to roughen pad surface as abrasives will stay in the pad material and damage the disc. A very fine flat file can be used, but pad replacement is suggested as a cure (see Chapter 7).
5 Disc warped. Can cause a chattering, clicking or intermittent squeal. Usually accompanied by a pulsating lever and uneven braking. Replace the disc (see Chapter 7).
6 Drum brake linings worn or contaminated. Can cause scraping or squealing. Replace the shoes (Chapter 7).
7 Drum brake linings warped or worn unevenly. Can cause chattering. Replace the linings (Chapter 7).
8 Brake drum out of round. Can cause chattering. Replace brake drum (Chapter 7).
9 Loose or worn wheel bearings. Check and replace as needed (Chapter 7).

Excessive exhaust smoke

39 White smoke

Oil/fuel mixture too rich. Drain fuel tank and refill with properly-mixed fuel.

40 Black smoke

1 Air cleaner clogged. Clean or replace the element (Chapter 1).
2 Main jet too large or loose. Compare the jet size to the Specifications (Chapter 4).
3 Choke (starter jet) stuck open (Chapter 4).
4 Fuel level too high. Check the float level and replace the float if necessary (Chapter 4).
5 Inlet needle held off needle seat. Clean the float chamber and fuel line and replace the needle and seat if necessary (Chapter 4).

41 Brown smoke

1 Main jet too small or clogged. Lean condition caused by wrong size main jet or by a restricted orifice. Clean float chamber and jets and compare jet size to Specifications (Chapter 4).
2 Fuel flow insufficient. Fuel inlet needle valve stuck closed due to chemical reaction with old fuel. Float level incorrect; check and replace float if necessary. Restricted fuel line. Clean line and float chamber.
3 Carburetor intake tube loose (Chapter 4).
4 Air cleaner poorly sealed or not installed (Chapter 1).

Poor handling or stability

42 Handlebar hard to turn

1   Steering stem adjusting nut too tight (Chapter 6).
2   Steering stem bearings damaged. Roughness can be felt as the bars are turned from side-to-side. Replace bearings and races (Chapter 6).
3   Races dented or worn. Denting results from wear in only one position (e.g. straight ahead), striking an immovable object or hole or from dropping the machine. Replace races and bearings (Chapter 6).
4   Steering stem bearing lubrication inadequate. Causes are grease getting hard from age or being washed out by high pressure car washes. Remove steering stem, clean and lubricate bearings (Chapter 6).
5   Steering stem bent. Caused by a collision, hitting a pothole or by dropping the machine. Replace damaged part. Don't try to straighten the steering stem (Chapter 6).
6   Front tire air pressure too low (Chapter 1).

43 Handlebar shakes or vibrates excessively

1   Tires worn or out of balance (Chapter 1 or 7).
2   Swingarm bearings worn. Replace worn bearings (Chapter 6).
3   Wheel rim(s) warped or damaged. Inspect wheels (Chapter 7).
4   Wheel bearings worn. Worn front or rear wheel bearings can cause poor tracking. Worn front bearings will cause wobble (Chapter 7).
5   Handlebar clamp bolts loose (Chapter 6).
6   Steering stem or triple clamps loose. Tighten them to the specified torque (Chapters 1 and 6).
7   Motor mount bolts loose. Will cause excessive vibration with increased engine rpm (Chapter 2).

44 Handlebar pulls to one side

1   Frame bent. Definitely suspect this if the machine has been dropped. May or may not be accompanied by cracking near the bend. Replace the frame (Chapter 8).
2   Front and rear wheels out of alignment. Caused by uneven adjustment of the drive chain adjusters (see Chapter 1). May also be caused by improper location of the axle spacers or from bent steering stem or frame (see Chapter 6).
3   Swingarm bent or twisted. Caused by age (metal fatigue) or impact damage. Replace the swingarm (Chapter 6).
4   Steering stem bent. Caused by impact damage or by dropping the motorcycle. Replace the steering stem (Chapter 6).

45 Poor shock absorbing qualities

1   Too hard:
  a) *Damping adjuster set too hard (see Chapter 6).*
  b) *Fork oil level excessive (see Chapter 6).*
  c) *Fork oil viscosity too high. Use a lighter oil (see the Specifications in Chapter 6).*
  d) *Fork tube bent. Causes a harsh, sticking feeling (see Chapter 6).*
  e) *Fork internal damage (see Chapter 6).*
  f) *Shock internal damage.*
  g) *Tire pressures too high (Chapter 1).*
2   Too soft:
  a) *Damping adjuster set too soft (see Chapter 6)..*
  b) *Fork or shock oil insufficient and/or leaking (Chapter 6).*
  d) *Fork oil level too low (see Chapter 6).*
  d) *Fork springs weak or broken (Chapter 6).*

Braking problems

46 Brakes are spongy or weak, don't hold

1   Air in brake line (disc brakes). Caused by inattention to master cylinder fluid level or by leakage. Locate problem and bleed brake (Chapter 7).
2   Pad or disc worn (Chapters 1 and 7).
3   Brake fluid leak. See paragraph 1.
4   Contaminated disc brake pads. Caused by contamination with oil, grease, brake fluid, etc. Clean or replace pads. Clean disc thoroughly with brake cleaner.
5   Brake fluid deteriorated (disc brakes). Fluid is old or contaminated. Drain system, replenish with new fluid and bleed the system (see Chapter 7).
6   Master cylinder internal parts worn or damaged, causing fluid to bypass (see Chapter 7).
7   Master cylinder bore scratched. From ingestion of foreign material or broken spring. Repair or replace master cylinder (see Chapter 7).
8   Disc warped. Replace disc (see Chapter 7).
9   Drum brake linings worn (Chapters 1 and 7).
10   Contaminated drum brake linings. Caused by contamination with oil, grease, etc. Clean or replace linings. Clean drum thoroughly with brake cleaner (Chapter 7).
11   Drum warped. Replace drum (Chapter 7).
12   Drum brake cable out of adjustment or stretched. Adjust or replace the cable (see Chapters 1 and 7).

47 Brake lever or pedal pulsates

1   Disc warped. Replace disc (see Chapter 7).
2   Axle bent. Replace axle (Chapter 6).
3   Brake caliper bolts loose (see Chapter 7).
4   Brake caliper shafts damaged or sticking, causing caliper to bind. Lube the shafts or replace them if they are corroded or bent (see Chapter 7).
5   Wheel warped or otherwise damaged (Chapter 7).
6   Wheel bearings damaged or worn (Chapter 7).
7   Brake drum out of round. Replace brake drum (Chapter 7).

48 Brakes drag

1   Master cylinder piston seized. Caused by wear or damage to piston or cylinder bore (see Chapter 7).
2   Lever or pedal balky or stuck. Check pivot and lubricate (see Chapter 7).
3   Brake caliper binds. Caused by inadequate lubrication or damage to caliper shafts (see Chapter 7).
4   Brake caliper piston seized in bore. Caused by wear or ingestion of dirt past deteriorated seal (see Chapter 7).
5   Brake pad or shoes damaged. Pad or lining material separated from backing plate or shoes. Usually caused by faulty manufacturing process or contact with chemicals. Replace pads (see Chapter 7).
6   Pads or shoes improperly installed (see Chapter 7).
7   Cable sticking. Lubricate or replace cable (see Chapters 1 and 7).
8   Shoes improperly installed (Chapter 7).
9   Brake pedal or lever freeplay insufficient (Chapter 1).
10   Drum brake springs weak. Replace brake springs (Chapter 7).

Chapter 1 Part A
Tune-up and routine maintenance (CR80R/85R and CR125R models)

Contents

Specifications

Engine

Spark plug type	
CR80R/85R	NGK BR10EG
CR125R	
Standard	NGK BR9EG, Champion QN-84 or ND W27ESR-V
Optional	NGK BR9EV, Champion QN59G or ND W27ESR-G
Spark plug gap	
CR80R/RB and CR85R/RB	
2004 and earlier	0.6 to 0.7 mm (0.024 to 0.028 inch)
2005 and later	0.5 to 0.6 mm (0.020 to 0.024 inch)
CR125R	0.5 to 0.6 mm (0.020 to 0.024 inch)
Cylinder compression	Not specified

Miscellaneous

Brake pad lining thickness limit	1.0 mm (3/64 inch)
Rear brake shoe lining limit (drum brakes)	1.0 mm (3/64 inch)
Front brake lever freeplay, at lever tip	
CR80R/RB and CR85R/RB	
1995 and 1996 (at adjuster gap)	1.0 to 1.4 mm (0.004 to 0.005 inch)
1995 and 1996 (at lever tip)	30 mm (1-1/4 inch or less)
1997 and later	20 mm (7/8 inch or less)
CR125R	
1986 through 1991	30 mm (1-1/4 inch) or less
1992-on	20 mm (25/32 inch) or less
Rear brake pedal freeplay (drum brake models)	20 to 30 mm (3/4 to 1-1/4 inch)

Miscellaneous (continued)

Rear master cylinder bolt length (1992 and later CR125R)	
2001 and earlier	75.0 mm (2.95 inches)
2002 and later	79.6 mm (3.13 inches)
Clutch lever freeplay...	10 to 20 mm (3/8 to 3/4 inch)
Throttle grip freeplay	3 to 5 mm (1/8 to 1/4 inch)
Minimum tire tread depth	8 mm (5/16 inch)
Tire pressures (cold)	
CR125R (2001 and earlier)...	15 psi front and rear
All others	14 psi front and rear
Tire sizes	
CR80R	
Front	70/100-17 40M
Rear	90/100-14 49M
CR80RB Expert	
Front	70/100-19 42M
Rear	90/100-16 52M
CR85R	
Front	70/100-17 40M
Rear	90/100-14 90M
CR85RB Expert	
Front	70/100-19 42M
Rear	90/100-16 52M
CR125R	
Front	80/100-21 51M
Rear	100/100-18 59M
Drive chain slack	
CR80R/RB and CR85R/RB	
1986 through 1995	30 to 35 mm (1-1/4 to 1-1/2 inches)
1996 on..	44 to 55 mm (1-3/4 to 2-1/8 inches)
CR125R	
1986 through 1992	35 to 40 mm (1-3/8 to 1-9/16 inches)
1993 through 1996	35 to 45 mm (1-3/8 to 1-3/4 inches)
1997	50 mm (2 inches)
1998 on..	25 to 35 mm (1 to 1-3/8 inches)
Chain slider groove depth limit (in top surface)	
CR80R/85R	
1986 through 1994	Not specified
1995	3.0 mm (1/8 inch)
1996 on..	4.0 mm (5/64 inch)
CR125R	
1986...	9.0 mm (3/8 inch)
1987 on..	5.0 mm (3/16 inch)
Chain roller diameter limit	
Upper roller	
CR80R/RB and CR85R/RB	Not applicable
2000 and earlier CR125R..	25 mm (1 inch)
2001 through 2004 CR125R..	35 mm (1.4 inches)
2005 and later CR125R	39 mm (1.54 inches)
Lower roller	
CR80R/RB and CR85R/RB	18 mm (0.7 inch)
2004 and earlier CR125R..	25 mm (1 inch)
2005 and later CR125R	39 mm (1.54 inches)

Torque specifications

Transmission oil check bolt	
CR80R/RB and CR85R/RB...	9 Nm (78 in-lbs)
CR125R...	10 Nm (84 in-lbs)
Transmission oil drain plug	
CR80R/RB and CR85R/RB...	25 Nm (18 ft-lbs)
CR125R...	30 Nm (22 ft-lbs)
Spark plug	18 Nm (156 in-lbs)
Wheel spokes	
CR80R/RB and CR85R/RB...	3.8 Nm (32 inch-lbs)
CR125R	
1986 through 1997	3.8 Nm (32 inch-lbs)
1998 on...	3.9 Nm (35 inch-lbs)
Rim lock locknut..	13 Nm (120 in-lbs)

Steering stem adjusting nut
  CR80R/RB and CR85R/RB
    1986 through 1994
      Initial torque.. 1 to 2 Nm (9 to 17 inch-lbs)
      Final torque .... Same as initial torque
    1995
      Initial torque.. 2 Nm (17 inch-lbs)
      Final torque .... Same as initial torque
    1996 on
      Initial torque.. 30 Nm (22 ft-lbs)
      Final torque .... 6 Nm (52 inch-lbs)
  CR125R
    1986 through 1989
      Initial torque.. 1 to 2 Nm (9 to 17 inch-lbs)
      Final torque .... Same as initial torque
    1990
      Initial torque.. 8 to 12 Nm (72 to 108 inch-lbs)
      Final torque .... Same as initial torque
    1991
      Initial torque.. 1 to 2 Nm (9 to 17 inch-lbs)
      Final torque .... Same as initial torque
    1992 and 1993
      Initial torque.. 2 Nm (17 inch-lbs)
      Final torque .... Same as initial torque
    1994 on.. 7 Nm (61 inch-lbs)

Recommended lubricants and fluids
Fuel
  1986 through 1991 CR125R .... 20:1 mix of gasoline (92 to 100 Research octane) and Honda two-stroke oil or equivalent
  All CR80/85R, 1992 and later CR125R............................ 32:1 mix of gasoline (90 or higher pump octane) and Honda two-stroke oil or equivalent
Transmission oil
  Type .... API grade SG or higher, meeting JASO Standard MA
  Viscosity
    CR80R/RB and CR85R/RB 10W-40
    CR125R
      2003 and earlier.. 10W-40
      2004 and later 10W-30
  Capacity at oil change*
    CR80R/RB and CR85R/RB
      1986 .... 500 cc (0.53 qt)
      1987 on .... 550 cc (0.58 qt)
    CR125R
      1986 .... 650 cc (22 fl oz)
      1987 on .... 570 cc (19 fl oz)
Air cleaner element oil .... Honda foam filter oil or equivalent
Coolant... Ethylene glycol antifreeze compatible with aluminum engines, mixed 50/50 with water
Brake fluid .... DOT 4
Drive chain lubricant... Chain lube

Miscellaneous
Wheel bearings... Medium weight, lithium-based multi-purpose grease
Swingarm pivot bushings... Molybdenum disulfide paste grease containing 40 percent or more molybdenum disulfide
Cables and lever pivots... Engine oil
Throttle grip, brake pedal/shift lever/throttle lever pivots ...... Medium weight, lithium-based multi-purpose grease

Approximate capacity; use oil check bolt to determine exact amount (see text).

1 Honda CR80R/85R and CR125R Routine maintenance intervals

Note: *This schedule was developed for your motorcycle's intended purpose, motocross competition. It's based on hours of running time or the equivalent number of races. The intervals listed below are the shortest intervals recommended by the manufacturer for each particular operation during the model years covered in this manual. Your owner's manual may have different intervals for your model.*

Every 2.5 hours of running time (or before each race)

Make sure the engine kill switch works properly
Check the throttle for smooth operation and correct free-play
Check clutch operation and freeplay
Inspect and lubricate the control cables
Check brake fluid level (hydraulic brakes)
Check the operation of both brakes - check the front brake lever and rear brake pedal for correct freeplay
Check the brake pads and shoes for wear
Check the tires for damage, the presence of foreign objects and correct air pressure
Lubricate and inspect the drive chain, sprockets and sliders
Check all fasteners, including axle nuts, for tightness
Inspect the front and rear suspensions
Check the coolant level and inspect the cooling system
Clean the air filter element*
Clean and gap the spark plug

Clean and inspect the Honda Power Port system (if equipped) (see Chapter 4)
Inspect the expansion chamber and muffler

Every 7.5 hours of running time (or before every third race)

Replace the spark plug
Change the transmission oil
Decarbonize the cylinder head (see Chapter 2)
Replace the piston and piston ring (see Chapter 2)
Replace the drive chain
Change the fork oil
Lubricate the swingarm bearings and shock linkage pivot points (see Chapter 6)

Every 22.5 running hours (or before every ninth race)

Replace the piston pin and connecting rod upper end bearing (see Chapter 2)
Inspect the steering head bearings

Every two years

Change the brake fluid (see Chapter 7)
Change the coolant
After every moto in dusty conditions.

2.1 Decals on the motorcycle include maintenance information such as drive chain adjustment

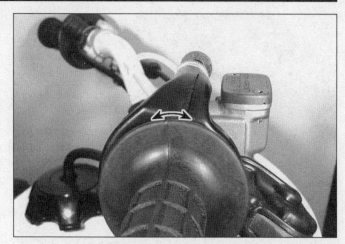

4.2 Measure throttle freeplay at the grip

2   Introduction to tune-up and routine maintenance

Refer to illustration 2.1

This Chapter covers in detail the checks and procedures necessary for the tune-up and routine maintenance of your motorcycle. Section 1 includes the routine maintenance schedule, which is designed to keep the machine in proper running condition and prevent possible problems. The remaining Sections contain detailed procedures for carrying out the items listed on the maintenance schedule, as well as additional maintenance information designed to increase reliability. Maintenance and safety information is also printed on decals, which are mounted in various locations on the motorcycle **(see illustration)**. Where information on the decals differs from that presented in this Chapter, use the decal information.

Since routine maintenance plays such an important role in the safe and efficient operation of your motorcycle, it is presented here as a comprehensive check list. For the rider who does all his own maintenance, these lists outline the procedures and checks that should be done on a routine basis.

Deciding where to start or plug into the routine maintenance schedule depends on several factors. If you have owned the bike for some time but have never performed any maintenance on it, then you may want to start at the nearest interval and include some additional procedures to ensure that nothing important is overlooked. If you have just had a major engine overhaul, then you may want to start the main-

tenance routine from the beginning. If you have a used machine and have no knowledge of its history or maintenance record, you may desire to combine all the checks into one large service initially and then settle into the maintenance schedule prescribed.

The Sections which outline the inspection and maintenance procedures are written as step-by-step comprehensive guides to the actual performance of the work. They explain in detail each of the routine inspections and maintenance procedures on the check list. References to additional information in applicable Chapters is also included and should not be overlooked.

Before beginning any actual maintenance or repair, the machine should be cleaned thoroughly, especially around the oil filler plug, radiator cap, engine covers, carburetor, etc. Cleaning will help ensure that dirt does not contaminate the engine and will allow you to detect wear and damage that could otherwise easily go unnoticed.

3   Engine kill switch - check

Start the engine, then use the kill switch to shut it off. If it doesn't shut off or if the engine doesn't start, refer to Chapter 5 and the wiring diagrams at the end of the book to test the switch.

4   Throttle and choke operation/grip freeplay - check and adjustment

Throttle check
Refer to illustration 4.2

1   Make sure the throttle twistgrip moves easily from fully closed to fully open with the front wheel turned at various angles. The grip should return automatically from fully open to fully closed when released. If the throttle sticks, check the throttle cable for cracks or kinks in the housings. Also, make sure the inner cable is clean and well-lubricated.

2   Check for a small amount of freeplay at the twistgrip **(see illustration)** and compare the freeplay to the value listed in this Chapter's Specifications.

Throttle adjustment
Refer to illustrations 4.4 and 4.5

3   Minor adjustments are made at the throttle lever end of the accelerator cable. Major adjustments are made at the carburetor end of the cable.

4   Pull back the rubber cover from the adjuster and loosen the lockwheel on the cable **(see illustration)**. Turn the adjuster until the desired freeplay is obtained, then retighten the lockwheel.

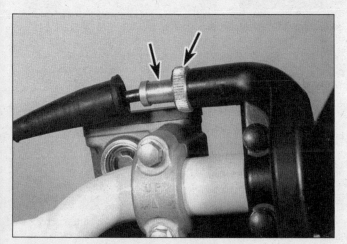

4.4 Loosen the lockwheel (right arrow) and turn the adjuster (left arrow) to make minor freeplay adjustments

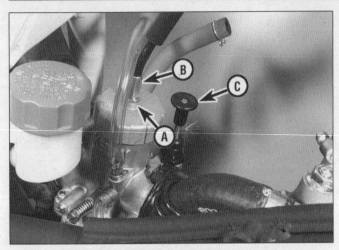

4.5 To make major adjustments, loosen the locknut (A) and turn the adjuster (B); the choke knob (C) should operate smoothly

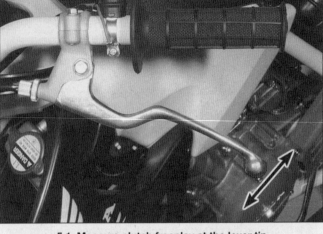

5.1 Measure clutch freeplay at the lever tip

5   If the freeplay can't be adjusted at the grip end, loosen the locknut at the carburetor end of the cable **(see illustration)**. Turn the adjuster to set freeplay, then tighten the locknuts securely.

Choke - operation check

6   Check that the choke knob moves smoothly **(see illustration 4.5)**. If not, refer to Chapter 4 and remove the choke plunger for inspection.

5   Clutch - check and freeplay adjustment

Refer to illustrations 5.1 and 5.2

1   Operate the clutch lever and measure freeplay at the tip of the lever **(see illustration)**. If it's not within the range listed in this Chapter's Specifications, adjust it as follows.

2   To make minor adjustments, pull back the rubber cover from the adjuster at the handlebar **(see illustration)**. Loosen the lockwheel and turn the adjuster to change freeplay.

3   If freeplay can't be brought within specifications by using the handlebar adjuster, turn the handlebar adjuster in all the way, then back it out one turn.

CR80R/85R

Refer to illustration 5.4

4   Loosen the locknut on the lower cable adjuster and turn the adjuster to set freeplay **(see illustration)**. Tighten the locknuts on the upper and lower adjusters.

CR125R

Refer to illustration 5.5

5   Loosen the locknut on the midline cable adjuster behind the number plate **(see illustration)**. Turn the adjuster to set freeplay, then tighten the locknuts on the upper and midline adjusters.

All models

6   If freeplay still can't be adjusted to within the specified range, the cable is probably stretched and should be replaced with a new one (see Chapter 2).

6   Lubrication - general

Refer to illustration 6.3

1   Since the controls, cables and various other components of a motorcycle are exposed to the elements, they should be lubricated

5.2 Loosen the lockwheel (right arrow) and turn the adjuster (left arrow) to make minor adjustments

5.4 To make major clutch cable adjustments on a CR80R/85R, loosen the locknut (right arrow) and turn the adjusting nut (left arrow)

5.5 To make major clutch cable adjustments on a CR125R, loosen the locknut (right arrow) and turn the adjuster (left arrow)

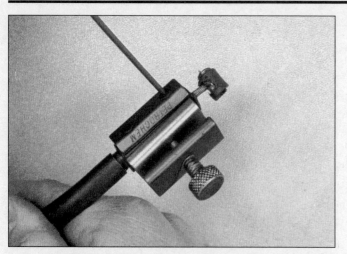

6.3 Lubricating a cable with a pressure lube adapter (make sure the tool seats around the inner cable)

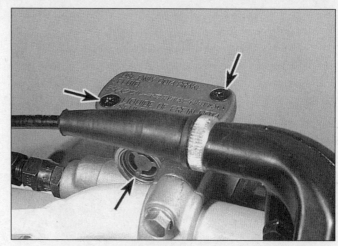

7.3 The front brake fluid level is visible in the window (lower arrow); remove the cover screws (upper arrows) and cover to add fluid

periodically to ensure safe and trouble-free operation.

2   The throttle twistgrip, brake lever, brake pedal and kickstarter pedal pivot should be lubricated frequently. In order for the lubricant to be applied where it will do the most good, the component should be disassembled. However, if chain and cable lubricant is being used, it can be applied to the pivot joint gaps and will usually work its way into the areas where friction occurs. If motor oil or light grease is being used, apply it sparingly as it may attract dirt (which could cause the controls to bind or wear at an accelerated rate). **Note:** *One of the best lubricants for the control lever pivots is a dry-film lubricant (available from many sources by different names).*

3   The throttle and clutch cables should be removed and treated with a commercially available cable lubricant which is specially formulated for use on motorcycle control cables. Small adapters for pressure lubricating the cables with spray can lubricants are available and ensure that the cable is lubricated along its entire length **(see illustration)**. When attaching the cable to the lever, be sure to lubricate the barrel-shaped fitting at the end with multi-purpose grease.

4   To lubricate the cables, disconnect them at the upper end, then lubricate the cable with a pressure lube adapter **(see illustration 6.3)**. See Chapter 4 (throttle cable) or Chapter 2 (clutch cable).

5   Lubrication of the swingarm and rear suspension linkage pivots requires removal of the components.

6   Refer to Chapter 6 for the following lubrication procedures:

a) *Swingarm bearings, dust seals and rear suspension linkage pivots*
b) *Steering head bearings*

7   Refer to Chapter 7 for the following lubrication procedures:

a) *Front and rear wheel bearings*
b) *Brake pedal pivot*

7   Brake fluid - check

Refer to illustrations 7.3 and 7.6

1   To ensure proper operation of the hydraulic disc brakes, the fluid level in the master cylinder reservoirs must be maintained within a safe range.

2   With the motorcycle supported in an upright position, turn the handlebars until the top of the front brake master cylinder is as level as possible.

3   The fluid level is visible in the window on the reservoir **(see illustration)**. Make sure the fluid level is above the Lower mark cast on the master cylinder body next to the reservoir.

4   If the fluid level is low, clean the area around the reservoir cover. Remove the cover screws and take off the cover, diaphragm retainer

and diaphragm **(see illustration 7.3)**. Add new brake fluid of the type listed in this Chapter's Specifications until the fluid level is even with the line cast inside the reservoir.

5   Install the diaphragm, retainer and cover, then tighten the cover screws securely.

6   The rear brake fluid level (on 2001 and earlier bikes with a rear disc brake) is visible through the master cylinder reservoir **(see illustration)**. If it's below the Lower mark cast in the reservoir body, the fluid must be replenished.

7   Unscrew the reservoir cap and pour in fluid to bring the level up to the Upper mark cast in the reservoir. Install the cap and tighten it securely.

8   The rear brake reservoir on 2002 and later models is integral with the master cylinder body. Remove three screws that secure the cap to the reservoir, then take off the cap and pull out the diaphragm. Fill the reservoir with fluid to the upper level line cast inside the reservoir.

9   Check the cover gasket for damage or deterioration, and replace it if necessary. Reinstall the cover and gasket, and install the screws.

8   Brake system - general check

1   A routine general check of the brakes will ensure that any problems are discovered and remedied before the rider's safety is jeopardized.

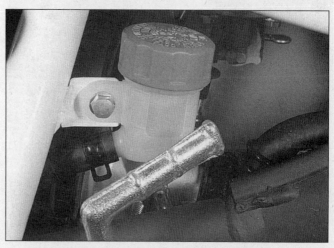

7.6 The rear brake fluid level is visible through the translucent reservoir

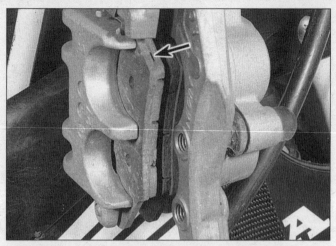

8.4a When the pad material is worn to or almost to the wear indicator groove, it's time for new pads (CR125R front caliper shown) . . .

8.4b . . . there's a similar groove at the back of the rear pads

2   Check the brake lever and pedal for loose connections, excessive play, bends, and other damage. Replace any damaged parts with new ones (see Chapter 7).
3   Make sure all brake fasteners are tight. Check the brakes for wear as described below.

Wear check

Disc brakes

Refer to illustrations 8.4a and 8.4b
4   There's a groove on the inside of each pad next to the metal backing **(see illustrations)**. When the friction material is nearly worn down to the groove, it's time to replace the pads (even if only one pad is worn that far).

Rear drum brakes

5   Operate the brake pedal. If operation is rough or sticky, refer to Section 6 and lubricate the cable.
6   With the rear brake lever and pedal freeplay properly adjusted (see Section 9), check the wear indicator triangular mark on the brake panel. If the slot in the brake arm lines up with the mark when the pedal is pressed, refer to Chapter 7 and replace the brake shoes.

9   Brake lever and pedal - check and adjustment

Front brake lever

1   Squeeze the front brake lever and note how far the lever travels (measure at the tip of the lever). If it exceeds the limit listed in this Chapter's Specifications, adjust the front brake.

CR80R/85R

Refer to illustration 9.2
2   Measure the gap between the adjusting screw and the steel ball inside the brake lever **(see illustration)**. If it's not within the range listed in this Chapter's Specifications, loosen the locknut, turn the adjusting screw to correct it and tighten the locknut. **Caution:** *Don't reduce the gap to less than the specified range.*

CR125R

Refer to illustration 9.3
3   Loosen the locknut and turn the adjusting screw **(see illustration)**. Tighten the locknut after making the adjustment.

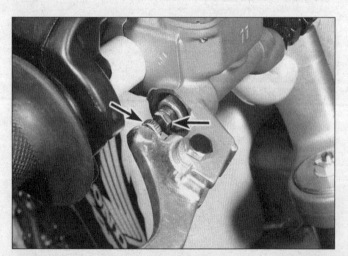

9.2 The CR80R/85R front brake lever should have a gap (left arrow) between the adjusting screw and the steel ball in the lever; loosen the locknut (right arrow) and turn the screw to change the gap

9.3 To adjust lever freeplay on a CR125R, loosen the locknut (right arrow) and turn the adjusting screw (left arrow)

All models

4   Recheck lever travel (see Step 1). If it's still not within the Specifications, refer to Chapter 7 and bleed the brakes.

Rear brake pedal

Drum brake models

5   To adjust brake pedal height, loosen the locknut and turn the adjusting bolt (they're mounted in a boss on the right side of the frame behind the brake pedal). Honda doesn't specify pedal height.
6   Check the play of the brake pedal. If it exceeds the limit listed in this Chapter's Specifications, adjust it with the wingnut at the rear end of the brake rod.

Disc brake models

Refer to illustration 9.7

7   To adjust pedal height, loosen the locknut and turn the pushrod on the rear master cylinder **(see illustration)**. Although pedal height isn't specified, Honda does specify a length for 1992 and later CR125R models; this is listed in this Chapter's Specifications.
8   Pedal freeplay on disc brake models is automatic and no means of manual adjustment is provided.

9.7 To adjust disc brake pedal height, loosen the locknut (lower arrow) and turn the master cylinder pushrod with the hex (upper arrow)

10   Tires/wheels - general check

Refer to illustrations 10.4, 10.5 and 10.7

1   Routine tire and wheel checks should be made with the realization that your safety depends to a great extent on their condition.
2   Check the tires carefully for cuts, tears, embedded nails or other sharp objects and excessive wear. Operation of the motorcycle with excessively worn tires is extremely hazardous, as traction and handling are directly affected. Check the tread depth at the center of the tire and compare it to the value listed in this Chapter's Specifications. Honda doesn't specify a minimum tread depth for some models, but as a general rule, tires should be replaced with new ones when the tread knobs are worn to 8 mm (5/16 inch) or less.
3   Repair or replace punctured tires as soon as damage is noted. Do not try to patch a torn tire, as wheel balance and tire reliability may be impaired.
4   Check the tire pressures when the tires are cold and keep them properly inflated **(see illustration)**. Proper air pressure will increase tire life and provide maximum stability and ride comfort. Keep in mind that low tire pressures may cause the tire to slip on the rim or come off, while high tire pressures will cause abnormal tread wear and unsafe handling.
5   The wheels should be kept clean and checked periodically for cracks, bending, loose spokes and rust. Never attempt to repair dam-

aged wheels; they must be replaced with new ones. Loose spokes can be tightened with a spoke wrench **(see illustration)**, but be careful not to overtighten and distort the wheel rim.
6   Check the valve stem locknuts to make sure they're tight. Also, make sure the valve stem cap is in place and tight. If it is missing, install a new one made of metal or hard plastic.
7   Check the tightness of the locknut on the rim lock **(see illustration)**. Tighten it if necessary to the torque listed in this Chapter's Specifications.

11   Drive chain and sprockets - check, adjustment and lubrication

Refer to illustrations 11.3, 11.6a, 11.6b, 11.6c, 11.7a and 11.7b

1   A neglected drive chain won't last long and can quickly damage the sprockets. Routine chain adjustment isn't difficult and will ensure maximum chain and sprocket life. **Note:** *The chain should be routinely replaced at the interval listed in Section 1.*
2   To check the chain, support the bike securely with the rear wheel off the ground. Place the transmission in neutral.
3   Push down and pull up on the top run of the chain and measure

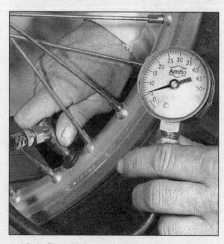

10.4 Check tire pressure with a gauge

10.5 Make sure the spokes are tight, but don't overtighten them

10.7 Tighten the locknut on the rim lock to the specified torque

11.3 Measure drive chain slack along the upper chain run; check the swingarm slider (arrow) for wear

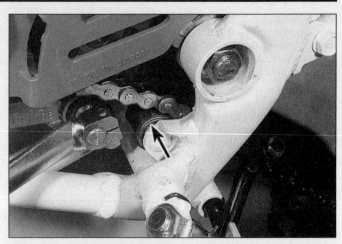

11.6a Later CR80R/85R models have a lower chain roller near the shift peal (arrow); early CR80R/85R models have a forward chain slider in the same area

the slack midway between the two sprockets **(see illustration)**, then compare the measurements to the value listed in this Chapter's Specifications. As wear occurs, the chain will actually stretch, which

11.6b On CR125R models, check the chain slider and lower roller for wear (arrows) . . .

means adjustment by removing some slack from the chain. In some cases where lubrication has been neglected, corrosion and galling may cause the links to bind and kink, which effectively shortens the chain's length. If the chain is tight between the sprockets, rusty or kinked, it's time to replace it with a new one. **Note:** *Repeat the chain slack measurement along the length of the chain - ideally, every inch or so. If you find a tight area, mark it with a felt pen or paint and repeat the measurement after the bike has been ridden. If the chain's still tight in the same areas, it may be damaged or worn. Because a tight or kinked chain can damage the transmission countershaft bearing, it's a good idea to replace it.*

4   Check the entire length of the chain for damaged rollers, loose links and loose pins.

5   Look through the slots in the engine sprocket cover and inspect the engine sprocket. Check the teeth on the engine sprocket and the rear sprocket for wear (see Chapter 6). Refer to Chapter 6 for the sprocket replacement procedure if the sprockets appear to be worn excessively.

6   Check the chain sliders and roller(s) **(see illustrations)**. If a slider is worn, measure its thickness. If it's less than the value listed in this Chapter's Specifications, replace it (see Chapter 6).

7   Look through the small hole in the chain slider bolted to the underside of the swingarm **(see illustrations)**. If you can see the chain through the hole, the slider is worn. Replace it. **Note:** *If you're working on a 1987 through 1989 CR125R, look through the upper hole in the*

11.6c . . . also check the upper chain roller

11.7a If the chain can be seen through the wear window on the lower chain slider, it's time for a new slider (this is a later CR80R) . . .

11.7b . . . and this is a later CR125R (other models similar)

11.9a Later CR80R/85R models use this type of chain adjuster; loosen the locknut and turn the bolt to make adjustments . . .

11.9b . . . later CR125R models use this design

slider if you're using a 49-tooth or 51-tooth rear sprocket; look through the lower hole if you're using a 53-tooth or 55-tooth rear sprocket.

Adjustment

Refer to illustrations 11.9a and 11.9b

8   Rotate the rear wheel until the chain is positioned with the least amount of slack present.

9   Loosen the rear axle nut (see Chapter 7). Loosen the locknut and turn the adjuster on each side of the swingarm evenly until the proper chain tension is obtained (get the adjuster on the chain side close, then set the adjuster on the opposite side) **(see illustrations)**. Be sure to turn the adjusters evenly to keep the wheel in alignment. If the adjusters reach the end of their travel, the chain is excessively worn and should be replaced with a new one (see Chapter 6).

10   When the chain has the correct amount of slack, make sure the marks on the adjusters correspond to the same relative marks on each side of the swingarm **(see illustrations 11.9a and 11.9b)**. Tighten the axle nut to the torque listed in the Chapter 7 Specifications.

Lubrication

Note: *If the chain is dirty, it should be removed and cleaned before it's lubricated (see Chapter 6).*

11   Use a good quality chain lubricant of the type listed in this Chapter's Specifications. Apply the lubricant along the top of the lower chain run, so that when the bike is ridden centrifugal force will move the lubricant into the chain, rather than throwing it off.

12   After applying the lubricant, let it soak in a few minutes before wiping off any excess.

12 Fasteners - check

1   Since vibration of the machine tends to loosen fasteners, all nuts, bolts, screws, etc. should be periodically checked for proper tightness. Also make sure all cotter pins or other safety fasteners are correctly installed.

2   Pay particular attention to the following:

Spark plug
Transmission oil drain plug and check bolt
Gearshift pedal
Brake lever and pedal
Kickstarter pedal
Footpegs
Engine mounting bolts
Steering stem locknut

Front axle nut
Rear axle nut
Skid plate bolts

3   If a torque wrench is available, use it along with the torque specifications at the beginning of this, or other, Chapters.

13 Suspension - check

Refer to illustration 13.4

1   The suspension components must be maintained in top operating condition to ensure rider safety. Loose, worn or damaged suspension parts decrease the motorcycle's stability and control.

2   Lock the front brake and push on the handlebars to compress the front forks several times. See if they move up-and-down smoothly without binding. If binding is felt, the forks should be disassembled and inspected as described in Chapter 6.

3   Check the tightness of all front suspension nuts and bolts to be sure none have worked loose.

4   With the front forks cold and fully extended (bike jacked up so the front wheel is off the ground), remove the air valve caps or pressure release screws from the forks and check air pressure with a pressure gauge **(see illustration)**. Compare with the reading listed in this Chapter's Specifications. **Note:** *Air will heat up and expand during a race, stiffening the forks.*

13.4 Remove the air valve cap to check fork pressure

14.1 Follow safety precautions when removing the radiator cap

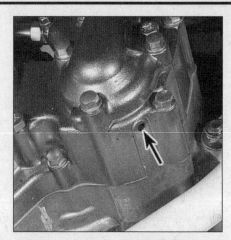

15.5 If coolant is leaking from the small hole under the water pump (arrow), it's time for a new water pump seal

16.1 Remove the water pump drain bolt (right arrow); the similar bolt behind it (left arrow) is used to check transmission oil level

5   Inspect the rear shock absorber for fluid leakage and tightness of the mounting nuts and bolts. If leakage is found, the shock should be replaced.

6   Support the motorcycle securely upright with its rear wheel off the ground. Grab the swingarm on each side, just ahead of the axle. Rock the swingarm from side to side - there should be no discernible movement at the rear. If there's a little movement or a slight clicking can be heard, make sure the swingarm pivot shaft is tight. If the pivot shaft is tight but movement is still noticeable, the swingarm will have to be removed and the bearings replaced as described in Chapter 6.

7   Inspect the tightness of the rear suspension nuts and bolts.

14   Coolant level - check

Refer to illustration 14.1

Warning: *Checking the coolant level on these bikes requires removal of the radiator cap. Always be sure the engine is cool before removing the radiator cap; otherwise, scalding coolant may spray out of the radiator opening, causing serious burns.*

1   With the engine cool, unscrew the radiator cap **(see illustration)**. Coolant should be up to the bottom of the filler neck.

2   If the coolant level is low, top up with the mixture of antifreeze and water listed in this Chapter's Specifications.

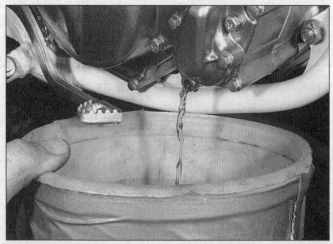

16.2 Remove the radiator cap so the coolant can drain freely

15   Cooling system - inspection

Refer to illustration 15.5

1   Refer to Chapter 3 and remove the radiator shrouds. Clean mud, leaves or other obstructions out of the radiator fins with low-pressure water or compressed air.

2   If any fins are bent, carefully straighten them with a small screwdriver, taking care not to puncture the coolant tubes in the radiator.

3   If more than 20 percent of the radiator's surface area is blocked, replace the radiator.

4   Check the coolant hoses for swelling, cracks, burns, cuts or other defects. Replace the hoses if their condition is doubtful. Make sure the hose clamps are tight and free of corrosion. Tighten loose clamps and replace corroded or damaged ones.

5   Check for leaks at the water pump weep hole **(see illustration)** and gaskets. Also check for leaks at the coolant drain plug(s). Replace water pump or drain plug gaskets if they've been leaking. If coolant has been leaking from the weep hole, it's time for a new water pump seal (see Chapter 3).

16   Coolant - change

Refer to illustrations 16.1, 16.2 and 16.3

Warning 1: *Do not allow antifreeze to come in contact with your skin or painted surfaces of the vehicle. Rinse off spills immediately with plenty of water. Antifreeze is highly toxic if ingested. Never leave antifreeze lying around in an open container or in puddles on the floor; children and pets are attracted by its sweet smell and may drink it. Check with local authorities about disposing of used antifreeze. Many communities have collection centers which will see that antifreeze is disposed of safely.*

Warning 2: *Don't remove the radiator cap or the drain bolts when the engine and radiator are hot. Scalding coolant and steam may be blown out under pressure, which could cause serious injury. To open the radiator cap or the drain bolts, place a thick rag, like a towel, over the radiator cap; slowly rotate the cap counterclockwise to the first stop. This procedure allows any residual pressure to escape. When the steam has stopped escaping, press down on the cap while turning it counterclockwise and remove it.*

1   Place a drain pan beneath the water pump drain bolt **(see illustration)**.

2   Remove the drain bolt. Coolant will dribble out until the radiator cap is removed, then it will flow **(see illustration)**.

3   Remove the cylinder drain bolt **(see illustration)** and let the coolant drain.

16.3 There's another drain bolt on the cylinder (arrow)

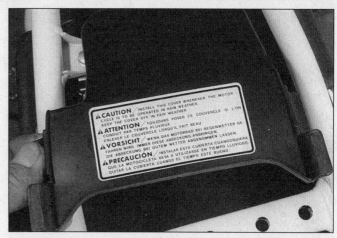

17.2 Remove the rain cover if it's in place; use the cover only in wet riding conditions and leave it off when it's dry

17.3a Unscrew the element bolt until it's loose . . .

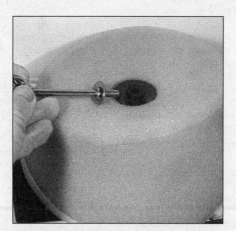

17.3b . . . then lift out the element and remove the bolt

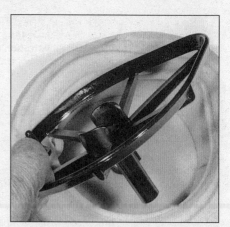

17.4 Separate the foam element from the holder for cleaning and re-oiling

4   Once the coolant has drained completely, place new gaskets on the drain screws and install them in the engine. Fill the cooling system with the antifreeze and water mixture listed in this Chapter's Specifications.

5   Lean the bike about twenty-degrees to one side, then the other, several times. This will allow air trapped in the coolant passages to make its way to the top of the coolant.

6   Check coolant level. It should be up to the bottom of the radiator filler neck. Add more antifreeze/water mixture if necessary.

7   Start the engine and check for leaks. Warm up the engine, then let it cool completely and recheck the coolant level.

17 Air cleaner element - replace

Refer to illustrations 17.2, 17.3a, 17.3b, 17.4, 17.8 and 17.10

1   Remove the seat (see Chapter 8).

2   If the rain cover is in place, lift it off **(see illustration)**.

3   Unscrew the filter element bolt **(see illustration)**. Lift out the element and pull the bolt out of it **(see illustration)**.

4   Separate the element holder from the foam element **(see illustration)**.

5   Thoroughly clean the element in high-flash point or non-flammable safety solvent. Do not use gasoline. After cleaning, squeeze out the solvent and allow the element to dry completely.

6   Coat the element with foam filter oil recommended in this Chapter's Specifications, then squeeze the element to work the oil through the foam. Once the element is soaked with oil, squeeze out the excess.

7   Place the holder on the element. On some models, there's an inner tab on the end foam piece; align this with the groove in the element holder.

8   Install the element in the case with its locating tab up **(see illustration)**. Some models have a triangular mark on the end of the air cleaner case; align the locating tab with this mark.

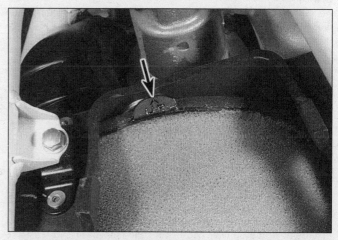

17.8 The holder tab (arrow) should be up when the element is installed

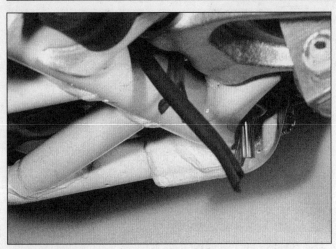

17.10 Clean the drain tubes if they're clogged

18.4 The transmission oil filler cap is on the upper right side of the crankcase

9   The remainder of installation is the reverse of the removal steps.

10   Check the drain tubes **(see illustration)**. If a tube is clogged, squeeze its clamp, remove it from the air cleaner housing and clean it out. Install the drain tube on the housing and secure it with the clamp.

18   Transmission oil level - check

Refer to illustration 18.4

1   Start the engine and run it for three minutes. **Warning:** *Do not run the engine in an enclosed space such as a garage or shop.*

2   Stop the engine and allow the bike to sit undisturbed in a level position for three minutes. Be sure it's upright.

3   With the engine off, unscrew the oil check bolt **(see illustration 16.1)**. A small amount of oil should flow out of the hole.

4   If no oil flows out of the hole, remove the oil filler cap **(see illustration)**. Add oil through the filler cap hole until it starts to flow from the check bolt hole. Let any excess drain, then reinstall the check bolt and filler cap.

19   Transmission oil - change

Refer to illustration 19.5

1   Consistent routine oil changes are the single most important maintenance procedure you can perform on these models. The oil not only lubricates the internal parts of the transmission and clutch, but it also acts as a coolant, a cleaner, a sealant, and a protectant. Because of these demands, the oil takes a terrific amount of abuse and should be replaced often with new oil of the recommended grade and type. Saving a little money on the difference in cost between a good oil and a cheap oil won't pay off if the engine is damaged. Honda recommends against using the following:

a) *Oils with graphite or molybdenum additives*
b) *Non-detergent oils*
c) *Castor or vegetable based oils*
d) *Oil additives*

2   Before changing the oil, warm up the engine by running it for three minutes so the oil will drain easily. Be careful when draining the oil, as the exhaust pipe, the engine and the oil itself can cause severe burns.

3   Park the motorcycle over a clean drain pan.

4   Remove the oil filler cap to vent the crankcase and act as a reminder that there is no oil in the engine. Also remove the oil check bolt **(see illustrations 16.1 and 18.4)**.

5   Next, remove the drain plug from the crankcase **(see illustration)** and allow the oil to drain into the pan. Do not lose the sealing washer on the drain plug.

6   Check the condition of the drain plug threads. Replace the plug if the threads are damaged.

7   Slip a new sealing washer over the drain plug, then install and tighten the plug to the torque listed in this Chapter's Specifications. Avoid overtightening, as damage to the threads or engine case will result.

8   Before refilling the engine, check the old oil carefully. If the oil was drained into a clean pan, small pieces of metal or other material can be easily detected. If the oil is very metallic colored, then the engine is experiencing wear from break-in (new engine) or from insufficient lubrication. If there are flakes or chips of metal in the oil, then something is drastically wrong internally and the engine will have to be disassembled for inspection and repair.

9   If there are pieces of fiber-like material in the oil, the clutch is experiencing excessive wear and should be checked.

10   If the inspection of the oil turns up nothing unusual, refill the engine as described below.

11   With the bike supported in an upright position, fill the crankcase until oil begins to flow from the check bolt hole. The specified capacity is only a guide; use the check bolt to determine the exact amount of oil to use.

12   Allow excess oil to flow from the check bolt hole, then install the

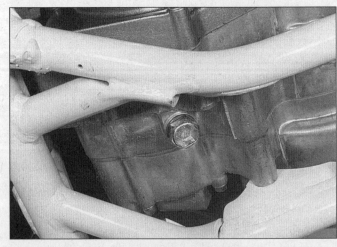

19.5 The transmission oil drain plug is on the bottom of the crankcase

check bolt with a new sealing washer and tighten it to the torque listed in this Chapter's Specifications. Install the filler cap.

13   Check around the drain plug and check bolt for leaks.

14   The old oil drained from the engine cannot be reused in its present state and should be disposed of. Check with your local refuse disposal company, disposal facility or environmental agency to see whether they will accept the oil for recycling. Don't pour used oil into drains or onto the ground. After the oil has cooled, it can be drained into a suitable container (capped plastic jugs, topped bottles, milk cartons, etc.) for transport to one of these disposal sites.

20   Spark plug - check and replacement

Refer to illustrations 20.1, 20.2, 20.6a and 20.6b

1   Twist the spark plug cap to break it free from the plug, then pull it off **(see illustration)**.

2   If available, use compressed air to blow any accumulated debris from around the spark plug. Remove the plug with a spark plug socket **(see illustration)**.

3   Inspect the electrodes for wear. Both the center and side electrodes should have square edges and the side electrode should be of uniform thickness. Look for excessive deposits (especially oil fouling) and evidence of a cracked or chipped insulator around the center electrode. Compare your spark plug to the color spark plug chart on the inside of the back cover. Check the threads, the washer and the ceramic insulator body for cracks and other damage.

4   If the electrodes are not excessively worn, and if the deposits can be easily removed with a wire brush, the plug can be regapped and reused (if no cracks or chips are visible in the insulator). If in doubt concerning the condition of the plug, replace it with a new one, as the expense is minimal. The plug should be replaced at the interval listed in the maintenance schedule.

5   Cleaning the spark plug by sandblasting is permitted, provided you clean the plug with a high flash-point solvent afterwards.

6   Before installing a new plug, make sure it is the correct type and heat range. Check the gap between the electrodes, as it is not preset. For best results, use a wire-type gauge rather than a flat gauge to check the gap **(see illustration)**. If the gap must be adjusted, bend the side electrode only and be very careful not to chip or crack the insulator nose **(see illustration)**. Make sure the washer is in place before installing the plug.

7   Since the cylinder head is made of aluminum, which is soft and easily damaged, thread the plug into the head by hand. Slip a short length of hose over the end of the plug to use as a tool to thread it into

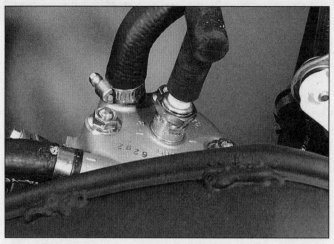

20.1 Twist the spark plug cap back and forth to free it, then pull it off the plug

place. The hose will grip the plug well enough to turn it, but will start to slip if the plug begins to cross-thread in the hole - this will prevent damaged threads and the accompanying repair costs.

8   Once the plug is finger tight, tighten the plug to the torque listed in this Chapter's Specifications.

9   Reconnect the spark plug cap.

21   Cylinder compression - check

1   Among other things, poor engine performance may be caused by a leaking head gasket, or worn piston, rings and/or cylinder wall. A cylinder compression check will help pinpoint these conditions and can also indicate the presence of excessive carbon deposits in the cylinder head.

2   The only tools required are a compression gauge, shown in the special tools section at the beginning of the book, and a spark plug wrench. Depending on the outcome of the initial test, a squirt-type oil can may also be needed.

3   Start the engine and allow it to reach normal operating temperature, then remove the spark plug (see Section 20, if necessary). Work carefully - don't strip the spark plug hole threads and don't burn your hands.

20.2 Remove the spark plug with a socket like this one

20.6a Spark plug manufacturers recommend using a wire type gauge when checking the gap - if the wire doesn't slide between the electrodes with a slight drag, adjustment is required

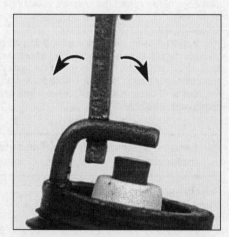

20.6b To change the gap, bend the side electrode only, as indicated by the arrows, and be very careful not to crack or chip the ceramic insulator surrounding the center electrode

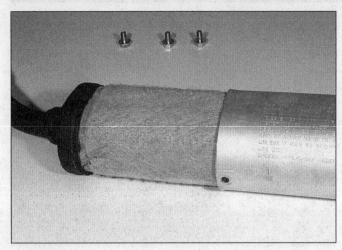

22.6a Pull the inner pipe and glass wool out of the muffler . . .

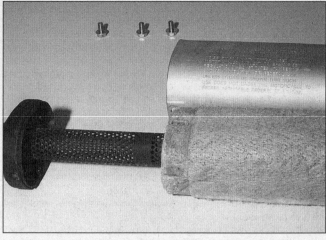

22.6b . . . and separate the inner pipe from the glass wool

4   Disable the ignition by disconnecting the primary (low tension) wires from the coil (see Chapter 5). Be sure to mark the locations of the wires before detaching them.

5   Install the compression gauge in the spark plug hole. Hold or block the throttle wide open.

6   Kick the engine over a minimum of four or five revolutions (or until the gauge reading stops increasing) and observe the initial movement of the compression gauge needle as well as the final total gauge reading. Note the reading. Although Honda doesn't specify cylinder compression pressure for these models, the reading can serve as a basis for comparison.

7   If the compression built up quickly and evenly, you can assume the engine upper end is in reasonably good mechanical condition. Worn or sticking piston rings and worn cylinders will produce very little initial movement of the gauge needle, but compression will tend to build up gradually as the engine spins over. Head gasket leakage, cylinder base leakage or crankcase compression leakage is indicated by low initial compression which does not tend to build up.

8   To further confirm your findings, add a small amount of engine oil to the cylinder by inserting the nozzle of a squirt-type oil can through the spark plug hole. The oil will tend to seal the piston ring if it is leaking.

9   If the compression increases significantly after the addition of the oil, the piston ring and/or cylinder are definitely worn. If the compression does not increase, the pressure is leaking past the head gasket or base gasket or the crankcase compression is low. Refer to Chapter 2 for crankcase compression testing.

10   If compression readings are considerably higher than normal, the combustion chamber is probably coated with excessive carbon deposits. It is possible (but not very likely) for carbon deposits to raise the compression enough to compensate for the effects of leakage. Refer to Chapter 2, remove the cylinder head and carefully decarbonize the combustion chamber.

22   Exhaust system - inspection and glass wool replacement

Refer to illustrations 22.6a and 22.6b
Warning: *Make sure the exhaust system is cool before doing this procedure.*

1   Periodically check the exhaust system for leaks and loose fasteners (see Chapter 4).

2   Check the expansion chamber springs at the cylinder to make sure they're unbroken and securely attached. Replace broken springs.

3   Check the expansion chamber for cracks or dents. The shape of the chamber has an important effect on engine performance, so dents

should not be ignored. Small dents can be removed or large dented areas replaced using body shop sheet metal repair techniques.

4   At the specified interval, clean the inner pipe and replace the glass wool in the muffler as described below.

5   If you're working on a 1986 through 1995 CR80R, remove the lower bolt from the rear end of the muffler. Loosen the upper bolt slightly, but don't remove it. Tap against the upper bolt with a plastic mallet to push the inner pipe out of the muffler, then pull out the glass wool insert.

6   If you're working on a 1996 or later CR80R/85R or a CR125R, place the muffler bracket in a padded vise. Remove the bolts from the rear end of the muffler, then pull out the inner pipe and glass wool insert. Pull the inner pipe out of the glass wool **(see illustrations)**.

7   Clean the small holes in the inner pipe with a wire brush.

8   Apply muffler sealant to the front and rear ends of the inner pipe where it contacts the muffler case. Install a new glass wool insert and the inner pipe in the case. Tighten the bolts to the torque listed in this Chapter's Specifications.

23   Steering head bearings - check and adjustment

Inspection

1   These motorcycles are equipped with ball-and-cone or roller-and-cone type steering head bearings, which can become dented, rough or loose during normal use of the machine. In extreme cases, worn or loose steering head bearings can cause steering wobble that is potentially dangerous.

2   To check the bearings, lift up the front end of the motorcycle and place a secure support beneath the engine so the front wheel is off the ground.

3   Point the wheel straight ahead and slowly move the handlebars from side-to-side. Dents or roughness in the bearing will be felt and the bars will not move smoothly. **Note:** *Make sure any hesitation in movement is not being caused by the cables and wiring harnesses that run to the handlebars.*

4   Next, grasp the fork legs and try to move the wheel forward and backward. Any looseness in the steering head bearing s will be felt. If play is felt in the bearings, adjust the steering head as follows.

Adjustment

Refer to illustrations 23.6 and 23.9

5   Remove the handlebars and upper triple clamp (see Chapter 6).

6   Loosen the bearing adjusting nut, then tighten it to the torque listed in this Chapter's Specifications **(see illustration)**.

7   Turn the lower triple clamp from lock-to-lock (all the way to the left

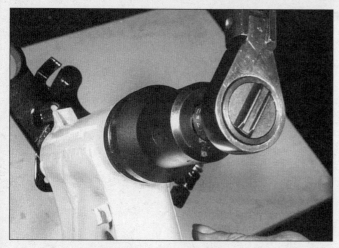

23.6 The best way to adjust the steering stem bearings is with a torque wrench and a special socket . . .

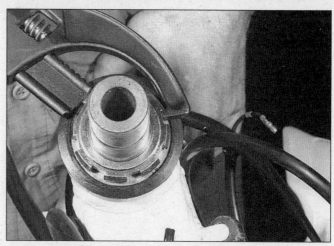

23.9 . . . but an adjustable spanner can also be used; be very sure there's no binding or looseness in the bearings

and all the way back to the right) four or five times to seat the bearings.
8   Loosen the adjusting nut all the way, then tighten it to the final torque listed in this Chapter's Specifications.
9   An adjustable wrench can be used to adjust the bearings if you don't have the special socket (see illustration). Since this tool can't be used with a torque wrench, it will be necessary to estimate the tightness of the nut. Be sure the final result is that the steering stem turns from side-to-side freely, but there is no side-to-side or vertical play of the steering stem in the bearings.

24   Front fork oil change

Refer to illustration 24.6
1   The following steps apply to the damper rod forks used on the 1986 through 1995 CR80R. On other models, which are equipped with cartridge forks, you'll need to disassemble the forks part-way to drain the oil (see Chapter 6).
2   Support the motorcycle securely upright.
3   Remove the handlebars (see Chapter 6).
4   Remove the fork cap bolts.
5   Wrap a rag around the top of the fork to catch dripping oil, the lift out the fork spring from each fork.
6   Place a pan under the fork drain bolt and remove the drain bolt and gasket (see illustration). Warning: *Do not allow the fork oil to drip onto the tire or brake disc. If it does, wash it off with soap and water before riding the motorcycle.*
7   After most of the oil has drained, slowly compress and release the forks to pump out the rest of the oil. An assistant may be needed to do this.
8   Check the drain bolt gasket for damage and replace it if necessary. Clean the threads of the drain bolt with solvent and let it dry, then reinstall the bolt and gasket, tightening it securely.
9   Pour the type and amount of fork oil listed in the Chapter 6 Specifications into the fork tube through the opening at the top. Slowly pump the forks a few times to purge air from the upper and lower chambers.

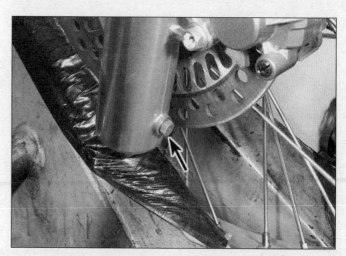

24.6 Some models have a fork oil drain bolt (arrow)

10   Fully compress the front forks (you may need an assistant to do this). Insert a stiff tape measure into the fork tube and measure the distance from the oil to the top of the fork tube (see Chapter 6). Compare your measurement to the value listed in the Chapter 6 Specifications, drain or add oil as necessary until the level is correct.
11   Check the O-ring on the fork cap bolt and replace it with a new one if it's deteriorated, broken or otherwise damaged. Install the fork spring. Install the cap bolt and tighten it to the Chapter 6 Specifications.
12   Repeat the procedure for the other fork. It is essential that the oil quantity and level are identical in each fork.
13   Install the handlebar, being sure to locate it correctly in the brackets, and tighten the handlebar bracket bolts to the torque listed in the Chapter 6 Specifications.

Notes

Chapter 1 Part B
Tune-up and routine maintenance (CR250R and CR500R models)

Contents

Specifications

Engine

Spark plug type
CR250R
1986	NGK BR8EG, Champion QN-86 or ND W24ESR-V
1987 and 1988	NGK BR9EG, Champion QN-84 or ND W27ESR-V
1989 through 2004	NGK BR8EG, Champion QN-86 or ND W24ESR-V
2005 and later	NGK BR9EG-N-8
CR500R	NGK BR8EG, Champion QN-86 or ND W24ESR-V

Spark plug gap
CR250R
2004 and earlier	0.5 to 0.6 mm (0.020 to 0.024 inch)
2005 and later	0.7 to 0.8 mm (0.027 to 0.031 inch)
CR500R	0.5 to 0.6 mm (0.020 to 0.024 inch)

Miscellaneous

Brake pad lining thickness limit	1.0 mm (3/64 inch), or bottom of wear groove
Rear brake shoe lining limit (drum brakes)	1.0 mm (3/64 inch)
Front brake lever freeplay	
At lever tip	
1986 through 1991	Less than 30 mm (1-1/4 inch)
1992 on	Less than 20 mm (3/4 inch)
At adjuster gap	0.1 to 1.4 mm (0.004 to 0.055 inch)
Rear brake pedal freeplay (drum brake models)	20 to 30 mm (3/4 to 1-1/4 inch)
Rear master cylinder bolt length (1992 and later CR250R)	
2001 and earlier	75.0 mm (2.95 inches)
2002 and later	79.6 mm (3.13 inches)
Clutch lever freeplay	10 to 20 mm (3/8 to 3/4 inch)
Throttle grip freeplay	3 to 5 mm (1/8 to 1/4 inch)
Fork air pressure	
1986 through 1989	
Standard	0 psi
Maximum	6 psi
1990 on	0 psi
Minimum tire tread depth	Not specified
Tire pressures (cold)	15 psi front and rear

Miscellaneous (continued)

Tire sizes
  CR250R
    Front
      1986 through 1997 .... 80/100-21 51M
      1998 and 1999 .... Not specified
      2000 and later 80/100-21 51M
    Rear
      1986 through 1996 .... 110/100-18 64M
      1997 .... 110/90-19 62M
      1998 and 1999 .... Not specified
      2000 and later 110/90-19 62M
  CR500R
    Front 80/100-21 51M
    Rear 110/100-18 64M
Drive chain slack
  CR250R
    1986 through 1991 .... 35 to 40 mm (1-3/8 to 1-9/16 inch)
    1992 through 1996 .... 45 to 55 mm (1-7/8 to 2-1/4 inch)
    1997 on .... 25 to 35 mm (1 to 1-3/8 inch)
  CR500R
    1986 through 1992 .... 35 to 40 mm (1-3/8 to 1-9/16 inch)
    1993 on .... 35 to 45 mm (1-3/8 to 1-49/64 inch)
Chain slider groove depth limit (in top surface)
  1986 CR500R .... 9.0 mm (0.35 inch)
  All others .... 5.0 mm(0.20 inch)
Chain roller diameter limit
  Upper roller .... 25 mm (1 inch)
  Lower roller
    1999 and earlier CR250R, all CR500R .... 25 mm (1 inch)
    2000 and later CR250R .... 39 mm (1.54 inch)

Torque specifications

Transmission oil check bolt .... 10 Nm (84 in-lbs)
Transmission oil drain plug .... 30 Nm (22 ft-lbs)
Spark plug .... 18 Nm (13 ft-lbs)
Wheel spokes .... 3.8 Nm (32 inch-lbs)
Rim lock locknut .... 13 Nm (108 in-lbs)
Steering stem adjusting nut
  CR250R
    1986 through 1991 .... 1 to 2 Nm (9 to 17 inch-lbs)
    1992 and 1993 .... 2 Nm (17 inch-lbs)
    1994 on .... 7 Nm (61 inch-lbs)
  CR500R
    1986 through 1989 .... 1 to 2 Nm (9 to 17 inch-lbs)
    1990 and 1991 .... 8 to 12 Nm (72 to 108 inch-lbs)
    1992 through 1994 .... 2 Nm (17 inch-lbs)
    1995 on .... 13 Nm (108 inch-lbs)

Recommended lubricants and fluids

Fuel
  1986 through 1991 .... 20:1 mix of gasoline (92 to 100 Research octane) and Honda two-stroke oil or equivalent
  1992 on .... 32:1 mix of gasoline (90 or higher pump octane) and Honda two-stroke oil or equivalent
Transmission oil
  Type .... API grade SF or SG multigrade four-stroke oil manufactured for use in motorcycles
  Viscosity
    All temperatures (recommended) 10W-40
    32-degrees F or above .... 20W-40 or 2W-50
    10 to 90-degrees F 10W-30
  Capacity at oil change*
    CR250R
      1986 through 1989 .... 550 cc (0.63 qt)
      1990 and 1991 .... 630 cc (0.67 qt)
      1992 .... 850 cc (0.9 qt)
      1993 through 2001 .... 750 cc (0.79 qt)
      2002 and later .... 650 cc (0.69 qt)

CR500R
    1986 through 1989 .... 650 cc (22 fl oz)
    1990 on... 680 cc (23 fl oz)
Air cleaner element oil .... Honda foam filter oil or equivalent
Coolant
    Type .... Ethylene glycol antifreeze compatible with aluminum engines, mixed 50/50 with water

Capacity (at coolant change)
    CR250R
        1986 and 1987 .... 0.96 liter (1.0 qt)
        1988 through 1991... 0.81 liter (0.85 qt)
        1992 through 1996... 1.10 liter (1.16 qt)
        1997 through 1999... 1.26 liter (1.32 qt)
        2000 on... 1.22 liter (1.29 qt)
    CR500R .... 1.08 liter (1.14 qt)
Brake fluid .... DOT 4
Drive chain lubricant.. Chain lube
Miscellaneous
    Wheel bearings .... Medium weight, lithium-based multi-purpose grease
    Swingarm pivot bearings .... Molybdenum disulfide paste grease containing 40 percent or more molybdenum disulfide

    Cables and lever pivots .... Engine oil
    Throttle grip... Engine oil
    Brake pedal/shift lever/throttle lever pivots .... Medium weight, lithium-based multi-purpose grease

*Approximate capacity; use oil check bolt to determine exact amount (see text).

1 Honda CR250R/500R Routine maintenance intervals

Note: *This schedule was developed for your motorcycle's intended purpose, motocross competition. It's based on hours of running time or the equivalent number of races. The intervals listed below are the shortest intervals recommended by the manufacturer for each particular operation during the model years covered in this manual. Your owner's manual may have different intervals for your model.*

Every 2.5 hours of running time (or before each race)

    Make sure the engine kill switch works properly
    Check the throttle for smooth operation and correct freeplay
    Check clutch operation and freeplay
    Inspect and lubricate the control cables
    Check the brake fluid level (hydraulic brakes)
    Check the operation of both brakes - check the front brake lever and rear brake pedal for correct freeplay
    Check the brake pads and shoes for wear
    Check the tires for damage, the presence of foreign objects and correct air pressure
    Lubricate and inspect the drive chain, sprockets, rollers and sliders
    Check all fasteners, including axle nuts, for tightness
    Inspect the front and rear suspensions
    Check the coolant level and inspect the cooling system
    Clean the air filter element*
    Clean and gap the spark plug
    Clean and inspect the Honda Power Port or Composite Racing Valve system (if equipped) (see Chapter 4)

    Inspect the reed valve (see Chapter 2)
    Inspect the expansion chamber and muffler

Every 7.5 hours of running time (or before every third race)

    Replace the spark plug
    Change the transmission oil
    Decarbonize the cylinder head (see Chapter 2)
    Replace the piston and piston ring (see Chapter 2)
    Replace the drive chain
    Change the fork oil
    Lubricate the swingarm bearings and shock linkage pivot points (see Chapter 6)

Every 22.5 running hours (or before every ninth race)

    Replace the piston pin and connecting rod upper end bearing (see Chapter 2)
    Inspect the steering head bearings

Every two years

    Change the brake fluid (see Chapter 7)
    Change the coolant
* After every moto in dusty conditions.

2   Introduction to tune-up and routine maintenance

Refer to illustration 2.1

This Chapter covers in detail the checks and procedures necessary for the tune-up and routine maintenance of your motorcycle. Section 1 includes the routine maintenance schedule, which is designed to keep the machine in proper running condition and prevent possible problems. The remaining Sections contain detailed procedures for carrying out the items listed on the maintenance schedule, as well as additional maintenance information designed to increase reliability. Maintenance and safety information is also printed on decals, which are mounted in various locations on the motorcycle **(see illustration)**. Where information on the decals differs from that presented in this Chapter, use the decal information.

Since routine maintenance plays such an important role in the safe and efficient operation of your motorcycle, it is presented here as a comprehensive check list. For the rider who does all his own maintenance, these lists outline the procedures and checks that should be done on a routine basis.

Deciding where to start or plug into the routine maintenance schedule depends on several factors. If you have owned the bike for some time but have never performed any maintenance on it, then you may want to start at the nearest interval and include some additional procedures to ensure that nothing important is overlooked. If you have just had a major engine overhaul, then you may want to start the maintenance routine from the beginning. If you have a used machine and have no knowledge of its history or maintenance record, you may desire to combine all the checks into one large service initially and then settle into the maintenance schedule prescribed.

The Sections which outline the inspection and maintenance procedures are written as step-by-step comprehensive guides to the actual performance of the work. They explain in detail each of the routine inspections and maintenance procedures on the check list. References to additional information in applicable Chapters is also included and should not be overlooked.

Before beginning any actual maintenance or repair, the machine should be cleaned thoroughly, especially around the oil filler plug, radiator cap, engine covers, carburetor, etc. Cleaning will help ensure that dirt does not contaminate the engine and will allow you to detect wear and damage that could otherwise easily go unnoticed.

3   Engine kill switch - check

Start the engine, then use the kill switch to shut it off. If it doesn't shut off (or if the engine doesn't start), refer to Chapter 5 and the wiring diagrams at the end of the book to test the switch.

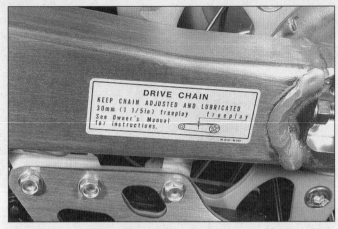

2.1 Decals on the motorcycle include maintenance information such as drive chain adjustment

4   Throttle and choke operation/grip freeplay - check and adjustment

Throttle check

Refer to illustration 4.2

1   Make sure the throttle twistgrip moves easily from fully closed to fully open with the front wheel turned at various angles. The grip should return automatically from fully open to fully closed when released. If the throttle sticks, check the throttle cable for cracks or kinks in the housings. Also, make sure the inner cable is clean and well-lubricated.

2   Check for a small amount of freeplay at the twistgrip **(see illustration)** and compare the freeplay to the value listed in this Chapter's Specifications.

Throttle adjustment

Refer to illustrations 4.4 and 4.5

3   Minor adjustments are made at the throttle lever end of the accelerator cable. Major adjustments are made at the carburetor end of the cable.

4   Pull back the rubber cover from the adjuster and loosen the lockwheel on the cable **(see illustration)**. Turn the adjuster until the desired freeplay is obtained, then retighten the lockwheel.

5   If the freeplay can't be adjusted at the grip end, loosen the locknut at the carburetor end of the cable **(see illustration)**. Turn the adjuster to set freeplay, then tighten the locknuts securely.

4.2 Measure throttle freeplay at the grip

4.4 Loosen the locknut (right arrow) and turn the adjuster (left arrow) to make minor freeplay adjustments

4.5 To make major adjustments, pull back the cover (right arrow), loosen the locknut and turn the adjuster; the choke knob (left arrow) should operate smoothly

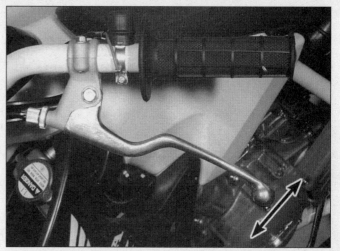

5.1 Measure clutch freeplay at the lever tip

Choke - operation check

6   Check that the choke knob moves smoothly **(see illustration 4.5)**. If not, refer to Chapter 4 and remove the choke plunger for inspection.

5   Clutch - check and freeplay adjustment

Refer to illustrations 5.1, 5.2 and 5.4

1   Operate the clutch lever and measure freeplay at the tip of the lever **(see illustration)**. If it's not within the range listed in this Chapter's Specifications, adjust it as follows.
2   To make minor adjustments, pull back the rubber cover from the adjuster at the handlebar **(see illustration)**. Loosen the lockwheel and turn the adjuster to change freeplay.
3   If freeplay can't be brought within specifications by using the handlebar adjuster, turn the handlebar adjuster in all the way, then back it out one turn.
4   Loosen the locknut on the midline cable adjuster behind the number plate **(see illustration)**. Turn the adjuster to set freeplay, then tighten the locknuts on the upper and midline adjusters.
5   If freeplay still can't be adjusted to within the specified range, the

cable is probably stretched and should be replaced with a new one (see Chapter 2).

6   Lubrication - general

Refer to illustration 6.3

1   Since the controls, cables and various other components of a motorcycle are exposed to the elements, they should be lubricated periodically to ensure safe and trouble-free operation.
2   The throttle twistgrip, brake lever, brake pedal and kickstarter pedal pivot should be lubricated frequently. In order for the lubricant to be applied where it will do the most good, the component should be disassembled. However, if chain and cable lubricant is being used, it can be applied to the pivot joint gaps and will usually work its way into the areas where friction occurs. If motor oil or light grease is being used, apply it sparingly as it may attract dirt (which could cause the controls to bind or wear at an accelerated rate). **Note:** *One of the best lubricants for the control lever pivots is a dry-film lubricant (available from many sources by different names).*
3   The throttle and clutch cables should be removed and treated with a commercially available cable lubricant which is specially formulated for use on motorcycle control cables. Small adapters for pressure lubricating the cables with spray can lubricants are available and

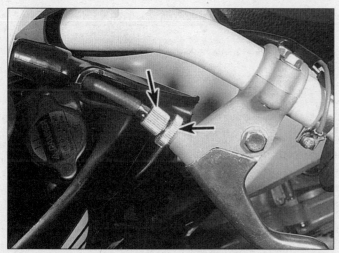

5.2 Loosen the lockwheel (right arrow) and turn the adjuster (left arrow) to make minor clutch cable adjustments

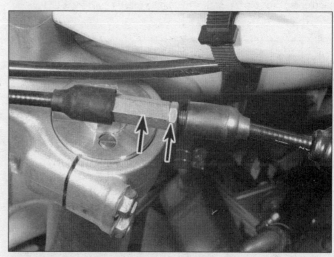

5.4 To make major clutch cable adjustments use the midline adjuster near the number plate; loosen the locknut (right arrow) and turn the adjuster (left arrow)

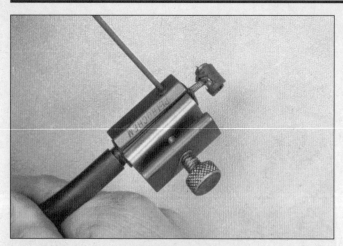

6.3 Lubricating a cable with a pressure lube adapter (make sure the tool seats around the inner cable)

7.3 The front brake fluid level is visible in the window (lower arrow); remove the cover screws (upper arrows) and cover to add fluid

ensure that the cable is lubricated along its entire length **(see illustration)**. When attaching the cable to the lever, be sure to lubricate the barrel-shaped fitting at the end with multi-purpose grease.

4   To lubricate the cables, disconnect them at the upper end, then lubricate the cable with a pressure lube adapter **(see illustration 6.3)**. See Chapter 4.

5   Lubrication of the swingarm and rear suspension linkage pivots requires removal of the components.

6   Refer to Chapter 6 for the following lubrication procedures:

a) *Swingarm bearings, dust seals and rear suspension linkage pivots*
b) *Steering head bearings*

7   Refer to Chapter 7 for the following lubrication procedures:

a) *Front and rear wheel bearings*
b) *Brake pedal pivot*

7   Brake fluid - check

Refer to illustrations 7.3 and 7.6

1   To ensure proper operation of the hydraulic disc brakes, the fluid level in the master cylinder reservoirs must be maintained within a safe range.

2   With the motorcycle supported in an upright position, turn the handlebars until the top of the front brake master cylinder is as level as possible.

7.6 The rear brake fluid level is visible through the translucent reservoir

3   The fluid level is visible in the window on the reservoir **(see illustration)**. Make sure the fluid level is above the Lower mark cast on the master cylinder body next to the reservoir.

4   If the fluid level is low, clean the area around the reservoir cover. Remove the cover screws and take off the cover, diaphragm retainer and diaphragm **(see illustration 7.3)**. Add new clean brake fluid of the type listed in this Chapter's Specifications until the fluid level is even with the line cast on the reservoir.

5   Install the diaphragm, retainer and cover, then tighten the cover screws securely.

6   The rear brake fluid level (on 2001 and earlier bikes with a rear disc brake) is visible through the master cylinder reservoir **(see illustration)**. If it's below the Lower mark cast in the reservoir body, the fluid must be replenished.

7   Unscrew the reservoir cap and pour in fluid to bring the level up to the Upper mark cast in the reservoir. Install the cap and tighten it securely.

8   The rear brake reservoir on 2002 and later models is integral with the master cylinder body. Remove three screws that secure the cap to the reservoir, then take off the cap and pull out the diaphragm. Fill the reservoir with fluid to the upper level line cast inside the reservoir.

9   Check the cover gasket for damage or deterioration, and replace it if necessary. Reinstall the cover and gasket, and install the screws.

8   Brake system - general check

1   A routine general check of the brakes will ensure that any problems are discovered and remedied before the rider's safety is jeopardized.

2   Check the brake lever and pedal for loose connections, excessive play, bends, and other damage. Replace any damaged parts with new ones (see Chapter 7).

3   Make sure all brake fasteners are tight. Check the brakes for wear as described below.

Wear check
Disc brakes
Refer to illustrations 8.4a and 8.4b

4   There's a groove on the inside of each pad next to the metal backing **(see illustrations)**. When the friction material is nearly worn down to the groove, it's time to replace the pads (even if only one pad is worn that far).

Rear drum brakes

5   Operate the brake pedal. If operation is rough or sticky, refer to Section 6 and lubricate the cable.

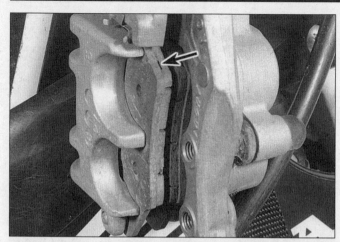

8.4a When the pad material is worn to or almost to the wear indicator groove, it's time for new pads (front caliper shown) . . .

8.4b . . . there's a similar groove at the back of the rear pads

6   With the rear brake lever and pedal freeplay properly adjusted (see Section 9), check the wear indicator triangular mark on the brake panel. If the slot in the brake arm lines up with the mark when the pedal is pressed, refer to Chapter 6 and replace the brake shoes.

9   Brake lever and pedal - check and adjustment

Front brake lever
Refer to illustration 9.2

1   Squeeze the front brake lever and note how far the lever travels (measure at the tip of the lever). If it exceeds the limit listed in this Chapter's Specifications, adjust the front brake as described below.
2   Loosen the locknut and turn the adjusting screw (**see illustration**). Tighten the locknut after making the adjustment.
3   Recheck lever travel (see Step 1). If it's still not within the Specifications, refer to Chapter 7 and bleed the brakes.

Rear brake pedal
Drum brake models

4   To adjust brake pedal height, loosen the locknut and turn the adjusting bolt (they're mounted in a boss on the right side of the frame behind the brake pedal). Honda doesn't specify pedal height.
5   Check the play of the brake pedal. If it exceeds the limit listed in

this Chapter's Specifications, adjust it with the wingnut at the rear end of the brake rod.

Disc brake models
Refer to illustration 9.6

6   To adjust pedal height, loosen the locknut and turn the pushrod on the rear master cylinder (**see illustration**). Although pedal height isn't specified, Honda does specify a pushrod length for 1992 and later CR250R models; this is listed in this Chapter's Specifications.
7   Pedal freeplay on disc brake models is automatic and no means of manual adjustment is provided.

10   Tires/wheels - general check

Refer to illustrations 10.4, 10.5 and 10.7

1   Routine tire and wheel checks should be made with the realization that your safety depends to a great extent on their condition.
2   Check the tires carefully for cuts, tears, embedded nails or other sharp objects and excessive wear. Operation of the motorcycle with excessively worn tires is extremely hazardous, as traction and handling are directly affected. Check the tread depth at the center of the tire. Honda doesn't specify a minimum tread depth for these models, but as a general rule, tires should be replaced with new ones when the tread knobs are worn to 8 mm (5/16 inch) or less.
3   Repair or replace punctured tires as soon as damage is noted. Do

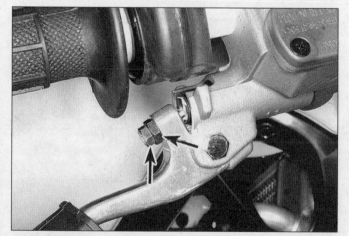

9.2 To adjust brake lever freeplay, loosen the locknut and turn the adjusting screw (arrows)

9.6 To adjust disc brake pedal height, loosen the locknut (lower arrow) and turn the master cylinder pushrod with the hex (upper arrow)

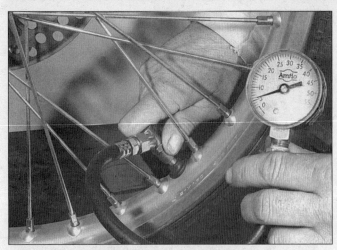

10.4 Check tire pressure with a gauge

10.5 Make sure the spokes are tight, but don't overtighten them

not try to patch a torn tire, as wheel balance and tire reliability may be impaired.

4   Check the tire pressures when the tires are cold and keep them properly inflated **(see illustration)**. Proper air pressure will increase tire life and provide maximum stability and ride comfort. Keep in mind that low tire pressures may cause the tire to slip on the rim or come off, while high tire pressures will cause abnormal tread wear and unsafe handling.

5   The wheels should be kept clean and checked periodically for cracks, bending, loose spokes and rust. Never attempt to repair damaged wheels; they must be replaced with new ones. Loose spokes can be tightened with a spoke wrench **(see illustration)**, but be careful not to overtighten and distort the wheel rim.

6   Check the valve stem locknuts to make sure they're tight. Also, make sure the valve stem cap is in place and tight. If it is missing, install a new one made of metal or hard plastic.

7   Check the tightness of the locknut on the rim lock **(see illustration)**. Tighten it if necessary to the torque listed in this Chapter's Specifications.

11   Drive chain and sprockets - check, adjustment and lubrication

Refer to illustrations 11.3, 11.6a and 11.6b

1   A neglected drive chain won't last long and can quickly damage the sprockets. Routine chain adjustment isn't difficult and will ensure

maximum chain and sprocket life. **Note:** *The chain should be routinely replaced at the interval listed in Section 1.*

2   To check the chain, support the bike securely with the rear wheel off the ground. Place the transmission in neutral.

3   Push down and pull up on the top run of the chain and measure the slack midway between the two sprockets **(see illustration)**, then compare the measurements to the value listed in this Chapter's Specifications. As wear occurs, the chain will actually stretch, which means adjustment is necessary by removing some slack from the chain. In some cases where lubrication has been neglected, corrosion and galling may cause the links to bind and kink, which effectively shortens the chain's length. If the chain is tight between the sprockets, rusty or kinked, it's time to replace it with a new one. **Note:** *Repeat the chain slack measurement along the length of the chain - ideally, every inch or so. If you find a tight area, mark it with felt pen or paint and repeat the measurement after the bike has been ridden. If the chain's still tight in the same areas, it may be damaged or worn. Because a tight or kinked chain can damage the transmission countershaft bearing, it's a good idea to replace it.*

4   Check the entire length of the chain for damaged rollers, loose links and loose pins.

5   Look through the slots in the engine sprocket cover and inspect the engine sprocket. Check the teeth on the engine sprocket and the rear sprocket for wear (see Chapter 6). Refer to Chapter 6 for the sprocket replacement procedure if the sprockets appear to be worn excessively.

6   Check the chain sliders and roller(s) **(see illustrations)**. If a slider is worn, measure its thickness. If it's less than the value listed in this

10.7 Tighten the locknut on the rim lock to the specified torque

11.3 Measure drive chain slack along the upper chain run

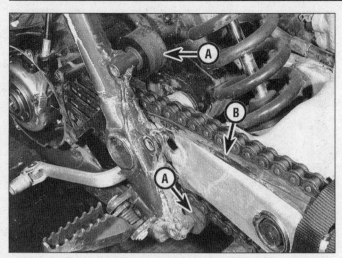

11.6a Check the upper and lower rollers (A) and the top surface of the slider (B) for wear

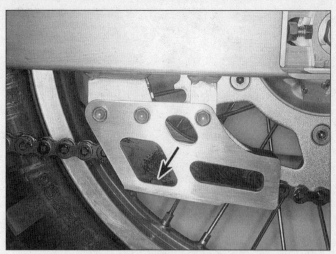

11.6b If the chain can be seen through the wear window on the lower chain slider, it's time for a new chain (this is a later CR250R; other models similar)

Chapter's Specifications, replace it (see Chapter 6).

7   Look through the hole in the chain guide bolted to the underside of the swingarm **(see illustration 11.6b)**. If you can see the chain through the hole, the slider is worn. Replace it.

Adjustment

Refer to illustration 11.9

8   Rotate the rear wheel until the chain is positioned with the least amount of slack present.

9   Loosen the rear axle nut (see *Wheels - inspection, removal and installation* in Chapter 7). Loosen the locknut and turn the adjuster on each side of the swingarm evenly until the proper chain tension is obtained (get the adjuster on the chain side close, then set the adjuster on the opposite side) **(see illustration)**. Be sure to turn the adjusters evenly to keep the wheel in alignment. If the adjusters reach the end of their travel, the chain is excessively worn and should be replaced with a new one (see Chapter 5).

10   When the chain has the correct amount of slack, make sure the marks on the adjusters correspond to the same relative marks on each side of the swingarm **(see illustration 11.9)**. Tighten the axle nut to the torque listed in the Chapter 7 Specifications.

Lubrication

Note: *If the chain is dirty, it should be removed and cleaned before it's lubricated (see Chapter 6).*

11   Use a good quality chain lubricant of the type listed in this Chapter's Specifications. Apply the lubricant along the top of the lower chain run, so that when the bike is ridden, centrifugal force will move the lubricant into the chain, rather than throwing it off.

12   After applying the lubricant, let it soak in for a few minutes before wiping off any excess.

12   Fasteners - check

1   Since vibration of the machine tends to loosen fasteners, all nuts, bolts, screws, etc. should be periodically checked for proper tightness. Also make sure all cotter pins or other safety fasteners are correctly installed.

2   Pay particular attention to the following:

Spark plug
Transmission oil drain plug and check bolt
Gearshift pedal
Brake lever and pedal
Kickstarter pedal
Footpegs

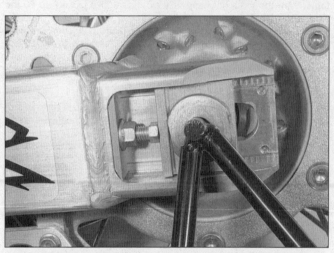

11.9 All 1987 and later models use this type of chain adjuster; loosen the locknut and turn the bolt to make adjustments

Engine mounting bolts
Steering stem locknut
Front axle nut
Rear axle nut

3   If a torque wrench is available, use it along with the torque specifications at the beginning of this, or other, Chapters.

13   Suspension - check

Refer to illustrations 13.5a and 13.5b

1   The suspension components must be maintained in top operating condition to ensure rider safety. Loose, worn or damaged suspension parts decrease the motorcycle's stability and control.

2   Lock the front brake and push on the handlebars to compress the front forks several times. See if they move up-and-down smoothly without binding. If binding is felt, the forks should be disassembled and inspected as described in Chapter 6.

3   On early models with fork boots, loosen the lower boot clamps. Slide the boot up the fork leg so you can inspect the dust seal. Remove any dirt that has built up on top of the dust seal, then lower the boot and tighten the clamp.

4   Check the tightness of all front suspension nuts and bolts to be sure none have worked loose.

13.5a On early models, remove the air valve cap and push the valve in to release built-up air pressure . . .

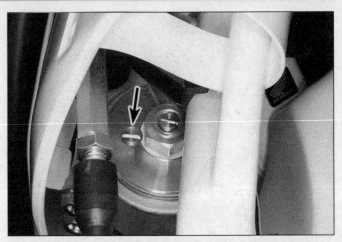

13.5b . . . on later models, remove the air relief screw

5   Air will heat up and expand during a race, stiffening the front forks. With the forks cold and fully extended (bike jacked up so the front wheel is off the ground), remove the air valve caps or pressure release screws from the forks and release built-up air pressure **(see illustrations). Note:** *Don't increase air pressure above zero on 1990 or later models. While adding air to 1986 through 1989 models may improve performance in some situations, the normal air pressure setting is zero. Never increase air pressure beyond the maximum listed in this Chapter's Specifications.*
6   Inspect the rear shock absorber for fluid leakage and tightness of the mounting nuts and bolts. If leakage is found, the shock should be replaced.
7   Support the motorcycle securely upright with its rear wheel off the ground. Grab the swingarm on each side, just ahead of the axle. Rock the swingarm from side to side - there should be no discernible movement at the rear. If there's a little movement or a slight clicking can be heard, make sure the swingarm pivot shaft is tight. If the pivot shaft is tight but movement is still noticeable, the swingarm will have to be removed and the bearings replaced as described in Chapter 6.
8   Inspect the tightness of the rear suspension nuts and bolts.

14   Coolant level - check

Refer to illustration 14.1
Warning: *Checking the coolant level on these bikes requires removal of*

the radiator cap. Always be sure the engine is cool before removing the radiator cap; otherwise, scalding coolant may spray out of the radiator opening, causing serious burns.
1   With the engine cool, unscrew the radiator cap **(see illustration)**. Coolant should be up to the bottom of the filler neck.
2   If the coolant level is low, top up with the mixture of antifreeze and water listed in this Chapter's Specifications.

15   Cooling system - inspection

Refer to illustration 15.5
1   Refer to Chapter 8 and remove the radiator shrouds. Clean mud, leaves or other obstructions out of the radiator fins with low-pressure water or compressed air.
2   If any fins are bent, carefully straighten them with a small screwdriver, taking care not to puncture the coolant tubes in the radiator.
3   If more than 20 percent of the radiator's surface area is blocked, replace the radiator.
4   Check the coolant hoses for swelling, cracks, burns, cuts or other defects. Replace the hoses if their condition is doubtful. Make sure the hose clamps are tight and free of corrosion. Tighten loose clamps and replace corroded or damaged ones.
5   Check for leaks at the water pump weep hole **(see illustration)** and gaskets. Also check for leaks at the coolant drain plug(s). Replace water pump or drain plug gaskets if they've been leaking. If coolant or

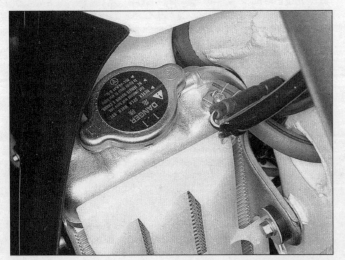

14.1 Follow safety precautions when removing the radiator cap

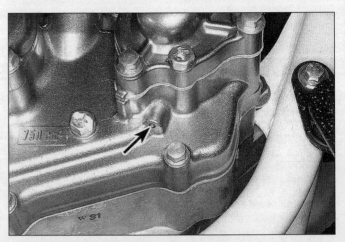

15.5 If coolant is leaking from the small hole under the water pump (arrow), it's time for a new water pump seal; if transmission oil is leaking, replace the oil seal

16.1 Remove the water pump drain bolt (right arrow); the similar bolt behind it (left arrow) is used to check transmission oil level

16.3 There's another drain bolt on the cylinder (arrow)

transmission oil has been leaking from the weep hole, it's time for new water pump seals (see Chapter 3).

16 Coolant - change

Refer to illustrations 16.1 and 16.3

Warning 1: *Do not allow antifreeze to come in contact with your skin or painted surfaces of the vehicle. Rinse off spills immediately with plenty of water. Antifreeze is highly toxic if ingested. Never leave antifreeze lying around in an open container or in puddles on the floor; children and pets are attracted by its sweet smell and may drink it. Check with local authorities about disposing of used antifreeze. Many communities have collection centers which will see that antifreeze is disposed of safely.*

Warning 2: *Don't remove the radiator cap when the engine and radiator are hot. Scalding coolant and steam may be blown out under pressure, which could cause serious injury. To open the radiator cap, place a thick rag, like a towel, over the radiator cap; slowly rotate the cap counterclockwise to the first stop. This procedure allows any residual pressure to escape. When the steam has stopped escaping, press down on the cap while turning it counterclockwise and remove it.*

1   Place a drain pan beneath the water pump drain screw **(see illustration)**.

2   Remove the drain screw. **Note:** *Coolant will dribble out until the*

radiator cap is removed, then it will shoot almost straight sideways, so position the drain pan accordingly.

3   Remove the cylinder drain screw **(see illustration)** and let the coolant drain.

4   Once the coolant has drained completely, place new gaskets on the drain screws and install them in the engine. Fill the cooling system with the antifreeze and water mixture listed in this Chapter's Specifications.

5   Lean the bike about twenty-degrees to one side, then the other, several times. This will allow air trapped in the coolant passages to make its way to the top of the coolant.

6   Check the coolant level. It should be up to the bottom of the radiator filler neck. Add more antifreeze-water mixture if necessary.

7   Start the engine and check for leaks. Warm up the engine, then let it cool completely and recheck the coolant level.

17 Air cleaner element - replacement

Refer to illustrations 17.2, 17.3a, 17.3b, 17.4, 17.8 and 17.10

1   Remove the seat (see Chapter 8).

2   If the rain cover is in place, lift it off **(see illustration)**.

3   Unscrew the filter element bolt **(see illustration)**. Lift out the element and pull the bolt out of it **(see illustration)**.

17.2 Remove the rain cover if it's in place; use the cover only in wet riding conditions and leave it off when it's dry

17.3a Unscrew the element bolt until it's loose . . .

17.3b . . . then lift out the element and remove the bolt

17.4 Separate the foam element from the holder for cleaning and re-oiling

17.8 The tab (arrow) should be up when the element is installed

17.10 Clean the drain tubes if they're clogged

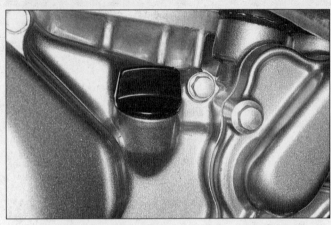

18.4 The transmission oil filler cap is on the upper right side of the crankcase

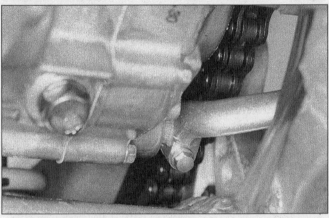

19.5 The transmission oil drain plug is on the bottom of the crankcase

4   Separate the element holder from the foam element **(see illustration)**. The inner and outer parts of the element can't be separated.
5   Thoroughly clean the element in high-flash point or non-flammable safety solvent. Do not use gasoline. After cleaning, squeeze out the solvent and allow the element to dry completely.
6   Coat the element with foam filter oil recommended in this Chapter's Specifications, then squeeze the element to work the oil through the foam. Once the element is soaked with oil, squeeze out the excess.
7   Place the holder on the element. On some models, there's an inner tab on the end foam piece; align this with the groove in the element holder.
8   Install the element in the case with its locating tab up **(see illustration)**. Some models have a triangular mark on the end of the air cleaner case; align the locating tab with this mark. The tab on 1997 through 1999 CR250R models fits in a notch in the air cleaner case.
9   The remainder of installation is the reverse of the removal steps.
10   Check the drain tubes **(see illustration)**. If a tube is clogged, squeeze its clamp, remove it from the air cleaner housing and clean it out. Install the drain tube on the housing and secure it with the clamp.

18   Transmission oil level - check

Refer to illustration 18.4
1   Start the engine and run it for three minutes. **Warning:** *Do not run the engine in an enclosed space such as a garage or shop.*
2   Stop the engine and allow the bike to sit undisturbed in a level position for three minutes. Be sure it's upright.
3   With the engine off, unscrew the oil check bolt **(see illustration 16.1)**. A small amount of oil should flow out of the hole.

4   If no oil flows out of the hole, remove the oil filler cap **(see illustration)**. Add oil through the filler cap hole until it starts to flow from the check bolt hole. Let any excess drain, then reinstall the check bolt and filler cap.

19   Transmission oil - change

Refer to illustration 19.5
1   Consistent routine oil changes are the single most important maintenance procedure you can perform on these models. The oil not only lubricates the internal parts of the transmission and clutch, but it also acts as a coolant, a cleaner, a sealant, and a protectant. Because of these demands, the oil takes a terrific amount of abuse and should be replaced often with new oil of the recommended grade and type. Saving a little money on the difference in cost between a good oil and a cheap oil won't pay off if the engine is damaged. Honda recommends against using the following:

a) *Oils with graphite or molybdenum additives*
b) *Non-detergent oils*
c) *Castor or vegetable based oils*
d) *Oil additives*

2   Before changing the oil, warm up the engine by running it for three minutes so the oil will drain easily. Be careful when draining the oil, as the exhaust pipe, the engine and the oil itself can cause severe burns.
3   Park the motorcycle over a clean drain pan.
4   Remove the oil filler cap to vent the crankcase and act as a reminder that there is no oil in the engine. Also remove the oil check bolt **(see illustrations 16.1 and 18.4)**.
5   Next, remove the drain plug from the crankcase **(see illustration)**

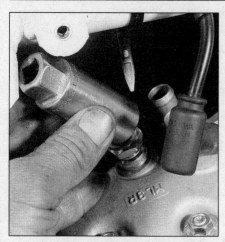

20.2 Remove the spark plug with a socket like this one

20.6a Spark plug manufacturers recommend using a wire type gauge when checking the gap - if the wire doesn't slide between the electrodes with a slight drag, adjustment is required

20.6b To change the gap, bend the side electrode only, as indicated by the arrows, and be very careful not to crack or chip the ceramic insulator surrounding the center electrode

and allow the oil to drain into the pan. Do not lose the sealing washer on the drain plug.

6   Check the condition of the drain plug threads. Replace the plug if the threads are damaged.

7   Slip a new sealing washer over the drain plug, then install and tighten the plug to the torque listed in this Chapter's Specifications. Avoid overtightening, as damage to the threads or engine case will result.

8   Before refilling the engine, check the old oil carefully. If the oil was drained into a clean pan, small pieces of metal or other material can be easily detected. If the oil is very metallic colored, then the transmission is experiencing wear from break-in (when new) or from insufficient lubrication. If there are flakes or chips of metal in the oil, then something is drastically wrong internally and the case will have to be disassembled for inspection and repair.

9   If there are pieces of fiber-like material in the oil, the clutch is experiencing excessive wear and should be checked.

10   If the inspection of the oil turns up nothing unusual, refill the transmission as described below.

11   With the bike supported in an upright position, fill the transmission until oil begins to flow from the check bolt hole. The specified capacity is only a guide; use the check bolt to determine the exact amount of oil to use.

12   Allow excess oil to flow from the check bolt hole, then install the check bolt with a new sealing washer and tighten it to the torque listed in this Chapter's Specifications. Install the filler cap.

13   Check around the drain plug and check bolt for leaks.

14   The old oil drained from the engine cannot be reused in its present state and should be disposed of. Check with your local refuse disposal company, disposal facility or environmental agency to see if they will accept the oil for recycling. Don't pour used oil into drains or onto the ground. After the oil has cooled, it can be drained into a suitable container (capped plastic jugs, topped bottles, milk cartons, etc.) for transport to one of these disposal sites.

20   Spark plug - check and replacement

Refer to illustrations 20.2, 20.6a and 20.6b

1   Twist the spark plug cap to break it free from the plug, then pull it off.

2   If available, use compressed air to blow any accumulated debris from around the spark plug. Remove the plug with a spark plug socket **(see illustration)**.

3   Inspect the electrodes for wear. Both the center and side electrodes should have square edges and the side electrode should be of

uniform thickness. Look for excessive deposits (especially oil fouling) and evidence of a cracked or chipped insulator around the center electrode. Compare your spark plugs to the color spark plug chart on the inside back cover of this manual. Check the threads, the washer and the ceramic insulator body for cracks and other damage.

4   If the electrodes are not excessively worn, and if the deposits can be easily removed with a wire brush, the plug can be regapped and reused (if no cracks or chips are visible in the insulator). If in doubt concerning the condition of the plug, replace it with a new one, as the expense is minimal. The plug should be replaced at the interval listed in the maintenance schedule.

5   Cleaning the spark plug by sandblasting is permitted, provided you clean the plug with a high flash-point solvent afterwards.

6   Before installing a new plug, make sure it is the correct type and heat range. Check the gap between the electrodes, as it is not preset. For best results, use a wire-type gauge rather than a flat gauge to check the gap **(see illustration)**. If the gap must be adjusted, bend the side electrode only and be very careful not to chip or crack the insulator nose **(see illustration)**. Make sure the washer is in place before installing the plug.

7   Since the cylinder head is made of aluminum, which is soft and easily damaged, thread the plug into the head by hand. Slip a short length of hose over the end of the plug to use as a tool to thread it into place. The hose will grip the plug well enough to turn it, but will start to slip if the plug begins to cross-thread in the hole - this will prevent damaged threads and the accompanying repair costs.

8   Once the plug is finger tight, tighten the plug to the torque listed in this Chapter's Specifications.

9   Reconnect the spark plug cap.

21   Exhaust system - inspection and glass wool replacement

Refer to illustrations 21.5a and 21.5b

Warning: *Make sure the exhaust system is cool before performing this procedure.*

1   Periodically check the exhaust system for leaks and loose fasteners (see Chapter 4).

2   Check the expansion chamber springs at the cylinder to make sure they're unbroken and securely attached. Replace broken springs.

3   Check the expansion chamber for cracks or dents. The shape of the chamber has an important effect on engine performance, so dents should not be ignored. Small dents can be removed or large dented areas replaced using body shop sheet metal repair techniques.

4   At the specified interval, clean the inner pipe and replace the glass wool in the muffler as described below.

21.5a Pull the inner pipe and glass wool out of the muffler . . .

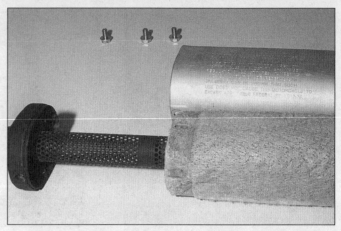

21.5b . . . and separate the inner pipe from the glass wool

5   Place the muffler bracket in a padded vise. Remove the small bolts from the front end of the muffler, then pull out the inner pipe and glass wool insert. Pull the inner pipe out of the glass wool **(see illustrations)**. If you're working on a 1989 or later CR500R, also remove the bolts from the rear of the muffler case and pull out the rear insert.

6   Clean the small holes in the inner pipe with a wire brush.

7   Apply muffler sealant to the front and rear ends of the inner pipe where it contacts the muffler case. Install a new glass wool insert and the inner pipe in the case. Tighten the bolts to the torque listed in this Chapter's Specifications.

22 Steering head bearings - check and adjustment

Inspection

1   These motorcycles are equipped with roller-and-cone type steering head bearings, which can become dented, rough or loose during normal use of the machine. In extreme cases, worn or loose steering head bearings can cause steering wobble that is potentially dangerous.

2   To check the bearings, lift up the front end of the motorcycle and place a secure support beneath the engine so the front wheel is off the ground.

3   Point the wheel straight ahead and slowly move the handlebars from side-to-side. Dents or roughness in the bearing will be felt and the bars will not move smoothly. **Note:** *Make sure any hesitation in movement is not being caused by the cables, brake hose and wiring harness that run to the handlebars.*

4   Next, grasp the fork legs and try to pull the wheel forward and push it backward. Any looseness in the steering head bearings will be felt as play in the forks. If play is felt in the bearings, adjust the steering head as follows.

Adjustment

Refer to illustrations 22.6 and 22.9

5   Remove the handlebars and upper triple clamp (see Chapter 5).

6   Loosen the bearing adjusting nut, then tighten it to the torque listed in this Chapter's Specifications **(see illustration)**.

7   Turn the lower triple clamp from lock-to-lock (all the way to the left and all the way back to the right) four or five times to seat the bearings.

8   Loosen the adjusting nut all the way, then tighten it to the final torque listed in this Chapter's Specifications.

9   An adjustable spanner wrench can be used to adjust the bearings if you don't have the special socket **(see illustration)**. Since this tool can't be used with a torque wrench, it will be necessary to estimate the tightness of the nut. Be sure the final result is that the steering stem turns from side-to-side freely, but there is no side-to-side or vertical play of the steering stem in the bearings.

23 Front fork oil change

Changing the front fork oil requires removal and partial disassembly of the forks. On some models, a special spacer tool is required to position the fork so oil level can be measured. Refer to Chapter 6 for details.

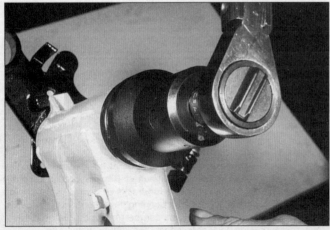

22.6 The best way to adjust the steering stem bearings is with a torque wrench and a special socket . . .

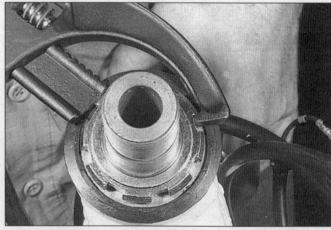

22.9 . . . but an adjustable spanner can also be used; be very sure there's no binding or looseness in the bearings

Chapter 2 Part A
Engine, clutch and transmission (CR80R/85R and CR125R models)

Contents

Specifications

CR80R/RB and CR85R/RB

Cylinder head warpage limit	0.10 mm (0.004 inch)

Cylinder

Bore
2002 and earlier	
Standard	46.980 to 46.995 mm (1.8496 to 1.8502 inches)
Limit	47.03 mm (1.852 inches)
2003 and later	
Standard	47.480 to 47.495 mm (1.8693 to 1.8699 inches)
Limit	47.53 mm (1.871 inches)
Taper and out-of-round limits	0.10 mm (0.004 inch)
Surface warpage limit	0.10 mm (0.004 inch)

Piston

Piston diameter
2002 and earlier	
Standard	46.945 to 46.980 mm (1.8482 to 1.8488 inches)
Limit	46.90 mm (1.846 inch)
2003 and later	
Standard	47.445 to 47.460 mm (1.8679 to 1.885 inches)
Limit	47.40 mm (1.866 inches)
Piston diameter measuring point (above bottom of piston)	10 mm (0.40 inch)

Piston-to-cylinder clearance
1086 through 1994	
Standard	0.04 to 0.07 mm (0.002 to 0.003 inch)
Limit	0.10 mm (0.004 inch)
1995 on	
Standard	0.02 to 0.05 mm (0.0008 to 0.0020 inch)
Limit	
1995 through 2002	0.10 mm (0.004 inch)
2003 and later	0.13 mm (0.005 inch)

Piston pin bore in piston
Standard	14.002 to 14.008 mm (0.5513 to 0.5515 inch)
Limit	14.02 mm (0.552 inch)

CR80R/RB and CR85R/RB (continued)

Piston (continued)

Piston pin outer diameter
  Standard .... 13.994 to 14.000 mm (0.5509 to 0.5512 inch)
  Limit .... 13.97 mm (0.550 inch)
Piston pin-to-piston clearance
  Standard .... 0.002 to 0.014 mm (0.0001 to 0.0006 inch)
  Limit .... 0.02 mm (0.001 inch)
Connecting rod small end bore
  Standard .... 18.005 to 18.017 mm (0.7089 to 0.7903 inch)
  Limit .... 18.03 mm (0.710 inch)
Ring end gap
  1986 through 1994
    Standard .... 0.2 to 0.4 mm (0.008 to 0.016 inch)
    Limit .... 0.5 mm (0.020 inch)
  1995 on
    Standard .... 0.27 to 0.42 mm (0.011 to 0.017 inch)
    Limit .... 0.52 mm (0.020 inch)

Clutch

Spring free length
  1986
    Standard .... 37.5 mm (1.48 inches)
    Limit .... 36.5 mm (1.44 inches)
  1987 on
    Standard .... 36.4 mm (1.43 inches)
    Limit .... 35.4 mm (1.39 inches)
Friction plate thickness
  2004 and earlier
    Standard .... 2.8 to 2.9 mm (0.110 to 0.114 inch)
    Limit .... 2.7 mm (0.11 inch)
  2005 and later
    Standard .... 2.92 to 3.08 mm (0.115 to 0.121 inch)
    Limit .... 2.85 mm (0.112 inch)
Metal plate warpage limit .... 0.15 mm (0.006 inch)
Clutch housing bushing
  Outside diameter
    Standard .... 21.964 to 21.985 mm (0.8647 to 0.8655 inch)
    Limit .... 21.95 mm (0.864 inch)
  Inside diameter
    Standard .... 17.000 to 17.018 mm (0.6693 to 0.6700 inch)
    Limit .... 17.03 mm (0.670 inch)
  Length
    Standard .... 30.40 to 30.50 mm (1.197 to 1.201 inches)
    Limit .... 30.35 mm (1.195 inches)
Clutch housing inside diameter
  Standard .... 22.000 to 22.021 mm (0.8661 to 0.8670 inch)
  Limit .... 22.04 mm (0.868 inch)
Mainshaft diameter at clutch housing bushing surface
  Standard .... 16.966 to 16.984 mm (0.6680 to 0.6686 inch)
  Limit .... 16.95 mm (0.667 inch)

Kickstarter

Spindle outside diameter
  Standard .... 16.978 to 16.989 mm (0.6684 to 0.6689 inch)
  Limit .... 16.96 mm (0.668 inch)
Pinion gear inside diameter
  Standard .... 19.020 to 19.041 mm (0.7488 to 0.7496 inch)
  Limit .... 19.05 mm (0.750 inch)
Pinion gear bushing inside diameter
  Standard .... 17.016 to 17.034 mm (0.6699 to 0.6706 inch)
  Limit .... 17.06 mm (0.672 inch)
Pinion gear bushing outside diameter
  Standard .... 18.982 to 18.995 mm (0.7473 to 0.7478 inch)
  Limit .... 18.96 mm (0.747 inch)
Idler gear inside diameter
  Standard .... 15.032 to 15.050 mm (0.5918 to 0.5925 inch)
  Limit .... 15.08 mm (0.594 inch)

Countershaft diameter at idler gear bushing surface
    Standard .... 14.982 to 15.000 mm (0.5898 to 0.5906 inch)
    Limit .... 14.96 mm (0.589 inch)

Shift drum and forks
Fork inside diameter
    1986 through 1995
        Standard .... 11.027 to 11.042 mm (0.4341 to 0.4347 inch)
        Limit .... 11.06 mm (0.435 inch)
    1996 on
        Standard .... 11.035 to 11.056 mm (0.4344 to 0.4353 inch)
        Limit .... 11.065 mm (0.4356 inch)
Fork shaft outside diameter
    Standard .... 10.969 to 10.980 mm (0.4318 to 0.4323 mm)
    Limit .... 10.95 mm (0.431 inch)
Fork finger thickness
    Standard .... 4.93 to 5.00 mm (0.194 to 0.197 inch)
    Limit .... 4.88 mm (0.192 inch)
Shift drum groove width limit .... Not specified

Transmission
Gear inside diameters
    Mainshaft fifth and sixth
        Standard .... 17.016 to 17.034 mm (0.6699 to 0.6706 inch)
        Limit .... 17.10 mm (0.673 inch)
    Countershaft first
        Standard .... 16.516 to 16.534 mm (0.6501 to 0.6509 inch)
        Limit .... 16.60 mm (0.654 inch)
    Countershaft second
        Standard .... 20.020 to 20.041 mm (0.7881 to 0.7890 inch)
        Limit .... 20.10 mm (0.791 inch)
    Countershaft third and fourth
        Standard .... 19.020 to 19.041 mm (0.7488 to 0.7496 inch)
        Limit .... 19.10 mm (0.752 inch)
Bushing diameters (countershaft second gear)
    Inside
        Standard .... 17.016 to 17.034 mm (0.6699 to 0.6706 inch)
        Limit .... 17.10 mm (0.673 inch)
    Outside
        Standard .... 19.984 to 19.995 mm (0.7868 to 0.7872 inch)
        Limit .... 19.92 mm (0.784 inch)
Mainshaft diameter (at fifth and sixth gears)
    Standard .... 16.966 to 16.984 mm (0.6679 to 0.6686 inch)
    Limit .... 16.95 mm (0.667 inch)
Countershaft diameter
    At first gear
        Standard .... 16.466 to 16.484 mm (0.6483 to 0.6489 inch)
        Limit .... 16.45 mm (0.648 inch)
    At second gear (1986 and 1987)
        Standard .... 16.978 to 16.989 mm (0.6684 to 0.6689 inch)
        Limit .... 16.96 mm (0.668 inch)
    At second gear (1988 on)
        Standard .... 16.981 to 16.992 mm (0.6685 to 0.6690 inch)
        Limit .... 16.96 mm (0.668 inch)
    At third and fourth gear
        Standard .... 18.959 to 18.980 mm (0.7464 to 0.7472 inch)
        Limit .... 18.94 mm (0.746 inch)

Crankshaft
Connecting rod side clearance
    Standard .... 0.15 to 0.55 mm (0.0059 to 0.0217 inch)
    Limit .... 0.7 mm (0.030 inch)
Connecting rod big end radial clearance
    Standard .... 0.013 to 0.027 mm (0.0005 to 0.0011 inch)
    Limit .... 0.034 mm (0.0013 inch)
Crankshaft V-block positions .... 28 mm (1.1 inch) on each side of centerline
Runout measuring points
    At alternator end .... 50 mm (2.0 inches) from centerline
    At clutch end .... 46 mm (1.8 inches) from centerline
Runout limit .... 0.1 mm (0.004 inch)

CR80R/RB and CR85R/RB (continued)

Torque specifications (continued)

Engine mounting bolts
  1986 .... 30 to 35 Nm (22 to 25 ft-lbs)
  1987 through 1995.. 47 Nm (34 ft-lbs)
  1996 on .... 33 Nm (24 ft-lbs)
Cylinder head nuts .... 27 Nm (20 ft-lbs)
Cylinder nuts .... 27 Nm (20 ft-lbs)
Carburetor intake tube bolts .... 7 to 11 Nm (60 to 96 inch-lbs)
Right crankcase cover bolts... Not specified
Clutch spring bolts .... Not specified
Clutch center bolt... 45 Nm (33 ft-lbs) (1)
Primary drive gear locknut .... 55 Nm (40 ft-lbs)
Shift cam plate to shift drum bolt
  1986 through 1994.. Not specified (2)
  1995 on .... 27 Nm (20 ft-lbs) (2)
Shift drum stopper arm bolt
  1986 through 1994.. Not specified
  1995 on .... 10 Nm (84 inch-lbs)
Shift pedal pinch bolt
  1986 through 1994.. Not specified
  1995 .... 10 Nm (84 inch-lbs)
  1996 through 2002.. 12 Nm (108 inch-lbs)
  2003 and later .... 16 Nm (144 inch-lbs)
Crankcase bolts .... Not specified

1. *Apply oil to the threads.*
2. *Apply non-permanent thread locking agent to the threads.*

CR125R

Cylinder head warpage limit.. 0.05 mm (0.002 inch)

Cylinder

Bore
  1986 through 1988
    Standard .... 54.000 to 54.015 mm (2.1259 to 2.1266 inches)
    Limit.. 54.05 mm (2.128 inches)
  1989 on (piston and bore coded A)
    Standard .... 53.976 to 53.983 mm (2.1250 to 2.1253 inches)
    Limit.. 54.01 mm (2.126 inches)
  1989 on (piston and bore coded B)
    Standard .... 53.968 to 53.976 mm (2.1247 to 2.1250 inches)
    Limit.. 54.01 mm (2.126 inches)
Taper and out-of-round limits .... 0.05 mm (0.002 inch)
Surface warpage limit... 0.05 mm (0.002 inch)

Piston

Piston diameter (1986)
  Standard .... 53.945 to 53.960 mm (2.1238 to 2.1244 inches)
  Limit.. 53.89 mm (2.122 inches)
Piston diameter (1987 and 1988)
  Standard .... 53.925 to 53.940 mm (2.1230 to 2.1236 inches)
  Limit.. 53.88 mm (2.121 inches)
Piston diameter (1989 on, coded A)
  Standard .... 53.933 to 53.940 mm (2.1233 to 2.1236 inches)
  Limit.. 53.88 mm (2.121 inches)
Piston diameter (1989 on, coded B)
  Standard .... 53.925 to 53.933 mm (2.1230 to 2.1233 inches)
  Limit.. 53.88 mm (2.121 inches)
Piston diameter measuring point (above bottom of piston)
  1986 through 1991.. 10 mm (0.40 inch)
  1992 through 1995.. 20 mm (0.79 inch)
  1996 through 2001.. 15 mm (0.59 inch)
  2002 through 2004.. 10 mm (0.039 inch)
  2005 and later .... 11 mm (0.43 inch)

Piston-to-cylinder clearance
  1986
    Standard .... 0.04 to 0.07 mm (0.0016 to 0.0028 inch)
    Limit .... 0.12 mm (0.005 inch)
  1987 and 1988
    Standard .... 0.06 to 0.09 mm (0.0024 to 0.0035 inch)
    Limit .... 0.12 mm (0.005 inch)
  1989 on
    Standard .... 0.035 to 0.050 mm (0.0014 to 0.0020 inch)
    Limit .... 0.07 mm (0.003 inch)
Piston pin bore in piston
  1986 and 1987
    Standard .... 14.002 to 14.008 mm (0.5513 to 0.5515 inch)
    Limit .... 14.02 mm (0.552 inch)
  1988 through 1995
    Standard .... 15.002 to 15.008 mm (0.5906 to 0.5909 inch)
    Limit .... 15.02 mm (0.5914 inch)
  1996 on
    Standard .... 15.002 to 15.015 mm (0.5906 to 0.5911 inch)
    Limit
      1996 and 1997 .... 15.02 mm (0.5914 inch)
      1998 on .... 15.035 mm (0.5919 inch)
Piston pin outer diameter
  1986 and 1987
    Standard .... 13.994 to 14.000 mm (0.5509 to 0.5512 inch)
    Limit .... 13.98 mm (0.5504 inch)
  1988 on
    Standard .... 14.994 to 15.000 mm (0.5903 to 0.5906 inch)
    Limit .... 14.980 mm (0.5898 inch)
Piston pin-to-piston clearance
  Standard
    1986 through 1995 .... 0.002 to 0.014 mm (0.0001 to 0.0006 inch)
    1996 on .... 0.002 to 0.020 mm (0.0001 to 0.0008 inch)
  Limit .... 0.03 mm (0.0012 inch)
Connecting rod small end bore
  1986 and 1987
    Standard .... 18.002 to 18.014 mm (0.7087 to 0.7092 inch)
    Limit .... 18.022 mm (0.7095 inch)
  1988 on
    Standard .... 19.002 to 19.014 mm (0.7481 to 0.7486 inch)
    Limit .... 19.022 mm (0.7489 inch)
Ring end gap
  1986 through 1988
    Standard .... 0.15 to 0.35 mm (0.006 to 0.014 inch)
    Limit .... 0.45 mm (0.018 inch)
  1989 on
    Standard .... 0.40 to 0.55 mm (0.016 to 0.022 inch)
    Limit .... 0.65 mm (0.026 inch)

Clutch

Spring free length
  1986 through 1999
    Standard .... 39.4 mm (1.55 inch)
    Limit .... 37.5 mm (1.48 inch)
  2000 through 2003
    Standard .... 37.1 mm (1.46 inch)
    Limit .... 35.2 mm (1.39 inch)
  2004 and later
    Standard .... 36.1 mm (1.42 inches)
    Limit .... 35.4 mm (1.39 inches)
Friction plate thickness
  Standard .... 2.92 to 3.08 mm (0.115 to 0.121 inch)
  Limit .... 2.85 mm (0.112 inch)
Metal plate warpage limit .... 0.15 mm (0.006 inch)
Clutch housing inside diameter
  1986 through 1991 and 1998 on
    Standard .... 20.000 to 20.021 mm (0.7874 to 0.7882 inch)
    Limit .... 20.050 mm (0.7894 inch)
  1992 through 1997 .... Not specified

CR125R (continued)

Clutch (continued)

Mainshaft diameter at clutch housing bushing surface
    1986 through 1991 and 1998 on
        Standard .... 19.959 to 19.980 mm (0.7858 to 0.7866 inch)
        Limit .... 19.940 mm (0.7850 inch)
    1992 through 1997 .... Not specified

Kickstarter
Spindle outside diameter
    1986 through 1991 and 1998 on
        Standard .... 16.466 to 16.484 mm (0.6483 to 0.6490 inch)
        Limit .... 16.450 mm (0.6476 inch)
    1992 through 1997 .... Not specified
Pinion gear inside diameter
    1986 through 1991 and 1998 on
        Standard .... 16.516 to 16.534 mm (0.6502 to 0.6509 inch)
        Limit .... 16.550 mm (0.6516 inch)
    1992 through 1997 .... Not specified
Idler gear inside diameter
    1986 through 1991 and 1998 on
        Standard .... 17.016 to 17.034 mm (0.6699 to 0.6706 inch)
        Limit .... 17.050 mm (0.6713 inch)
    1992 through 1997 .... Not specified
Countershaft diameter at idler gear bushing surface
    1986 through 1991 and 1998 on
        Standard .... 16.988 to 16.994 mm (0.6682 to 0.6691 inch)
        Limit .... 16.97 mm (0.6681 inch)
    1992 through 1997 .... Not specified

Shift drum and forks

Fork inside diameter
    1986 through 1995
        Standard .... 11.041 to 11.056 mm (0.4347 to 0.4353 inch)
        Limit .... 11.065 mm (0.4356 inch)
    1996 on
        Standard .... 11.035 to 11.056 mm (0.4344 to 0.4353 inch)
        Limit .... 11.065 mm (0.4356 inch)
Fork shaft outside diameter
    1986 through 1991
        Standard .... 10.980 to 10.994 mm (0.4323 to 0.4328 mm)
        Limit .... 10.973 mm (0.4320 inch)
    1992 on
        Standard .... 10.983 to 10.994 mm (0.4324 to 0.4328 inch)
        Limit .... 10.973 mm (0.4320 inch)
Fork finger thickness
    Standard .... 4.93 to 5.00 mm (0.194 to 0.197 inch)
    Limit .... 4.88 mm (0.192 inch)
Shift drum groove width limit .... Not specified

Transmission

Gear inside diameters
    Mainshaft fifth
        1986 through 1988
            Standard .... 20.020 to 20.041 mm (0.7882 to 0.7890 inch)
            Limit .... 20.060 mm (0.7898 inch)
        1989 on
            Standard .... 23.020 to 23.041 mm (0.9063 to 0.9071 inch)
            Limit .... 23.060 mm (0.9079 inch)
    Mainshaft sixth
        1986 through 1988
            Standard .... 23.007 to 23.028 mm (0.9058 to 0.9066 inch)
            Limit .... 23.050 mm (0.9075 inch)
        1989 on
            Standard .... 23.020 to 23.041 mm (0.9063 to 0.9071 inch)
            Limit .... 23.060 mm (0.9079 inch)
    Countershaft first
        1986 through 1988
            Standard .... 17.000 to 17.018 mm (0.6693 to 0.6700 inch)
            Limit .... 17.030 (0.6705 inch)

1989 on
  Standard.. 20.020 to 20.041 mm (0.7882 to 0.7890 inch)
  Limit... 20.060 mm (0.7898 inch)
Countershaft second
  1986 through 1988
    Standard.. 22.020 to 22.041 mm (0.8669 to 0.8678 inch)
    Limit... 22.060 mm (0.8685 inch)
  1989 through 2003
    Standard.. 25.020 to 25.041 mm (0.9850 to 0.9852 inch)
    Limit... 25.060 mm (0.9866 inch)
  2004 and later
    Standard.. 27.020 to 27.041 mm (1.0638 to 1.0646 inches)
    Limit... 26.95 mm (1.061 inches)
Countershaft third
  1986 through 1988
    Standard.. 22.010 to 22.025 mm (0.8665 to 0.8671 inch)
    Limit... 22.045 mm (0.8679 inch)
  1989 on
    Standard.. 25.020 to 25.041 mm (0.9850 to 0.9852 inch)
    Limit... 25.060 mm (0.9866 inch)
Countershaft fourth
  1986 through 1988
    Standard.. 22.020 to 22.041 mm (0.8669 to 0.8678 inch)
    Limit... 22.060 mm (0.8685 inch)
  1989 through 1991
    Standard.. 25.020 to 25.041 mm (0.9850 to 0.9852 inch)
    Limit... 25.060 mm (0.9866 inch)
Bushing diameters
  Mainshaft sixth (outside only)
    Standard.. 22.959 to 22.980 mm (0.9039 to 0.9047 inch)
    Limit... 22.940 mm (0.9031 inch)
  Mainshaft fifth
    Inside
      Standard.. 20.000 to 20.021 mm (0.7874 to 0.7882 inch)
      Limit... 20.040 mm (0.7890 inch)
    Outside
      Standard.. 22.979 to 23.000 mm (0.9047 to 0.9055 inch)
      Limit... 22.950 mm (0.9035 inch)
  Countershaft first
    Inside
      Standard.. 17.000 to 17.018 mm (0.6693 to 0.6700 inch)
      Limit... 17.030 mm (0.6705 inch)
    Outside
      Standard.. 19.979 to 20.000 mm (0.7866 to 0.7874 inch)
      Limit... 19.950 mm (0.7854 inch)
  Countershaft second
    2003 and earlier
      Inside
        Standard.. 22.000 to 22.021 mm (0.8661 to 0.8670 inch)
        Limit... 22.040 mm (0.8677 inch)
      Outside
        Standard.. 24.979 to 25.000 mm (0.9834 to 0.9843 inch)
        Limit... 24.950 mm (0.9823 inch)
    2004 and later
      Inside
        Standard.. 24.000 to 24.021 mm (0.9449 to 0.9457 inch)
        Limit... 24.204 mm (0.946 inch)
      Outside
        Standard.. 26.979 to 27.000 mm (1.0622 to 1.0630 inches)
        Limit... 26.95 mm (1.061 inch)
  Countershaft third (outside only)
    Standard.. 24.979 to 25.000 mm (0.9834 to 0.9843 inch)
    Limit... 24.950 mm (0.9823 inch)
  Countershaft fourth
    Inside
      Standard.. 22.000 to 22.021 mm (0.8661 to 0.8670 inch)
      Limit... 22.040 mm (0.8677 inch)
    Outside
      Standard.. 24.979 to 25.000 mm (0.9834 to 0.9843 inch)
      Limit... 24.950 mm (0.9823 inch)

CR125R (continued)

Transmission (continued)

Mainshaft diameter at fifth gear
  Standard .... 19.959 to 19.980 mm (0.7858 to 0.7866 inch)
  Limit .... 19.940 mm (0.7850 inch)
Countershaft diameter
  At first gear and kickstarter idler gear
    1986
      Standard.. 16.988 to 16.994 mm (0.6682 to 0.6691 inch)
      Limit.. 16.970 mm (0.6681 inch)
    1987 on
      Standard.. 16.983 to 16.994 mm (0.6686 to 0.6691 inch)
      Limit.. 16.970 mm (0.6681 inch)
  At second gear
    2003 and earlier
      Standard.. 21.959 to 21.980 mm (0.8645 to 0.8654 inch)
      Limit.. 21.94 mm (0.8638 inch)
    2004 and later
      Standard.. 23.959 to 23.980 mm (0.9433 to 0.9441 inch)
      Limit.. 23.94 mm (0.943 inch)
  At third (1998 and later five-speed) or fourth (six-speed)
    Standard.. 21.959 to 21.980 mm (0.8645 to 0.8654 inch)
    Limit.. 21.94 mm (0.8638 inch)
  At third gear (1986 and 1987)
    Standard.. 21.959 to 21.980 mm (0.8645 to 0.8654 inch)
    Limit.. 21.94 mm (0.8638 inch)

Crankshaft

Connecting rod side clearance
  1986 through 1988
    Standard.. 0.15 to 0.60 mm (0.006 to 0.024 inch)
    Limit.. 0.7 mm (0.028 inch)
  1989
    Standard.. 0.20 to 0.65 mm (0.007 to 0.024 inch)
    Limit.. 0.75 mm (0.030 inch)
Connecting rod side clearance (continued)
  1990 on
    Standard.. 0.4 to 0.8 mm (0.016 to 0.031 inch)
    Limit.. 0.9 mm (0.035 inch)
Connecting rod big end radial clearance
  1986 through 1988
    Standard.. 0.012 to 0.024 mm (0.0005 to 0.0009 inch)
    Limit.. 0.034 mm (0.0013 inch)
  1989 through 1991
    Standard.. 0.022 to 0.034 mm (0.0008 to 0.0013 inch)
    Limit.. 0.044 mm (0.0017 inch)
  1992 on
    Standard.. 0.010 to 0.022 mm (0.0004 to 0.0009 inch)
    Limit.. 0.032 mm (0.0013 inch)
Crankshaft V-block positions
  1986 through 1991 and 1998 on.. 8 mm (0.3 inch) outboard of outer crank throw surfaces (centered on bearing journals)
  1992 through 1997... Not specified
Runout measuring points
  At alternator end
    1986 and 1987... 35 mm (1.38 inches) outboard of crank throw surface (in alternator rotor area)
    1988 through 1991 and 1998 on .... 32 mm (1.26 inches) outboard of crank throw surface (in alternator rotor area)
    1992 through 1997 .... Not specified
  At clutch end
    1986 through 1991 and 1998 on..................................... 19 mm (0.75 inch) outboard of crank throw surface (in clutch housing area)
    1992 through 1997 .... Not specified
Runout limit
  1986 and 1987 .... 0.02 mm (0.0008 inch)
  1988 on .... 0.05 mm (0.002 inch)

Torque specifications

Engine mounting through-bolts
  1986 through 1992 .... 27 Nm (20 ft-lbs)
  1993 through 1997 .... 33 Nm (24 ft-lbs)
  1998 and 1999 .... 37 Nm (27 ft-lbs)
  2000 on .... 54 Nm (40 ft-lbs)
Engine mounting bracket bolts
  1986 through 1989 .... 38 to 48 Nm (27 to 35 ft-lbs)
  1990 through 1998 .... 27 Nm (20 ft-lbs)
  1999 .... 64 Nm (47 ft-lbs)
  2000 on .... 34 Nm (25 ft-lbs)
Cylinder head nuts .... 27 Nm (20 ft-lbs)
Cylinder nuts .... 27 Nm (20 ft-lbs)
Cylinder studs .... 12 Nm (108 inch-lbs) (1)
Outer clutch cover bolts (1992 on) .... 9 Nm (78 inch-lbs)
Right crankcase cover bolts .... 9 Nm (78 inch-lbs)
Clutch spring bolts .... 10 Nm (84 inch-lbs)
Clutch center nut
  1986 and 1987 .... 40 to 50 Nm (ft-lbs) (2)
  1988 through 1999 .... 60 Nm (43 ft-lbs) (2)
  2000 on .... 69 Nm (51 ft-lbs) (2)
Primary drive gear bolt
  1986 through 1993 .... 45 Nm (33 ft-lbs)
  1994 on .... 65 Nm (47 ft-lbs)
Shift cam plate to shift drum bolt .... 22 Nm (16 ft-lbs) (1)
Shift drum stopper arm bolt .... 12 Nm (108 inch-lbs)
Shift pedal pinch bolt .... Not specified
Crankcase bolts .... Not specified
Case bearing retainer screws or bolts.................................. 10 Nm 84 inch-lbs) (1)

1. *Apply non-permanent thread locking agent to the threads.*
2. *Use a new lockwasher.*

1   General information

The engine/transmission unit is of the liquid-cooled, single-cylinder two-stroke design. The engine/transmission assembly is constructed from aluminum alloy. The crankcase is divided vertically.

The cylinder, piston, crankshaft bearings and connecting rod lower end bearing are lubricated by the fuel, which is a mixture of gasoline and two-stroke oil (20:1 for 1986 through 1991 CR125R models; 32:1 for 1992 and later CR125R and all CR80R/85R models). The transmission and clutch are lubricated by four-stroke engine oil, which is contained in a sump within the crankcase. Power from the crankshaft is routed to the transmission via a wet, multi-plate type clutch. The transmission on 1986 through 1997 models has six forward gears. On 1998 and later models it has five forward gears.

2   Operations possible with the engine in the frame

The components and assemblies listed below can be removed without having to remove the engine from the frame. If, however, a number of areas require attention at the same time, removal of the engine is recommended.

Cylinder and piston
External shift mechanism
Clutch and primary drive gear
Kickstarter

3   Operations requiring engine removal

It is necessary to remove the engine/transmission assembly from the frame and separate the crankcase halves to gain access to the following components:

Crankshaft and connecting rod
Transmission shafts
Internal shift mechanism (gearshift spindle, shift drum and forks)
Crankcase bearings

4   Major engine repair - general note

1   It is not always easy to determine when or if an engine should be completely overhauled, as a number of factors must be considered.
2   High mileage is not necessarily an indication that an overhaul is needed, while low mileage, on the other hand, does not preclude the need for an overhaul. Regular maintenance is probably the single most important consideration. This is especially true if the bike is used in competition. An engine that has regular and frequent oil changes, as well as other required maintenance, will most likely give many hours of reliable service. Conversely, a neglected engine, or one which has not been broken in properly, may require an overhaul very early in its life.
3   Poor running that can't be accounted for by seemingly obvious causes (fouled spark plug, leaking head or cylinder base gasket, worn piston ring, carburetor problems) may be due to leaking crankshaft seals. In two-stroke engines, the crankcase acts as a suction pump to draw in fuel mixture and as a compressor to force it into the cylinder. If the crankcase seals are leaking, the pressure drop will cause a loss of performance.
4   If the engine is making obvious knocking or rumbling noises, the connecting rod and/or main bearings are probably at fault. The upper connecting rod bearing should be replaced at the maintenance interval listed in Chapter 1.
5   A top-end overhaul, part of regularly scheduled maintenance on these machines, consists of replacing the piston and ring and inspecting the cylinder bore. The cylinder on some models can be bored for an oversize piston if necessary; on others, the cylinder and piston must be replaced with new ones if they're worn.
6   A lower-end engine overhaul generally involves inspecting the

crankshaft, transmission and crankcase bearings and seals. Unlike four-stroke engines equipped with plain main and connecting rod bearings, there isn't much in the way of machine work that can be done to refurbish existing parts. Worn bearings, gears, seals and shift mechanism parts should be replaced with new ones. The crankshaft and connecting rod are permanently assembled, so if one of these components (or the connecting rod lower end bearing) needs to be replaced, both must be. While the engine is being overhauled, other components such as the carburetor can be rebuilt also. The end result should be a like-new engine that will give as many trouble-free hours as the original.
7   Before beginning the engine overhaul, read through all of the related procedures to familiarize yourself with the scope and requirements of the job. Overhauling an engine is not all that difficult, but it is time consuming. Plan on the motorcycle being tied up for a minimum of two weeks. Check on the availability of parts and make sure that any necessary special tools, equipment and supplies are obtained in advance.
8   Most work can be done with typical shop hand tools, although a number of precision measuring tools are required for inspecting parts to determine if they must be replaced. Often a dealer service department or repair shop will handle the inspection of parts and offer advice concerning reconditioning and replacement. As a general rule, time is the primary cost of an overhaul so it doesn't pay to install worn or substandard parts.
9   As a final note, to ensure maximum life and minimum trouble from a rebuilt engine, everything must be assembled with care in a spotlessly clean environment.

5   Crankcase pressure and vacuum - check

This test can pinpoint the cause of otherwise unexplained poor running. It can also prevent piston seizures by detecting air leaks that can cause a lean mixture. It requires special equipment, but can easily be done by a Honda dealer or other motorcycle shop. If you regularly work on two-stroke engines, you might want to consider purchasing the tester for yourself (or with a group of other riders). You may also be able to fabricate the tester.

The test involves sealing off the intake and exhaust ports (and the Honda Power Port openings on models equipped with an HPP system), then applying vacuum and pressure to the spark plug hole with a hand vacuum/pressure pump, similar to the type used for brake bleeding and automotive vacuum testing.

First, remove the carburetor and exhaust system. Block off the carburetor opening with a rubber plug, clamped securely in position. Place a rubber sheet (cut from a tire tube or similar material) over the exhaust port and secure it with a metal plate. If the bike has a Honda Power Port system, you'll need to seal these openings as well, using rubber gaskets and special adapters.

Apply air pressure to the spark plug hole with the vacuum/pressure pump. Check for leaks at the crankcase gasket, intake manifold, reed valve gasket, cylinder base gasket and head gasket. If the crankcase gasket leaks between the transmission sump and the crankcase (the area where the crankshaft spins), transmission oil will be sucked into the crankcase, causing the fuel mixture to be oil-rich. Also check the seal at the alternator end of the crankshaft. If the leaks are large, air will hiss as it passes through them. Small leaks can be detected by pouring soapy water over the suspected area and looking for bubbles.

After checking for air leaks, apply vacuum with the pump. If vacuum leaks down quickly, the crankshaft seals are leaking.

6   Engine - removal and installation

Note: *Engine removal and installation should be done with the aid of an assistant to avoid damage or injury that could occur if the engine is dropped.*

Removal

Refer to illustrations 6.13, 6.14, 6.15a and 6.15b
1   Drain the transmission oil and coolant (see Chapter 1).

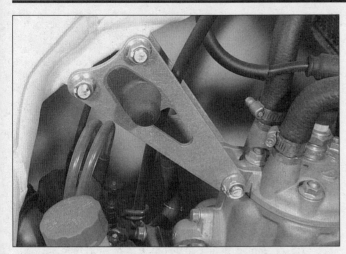

6.13 **Remove the upper mounting bracket (CR125R only) . . .**

6.14 **. . . the two through-bolts under the engine . . .**

2   Remove the seat and right side cover (see Chapter 8).
3   If you're working on a 1986 CR125R, remove the subframe from the rear of the bike (see Chapter 8).
4   If you're working on a 1992 or later CR125R, remove the brake pedal (see Chapter 7).
5   Remove the fuel tank, exhaust system and carburetor (see Chapter 4).
6   Disconnect the spark plug wire (see Chapter 1).
7   Disconnect the coolant hoses from the engine (see Chapter 3).
8   On 1986 through 1998 models, label and disconnect the alternator and pulse generator wires (refer to Chapter 5 for component location if necessary). On 1999 and later models, label and disconnect the wires for the ignition coil (primary and ground), ignition control unit and engine kill switch. Detach the wires from their retainers.
9   Remove the drive chain and sprocket (see Chapter 6).
10   Disconnect the clutch cable (see Section 12).
11   If you're working on a 1995 or later CR80R/85R, free the crankcase breather hose from its clip on top of the engine.
12   Support the bike securely upright so it can't fall over during the remainder of this procedure. Support the engine with a jack, if necessary, using a block of wood between the jack and the engine to protect the crankcase.
13   If you're working on a CR125R, remove the upper engine mount **(see illustration)**.
14   Remove the engine mounting bolts and nuts at the front and bot-

tom **(see illustration)**.
15   Remove the swingarm pivot bolt nut (see Chapter 6). The pivot bolt passes through the rear of the crankcase to act as an engine support **(see illustration)**, so it needs to be pulled out of the crankcase. To avoid removing the swingarm completely, pull the bolt only until it clears the engine. Leave the bolt in the right swingarm pivot while you lift the engine out **(see illustration)**.
16   Have an assistant help you lift the engine out of the frame, if necessary.
17   Slowly lower the engine to a suitable work surface.

Installation

18   Have an assistant help lift the engine into the frame, then align the mounting bolt holes and install the bolts, nuts and upper bracket (CR125R). Tighten them to the torques listed in this Chapter's Specifications. Refer to the Chapter 6 Specifications for the swingarm pivot bolt torque.
19   The remainder of installation is the reverse of the removal steps, with the following additions:
a) Use new gaskets at all exhaust pipe connections.
b) Adjust the throttle cable and clutch cable following the procedures in Chapter 1.
c) Fill the engine with oil and coolant, also following the procedures in Chapter 1.
d) Run the engine and check for oil, coolant or exhaust leaks.

6.15a **. . . and the swingarm pivot bolt where it passes through the crankcase casting . . .**

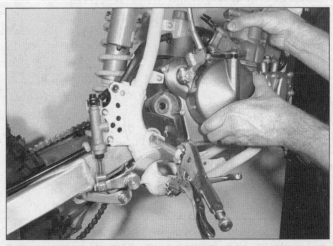

6.15b **. . . if you pull the pivot bolt out just far enough to clear the engine, you won't have to remove the swingarm from the bike**

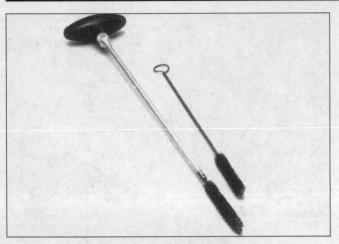

7.2 A selection of brushes is required for cleaning holes and passages in the engine components

7.3 An engine stand can be made from short lengths of lumber and lag bolts or nails

7 Engine disassembly and reassembly - general information

Refer to illustrations 7.2 and 7.3

1 Before disassembling the engine, clean the exterior with a degreaser and rinse it with water. A clean engine will make the job easier and prevent the possibility of getting dirt into the internal areas of the engine.

2 In addition to the precision measuring tools mentioned earlier, you will need a torque wrench and oil gallery brushes **(see illustration)**. Some new, clean engine oil of the correct grade and type (two-stroke oil, four-stroke oil or both, depending on whether it's a top-end or bottom-end overhaul), some engine assembly lube (or moly-based grease) and a tube of RTV (silicone) sealant will also be required.

3 An engine support stand made from short lengths of 2 x 4's bolted together will facilitate the disassembly and reassembly procedures **(see illustration)**. If you have an automotive-type engine stand, an adapter plate can be made from a piece of plate, some angle iron and some nuts and bolts.

4 When disassembling the engine, keep "mated" parts together (including gears, shift forks and shafts, etc.) that have been in contact with each other during engine operation. These "mated" parts must be reused or replaced as an assembly.

5 Engine/transmission disassembly should be done in the following general order with reference to the appropriate Sections.

> *Remove the cylinder head*
> *Remove the cylinder*
> *Remove the piston*
> *Remove the water pump*
> *Remove the clutch*
> *Remove the primary drive gear*
> *Remove the kickstarter*
> *Remove the external shift mechanism*
> *Remove the alternator rotor*
> *Separate the crankcase halves*
> *Remove the internal shift mechanism*
> *Remove the transmission shafts and gears*
> *Remove the crankshaft and connecting rod*

6 Reassembly is accomplished by reversing the general disassembly sequence.

8 Cylinder head - removal, inspection and installation

Caution: *The engine must be completely cool before beginning this procedure, or the cylinder head may become warped.*

Note: *This procedure is described with the engine in the frame. If the engine has been removed, ignore the steps which don't apply.*

Removal

Refer to illustrations 8.6a, 8.6b, 8.8a and 8.8b

1 Drain the coolant system (see Chapter 1) and disconnect the radiator hoses from the cylinder head (see Chapter 3).

2 Disconnect the spark plug wire (see Chapter 1).

CR125R

3 Remove the seat and right side cover (see Chapter 8).

4 Remove the top engine mount (see Section 6).

5 Remove the expansion chamber (see Chapter 4).

All models

6 Loosen the cylinder head nuts in two or three stages, in a crisscross pattern **(see illustrations)**. Remove the nuts once they're all loose.

7 Lift the cylinder head off the cylinder. If the head is stuck, use a wooden dowel inserted into the spark plug hole to lever the head off. Don't attempt to pry the head off by inserting a screwdriver between the head and the cylinder - you'll damage the sealing surfaces. If you're working on a 2000 or later model, locate the two cylinder head dowels - they may have come off with the head or remained in the cylinder.

8 Rotate the piston to the top of the cylinder or stuff a clean rag into the cylinder to prevent the entry of debris. Once this is done, remove the gasket from the cylinder **(see illustrations)**.

Inspection

Refer to illustrations 8.12a and 8.12b

9 Check the cylinder head gasket and the mating surfaces on the cylinder head and cylinder for leakage, which could indicate warpage.

10 Clean all traces of old gasket material from the cylinder head and cylinder. Be careful not to let any of the gasket material fall into the cylinder or coolant passages.

11 Inspect the head very carefully for cracks and other damage. If cracks are found, a new head will be required

12 Using a precision straightedge and a feeler gauge, check the head gasket mating surface for warpage. Lay the straightedge across the head, intersecting the head bolt holes, and try to slip a feeler gauge under it, on either side of the combustion chamber **(see illustrations)**. The feeler gauge thickness should be the same as the cylinder head warpage limit listed in this Chapter's Specifications. If the feeler gauge can be inserted between the head and the straightedge, the head is warped and must either be machined or, if warpage is excessive, replaced with a new one.

8.6a The CR80R/85R cylinder head is secured by four nuts; the triangular mark (arrow) points to the front of the engine

8.6b The CR125R cylinder head is secured by five nuts

8.8a The tab with the UP mark goes toward the rear of the engine; the cylinder is secured by four nuts (arrows)

8.8b Make sure the small coolant passages are clear

Installation

13   Lay the new gasket in place on the cylinder **(see illustration 8.8a or 8.8b)**. Never reuse the old gasket and don't use any type of gasket sealant.

14   Carefully lower the cylinder head over the studs.

15   Install the cylinder head nuts and tighten them evenly, in a criss-cross pattern, to the torque listed in this Chapter's Specifications.

16   The remainder of installation is the reverse of the removal steps. Be sure to refill the cooling system (see Chapter 1).

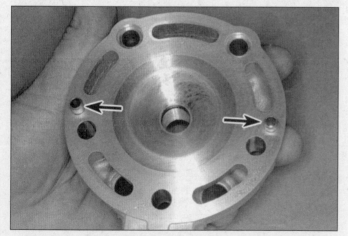

8.12a On 2000 and later CR125R models, remove the two dowels (arrows) . . .

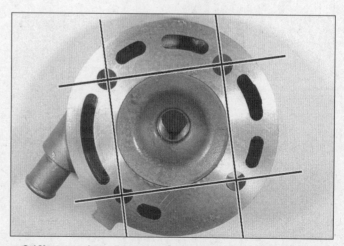

8.12b . . . and on all models, measure cylinder head warpage along the bolt holes

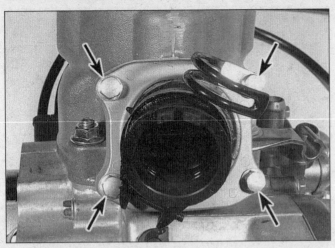

9.2 Unbolt the carburetor intake tube and remove it from the cylinder with its O-ring . . .

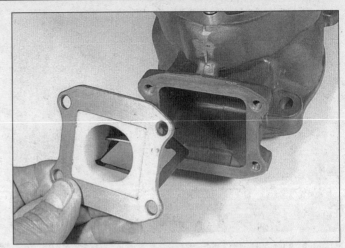

9.3 . . . then pull out the reed valve and remove the gasket

9   Reed valve - removal, inspection and installation

Removal

Refer to illustrations 9.2 and 9.3

1   Remove the carburetor (see Chapter 4).
2   Unbolt the carburetor intake tube from the cylinder **(see illustration)**. Take off the intake tube and its O-ring.
3   Pull the reed valve out of the cylinder and remove the gasket **(see illustration)**.

Inspection

Refer to illustrations 9.6a and 9.6b

4   Check the reed valve for obvious damage, such as cracked or broken reeds or stoppers. Also make sure there's no clearance between the reeds and the edges where they make contact with the seats.
5   If you're working on a 1986 through 1994 model, the reed valve must be replaced as an assembly if any problems are found.
6   1995 and later reed valves can be disassembled and the reeds replaced. Remove the screws and stoppers **(see illustration)**. The screws have locking agent on the threads, so you may need to use an impact driver. Remove the reeds and install new ones. Install the

stoppers, aligning the cutout in the stopper with the cutout in the reed. Coat the screw threads with non-permanent thread locking agent, then tighten securely. After assembly, check the clearance between the reeds and reed stoppers (CR80R/85R models) **(see illustration)**. It should be 7.4 ± 0.2 mm (0.29 ± 0.01 inch). On CR125 models, check the reed valve opening clearance. It should be 0.2 mm (0.01 inch).

Installation

7   Installation is the reverse of the removal steps, with the following additions:

a) *Use a new gasket between the reed valve assembly and cylinder.*
b) *Use a new O-ring between the carburetor intake tube and the reed valve assembly.*
c) *Tighten the intake tube bolts in a criss-cross pattern to the torque listed in this Chapter's Specifications.*

10   Cylinder - removal, inspection and installation

Note: *For bikes used in competition, periodic replacement of the cylinder is a routine maintenance procedure that should be done at the intervals listed in Chapter 1.*

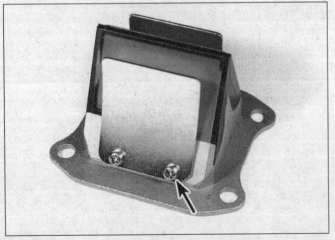

9.6a Remove the screws to detach the reed stoppers from the reed valve; on installation, align the diagonally cut corners of the reed and stopper (arrow)

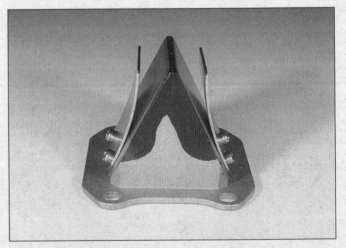

9.6b Measure the gap between the reed stoppers and reeds (CR80R/85R models)

10.3 Tap the cylinder with a soft-faced mallet to free it from the crankcase

10.4a CR80R/85R models have a single dowel (arrow) . . .

Removal

Refer to illustrations 10.3, 10.4a, 10.4b and 10.4c

1   Remove the cylinder head (see Section 8). Make sure the crankshaft is positioned at top dead center (TDC). If you're working on a CR125R model, disconnect the pinion rod for the HPP, CRV or RC system (see Chapter 4).

2   Remove four nuts securing the cylinder to the crankcase **(see illustration 8.8a)**.

3   Lift the cylinder straight up off the piston. If it's stuck, tap around its perimeter with a soft-faced hammer **(see illustration)**. Don't attempt to pry between the cylinder and the crankcase, as you'll ruin the sealing surfaces.

4   Locate the dowel pins (they may have come off with the cylinder or still be in the crankcase) **(see illustrations)**. Be careful not to let these drop into the engine. Stuff clean shop rags around the piston and remove the gasket and all traces of old gasket material from the surfaces of the cylinder and the crankcase **(see illustration)**.

Inspection

Refer to illustrations 10.5a, 10.5b, 10.6, 10.7a, 10.7b and 10.8
Caution: *Don't attempt to separate the liner from the cylinder.*

5   Check the top surface of the cylinder for warpage. Measure along the sides, across the stud holes **(see illustrations)**.

10.4b . . . CR125R models have two dowels (right arrows) - the piston IN mark faces the rear of the engine on installation; the letter is a bore size code that should match the one on the cylinder

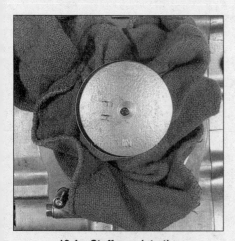

10.4c Stuff rags into the crankcase opening

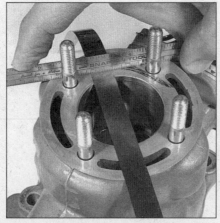

10.5a Measure cylinder surface warpage with a straightedge and feeler gauge . . .

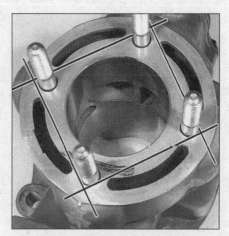

10.5b . . . in the directions shown

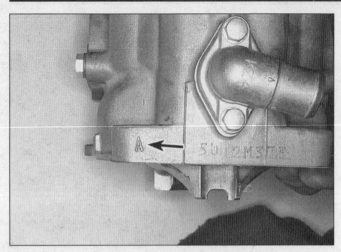

10.6 The bore size code on the cylinder (arrow) should match the one on the piston crown

10.7a Remove the cylinder coolant drain plug (arrow) if it's still installed and unbolt the exhaust headpipe (if equipped) . . .

6   If you're working on a 1989 or later CR125R, look for the bore size code on the base of the cylinder **(see illustration)**. This should match the letter code on the piston crown.

7   Check the cylinder walls carefully for scratches and score marks. Remove the coolant drain screw and sealing washer (if you haven't already done so). Unbolt the exhaust headpipe (CR80R/85R, 1990 and later CR125R) and remove its gasket **(see illustrations)**. If you're working on a 1986 through 1989 CR125R, remove the ATAC headpipe or chamber (see Chapter 4).

8   Using the appropriate precision measuring tools, check the cylinder's diameter at the top, center and bottom of the cylinder bore, parallel to the crankshaft axis **(see illustration)**. Next, measure the cylinder's diameter at the same three locations across the crankshaft axis. Compare the results to this Chapter's Specifications.

9   If you're working on a 1986 through 1988 CR125R and the cylinder walls are tapered, out-of-round, worn beyond the specified limits, or badly scuffed or scored, you can have the cylinder rebored and honed by a dealer service department or a motorcycle repair shop. If a rebore is done, oversize pistons and rings will be required as well. **Note:** *Honda supplies pistons in two oversizes for these models.*

10   If you're working on a CR80R/85R or a 1989 or later CR125R, the cylinder will have to be replaced if the conditions described in Step 9 are found.

11   As an alternative, if the precision measuring tools are not available, a dealer service department or repair shop will make the measurements and offer advice concerning servicing of the cylinder.

12   If it's in reasonably good condition and not worn to the outside of the limits, and if the piston-to-cylinder clearance can be maintained properly, then the cylinder does not have to be rebored; honing is all that is necessary.

13   To perform the honing operation you will need the proper size flexible hone with fine stones as shown in *Maintenance techniques, tools and working facilities* at the front of this book, or a "bottle brush" type hone, plenty of light oil or honing oil, some shop towels and an electric drill motor. Hold the cylinder in a vise (cushioned with soft jaws or wood blocks) when performing the honing operation. Mount the hone in the drill motor, compress the stones and slip the hone into the cylinder. Lubricate the cylinder thoroughly, turn on the drill and move the hone up and down in the cylinder at a pace which will produce a fine crosshatch pattern on the cylinder wall with the crosshatch lines intersecting at approximately a 60-degree angle. Be sure to use plenty of lubricant and do not take off any more material than is absolutely necessary to produce the desired effect. Do not withdraw the hone from the cylinder while it is running. Instead, shut off the drill and continue moving the hone up and down in the cylinder until it comes to a complete stop, then compress the stones and withdraw

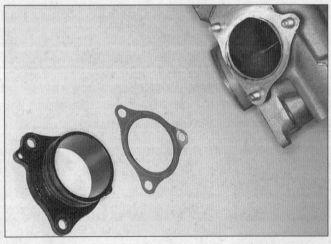

10.7b . . . then remove the headpipe and its gasket

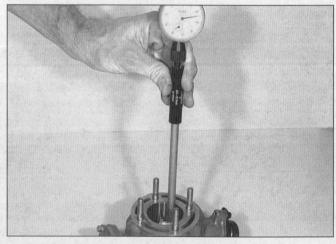

10.8 Measure bore diameter with a bore gauge

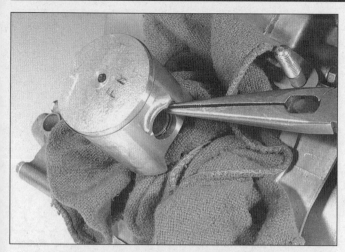

11.3 Wear eye protection and remove the circlip with a pointed tool or needle-nosed pliers

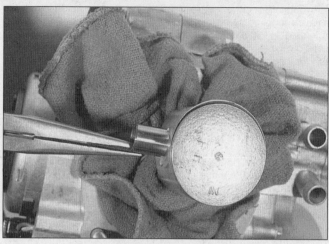

11.4a Push the piston pin partway out, then pull it the rest of the way

the hone. Wipe the oil out of the cylinder. Remember, do not remove too much material from the cylinder wall. If you do not have the tools, or do not desire to perform the honing operation, a dealer service department or motorcycle repair shop will generally do it for a reasonable fee.

14 Next, the cylinder must be thoroughly washed with warm soapy water to remove all traces of the abrasive grit produced during the honing operation. Be sure to run a brush through the bolt holes and flush them with running water. After rinsing, dry the cylinder thoroughly and apply a coat of light, rust-preventative oil to all machined surfaces.

Installation

15 Lubricate the piston with plenty of clean two-stroke engine oil.
16 Install the dowel pins, then lower a new cylinder base gasket over them **(see illustration 10.4a or 10.4b)**.
17 Install the cylinder over the studs and carefully lower it down until the piston crown fits into the cylinder liner. Push down on the cylinder, making sure the piston doesn't get cocked sideways, until the bottom of the cylinder liner slides down past the piston ring. Be sure not to rotate the cylinder, as this may snag the piston ring on the exhaust port. A wood or plastic hammer handle can be used to gently tap the cylinder down, but don't use too much force or the piston will be damaged.
18 The remainder of installation is the reverse of the removal steps.

11 Piston and ring - removal, inspection and installation

Note: *For bikes used in competition, periodic replacement of the piston and ring is a routine maintenance procedure that should be done at the intervals listed in Chapter 1.*
1 The piston is attached to the connecting rod with a piston pin that is a slip fit in the piston and connecting rod needle bearing.
2 Before removing the piston from the rod, stuff a clean shop towel into the crankcase hole, around the connecting rod. This will prevent the circlips from falling into the crankcase if they are inadvertently dropped.

Removal

Refer to illustrations 11.3, 11.4a and 11.4b
3 The piston should have an IN mark on its crown that goes toward

11.4b The piston pin should come out with hand pressure - if it doesn't, this removal tool can be fabricated from readily available parts

1	Bolt	7	Nut (B)
2	Washer	A	Large enough for piston pin to fit inside
3	Pipe (A)		
4	Padding (A)	B	Small enough to fit through piston pin bore
5	Piston		
6	Washer (B)		

the intake (rear) side of the engine **(see illustration 10.4b)**. If this mark is not visible due to carbon buildup, scribe an arrow into the piston crown before removal. Support the piston and pry the circlip out with a pointed tool or needle-nosed pliers **(see illustration)**.
4 Push the piston pin out from the opposite end to free the piston from the rod **(see illustration)**. You may have to deburr the area around the groove to enable the pin to slide out (use a triangular file for this procedure). If the pin won't come out, you can fabricate a piston pin removal tool from a long bolt, a nut, a piece of tubing and washers **(see illustration)**.

Inspection

Refer to illustrations 11.6, 11.9, 11.14, 11.15a, 11.15b and 11.16
5 Before the inspection process can be carried out, the piston must be cleaned and the old piston ring removed.

6   Carefully remove the ring from the piston **(see illustration)**. Do not nick or gouge the pistons in the process. A ring removal and installation tool will make this easier, but you can use your fingers if you don't have one - just be sure not to cut yourself.

7   Scrape all traces of carbon from the top of the piston. A hand-held wire brush or a piece of fine emery cloth can be used once most of the deposits have been scraped away. Do not, under any circumstances, use a wire brush mounted in a drill motor to remove deposits from the piston; the piston material is soft and will be eroded away by the wire brush.

8   Use a piston ring groove cleaning tool to remove any carbon deposits from the ring groove. If a tool is not available, a piece broken off the old ring will do the job. Be very careful to remove only the carbon deposits. Do not remove any metal and do not nick or gouge the sides of the ring grooves.

9   Once the deposits have been removed, clean the piston with solvent and dry it thoroughly. Make sure the oil return holes inside the piston are clear **(see illustration)**.

10   Normal piston wear appears as even, vertical wear on the thrust surfaces of the piston and slight looseness of the ring in its groove.

11   Carefully inspect each piston for cracks around the skirt, at the pin bosses and at the ring lands.

12   Look for scoring and scuffing on the thrust faces of the skirt, holes in the piston crown and burned areas at the edge of the crown. If the skirt is scored or scuffed, the engine may have been suffering from overheating and/or abnormal combustion, which caused excessively high operating temperatures. A hole in the piston crown, an extreme to be sure, is an indication that abnormal combustion (pre-ignition) was occurring. Burned areas at the edge of the piston crown are usually evidence of spark knock (detonation). If any of the above problems exist, the causes must be corrected or the damage will occur again.

13   If you're working on a CR125R, measure the piston ring-to-groove clearance (side clearance) by laying a new piston ring in the ring groove and slipping a feeler gauge in beside it. Ring side clearance isn't specified for CR80R/85R models. Check the clearance at three or four locations around the groove. If the clearance is greater than specified, a new piston will have to be used when the engine is reassembled.

14   Check the piston-to-bore clearance by measuring the bore (see Section 10) and the piston diameter **(see illustration)**. Measure the piston across the skirt on the thrust faces at a 90-degree angle to the piston pin, at the specified distance up from the bottom of the skirt. Subtract the piston diameter from the bore diameter to obtain the clearance. If it is greater than specified, the cylinder will have to be rebored and a new oversized piston and ring installed (1986 through 1988 CR125R) or the cylinder and piston will have to be replaced (all other models). If the appropriate precision measuring tools are not

11.6 Remove the piston rings with a ring removal and installation tool if you have one; you can use fingers instead if you're careful

available, the piston-to-cylinder clearance can be obtained, though not quite as accurately, using feeler gauge stock. Feeler gauge stock comes in 12-inch lengths and various thickness and is generally available at auto parts stores. To check the clearance, slip a piece of feeler gauge stock of the same thickness as the specified piston clearance into the cylinder along with appropriate piston. The cylinder should be upside down and the piston must be positioned exactly as it normally would be. Place the feeler gauge between the piston and cylinder on one of the thrust faces (90-degrees to the piston pin bore). The piston should slip through the cylinder (with the feeler gauge in place) with moderate pressure. If it falls through, or slides through easily, the clearance is excessive and a new piston will be required. If the piston binds at the lower end of the cylinder and is loose toward the top, the cylinder is tapered, and if tight spots are encountered as the piston/feeler gauge is rotated in the cylinder, the cylinder is out-of-round. Be sure to have the cylinder and piston checked by a dealer service department or a repair shop to confirm your findings before purchasing new parts.

15   Apply clean two-stroke oil to the pin, insert it into the piston and check for freeplay by rocking the pin back-and-forth **(see illustration)**. If the pin is loose, a new piston and possibly new pin must be installed. To determine which, measure the pin diameter and the pin bore in the piston (or have this done by a dealer or repair shop) **(see illustration)**.

16   Repeat Step 15, this time inserting the piston pin into the connecting rod needle bearing **(see illustration)**. If it wobbles and the pin diameter is within specifications, replace the needle bearing.

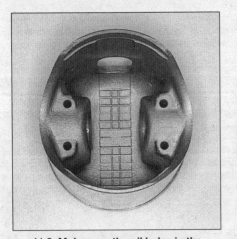

11.9 Make sure the oil holes in the underside of the piston are clear

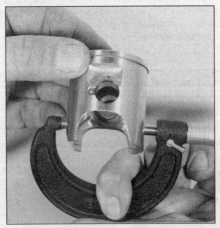

11.14 Measure the piston diameter with a micrometer

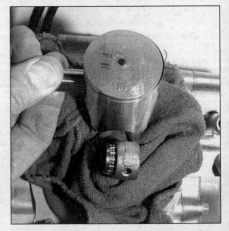

11.15a Slip the pin into the piston and try to wiggle it back-and-forth; if it's loose, replace the piston and pin; the needle bearing in the rod should be replaced if its condition is in doubt

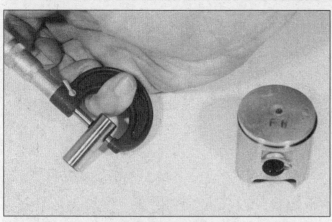

11.15b Measure pin diameter and the diameter of the pin hole in the piston

Installation

Refer to illustrations 11.19a and 11.19b

17   Install the piston with its IN mark toward the intake side (rear) of the engine. **Note:** *On 1990 and later CR125R models, there's a hole in the intake side of the piston skirt. If you can't see the IN mark, install the piston with its intake hole to the rear.* Lubricate the pin and the rod needle bearing with two-stroke oil of the type listed in the Chapter 1 Specifications.

18   Install a new circlip in the groove in one side of the piston (don't reuse the old circlips). Push the pin into position from the opposite side and install another new circlip. Compress the circlips only enough for them to fit in the piston. Make sure the clips are properly seated in the grooves.

19   Locate the manufacturer's mark on the piston ring near one of the ends **(see illustration)**. Turn the ring so this mark is upward, then carefully spread it and install it in the ring groove. Make sure the end gap is positioned over the dowel pin in the ring groove **(see illustration)**.

12   Clutch - removal, inspection and installation

Cable

Removal

Refer to illustrations 12.2, 12.3a and 12.3b

1   Loosen the cable adjuster at the handlebar grip all the way (see Chapter 1). Rotate the cable so the inner cable aligns with the slot in the lever, then slip the cable end fitting out of the lever.

2   If you're working on a CR80R/85R, loosen the locknut and adjusting nut at the engine bracket (see Chapter 1). Disengage the cable from the lifter lever in the right engine cover, then pull the outer cable out of the bracket and slip the inner cable through the slot in the bracket **(see illustration)**.

3   If you're working on a CR125R, remove the left crankcase cover (see Chapter 5). You may need to spread the gap in the lifter lever slightly so the cable will fit through it **(see illustration)**. Turn the lifter lever to slacken the cable, then slip the cable end through the gap and pull it out of the crankcase **(see illustration)**.

11.16 The needle bearing should be replaced if the pin wobbles inside it

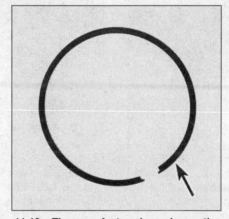

11.19a The manufacturer's mark near the ring gap (arrow) should be facing up when the ring is installed

11.19b Position the ring ends on either side of the dowel pin in the ring groove (arrow)

12.2 Rotate the lever arm against spring tension and slip the cable out of its slot (CR80R/85R)

12.3a You may need to widen the slot to make room for the cable (CR125R)

12.3b Rotate the lever arm against spring tension and slip the cable out of its slot (CR125R)

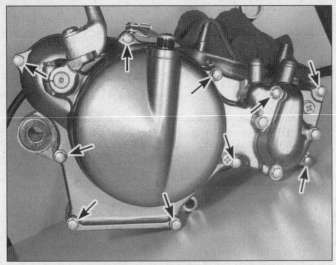

12.11a Right crankcase cover bolts - CR80R/85R

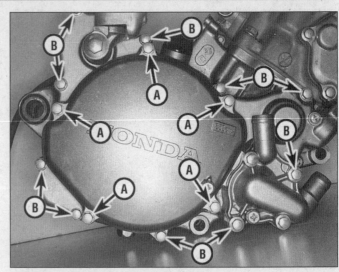

12.11b The CR125R clutch is accessible by removing the outer cover bolts (A); to remove the entire crankcase cover, remove its bolts (B)

12.11c CR80R/85R cover dowels

12.11d Later CR125R cover dowels (A); early models have one dowel at the rear of the engine, as shown, and one at the top near the front of the engine (B)

Inspection

4   Slide the inner cable back and forth in the housing and make sure it moves freely. If it doesn't, try lubricating it as described in Chapter 1. If that doesn't help, replace the cable. Inspect the O-ring on the end of the cable that fits into the crankcase and replace it if necessary.

Installation

5   Installation is the reverse of the removal steps. Refer to Chapter 1 and adjust clutch freeplay.

Right crankcase cover

Refer to illustrations 12.11a, 12.11b, 12.11c and 12.11d

Note: *If you're working on a 1992 or later CR125R, you can service the clutch (discs, plates, center and housing) by removing just the outer clutch cover. It isn't necessary to remove the entire crankcase cover.*

6   Drain the transmission oil and coolant oil (see Chapter 1).
7   Disconnect the hoses from the water pump (see Chapter 3).
8   Remove the brake pedal (see Chapter 7).
9   Remove the kickstarter pedal (see Section 15).
10   If you're working on a CR80R/85R, disconnect the clutch cable from the lifter lever as described above.
11   Remove the cover bolts and pull the cover off the engine **(see illustrations)**. The upper rear bolt on 20000 and later CR125R models secures a harness retainer. Tap gently with a rubber mallet if necessary

to break the gasket seal. Don't pry against the mating surfaces of the cover and crankcase.
12   Once the cover is off, locate the dowels; they may have stayed in the crankcase or come off with the cover.

Lifter lever

CR80R/85R models

Refer to illustrations 12.14a, 12.14b, 12.14c and 12.17

13   Remove the right crankcase cover as described above.
14   Note how the spring is installed, then turn the lifter lever and pull the lifter pin out of the lever notch **(see illustrations)**.
15   Pull out the lifter lever shaft out of the cover.
16   Check for visible wear or damage at the contact points of the lifter lever and push piece. Replace any parts that show problems.
17   Pry the lifter shaft seal out of the cover **(see illustration)**. If the needle bearing is worn or damaged, drive it out with a shouldered drift the same diameter as the bearing, then use the same tool to drive in a new one. Pack the needle bearing with grease and press in a new seal.
18   Installation is the reverse of the removal steps. Engage the notch in the lever shaft with the lifter pin and hook the spring to the lever and cover.

12.14a CR80R/85R clutch lifter lever spring

12.14b Pull the push piece out of the cover . . .

12.14c . . . on installation, engage the push piece with the notch in the lever shaft

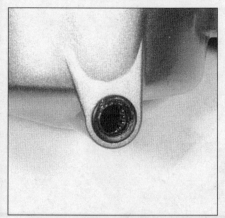

12.17 The lifter lever shaft rides in this bearing; replace the seal if it's worn

12.21 Some CR125R models have a spring and washer on the lifter lever shaft

12.24a Wedge a copper washer or penny between the gears to prevent the clutch from turning

12.24b Unscrew the bolts and remove the lifter plate together with its ball bearing

12.24c Take the clutch springs off their posts

12.24d Remove the bolt and washer; if there's an OUT mark on the washer, it faces away from the engine on installation

CR125R models
Refer to illustration 12.21

19 Remove the alternator cover (see Chapter 5).
20 Disconnect the clutch cable as described above.
21 Slide the lever (and its spring and washer if equipped) out of the pivot bore in the crankcase **(see illustration)**.
22 Installation is the reverse of the removal steps.

Clutch
Removal (CR80R/85R)
Refer to illustrations 12.24a through 12.24g

23 Remove the right crankcase cover as described above.
24 Refer to the accompanying illustrations to remove the clutch **(see illustrations)**.

12.24e Pull off the pressure plate, clutch discs and clutch center . . .

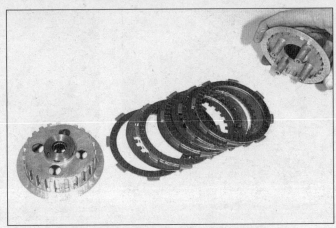

12.24f . . . then separate the parts for inspection

12.24g Pull off the thrust washer, clutch housing and the bushing (arrow)

12.26a Remove the CR125R clutch outer cover and its O-ring

Removal (CR125R)

Refer to illustrations 12.26a through 12.26i

25   Remove the clutch cover or right crankcase cover as described above.

26   Refer to the accompanying illustrations to remove the clutch components **(see illustrations)**.

Inspection

Refer to illustrations 12.28, 12.32, 12.33 and 12.34

27   If you're working on a CR80R/85R, rotate the release bearing and

check it for rough, loose or noisy operation **(see illustration 12.24b)**. If the bearing's condition is in doubt, push it out of the lifter plate and install a new one.

28   Check the friction surface on the pressure plate for scoring or wear **(see illustration)**. Replace the pressure plate if any defects are found.

29   Check the edges of the slots in the clutch housing for indentations made by the friction plate tabs. If the indentations are deep they can prevent clutch release, so the housing should be replaced with a new one. If the indentations can be removed easily with a file, the life of the housing can be prolonged to an extent. Also, check the driven gear teeth for cracks, chips and excessive wear and the springs on the back side (if

12.26b Remove the bolts and take off the pressure plate

12.26c The lifter fits in the center of the clutch . . .

12.26d . . . pull it out, followed by its steel ball and the clutch pushrod

12.26e Bend the clutch lockwasher away from the nut

12.26f Hold the clutch from turning with a tool like this one and unscrew the nut . . .

12.26g . . . then remove the washer and pull off the clutch center and discs

12.26h Remove the thrust washer and clutch housing . . .

12.26i . . . the needle bearing and bushing

equipped) for breakage. If the gear is worn or damaged or the springs are broken, the clutch housing must be replaced with a new one.

30   Check the bearing surface in the center of the clutch housing for score marks, scratches and excessive wear. Measure the inside diameter of the bearing surface, the inside and outside diameters of the clutch housing bushing and the bushing's mounting surface on the transmission mainshaft. Compare these to the values listed in this Chapter's Specifications. Replace any parts worn beyond the service limits. If the bushing mounting surface on the mainshaft is worn excessively, the mainshaft will have to be replaced.

31   Check the clutch center's friction surface and slots for scoring, wear and indentations (see illustration 12.28). Also check the splines in the middle of the clutch center. Replace the clutch center if problems are found.

32   Measure the free length of the clutch springs (see illustration) and compare the results to this Chapter's Specifications. If the springs have sagged, or if cracks are noted, replace them with new ones as a set.

12.28 Clutch inspection points (CR80R/85R shown; CR125R similar)

A   Spring posts
B   Friction surfaces
C   Splines
D   Driven gear
E   Clutch housing bushing surface
F   Clutch housing slots

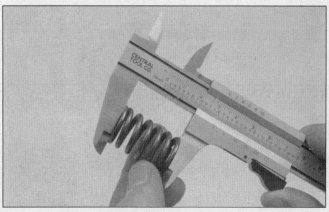

12.32 Measure the clutch spring free length

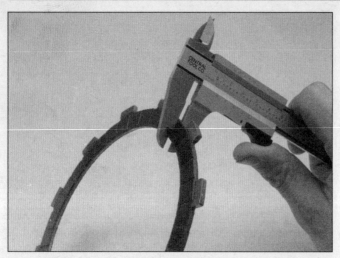

12.33 Measure the thickness of the friction plates

12.34 Check the metal plates for warpage

33   If the lining material of the friction plates smells burnt or if it is glazed, new parts are required. If the metal clutch plates are scored or discolored, they must be replaced with new ones. Measure the thickness of the friction plates **(see illustration)** and replace with new parts any friction plates that are worn.

13.2a Wedge a copper washer or penny between the gears, then unscrew the nut (CR80R/85R) . . .

13.2b . . . or bolt (CR125R)

34   Lay the metal plates, one at a time, on a perfectly flat surface (such as a piece of plate glass) and check for warpage by trying to slip a feeler gauge between the flat surface and the plate **(see illustration)**. The feeler gauge should be the same thickness as the maximum warp listed in this Chapter's Specifications. Do this at several places around the plate's circumference. If the feeler gauge can be slipped under the plate, it is warped and should be replaced with a new one.
35   Check the tabs on the friction plates for excessive wear and mushroomed edges. They can be cleaned up with a file if the deformation is not severe. Check the friction plates for warpage as described in Step 33.

Installation
36   Installation is the reverse of the removal steps, with the following additions:
   a) *If you're working on a CR80R/85R, install the lockwasher with its OUT mark (if it has one) facing away from the engine, then install the clutch bolt and tighten it to the torque listed in this Chapter's Specifications.*
   b) *If you're working on a CR125R, install a new lockwasher and position its tabs between the ribs of the clutch center. Tighten the clutch nut to the torque listed in this Chapter's Specifications, then bend the lockwasher against two of the flats on the nut.*
   c) *Coat the friction plates with clean engine oil before you install them.*
   d) *Install a friction plate, then alternate the remaining metal and friction plates until they're all installed. Friction plates go on first and last, so the friction material contacts the metal surfaces of the clutch center and the pressure plate.*
   e) *If you're working on a CR125R, apply grease to the ends of the clutch pushrod and the pushrod's steel ball.*

---

13   Primary drive gear - removal, inspection and installation

---

Removal
Refer to illustrations 13.2a, 13.2b and 13.4
1   Remove the right crankcase cover (see Section 12).
2   Wedge a copper washer or penny between the teeth of the primary drive gear and the primary driven gear on the clutch housing. Unscrew the primary drive gear locknut (CR80R/85R) or bolt (CR125R), then remove the lockwasher **(see illustrations)**.
3   Remove the clutch (Section 12).
4   Slide the water pump drive gear (CR80R/85R only) and primary drive gear off the crankshaft **(see illustration)**. If you're working on a CR125R, pull the collar off the crankshaft.

13.4 Remove the nut or bolt, lockwasher, water pump drive gear (CR80R/85R only) and primary drive gear; on CR125R models, remove the collar from the shaft

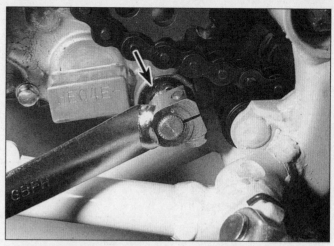

14.1 If you don't see a punch mark on the pedal and the end of the spindle, make your own; check the seal for leaks (arrow)

14.8a The ends of the return spring fit over the post (left arrow); there's a bushing in the spindle arm slot (right arrow) - this is the CR80R/85R shift mechanism . . .

14.8b . . . the CR125R mechanism is similar but uses three bolts on the guide plate

Inspection

5   Check the drive gear(s) for obvious damage such as chipped or broken teeth. Replace it if any of these problems are found.

Installation

6   Installation is the reverse of the removal steps, with the following additions:

 a) If there's an OUT mark on the lockwasher, face it away from the engine.
 b) Wedge the underside of the gear using the same method used for removal, then tighten the locknut or bolt to the torque listed in this Chapter's Specifications.

14 External shift mechanism - removal, inspection and installation

Shift pedal

Removal

Refer to illustration 14.1

1   Look for alignment marks on the end of the shift pedal and gearshift spindle (**see illustration**). If they aren't visible, make your own marks with a sharp punch.

2   Remove the shift pedal pinch bolt and slide the pedal off the shaft.

Inspection

3   Check the shift pedal for wear or damage such as bending. Check the splines on the shift pedal and gearshift spindle for stripping or step wear. Replace the pedal or spindle if these problems are found.

4   Check the gearshift spindle seal for signs of oil leakage (**see illustration 14.1**). If it has been leaking, remove the gearshift spindle as described below. Pry the seal out of the cover and install a new one. You may be able to push the seal in with your thumbs; if not, tap it in with a hammer and block of wood or a socket the same diameter as the seal.

Installation

5   Line up the punch marks, install the shift pedal and tighten the pinch bolt.

External shift linkage

Removal

Refer to illustrations 14.8a, 14.8b, 14.9, 14.10a and 14.10b

6   Remove the shift pedal as described above.

7   Remove the clutch (Section 12).

8   Note how the gearshift spindle's return spring fits over its pin and how the gearshift spindle's arm fits over the shifter collar (**see illustrations**). Pull the gearshift spindle out of the crankcase.

14.9 Pull the gearshift spindle out of the case, then remove the bushing from the guide plate

14.10a Note how the ends of the spring are positioned, (right arrows) then loosen the stopper arm bolt and remove the bolt (left arrow) from the center of the shift drum cam

14.10b Pull the stopper arm away from the cam and take the cam off; align its notch (arrow) with the pin in the shift drum (arrow) on installation

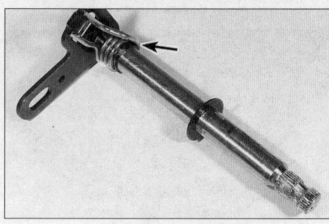

14.11 The return spring is held on the shaft by a snap-ring (arrow)

9   Remove the shifter collar from the drum shifter. Unbolt the guide plate from the crankcase and remove it together with the pawl assembly **(see illustration)**.
10   Remove the bolt from the shift drum cam **(see illustration)**. Note how the stopper arm spring presses against the case post and hooks around the stopper arm **(see illustration)**. Pull the stopper arm away from the shift drum cam, then pull the cam off the shift drum. Remove the bolt and take the stopper arm and spring off the crankcase.

Inspection
Refer to illustrations 14.11, 14.13a, 14.13b and 14.13c
11   Check the gearshift spindle return spring and splines for damage **(see illustration)**. The return spring can be replaced separately, but if the splines are damaged the complete shaft must be replaced. To replace the return spring, remove the snap-ring and slide the spring off the spindle. Install the new spring with its ends toward the spindle arm, so they fit securely over the tab when the spring is installed. **Note:** *The snap-ring should be installed with its chamfered edge facing the spring*

14.13a This is the crankcase side of the pawl assembly; the rounded ends of the pawls fit into the notches of the drum shifter

14.13b Pawl assembly details

14.13c The plungers fit into the pawl grooves; note how the grooves are offset in the pawls

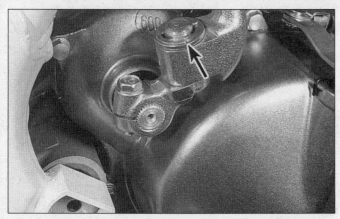

15.2 Look for alignment marks on the pedal and shaft; if you don't see them, make a punch mark on the end of the shaft that aligns with the slit in the pedal - the pedal is attached to the pivot with a snap-ring (CR80R/85R, arrow) or a bolt (CR125R)

15.6a Unhook the spring and pull off the idler gear (arrows) - this is a CR80R/85R . . .

and must be securely engaged with its groove.

12   Check the condition of the stopper arm and spring. Replace the stopper arm if it's worn where it contacts the shift cam. Replace the spring if it's bent.

13   Inspect the shifter pawls and the shift cam for wear on their contact surfaces (see illustrations). If they're worn or damaged, replace the cam and both pawls. Replace the pawl springs if there's any doubt about their condition.

Installation

14   Install the stopper arm and spring on the crankcase. Place the straight end of the spring against the post on the crankcase and the hooked end over the stopper arm. Tighten the stopper arm bolt securely, but don't overtighten it and strip the threads.

15   Pull the stopper arm down and position the shift drum cam on the shift drum, aligning the hole in the back of the cam with the pin on the shift drum. Apply non-permanent thread locking agent to the threads of the bolt, then tighten it to the torque listed in this Chapter's Specifications. Engage the roller end of the stopper arm with the neutral notch in the shift drum cam.

16   Place the plungers and springs in the shifter. Install the pawls, making sure the slots are offset in the proper direction (see illustration 14.13c). Place the assembly in the guide plate so the guide plate holds it together (see illustration 14.13a).

17   Place the drum shifter assembly the crankcase, engaging the ratchet pawls with the shift drum cam (see illustration 14.9). Tighten the guide plate bolts securely, but don't overtighten them and strip the threads.

18   Place the shifter collar on the drum shifter (see illustration 14.9).

19   Make sure the thrust washer is in place on the gearshift spindle, then carefully slide the spindle into the crankcase, taking care not to damage the seal on the other side.

20   The remainder of installation is the reverse of the removal steps.

21   Check the transmission oil level and add some, if necessary (see Chapter 1).

15   Kickstarter - removal, inspection and installation

Removal

Pedal

Refer to illustration 15.2

1   The kickstarter pedal is accessible from outside the engine. The kickstarter mechanism can be reached by removing the right crankcase cover (see Section 12).

2   To remove the pedal from the shaft, remove the snap-ring (CR80R/85R) or bolt (CR125R) and slip the pedal off (see illustration).

3   Look for a punch mark on the end of the kickstarter spindle (see illustration 15.2). If you can't see one, make your own to align with the slit in the pedal shaft. Remove the pinch bolt and slide the pedal off the spindle.

Kickstarter mechanism

Refer to illustrations 15.6a, 15.6b, 15.6c, 15.7a, 15.7b, 15.8a, 15.8b and 15.8c

4   Remove the kickstarter pedal (see Step 3 above).

5   Remove the right crankcase cover and the clutch (Section 12).

6   Slip the idler gear off its shaft (see illustrations). If you're working on a CR125R, take the idler gear thrust washer off (see illustration).

15.6b . . . and this is a CR125R

15.6c . . . there's a thrust washer behind the idler gear on CR125R models

15.7a Take the thrust washer (not shown) off the outer end of the kickstarter spindle, then turn the kickstarter so the pawl clears the guide on the crankcase (arrows) - this is a CR80R/85R ...

15.7b ... and this is a CR125R

15.8a The return spring passes through a plastic collar and fits in the hole in the shaft; all CR80R/85R and 1997-on CR125R collars are slotted like this one ...

7   Unhook the spring from the crankcase. Turn the kickstarter mechanism counterclockwise until the ratchet pawl clears the guide, then pull the kickstarter out of the engine **(see illustrations)**.

8   Disengage the return spring from the hole in the shaft **(see illustrations)**. Slide off the return spring and collar, pinion gear, thrust washers, ratchet spring and ratchet **(see illustration)**.

9   If necessary, unbolt the guide from the engine. If you're working on a 1986 through 1994 CR80R/85R, you'll need to bend back the tabs of the guide bolt lockwasher.

Inspection

Refer to illustration 15.10

10   If the snap-ring is damaged, remove it from the spindle and install a new one **(see illustration)**.

11   Check all parts for wear or damage, paying special attention to the teeth on the ratchet and the matching teeth on the pinion gear. Replace worn or damaged parts.

12   Measure the inside diameter of the pinion gear and idle gear.

13   If you're working on a CR80R/85R, measure the inside and outside diameters of the pinion gear bushing.

14   Measure the outside diameter of the shaft where the pinion gear

bushing rides. Replace any parts that are worn beyond the limit listed in this Chapter's Specifications.

Installation

Refer to illustration 15.15

15   Installation is the reverse of the removal steps, with the following additions:

a) *Use a new snap-ring if the old one was removed.*
b) *Align the punch marks on the ratchet and shaft* **(see illustration)**.

15.8b ... and the collar on 1986 through 1996 CR125R models has a notch

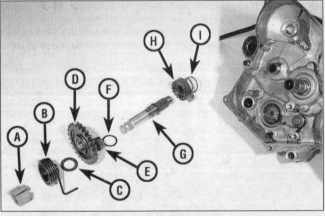

15.8c Kickstarter details

A	Collar (slotted type shown)	F	Removable bushing (CR80R/85R only)
B	Return spring	G	Kickstarter spindle
C	Thrust washer	H	Ratchet
D	Washer and snap-ring	I	Spring
E	Pinion gear		

15.10 Remove the snap-ring with snap-ring pliers - use a new one on installation

15.15 Align the ratchet punch mark with the mark on the spindle

c) *Place the end of the return spring through the notch or slot in the collar and into the hole in the shaft* (**see illustration 15.8a or 15.8b**).

d) *Make sure the pawl on the kickstarter ratchet fits behind the guide on the crankcase* (**see illustrations 15.7a and 15.7b**).

Pedal

16 Slip the pedal onto the kickstarter spindle, aligning the marks. Install the pinch bolt and tighten it securely.

16 Crankcase - disassembly and reassembly

1 To examine and repair or replace the crankshaft, connecting rod, bearings and transmission components, the crankcase must be split into two parts.

Disassembly

Refer to illustrations 16.10a, 16.10b, 16.11a, 16.11b, 16.11c, 16.12a and 16.12b

2 Remove the engine from the motorcycle (see Section 6).

3 Remove the carburetor (see Chapter 3).

4 Remove the alternator rotor (see Chapter 4).

5 Remove the clutch (see Section 12).

6 Remove the external shift mechanism (see Section 14).

7 Remove the cylinder head, cylinder and piston (see Sections 8, 10 and 11).

8 Remove the kickstarter (see Section 15).

9 Check carefully to make sure there aren't any remaining components that attach the halves of the crankcase together.

10 Loosen the crankcase bolts evenly in two or three stages, then remove them (**see illustrations**).

11 Place the crankcase with its right side down on a workbench. Attach a puller to the crankcase (**see illustration**). As you slowly tighten the puller, carefully tap the crankcase apart and lift the left half off the right half (**see illustrations**). Don't pry against the mating surfaces or they'll develop leaks.

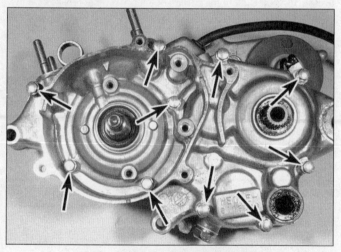

16.10a Crankcase bolts (CR80R/85R)

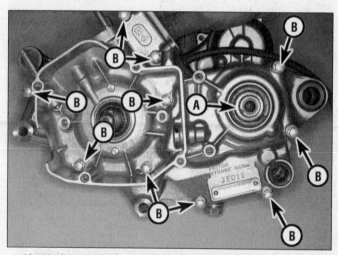

16.10b Remove the collar (A) from the CR125R countershaft and remove the crankcase bolts (B)

16.11a Use a tool like this one to push the crankshaft out of the left case half . . .

16.11b . . . and lift the left case half off the right half . . .

16.11c ... the crankshaft and transmission shafts will stay in the right case half

12   Locate the two crankcase dowels (see illustrations).
13   Refer to Sections 17 through 20 for information on the internal components of the crankcase.

Reassembly

Refer to illustration 16.15

14   Remove all traces of old gasket and sealant from the crankcase mating surfaces with a sharpening stone or similar tool. Be careful not to let any fall into the case as this is done and be careful not to damage the mating surfaces.

16.12b CR125R case dowels and breather hose (behind gasket); you'll need an impact driver to remove the bearing retainer screws

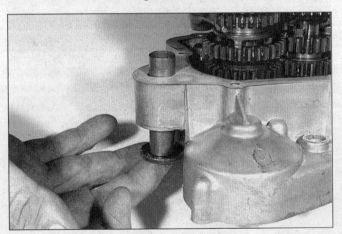

16.15 Don't lose track of the swingarm pivot bolt bushings (CR80R/85R shown)

16.12a CR80R/85R case dowels and breather hose

15   Check to make sure the two dowel pins are in place in their holes in the mating surface of the left crankcase half (see illustration 16.12a or 16.12b). Make sure the collars for the swingarm pivot bolt are in their bores (see illustration).
16   Pour some engine oil over the transmission gears. Don't get any oil in the crankshaft cavity or on the crankcase mating surface.
17   Install a new gasket on the crankcase mating surface (see illustration 16.12b). Cut out the portion of the gasket that crosses the cylinder opening.
18   Carefully place the right crankcase half onto the left crankcase half. While doing this, make sure the transmission shafts, shift drum and crankshaft fit into their bearings in the right crankcase half.
19   Install the crankcase bolts and tighten them so they are just snug. Then tighten them evenly in two or three stages to the torque listed in this Chapter's Specifications.
20   Turn the transmission mainshaft to make sure it turns freely. Also make sure the crankshaft turns freely.
21   The remainder of assembly is the reverse of disassembly.

17   Crankcase components - inspection and servicing

Refer to illustrations 17.3a, 17.3b and 17.3c

1   Separate the crankcase and remove the following:
   a) *Shift drum and forks (Section 18).*
   b) *Transmission shafts and gears (Section 19).*
   c) *Crankshaft (Section 20).*

2   Clean the crankcase halves thoroughly with new solvent and dry them with compressed air. All oil passages should be blown out with compressed air and all traces of old gasket should be removed from

17.3a The mainshaft bearing in the right side of the CR80R/85R transmission case is secured by retainers ...

17.3b . . . as is the shift drum bearing in the CR125R right case half

bearing outer race. Before installing the bearings, allow them to sit in the freezer overnight, and about fifteen-minutes before installation, place the case half in an oven, set to about 200-degrees F, and allow it to heat up. The bearings are an interference fit, and this will ease installation. **Warning:** *Before heating the case, wash it thoroughly with soap and water so no explosive fumes are present. Also, don't use a flame to heat the case. Install the ball bearings with a socket or bearing driver that bears against the bearing outer race.*

4   Replace the oil seals whenever the crankcase is disassembled. The crankshaft seals are critical to the performance of two-stroke engines, so they should be replaced whenever the crankcase is disassembled, even if they look perfectly alright.

5   If any damage is found that can't be repaired, replace the crankcase halves as a set.

6   Assemble the case halves (see Section 16) and check to make sure the crankshaft and the transmission shafts turn freely.

the mating surfaces. **Caution:** *Be very careful not to nick or gouge the crankcase mating surfaces or leaks will result.* Check both crankcase halves very carefully for cracks and other damage.

3   Check the bearings in the case halves **(see illustrations 16.12a, 16.12b and the accompanying illustrations)**. If the bearings don't turn smoothly, replace them. For bearings which aren't accessible from the outside, a blind hole puller will be needed for removal **(see illustrations)**. Drive the remaining bearings out with a bearing driver or a socket having an outside diameter slightly smaller than that of the

18 Shift drum and forks - removal, inspection and installation

1   Refer to Section 16 and separate the crankcase halves.

Removal
Refer to illustrations 18.2a through 18.2e

2   Pull up on each shift rod until it clears the case, then move the rods and forks away from the gears and shift drum **(see illustrations)**.

3   Lift the shift drum out of the case.

17.3c A blind hole puller like this one is needed to remove bearings which are only accessible from one side

18.2a Before removing the shift forks, check for the letters L, C and R (left, center and right); on some models, they're included in a number and face the left side of the case, as shown here . . .

18.2b . . . if the letters aren't visible on the left sides of the forks, as shown here, they're on the right side; pull out the right-left fork shaft and remove the forks . . .

18.2c . . . then pull out the center fork shaft and remove its fork . . .

18.2d . . . lift the shift drum out of the case . . .

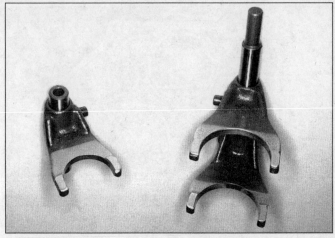

18.2e . . . and reassemble the forks on the shafts so you don't forget how they go

Inspection

Refer to illustrations 18.6a, 18.6b and 18.8

4   Wash all of the components in clean solvent and dry them off.

5   Inspect the shift fork grooves in the gears. If a groove is worn or scored, replace the affected gear (see Section 19) and inspect its corresponding shift fork.

6   Check the shift forks for distortion and wear, especially at the fork fingers **(see illustrations)**. Measure the thickness of the fork fingers and compare your findings with this Chapter's Specifications. If they are discolored or severely worn they are probably bent. Inspect the guide pins for excessive wear and distortion and replace any defective parts with new ones.

7   Measure the inside diameter of the forks and the outside diameter of the fork shaft and compare to the values listed in this Chapter's Specifications. Replace any parts that are worn beyond the limits. Check the shift fork shaft for evidence of wear, galling and other damage. Make sure the shift forks move smoothly on the shaft. If the shaft is worn or bent, replace it with a new one.

8   Check the edges of the grooves in the drum for signs of excessive wear **(see illustration)**.

9   Spin the shift drum bearing with fingers and replace it if it's rough, loose or noisy.

Installation

Refer to illustration 18.10

10   Installation is the reverse of the removal steps. Refer to the identifying letters (R, C and L) on the forks and make sure they're installed in the correct positions, with the letters facing in the proper direction.

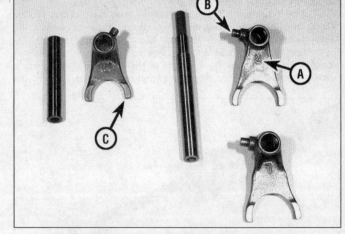

18.6a These forks have L, C and R identifying letters facing the right side of the case (A); check the forks for wear on the pins (B) and the fingers (C)

Engage the fork fingers with the gear grooves **(see illustration)**. **Note:** *The forks on some models are identified by a single letter, which faces the right side of the engine when the fork is installed. On other models, the position letter is incorporated into a number, which faces the left side of the engine when the fork is installed.*

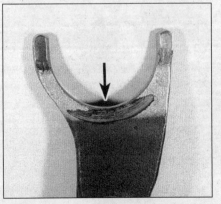

18.6b An arc-shaped burn mark like this means the fork was rubbing against a gear, probably due to bending or worn fork fingers

18.8 Check the shift drum grooves for wear, especially at the points; this is where the most friction occurs

18.10 The fork fingers engage the gear grooves like this (shift drum removed for clarity)

19.4 Both transmission shafts have a thrust washer on the left side; on the right side, the countershaft has a thrust washer

19 Transmission shafts - removal, disassembly, inspection, assembly and installation

Note: *When disassembling the transmission shafts, place the parts on a long rod or thread a wire through them to keep them in order and facing the proper direction.*

Removal

Refer to illustration 19.4

1   Remove the engine, then separate the case halves (see Sections 6 and 16).
2   The transmission components remain in the right case half when the case is separated **(see illustration 16.11c)**.
3   Refer to Section 18 and remove the shift drum and forks.
4   Take the thrust washers off the transmission shafts **(see illustration)**. Lift the transmission shafts out of the case together, then remove the thrust washers from the case.

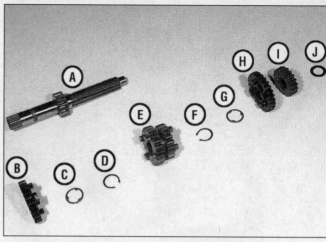

19.6a Mainshaft details (CR80R/85R)

A	Mainshaft	F	Snap-ring
B	Fifth gear	G	Splined washer
C	Splined washer	H	Sixth gear
D	Snap-ring	I	Second gear
E	Third-fourth gear	J	Thrust washer

5   Separate the shafts once they're lifted out. If you're not planning to disassemble them right away, reinstall the thrust washers and place a large rubber band over both ends of each shaft so the gears won't slide off.

Disassembly

Six-speed transmission

Refer to illustrations 19.6a, 196.b, 19.6c and 19.6d

6   To disassemble the shafts, remove the snap-rings and slide the gears, bushings and thrust washers off **(see illustrations)**.

Five-speed transmission

7   The five-speed transmission was introduced on 1998 models.

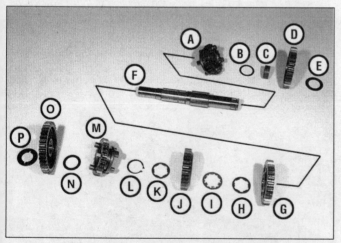

19.6b Countershaft details (CR80R/85R)

A	Sixth gear	I	Lockwasher
B	Thrust washer	J	Fourth gear
C	Bushing	K	Splined washer
D	Second gear	L	Snap-ring
E	Thrust washer	M	Fifth gear
F	Countershaft	N	Thrust washer
G	Third gear	O	First gear
H	Splined washer	P	Thrust washer

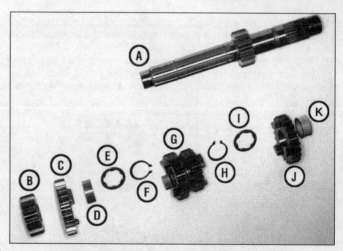

19.6c Mainshaft details (CR125R six-speed)

A	Mainshaft	G	Third-fourth gear
B	Second gear	H	Snap-ring
C	Sixth gear	I	Splined washer
D	Splined bushing	J	Fifth gear
E	Splined washer	K	Bushing (1989 on)
F	Snap-ring		

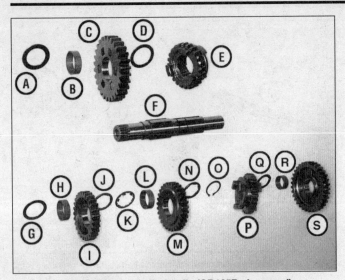

19.6d Countershaft details (CR125R six-speed)

A	Thrust washer	K	Lockwasher
B	Bushing (1989 on)	L	Bushing (1989 on)
C	Second gear	M	Third gear
D	Thrust washer	N	Splined washer
E	Sixth gear	O	Snap-ring
F	Countershaft	P	Fifth gear
G	Thrust washer	Q	Thrust washer
H	Bushing (1989 on)	R	Bushing (1989 on)
I	Fourth gear	S	First gear
J	Splined washer		

8   Its countershaft is basically the same as the CR250R counter-shaft, described in Part B of this Chapter. To disassemble the five-speed countershaft, refer to Section 19 of Chapter 2B.
9   The mainshaft is similar to the mainshaft of the CR250R transmis-sion, but with some important differences. To disassemble the main-shaft, refer to illustration 19.6a in Chapter 2B and refer to the following Steps.
10   Slide second gear (15 teeth) off the mainshaft, noting which direc-tion it faces.
11   Pull fourth gear (21 teeth) partway off and push it back on, so the "hat brim" section of the fourth gear splined bushing is exposed. Slide off the bushing, thrust washer and fourth gear.
12   Slide off the splined thrust washer, then remove the snap-ring that secures third gear (19 teeth). Slide third gear off the shaft, noting that its shift fork groove faces onto the shaft (toward the integral first gear).

13   Remove a second snap-ring, then slide of the remaining splined washer and fifth gear (23 teeth). Note that the three shift dogs on fifth gear face off of the shaft (away from the integral first gear).

Inspection
Refer to illustration 19.17
14   Wash all of the components in clean solvent and dry them off.
15   Inspect the shift fork grooves in gears so equipped. If a groove is worn or scored, replace the affected gear and inspect its correspond-ing shift fork.
16   Check the gear teeth for cracking and other obvious damage. Check the bushing or surface in the inner diameter of the freewheeling gears for scoring or heat discoloration. Measure the inside diameters of the gears and compare them to the values listed in this Chapter's Specifications. Replace parts that are damaged or worn beyond the limits.
17   Inspect the engagement dogs and dog holes on gears so equipped for excessive wear or rounding off **(see illustration)**. Replace the paired gears as a set if necessary.
18   Measure the transmission shaft diameters at the points listed in this Chapter's Specifications. If they're worn beyond the limits, replace the shaft(s).
19   Measure the inner and outer diameters of the gear bushings and replace any that are worn beyond the limit listed in this Chapter's Specifications.
20   Inspect the thrust washers. Honda doesn't specify wear limits, but they should be replaced if they show any visible wear or scoring. It's a good idea to replace them whenever the transmission is disas-sembled.
21   Check the transmission shaft bearings in the crankcase for rough-ness, looseness or noise and replace them if necessary.
22   Discard the snap-rings and use new ones on reassembly.

Assembly and installation
Refer to illustrations 19.23, 19.24a and 19.24b
23   Assembly and installation are the reverse of the removal proce-dure, but take note of the following points:
a) Align the lockwasher tabs with the notches in the spline washer next to it (see illustration).
b) Make sure the snap-rings are securely seated in their grooves, with their rounded sides facing the direction of thrust (toward the gears they hold on the shafts). The ends of the snap rings must fit in raised splines, so the gap in the snap-ring aligns with a spline groove.
c) Lubricate the components with engine oil before assembling them.
24   After assembly, check the gears to make sure they're installed correctly **(see illustrations)**.

19.17 Check the slots (left arrow) and dogs (right arrow) for wear, especially at the edges; rounded corners cause the transmission to jump out of gear - new gears (bottom) have sharp corners

19.23 Place the lockwasher against the splined washer and push its tabs into the notches

19.24a The assembled CR80R/85R shafts and gears should look like this . . .

19.24b . . . and the assembled CR125R six-speed shafts and gears should look like this

20.1a Press the crankshaft out of the crankcase . . .

20.1b . . . you can also use a puller if you have the correct adapters

20 Crankshaft and connecting rod - removal, inspection and installation

Crankshaft

Removal

Refer to illustrations 20.1a, 20.1b and 20.1c

Note: *Removal and installation of the crankshaft require a press and some special tools. If you don't have the necessary equipment or suitable substitutes, have the crankshaft removed and installed by a Honda dealer.*

1 Place the left crankcase half in a press and press out the crankshaft, or remove it with a puller **(see illustrations)**. The ball bearing may remain in the crankcase or come out with the crankshaft. If it stays on the crankshaft, remove it with a bearing splitter **(see illustration)**. Discard the bearing, no matter what its apparent condition, and use a new one on installation.

Inspection

Refer to illustrations 20.2 and 20.3

2 Measure the side clearance between connecting rod and crankshaft with a feeler gauge **(see illustration)**. If it's more than the limit listed in this Chapter's Specifications, replace the crankshaft and connecting rod as an assembly.

3 Set up the crankshaft in V-blocks with a dial indicator contacting the big end of the connecting rod **(see illustration)**. Move the connect-

20.1c If the bearing stays on the crankshaft, remove it with a bearing splitter and a puller

20.2 Check the connecting rod side clearance with a feeler gauge

20.3 Check the connecting rod radial clearance with a dial indicator

20.6 The crankshaft seals have a major effect on two-stroke engine performance

20.7 Thread the adapter into the end of the crankshaft . . .

ing rod up-and-down against the indicator pointer and compare the reading to the value listed in this Chapter's Specifications. If it's beyond the limit, replace the crankshaft and connecting rod as an assembly.

4   Check the crankshaft and splines for visible wear or damage, such as step wear of the splines or scoring. If any of these conditions are found, replace the crankshaft and connecting rod as an assembly.

5   Set the crankshaft in a pair of V-blocks, with a dial indicator contacting each end. Rotate the crankshaft and note the runout. If the runout at either end is beyond the limit listed in this Chapter's Specifications, replace the crankshaft and connecting rod as an assembly.

Installation

Refer to illustrations 20.6, 20.7 and 20.8

6   Pry out the crankshaft seals, then install new ones with a seal driver or a socket the same diameter as the seal **(see illustration)**.

7   Thread a puller adapter into the end of the crankshaft **(see illustration)**.

8   Install the crankshaft puller and collar on the end of the crankshaft **(see illustration)**.

9   Hold the puller shaft with one wrench and turn the nut with another wrench to pull the crankshaft into the center race of the ball bearing.

10   Remove the special tools from the crankshaft.

11   Installation is the reverse of the removal steps.

---

21   Recommended start-up and break-in procedure

1   This procedure should be followed each time the piston and ring, cylinder, crankshaft or crankshaft bearings are replaced. Make sure the transmission and controls, especially the brakes, function properly before riding the machine.

2   Place pieces of tape on the throttle twist grip and the handlebar next to it to indicate the half throttle and three-quarter throttle positions.

20.8 . . . and attach the puller to the adapter

3   Make sure there is fuel in the tank, then operate the choke.

4   Start the engine and ride for ten minutes, using no more than half throttle. Use the transmission to keep from lugging or over-revving the engine.

5   Shut the engine off and let it cool completely. Once the engine has cooled, ride for another ten minutes, again using no more than half throttle, without lugging or over-revving the engine.

6   Let the engine cool again, then ride for 10 minutes using no more than three-quarters throttle. Again, do not lug or over-rev the engine.

7   Let the engine cool, then ride for three more ten-minute periods, again using no more than three-quarters throttle, letting the engine cool completely between each period.

8   Check carefully for transmission oil and coolant leaks.

9   Upon completion of the break-in rides, and after the engine has cooled down completely, recheck the transmission oil and coolant level (see Chapter 1).

Chapter 2 Part B
Engine, clutch and transmission
(CR250R and CR500R models)

Contents

Specifications

CR250R
Cylinder head warpage limit ... 0.05 mm (0.002 inch)

Cylinder
Bore
1986 through 1996
Standard ... 66.390 to 66.405 mm (2.6138 to 2.6144 inches)
Limit ... 66.44 mm (2.616 inches)
1997 and later (bore code A)
Standard ... 66.398 to 66.405 mm (2.6141 to 2.6144 inches)
Limit ... 66.43 mm (2.615 inches)
1997 and later (bore code B)
Standard ... 66.390 to 66.398 mm (2.6138 to 2.6141 inches)
Limit ... 66.428 mm (2.615 inches)
Taper and out-of-round limits ... 0.05 mm (0.002 inch)
Surface warpage limit ... 0.05 mm (0.002 inch)

Piston
Piston diameter
1986 through 1996
Standard ... 66.33 to 66.35 mm (2.6114 to 2.6122 inches)
Limit ... 66.28 mm (2.609 inches)
1997 through 2004 (bore code A)
Standard ... 66.330 to 66.338 mm (2.6114 to 2.6117 inches)
Limit ... 66.28 mm (2.6094 inches)
1997 through 2004 (bore code B)
Standard ... 66.323 to 66.338 mm (2.6111 to 2.6117 inches)
Limit ... 66.273 mm (2.6092 inches)
2005 and later (bore code A) ... 66.398 to 66.405 mm (2.6141 to 2.6244 inches)
2005 and later (bore code B) ... 66.390 to 66.398 mm (2.6138 to 2.6141 inches)
Piston diameter measuring point (above bottom of piston)
1986 through 1991 ... 25 to 30 mm (0.98 to 0.118 inch)
1992 through 2004 ... 15 to 25 mm (0.59 to 0.98 inch)
2005 and later ... 13.5 to 28.5 mm (0.53 to 1.12 inches) from bottom of skirt

CR250R (continued)
Piston (continued)
Piston-to-cylinder clearance
  1986 through 1991
    Standard .... 0.040 to 0.075 mm (0.0016 to 0.0030 inch)
    Limit .... 0.10 mm (0.004 inch)
  1992 through 1996
    Standard .... 0.007 to 0.019 mm (0.0003 to 0.0007 inch)
    Limit .... 0.04 mm (0.0016 inch)
  1997 through 2004
    Standard .... 0.060 to 0.075 mm (0.0024 to 0.0029 inch)
    Limit .... 0.09 mm (0.0035 inch)
  2005 and later .... 0.050 to 0.065 mm (0.0020 to 0.0026 inch)
Piston pin bore in piston
  1986 through 1988
    Standard .... 18.007 to 18.013 mm (0.7089 to 0.7092 inch)
    Limit .... 18.03 mm (0.710 inch)
  1989 through 1991
    Standard .... 18.002 to 18.008 mm (0.7087 to 0.7090 inch)
    Limit .... 18.02 mm (0.709 inch)
  1992 on .... 18.007 to 18.013 mm (0.7089 to 0.7092 inch)
Piston pin outer diameter
  Standard .... 17.994 to 18.000 mm (0.7084 to 0.7087 inch)
  Limit .... 17.98 mm (0.708 inch)
Piston pin-to-piston clearance
  1986 through 1991
    Standard .... 0.007 to 0.019 mm (0.0003 to 0.0008 inch)
    Limit .... 0.03 mm (0.001 inch)
  1992 through 1996
    Standard .... 0.002 to 0.014 mm (0.0001 to 0.0005 inch)
    Limit .... 0.02 mm (0.001 inch)
  1997 on
    Standard .... 0.007 to 0.019 mm (0.0003 to 0.0007 inch)
    Limit .... 0.04 mm (0.0016 inch)
Connecting rod small end bore
  1986 through 1991
    Standard .... 22.002 to 22.014 mm (0.8662 to 0.8667 inch)
    Limit .... 22.03 mm (0.867 inch)
  1992 on
    Standard .... 21.997 to 22.009 mm (0.8660 to 0.8665 inch)
    Limit .... 22.02 mm (0.867 inch)
Ring end gap
  1986
    Standard .... 0.2 to 0.4 mm (0.008 to 0.016 inch)
    Limit .... 0.5 mm (0.020 inch)
  1987 through 1989
    Standard .... 0.3 to 0.5 mm (0.011 to 0.017 inch)
    Limit .... 0.6 mm (0.024 inch)
  1990 through 2004
    Standard .... 0.40 to 0.55 mm (0.016 to 0.022 inch)
    Limit .... 0.65 mm (0.026 inch)
  2005 and later .... Not specified

Clutch
Spring free length
  1986
    Standard .... 43.3 mm (1.705 inches)
    Limit .... 41.5 mm (1.634 inches)
  1987 and 1988
    Standard .... 43.1 mm (1.697 inches)
    Limit .... 41.3 mm (1.626 inches)
  1989
    Standard .... 44.8 mm (1.76 inches)
    Limit .... 43.0 mm (1.69 inches)
  1990 and 1991
    Standard .... 44.2 mm (1.74 inches)
    Limit .... 42.4 mm (1.67 inches)
  1992 and 1993
    Standard .... 44.7 mm (1.76 inches)
  1994 on .... 45.7 mm (1.83 inches)

Friction plate thickness
  Standard .... 2.92 to 3.08 mm (0.114 to 0.121 inch)
  Limit .... 2.85 mm (0.112 inch)
Metal plate warpage limit .... 0.20 mm (0.008 inch)
Clutch housing bushing outside diameter
  2001 and earlier
    Standard .... 27.987 to 28.000 mm (1.1018 to 1.1024 inches)
    Limit .... 27.97 mm (1.101 inches)
  2002 and later
    Standard .... 23.000 to 23.021 mm (0.9055 to 0.9063 inch)
    Limit .... 23.03 mm (0.907 inch)
Clutch housing inside diameter limit
  1986 through 1991 .... 32.05 mm (1.262 inches)
  1992 on .... Not specified

Kickstarter
Spindle outside diameter
  Standard .... 21.959 to 21.980 mm (0.8645 to 0.8654 inch)
  Limit .... 21.95 mm (0.864 inch)
Pinion gear inside diameter
  1986 through 1994
    Standard .... 22.020 to 22.041 mm (0.8669 to 0.8678 inch)
    Limit .... 22.06 mm (0.869 inch)
  1995 on
    Standard .... 22.007 to 22.028 mm (0.8664 to 0.8672 inch)
    Limit .... 22.05 mm (0.868 inch)
Idler gear inside diameter
  Standard .... 20.020 to 20.041 mm (0.7882 to 0.7890 inch)
  Limit .... 20.07 mm (0.790 inch)
Idler gear bushing inside diameter
  Standard .... 17.000 to 17.018 mm (0.6693 to 0.6700 inch)
  Limit .... 17.04 mm (0.671 inch)
Idler gear bushing outside diameter
  Standard .... 19.979 to 20.000 mm (0.7866 to 0.7874 inch)
  Limit .... 19.96 mm (0.786 inch)
Countershaft diameter at idler gear bushing surface
  Standard .... 16.966 to 16.984 mm (0.6680 to 0.6687 inch)
  Limit .... 16.95 mm (0.667 inch)

Shift drum and forks
Fork inside diameter wear limits
  Center .... 11.04 mm (0.435 inch)
  Left-right .... 12.07 mm (0.475 inch)
Fork shaft outside diameter wear limits
  1986 through 1994
    Center .... 10.95 mm (0.431 inch)
    Left-right .... 11.98 mm (0.472 inch)
  1995 on
    Center .... 10.97 mm (0.432 inch)
    Left-right .... 11.95 mm (0.470 inch)
Fork finger thickness
  Standard .... 4.93 to 5.00 mm (0.194 to 0.197 inch)
  Limit .... 4.8 mm (0.19 inch)
Shift drum groove width limit .... Not specified

Transmission
Gear inside diameters
  Mainshaft fourth
    Standard .... 28.007 to 28.028 mm (1.1026 to 1.1035 inches)
    Limit .... 28.05 mm (1.104 inches)
  Mainshaft fifth
    Standard .... 25.020 to 25.041 mm (0.9850 to 0.9859 inch)
    Limit .... 25.07 mm (0.987 inch)
  Countershaft first
    Standard .... 22.020 to 22.041 mm (0.8669 to 0.8678 inch)
    Limit .... 22.07 mm (0.869 inch)
  Countershaft second
    Standard .... 30.020 to 30.041 mm (1.1819 to 1.1827 inches)
    Limit .... 30.07 mm (1.184 inches)

CR250R (continued)

Transmission (continued)
Gear inside diameters
  Countershaft third
    Standard .... 25.020 to 25.041 mm (0.9850 to 0.9859 inch)
    Limit .... 25.07 mm (0.987 inch)
Bushing diameters
  Countershaft first gear
    Inside
      Standard .... 19.000 to 19.021 mm (0.7480 to 0.7489 inch)
      Limit .... 19.04 mm (0.750 inch)
    Outside
      Standard .... 21.979 to 22.000 mm (0.8653 to 0.8661 inch)
      Limit .... 21.95 mm (0.864 inch)
  Countershaft second gear
    Inside
      Standard .... 26.959 to 26.980 mm (1.0614 to 1.0622 inches)
      Limit .... 26.94 mm (1.061 inches)
    Outside
      Standard .... 29.979 to 30.000 mm (1.1802 to 1.1811 inches)
      Limit .... 29.95 mm (1.179 inches)
  Mainshaft fourth gear (outside diameter)
    Standard .... 27.959 to 27.980 mm (1.1007 to 1.1015 inches)
    Limit .... 27.94 mm (1.100 inches)
Mainshaft diameter (at fifth gear)
  Standard .... 24.959 to 24.980 mm (0.9826 to 0.9835 inch)
  Limit .... 24.94 mm (0.982 inch)
Countershaft diameter
  At third gear
    Standard .... 24.959 to 24.979 mm (0.9826 to 0.9834 inch)
    Limit .... 24.96 mm (0.983 inch)
  At second gear bushing
    Standard .... 26.959 to 26.980 mm (1.1064 to 1.0622 inches)
    Limit .... 26.94 mm (1.061 inches)
  At first gear bushing
    Standard .... 18.959 to 18.980 mm (0.7464 to 0.7472 inch)
    Limit .... 18.94 mm (0.746 inch)

Crankshaft
Connecting rod side clearance
  1986 through 1991
    Standard .... 0.2 to 0.6 mm (0.008 to 0.024 inch)
    Limit .... 0.7 mm (0.027 inch)
  1992 on
    Standard .... 0.4 to 0.8 mm (0.016 to 0.031 inch)
    Limit .... 0.9 mm (0.035 inch)
Connecting rod big end radial clearance
  1986 and 1987
    Standard .... 0.008 to 0.020 mm (0.0003 to 0.0008 inch)
    Limit .... 0.03 mm (0.001 inch)
  1988 on
    Standard .... 0.010 to 0.022 mm (0.0004 to 0.0009 inch)
    Limit .... 0.03 mm (0.001 inch)
Crankshaft V-block positions .... At center of each main bearing journal
Runout measuring points
  From alternator end .... 44 mm (1.7 inches) from outer surface of crank throw
  From clutch end .... 22 mm (0.9 inch) from outer surface of crank throw
Runout limit .... 0.05 mm (0.002 inch)

Torque specifications
Engine mounting bolts
  1986 through 1988 .... 38 to 48 Nm (27 to 35 ft-lbs)
  1989 through 1991 .... 24 to 29 Nm (17 to 21 ft-lbs)
  1992 through 1996
    Upper .... 43 Nm (31 ft-lbs)
    Lower .... 65 Nm (47 ft-lbs)
  1997
    Upper .... 39 Nm (29 ft-lbs)
    Lower .... 49 Nm (36 ft-lbs)

1998 and 1999
    Upper .... 39 Nm (29 ft-lbs)
    Lower .... 64 Nm (47 ft-lbs)
2000 on
    Upper and lower .... 54 Nm (40 ft-lbs)
Engine hanger plate bolts
    1986 through 1991
        10 mm .... 38 to 48 Nm (27 to 35 ft-lbs)
        8 mm .... 24 to 29 Nm (17 to 21 ft-lbs)
    1992 on
        Upper .... 27 Nm (20 ft-lbs)
        Lower
            1992 and 1993 .... 43 Nm (31 ft-lbs)
            1994 on .... 40 Nm (29 ft-lbs)
Cylinder head nuts
    1986 through 1993 .... 27 Nm (20 ft-lbs)
    1994 through 1996 .... 28 Nm (21 ft-lbs)
    1997 on .... 27 Nm (20 ft-lbs)
Cylinder nuts
    1986 through 1988 .... 38 to 48 Nm (27 to 35 ft-lbs)
    1989 on .... 40 Nm (29 ft-lbs)
Cylinder studs .... 12 Nm (84 to 120 in-lbs)*
Honda Power Port cover bolts .... 10 Nm (84 in-lbs)
Reed valve case bolts .... Not specified
Right crankcase cover bolts .... 10 Nm (84 in-lbs)
Clutch cover bolts .... 10 Nm (84 in-lbs)
Clutch pressure plate bolts .... 10 Nm (84 in-lbs)
Clutch locknut
    1986 through 1989 .... 55 to 65 Nm (40 to 47 ft-lbs)
    1990 through 1996 .... 82 Nm (60 ft-lbs)
    1997 on .... 80 Nm (59 ft-lbs)
Primary drive gear bolt
    1986 through 1993 .... 45 Nm (33 ft-lbs)
    1994 .... 95 Nm (70 ft-lbs)
    1995 on .... 65 Nm (47 ft-lbs)
Shift drum center pin .... 22 Nm (16 ft-lbs) (2)
Shift drum stopper arm bolt .... 12 Nm (108 in-lbs)
Kickstarter pedal bolt
    1986 through 2000 .... 27 Nm (20 ft-lbs)
    2001 .... 38 Nm (28 ft-lbs)
Shift pedal pinch bolt
    1986 through 1991 .... 18 to 25 Nm (13 to 18 ft-lbs)
    1992 through 1996 .... Not specified
    1997 on .... 12 Nm (108 inch-lbs)
Crankcase bolts .... Not specified
Countershaft bearing retainer plate bolts .... 10 Nm (84 in-lbs) (2)

1. Apply anaerobic thread locking agent to the threads.
2. Apply non-permanent thread locking agent to the threads.

CR500R
Cylinder head warpage limit .... 0.05 mm (0.002 inch)

Cylinder
Bore
    1986
        Standard .... 89.000 to 89.015 mm (3.5039 to 3.5045 inches)
        Limit .... 89.05 mm (3.506 inches)
    1987 on
        Standard .... 89.020 to 89.035 mm (3.5047 to 3.5053 inches)
        Limit .... 89.07 mm (3.507 inches)
Taper and out-of-round limits .... 0.05 mm (0.002 inch)
Surface warpage limit .... 0.05 mm (0.002 inch)

Piston
Piston diameter
    Standard .... 88.93 to 88.95 mm (3.501 to 3.502 inches)
    Limit .... 88.88 mm (3.499 inches)
Piston diameter measuring point
    (above bottom of piston) .... 25 mm (0.98 inch)

CR500R (continued)

Piston (continued)

Piston-to-cylinder clearance
  1986
    Standard .... 0.050 to 0.085 mm (0.0020 to 0.0033 inch)
    Limit .... 0.10 mm (0.004 inch)
  1987 on
    Standard .... 0.070 to 0.105 mm (0.00027 to 0.0041 inch)
    Limit .... 0.12 mm (0.005 inch)
Piston pin bore in piston
  1986 through 1988
    Standard .... 20.007 to 20.013 mm (0.7876 to 0.7879 inch)
    Limit .... 20.03 mm (0.789 inch)
  1989 on
    Standard .... 20.002 to 20.008 mm (0.7875 to 0.7877 inch)
    Limit .... 20.02 mm (0.788 inch)
Piston pin outer diameter
  Standard .... 19.994 to 20.000 mm (0.7871 to 0.7874 inch)
  Limit .... 19.98 mm (0.787 inch)
Piston pin-to-piston clearance
  1986 through 1988
    Standard .... 0.007 to 0.019 mm (0.0003 to 0.0008 inch)
    Limit .... 0.03 mm (0.001 inch)
  1989 on
    Standard .... 0.002 to 0.014 mm (0.0001 to 0.0005 inch)
    Limit .... 0.02 mm (0.001 inch)
Connecting rod small end bore
  Standard .... 25.002 to 25.014 mm (0.9846 to 0.9848 inch)
  Limit .... 25.025 mm (0.9852 inch)
Ring end gap
  Standard .... 0.3 to 0.5 mm (0.011 to 0.017 inch)
  Limit .... 0.6 mm (0.024 inch)

Clutch

Spring free length
  1986 through 1989
    Standard .... 44.5 mm (1.752 inches)
    Limit .... 42.5 mm (1.67 inches)
  1990 on
    Standard .... 44.2 mm (1.74 inches)
    Limit .... 42.2 mm (1.66 inches)
Friction plate thickness
  Standard .... 2.92 to 3.08 mm (0.114 to 0.121 inch)
  Limit .... 2.85 mm (0.112 inch)
Metal plate warpage limit .... 0.20 mm (0.008 inch)
Clutch housing bushing outside diameter
  Standard .... 27.987 to 28.000 mm (1.1018 to 1.1024 inches)
  Limit .... 27.97 mm (1.101 inches)
Clutch housing inside diameter limit
  Standard .... 32.009 to 342.034 mm (1.2602 to 1.2612 inches)
  Limit .... 32.054 mm (1.2620 inches)

Kickstarter

Spindle outside diameter
  Standard .... 21.959 to 21.980 mm (0.8645 to 0.8654 inch)
  Limit .... 21.95 mm (0.864 inch)
Pinion gear inside diameter
  Standard .... 20.020 to 20.041 mm (0.7882 to 0.7890 inch)
  Limit .... 20.06 mm (0.790 inch)
Idler gear inside diameter
  Standard .... 20.020 to 20.041 mm (0.7882 to 0.7890 inch)
  Limit .... 0.07 mm (0.790 inch)
Idler gear bushing inside diameter
  Standard .... 17.000 to 17.018 mm (0.6693 to 0.6700 inch)
  Limit .... 17.04 mm (0.671 inch)
Idler gear bushing outside diameter
  Standard .... 19.979 to 20.000 mm (0.7866 to 0.7874 inch)
  Limit .... 19.94 mm (0.785 inch)
Countershaft diameter at idler gear bushing surface .... Not specified

Shift drum and forks

Fork inside diameter wear limits
Center .... 11.04 mm (0.435 inch)
Left-right .... 12.07 mm (0.475 inch)
Fork shaft outside diameter wear limits
Center .... 0.95 mm (0.431 inch)
Left-right .... 11.98 mm (0.472 inch)
Fork finger thickness
Standard .... 4.93 to 5.00 mm (0.194 to 0.197 inches)
Limit .... 4.8 mm (0.19 inch)
Shift drum groove width limit .... Not specified

Transmission

Gear inside diameters
Mainshaft fourth (1986 through 1992)
Standard .... 28.007 to 28.028 mm (1.1026 to 1.1035 inches)
Limit .... 28.05 mm (1.104 inch)
Mainshaft fourth (1993 on)
Standard .... 28.000 to 28.021 mm (1.1024 to 1.032 inches)
Limit .... 28.05 mm (1.104 inch)
Mainshaft fifth
Standard .... 25.020 to 25.041 mm (0.9850 to 0.9859 inch)
Limit
1986 through 1991 .... 25.05 mm (0.986 inch)
1992 on .... 25.07 mm (0.987 inch)
Countershaft first
Standard .... 22.020 to 22.041 mm (0.8669 to 0.8678 inch)
Limit .... 22.07 mm (0.869 inch)
Countershaft second (1986, 1987 and 1992 on)
Standard .... 27.020 to 27.041 mm (1.0638 to 1.0646 inches)
Limit .... 27.05 mm (1.065 inch)
Countershaft second (1988 through 1991)
Standard .... 30.020 to 30.041 mm (1.1819 to 1.1827 inches)
Limit .... 30.05 mm (1.183 inches)
Countershaft third
Standard .... 25.020 to 25.041 mm (0.9850 to 0.9859 inch)
Limit
1986 through 1991 .... 25.05 mm (0.986 inch)
1992 on .... 25.07 mm (0.987 inch)
Bushing diameters
Countershaft first gear
Inside
Standard .... 19.000 to 19.021 mm (0.7480 to 0.7489 inch)
Limit .... 19.04 mm (0.750 inch)
Outside
Standard .... 21.979 to 22.000 mm (0.8653 to 0.8661 inch)
Limit .... 21.95 mm (0.864 inch)
Countershaft second gear (1986, 1987 and 1992 on)
Inside
Standard .... 24.000 to 24.021 mm (0.9449 to 0.9457 inch)
Limit .... 24.04 mm (0.946 inch)
Outside
Standard .... 26.979 to 27.000 mm (1.0622 to 1.0630 inches)
Limit .... 26.95 mm (1.061 inches)
Countershaft second gear (1988 through 1991)
Inside
Standard .... 27.000 to 27.021 mm (1.0630 to 1.0638 inches)
Limit .... 27.04 mm (1.065 inches)
Outside
Standard .... 29.979 to 30.000 mm (1.1803 to 1.1811 inches)
Limit .... 29.95 mm (1.179 inches)
Mainshaft fourth gear (outside diameter)
Standard .... 27.959 to 27.980 mm (1.1007 to 1.1015 inches)
Limit .... 27.94 mm (1.100 inches)
Mainshaft diameter (at fifth gear)
Standard .... 24.959 to 24.980 mm (0.9826 to 0.9835 inch)
Limit .... 24.94 mm (0.982 inch)

CR500R (continued)

Transmission (continued)
Countershaft diameter
  At third gear
    Standard .... 24.959 to 24.980 mm (0.9826 to 0.9835 inch)
    Limit .... 24.94 mm (0.982 inch)
  At second gear bushing (1986 and 1987)
    Standard .... 23.959 to 23.980 mm (0.9433 to 0.9441 inch)
    Limit .... 23.94 mm (0.943 inch)
  At second gear bushing (1988 on)
    Standard .... 26.959 to 26.980 mm (1.1064 to 1.0622 inches)
    Limit .... 26.94 mm (1.061 inches)
  At first gear bushing
    Standard .... 18.959 to 18.980 mm (0.7464 to 0.7472 inch)
    Limit .... 18.94 mm (0.746 inch)

Crankshaft
Connecting rod side clearance
  1986 through 1989
    Standard .... 0.2 to 0.6 mm (0.008 to 0.024 inch)
    Limit .... 0.7 mm (0.027 inch)
  1990 on
    Standard .... 0.4 to 0.8 mm (0.016 to 0.031 inch)
    Limit .... 0.9 mm (0.035 inch)
Connecting rod big end radial clearance
  Standard .... 0.008 to 0.020 mm (0.0003 to 0.0008 inch)
  Limit .... 0.03 mm (0.001 inch)
Crankshaft V-block positions .... At center of each main bearing journal
Runout measuring points
  1986 through 1991
    From alternator end .... 43 mm (1.7 inch) from outer surface of crank throw
    From clutch end .... 25 mm (0.9 inch) from outer surface of crank throw
  1992 on .... Not specified
Runout limit .... 0.05 mm (0.002 inch)

Torque specifications
Engine mounting bolts
  1986 through 1988
    10 mm .... 38 to 48 Nm (27 to 35 ft-lbs)
    8 mm .... 24 to 29 Nm (17 to 21 ft-lbs)
  1989 .... 38 to 48 Nm (27 to 35 ft-lbs)
  1990 and 1991 .... 60 to 70 Nm (43 to 51 ft-lbs)
  1992
    Upper .... 43 Nm (31 ft-lbs)
    Lower .... 65 Nm (47 ft-lbs)
  1993 on
    Upper .... 40 Nm (29 ft-lbs)
    Lower .... 65 Nm (47 ft-lbs)
Engine hanger plate bolts
  1986 through 1989
    To engine .... 38 to 48 Nm (27 to 35 ft-lbs)
    To frame .... 24 to 29 Nm (17 to 21 ft-lbs)
  1990 and 1991
    To engine .... 60 to 70 Nm (43 to 51 ft-lbs)
    To frame .... 24 to 29 Nm (17 to 21 ft-lbs)
  1992
    To engine .... 43 Nm (31 ft-lbs)
    To frame .... 27 Nm (20 ft-lbs)
  1993 on
    To engine .... 40 Nm (29 ft-lbs)
    To frame .... 27 Nm (20 ft-lbs)
Cylinder head nuts .... 27 Nm (20 ft-lbs)
Cylinder nuts
  1986 through 1988 .... 38 to 48 Nm (27 to 35 ft-lbs)
  1989 on .... 40 Nm (29 ft-lbs)
Cylinder studs .... 12 Nm (84 to 120 in-lbs)*
Reed valve case bolts .... Not specified
Right crankcase cover bolts .... 10 Nm (84 in-lbs)
Clutch cover bolts .... 10 Nm (84 in-lbs)

Clutch pressure plate bolts	
1986 through 1991	Not specified
1992 on	10 Nm (84 in-lbs)
Clutch locknut	
1986 through 1988	55 to 65 Nm (40 to 47 ft-lbs)
1989 on	82 Nm (60 ft-lbs)
Primary drive gear bolt	45 Nm (33 ft-lbs)
Shift drum center pin	22 Nm (16 ft-lbs) (2)
Shift drum stopper arm bolt	
1986 through 1991	Not specified
1992 on	12 Nm (108 in-lbs)
Kickstarter pedal bolt	27 Nm (20 ft-lbs)
Shift pedal pinch bolt	12 Nm (108 in-lbs)
Crankcase bolts	Not specified
Countershaft bearing retainer plate bolts..............................	10 Nm (84 in-lbs) (2)
Shift drum retainer plate bolts...	10 Nm (84 in-lbs) (2)

1. *Apply anaerobic thread locking agent to the threads.*
2. *Apply non-permanent thread locking agent to the threads.*

1   General information

The engine/transmission unit is of the liquid-cooled, single-cylinder two-stroke design. The engine/transmission assembly is constructed from aluminum alloy. The crankcase is divided vertically.

The cylinder, piston, crankshaft bearings and connecting rod lower end bearing are lubricated by the fuel, which is a mixture of gasoline and two-stroke oil. The transmission and clutch are lubricated by four-stroke engine oil, which is contained in a sump within the crankcase. Power from the crankshaft is routed to the transmission via a wet, multi-plate type clutch. The transmission has five forward gears.

2   Operations possible with the engine in the frame

The components and assemblies listed below can be removed without having to remove the engine from the frame. If, however, a number of areas require attention at the same time, removal of the engine is recommended.

Cylinder and piston
External shift mechanism
Clutch and primary drive gear
Kickstarter

3   Operations requiring engine removal

It is necessary to remove the engine/transmission assembly from the frame and separate the crankcase halves to gain access to the following components:

Crankshaft and connecting rod
Transmission shafts
Internal shift mechanism (gearshift spindle, shift drum and forks)
Crankcase bearings

4   Major engine repair - general note

1   It is not always easy to determine when or if an engine should be completely overhauled, as a number of factors must be considered.
2   High mileage is not necessarily an indication that an overhaul is needed, while low mileage, on the other hand, does not preclude the need for an overhaul. Regular maintenance is probably the single most important consideration. This is especially true if the bike is used in competition. An engine that has regular and frequent oil changes, as well as other required maintenance, will most likely give many hours of reliable service. Conversely, a neglected engine, or one which has not been broken in properly, may require an overhaul very early in its life.
3   Poor running that can't be accounted for by seemingly obvious causes (fouled spark plug, leaking head or cylinder base gasket, worn piston rings, carburetor problems) may be due to leaking crankshaft seals. In two-stroke engines, the crankcase acts as a suction pump to draw in fuel mixture and as a compressor to force it into the cylinder. If the crankcase seals are leaking, the pressure drop will cause a loss of performance.
4   If the engine is making obvious knocking or rumbling noises, the connecting rod and/or main bearings are probably at fault. The upper connecting rod bearing should be replaced at the maintenance interval listed in Chapter 1.
5   A top-end overhaul, part of regularly scheduled maintenance on these machines, consists of replacing the piston and rings and inspecting the cylinder bore. The cylinder on CR500R models can be bored for an oversize piston if necessary; on CR250R models, the Nikasil coating on the cylinder wall can't be honed or bored, so the cylinder and piston must be replaced with new ones if they're worn.
6   A lower-end engine overhaul generally involves inspecting the crankshaft, transmission and crankcase bearings and seals. Unlike four-stroke engines equipped with plain main and connecting rod bearings, there isn't much in the way of machine work that can be done to refurbish existing parts. Worn bearings, gears, seals and shift mechanism parts should be replaced with new ones. The crankshaft and connecting rod are permanently assembled, so if one of these components (or the connecting rod lower end bearing) needs to be replaced, both must be. While the engine is being overhauled, other components such as the carburetor can be rebuilt also. The end result should be a like-new engine that will give as many trouble-free hours as the original.
7   Before beginning the engine overhaul, read through all of the related procedures to familiarize yourself with the scope and requirements of the job. Overhauling an engine is not all that difficult, but it is time consuming. Plan on the motorcycle being tied up for a minimum of two (2) weeks. Check on the availability of parts and make sure that any necessary special tools, equipment and supplies are obtained in advance.
8   Most work can be done with typical shop hand tools, although a number of precision measuring tools are required for inspecting parts to determine if they must be replaced. Often a dealer service department or repair shop will handle the inspection of parts and offer advice concerning reconditioning and replacement. As a general rule, time is

6.12a Remove the upper mounting bracket; this is a 1997 CR250R . . .

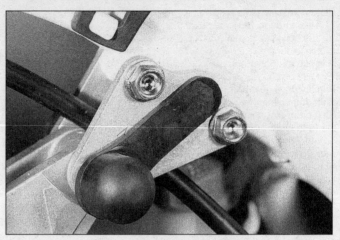

6.12b . . . and this is a CR500R

the primary cost of an overhaul so it doesn't pay to install worn or sub-standard parts.

9   As a final note, to ensure maximum life and minimum trouble from a rebuilt engine, everything must be assembled with care in a spotlessly clean environment.

5   Crankcase pressure and vacuum - check

This test can pinpoint the cause of otherwise unexplained poor running. It can also prevent piston seizures by detecting air leaks that can cause a lean mixture. It requires special equipment, but can easily be done by a Honda dealer or other motorcycle shop. If you regularly work on two-stroke engines, you might want to consider purchasing the tester for yourself (or with a group of other riders). You may also be able to fabricate the tester.

The test involves sealing off the intake and exhaust ports (and the Honda Power Port or Composite Racing Valve openings on models so equipped), then applying vacuum and pressure to the spark plug hole with a hand vacuum/pressure pump, similar to the type used for brake bleeding and automotive vacuum testing.

First, remove the carburetor and exhaust system. Block off the carburetor opening with a rubber plug, clamped securely in position. Place a rubber sheet (cut from a tire tube or similar material) over the exhaust port and secure it with a metal plate. If the bike has a Honda Power Port or Composite Racing Valve system, you'll need to seal these openings as well, using rubber gaskets and special adapters.

Apply air pressure to the spark plug hole with the vacuum/pressure pump. Check for leaks at the crankcase gasket, intake manifold, reed valve gasket, cylinder base gasket and head gasket. If the crankcase gasket leaks between the transmission sump and the crankcase (the area where the crankshaft spins), transmission oil will be sucked into the crankcase, causing the fuel mixture to be oil-rich. Also check the seal at the alternator end of the crankshaft. If the leaks are large, air will hiss as it passes through them. Small leaks can be detected by pouring soapy water over the suspected area and looking for bubbles.

After checking for air leaks, apply vacuum with the pump. If vacuum leaks down quickly, the crankshaft seals are leaking.

6   Engine - removal and installation

Warning: *Engine removal and installation should be done with the aid of an assistant to avoid damage or injury that could occur if the engine is dropped. A hydraulic floor jack should be used to support and lift the engine if possible (they can be rented at low cost).*

Removal

Refer to illustrations 6.12a, 6.12b, 6.14 and 6.15

1   Drain the transmission oil and coolant (see Chapter 1).
2   Remove the seat (see Chapter 8). If you're working on a 1986 or 1987 CR250R or a 1986 through 1991 CR500R, remove the right side cover.
3   If you're working on a 1992 or later CR250R, remove the brake pedal (see Chapter 7).
4   Remove the fuel tank, exhaust system and carburetor (see Chapter 4).
5   Disconnect the spark plug wire (see Chapter 1).
6   Disconnect the coolant hoses from the engine (see Chapter 3). If you're working on a 1989 through 1991 CR250R or a 1989 or later CR500R, remove the radiator(s).
7   Label and disconnect the alternator and pulse generator wires (refer to Chapter 5 for component location if necessary). If you're working on a 1999 or later model, disconnect the connectors for the coil primary and ground wires, ignition control unit and kill switch. Detach the wires from their retainers.
8   Remove the drive chain and sprocket (see Chapter 6).
9   Disconnect the clutch cable (see Section 12).
10   If you're working on a 1997 or later CR250R, remove the rear master cylinder reservoir (see Chapter 7).
11   Support the bike securely upright so it can't fall over during the remainder of this procedure. Support the engine with a jack, using a block of wood between the jack and the engine to protect the crankcase.
12   Remove the upper engine mount **(see illustrations)**.
13   If you're working on a 1992 or later CR500R, remove the shock

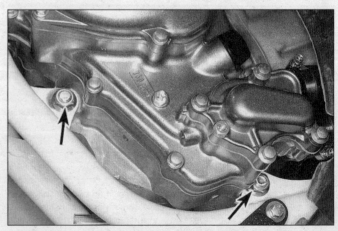

6.14 Remove the two through-bolts at the bottom and front of the engine (1997 CR500R shown). . .

6.15 . . . and the swingarm pivot bolt where it passes through the crankcase casting

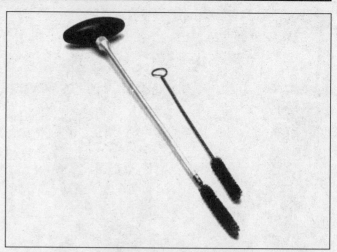

7.2 A selection of brushes is required for cleaning holes and passages in the engine components

absorber lower mounting bolt (see Chapter 6).

14 Remove the engine mounting bolts and nuts at the front and bottom **(see illustration)**. **Note:** *Raise and lower the jack as needed to relieve strain on the mounting bolts.*

15 Remove the swingarm pivot bolt nut (see Chapter 5). The pivot bolt passes through the rear of the crankcase to act as an engine support **(see illustration)**, so it needs to be pulled out of the crankcase. Pull the swingarm back about half the diameter of the bolt hole to provide removal clearance for the engine.

16 Have an assistant help you lift the engine out of the frame.

17 Slowly lower the engine to a suitable work surface.

Installation

18 Have an assistant help lift the engine into the frame so it rests on the jack and block of wood. Use the jack to align the mounting bolt holes, then install the bolts, nuts and upper bracket. Tighten them to the torques listed in this Chapter's Specifications. Refer to the Chapter 5 Specifications for the swingarm pivot bolt torque.

19 The remainder of installation is the reverse of the removal steps, with the following additions:

a) *Use new gaskets at all exhaust pipe connections.*

b) *Adjust the throttle cable and clutch cable following the procedures in Chapter 1.*

c) *Fill the engine with oil and coolant, also following the procedures in Chapter 1.*

d) *Run the engine and check for oil, coolant or exhaust leaks.*

7 Engine disassembly and reassembly - general information

Refer to illustrations 7.2 and 7.3

1 Before disassembling the engine, clean the exterior with a degreaser and rinse it with water. A clean engine will make the job easier and prevent the possibility of getting dirt into the internal areas of the engine.

2 In addition to the precision measuring tools mentioned earlier, you will need a torque wrench and oil gallery brushes **(see illustration)**. Some new, clean engine oil of the correct grade and type (two-stroke oil, four-stroke oil or both, depending on whether it's a top-end or bottom-end overhaul), some engine assembly lube (or moly-based grease) and a tube of RTV (silicone) sealant will also be required.

3 An engine support stand made from short lengths of 2 x 4's bolted together will facilitate the disassembly and reassembly procedures **(see illustration)**. If you have an automotive-type engine stand, an adapter plate can be made from a piece of plate, some angle iron and some nuts and bolts.

7.3 An engine stand can be made from short lengths of lumber and lag bolts or nails

4 When disassembling the engine, keep "mated" parts together (including gears, shift forks and shafts, etc.) that have been in contact with each other during engine operation. These "mated" parts must be reused or replaced as an assembly.

5 Engine/transmission disassembly should be done in the following general order with reference to the appropriate Sections.

Remove the cylinder head
Remove the cylinder
Remove the piston
Remove the water pump
Remove the clutch
Remove the primary drive gear
Remove the kickstarter
Remove the external shift mechanism
Remove the alternator rotor
Separate the crankcase halves
Remove the internal shift mechanism
Remove the transmission shafts and gears
Remove the crankshaft and connecting rod

6 Reassembly is accomplished by reversing the general disassembly sequence.

8 Cylinder head - removal, inspection and installation

Caution: *The engine must be completely cool before beginning this procedure, or the cylinder head may become warped.*

Note: *This procedure is described with the engine in the frame. If the engine has been removed, ignore the steps which don't apply.*

8.6 Loosen the cylinder head nuts evenly, in a criss-cross pattern, in stages

8.8 Make sure the small coolant passages are clear; on installation, place the UP mark on the gasket upward (arrow)

Removal

Refer to illustrations 8.6 and 8.8

1   Drain the cooling system (see Chapter 1) and disconnect the coolant hose from the cylinder head (see Chapter 3).

2   Disconnect the spark plug wire (see Chapter 1).

3   Remove the seat (see Chapter 8).

4   Remove the fuel tank and the expansion chamber (see Chapter 4).

5   Remove the top engine mount (see Section 6).

6   Loosen the cylinder head nuts in two or three stages, in a criss-cross pattern **(see illustration)**. Remove the nuts once they're all loose.

7   Lift the cylinder head off the cylinder. If the head is stuck, use a wooden dowel inserted into the spark plug hole to lever the head off. Don't attempt to pry the head off by inserting a screwdriver between the head and the cylinder - you'll damage the sealing surfaces.

8   Rotate the piston to the top of the cylinder or stuff a clean rag into the cylinder to prevent the entry of debris. Once this is done, remove the gasket from the cylinder **(see illustration)**.

Inspection

Refer to illustrations 8.12a and 8.12b

9   Check the cylinder head gasket and the mating surfaces on the cylinder head and cylinder for leakage, which could indicate warpage.

10   Clean all traces of old gasket material from the cylinder head and cylinder. Be careful not to let any of the gasket material fall into the cylinder or coolant passages.

11   Inspect the head very carefully for cracks and other damage. If cracks are found, a new head will be required

12   Using a precision straightedge and a feeler gauge, check the head gasket mating surface for warpage. Lay the straightedge across the head, intersecting the head bolt holes, and try to slip a feeler gauge under it, on either side of the combustion chamber **(see illustrations)**. The feeler gauge thickness should be the same as the cylinder head warpage limit listed in this Chapter's Specifications. If the feeler gauge can be inserted between the head and the straightedge, the head is warped and must either be machined or, if warpage is excessive, replaced with a new one.

Installation

13   Lay the new gasket in place on the cylinder **(see illustration 8.8)**. Never reuse the old gasket and don't use any type of gasket sealant.

14   Carefully lower the cylinder head over the studs.

15   Install the cylinder head nuts and tighten them evenly, in a criss-cross pattern, to the torque listed in this Chapter's Specifications.

16   The remainder of installation is the reverse of the removal steps. Be sure to refill the cooling system (see Chapter 1).

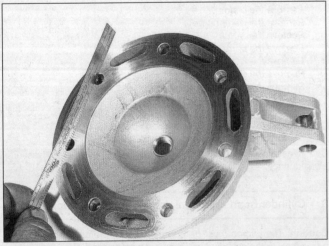

8.12a Check for head warpage with a straightedge and feeler gauge . . .

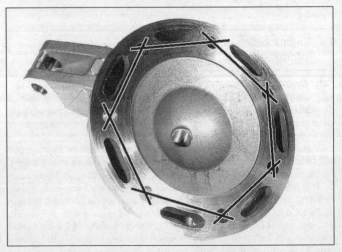

8.12b . . . in the directions shown

9.2 Unbolt the reed valve body and remove it from the cylinder with its O-ring . . .

9.3 . . . then pull out the reed valve and remove the gasket; some models have a tab that goes upward on installation (arrow)

9 Reed valve - removal, inspection and installation

Removal
Refer to illustrations 9.2 and 9.3
1 Remove the carburetor (see Chapter 4).
2 Unbolt the carburetor intake tube from the cylinder **(see illustration)**. Take off the intake tube and its O-ring.
3 Pull the reed valve out of the cylinder and remove the gasket **(see illustration)**.

Inspection
Refer to illustrations 9.6a and 9.6b
4 Check the reed valve for obvious damage, such as cracked or broken reeds or stoppers. Also make sure there's no clearance between the reeds and the edges where they make contact with the seats.
5 If you're working on a 1986 through 1994 model, the reed valve must be replaced as an assembly if any problems are found.
6 1995 and later reed valves can be disassembled and the reeds replaced. Remove the screws and stoppers **(see illustration)**. The screws have locking agent on the threads, so you may need to use an impact driver. Remove the reeds and install new ones. Install the stoppers, aligning the cutout in the stopper with the cutout in the reed. Coat the screw threads with non-permanent thread locking agent, then tighten them to the torque listed in this Chapter's Specifications. After

assembly, check the clearance between the reeds and reed stoppers **(see illustration)**.

Installation
7 Installation is the reverse of the removal steps, with the following additions:
a) *Use a new gasket between the reed valve assembly and cylinder.*
b) *If you're working on a 1994 or later CR250R, install the reed valve with its tab upward* **(see illustration 9.3)**.
c) *Use a new O-ring (if equipped) between the carburetor intake tube and the reed valve assembly.*
d) *Tighten the intake tube bolts in a criss-cross pattern to the torque listed in this Chapter's Specifications.*

10 Cylinder - removal, inspection and installation

Note: *For bikes used in competition, periodic replacement of the cylinder is a routine maintenance procedure that should be done at the intervals listed in Chapter 1.*

Removal
Refer to illustrations 10.2a, 10.2b, 10.2c, 10.3, 10.4a and 10.4b
1 Remove the cylinder head (see Section 8). Make sure the crankshaft is positioned at top dead center (TDC).

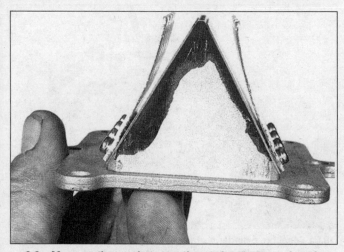

9.6a Measure the gap between the reed stoppers and reeds

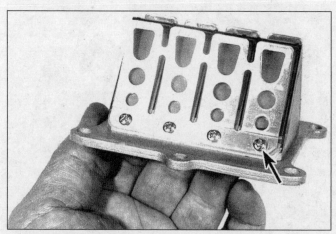

9.6b Remove the screws to detach the reed stoppers from the reed valve; on installation, align the diagonally cut corners of the reed and stopper (arrow)

10.2a Remove the cylinder base nuts from the right side of the cylinder . . .

10.2b . . . and from the left side; you'll need a box-end wrench to unscrew the forward nuts

10.2c Unbolt the CR500R coolant fitting and remove its O-ring

10.3 Tap the cylinder with a soft-faced mallet to free it from the crankcase

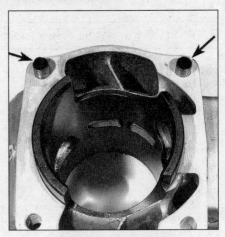

10.4a Locate the cylinder dowels (arrows) . . .

2   Remove four nuts securing the cylinder to the crankcase **(see illustrations)**. If you're working on a CR500R, unbolt the coolant hose fitting and remove its O-ring **(see illustration)**.
3   Lift the cylinder straight up off the piston **(see illustration)**. If it's stuck, tap around its perimeter with a soft-faced hammer. Don't attempt to pry between the cylinder and the crankcase, as you'll ruin

the sealing surfaces.
4   Locate the dowel pins (they may have come off with the cylinder or still be in the crankcase) **(see illustration)**. Be careful not to let these drop into the engine. Stuff clean shop rags around the piston and remove the gasket and all traces of old gasket material from the surfaces of the cylinder and the crankcase **(see illustration)**.

10.4b Stuff rags into the crankcase opening; on assembly, the IN mark faces the rear (intake side) of the engine - the letter mark on top of the piston is a bore grade

10.5a Measure cylinder surface warpage with a straightedge and feeler gauge along the bolt hole lines

10.5b The bore grade mark on the cylinder (arrow) should match the one on the piston

10.6a Note how the spring bracket is installed (if equipped) and unbolt the exhaust headpipe

Inspection

Refer to illustrations 10.5a, 10.5b, 10.6a, 10.6b and 10.7

Caution: *Don't attempt to separate the liner from the cylinder.*

5   Check the top surface of the cylinder for warpage, using the same method as for the cylinder head (see Section 10). Measure along the sides, across the stud holes **(see illustration)**. Look for the bore code on the outside of the cylinder **(see illustration)**. It should match the one on the piston **(see illustration 10.4b)**.

6   Check the cylinder walls carefully for scratches and score marks. Remove the coolant drain screw and sealing washer (if you haven't already done so). Unbolt the exhaust headpipe and remove its gasket **(see illustrations)**.

7   Using the appropriate precision measuring tools, check the cylinder's diameter at the top, center and bottom of the cylinder bore, parallel to the crankshaft axis **(see illustration)**. Next, measure the cylinder's diameter at the same three locations across the crankshaft axis. Compare the results to this Chapter's Specifications.

8   As an alternative, if the precision measuring tools are not available, a dealer service department or repair shop will make the measurements and offer advice concerning servicing of the cylinder.

9   If you're working on a CR500R and the cylinder walls are tapered, out-of-round, worn beyond the specified limits, or badly scuffed or scored, you can have the cylinder rebored and honed by a dealer service department or a motorcycle repair shop. If a rebore is done, an oversize piston and rings will be required as well. **Note:** *Honda supplies pistons in two oversizes for these models.*

10   CR250R models have a Nikasil coating on the cylinder wall. Bor-

ing or honing will remove the coating, so the cylinder will have to be replaced if the conditions described in Step 8 are found.

11   If a CR500R cylinder in reasonably good condition and not worn to the outside of the limits, and if the piston-to-cylinder clearance can be maintained properly, then the cylinder does not have to be rebored; honing is all that is necessary.

12   To perform the honing operation you will need the proper size flexible hone with fine stones as shown in *Maintenance techniques, tools and working facilities* at the front of this book, or a "bottle brush" type hone, plenty of light oil or honing oil, some shop towels and an electric drill motor. Hold the cylinder in a vise (cushioned with soft jaws or wood blocks) when performing the honing operation. Mount the hone in the drill motor, compress the stones and slip the hone into the cylinder. Lubricate the cylinder thoroughly, turn on the drill and move the hone up and down in the cylinder at a pace which will produce a fine crosshatch pattern on the cylinder wall with the crosshatch lines intersecting at approximately a 60-degree angle. Be sure to use plenty of lubricant and do not take off any more material than is absolutely necessary to produce the desired effect. Do not withdraw the hone from the cylinder while it is running. Instead, shut off the drill and continue moving the hone up and down in the cylinder until it comes to a complete stop, then compress the stones and withdraw the hone. Wipe the oil out of the cylinder. Remember, do not remove too much material from the cylinder wall. If you do not have the tools, or do not desire to perform the honing operation, a dealer service department or other repair shop will generally do it for a reasonable fee.

13   Next, the cylinder must be thoroughly washed with warm soapy

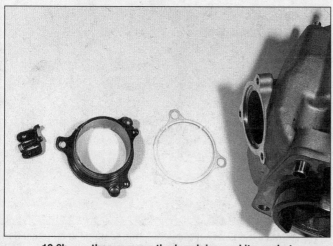

10.6b . . . then remove the headpipe and its gasket

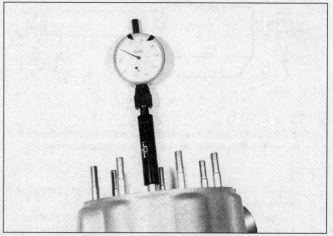

10.7 Measure bore diameter with a bore gauge

11.3 Wear eye protection and remove the circlip with a pointed tool or needle-nosed pliers

11.4a Push the piston pin partway out, then pull it the rest of the way

water to remove all traces of the abrasive grit produced during the honing operation. Be sure to run a brush through the bolt holes and flush them with running water. After rinsing, dry the cylinder thoroughly and apply a coat of light, rust-preventative oil to all machined surfaces.

Installation

14   Lubricate the piston with plenty of clean two-stroke engine oil.

15   Install the dowel pins, then lower a new cylinder base gasket over them **(see illustration 10.4a)**.

16   Install the cylinder over the studs and carefully lower it down until the piston crown fits into the cylinder liner. Push down on the cylinder, making sure the piston doesn't get cocked sideways, until the bottom of the cylinder liner slides down past the piston rings. Be sure not to rotate the cylinder, as this may snag the piston rings on the exhaust port. A wood or plastic hammer handle can be used to gently tap the cylinder down, but don't use too much force or the piston will be damaged.

17   The remainder of installation is the reverse of the removal steps.

---

11   Piston and rings - removal, inspection and installation

Note: *For bikes used in competition, periodic replacement of the pis-*

ton and rings is a routine maintenance procedure that should be done at the intervals listed in Chapter 1.

1   The piston is attached to the connecting rod with a piston pin that is a slip fit in the piston and connecting rod needle bearing.

2   Before removing the piston from the rod, stuff a clean shop towel into the crankcase hole, around the connecting rod. This will prevent the circlips from falling into the crankcase if they are inadvertently dropped.

Removal

Refer to illustrations 11.3, 11.4a and 11.4b

3   The piston should have an IN mark on its crown that goes toward the intake (rear) side of the engine **(see illustration 10.4)**. If this mark is not visible due to carbon buildup, scribe an arrow into the piston crown before removal. Support the piston and pry the circlip out with a pointed tool or needle-nosed pliers **(see illustration)**.

4   Push the piston pin out from the opposite end to free the piston from the rod **(see illustration)**. You may have to deburr the area around the groove to enable the pin to slide out (use a triangular file for this procedure). If the pin won't come out, you can fabricate a piston pin removal tool from a long bolt, a nut, a piece of tubing and washers **(see illustration)**.

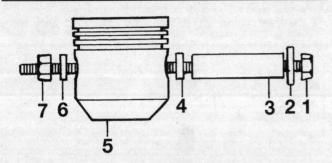

11.4b The piston pin should come out with hand pressure - if it doesn't, this removal tool can be fabricated from readily available parts

1	Bolt	7	Nut (B)
2	Washer	A	Large enough for piston
3	Pipe (A)		pin to fit inside
4	Padding (A)	B	Small enough to fit
5	Piston		through piston pin bore
6	Washer (B)		

11.6 Remove the piston rings with a ring removal and installation tool if you have one; you can use fingers instead if you're careful

11.9 Make sure the oil holes (if equipped) in the underside of the piston are clear

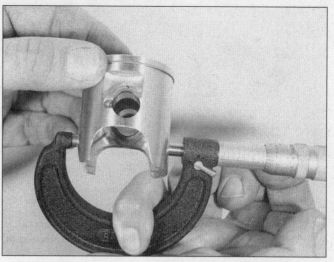

11.14 Measure the piston diameter with a micrometer

Inspection

Refer to illustrations 11.6, 11.9, 11.14, 11.15a, 11.15b and 11.16

5   Before the inspection process can be carried out, the piston must be cleaned and the old piston rings removed.

6   Carefully remove the rings from the piston **(see illustration)**. Do not nick or gouge the pistons in the process. A ring removal and installation tool will make this easier, but you can use fingers if you don't have one - just be sure not to cut yourself.

7   Scrape all traces of carbon from the top of the piston. A hand-held wire brush or a piece of fine emery cloth can be used once most of the deposits have been scraped away. Do not, under any circumstances, use a wire brush mounted in a drill motor to remove deposits from the piston; the piston material is soft and will be eroded away by the wire brush.

8   Use a piston ring groove cleaning tool to remove any carbon deposits from the ring groove. If a tool is not available, a piece broken off the old ring will do the job. Be very careful to remove only the carbon deposits. Do not remove any metal and do not nick or gouge the sides of the ring grooves.

9   Once the deposits have been removed, clean the piston with solvent and dry it thoroughly. Make sure the oil return holes inside the piston (if equipped) are clear **(see illustration)**.

10   Normal piston wear appears as even, vertical wear on the thrust surfaces of the piston and slight looseness of the ring in its groove.

11   Carefully inspect each piston for cracks around the skirt, at the pin bosses and at the ring lands.

12   Look for scoring and scuffing on the thrust faces of the skirt, holes in the piston crown and burned areas at the edge of the crown. If the skirt is scored or scuffed, the engine may have been suffering from overheating and/or abnormal combustion, which caused excessively high operating temperatures. A hole in the piston crown, an extreme to be sure, is an indication that abnormal combustion (pre-ignition) was occurring. Burned areas at the edge of the piston crown are usually evidence of spark knock (detonation). If any of the above problems exist, the causes must be corrected or the damage will occur again.

13   Measure the piston ring-to-groove clearance (side clearance) by laying a new piston ring in the ring groove and slipping a feeler gauge in beside it. Check the clearance at three or four locations around the groove. If the clearance is greater than specified, a new piston will have to be used when the engine is reassembled.

14   Check the piston-to-bore clearance by measuring the bore (see Section 10) and the piston diameter **(see illustration)**. Measure the piston across the skirt on the thrust faces at a 90-degree angle to the piston pin, at the specified distance up from the bottom of the skirt. Subtract the piston diameter from the bore diameter to obtain the clearance. If it is greater than specified, the cylinder will have to be

rebored and a new oversized piston and rings installed (CR500R) or the cylinder and piston will have to be replaced (CR250R). If the appropriate precision measuring tools are not available, the piston-to-cylinder clearance can be obtained, though not quite as accurately, using feeler gauge stock. Feeler gauge stock comes in 12-inch lengths and various thickness and is generally available at auto parts stores. To check the clearance, slip a piece of feeler gauge stock of the same thickness as the specified piston clearance into the cylinder along with appropriate piston. The cylinder should be upside down and the piston must be positioned exactly as it normally would be. Place the feeler gauge between the piston and cylinder on one of the thrust faces (90-degrees to the piston pin bore). The piston should slip through the cylinder (with the feeler gauge in place) with moderate pressure. If it falls through, or slides through easily, the clearance is excessive and a new piston will be required. If the piston binds at the lower end of the cylinder and is loose toward the top, the cylinder is tapered, and if tight spots are encountered as the piston/feeler gauge is rotated in the cylinder, the cylinder is out-of-round. Be sure to have the cylinder and piston checked by a dealer service department or a repair shop to confirm your findings before purchasing new parts.

15   Apply clean two-stroke oil to the pin, insert it into the piston and check for freeplay by rocking the pin back-and-forth **(see illustration)**. If the pin is loose, a new piston and possibly new pin must be installed. To determine which, measure the pin diameter and the pin bore in the piston

11.15a Slip the pin into the piston and try to wiggle it back-and-forth; if it's loose, replace the piston and pin; the needle bearing in the rod should be replaced if its condition is in doubt

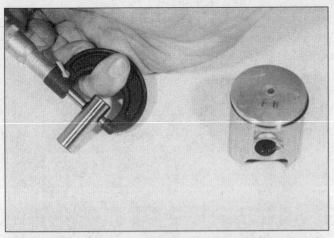

11.15b Measure pin diameter and the diameter of the pin hole in the piston

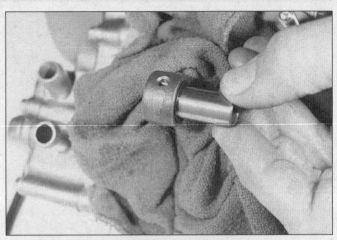

11.16 The needle bearing should be replaced if the pin wobbles inside it

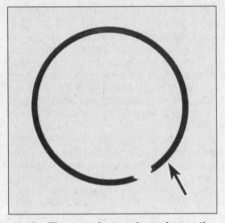

11.19a The manufacturer's mark near the ring gap (arrow) should be upward when the ring is installed

11.19b Position the ring ends on either side of the dowel pin in each ring groove (arrow)

12.2a Unhook the spring from the lifter lever

(or have this done by a dealer or other repair shop) **(see illustration)**.
16   Repeat Step 15, this time inserting the piston pin into the connecting rod needle bearing **(see illustration)**. If it wobbles and the pin diameter is within specifications, replace the needle bearing.

Installation
Refer to illustrations 11.19a and 11.19b
17   Install the piston with its IN mark toward the intake side (rear) of

12.2b You may need to widen the slot to make room for the cable

the engine. Lubricate the pin and the rod needle bearing with two-stroke oil of the type listed in the Chapter 1 Specifications.
18   Install a new circlip in the groove in one side of the piston (don't reuse the old circlips). Push the pin into position from the opposite side and install another new circlip. Compress the circlips only enough for them to fit in the piston. Make sure the clips are properly seated in the grooves.
19   Locate the manufacturer's mark on the lower piston ring near one of the ends **(see illustration)**. Turn the ring so this mark is upward, then carefully spread it and install it in the ring groove. Make sure the end gap is positioned over the ring stoppers in the ring groove **(see illustration)**. Install the upper ring in the same way.

12 Clutch - removal, inspection and installation

Cable
Removal
Refer to illustrations 12.2a, 12.2b and 12.2c
1   Loosen the cable adjuster at the handlebar grip all the way (see Chapter 1). Rotate the cable so the inner cable aligns with the slot in the lever, then slip the cable end fitting out of the lever.
2   Remove the left crankcase cover (see Chapter 5). Unhook the lifter lever spring **(see illustration)**. You may need to spread the gap in the lifter lever slightly so the cable will fit through it **(see illustration)**. Turn the lifter lever to slacken the cable, then slip the cable through the gap **(see illustration)**.

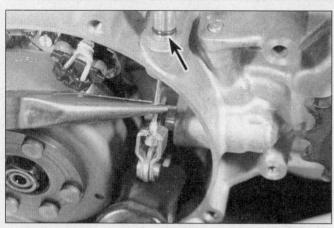

12.2c Rotate the lever arm against spring tension (you can pry it up with a large screwdriver handle) and slip the cable out of its slot

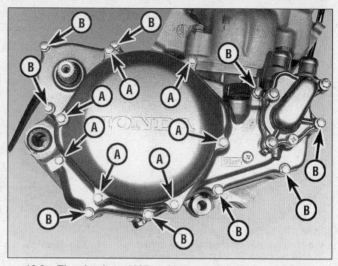

12.9a The clutch on 1987 and later models is accessible by removing the outer cover bolts (A); to remove the entire crankcase cover, remove its bolts (B)

12.9b In this case, the rear cover dowel (left arrow) stayed in the crankcase, while the front dowel pulled out of its hole (right arrow) . . .

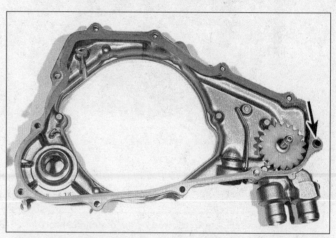

12.9c . . . and can be found in the crankcase cover (arrow)

Inspection

3   Slide the inner cable back and forth in the housing and make sure it moves freely. If it doesn't, try lubricating it as described in Chapter 1. If that doesn't help, replace the cable.

Installation

4   Installation is the reverse of the removal steps. Refer to Chapter 1 and adjust clutch freeplay.

Right crankcase cover

Refer to illustrations 12.9a, 12.9b and 12.9c

Note: *If you're working on a 1987 or later model, you can service the clutch (discs, plates, center and housing) by removing just the outer clutch cover. It isn't necessary to remove the entire crankcase cover.*

5   Drain the transmission oil and engine coolant (see Chapter 1).
6   Disconnect the hoses from the water pump (see Chapter 3).
7   Remove the brake pedal (see Chapter 7).
8   Remove the kickstarter pedal (see Section 15).
9   Remove the cover bolts and pull the cover off the engine **(see illustrations)**. Tap gently with a rubber mallet if necessary to break the O-ring or gasket seal. Don't pry against the mating surfaces of the cover and crankcase. Once the cover is off, locate the dowels; they may have stayed in the crankcase or come off with the cover.

Lifter lever

Refer to illustration 12.12

10   Remove the alternator cover (see Chapter 5).

12.12 Pull the lifter lever shaft out of the crankcase; the notch in the end of the lever engages the clutch pushrod

11   Disconnect the clutch cable as described above.
12   Slide the lever (and its spring and washer if equipped) out of the pivot bore in the crankcase **(see illustration)**.
13   Installation is the reverse of the removal steps.

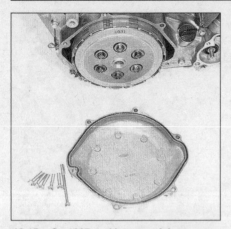

12.15a On 1987 and later models, remove the clutch outer cover and its O-ring; if you're working on a 1986 model you'll need to remove the entire crankcase cover

12.15b Remove the bolts and springs and take off the pressure plate

12.15c The lifter fits in the center of the clutch . . .

12.15d . . . pull it out, followed by the clutch pushrod

12.15e Pull the clutch plates out of the housing

Clutch

Removal

Refer to illustrations 12.15a through 12.15j

14   Remove the clutch cover or right crankcase cover as described above.

15   Refer to the accompanying illustrations to remove the clutch components **(see illustrations)**.

Inspection

Refer to illustrations 12.16, 12.17, 12.21, 12.22 and 12.23

16   Rotate the clutch lifter needle bearing and check it for rough,

12.15f Bend the lockwasher tab away from the nut

12.15g Hold the clutch from turning with a tool like this one and unscrew the nut . . .

12.15h . . . then remove the washer and pull off the clutch center

12.15i Remove the thrust washer and clutch housing . . .

12.15j . . . followed by the needle bearing and bushing

12.16 Remove the circlip and washer for access to the lifter bearing

loose or noisy operation **(see illustration)**. If the bearing's condition is in doubt, remove it from the lifter plate and install a new one.

17   Check the friction surface on the pressure plate for scoring or wear **(see illustration)**. Replace the pressure plate if any defects are found.

18   Check the edges of the slots in the clutch housing for indentations made by the friction plate tabs. If the indentations are deep they can prevent clutch release, so the housing should be replaced with a new one. If the indentations can be removed easily with a file, the life of the housing can be prolonged to an extent. Also, check the driven gear teeth for cracks, chips and excessive wear and the springs on the back side (if equipped) for breakage. If the gear is worn or damaged or the springs are broken, the clutch housing must be replaced with a new one.

19   Check the bearing surface in the center of the clutch housing for score marks, scratches and excessive wear. Measure the inside diam eter of the bearing surface, the inside and outside diameters of the clutch housing bushing and the bushing's mounting surface on the transmission mainshaft. Compare these to the values listed in this Chapter's Specifications. Replace any parts worn beyond the service limits. If the bushing mounting surface on the mainshaft is worn excessively, the mainshaft will have to be replaced.

20   Check the clutch center's friction surface and slots for scoring, wear and indentations **(see illustration 12.17)**. Also check the splines in the middle of the clutch center. Replace the clutch center if problems are found.

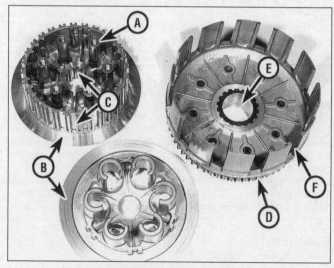

12.17 Clutch inspection points

A	Spring posts	E	Clutch housing bushing
B	Friction surfaces		surface
C	Splines	F	Clutch housing slots
D	Driven gear		

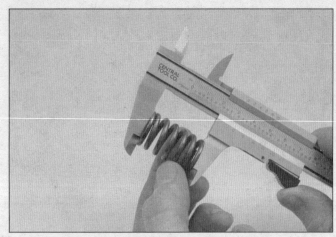

12.21 Measure the clutch spring free length

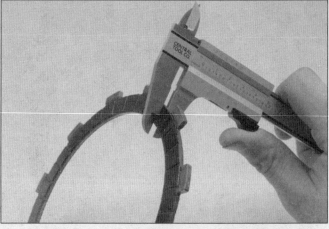

12.22 Measure the thickness of the friction plates

12.23 Check the metal plates for warpage

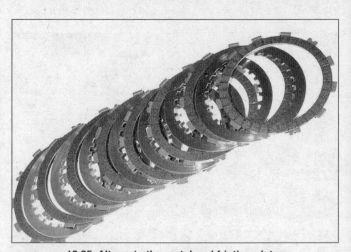

12.25 Alternate the metal and friction plates

21   Measure the free length of the clutch springs **(see illustration)** and compare the results to this Chapter's Specifications. If the springs have sagged, or if cracks are noted, replace them with new ones as a set.

22   If the lining material of the friction plates smells burnt or if it is glazed, new parts are required. If the metal clutch plates are scored or discolored, they must be replaced with new ones. Measure the thickness of the friction plates **(see illustration)** and replace with new parts any friction plates that are worn.

23   Lay the metal plates, one at a time, on a perfectly flat surface (such as a piece of plate glass) and check for warpage by trying to slip a feeler gauge between the flat surface and the plate **(see illustration)**. The feeler gauge should be the same thickness as the maximum warp listed in this Chapter's Specifications. Do this at several places around the plate's circumference. If the feeler gauge can be slipped under the plate, it is warped and should be replaced with a new one.

24   Check the tabs on the friction plates for excessive wear and mushroomed edges. They can be cleaned up with a file if the deformation is not severe. Check the friction plates for warpage as described in Step 23.

Installation

Refer to illustration 12.25

25   Installation is the reverse of the removal steps, with the following additions:

a) *Install a new lockwasher and position its tabs between the ribs of the clutch center. Tighten the clutch nut to the torque listed in this Chapter's Specifications, then bend the lockwasher against two of the flats on the nut.*

b) *Coat the friction plates with clean engine oil before you install them.*

c) *Install a friction plate, then alternate the remaining metal and friction plates until they're all installed* **(see illustration)**. *Friction plates go on first and last, so the friction material contacts the metal surfaces of the clutch center and the pressure plate.*

d) *Apply grease to the ends of the clutch pushrod and the pushrod's steel ball.*

13   Primary drive gear - removal, inspection and installation

Removal

Refer to illustrations 13.2 and 13.4

1   Remove the right crankcase cover (see Section 16).

2   Wedge a copper washer or penny between the teeth of the primary drive gear and the primary driven gear on the clutch housing. Unscrew the primary drive gear bolt, then remove the lockwasher **(see illustration)**.

3   Remove the clutch (Section 12).

4   Slide the primary drive gear off the crankshaft **(see illustration)**. Pull the collar (if equipped) off the crankshaft.

Inspection

5   Check the drive gear for obvious damage such as chipped or broken teeth. Replace it if any of these problems are found.

13.2 Wedge a copper washer or penny between the gears, then unscrew the bolt

13.4 Remove the bolt, lockwasher and primary drive gear, then remove the collar from the crankshaft

14.1 If you don't see a punch mark on the pedal and the end of the spindle, make your own; check the seal behind the pedal for leaks

14.8 The ends of the return spring fit over the post (left arrow); there's a collar in the spindle arm slot (right arrow)

14.9 Pull the gearshift spindle out of the case, then remove the collar from the guide plate

Installation

6   Installation is the reverse of the removal steps, with the following additions:

a) *If there's an OUT mark on the lockwasher, face it away from the engine.*

b) *Wedge the underside of the gear using the same method used for removal, then tighten the bolt to the torque listed in this Chapter's Specifications.*

14 External shift mechanism - removal, inspection and installation

Shift pedal

Removal

Refer to illustration 14.1

1   Look for alignment marks on the end of the shift pedal and gearshift spindle **(see illustration)**. If they aren't visible, make your own marks with a sharp punch.

2   Remove the shift pedal pinch bolt and slide the pedal off the shaft.

Inspection

3   Check the shift pedal for wear or damage such as bending. Check the splines on the shift pedal and gearshift spindle for stripping or step wear. Replace the pedal or spindle if these problems are found.

4   Check the gearshift spindle seal for signs of oil leakage **(see illustration 14.1)**. If it has been leaking, remove the gearshift spindle as described below. Pry the seal out of the cover and install a new one. You may be able to push the seal in with your thumbs; if not, tap it in with a hammer and block of wood or a socket the same diameter as the seal.

Installation

5   Line up the punch marks, install the shift pedal and tighten the pinch bolt.

External shift linkage

Removal

Refer to illustrations 14.8, 14.9, 14.10a and 14.10b

6   Remove the shift pedal as described above.

7   Remove the clutch (Section 12).

8   Note how the gearshift spindle's return spring fits over its pin and how the gearshift spindle's arm fits over the shifter collar **(see illustration)**. Pull the gearshift spindle out of the crankcase.

9   Remove the shifter collar from the drum shifter. Unbolt the guide plate from the crankcase and remove it together with the pawl assembly **(see illustration)**.

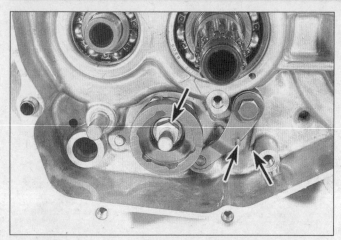

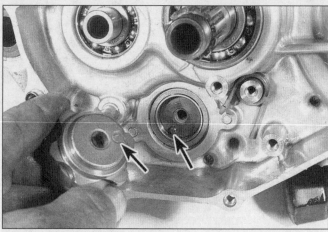

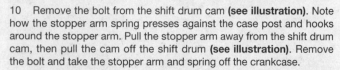

14.10a Note how the ends of the spring are positioned, (right arrows) then loosen the stopper arm bolt and washer; remove the bolt (left arrow) from the center of the shift drum cam

14.10b Pull the stopper arm away from the cam and take the cam off; its notch (arrow) aligns with the pin in the shift drum (arrow) on installation

10   Remove the bolt from the shift drum cam **(see illustration)**. Note how the stopper arm spring presses against the case post and hooks around the stopper arm. Pull the stopper arm away from the shift drum cam, then pull the cam off the shift drum **(see illustration)**. Remove the bolt and take the stopper arm and spring off the crankcase.

Inspection

Refer to illustrations 14.11, 14.13a, 14.13b and 14.13c

11   Check the gearshift spindle return spring and splines for damage **(see illustration)**. The return spring can be replaced separately, but if the splines are damaged the complete shaft must be replaced. To replace the return spring, remove the snap-ring and slide the spring off the spindle. Install the new spring with its ends toward the spindle arm, so they fit securely over the tab when the spring is installed. **Note:** *The snap-ring should be installed with its chamfered edge facing the spring and must be securely engaged with its groove.*

12   Check the condition of the stopper arm and spring. Replace the stopper arm if it's worn where it contacts the shift cam. Replace the spring if it's bent.

13   Inspect the shifter pawls and the shift cam for wear on their contact surfaces **(see illustrations)**. If they're worn or damaged, replace the cam and both pawls. Replace the pawl springs if there's any doubt about their condition.

Installation

14   Install the stopper arm and spring on the crankcase. Place the straight end of the spring against the post on the crankcase and the

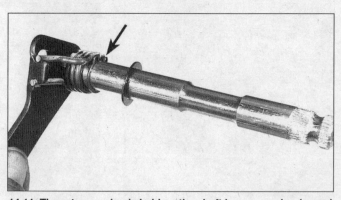

14.11 The return spring is held on the shaft by a snap-ring (arrow)

hooked end over the stopper arm. Install the washer and tighten the stopper arm bolt securely, but don't overtighten it and strip the threads.

15   Pull the stopper arm down and position the shift drum cam on the shift drum, aligning the hole in the back of the cam with the pin on the shift drum. Apply non-permanent thread locking agent to the threads of the bolt, then tighten it to the torque listed in this Chapter's Specifications. Engage the roller end of the stopper arm with the neutral notch in the shift drum cam.

16   Place the plungers and springs in the shifter. Install the pawls, making sure the slots are offset in the proper direction **(see illustration 14.13c)**. Place the assembly in the guide plate so the guide plate holds

14.13a This is the crankcase side of the pawl assembly; the rounded ends of the pawls fit into the notches of the drum shifter

14.13b Pawl assembly details

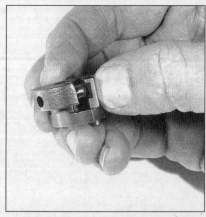

14.13c The plungers fit into the pawl grooves; note how the grooves are offset in the pawls

15.2 The kickstarter pedal is attached to the pivot with a screw

15.6a Unhook the spring and pull off the idler gear (arrows)

it together **(see illustration 14.13a)**.

17 Place the drum shifter assembly the crankcase, engaging the ratchet pawls with the shift drum cam **(see illustration 14.9)**. Tighten the guide plate bolts securely, but don't overtighten them and strip the threads.

18 Place the shifter collar on the drum shifter **(see illustration 14.9)**.

19 Make sure the thrust washer is in place on the gearshift spindle, then carefully slide the spindle into the crankcase, taking care not to damage the seal on the other side.

20 The remainder of installation is the reverse of the removal steps.

21 Check the transmission oil level and add some, if necessary (see Chapter 1).

15.6b There's a bushing behind the idler gear

---

15 Kickstarter - removal, inspection and installation

Removal

Pedal

Refer to illustration 15.2

1 The kickstarter pedal is accessible from outside the engine. The kickstarter mechanism can be reached by removing the right crankcase cover (see Section 16).

2 To remove the pedal from the shaft, remove the screw and slip the pedal off **(see illustration)**.

3 Look for a punch mark on the end of the kickstarter spindle. If you can't see one, make your own to align with the slit in the pedal shaft. Remove the pinch bolt and slide the pedal off the spindle.

Kickstarter mechanism

Refer to illustrations 15.6a, 15.6b, 15.7, 15.8a and 15.8b

4 Remove the kickstarter pedal (see Step 3 above).

5 Remove the right crankcase cover and the clutch (Section 12).

6 Slip the idler gear off its shaft and remove the idler gear bushing **(see illustrations)**.

7 Unhook the spring from the crankcase. Turn the kickstarter mechanism counterclockwise until the ratchet pawl clears the guide, then pull the kickstarter out of the engine **(see illustration)**.

8 Disengage the return spring from the hole in the shaft **(see illus-**

15.7 Take the thrust washer off the outer end of the kickstarter spindle, then turn the kickstarter so the tab clears the guide on the crankcase (arrows)

15.8a The return spring passes through a collar and fits in the hole in the shaft

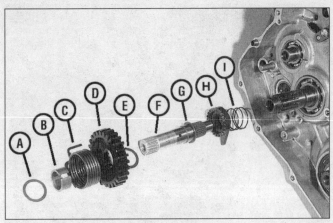

15.8b Kickstarter details

A Thrust washer	F Kickstarter spindle
B Collar	G Snap-ring
C Return spring	H Ratchet
D Pinion gear	I Spring
E Thrust washer	

tration). Slide off the return spring and collar, pinion gear, thrust washers, ratchet spring and ratchet **(see illustration)**.

9   If necessary, unbolt the guide from the engine.

Inspection

Refer to illustration 15.10

10   If the snap-ring is damaged, remove it from the spindle and install a new one **(see illustration)**.

11   Check all parts for wear or damage, paying special attention to the teeth on the ratchet and the matching teeth on the pinion gear. Replace worn or damaged parts.

12   Measure the inside diameter of the pinion gear and idler gear.

13   Measure the inside and outside diameters of the idler gear bushing.

14   Measure the outside diameter of the transmission shaft where the idler gear bushing rides. Replace any parts that are worn beyond the limit listed in this Chapter's Specifications.

Installation

Refer to illustration 15.15

15   Installation is the reverse of the removal steps, with the following additions:

a)   *Use a new snap-ring if the old one was removed.*

b)   *Align the punch marks on the ratchet and shaft* **(see illustration)**.

15.10 Remove the snap-ring with snap-ring pliers - use a new one on installation

c)   *Place the end of the return spring through the notch or slot in the collar and into the hole in the shaft* **(see illustration 15.8a or 15.8b)**.

d)   *Make sure the pawl on the kickstarter ratchet fits behind the guide on the crankcase* **(see illustration 15.7)**.

Pedal

16   Slip the pedal onto the kickstarter spindle, aligning the marks. Install the pinch bolt and tighten it securely.

16   Crankcase - disassembly and reassembly

1   To examine and repair or replace the crankshaft, connecting rod, bearings and transmission components, the crankcase must be split into two parts.

Disassembly

Refer to illustrations 16.9a, 16.9b, 16.10, 16.11a, 16.11b, 16.11c and 16.12

2   Remove the engine from the motorcycle (see Section 6).

3   Remove the carburetor (see Chapter 3).

4   Remove the alternator rotor (see Chapter 5).

5   Remove the clutch (see Section 12).

6   Remove the external shift mechanism (see Section 14).

7   Remove the cylinder head, cylinder and piston (see Sections 8, 10 and 11).

8   Remove the kickstarter (see Section 15).

9   Pull off the countershaft collar and rubber ring and the crankshaft collar **(see illustrations)**. Check carefully to make sure there aren't any remaining components that attach the halves of the crankcase together.

15.15 Align the ratchet punch mark with the mark on the spindle

16.9a Note which way the narrow end of the collar faces, then pull it out

16.9b There's an O-ring inside the inner end of the countershaft collar

16.10 Crankcase bolts (1997 CR500R shown)

16.11a Use a tool like this one to push the crankshaft out of the left case half . . .

16.11b . . . and lift the left case half off the right half . . .

16.11c . . . the crankshaft and transmission shafts will usually stay in the right case half

10 Loosen the crankcase bolts evenly in two or three stages, then remove them **(see illustration)**.

11 Place the crankcase with its right side down on a workbench. Attach a puller to the crankcase **(see illustration)**. As you slowly tighten the puller, carefully tap the crankcase apart and lift the left half off the right half **(see illustrations)**. Don't pry against the mating surfaces or they'll develop leaks.

12 Locate the crankcase dowels **(see illustration)**.

13 Refer to Sections 17 through 20 for information on the internal components of the crankcase.

Reassembly

Refer to illustration 16.15

14 Remove all traces of old gasket and sealant from the crankcase mating surfaces with a sharpening stone or similar tool. Be careful not to let any fall into the case as this is done and be careful not to damage the mating surfaces.

15 Check to make sure the dowel pins are in place in their holes in the mating surface of the left crankcase half **(see illustration 16.12)**. Make sure the collars for the swingarm pivot bolt are in their bores **(see illustration)**.

16.12 Case dowels and breather hose

16.15 Don't lose track of the swingarm pivot bolt bushings

17.3a The countershaft bearing in the left side of the transmission case is secured by retainers . . .

16   Pour some engine oil over the transmission gears. Don't get any oil in the crankshaft cavity or on the crankcase mating surface.
17   Install a new gasket on the crankcase mating surface (**see illustration 16.12**). Cut out the portion of the gasket that crosses the cylinder opening.
18   Carefully place the right crankcase half onto the left crankcase half. While doing this, make sure the transmission shafts, shift drum and crankshaft fit into their bearings in the right crankcase half.
19   Install the crankcase bolts and tighten them so they are just snug. Then tighten them evenly in two or three stages to the torque listed in this Chapter's Specifications.
20   Turn the transmission mainshaft to make sure it turns freely. Also make sure the crankshaft turns freely.
21   The remainder of assembly is the reverse of disassembly.

17 Crankcase components - inspection and servicing

Refer to illustrations 17.3a, 17.3b and 17.3c
1   Separate the crankcase and remove the following:

 a) *Shift drum and forks*
 b) *Transmission shafts and gears*
 c) *Crankshaft*

2   Clean the crankcase halves thoroughly with new solvent and dry them with compressed air. All oil passages should be blown out with compressed air and all traces of old gasket should be removed from the mating surfaces. **Caution:** *Be very careful not to nick or gouge the crankcase mating surfaces or leaks will result. Check both crankcase halves very carefully for cracks and other damage.*
3   Check the bearings in the case halves (**see illustration 16.12 and**

17.3c A blind hole puller like this one is needed to remove bearings which are only accessible from one side

17.3b . . . as is the shift drum bearing in the right case half

the accompanying illustrations). If the bearings don't turn smoothly, replace them. For bearings which aren't accessible from the outside, a blind hole puller will be needed for removal (**see illustration**). Drive the remaining bearings out with a bearing driver or a socket having an outside diameter slightly smaller than that of the bearing outer race. Before installing the bearings, allow them to sit in the freezer overnight, and about fifteen-minutes before installation, place the case half in an oven, set to about 200-degrees F, and allow it to heat up. The bearings are an interference fit, and this will ease installation. **Warning:** *Before heating the case, wash it thoroughly with soap and water so no explosive fumes are present. Also, don't use a flame to heat the case. Install the ball bearings with a socket or bearing driver that bears against the bearing outer race.*
4   Replace the oil seals whenever the crankcase is disassembled. The crankshaft seals are critical to the performance of two-stroke engines, so they should be replaced whenever the crankcase is disassembled, even if they look perfectly alright.
5   If any damage is found that can't be repaired, replace the crankcase halves as a set.
6   Assemble the case halves (see Section 16) and check to make sure the crankshaft and the transmission shafts turn freely.

18 Shift drum and forks - removal, inspection and installation

1   Refer to Section 16 and separate the crankcase halves.

Removal
Refer to illustrations 18.2a through 18.2e
2   Pull up on each shift rod until it clears the case, then move the rods and forks away from the gears and shift drum (**see illustrations**).
3   Lift the shift drum out of the case.

Inspection
Refer to illustrations 18.6 and 18.8
4   Wash all of the components in clean solvent and dry them off.
5   Inspect the shift fork grooves in the gears. If a groove is worn or scored, replace the affected gear (see Section 19) and inspect its corresponding shift fork.
6   Check the shift forks for distortion and wear, especially at the fork fingers (**see illustration 18.2e and the accompanying illustration**). Measure the thickness of the fork fingers and compare your findings with this Chapter's Specifications. If they are discolored or severely worn they are probably bent. Inspect the guide pins for excessive wear and distortion and replace any defective parts with new ones.
7   Measure the inside diameter of the forks and the outside diameter of the fork shaft and compare to the values listed in this Chapter's Specifications. Replace any parts that are worn beyond the limits.

18.2a The assembled shift forks and shafts should look like this

18.2b Pull out the right-left fork shaft. . .

18.2c . . . then pull out the center fork shaft and remove the forks; each fork has a letter indicating its position (left, center or right) . . .

18.2d . . . lift the shift drum out of the case . . .

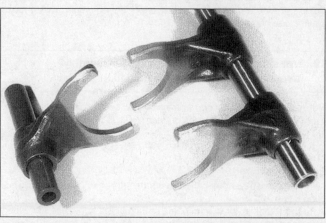

18.2e . . . and reassemble the forks on the shafts so you don't forget how they go; check the forks for wear on the pins and fingers

Check the shift fork shaft for evidence of wear, galling and other damage. Make sure the shift forks move smoothly on the shaft. If the shaft is worn or bent, replace it with a new one.

8   Check the edges of the grooves in the drum for signs of excessive wear **(see illustration)**.

9   Spin the shift drum bearing with fingers and replace it if it's rough, loose or noisy.

Installation

Refer to illustration 18.10

10   Installation is the reverse of the removal steps. Refer to the identifying letters (R, C and L) on the forks and make sure they're installed in the correct positions, with the letters facing in the proper direction. Engage the fork fingers with the gear grooves **(see illustration)**.

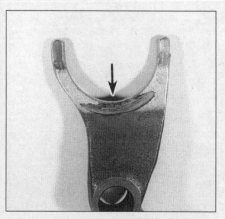

18.6 An arc-shaped burn mark like this means the fork was rubbing against a gear, probably due to bending or worn fork fingers

18.8 Check the shift drum grooves for wear, especially at the points; this is where the most friction occurs

18.10 The fork fingers engage the gear grooves like this (shift drum removed for clarity)

19.4 Both transmission shafts have a thrust washer on the left side

Note: *The forks on some models are identified by a single letter, which faces the right side of the engine when the fork is installed. On other models, the position letter is incorporated into a number, which faces the left side of the engine when the fork is installed.*

19 Transmission shafts - removal, disassembly, inspection, assembly and installation

Note: *When disassembling the transmission shafts, place the parts on a long rod or thread a wire through them to keep them in order and facing the proper direction.*

Removal

Refer to illustration 19.4

1   Remove the engine, then separate the case halves (see Sections 6 and 16).

2   The transmission components remain in the right case half when the case is separated **(see illustration 16.11c)**.

3   Refer to Section 18 and remove the shift drum and forks.

4   Take the thrust washers off the transmission shafts **(see illustration)**. Lift the transmission shafts out of the case together, then remove

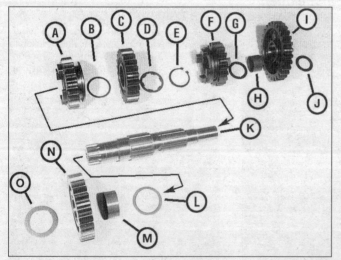

19.6b Countershaft details

A	Fourth gear	F	Fifth gear	K	Countershaft
B	Thrust washer	G	Thrust washer	L	Thrust washer
C	Third gear	H	Bushing	M	Bushing
D	Splined washer	I	First gear	N	Second gear
E	Snap-ring	J	Thrust washer	O	Thrust washer

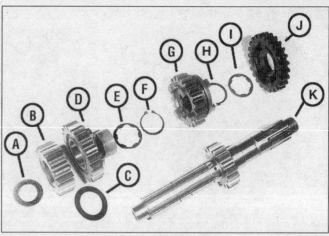

19.6a Mainshaft details

A	Thrust washer	E	Splined washer	I	Splined washer
B	Second gear	F	Snap-ring	J	Fifth gear
C	Thrust washer	G	Third gear	K	Mainshaft
D	Splined bushing	H	Snap-ring		

the thrust washers from the case.

5   Separate the shafts once they're lifted out. If you're not planning to disassemble them right away, reinstall the thrust washers and place a large rubber band over both ends of each shaft so the gears won't slide off.

Disassembly

Refer to illustrations 19.6a and 19.6b

6   To disassemble the shafts, remove the snap-rings and slide the gears, bushings and thrust washers off **(see illustrations)**.

Inspection

Refer to illustration 19.10

7   Wash all of the components in clean solvent and dry them off.

8   Inspect the shift fork grooves in gears so equipped. If a groove is worn or scored, replace the affected gear and inspect its corresponding shift fork.

9   Check the gear teeth for cracking and other obvious damage. Check the bushing or surface in the inner diameter of the freewheeling gears for scoring or heat discoloration. Measure the inside diameters of the gears and compare them to the values listed in this Chapter's Specifications. Replace parts that are damaged or worn beyond the limits.

19.10 Check the slots (left arrow) and dogs (right arrow) for wear, especially at the edges; rounded corners cause the transmission to jump out of gear - new gears (bottom) have sharp corners

19.17 The assembled shafts and gears should look like this

20.1a Press the crankshaft out of the crankcase . . .

10   Inspect the engagement dogs and dog holes on gears so equipped for excessive wear or rounding off **(see illustration)**. Replace the paired gears as a set if necessary.

11   Measure the transmission shaft diameters at the points listed in this Chapter's Specifications. If they're worn beyond the limits, replace the shaft(s).

12   Measure the inner and outer diameters of the gear bushings and replace any that are worn beyond the limit listed in this Chapter's Specifications.

13   Inspect the thrust washers. Honda doesn't specify wear limits, but they should be replaced if they show any visible wear or scoring. It's a good idea to replace them whenever the transmission is disassembled.

14   Check the transmission shaft bearings in the crankcase for roughness, looseness or noise and replace them if necessary.

15   Discard the snap-rings and use new ones on reassembly.

Assembly and installation

Refer to illustration 19.17

16   Assembly and installation are the reverse of the removal procedure, but take note of the following points:

a) *Make sure the snap-rings are securely seated in their grooves, with their rounded sides facing the direction of thrust (toward the gears they hold on the shafts). The ends of the snap-rings must fit in raised splines, so the gap in the snap-ring aligns with a spline groove.*

b) *Lubricate the components with engine oil before assembling them.*

17   After assembly, check the gears to make sure they're installed correctly **(see illustration)**.

---

20   Crankshaft and connecting rod - removal, inspection and installation

---

Crankshaft

Removal

Refer to illustrations 20.1a, 20.1b and 20.1c

Note: *Removal and installation of the crankshaft require a press and some special tools. If you don't have the necessary equipment or suitable substitutes, have the crankshaft removed and installed by a Honda dealer.*

1   Place the left crankcase half in a press and press out the crankshaft, or remove it with a puller **(see illustrations)**. The ball bearing may remain in the crankcase or come out with the crankshaft. If it stays on the crankshaft, remove it with a bearing splitter **(see illustration)**. Discard the bearing, no matter what its apparent condition, and use a new one on installation.

Inspection

Refer to illustrations 20.2 and 20.3

2   Measure the side clearance between connecting rod and crankshaft with a feeler gauge **(see illustration)**. If it's more than the limit listed in this Chapter's Specifications, replace the crankshaft and connecting rod as an assembly.

20.1b . . . you can also use a puller if you have the correct adapters

20.1c If the bearing stays on the crankshaft, remove it with a press and bearing splitter

20.2 Check the connecting rod side clearance with a feeler gauge

20.3 Check the connecting rod radial clearance with a dial indicator

20.6 The crankshaft seals have a major effect on two-stroke engine performance

20.7 Thread the adapter into the end of the crankshaft . . .

20.8 . . . and attach the puller to the adapter

3   Set up the crankshaft in V-blocks with a dial indicator contacting the big end of the connecting rod **(see illustration)**. Move the connecting rod up-and-down against the indicator pointer and compare the reading to the value listed in this Chapter's Specifications. If it's beyond the limit, replace the crankshaft and connecting rod as an assembly.

4   Check the crankshaft and splines for visible wear or damage, such as step wear of the splines or scoring. If any of these conditions are found, replace the crankshaft and connecting rod as an assembly.

5   Set the crankshaft in a pair of V-blocks, with a dial indicator contacting each end. Rotate the crankshaft and note the runout. If the runout at either end is beyond the limit listed in this Chapter's Specifications, replace the crankshaft and connecting rod as an assembly.

Installation

Refer to illustrations 20.6, 20.7 and 20.8

6   Pry out the crankshaft seals, then install new ones with a seal driver or a socket the same diameter as the seal **(see illustration)**.

7   Thread a puller adapter into the end of the crankshaft **(see illustration)**.

8   Install the crankshaft puller and collar on the end of the crankshaft **(see illustration)**.

9   Hold the puller shaft with one wrench and turn the nut with another wrench to pull the crankshaft into the center race of the ball bearing.

10   Remove the special tools from the crankshaft.

11   Installation is the reverse of the removal steps.

21   Recommended start-up and break-in procedure

1   This procedure should be followed each time the piston and rings, cylinder, crankshaft or crankshaft bearings are replaced. Make sure the transmission and controls, especially the brakes, function properly before riding the machine.

2   Place pieces of tape on the throttle twist grip and the handlebar next to it to indicate the half throttle and three-quarter throttle positions.

3   Make sure there is fresh fuel in the tank, then operate the choke.

4   Start the engine and ride for ten minutes, using no more than half throttle. Use the transmission to keep from lugging or over-revving the engine.

5   Shut the engine off and let it cool completely. Once the engine has cooled, ride for another ten minutes, again using no more than half throttle, without lugging or over-revving the engine.

6   Let the engine cool again, then ride for 10 minutes using no more than three-quarters throttle. Again, do not lug or over-rev the engine.

7   Let the engine cool, then ride for three more ten-minute periods, again using no more than three-quarters throttle, letting the engine cool completely between each period.

8   Check carefully for transmission oil and coolant leaks.

9   Upon completion of the break-in rides, and after the engine has cooled down completely, recheck the transmission oil and coolant level (see Chapter 1).

Chapter 3 Part A
Cooling systems
(CR80R/85R and CR125R models)

Contents

Specifications

General
Radiator cap relief pressure .... 16 to 20 psi

Torque settings
Water pump impeller
   CR80R/85R .... 10 Nm (84 inch-lbs)
   CR125R .... 12 Nm (108 inch-lbs)
Water pump bolts
   CR80R/85R .... Not specified
   CR125R
      1986 through 1991 .... 8 to 12 Nm (72 to 108 inch-lbs)
      1992 on.. 12 Nm (108 inch-lbs)

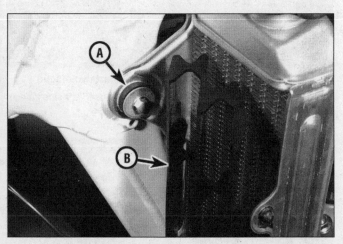

1.1a CR80R/85R cooling system details (part one of three)

   A   *Radiator front mounting bolt and grommet*
   B   *Radiator grille*

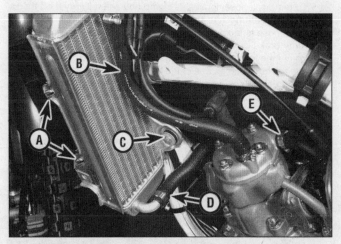

1.1b CR80R/85R cooling system details (part two of three)

   A   *Grille mounting tabs*
   B   *Coolant hose - radiator-to-cylinder head*
   C   *Radiator rear mounting bolt and grommet*
   D   *Coolant hose - radiator-to-water pump front fitting*

1 General information

Refer to illustrations 1.1a through 1.1g

The motorcycles covered by this manual are equipped with a liquid cooling system which utilizes a water/antifreeze mixture to carry away excess heat produced during the combustion process **(see illustrations)**. The cylinder is surrounded by a water jacket, through which the coolant is circulated by the water pump. The pump is mounted to the right side of the crankcase and is driven by a gear. The coolant is pumped through the radiator (both radiators on all except 1998 and 1999 CR125R models) where it is cooled, then out of the radiator(s) and through the cylinder and head.

Because these bikes are intended for competition, the cooling system is a very basic one, without a temperature gauge or light, fan, coolant reservoir or thermostat.

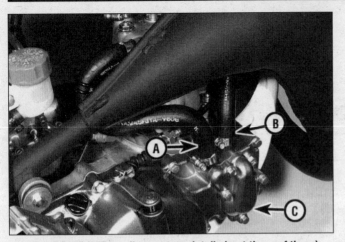

1.1c CR80R/85R cooling system details (part three of three)

A   *Coolant hose - cylinder head rear fitting-to-water pump*
B   *Coolant hose - water pump-to-radiator*
C   *Water pump*

2   Radiator cap - check

If problems such as overheating or loss of coolant occur, check the entire system as described in Chapter 1. The radiator cap opening pressure should be checked by a dealer service department or service station equipped with the special tester required to do the job. If the cap is defective, replace it with a new one.

3   Coolant hoses - removal and installation

1   The coolant hoses are all secured by screw-type clamps to fittings on the engine and radiator.
2   To remove a hose, loosen its clamp and carefully pry it off the fitting **(see illustrations 1.1b through 1.1g)**.
3   If the hose is stuck, pry the edge up slightly with a pointed tool and spray brake or electrical contact cleaner into the gap. Work the tool around the fitting, lifting the edge of the hose and spraying into the gap until the hose comes free of the fitting.
4   In extreme cases, you may have to slit the hose and cut it off the fitting with a knife. Make sure you can get a replacement hose before doing this.

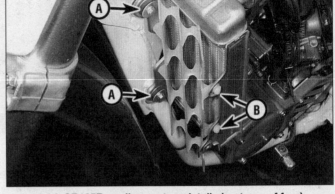

1.1d CR125R cooling system details (part one of four)

A   *Radiator front mounting bolts and grommets*
B   *Radiator grille mounting tabs*

1.1e CR125R cooling system details (part two of four)

A   *Coolant hose - left radiator-to-cylinder head left-side fitting*
B   *Radiator rear mounting bolt and grommet*

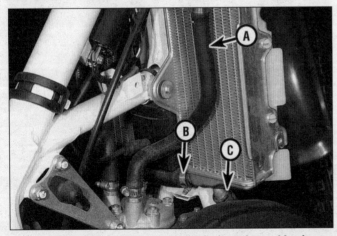

1.1f CR125R cooling system details (part three of four)

A   *Coolant hose - right radiator-to-cylinder head right-side fitting*
B   *Coolant hose - right radiator-to-left radiator (later models)*
C   *Coolant hose - radiator-to-water pump front fitting*

1.1g CR125R cooling system details (part four of four)

A   *Coolant hose - cylinder hose fitting-to-water pump*
B   *Coolant hose - water pump-to-radiator (later model shown)*
C   *Water pump*

5.2 Detach the hose and remove the hose fitting bolts (arrow) (upper bolt shown; lower bolt hidden)

4 Radiator(s) - removal and installation

Warning: *The engine must be completely cool before beginning this procedure.*

Removal

1   Support the bike securely upright. Remove the radiator shroud(s) (see Chapter 8) and drain the cooling system (see Chapter 1).
2   Squeeze the grille tabs and separate the grille from the radiator **(see illustration 1.1b or 1.1d)**.
3   Disconnect the hoses at the top and bottom of the radiator.
4   If you're working on a CR80R/85R, remove the mounting bolts at the front and rear of the radiator **(see illustrations 1.1a and 1.1b)**.
5   If you're working on a CR125R, remove two mounting bolts at the front and one at the rear of the radiator **(see illustrations 1.1d and 1.1e)**.
6   Lift the radiator away from the frame. Inspect the mounting bolt grommets and replace them of they're worn or deteriorated.
7   Installation is the reverse of the removal steps, with the following additions:

a) *Tighten the mounting bolts securely, but don't overtighten them and distort the grommets.*
b) *Fill the cooling system (see Chapter 1).*
c) *Run the engine and check for coolant leaks.*

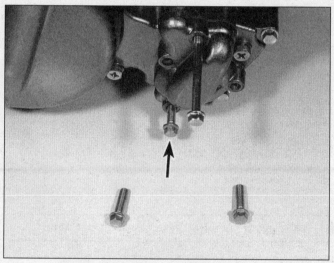

6.3a CR80R/85R water pump bolts - the lower bolt has a copper washer (arrow)

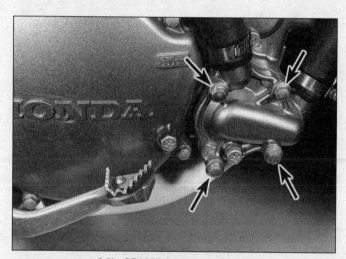

6.3b CR125R water pump bolts

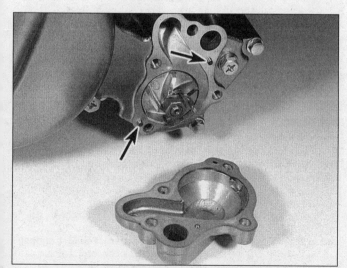

6.4a Take off the cover and gasket and locate the dowels (arrows) (CR80R/85R shown)

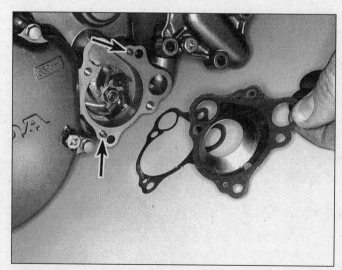

6.4b 2004 and earlier CR125R models also use a spacer with a gasket on each side

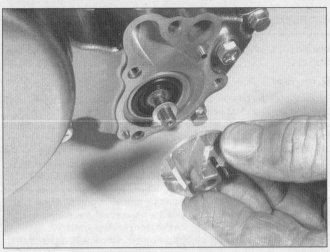

6.5 Unscrew the impeller and slide the copper washer off the shaft; the seal can then be inspected

6.7a The CR80R/85R water pump shaft fits in its outer bearing like this

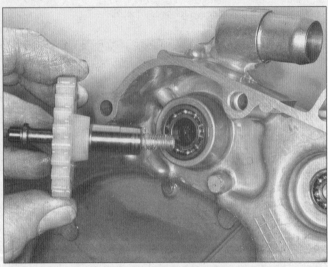

6.7b The CR125R water pump shaft fits in its outer bearing like this

6.8 The inner water pump shaft bearing is mounted in the crankcase (CR80R/85R shown)

5   Cylinder hose fitting (CR125R) - removal and installation

Refer to illustration 5.2

1   Drain the cooling system (see Chapter 3).
2   Disconnect the hose from the fitting, then unbolt the fitting from the cylinder **(see illustration)**.
3   Pull the fitting off the cylinder. Remove its O-ring and clean the O-ring groove.
4   Installation is the reverse of the removal steps, with the following additions:

   a) *Use a new O-ring.*
   b) *Tighten the mounting bolts securely, but don't overtighten them and strip the threads.*
   c) *Fill the cooling system (see Chapter 1).*
   d) *Run the engine and check for coolant leaks.*

6   Water pump - removal, inspection and installation

Removal

Refer to illustrations 6.3a, 6.3b, 6.4a, 6.4b and 6.5

1   Drain the cooling system (see Chapter 3).
2   Disconnect the hoses from the water pump.
3   Remove the pump mounting bolts **(see illustrations)**. The bolts are different lengths, so tag them for reinstallation. One bolt on CR80R/85R models has a copper washer.
4   Take off the pump cover and gasket **(see illustrations)**. If you're working on a CR125R, remove the inner cover and its gasket as well.
5   Unscrew the impeller from its shaft and remove the copper washer **(see illustration)**.

Inspection

Refer to illustrations 6.7a, 6.7b and 6.8

6   Check the impeller seal for wear or damage **(see illustration 6.5)**. This seal separates the coolant from the oil supply used by the transmission and clutch. If the transmission oil is milky or foamy, coolant may have been leaking into it past the seal. Refer to Section 7 and replace it.
7   To inspect the bearings and water pump shaft and gear, you'll need to remove the right crankcase cover (see Chapter 2). Lift the water pump shaft out of the bearing in the cover **(see illustrations)**. Spin the bearing and check it for roughness, looseness or noise and replace it if any problems are found.
8   Also check the water pump shaft bearing in the crankcase **(see illustration)**. If it's rough, loose or noisy, replace it (See Section 7).

7.2a Remove the water pump shaft bearings with a small slide hammer and puller attachment; the puller fits inside the bearing and expands to grasp the inner race

7.2b Drive in new bearings with a drift that applies pressure to the outer race

Installation

9   Installation is the reverse of the removal steps, with the following additions:

a) *Use a new gasket(s).*
b) *Tighten the water pump bolts to the torque listed in this Chapter's Specifications.*
c) *Fill the cooling system (see Chapter 1).*
d) *Run the engine and check for coolant leaks.*

7   Water pump seal and bearings - replacement

Refer to illustrations 7.2a, 7.2b, 7.3a, 7.3b and 7.3c

1   Remove the water pump (Section 6) and the right crankcase cover (Chapter 2).

2   Remove the bearing from the cover or crankcase with a slide hammer and bearing puller attachment **(see illustration)**. Drive in a new bearing with a bearing driver or socket that bears against the bearing outer race **(see illustration)**.

3   Pry the seal out of its bore **(see illustration)**. Install a new one with Honda tool 07965-45000A or equivalent **(see illustrations)**.

7.3a Pry the impeller seal (arrow) out of the right crankcase cover

7.3b Install a new seal with a tool like this one . . .

7.3c . . . place the bolt and collar over the seal like this; install the washer and nut on the other side, then tighten the bolt and nut to draw the seal into its bore

Notes

Chapter 3 Part B
Cooling systems
(CR250R and CR500R models)

Contents

Specifications

General
Radiator cap relief pressure .... 16 to 20 psi

Torque specifications
Water pump impeller .... 12 Nm (9 ft-lbs)
Water pump bolts .... 12 Nm (9 ft-lbs)

1   General information

The motorcycles covered by this manual are equipped with a liquid cooling system which utilizes a water/antifreeze mixture to carry away excess heat produced during the combustion process. The cylinder is surrounded by a water jacket, through which the coolant is circulated by the water pump. The pump is mounted to the right side of the crankcase and is driven by a gear. The 1997 through 1999 CR250R uses a single radiator; all other models have two radiators. The coolant is pumped through the radiator(s) where it is cooled, then out of the radiator(s) and through the cylinder and head.

Because these bikes are intended for motocross competition, the cooling system is a very basic one, without a temperature gauge or light, fan, coolant reservoir or thermostat.

2   Radiator cap - check

If problems such as overheating or loss of coolant occur, check the entire system as described in Chapter 1. The radiator cap opening pressure should be checked by a dealer service department or service station equipped with the special tester required to do the job. If the cap is defective, replace it with a new one.

3   Coolant hoses - removal and installation

Refer to illustration 3.2
1   The coolant hoses are all secured by screw-type clamps to fittings on the engine and radiator.

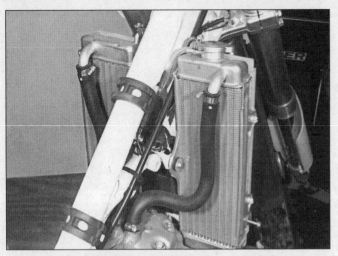

3.2 Coolant hoses (dual-radiator models)

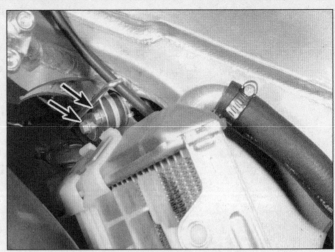

4.4a The 1997 through 1999 CR250R has a single radiator; its upper mounting bolts are accessible from the top front . . .

2   To remove a hose, loosen its clamp and carefully pry it off the fitting **(see illustration)**.

3   If the hose is stuck, pry the edge up slightly with a pointed tool and spray brake or electrical contact cleaner into the gap. Work the tool around the fitting, lifting the edge of the hose and spraying into the gap until the hose comes free of the fitting.

4   In extreme cases, you may have to slit the hose and cut it off the fitting with a knife. Make sure you can get a replacement hose before doing this.

---

4   Radiator(s) - removal and installation

Warning: *The engine must be completely cool before beginning this procedure.*

Removal

Refer to illustrations 4.4a and 4.4b

1   Support the bike securely upright. Remove the radiator shroud(s) (see Chapter 8) and drain the cooling system (see Chapter 1).

2   Squeeze the grille tabs and separate the grille from the radiator.

3   Disconnect the hoses at the top and bottom of the radiator.

4   Remove the radiator mounting bolts **(see illustration 3.2 and the accompanying illustrations)**.

5   Lift the radiator away from the frame. Inspect the mounting bolt grommets and replace them of they're worn or deteriorated.

6   Installation is the reverse of the removal steps, with the following additions:

    a) *Tighten the mounting bolts securely, but don't overtighten them and distort the grommets.*

    b) *Fill the cooling system (see Chapter 1).*

    c) *Run the engine and check for coolant leaks.*

---

5   Water pump - removal, inspection and installation

Removal

Refer to illustrations 5.3a, 5.3b, 5.4 and 5.5

1   Drain the cooling system (see Chapter 1).

2   Disconnect the hoses from the water pump.

3   Remove the pump mounting bolts **(see illustrations)**. The bolts are different lengths, so tag them for reinstallation.

4   Take off the pump cover and gasket, then remove the inner cover and gasket **(see illustration)**.

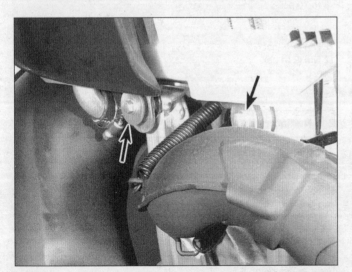

4.4b   . . . and its lower mounting bolts are accessible from the bottom front

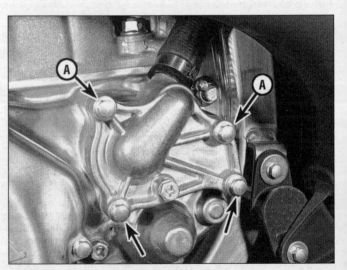

5.3a Water pump bolts (CR250R)

A   Dowel locations

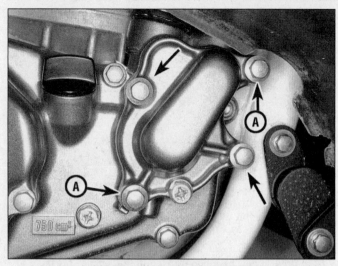

5.3b Water pump bolts (CR500R)

A Dowel locations

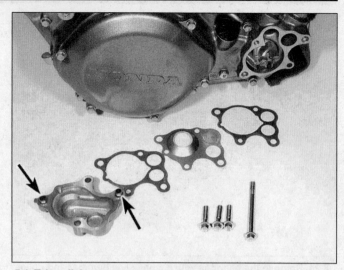

5.4 Take off the cover, spacer and gaskets and locate the dowels (arrows) (1997 CR500R shown)

5.5 Unscrew the impeller and slide the copper washer off the shaft; the seal can then be inspected

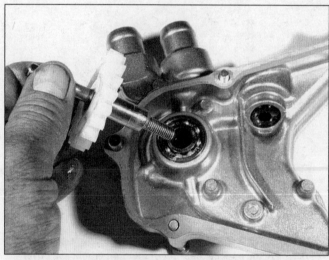

5.7 The impeller shaft fits in its outer bearing like this

5   Unscrew the impeller from its shaft and remove the copper washer **(see illustration)**.

Inspection

Refer to illustrations 5.7 and 5.8

6   Check the impeller seal for wear or damage **(see illustration 5.5)**. This seal separates the coolant from the oil supply used by the transmission and clutch. If the transmission oil is milky or foamy, coolant may have been leaking into it past the seal. Refer to Section 6 and replace it.

7   To inspect the bearings and impeller driven gear, you'll need to remove the right crankcase cover (see Chapter 2). If you're working on a 1986 through 1991 CR250R, you'll also need to remove the Honda Power Port governor (see Chapter 4). Lift the impeller shaft out of the bearing in the cover **(see illustration)**. Spin the bearing and check it for roughness, looseness or noise and replace it if any problems are found.

8   Also check the impeller bushing (CR250R) or bearing (CR500R) in the crankcase **(see illustration)**. If it's rough, loose or noisy, replace it (see Section 6).

5.8 The inner impeller bushing or bearing is mounted in the crankcase (1997 CR500R shown)

6.2a   Remove the bearings with a small slide hammer and puller attachment; the puller fits inside the bearing and expands to grasp the inner race

6.2b   Drive in new bearings with a drift that applies pressure to the outer race

6.3a   Pry the impeller seal out of the right crankcase cover

6.3b   Install a new seal with a tool like this one . . .

Installation

9   Installation is the reverse of the removal steps, with the following additions:

a) *Use a new gasket(s).*
b) *Tighten the water pump bolts to the torque listed in this Chapter's Specifications.*
c) *Fill the cooling system (see Chapter 1).*
d) *Run the engine and check for coolant leaks.*

6   Water pump seal and bearings - replacement

Refer to illustrations 6.2a, 6.2b, 6.3a, 6.3b and 6.3c

1   Remove the water pump (see Section 5) and the right crankcase cover (Chapter 2).
2   Remove the cover bearing, or the crankcase bushing or bearing, with a slide hammer and bearing puller attachment **(see illustration)**. Drive in a new bearing with a bearing driver or socket that bears against the bearing outer race **(see illustration)**.
3   Pry the seal out of its bore **(see illustration)**. Install a new one with Honda tool 07965-45000A or equivalent **(see illustrations)**.

6.3c   . . . place the bolt and collar over the seal like this; install the washer and nut on the other side, then tighten the bolt and nut to draw the seal into its bore

Chapter 4 Part A
Fuel and exhaust systems
(CR80R/85R and CR125R models)

Contents

Specifications

General
Fuel type.. See Chapter 1

Carburetor (CR80R/RB and CR85R/RB)
Standard air screw setting
2002 and earlier .... 2 turns out
2003 and 2004 .... 1-5/8 turns out
2005 and later .... 2 turns out
Maximum air screw range .... 1 to 3 turns out
Identification mark
1986 and 1987 .... PE68A
1988 through 1995 .... PE68B
1996 through 2002 .... PE68D

Carburetor (CR80R/RB and CR85R/RB) (continued)

Jet sizes
  Standard main jet
    1986 128
    1987 through 2004 125
    2005 and later 142
  Slow jet
    1986 through 1995 52
    1996 through 2004 50
    2005 and later 45
  Jet needle clip position
    1986 through 1995 .... 2nd groove from top
    1996 through 2002 .... 3rd groove from top
    2003 and 2004 .... 2nd groove from top
    2005 and later .... 3rd groove from top
Float level .... 19.0 mm (3/4 inch)
Correction factor, needle clip position and air screw setting
  0.94 or below
    Needle clip position .... One groove above standard
    Air screw setting .... 1 turn out from standard
  0.94 to 0.98
    Needle clip position .... Standard
    Air screw setting .... 1/2 turn out from standard
  0.98 to 1.02
    Needle clip position .... Standard
    Air screw setting .... Standard
  1.02 to 1.06
    Needle clip position .... Standard
    Air screw setting .... 1/2 turn in from standard
  1.06 or above
    Needle clip position .... One groove below standard
    Air screw opening .... 1 turn in from standard

Carburetor (CR125R)

Standard air screw setting
  1986 through 1988 .... 1-1/2 turns out
  1989 .... 1-3/4 turns out
  1990 through 1992 .... 2 turns out
  1993 and 1994 .... 1-1/2 turns out
  1995 .... 2 turns out
  1996 .... 1-3/4 turns out
  1997 .... 2-1/8 turns out
  1998 .... 2 turns out
  1999 .... 2-3/4 turns out
  2000 .... 1-3/4 turns out
  2001 .... 2-1/4 turns out
  2002 .... 2-1/8 turns out
  2003 .... 1-3/4 turns out
  2004 .... 2 turns out
  2005 and later .... 1-3/4 turns out
Maximum air screw range .... 1 to 3 turns out
Idle speed knob minimum setting .... 4 turns out (24 clicks) from seated position
Identification mark
  1986 .... PJ04A
  1987 .... PJ08A
  1988 .... PJ08B
  1989 .... PJ08C
  1990 .... PJ15A
  1991 .... Not available
  1992 .... PJ15E
  1993 .... PJ15G
  1994 .... PJ15H
  1995 .... PJ15J
  1996 .... PJ15K
  1997 .... PJ15L
  1998 .... PJ15M
  1999 .... PJ16N
  2000 .... TMX01A
  2001 .... TMX01B
  2002 .... TMX02A

2003	TMX03A
2004	TMX04A
2005 and later	TMX05A

Jet sizes
Standard main jet

1986	152
1987 through 1989	165
1990	168
1991 through 1997	172
1998	175
1999	178
2000	360
2001	380
2002	400
2003	430
2004	420
2005 and later	430

Slow jet

1986	65
1987 through 1989	60
1990 through 1994	58
1995	55
1996 and 1997	50
1998	52
1999	55
2000	50
2001	45
2002	32.5
2003	30
2004	40
2005	45

Jet needle clip position

All except 1987 and 1998	3rd groove from top
1987 and 1998	4th groove from top

Float level

1986 through 1999	16.0 mm (5/8 inch)
2000 and 2001	15.0 mm (19/32 inch)
2002 and later	7.5 mm (19/64 inch)

Carburetor settings

1995 CR80R

Sea level to 999 feet (299 meters)
Minus 21 to 0-degrees F (minus 35 to minus 18-degrees C)

Air screw	1 turn out
Slow jet	58
Needle clip position	3rd groove
Main jet	135

Minus 1 to 20-degrees F (minus 17 to minus 7-degrees C)

Air screw	1 turn out
Slow jet	55
Needle clip position	3rd groove
Main jet	132

19 to 40-degrees F (minus 6 to 4-degrees C)

Air screw	1-1/2 turns out
Slow jet	55
Needle clip position	3rd groove
Main jet	130

39 to 60-degrees F (3 to 15-degrees C)

Air screw	1-3/4 turns out
Slow jet	52
Needle clip position	2nd groove
Main jet	128

59 to 80-degrees F (14 to 26-degrees C)*

Air screw	2 turns out
Slow jet	52
Needle clip position	2nd groove
Main jet	125

* Standard jetting

Carburetor settings (continued)

1995 CR80R (continued)

Sea level to 999 feet (299 meters)

  79 to 100-degrees F (25 to 38-degrees C)

Air screw	2-1/2 turns out
Slow jet	50
Needle clip position	2nd groove
Main jet	122

  99 to 120-degrees F (37 to 49-degrees C)

Air screw	2-1/2 turns out
Slow jet	50
Needle clip position	2nd groove
Main jet	122

1000 to 2499 feet (300 to 749 meters)

  Minus 21 to 0-degrees F (minus 35 to minus 18-degrees C)

Air screw	1 turn out
Slow jet	55
Needle clip position	3rd groove
Main jet	135

  Minus 1 to 20-degrees F (minus 17 to minus 7-degrees C)

Air screw	1-1/2 turn out
Slow jet	55
Needle clip position	3rd groove
Main jet	132

  19 to 40-degrees F (minus 6 to 4-degrees C)

Air screw	1-1/2 turns out
Slow jet	55
Needle clip position	3rd groove
Main jet	128

  39 to 60-degrees F (3 to 15-degrees C)

Air screw	2 turns out
Slow jet	55
Needle clip position	2nd groove
Main jet	125

  59 to 80-degrees F (14 to 26-degrees C)

Air screw	2-1/4 turns out
Slow jet	52
Needle clip position	2nd groove
Main jet	122

  79 to 100-degrees F (25 to 38-degrees C)

Air screw	2-1/2 turns out
Slow jet	50
Needle clip position	2nd groove
Main jet	120

  99 to 120-degrees F (37 to 49-degrees C)

Air screw	2-3/4 turns out
Slow jet	48
Needle clip position	2nd groove
Main jet	118

2500 to 4999 feet (750 to 1499 meters)

  Minus 21 to 0-degrees F (minus 35 to minus 18-degrees C)

Air screw	1 turn out
Slow jet	55
Needle clip position	3rd groove
Main jet	132

  Minus 1 to 20-degrees F (minus 17 to minus 7-degrees C)

Air screw	1-1/2 turn out
Slow jet	55
Needle clip position	3rd groove
Main jet	130

  19 to 40-degrees F (minus 6 to 4-degrees C)

Air screw	1-3/4 turns out
Slow jet	52
Needle clip position	2nd groove
Main jet	128

  39 to 60-degrees F (3 to 15-degrees C)

Air screw	2 turns out
Slow jet	52

Needle clip position.. 2nd groove
Main jet.. 125
  59 to 80-degrees F (14 to 26-degrees C)
    Air screw... 2 turns out
    Slow jet.. 50
    Needle clip position.. 2nd groove
    Main jet.. 122
  79 to 100-degrees F (25 to 38-degrees C)
    Air screw... 2-1/2 turns out
    Slow jet.. 50
    Needle clip position.. 2nd groove
    Main jet.. 118
  99 to 120-degrees F (37 to 49-degrees C)
    Air screw... 2-3/4 turns out
    Slow jet.. 48
    Needle clip position.. 1st groove
    Main jet.. 115
5000 to 7499 feet (1500 to 2299 meters)
  Minus 21 to 0-degrees F (minus 35 to minus 18-degrees C)
    Air screw... 1-1/2 turns out
    Slow jet.. 55
    Needle clip position.. 3rd groove
    Main jet.. 130
  Minus 1 to 20-degrees F (minus 17 to minus 7-degrees C)
    Air screw... 1-3/4 turns out
    Slow jet.. 52
    Needle clip position.. 3rd groove
    Main jet.. 125
  19 to 40-degrees F (minus 6 to 4-degrees C)
    Air screw... 2 turns out
    Slow jet.. 52
    Needle clip position.. 2nd groove
    Main jet.. 125
  39 to 60-degrees F (3 to 15-degrees C)
    Air screw... 2-1/4 turns out
    Slow jet.. 50
    Needle clip position.. 2nd groove
    Main jet.. 122
  59 to 80-degrees F (14 to 26-degrees C)
    Air screw... 2-1/2 turns out
    Slow jet.. 48
    Needle clip position.. 1st groove
    Main jet.. 118
  79 to 100-degrees F (25 to 38-degrees C)
    Air screw... 2-3/4 turns out
    Slow jet.. 48
    Needle clip position.. 1st groove
    Main jet.. 115
  99 to 120-degrees F (37 to 49-degrees C)
    Air screw... 3.0 turns out
    Slow jet.. 48
    Needle clip position.. 1st groove
    Main jet.. 112
7500 to 10,000 feet (2300 to 3000 meters)
  Minus 21 to 0-degrees F (minus 35 to minus 18-degrees C)
    Air screw... 1-3/4 turns out
    Slow jet.. 52
    Needle clip position.. 2nd groove
    Main jet.. 128
  Minus 1 to 20-degrees F (minus 17 to minus 7-degrees C)
    Air screw... 2 turns out
    Slow jet.. 52
    Needle clip position.. 2nd groove
    Main jet.. 125
  19 to 40-degrees F (minus 6 to 4-degrees C)
    Air screw... 1-1/4 turns out
    Slow jet.. 50
    Needle clip position.. 2nd groove
    Main jet.. 122

Carburetor settings (continued)

1995 CR80R (continued)

7500 to 10,000 feet (2300 to 3000 meters)
  39 to 60-degrees F (3 to 15-degrees C)
    Air screw .... 1-1/2 turns out
    Slow jet 50
    Needle clip position .... 2nd groove
    Main jet 118
  59 to 80-degrees F (14 to 26-degrees C)
    Air screw .... 2-3/4 turns out
    Slow jet 48
    Needle clip position .... 1st groove
    Main jet 115
  79 to 100-degrees F (25 to 38-degrees C)
    Air screw .... 3 turns out
    Slow jet 48
    Needle clip position .... 1st groove
    Main jet 112
  99 to 120-degrees F (37 to 49-degrees C)
    Air screw .... 3 turns out
    Slow jet 48
    Needle clip position .... 1st groove
    Main jet 110

1996 and later CR80R

Sea level to 999 feet (299 meters)
  Minus 21 to 0-degrees F (minus 35 to minus 18-degrees C)
    Air screw .... 1 turn out
    Slow jet 58
    Needle clip position .... 4th groove
    Main jet 135
  Minus 1 to 20-degrees F (minus 17 to minus 7-degrees C)
    Air screw .... 1 turn out
    Slow jet 55
    Needle clip position .... 4th groove
    Main jet 132
  19 to 40-degrees F (minus 6 to 4-degrees C)
    Air screw .... 1-1/2 turns out
    Slow jet 55
    Needle clip position .... 4th groove
    Main jet 130
  39 to 60-degrees F (3 to 15-degrees C)
    Air screw .... 1-3/4 turns out
    Slow jet 52
    Needle clip position .... 3rd groove
    Main jet 128
  59 to 80-degrees F (14 to 26-degrees C)*
    Air screw .... 2 turns out
    Slow jet 50
    Needle clip position .... 3rd groove
    Main jet 125
  79 to 100-degrees F (25 to 38-degrees C)
    Air screw .... 2-1/2 turns out
    Slow jet 50
    Needle clip position .... 3rd groove
    Main jet 122
  99 to 120-degrees F (37 to 49-degrees C)
    Air screw .... 2-3/4 turns out
    Slow jet 48
    Needle clip position .... 3rd groove
    Main jet 118
1000 to 2499 feet (300 to 749 meters)
  Minus 21 to 0-degrees F (minus 35 to minus 18-degrees C)
    Air screw .... 1 turn out
    Slow jet 55
    Needle clip position .... 4th groove
    Main jet 135

Standard jetting

Minus 1 to 20-degrees F (minus 17 to minus 7-degrees C)
Air screw..	1-1/2 turns out
Slow jet...	55
Needle clip position...	4th groove
Main jet...	132

19 to 40-degrees F (minus 6 to 4-degrees C)
Air screw..	1-1/2 turns out
Slow jet...	55
Needle clip position...	4th groove
Main jet...	128

39 to 60-degrees F (3 to 15-degrees C)
Air screw..	2 turns out
Slow jet...	52
Needle clip position...	3rd groove
Main jet...	125

59 to 80-degrees F (14 to 26-degrees C)
Air screw..	2-1/4 turns out
Slow jet...	50
Needle clip position...	3rd groove
Main jet...	122

79 to 100-degrees F (25 to 38-degrees C)
Air screw..	2-1/2 turns out
Slow jet...	50
Needle clip position...	3rd groove
Main jet...	120

99 to 120-degrees F (37 to 49-degrees C)
Air screw..	2-3/4 turns out
Slow jet...	48
Needle clip position...	2nd groove
Main jet...	118

2500 to 4999 feet (750 to 1499 meters)
Minus 21 to 0-degrees F (minus 35 to minus 18-degrees C)
Air screw..	1 turn out
Slow jet...	55
Needle clip position...	4th groove
Main jet...	132

Minus 1 to 20-degrees F (minus 17 to minus 7-degrees C)
Air screw..	1-1/2 turn out
Slow jet...	55
Needle clip position...	4th groove
Main jet...	130

19 to 40-degrees F (minus 6 to 4-degrees C)
Air screw..	1-3/4 turns out
Slow jet...	52
Needle clip position...	3rd groove
Main jet...	128

39 to 60-degrees F (3 to 15-degrees C)
Air screw..	2 turns out
Slow jet...	52
Needle clip position...	3rd groove
Main jet...	125

59 to 80-degrees F (14 to 26-degrees C)
Air screw..	2 turns out
Slow jet...	48
Needle clip position...	2nd groove
Main jet...	122

79 to 100-degrees F (25 to 38-degrees C)
Air screw..	2-1/2 turns out
Slow jet...	48
Needle clip position...	2nd groove
Main jet...	118

99 to 120-degrees F (37 to 49-degrees C)
Air screw..	2-3/4 turns out
Slow jet...	48
Needle clip position...	2nd groove
Main jet...	115

Carburetor settings (continued)

1996 and later CR80R (continued)

5000 to 7499 feet (1500 to 2299 meters)

 Minus 21 to 0-degrees F (minus 35 to minus 18-degrees C)

  Air screw .... 1-1/2 turns out

  Slow jet 55

  Needle clip position .... 4th groove

  Main jet 130

 Minus 1 to 20-degrees F (minus 17 to minus 7-degrees C)

  Air screw .... 1-3/4 turns out

  Slow jet 52

  Needle clip position .... 4th groove

  Main jet 125

 19 to 40-degrees F (minus 6 to 4-degrees C)

  Air screw .... 2 turns out

  Slow jet 52

  Needle clip position .... 3rd groove

  Main jet 125

 39 to 60-degrees F (3 to 15-degrees C)

  Air screw .... 2-1/4 turns out

  Slow jet 50

  Needle clip position .... 2nd groove

  Main jet 122

 59 to 80-degrees F (14 to 26-degrees C)

  Air screw .... 2-1/2 turns out

  Slow jet 48

  Needle clip position .... 2nd groove

  Main jet 118

 79 to 100-degrees F (25 to 38-degrees C)

  Air screw .... 2-3/4 turns out

  Slow jet 48

  Needle clip position .... 2nd groove

  Main jet 115

 99 to 120-degrees F (37 to 49-degrees C)

  Air screw .... 3 turns out

  Slow jet 48

  Needle clip position .... 2nd groove

  Main jet 112

7500 to 10,000 feet (2300 to 3000 meters)

 Minus 21 to 0-degrees F (minus 35 to minus 18-degrees C)

  Air screw .... 1-3/4 turns out

  Slow jet 52

  Needle clip position .... 3rd groove

  Main jet 128

 Minus 1 to 20-degrees F (minus 17 to minus 7-degrees C)

  Air screw .... 2 turns out

  Slow jet 52

  Needle clip position .... 3rd groove

  Main jet 125

 19 to 40-degrees F (minus 6 to 4-degrees C)

  Air screw .... 2-1/4 turns out

  Slow jet 50

  Needle clip position .... 3rd groove

  Main jet 122

 39 to 60-degrees F (3 to 15-degrees C)

  Air screw .... 2-1/2 turns out

  Slow jet 50

  Needle clip position .... 2nd groove

  Main jet 118

 59 to 80-degrees F (14 to 26-degrees C)

  Air screw .... 2-3/4 turns out

  Slow jet 48

  Needle clip position .... 2nd groove

  Main jet 115

79 to 100-degrees F (25 to 38-degrees C)
Air screw .... 3 turns out
Slow jet 48
Needle clip position .... 2nd groove
Main jet 112
99 to 120-degrees F (37 to 49-degrees C)
Air screw .... 3 turns out
Slow jet 48
Needle clip position .... 1st groove
Main jet 110

2003 and 2004 CR85R
Sea level to 999 feet (299 meters)
Minus 21 to 0-degrees F (minus 35 to minus 18-degrees C)
Air screw 1-1/8
Slow jet 52
Needle clip position 3
Main jet 135
Minus 1 to 20-degrees F (minus 17 to minus 7-degrees C)
Air screw 1-3/8
Slow jet 52
Needle clip position 3
Main jet 132
19 to 40-degrees F (minus 6 to 4-degrees C)
Air screw 1-1/8
Slow jet 50
Needle clip position 3
Main jet 130
39 to 60-degrees F (3 to 15-degrees C)
Air screw 1-3/8
Slow jet 50
Needle clip position 2
Main jet 128
59 to 80-degrees F (14 to 26-degrees C)
Air screw 1-5/8
Slow jet 50
Needle clip position 2
Main jet 125
79 to 100-degrees F (25 to 38-degrees C)
Air screw 1-7/8
Slow jet 50
Needle clip position 2
Main jet 122
99 to 120-degrees F (37 to 49-degrees C)
Air screw 2-1/8
Slow jet 50
Needle clip position 2
Main jet 120
1000 to 2499 feet (300 to 749 meters)
Minus 21 to 0-degrees F (minus 35 to minus 18-degrees C)
Air screw 1-3/8
Slow jet 52
Needle clip position 3
Main jet 132
Minus 1 to 20-degrees F (minus 17 to minus 7-degrees C)
Air screw 1-1/8
Slow jet 50
Needle clip position 3
Main jet 130
19 to 40-degrees F (minus 6 to 4-degrees C)
Air screw 1-3/8
Slow jet 50
Needle clip position 2
Main jet 128
39 to 60-degrees F (3 to 15-degrees C)
Air screw 1-5/8
Slow jet 50
Needle clip position 2
Main jet 125

Carburetor settings (continued)

2003 and 2004 CR85R (continued)

1000 to 2499 feet (300 to 749 meters)

59 to 80-degrees F (14 to 26-degrees C)

Air screw	1-7/8
Slow jet	50
Needle clip position	2
Main jet	122

79 to 100-degrees F (25 to 38-degrees C)

Air screw	2-1/8
Slow jet	50
Needle clip position	2
Main jet	120

99 to 120-degrees F (37 to 49-degrees C)

Air screw	2-3/8
Slow jet	50
Needle clip position	2
Main jet	118

2500 to 4999 feet (750 to 1499 meters)

Minus 21 to 0-degrees F (minus 35 to minus 18-degrees C)

Air screw	1-1/8
Slow jet	50
Needle clip position	3
Main jet	130

Minus 1 to 20-degrees F (minus 17 to minus 7-degrees C)

Air screw	1-/8
Slow jet	50
Needle clip position	2
Main jet	128

19 to 40-degrees F (minus 6 to 4-degrees C)

Air screw	1-5/8
Slow jet	50
Needle clip position	2
Main jet	125

39 to 60-degrees F (3 to 15-degrees C)

Air screw	1-7/8
Slow jet	50
Needle clip position	2
Main jet	122

59 to 80-degrees F (14 to 26-degrees C)

Air screw	2-1/8
Slow jet	50
Needle clip position	2
Main jet	120

79 to 100-degrees F (25 to 38-degrees C)

Air screw	2-3/8
Slow jet	50
Needle clip position	2
Main jet	118

99 to 120-degrees F (37 to 49-degrees C)

Air screw	2-3/8
Slow jet	48
Needle clip position	1
Main jet	115

5000 to 7499 feet (1500 to 2299 meters)

Minus 21 to 0-degrees F (minus 35 to minus 18-degrees C)

Air screw	1-3/8
Slow jet	50
Needle clip position	2
Main jet	128

Minus 1 to 20-degrees F (minus 17 to minus 7-degrees C)

Air screw	1-5/8
Slow jet	50
Needle clip position	2
Main jet	125

19 to 40-degrees F (minus 6 to 4-degrees C)

Air screw	1-7/8
Slow jet	50
Needle clip position	2
Main jet	122

39 to 60-degrees F (3 to 15-degrees C)
    Air screw 2-1/8
    Slow jet 50
    Needle clip position 2
    Main jet 120
59 to 80-degrees F (14 to 26-degrees C)
    Air screw 2-3/8
    Slow jet 50
    Needle clip position 2
    Main jet 118
79 to 100-degrees F (25 to 38-degrees C)
    Air screw 2-1/8
    Slow jet 48
    Needle clip position 2
    Main jet 115
99 to 120-degrees F (37 to 49-degrees C)
    Air screw 2-3/8
    Slow jet 48
    Needle clip position 1
    Main jet 112
7500 to 10,000 feet (2300 to 3050 meters)
  Minus 21 to 0-degrees F (minus 35 to minus 18-degrees C)
    Air screw 1-1/8
    Slow jet 50
    Needle clip position 2
    Main jet 125
  Minus 1 to 20-degrees F (minus 17 to minus 7-degrees C)
    Air screw 1-7/8
    Slow jet 50
    Needle clip position 2
    Main jet 122
  19 to 40-degrees F (minus 6 to 4-degrees C)
    Air screw 2-1/8
    Slow jet 50
    Needle clip position 2
    Main jet 120
  39 to 60-degrees F (3 to 15-degrees C)
    Air screw 2-3/8
    Slow jet 50
    Needle clip position 2
    Main jet 118
  59 to 80-degrees F (14 to 26-degrees C)
    Air screw 2-1/8
    Slow jet 48
    Needle clip position 1
    Main jet 115
  79 to 100-degrees F (25 to 38-degrees C)
    Air screw 2-3/8
    Slow jet 48
    Needle clip position 1
    Main jet 112
  99 to 120-degrees F (37 to 49-degrees C)
    Air screw 2-5/8
    Slow jet 48
    Needle clip position 1
    Main jet 110

2005 and later CR85R
Sea level to 999 feet (299 meters)
  Minus 21 to 0-degrees F (minus 35 to minus 18-degrees C)
    Air screw 1-1/2
    Slow jet 48
    Needle clip position 4
    Main jet 152
  Minus 1 to 20-degrees F (minus 17 to minus 7-degrees C)
    Air screw 1-3/4
    Slow jet 48
    Needle clip position 4
    Main jet 150

Carburetor settings (continued)

2005 and later CR85R (continued)

Sea level to 999 feet (299 meters)

  19 to 40-degrees F (minus 6 to 4-degrees C)

Air screw	2
Slow jet	48
Needle clip position	3
Main jet	148

  39 to 60-degrees F (3 to 15-degrees C)

Air screw	1-3/4
Slow jet	45
Needle clip position	3
Main jet	145

  59 to 80-degrees F (14 to 26-degrees C)

Air screw	2
Slow jet	45
Needle clip position	3
Main jet	142

  79 to 100-degrees F (25 to 38-degrees C)

Air screw	2
Slow jet	45
Needle clip position	3
Main jet	142

  99 to 120-degrees F (37 to 49-degrees C)

Air screw	2-1/2
Slow jet	45
Needle clip position	2
Main jet	140

1000 to 2499 feet (300 to 749 meters)

  Minus 21 to 0-degrees F (minus 35 to minus 18-degrees C)

Air screw	1-3/4
Slow jet	48
Needle clip position	4
Main jet	150

  Minus 1 to 20-degrees F (minus 17 to minus 7-degrees C)

Air screw	2
Slow jet	48
Needle clip position	3
Main jet	148

  19 to 40-degrees F (minus 6 to 4-degrees C)

Air screw	1-3/4
Slow jet	45
Needle clip position	3
Main jet	145

  39 to 60-degrees F (3 to 15-degrees C)

Air screw	2
Slow jet	45
Needle clip position	3
Main jet	142

  59 to 80-degrees F (14 to 26-degrees C)

Air screw	2
Slow jet	45
Needle clip position	3
Main jet	142

  79 to 100-degrees F (25 to 38-degrees C)

Air screw	2-1/4
Slow jet	45
Needle clip position	2
Main jet	140

  99 to 120-degrees F (37 to 49-degrees C)

Air screw	2-1/2
Slow jet	45
Needle clip position	2
Main jet	138

2500 to 4999 feet (750 to 1499 meters)

  Minus 21 to 0-degrees F (minus 35 to minus 18-degrees C)

Air screw	2
Slow jet	48
Needle clip position	3
Main jet	148

Minus 1 to 20-degrees F (minus 17 to minus 7-degrees C)

Air screw	1-3/4
Slow jet	45
Needle clip position	3
Main jet	145

19 to 40-degrees F (minus 6 to 4-degrees C)

Air screw	2
Slow jet	45
Needle clip position	3
Main jet	142

39 to 60-degrees F (3 to 15-degrees C)

Air screw	2
Slow jet	45
Needle clip position	3
Main jet	142

59 to 80-degrees F (14 to 26-degrees C)

Air screw	2-1/4
Slow jet	45
Needle clip position	2
Main jet	140

79 to 100-degrees F (25 to 38-degrees C)

Air screw	2-1/2
Slow jet	45
Needle clip position	2
Main jet	138

99 to 120-degrees F (37 to 49-degrees C)

Air screw	2-3/4
Slow jet	45
Needle clip position	2
Main jet	135

5000 to 7499 feet (1500 to 2299 meters)

Minus 21 to 0-degrees F (minus 35 to minus 18-degrees C)

Air screw	1-3/4
Slow jet	45
Needle clip position	3
Main jet	145

Minus 1 to 20-degrees F (minus 17 to minus 7-degrees C)

Air screw	2
Slow jet	45
Needle clip position	3
Main jet	142

19 to 40-degrees F (minus 6 to 4-degrees C)

Air screw	2
Slow jet	45
Needle clip position	3
Main jet	142

39 to 60-degrees F (3 to 15-degrees C)

Air screw	2-1/4
Slow jet	45
Needle clip position	2
Main jet	140

59 to 80-degrees F (14 to 26-degrees C)

Air screw	2-1/2
Slow jet	45
Needle clip position	2
Main jet	138

79 to 100-degrees F (25 to 38-degrees C)

Air screw	2-3/4
Slow jet	45
Needle clip position	2
Main jet	135

99 to 120-degrees F (37 to 49-degrees C)

Air screw	3
Slow jet	45
Needle clip position	2
Main jet	132

Carburetor settings (continued)

2005 and later CR85R (continued)

7500 to 10,000 feet (2300 to 3050 meters)

Minus 21 to 0-degrees F (minus 35 to minus 18-degrees C)

Air screw	2
Slow jet	45
Needle clip position	3
Main jet	142

Minus 1 to 20-degrees F (minus 17 to minus 7-degrees C)

Air screw	2
Slow jet	45
Needle clip position	3
Main jet	142

19 to 40-degrees F (minus 6 to 4-degrees C)

Air screw	2-1/4
Slow jet	45
Needle clip position	2
Main jet	140

39 to 60-degrees F (3 to 15-degrees C)

Air screw	2-1/2
Slow jet	45
Needle clip position	2
Main jet	138

59 to 80-degrees F (14 to 26-degrees C)

Air screw	2-1/2
Slow jet	45
Needle clip position	2
Main jet	135

79 to 100-degrees F (25 to 38-degrees C)

Air screw	3
Slow jet	45
Needle clip position	2
Main jet	132

99 to 120-degrees F (37 to 49-degrees C)

Air screw	3
Slow jet	42
Needle clip position	1
Main jet	130

1990 CR125R

Sea level to 999 feet (299 meters)

Minus 21 to 0-degrees F (minus 35 to minus 18-degrees C)

Air screw	1 turn out
Slow jet	62
Needle clip position	4th groove
Main jet	182

Minus 1 to 20-degrees F (minus 17 to minus 7-degrees C)

Air screw	1-1/4 turns out
Slow jet	62
Needle clip position	4th groove
Main jet	178

19 to 40-degrees F (minus 6 to 4-degrees C)

Air screw	1-1/2 turns out
Slow jet	60
Needle clip position	4th groove
Main jet	175

39 to 60-degrees F (3 to 15-degrees C)

Air screw	1-3/4 turns out
Slow jet	60
Needle clip position	3rd groove
Main jet	170

59 to 80-degrees F (14 to 26-degrees C)*

Air screw	2 turns out
Slow jet	58
Needle clip position	3rd groove
Main jet	168

* Standard jetting

79 to 100-degrees F (25 to 38-degrees C)

Air screw	2-1/4 turns out
Slow jet	58
Needle clip position	3rd groove
Main jet	165

99 to 120-degrees F (37 to 49-degrees C)

Air screw	2-1/2 turns out
Slow jet	55
Needle clip position	3rd groove
Main jet	162

1000 to 2499 feet (300 to 749 meters)

Minus 21 to 0-degrees F (minus 35 to minus 18-degrees C)

Air screw	1-1/4 turn out
Slow jet	62
Needle clip position	4th groove
Main jet	180

Minus 1 to 20-degrees F (minus 17 to minus 7-degrees C)

Air screw	1-1/2 turn out
Slow jet	62
Needle clip position	4th groove
Main jet	178

19 to 40-degrees F (minus 6 to 4-degrees C)

Air screw	1-3/4 turns out
Slow jet	60
Needle clip position	4th groove
Main jet	172

39 to 60-degrees F (3 to 15-degrees C)

Air screw	2 turns out
Slow jet	58
Needle clip position	3rd groove
Main jet	170

59 to 80-degrees F (14 to 26-degrees C)

Air screw	2-1/4 turns out
Slow jet	58
Needle clip position	3rd groove
Main jet	165

79 to 100-degrees F (25 to 38-degrees C)

Air screw	2-1/2 turns out
Slow jet	58
Needle clip position	3rd groove
Main jet	162

99 to 120-degrees F (37 to 49-degrees C)

Air screw	2-3/4 turns out
Slow jet	55
Needle clip position	3rd groove
Main jet	160

2500 to 4999 feet (750 to 1499 meters)

Minus 21 to 0-degrees F (minus 35 to minus 18-degrees C)

Air screw	1-1/2 turns out
Slow jet	62
Needle clip position	4th groove
Main jet	178

Minus 1 to 20-degrees F (minus 17 to minus 7-degrees C)

Air screw	1-3/4 turn out
Slow jet	60
Needle clip position	4th groove
Main jet	172

19 to 40-degrees F (minus 6 to 4-degrees C)

Air screw	2 turns out
Slow jet	58
Needle clip position	3rd groove
Main jet	170

39 to 60-degrees F (3 to 15-degrees C)

Air screw	2-1/4 turns out
Slow jet	58
Needle clip position	3rd groove
Main jet	165

Carburetor settings (continued)

1990 CR125R (continued)

2500 to 4999 feet (750 to 1499 meters)
  59 to 80-degrees F (14 to 26-degrees C)
    Air screw .... 2-1/2 turns out
    Slow jet 58
    Needle clip position .... 3rd groove
    Main jet 162
  79 to 100-degrees F (25 to 38-degrees C)
    Air screw .... 2-3/4 turns out
    Slow jet 55
    Needle clip position .... 2nd groove
    Main jet 160
  99 to 120-degrees F (37 to 49-degrees C)
    Air screw .... 3 turns out
    Slow jet 55
    Needle clip position .... 2nd groove
    Main jet 155
5000 to 7499 feet (1500 to 2299 meters)
  Minus 21 to 0-degrees F (minus 35 to minus 18-degrees C)
    Air screw .... 1-3/4 turns out
    Slow jet 60
    Needle clip position .... 4th groove
    Main jet 175
  Minus 1 to 20-degrees F (minus 17 to minus 7-degrees C)
    Air screw .... 2 turns out
    Slow jet 58
    Needle clip position .... 4th groove
    Main jet 170
  19 to 40-degrees F (minus 6 to 4-degrees C)
    Air screw .... 2-1/4 turns out
    Slow jet 58
    Needle clip position .... 3rd groove
    Main jet 165
  39 to 60-degrees F (3 to 15-degrees C)
    Air screw .... 2-1/2 turns out
    Slow jet 55
    Needle clip position .... 3rd groove
    Main jet 162
  59 to 80-degrees F (14 to 26-degrees C)
    Air screw .... 2-3/4 turns out
    Slow jet 55
    Needle clip position .... 2nd groove
    Main jet 160
  79 to 100-degrees F (25 to 38-degrees C)
    Air screw .... 3 turns out
    Slow jet 52
    Needle clip position .... 2nd groove
    Main jet 155
  99 to 120-degrees F (37 to 49-degrees C)
    Air screw .... 3-1/4 turns out
    Slow jet 52
    Needle clip position .... 2nd groove
    Main jet 152
7500 to 10,000 feet (2300 to 3000 meters)
  Minus 21 to 0-degrees F (minus 35 to minus 18-degrees C)
    Air screw .... 2 turns out
    Slow jet 60
    Needle clip position .... 3rd groove
    Main jet 172
  Minus 1 to 20-degrees F (minus 17 to minus 7-degrees C)
    Air screw .... 2-1/4 turns out
    Slow jet 58
    Needle clip position .... 3rd groove
    Main jet 165
  19 to 40-degrees F (minus 6 to 4-degrees C)
    Air screw .... 2-1/2 turns out
    Slow jet 58
    Needle clip position .... 3rd groove
    Main jet 162

39 to 60-degrees F (3 to 15-degrees C)
Air screw .... 2-3/4 turns out
Slow jet 55
Needle clip position .... 2nd groove
Main jet 160
59 to 80-degrees F (14 to 26-degrees C)
Air screw .... 3 turns out
Slow jet 52
Needle clip position .... 2nd groove
Main jet 155
79 to 100-degrees F (25 to 38-degrees C)
Air screw .... 3-1/4 turns out
Slow jet 52
Needle clip position .... 1st groove
Main jet 152
99 to 120-degrees F (37 to 49-degrees C)
Air screw .... 3-1/2 turns out
Slow jet 52
Needle clip position .... 1st groove
Main jet 148

1991 and 1992 CR125R
Sea level to 999 feet (299 meters)
Minus 21 to 0-degrees F (minus 35 to minus 18-degrees C)
Air screw .... 1 turn out
Slow jet 62
Needle clip position .... 4th groove
Main jet 188
Minus 1 to 20-degrees F (minus 17 to minus 7-degrees C)
Air screw .... 1-1/4 turns out
Slow jet 62
Needle clip position .... 4th groove
Main jet 182
19 to 40-degrees F (minus 6 to 4-degrees C)
Air screw .... 1-1/2 turns out
Slow jet 60
Needle clip position .... 4th groove
Main jet 178
39 to 60-degrees F (3 to 15-degrees C)
Air screw .... 1-3/4 turns out
Slow jet 60
Needle clip position .... 3rd groove
Main jet 175
59 to 80-degrees F (14 to 26-degrees C)*
Air screw .... 2 turns out
Slow jet 58
Needle clip position .... 3rd groove
Main jet 172
79 to 100-degrees F (25 to 38-degrees C)
Air screw .... 2-1/4 turns out
Slow jet 58
Needle clip position .... 3rd groove
Main jet 170
99 to 120-degrees F (37 to 49-degrees C)
Air screw .... 2-1/2 turns out
Slow jet 55
Needle clip position .... 3rd groove
Main jet 168
1000 to 2499 feet (300 to 749 meters)
Minus 21 to 0-degrees F (minus 35 to minus 18-degrees C)
Air screw .... 1-1/4 turns out
Slow jet 62
Needle clip position .... 4th groove
Main jet 185
Minus 1 to 20-degrees F (minus 17 to minus 7-degrees C)
Air screw .... 1-1/2 turn out
Slow jet 62
Needle clip position .... 4th groove
Main jet 182

* *Standard jetting*

Carburetor settings (continued)

1991 and 1992 CR125R (continued)

1000 to 2499 feet (300 to 749 meters)

19 to 40-degrees F (minus 6 to 4-degrees C)

Air screw	1-3/4 turns out
Slow jet	60
Needle clip position	4th groove
Main jet	178

39 to 60-degrees F (3 to 15-degrees C)

Air screw	2 turns out
Slow jet	58
Needle clip position	3rd groove
Main jet	175

59 to 80-degrees F (14 to 26-degrees C)

Air screw	2-1/4 turns out
Slow jet	58
Needle clip position	3rd groove
Main jet	170

79 to 100-degrees F (25 to 38-degrees C)

Air screw	2-1/2 turns out
Slow jet	58
Needle clip position	3rd groove
Main jet	168

99 to 120-degrees F (37 to 49-degrees C)

Air screw	2-3/4 turns out
Slow jet	55
Needle clip position	3rd groove
Main jet	165

2500 to 4999 feet (750 to 1499 meters)

Minus 21 to 0-degrees F (minus 35 to minus 18-degrees C)

Air screw	1-1/2 turns out
Slow jet	62
Needle clip position	4th groove
Main jet	182

Minus 1 to 20-degrees F (minus 17 to minus 7-degrees C)

Air screw	1-3/4 turn out
Slow jet	60
Needle clip position	4th groove
Main jet	178

19 to 40-degrees F (minus 6 to 4-degrees C)

Air screw	2 turns out
Slow jet	58
Needle clip position	3rd groove
Main jet	175

39 to 60-degrees F (3 to 15-degrees C)

Air screw	2-1/4 turns out
Slow jet	58
Needle clip position	3rd groove
Main jet	170

59 to 80-degrees F (14 to 26-degrees C)

Air screw	2-1/2 turns out
Slow jet	58
Needle clip position	3rd groove
Main jet	168

79 to 100-degrees F (25 to 38-degrees C)

Air screw	2-3/4 turns out
Slow jet	55
Needle clip position	2nd groove
Main jet	165

99 to 120-degrees F (37 to 49-degrees C)

Air screw	3 turns out
Slow jet	55
Needle clip position	2nd groove
Main jet	160

5000 to 7499 feet (1500 to 2299 meters)

Minus 21 to 0-degrees F (minus 35 to minus 18-degrees C)

Air screw...	1-3/4 turns out
Slow jet..	60
Needle clip position...	4th groove
Main jet..	180

Minus 1 to 20-degrees F (minus 17 to minus 7-degrees C)

Air screw...	2 turns out
Slow jet..	58
Needle clip position...	4th groove
Main jet..	175

19 to 40-degrees F (minus 6 to 4-degrees C)

Air screw...	2-1/4 turns out
Slow jet..	58
Needle clip position...	3rd groove
Main jet..	170

39 to 60-degrees F (3 to 15-degrees C)

Air screw...	2-1/2 turns out
Slow jet..	55
Needle clip position...	3rd groove
Main jet..	168

59 to 80-degrees F (14 to 26-degrees C)

Air screw...	2-3/4 turns out
Slow jet..	55
Needle clip position...	2nd groove
Main jet..	165

79 to 100-degrees F (25 to 38-degrees C)

Air screw...	3 turns out
Slow jet..	52
Needle clip position...	2nd groove
Main jet..	160

99 to 120-degrees F (37 to 49-degrees C)

Air screw...	3-1/4 turns out
Slow jet..	52
Needle clip position...	2nd groove
Main jet..	158

7500 to 10,000 feet (2300 to 3000 meters)

Minus 21 to 0-degrees F (minus 35 to minus 18-degrees C)

Air screw...	2 turns out
Slow jet..	60
Needle clip position...	3rd groove
Main jet..	178

Minus 1 to 20-degrees F (minus 17 to minus 7-degrees C)

Air screw...	2-1/4 turns out
Slow jet..	58
Needle clip position...	3rd groove
Main jet..	170

19 to 40-degrees F (minus 6 to 4-degrees C)

Air screw...	2-1/2 turns out
Slow jet..	58
Needle clip position...	3rd groove
Main jet..	168

39 to 60-degrees F (3 to 15-degrees C)

Air screw...	2-3/4 turns out
Slow jet..	55
Needle clip position...	2nd groove
Main jet..	165

59 to 80-degrees F (14 to 26-degrees C)

Air screw...	3 turns out
Slow jet..	52
Needle clip position...	2nd groove
Main jet..	160

79 to 100-degrees F (25 to 38-degrees C)

Air screw...	3-1/4 turns out
Slow jet..	52
Needle clip position...	1st groove
Main jet..	158

Carburetor settings (continued)

1991 and 1992 CR125R (continued)

7500 to 10,000 feet (2300 to 3000 meters)
  99 to 120-degrees F (37 to 49-degrees C)

Air screw	3-1/2 turns out
Slow jet	52
Needle clip position	1st groove
Main jet	152

1993 and 1994 CR125R

Sea level to 999 feet (299 meters)
  Minus 21 to 0-degrees F (minus 35 to minus 18-degrees C)

Air screw	1/2 turn out
Slow jet	62
Needle clip position	4th groove
Main jet	188

  Minus 1 to 20-degrees F (minus 17 to minus 7-degrees C)

Air screw	3/4 turn out
Slow jet	62
Needle clip position	4th groove
Main jet	182

  19 to 40-degrees F (minus 6 to 4-degrees C)

Air screw	1 turn out
Slow jet	60
Needle clip position	4th groove
Main jet	178

  39 to 60-degrees F (3 to 15-degrees C)

Air screw	1-1/4 turns out
Slow jet	60
Needle clip position	3rd groove
Main jet	175

  59 to 80-degrees F (14 to 26-degrees C)*

Air screw	1-1/2 turns out
Slow jet	58
Needle clip position	3rd groove
Main jet	172

  79 to 100-degrees F (25 to 38-degrees C)

Air screw	1-3/4 turns out
Slow jet	58
Needle clip position	3rd groove
Main jet	170

  99 to 120-degrees F (37 to 49-degrees C)

Air screw	2 turns out
Slow jet	55
Needle clip position	3rd groove
Main jet	168

1000 to 2499 feet (300 to 749 meters)
  Minus 21 to 0-degrees F (minus 35 to minus 18-degrees C)

Air screw	3/4 turn out
Slow jet	62
Needle clip position	4th groove
Main jet	185

  Minus 1 to 20-degrees F (minus 17 to minus 7-degrees C)

Air screw	1 turn out
Slow jet	62
Needle clip position	4th groove
Main jet	182

  19 to 40-degrees F (minus 6 to 4-degrees C)

Air screw	1-1/4 turns out
Slow jet	60
Needle clip position	4th groove
Main jet	178

  39 to 60-degrees F (3 to 15-degrees C)

Air screw	1-1/2 turns out
Slow jet	58
Needle clip position	3rd groove
Main jet	175

* Standard jetting

59 to 80-degrees F (14 to 26-degrees C)
- Air screw .... 1-3/4 turns out
- Slow jet 58
- Needle clip position .... 3rd groove
- Main jet 170

79 to 100-degrees F (25 to 38-degrees C)
- Air screw .... 2 turns out
- Slow jet 58
- Needle clip position .... 3rd groove
- Main jet 168

99 to 120-degrees F (37 to 49-degrees C)
- Air screw .... 2-1/4 turns out
- Slow jet 55
- Needle clip position .... 3rd groove
- Main jet 165

2500 to 4999 feet (750 to 1499 meters)

Minus 21 to 0-degrees F (minus 35 to minus 18-degrees C)
- Air screw .... 1 turn out
- Slow jet 62
- Needle clip position .... 4th groove
- Main jet 182

Minus 1 to 20-degrees F (minus 17 to minus 7-degrees C)
- Air screw .... 1-1/4 turn out
- Slow jet 60
- Needle clip position .... 4th groove
- Main jet 178

19 to 40-degrees F (minus 6 to 4-degrees C)
- Air screw .... 1-1/2 turns out
- Slow jet 58
- Needle clip position .... 3rd groove
- Main jet 175

39 to 60-degrees F (3 to 15-degrees C)
- Air screw .... 1-3/4 turns out
- Slow jet 58
- Needle clip position .... 3rd groove
- Main jet 170

59 to 80-degrees F (14 to 26-degrees C)*
- Air screw .... 2 turns out
- Slow jet 58
- Needle clip position .... 3rd groove
- Main jet 168

79 to 100-degrees F (25 to 38-degrees C)
- Air screw .... 2-1/4 turns out
- Slow jet 55
- Needle clip position .... 2nd groove
- Main jet 165

99 to 120-degrees F (37 to 49-degrees C)
- Air screw .... 2-1/2 turns out
- Slow jet 55
- Needle clip position .... 2nd groove
- Main jet 160

5000 to 7499 feet (1500 to 2299 meters)

Minus 21 to 0-degrees F (minus 35 to minus 18-degrees C)
- Air screw .... 1-1/4 turns out
- Slow jet 60
- Needle clip position .... 4th groove
- Main jet 180

Minus 1 to 20-degrees F (minus 17 to minus 7-degrees C)
- Air screw .... 1-1/2 turns out
- Slow jet 58
- Needle clip position .... 4th groove
- Main jet 175

19 to 40-degrees F (minus 6 to 4-degrees C)
- Air screw .... 1-3/4 turns out
- Slow jet 58
- Needle clip position .... 3rd groove
- Main jet 170

* Standard jetting

Carburetor settings (continued)

1993 and 1994 CR125R (continued)

5000 to 7499 feet (1500 to 2299 meters)

39 to 60-degrees F (3 to 15-degrees C)

Air screw	2 turns out
Slow jet	55
Needle clip position	3rd groove
Main jet	168

59 to 80-degrees F (14 to 26-degrees C)

Air screw	2-1/4 turns out
Slow jet	55
Needle clip position	2nd groove
Main jet	165

79 to 100-degrees F (25 to 38-degrees C)

Air screw	2-1/2 turns out
Slow jet	52
Needle clip position	2nd groove
Main jet	160

99 to 120-degrees F (37 to 49-degrees C)

Air screw	2-3/4 turns out
Slow jet	52
Needle clip position	2nd groove
Main jet	158

7500 to 10,000 feet (2300 to 3000 meters)

Minus 21 to 0-degrees F (minus 35 to minus 18-degrees C)

Air screw	1-1/2 turns out
Slow jet	60
Needle clip position	3rd groove
Main jet	178

Minus 1 to 20-degrees F (minus 17 to minus 7-degrees C)

Air screw	1-3/4 turns out
Slow jet	58
Needle clip position	3rd groove
Main jet	170

19 to 40-degrees F (minus 6 to 4-degrees C)

Air screw	2 turns out
Slow jet	58
Needle clip position	3rd groove
Main jet	168

39 to 60-degrees F (3 to 15-degrees C)

Air screw	2-1/4 turns out
Slow jet	55
Needle clip position	2nd groove
Main jet	165

59 to 80-degrees F (14 to 26-degrees C)*

Air screw	2-1/2 turns out
Slow jet	52
Needle clip position	2nd groove
Main jet	160

79 to 100-degrees F (25 to 38-degrees C)

Air screw	2-3/4 turns out
Slow jet	52
Needle clip position	1st groove
Main jet	158

99 to 120-degrees F (37 to 49-degrees C)

Air screw	3 turns out
Slow jet	52
Needle clip position	1st groove
Main jet	152

1995 CR125R

Sea level to 999 feet (299 meters)

Minus 21 to 0-degrees F (minus 35 to minus 18-degrees C)

Air screw	1 turn out
Slow jet	62
Needle clip position	4th groove
Main jet	188

* Standard jetting

Minus 1 to 20-degrees F (minus 17 to minus 7-degrees C)

Air screw	1-1/4 turn out
Slow jet	62
Needle clip position	4th groove
Main jet	182

19 to 40-degrees F (minus 6 to 4-degrees C)

Air screw	1-1/2 turns out
Slow jet	58
Needle clip position	4th groove
Main jet	178

39 to 60-degrees F (3 to 15-degrees C)

Air screw	1-3/4 turns out
Slow jet	55
Needle clip position	3rd groove
Main jet	175

59 to 80-degrees F (14 to 26-degrees C)*

Air screw	2 turns out
Slow jet	55
Needle clip position	3rd groove
Main jet	172

79 to 100-degrees F (25 to 38-degrees C)

Air screw	2-1/4 turns out
Slow jet	55
Needle clip position	3rd groove
Main jet	170

99 to 120-degrees F (37 to 49-degrees C)

Air screw	2-1/2 turns out
Slow jet	52
Needle clip position	3rd groove
Main jet	168

1000 to 2499 feet (300 to 749 meters)

Minus 21 to 0-degrees F (minus 35 to minus 18-degrees C)

Air screw	1-1/4 turns out
Slow jet	60
Needle clip position	4th groove
Main jet	185

Minus 1 to 20-degrees F (minus 17 to minus 7-degrees C)

Air screw	1-1/2 turn out
Slow jet	60
Needle clip position	4th groove
Main jet	182

19 to 40-degrees F (minus 6 to 4-degrees C)

Air screw	1-3/4 turns out
Slow jet	58
Needle clip position	4th groove
Main jet	178

39 to 60-degrees F (3 to 15-degrees C)

Air screw	2 turns out
Slow jet	55
Needle clip position	3rd groove
Main jet	175

59 to 80-degrees F (14 to 26-degrees C)*

Air screw	2-1/4 turns out
Slow jet	55
Needle clip position	3rd groove
Main jet	170

79 to 100-degrees F (25 to 38-degrees C)

Air screw	2-1/2 turns out
Slow jet	55
Needle clip position	3rd groove
Main jet	168

99 to 120-degrees F (37 to 49-degrees C)

Air screw	2-3/4 turns out
Slow jet	52
Needle clip position	3rd groove
Main jet	165

* Standard jetting

Carburetor settings (continued)

1995 CR125R (continued)

2500 to 4999 feet (750 to 1499 meters)

Minus 21 to 0-degrees F (minus 35 to minus 18-degrees C)
- Air screw .... 1-1/2 turn out
- Slow jet 60
- Needle clip position .... 4th groove
- Main jet 182

Minus 1 to 20-degrees F (minus 17 to minus 7-degrees C)
- Air screw .... 1-3/4 turn out
- Slow jet 58
- Needle clip position .... 4th groove
- Main jet 178

19 to 40-degrees F (minus 6 to 4-degrees C)
- Air screw .... 2 turns out
- Slow jet 55
- Needle clip position .... 3rd groove
- Main jet 175

39 to 60-degrees F (3 to 15-degrees C)
- Air screw .... 2-3/4 turns out
- Slow jet 55
- Needle clip position .... 3rd groove
- Main jet 170

59 to 80-degrees F (14 to 26-degrees C)
- Air screw .... 2-1/2 turns out
- Slow jet 55
- Needle clip position .... 3rd groove
- Main jet 168

79 to 100-degrees F (25 to 38-degrees C)
- Air screw .... 2-3/4 turns out
- Slow jet 52
- Needle clip position .... 2nd groove
- Main jet 165

99 to 120-degrees F (37 to 49-degrees C)
- Air screw .... 3 turns out
- Slow jet 52
- Needle clip position .... 2nd groove
- Main jet 160

5000 to 7499 feet (1500 to 2299 meters)

Minus 21 to 0-degrees F (minus 35 to minus 18-degrees C)
- Air screw .... 1-3/4 turns out
- Slow jet 58
- Needle clip position .... 4th groove
- Main jet 180

Minus 1 to 20-degrees F (minus 17 to minus 7-degrees C)
- Air screw .... 2 turns out
- Slow jet 55
- Needle clip position .... 4th groove
- Main jet 175

19 to 40-degrees F (minus 6 to 4-degrees C)
- Air screw .... 2-1/4 turns out
- Slow jet 55
- Needle clip position .... 3rd groove
- Main jet 170

39 to 60-degrees F (3 to 15-degrees C)
- Air screw .... 2-1/2 turns out
- Slow jet 52
- Needle clip position .... 3rd groove
- Main jet 168

59 to 80-degrees F (14 to 26-degrees C)
- Air screw .... 2-3/4 turns out
- Slow jet 52
- Needle clip position .... 2nd groove
- Main jet 165

79 to 100-degrees F (25 to 38-degrees C)
- Air screw .... 3 turns out
- Slow jet 50

Needle clip position .... 2nd groove
Main jet 160
99 to 120-degrees F (37 to 49-degrees C)
   Air screw .... 3-1/4 turns out
   Slow jet 50
   Needle clip position .... 2nd groove
   Main jet 158
7500 to 10,000 feet (2300 to 3000 meters)
  Minus 21 to 0-degrees F (minus 35 to minus 18-degrees C)
   Air screw .... 2 turns out
   Slow jet 58
   Needle clip position .... 3rd groove
   Main jet 178
  Minus 1 to 20-degrees F (minus 17 to minus 7-degrees C)
   Air screw .... 2-1/4 turns out
   Slow jet 55
   Needle clip position .... 3rd groove
   Main jet 170
  19 to 40-degrees F (minus 6 to 4-degrees C)
   Air screw .... 2-1/2 turns out
   Slow jet 55
   Needle clip position .... 3rd groove
   Main jet 168
  39 to 60-degrees F (3 to 15-degrees C)
   Air screw .... 2-3/4 turns out
   Slow jet 52
   Needle clip position .... 2nd groove
   Main jet 165
  59 to 80-degrees F (14 to 26-degrees C)*
   Air screw .... 3 turns out
   Slow jet 50
   Needle clip position .... 2nd groove
   Main jet 160
  79 to 100-degrees F (25 to 38-degrees C)
   Air screw .... 3-1/4 turns out
   Slow jet 50
   Needle clip position .... 1st groove
   Main jet 158
  99 to 120-degrees F (37 to 49-degrees C)
   Air screw .... 3-1/2 turns out
   Slow jet 50
   Needle clip position .... 1st groove
   Main jet 152

1996 CR125R

Sea level to 999 feet (299 meters)
  Minus 21 to 0-degrees F (minus 35 to minus 18-degrees C)
   Air screw .... 3/4 turn out
   Slow jet 58
   Needle clip position .... 4th groove
   Main jet 188
  Minus 1 to 20-degrees F (minus 17 to minus 7-degrees C)
   Air screw .... 1 turn out
   Slow jet 55
   Needle clip position .... 4th groove
   Main jet 182
  19 to 40-degrees F (minus 6 to 4-degrees C)
   Air screw .... 1-1/4 turn out
   Slow jet 52
   Needle clip position .... 4th groove
   Main jet 178
  39 to 60-degrees F (3 to 15-degrees C)
   Air screw .... 1-1/2 turns out
   Slow jet 50
   Needle clip position .... 3rd groove
   Main jet 175

* Standard jetting

Carburetor settings (continued)

1996 CR125R (continued)

Sea level to 999 feet (299 meters)

59 to 80-degrees F (14 to 26-degrees C)*

Air screw	1-3/4 turns out
Slow jet	50
Needle clip position	3rd groove
Main jet	172

79 to 100-degrees F (25 to 38-degrees C)

Air screw	2 turns out
Slow jet	50
Needle clip position	3rd groove
Main jet	170

99 to 120-degrees F (37 to 49-degrees C)

Air screw	2-1/4 turns out
Slow jet	48
Needle clip position	3rd groove
Main jet	168

1000 to 2499 feet (300 to 749 meters)

Minus 21 to 0-degrees F (minus 35 to minus 18-degrees C)

Air screw	1 turn out
Slow jet	55
Needle clip position	4th groove
Main jet	185

Minus 1 to 20-degrees F (minus 17 to minus 7-degrees C)

Air screw	1-1/4 turns out
Slow jet	55
Needle clip position	4th groove
Main jet	182

19 to 40-degrees F (minus 6 to 4-degrees C)

Air screw	1-1/2 turns out
Slow jet	52
Needle clip position	4th groove
Main jet	178

39 to 60-degrees F (3 to 15-degrees C)

Air screw	1-3/4 turns out
Slow jet	50
Needle clip position	3rd groove
Main jet	175

59 to 80-degrees F (14 to 26-degrees C)

Air screw	2 turns out
Slow jet	50
Needle clip position	3rd groove
Main jet	170

79 to 100-degrees F (25 to 38-degrees C)

Air screw	2-1/4 turns out
Slow jet	50
Needle clip position	3rd groove
Main jet	168

99 to 120-degrees F (37 to 49-degrees C)

Air screw	2-1/2 turns out
Slow jet	48
Needle clip position	3rd groove
Main jet	165

2500 to 4999 feet (750 to 1499 meters)

Minus 21 to 0-degrees F (minus 35 to minus 18-degrees C)

Air screw	1-1/4 turns out
Slow jet	55
Needle clip position	4th groove
Main jet	182

Minus 1 to 20-degrees F (minus 17 to minus 7-degrees C)

Air screw	1-1/2 turn out
Slow jet	52
Needle clip position	4th groove
Main jet	178

19 to 40-degrees F (minus 6 to 4-degrees C)

Air screw	1-3/4 turns out
Slow jet	50

Standard jetting

Needle clip position	3rd groove
Main jet	175

39 to 60-degrees F (3 to 15-degrees C)

Air screw	2 turns out
Slow jet	50
Needle clip position	3rd groove
Main jet	170

59 to 80-degrees F (14 to 26-degrees C)

Air screw	2-3/4 turns out
Slow jet	50
Needle clip position	3rd groove
Main jet	168

79 to 100-degrees F (25 to 38-degrees C)

Air screw	2-1/2 turns out
Slow jet	48
Needle clip position	2nd groove
Main jet	165

99 to 120-degrees F (37 to 49-degrees C)

Air screw	2-3/4 turns out
Slow jet	48
Needle clip position	2nd groove
Main jet	160

5000 to 7499 feet (1500 to 2299 meters)

Minus 21 to 0-degrees F (minus 35 to minus 18-degrees C)

Air screw	1-1/2 turns out
Slow jet	52
Needle clip position	4th groove
Main jet	180

Minus 1 to 20-degrees F (minus 17 to minus 7-degrees C)

Air screw	1-3/4 turns out
Slow jet	50
Needle clip position	4th groove
Main jet	175

19 to 40-degrees F (minus 6 to 4-degrees C)

Air screw	2 turns out
Slow jet	50
Needle clip position	3rd groove
Main jet	170

39 to 60-degrees F (3 to 15-degrees C)

Air screw	2-1/4 turns out
Slow jet	48
Needle clip position	3rd groove
Main jet	168

59 to 80-degrees F (14 to 26-degrees C)

Air screw	2-1/2 turns out
Slow jet	48
Needle clip position	2nd groove
Main jet	165

79 to 100-degrees F (25 to 38-degrees C)

Air screw	2-3/4 turns out
Slow jet	45
Needle clip position	2nd groove
Main jet	160

99 to 120-degrees F (37 to 49-degrees C)

Air screw	3 turns out
Slow jet	45
Needle clip position	2nd groove
Main jet	158

7500 to 10,000 feet (2300 to 3000 meters)

Minus 21 to 0-degrees F (minus 35 to minus 18-degrees C)

Air screw	1-3/4 turns out
Slow jet	52
Needle clip position	3rd groove
Main jet	178

Minus 1 to 20-degrees F (minus 17 to minus 7-degrees C)

Air screw	2 turns out
Slow jet	50
Needle clip position	3rd groove
Main jet	170

Carburetor settings (continued)

1996 CR125R (continued)

7500 to 10,000 feet (2300 to 3000 meters)

19 to 40-degrees F (minus 6 to 4-degrees C)

Air screw	2-1/4 turns out
Slow jet	50
Needle clip position	3rd groove
Main jet	168

39 to 60-degrees F (3 to 15-degrees C)

Air screw	2-1/2 turns out
Slow jet	48
Needle clip position	2nd groove
Main jet	165

59 to 80-degrees F (14 to 26-degrees C)

Air screw	2-3/4 turns out
Slow jet	45
Needle clip position	2nd groove
Main jet	160

79 to 100-degrees F (25 to 38-degrees C)

Air screw	3 turns out
Slow jet	45
Needle clip position	1st groove
Main jet	158

99 to 120-degrees F (37 to 49-degrees C)

Air screw	3-1/4 turns out
Slow jet	45
Needle clip position	1st groove
Main jet	152

1997 CR125R

Sea level to 999 feet (299 meters)

Minus 21 to 0-degrees F (minus 35 to minus 18-degrees C)

Air screw	1-1/8 turns out
Slow jet	58
Needle clip position	4th groove
Main jet	188

Minus 1 to 20-degrees F (minus 17 to minus 7-degrees C)

Air screw	1-3/8 turns out
Slow jet	55
Needle clip position	4th groove
Main jet	182

19 to 40-degrees F (minus 6 to 4-degrees C)

Air screw	1-5/8 turns out
Slow jet	6052
Needle clip position	4th groove
Main jet	178

39 to 60-degrees F (3 to 15-degrees C)

Air screw	1-7/8 turns out
Slow jet	50
Needle clip position	3rd groove
Main jet	175

59 to 80-degrees F (14 to 26-degrees C)*

Air screw	2-1/8 turns out
Slow jet	50
Needle clip position	3rd groove
Main jet	172

79 to 100-degrees F (25 to 38-degrees C)

Air screw	2-3/8 turns out
Slow jet	50
Needle clip position	3rd groove
Main jet	170

99 to 120-degrees F (37 to 49-degrees C)

Air screw	2-5/8 turns out
Slow jet	48
Needle clip position	3rd groove
Main jet	168

* Standard jetting

1000 to 2499 feet (300 to 749 meters)

    Minus 21 to 0-degrees F (minus 35 to minus 18-degrees C)

Air screw	1-3/8 turns out
Slow jet	55
Needle clip position	4th groove
Main jet	185

    Minus 1 to 20-degrees F (minus 17 to minus 7-degrees C)

Air screw	1-5/8 turn out
Slow jet	55
Needle clip position	4th groove
Main jet	182

    19 to 40-degrees F (minus 6 to 4-degrees C)

Air screw	1-7/8 turns out
Slow jet	52
Needle clip position	4th groove
Main jet	178

    39 to 60-degrees F (3 to 15-degrees C)

Air screw	2-1/8 turns out
Slow jet	50
Needle clip position	3rd groove
Main jet	175

    59 to 80-degrees F (14 to 26-degrees C)

Air screw	2-3/8 turns out
Slow jet	50
Needle clip position	3rd groove
Main jet	170

    79 to 100-degrees F (25 to 38-degrees C)

Air screw	2-5/8 turns out
Slow jet	50
Needle clip position	3rd groove
Main jet	168

    99 to 120-degrees F (37 to 49-degrees C)

Air screw	2-7/8 turns out
Slow jet	48
Needle clip position	3rd groove
Main jet	165

2500 to 4999 feet (750 to 1499 meters)

    Minus 21 to 0-degrees F (minus 35 to minus 18-degrees C)

Air screw	1-5/8 turns out
Slow jet	55
Needle clip position	4th groove
Main jet	182

    Minus 1 to 20-degrees F (minus 17 to minus 7-degrees C)

Air screw	1-7/8 turns out
Slow jet	52
Needle clip position	4th groove
Main jet	178

    19 to 40-degrees F (minus 6 to 4-degrees C)

Air screw	2-1/8 turns out
Slow jet	50
Needle clip position	3rd groove
Main jet	175

    39 to 60-degrees F (3 to 15-degrees C)

Air screw	2-3/8 turns out
Slow jet	50
Needle clip position	3rd groove
Main jet	170

    59 to 80-degrees F (14 to 26-degrees C)

Air screw	2-5/8 turns out
Slow jet	50
Needle clip position	3rd groove
Main jet	168

    79 to 100-degrees F (25 to 38-degrees C)

Air screw	2-7/8 turns out
Slow jet	48
Needle clip position	2nd groove
Main jet	165

Carburetor settings (continued)

1997 CR125R (continued)

2500 to 4999 feet (750 to 1499 meters)

99 to 120-degrees F (37 to 49-degrees C)

Air screw	3-1/8 turns out
Slow jet	48
Needle clip position	2nd groove
Main jet	160

5000 to 7499 feet (1500 to 2299 meters)

Minus 21 to 0-degrees F (minus 35 to minus 18-degrees C)

Air screw	1-7/8 turns out
Slow jet	52
Needle clip position	4th groove
Main jet	180

Minus 1 to 20-degrees F (minus 17 to minus 7-degrees C)

Air screw	2-1/8 turns out
Slow jet	50
Needle clip position	4th groove
Main jet	175

19 to 40-degrees F (minus 6 to 4-degrees C)

Air screw	2-3/8 turns out
Slow jet	50
Needle clip position	3rd groove
Main jet	170

39 to 60-degrees F (3 to 15-degrees C)

Air screw	2-5/8 turns out
Slow jet	48
Needle clip position	3rd groove
Main jet	168

59 to 80-degrees F (14 to 26-degrees C)

Air screw	2-7/8 turns out
Slow jet	48
Needle clip position	2nd groove
Main jet	165

79 to 100-degrees F (25 to 38-degrees C)

Air screw	3-1/8 turns out
Slow jet	45
Needle clip position	2nd groove
Main jet	160

99 to 120-degrees F (37 to 49-degrees C)

Air screw	3-3/8 turns out
Slow jet	45
Needle clip position	2nd groove
Main jet	158

7500 to 10,000 feet (2300 to 3000 meters)

Minus 21 to 0-degrees F (minus 35 to minus 18-degrees C)

Air screw	2-1/8 turns out
Slow jet	52
Needle clip position	3rd groove
Main jet	178

Minus 1 to 20-degrees F (minus 17 to minus 7-degrees C)

Air screw	2-3/8 turns out
Slow jet	50
Needle clip position	3rd groove
Main jet	170

19 to 40-degrees F (minus 6 to 4-degrees C)

Air screw	2-5/8 turns out
Slow jet	50
Needle clip position	3rd groove
Main jet	168

39 to 60-degrees F (3 to 15-degrees C)

Air screw	2-7/8 turns out
Slow jet	48
Needle clip position	2nd groove
Main jet	165

59 to 80-degrees F (14 to 26-degrees C)
  Air screw .... 3-1/8 turns out
  Slow jet 45
  Needle clip position.. 2nd groove
  Main jet 160
79 to 100-degrees F (25 to 38-degrees C)
  Air screw .... 3-3/8 turns out
  Slow jet 45
  Needle clip position.. 1st groove
  Main jet 158
99 to 120-degrees F (37 to 49-degrees C)
  Air screw .... 3-5/8 turns out
  Slow jet 45
  Needle clip position.. 1st groove
  Main jet 152

1998 CR125R

Sea level to 999 feet (299 meters)
  Minus 21 to 0-degrees F (minus 35 to minus 18-degrees C)
    Air screw .... 1 turn out
    Slow jet.. 60
    Needle clip position.. 4th groove
    Main jet.. 190
  Minus 1 to 20-degrees F (minus 17 to minus 7-degrees C)
    Air screw .... 1-1/4 turns out
    Slow jet.. 58
    Needle clip position.. 4th groove
    Main jet.. 185
  19 to 40-degrees F (minus 6 to 4-degrees C)
    Air screw .... 1-1/2 turns out
    Slow jet.. 55
    Needle clip position.. 4th groove
    Main jet.. 180
  39 to 60-degrees F (3 to 15-degrees C)
    Air screw .... 1-3/4 turns out
    Slow jet.. 52
    Needle clip position.. 3rd groove
    Main jet.. 178
  59 to 80-degrees F (14 to 26-degrees C)
    Air screw .... 2 turns out
    Slow jet.. 52
    Needle clip position.. 3rd groove
    Main jet.. 175
  79 to 100-degrees F (25 to 38-degrees C)
    Air screw .... 2-1/4 turns out
    Slow jet.. 52
    Needle clip position.. 3rd groove
    Main jet.. 172
  99 to 120-degrees F (37 to 49-degrees C)
    Air screw .... 2-1/2 turns out
    Slow jet.. 50
    Needle clip position.. 3rd groove
    Main jet.. 170
1000 to 2499 feet (300 to 749 meters)
  Minus 21 to 0-degrees F (minus 35 to minus 18-degrees C)
    Air screw .... 1-1/4 turns out
    Slow jet.. 58
    Needle clip position.. 4th groove
    Main jet.. 188
  Minus 1 to 20-degrees F (minus 17 to minus 7-degrees C)
    Air screw .... 1-1/2 turns out
    Slow jet.. 58
    Needle clip position.. 4th groove
    Main jet.. 185
  19 to 40-degrees F (minus 6 to 4-degrees C)
    Air screw .... 1-3/4 turns out
    Slow jet.. 55
    Needle clip position.. 4th groove
    Main jet.. 180

Carburetor settings (continued)
1998 CR125R (continued)
  1000 to 2499 feet (300 to 749 meters)
    39 to 60-degrees F (3 to 15-degrees C)

Air screw	2 turns out
Slow jet	52
Needle clip position	3rd groove
Main jet	178

    59 to 80-degrees F (14 to 26-degrees C)

Air screw	2-1/4urns out
Slow jet	52
Needle clip position	3rd groove
Main jet	172

    79 to 100-degrees F (25 to 38-degrees C)

Air screw	2-1/2 turns out
Slow jet	52
Needle clip position	3rd groove
Main jet	170

    99 to 120-degrees F (37 to 49-degrees C)

Air screw	2-3/4 turns out
Slow jet	50
Needle clip position	3rd groove
Main jet	168

  2500 to 4999 feet (750 to 1499 meters)
    Minus 21 to 0-degrees F (minus 35 to minus 18-degrees C)

Air screw	1-1/2 turns out
Slow jet	58
Needle clip position	4th groove
Main jet	188

    Minus 1 to 20-degrees F (minus 17 to minus 7-degrees C)

Air screw	1-3/4 turns out
Slow jet	55
Needle clip position	4th groove
Main jet	180

    19 to 40-degrees F (minus 6 to 4-degrees C)

Air screw	2 turns out
Slow jet	52
Needle clip position	3rd groove
Main jet	178

    39 to 60-degrees F (3 to 15-degrees C)

Air screw	2-1/4 turns out
Slow jet	52
Needle clip position	3rd groove
Main jet	172

    59 to 80-degrees F (14 to 26-degrees C)

Air screw	2-1/2 turns out
Slow jet	52
Needle clip position	3rd groove
Main jet	170

    79 to 100-degrees F (25 to 38-degrees C)

Air screw	2-3/4 turns out
Slow jet	50
Needle clip position	2nd groove
Main jet	168

    99 to 120-degrees F (37 to 49-degrees C)

Air screw	3 turns out
Slow jet	50
Needle clip position	2nd groove
Main jet	162

  5000 to 7499 feet (1500 to 2299 meters)
    Minus 21 to 0-degrees F (minus 35 to minus 18-degrees C)

Air screw	1-3/4 turns out
Slow jet	54
Needle clip position	4th groove
Main jet	182

    Minus 1 to 20-degrees F (minus 17 to minus 7-degrees C)

Air screw	2 turns out
Slow jet	52
Needle clip position	4th groove
Main jet	178

19 to 40-degrees F (minus 6 to 4-degrees C)
  Air screw .... 2-1/4 turns out
  Slow jet.. 52
  Needle clip position.. 3rd groove
  Main jet.. 172
39 to 60-degrees F (3 to 15-degrees C)
  Air screw .... 2-1/2 turns out
  Slow jet.. 50
  Needle clip position.. 3rd groove
  Main jet.. 170
59 to 80-degrees F (14 to 26-degrees C)
  Air screw .... 2-3/4 turns out
  Slow jet.. 50
  Needle clip position.. 2nd groove
  Main jet.. 168
79 to 100-degrees F (25 to 38-degrees C)
  Air screw .... 3 turns out
  Slow jet.. 48
  Needle clip position.. 2nd groove
  Main jet.. 162
99 to 120-degrees F (37 to 49-degrees C)
  Air screw .... 3-1/4 turns out
  Slow jet.. 48
  Needle clip position.. 2nd groove
  Main jet.. 160
7500 to 10,000 feet (2300 to 3000 meters)
  Minus 21 to 0-degrees F (minus 35 to minus 18-degrees C)
    Air screw .... 2 turns out
    Slow jet.. 54
    Needle clip position.. 3rd groove
    Main jet.. 180
  Minus 1 to 20-degrees F (minus 17 to minus 7-degrees C)
    Air screw .... 2-1/4 turns out
    Slow jet.. 52
    Needle clip position.. 3rd groove
    Main jet.. 172
  19 to 40-degrees F (minus 6 to 4-degrees C)
    Air screw .... 2-1/2 turns out
    Slow jet.. 52
    Needle clip position.. 3rd groove
    Main jet.. 170
  39 to 60-degrees F (3 to 15-degrees C)
    Air screw .... 2-3/4 turns out
    Slow jet.. 50
    Needle clip position.. 2nd groove
    Main jet.. 168
  59 to 80-degrees F (14 to 26-degrees C)
    Air screw .... 3 turns out
    Slow jet.. 48
    Needle clip position.. 2nd groove
    Main jet.. 162
  79 to 100-degrees F (25 to 38-degrees C)
    Air screw .... 3-1/4 turns out
    Slow jet.. 48
    Needle clip position.. 1st groove
    Main jet.. 160
  99 to 120-degrees F (37 to 49-degrees C)
    Air screw .... 3-1/2 turns out
    Slow jet.. 48
    Needle clip position.. 1st groove
    Main jet.. 155

1999 CR125R
Sea level to 999 feet (299 meters)
  Minus 21 to 0-degrees F (minus 35 to minus 18-degrees C)
    Air screw .... 1-3/4 turns out
    Slow jet.. 55
    Needle clip position.. 5th groove
    Main jet.. 192

Carburetor settings (continued)

1999 CR125R (continued)

Sea level to 999 feet (299 meters)

Minus 1 to 20-degrees F (minus 17 to minus 7-degrees C)

Air screw	2 turns out
Slow jet	55
Needle clip position	5th groove
Main jet	188

19 to 40-degrees F (minus 6 to 4-degrees C)

Air screw	2-1/4 turns out
Slow jet	55
Needle clip position	4th groove
Main jet	185

39 to 60-degrees F (3 to 15-degrees C)

Air screw	2-1/2 turns out
Slow jet	55
Needle clip position	4th groove
Main jet	180

59 to 80-degrees F (14 to 26-degrees C)

Air screw	2-3/4 turns out
Slow jet	55
Needle clip position	4th groove
Main jet	178

79 to 100-degrees F (25 to 38-degrees C)

Air screw	3 turns out
Slow jet	55
Needle clip position	4th groove
Main jet	175

99 to 120-degrees F (37 to 49-degrees C)

Air screw	3-1/4 turns out
Slow jet	55
Needle clip position	4th groove
Main jet	170

1000 to 2499 feet (300 to 749 meters)

Minus 21 to 0-degrees F (minus 35 to minus 18-degrees C)

Air screw	1-3/4 turns out
Slow jet	55
Needle clip position	5th groove
Main jet	192

Minus 1 to 20-degrees F (minus 17 to minus 7-degrees C)

Air screw	2 turns out
Slow jet	55
Needle clip position	4th groove
Main jet	185

19 to 40-degrees F (minus 6 to 4-degrees C)

Air screw	2-1/4 turns out
Slow jet	55
Needle clip position	4th groove
Main jet	182

39 to 60-degrees F (3 to 15-degrees C)

Air screw	2-3/4 turns out
Slow jet	55
Needle clip position	4th groove
Main jet	178

59 to 80-degrees F (14 to 26-degrees C)

Air screw	3 turns out
Slow jet	55
Needle clip position	4th groove
Main jet	175

79 to 100-degrees F (25 to 38-degrees C)

Air screw	3-1/4 turns out
Slow jet	55
Needle clip position	4th groove
Main jet	170

99 to 120-degrees F (37 to 49-degrees C)

Air screw	3-1/2 turns out
Slow jet	55
Needle clip position	3rd groove
Main jet	168

2500 to 4999 feet (750 to 1499 meters)

Minus 21 to 0-degrees F (minus 35 to minus 18-degrees C)

Air screw	2 turns out
Slow jet	55
Needle clip position	4th groove
Main jet	188

Minus 1 to 20-degrees F (minus 17 to minus 7-degrees C)

Air screw	2-1/4 turns out
Slow jet	55
Needle clip position	4th groove
Main jet	182

19 to 40-degrees F (minus 6 to 4-degrees C)

Air screw	2-1/2 turns out
Slow jet	55
Needle clip position	4th groove
Main jet	178

39 to 60-degrees F (3 to 15-degrees C)

Air screw	2-3/4 turns out
Slow jet	55
Needle clip position	4th groove
Main jet	175

59 to 80-degrees F (14 to 26-degrees C)

Air screw	3-1/4 turns out
Slow jet	55
Needle clip position	4th groove
Main jet	172

79 to 100-degrees F (25 to 38-degrees C)

Air screw	3-1/2 turns out
Slow jet	55
Needle clip position	4th groove
Main jet	168

99 to 120-degrees F (37 to 49-degrees C)

Air screw	3 turns out
Slow jet	52
Needle clip position	3rd groove
Main jet	162

5000 to 7499 feet (1500 to 2299 meters)

Minus 21 to 0-degrees F (minus 35 to minus 18-degrees C)

Air screw	2-1/4 turns out
Slow jet	55
Needle clip position	4th groove
Main jet	185

Minus 1 to 20-degrees F (minus 17 to minus 7-degrees C)

Air screw	2-1/2 turns out
Slow jet	55
Needle clip position	4th groove
Main jet	180

19 to 40-degrees F (minus 6 to 4-degrees C)

Air screw	2-1/4 turns out
Slow jet	55
Needle clip position	4th groove
Main jet	178

39 to 60-degrees F (3 to 15-degrees C)

Air screw	3-1/4 turns out
Slow jet	55
Needle clip position	4th groove
Main jet	172

59 to 80-degrees F (14 to 26-degrees C)

Air screw	3-1/2 turns out
Slow jet	55
Needle clip position	4th groove
Main jet	170

79 to 100-degrees F (25 to 38-degrees C)

Air screw	3 turns out
Slow jet	52
Needle clip position	3rd groove
Main jet	165

Carburetor settings (continued)

1999 CR125R (continued)

5000 to 7499 feet (1500 to 2299 meters)

99 to 120-degrees F (37 to 49-degrees C)

Air screw	3-1/4 turns out
Slow jet	52
Needle clip position	3rd groove
Main jet	160

7500 to 10,000 feet (2300 to 3000 meters)

Minus 21 to 0-degrees F (minus 35 to minus 18-degrees C)

Air screw	2-1/2 turns out
Slow jet	55
Needle clip position	4th groove
Main jet	182

Minus 1 to 20-degrees F (minus 17 to minus 7-degrees C)

Air screw	2-3/4 turns out
Slow jet	55
Needle clip position	4th groove
Main jet	178

19 to 40-degrees F (minus 6 to 4-degrees C)

Air screw	3-1/4 turns out
Slow jet	55
Needle clip position	4th groove
Main jet	175

39 to 60-degrees F (3 to 15-degrees C)

Air screw	3-1/2 turns out
Slow jet	55
Needle clip position	4th groove
Main jet	168

59 to 80-degrees F (14 to 26-degrees C)

Air screw	3 turns out
Slow jet	52
Needle clip position	3rd groove
Main jet	165

79 to 100-degrees F (25 to 38-degrees C)

Air screw	3-1/4 turns out
Slow jet	52
Needle clip position	3rd groove
Main jet	160

99 to 120-degrees F (37 to 49-degrees C)

Air screw	3-1/2 turns out
Slow jet	52
Needle clip position	3rd groove
Main jet	155

2000 CR125R

Sea level to 999 feet (299 meters)

Minus 21 to 0-degrees F (minus 35 to minus 18-degrees C)

Air screw	1-1/2 turns out
Slow jet	55
Needle clip position	4th groove
Main jet	420

Minus 1 to 20-degrees F (minus 17 to minus 7-degrees C)

Air screw	1 turns out
Slow jet	50
Needle clip position	4th groove
Main jet	400

19 to 40-degrees F (minus 6 to 4-degrees C)

Air screw	1-1/4 turns out
Slow jet	50
Needle clip position	3rd groove
Main jet	390

39 to 60-degrees F (3 to 15-degrees C)

Air screw	1-1/2 turns out
Slow jet	50
Needle clip position	3rd groove
Main jet	370

59 to 80-degrees F (14 to 26-degrees C)*
- Air screw .... 1-3/4 turns out
- Slow jet... 50
- Needle clip position.. 3rd groove
- Main jet... 360

79 to 100-degrees F (25 to 38-degrees C)
- Air screw .... 2 turns out
- Slow jet... 50
- Needle clip position.. 3rd groove
- Main jet... 350

99 to 120-degrees F (37 to 49-degrees C)
- Air screw .... 2-1/4 turns out
- Slow jet... 50
- Needle clip position.. 3rd groove
- Main jet... 340

1000 to 2499 feet (300 to 749 meters)

Minus 21 to 0-degrees F (minus 35 to minus 18-degrees C)
- Air screw .... 1 turn out
- Slow jet... 50
- Needle clip position.. 4th groove
- Main jet... 410

Minus 1 to 20-degrees F (minus 17 to minus 7-degrees C)
- Air screw .... 1-1/4 turns out
- Slow jet... 50
- Needle clip position.. 4th groove
- Main jet... 390

19 to 40-degrees F (minus 6 to 4-degrees C)
- Air screw .... 1-1/2 turns out
- Slow jet... 50
- Needle clip position.. 3rd groove
- Main jet... 380

39 to 60-degrees F (3 to 15-degrees C)
- Air screw .... 1-3/4 turns out
- Slow jet... 50
- Needle clip position.. 3rd groove
- Main jet... 360

59 to 80-degrees F (14 to 26-degrees C)
- Air screw .... 2 turns out
- Slow jet... 50
- Needle clip position.. 3rd groove
- Main jet... 350

79 to 100-degrees F (25 to 38-degrees C)
- Air screw .... 2-1/4 turns out
- Slow jet... 50
- Needle clip position.. 3rd groove
- Main jet... 340

99 to 120-degrees F (37 to 49-degrees C)
- Air screw .... 2-1/2 turns out
- Slow jet... 50
- Needle clip position.. 3rd groove
- Main jet... 330

2500 to 4999 feet (750 to 1499 meters)

Minus 21 to 0-degrees F (minus 35 to minus 18-degrees C)
- Air screw .... 1-1/4 turns out
- Slow jet... 50
- Needle clip position.. 4th groove
- Main jet... 390

Minus 1 to 20-degrees F (minus 17 to minus 7-degrees C)
- Air screw .... 1-1/2 turns out
- Slow jet... 50
- Needle clip position.. 3rd groove
- Main jet... 380

19 to 40-degrees F (minus 6 to 4-degrees C)
- Air screw .... 1-3/4 turns out
- Slow jet... 50
- Needle clip position.. 3rd groove
- Main jet... 370

* Standard jetting

Carburetor settings (continued)

2000 CR125R (continued)

2500 to 4999 feet (750 to 1499 meters)
39 to 60-degrees F (3 to 15-degrees C)
Air screw .... 2 turns out
Slow jet.. 50
Needle clip position... 3rd groove
Main jet.. 350

59 to 80-degrees F (14 to 26-degrees C)
Air screw .... 2-1/4 turns out
Slow jet.. 50
Needle clip position... 3rd groove
Main jet.. 340

79 to 100-degrees F (25 to 38-degrees C)
Air screw .... 2-1/2 turns out
Slow jet.. 50
Needle clip position... 2nd groove
Main jet.. 330

99 to 120-degrees F (37 to 49-degrees C)
Air screw .... 2-3/4 turns out
Slow jet.. 50
Needle clip position... 2nd groove
Main jet.. 320

5000 to 7499 feet (1500 to 2299 meters)
Minus 21 to 0-degrees F (minus 35 to minus 18-degrees C)
Air screw .... 1-1/2 turns out
Slow jet.. 50
Needle clip position... 3rd groove
Main jet.. 370

Minus 1 to 20-degrees F (minus 17 to minus 7-degrees C)
Air screw .... 1-3/4 turns out
Slow jet.. 50
Needle clip position... 3rd groove
Main jet.. 360

19 to 40-degrees F (minus 6 to 4-degrees C)
Air screw .... 2 turns out
Slow jet.. 50
Needle clip position... 3rd groove
Main jet.. 350

39 to 60-degrees F (3 to 15-degrees C)
Air screw .... 2-1/4 turns out
Slow jet.. 50
Needle clip position... 3rd groove
Main jet.. 340

59 to 80-degrees F (14 to 26-degrees C)
Air screw .... 2-1/2 turns out
Slow jet.. 50
Needle clip position... 2nd groove
Main jet.. 330

79 to 100-degrees F (25 to 38-degrees C)
Air screw .... 2-3/4 turns out
Slow jet.. 50
Needle clip position... 2nd groove
Main jet.. 320

99 to 120-degrees F (37 to 49-degrees C)
Air screw .... 3 turns out
Slow jet.. 50
Needle clip position... 2nd groove
Main jet.. 310

7500 to 10,000 feet (2300 to 3000 meters)
Minus 21 to 0-degrees F (minus 35 to minus 18-degrees C)
Air screw .... 1-3/4 turns out
Slow jet.. 50
Needle clip position... 3rd groove
Main jet.. 360

Minus 1 to 20-degrees F (minus 17 to minus 7-degrees C)
Air screw .... 2 turns out
Slow jet.. 50
Needle clip position... 3rd groove
Main jet.. 350

19 to 40-degrees F (minus 6 to 4-degrees C)
  Air screw .... 2-1/4 turns out
  Slow jet.. 50
  Needle clip position.. 3rd groove
  Main jet.. 340
39 to 60-degrees F (3 to 15-degrees C)
  Air screw .... 2-1/2 turns out
  Slow jet.. 50
  Needle clip position.. 3rd groove
  Main jet.. 330
59 to 80-degrees F (14 to 26-degrees C)
  Air screw .... 2-3/4 turns out
  Slow jet.. 50
  Needle clip position.. 2nd groove
  Main jet.. 320
79 to 100-degrees F (25 to 38-degrees C)
  Air screw .... 3 turns out
  Slow jet.. 50
  Needle clip position.. 2nd groove
  Main jet.. 310
99 to 120-degrees F (37 to 49-degrees C)
  Air screw .... 2-1/2 turns out
  Slow jet.. 45
  Needle clip position.. 2nd groove
  Main jet.. 300

2001 CR125R

Sea level to 999 feet (299 meters)
  Minus 21 to 0-degrees F (minus 35 to minus 18-degrees C)
    Air screw .... 1-1/4 turns out
    Slow jet.. 45
    Jet needle... 6BEG20-68
    Needle clip position.. 4th groove
    Main jet.. 430
  Minus 1 to 20-degrees F (minus 17 to minus 7-degrees C)
    Air screw .... 1-1/2 turns out
    Slow jet.. 45
    Jet needle... 6BEG21-68
    Needle clip position.. 3rd groove
    Main jet.. 420
  19 to 40-degrees F (minus 6 to 4-degrees C)
    Air screw .... 1-3/4 turns out
    Slow jet.. 45
    Jet needle... 6BEG20-68
    Needle clip position.. 3rd groove
    Main jet.. 410
  39 to 60-degrees F (3 to 15-degrees C)
    Air screw .... 2 turns out
    Slow jet.. 45
    Jet needle... 6BEG20-68
    Needle clip position.. 3rd groove
    Main jet.. 390
  59 to 80-degrees F (14 to 26-degrees C)
    Air screw .... 2-1/4 turns out
    Slow jet.. 45
    Jet needle... 6BEG20-68
    Needle clip position.. 3rd groove
    Main jet.. 380
  79 to 100-degrees F (25 to 38-degrees C)
    Air screw .... 2 1/2 turns out
    Slow jet.. 45
    Jet needle... 6BEG20-68
    Needle clip position.. 3rd groove
    Main jet.. 370
  99 to 120-degrees F (37 to 49-degrees C)
    Air screw .... 2-3/4 turns out
    Slow jet.. 45
    Jet needle... 6BEG21-68
    Needle clip position.. 2nd groove
    Main jet.. 360

Carburetor settings (continued)

2001 CR125R (continued)

1000 to 2499 feet (300 to 749 meters)

Minus 21 to 0-degrees F (minus 35 to minus 18-degrees C)

Air screw	1-1/2 turns out
Slow jet	45
Jet needle	6BEG20-68
Needle clip position	4th groove
Main jet	420

Minus 1 to 20-degrees F (minus 17 to minus 7-degrees C)

Air screw	1-3/4 turns out
Slow jet	45
Jet needle	6BEG21-68
Needle clip position	3rd groove
Main jet	410

19 to 40-degrees F (minus 6 to 4-degrees C)

Air screw	2 turns out
Slow jet	45
Jet needle	6BEG21-68
Needle clip position	3rd groove
Main jet	400

39 to 60-degrees F (3 to 15-degrees C)

Air screw	2-1/4 turns out
Slow jet	45
Jet needle	6BEG20-68
Needle clip position	3rd groove
Main jet	380

59 to 80-degrees F (14 to 26-degrees C)

Air screw	2-1/2 turns out
Slow jet	45
Jet needle	6BEG20-68
Needle clip position	3rd groove
Main jet	370

79 to 100-degrees F (25 to 38-degrees C)

Air screw	2-3/4 turns out
Slow jet	45
Jet needle	6BEG21-68
Needle clip position	2nd groove
Main jet	360

99 to 120-degrees F (37 to 49-degrees C)

Air screw	3 turns out
Slow jet	45
Jet needle	6BEG21-68
Needle clip position	2nd groove
Main jet	350

2500 to 4999 feet (750 to 1499 meters)

Minus 21 to 0-degrees F (minus 35 to minus 18-degrees C)

Air screw	1-3/4 turns out
Slow jet	45
Jet needle	6BEG21-68
Needle clip position	3rd groove
Main jet	410

Minus 1 to 20-degrees F (minus 17 to minus 7-degrees C)

Air screw	2 turns out
Slow jet	45
Jet needle	6BEG21-68
Needle clip position	3rd groove
Main jet	400

19 to 40-degrees F (minus 6 to 4-degrees C)

Air screw	2-1/4 turns out
Slow jet	45
Jet needle	6BEG20-68
Needle clip position	3rd groove
Main jet	390

39 to 60-degrees F (3 to 15-degrees C)

Air screw	2-1/2 turns out
Slow jet	45
Jet needle	6BEG20-68

Needle clip position	3rd groove
Main jet	370
59 to 80-degrees F (14 to 26-degrees C)	
Air screw	2-3/4 turns out
Slow jet	45
Jet needle	6BEG21-68
Needle clip position	2nd groove
Main jet	360
79 to 100-degrees F (25 to 38-degrees C)	
Air screw	3 turns out
Slow jet	45
Jet needle	6BEG21-68
Needle clip position	2nd groove
Main jet	350
99 to 120-degrees F (37 to 49-degrees C)	
Air screw	2-1/2 turns out
Slow jet	40
Jet needle	6BEG21-68
Needle clip position	2nd groove
Main jet	340
5000 to 7499 feet (1500 to 2299 meters)	
Minus 21 to 0-degrees F (minus 35 to minus 18-degrees C)	
Air screw	2 turns out
Slow jet	45
Jet needle	6BEG21-68
Needle clip position	3rd groove
Main jet	390
Minus 1 to 20-degrees F (minus 17 to minus 7-degrees C)	
Air screw	2-1/4 turns out
Slow jet	45
Jet needle	6BEG20-68
Needle clip position	3rd groove
Main jet	380
19 to 40-degrees F (minus 6 to 4-degrees C)	
Air screw	2-1/2 turns out
Slow jet	45
Jet needle	6BEG20-68
Needle clip position	3rd groove
Main jet	370
39 to 60-degrees F (3 to 15-degrees C)	
Air screw	2-3/4 turns out
Slow jet	45
Jet needle	6BEG21-68
Needle clip position	2nd groove
Main jet	360
59 to 80-degrees F (14 to 26-degrees C)	
Air screw	3 turns out
Slow jet	45
Jet needle	6BEG21-68
Needle clip position	2nd groove
Main jet	350
79 to 100-degrees F (25 to 38-degrees C)	
Air screw	2-1/2 turns out
Slow jet	40
Jet needle	6BEG20-68
Needle clip position	2nd groove
Main jet	340
99 to 120-degrees F (37 to 49-degrees C)	
Air screw	2-3/4 turns out
Slow jet	40
Jet needle	6BEG20-68
Needle clip position	2nd groove
Main jet	330
7500 to 10,000 feet (2300 to 3000 meters)	
Minus 21 to 0-degrees F (minus 35 to minus 18-degrees C)	
Air screw	2-1/4 turns out
Slow jet	45
Jet needle	6BEG20-68
Needle clip position	3rd groove
Main jet	380

Carburetor settings (continued)
2001 CR125R (continued)
7500 to 10,000 feet (2300 to 3000 meters)

Minus 1 to 20-degrees F (minus 17 to minus 7-degrees C)

Air screw	2-1/2 turns out
Slow jet	45
Jet needle	6BEG20-68
Needle clip position	3rd groove
Main jet	370

19 to 40-degrees F (minus 6 to 4-degrees C)

Air screw	2-3/4 turns out
Slow jet	45
Jet needle	6BEG20-68
Needle clip position	3rd groove
Main jet	360

39 to 60-degrees F (3 to 15-degrees C)

Air screw	3 turns out
Slow jet	45
Jet needle	6BEG21-68
Needle clip position	2nd groove
Main jet	350

59 to 80-degrees F (14 to 26-degrees C)

Air screw	2-1/2 turns out
Slow jet	40
Jet needle	6BEG21-68
Needle clip position	2nd groove
Main jet	340

79 to 100-degrees F (25 to 38-degrees C)

Air screw	2-3/4 turns out
Slow jet	40
Jet needle	6BEG20-68
Needle clip position	2nd groove
Main jet	330

99 to 120-degrees F (37 to 49-degrees C)

Air screw	3 turns out
Slow jet	40
Jet needle	6BEG20-68
Needle clip position	2nd groove
Main jet	320

2002 CR125R
Sea level to 999 feet (299 meters)

Minus 21 to 0-degrees F (minus 35 to minus 18-degrees C)

Air screw	1
Slow jet	37.5
Needle clip position	4
Main jet	450

Minus 1 to 20-degrees F (minus 17 to minus 7-degrees C)

Air screw	1-1/4
Slow jet	35
Needle clip position	3
Main jet	440

19 to 40-degrees F (minus 6 to 4-degrees C)

Air screw	1-1/2
Slow jet	32.5
Needle clip position	3
Main jet	430

39 to 60-degrees F (3 to 15-degrees C)

Air screw	1-3/4
Slow jet	32.5
Needle clip position	3
Main jet	410

59 to 80-degrees F (14 to 26-degrees C)

Air screw	2-1/8
Slow jet	32.5
Needle clip position	3
Main jet	400

79 to 100-degrees F (25 to 38-degrees C)

Air screw	2-1/4
Slow jet	32.5

Needle clip position	3
Main jet	390

99 to 120-degrees F (37 to 49-degrees C)

Air screw	2-1/2
Slow jet	32.5
Needle clip position	2
Main jet	380

1000 to 2499 feet (300 to 749 meters)

Minus 21 to 0-degrees F (minus 35 to minus 18-degrees C)

Air screw	1-1/4
Slow jet	35
Needle clip position	4
Main jet	440

Minus 1 to 20-degrees F (minus 17 to minus 7-degrees C)

Air screw	1-1/2
Slow jet	32.5
Needle clip position	3
Main jet	430

19 to 40-degrees F (minus 6 to 4-degrees C)

Air screw	1-3/4
Slow jet	32.5
Needle clip position	3
Main jet	420

39 to 60-degrees F (3 to 15-degrees C)

Air screw	2
Slow jet	32.5
Needle clip position	3
Main jet	400

59 to 80-degrees F (14 to 26-degrees C)

Air screw	2-1/4
Slow jet	32.5
Needle clip position	3
Main jet	390

79 to 100-degrees F (25 to 38-degrees C)

Air screw	2-1/2
Slow jet	32.5
Needle clip position	2
Main jet	380

99 to 120-degrees F (37 to 49-degrees C)

Air screw	2-3/4
Slow jet	32.5
Needle clip position	2
Main jet	370

2500 to 4999 feet (750 to 1499 meters)

Minus 21 to 0-degrees F (minus 35 to minus 18-degrees C)

Air screw	1-1/2
Slow jet	32.5
Needle clip position	3
Main jet	430

Minus 1 to 20-degrees F (minus 17 to minus 7-degrees C)

Air screw	1-3/4
Slow jet	32.5
Needle clip position	3
Main jet	420

19 to 40-degrees F (minus 6 to 4-degrees C)

Air screw	2
Slow jet	32.5
Needle clip position	3
Main jet	410

39 to 60-degrees F (3 to 15-degrees C)

Air screw	2-1/4
Slow jet	32.5
Needle clip position	3
Main jet	390

59 to 80-degrees F (14 to 26-degrees C)

Air screw	2-1/2
Slow jet	32.5
Needle clip position	2
Main jet	380

Carburetor settings (continued)

2002 CR125R (continued)

2500 to 4999 feet (750 to 1499 meters)

    79 to 100-degrees F (25 to 38-degrees C)

Air screw	2-3/4
Slow jet	32.5
Needle clip position	2
Main jet	370

    99 to 120-degrees F (37 to 49-degrees C)

Air screw	2-1/4
Slow jet	27.5
Needle clip position	2
Main jet	360

5000 to 7499 feet (1500 to 2299 meters)

    Minus 21 to 0-degrees F (minus 35 to minus 18-degrees C)

Air screw	1-1/2
Slow jet	32.5
Needle clip position	3
Main jet	430

    Minus 1 to 20-degrees F (minus 17 to minus 7-degrees C)

Air screw	1-3/4
Slow jet	32.5
Needle clip position	3
Main jet	420

    19 to 40-degrees F (minus 6 to 4-degrees C)

Air screw	2
Slow jet	32.5
Needle clip position	3
Main jet	410

    39 to 60-degrees F (3 to 15-degrees C)

Air screw	2-1/4
Slow jet	32.5
Needle clip position	3
Main jet	390

    59 to 80-degrees F (14 to 26-degrees C)

Air screw	2-1/2
Slow jet	32.5
Needle clip position	2
Main jet	380

    79 to 100-degrees F (25 to 38-degrees C)

Air screw	2-3/4
Slow jet	32.5
Needle clip position	2
Main jet	370

    99 to 120-degrees F (37 to 49-degrees C)

Air screw	2-1/4
Slow jet	27.5
Needle clip position	2
Main jet	360

7500 to 10,000 feet (2300 to 3050 meters)

    Minus 21 to 0-degrees F (minus 35 to minus 18-degrees C)

Air screw	2
Slow jet	32.5
Needle clip position	3
Main jet	400

    Minus 1 to 20-degrees F (minus 17 to minus 7-degrees C)

Air screw	2-1/4
Slow jet	32.5
Needle clip position	3
Main jet	390

    19 to 40-degrees F (minus 6 to 4-degrees C)

Air screw	2-1/2
Slow jet	32.5
Needle clip position	3
Main jet	380

    39 to 60-degrees F (3 to 15-degrees C)

Air screw	2-3/4
Slow jet	32.5
Needle clip position	2
Main jet	370

59 to 80-degrees F (14 to 26-degrees C)
Air screw	2-1/4
Slow jet	27.5
Needle clip position	2
Main jet	360

79 to 100-degrees F (25 to 38-degrees C)
Air screw	2-1/2
Slow jet	27.5
Needle clip position	2
Main jet	350

99 to 120-degrees F (37 to 49-degrees C)
Air screw	2-3/4
Slow jet	27.5
Needle clip position	2
Main jet	340

2003 CR125R

Sea level to 999 feet (299 meters)

Minus 21 to 0-degrees F (minus 35 to minus 18-degrees C)
Air screw	1-1/2
Slow jet	32.5
Needle clip position	4
Main jet	470

Minus 1 to 20-degrees F (minus 17 to minus 7-degrees C)
Air screw	1-3/4
Slow jet	32.5
Needle clip position	4
Main jet	460

19 to 40-degrees F (minus 6 to 4-degrees C)
Air screw	1-1/4
Slow jet	30
Needle clip position	3
Main jet	450

39 to 60-degrees F (3 to 15-degrees C)
Air screw	1-1/2
Slow jet	30
Needle clip position	3
Main jet	440

59 to 80-degrees F (14 to 26-degrees C)
Air screw	1-3/4
Slow jet	30
Needle clip position	3
Main jet	430

79 to 100-degrees F (25 to 38-degrees C)
Air screw	2
Slow jet	30
Needle clip position	3
Main jet	420

99 to 120-degrees F (37 to 49-degrees C)
Air screw	2-1/4
Slow jet	30
Needle clip position	2
Main jet	410

1000 to 2499 feet (300 to 749 meters)

Minus 21 to 0-degrees F (minus 35 to minus 18-degrees C)
Air screw	1-3/4
Slow jet	32.5
Needle clip position	4
Main jet	460

Minus 1 to 20-degrees F (minus 17 to minus 7-degrees C)
Air screw	1-1/4
Slow jet	30
Needle clip position	3
Main jet	450

19 to 40-degrees F (minus 6 to 4-degrees C)
Air screw	1-1/2
Slow jet	30
Needle clip position	3
Main jet	440

Carburetor settings (continued)

2003 CR125R (continued)
1000 to 2499 feet (300 to 749 meters)
  39 to 60-degrees F (3 to 15-degrees C)
    Air screw... 1-3/4
    Slow jet... 30
    Needle clip position.. 3
    Main jet... 430
  59 to 80-degrees F (14 to 26-degrees C)
    Air screw... 2
    Slow jet... 30
    Needle clip position.. 3
    Main jet... 420
  79 to 100-degrees F (25 to 38-degrees C)
    Air screw... 2-1/4
    Slow jet... 30
    Needle clip position.. 2
    Main jet... 410
  99 to 120-degrees F (37 to 49-degrees C)
    Air screw... 2-1/2
    Slow jet... 30
    Needle clip position.. 2
    Main jet... 400
2500 to 4999 feet (750 to 1499 meters)
  Minus 21 to 0-degrees F (minus 35 to minus 18-degrees C)
    Air screw... 1-1/4
    Slow jet... 30
    Needle clip position.. 3
    Main jet... 450
  Minus 1 to 20-degrees F (minus 17 to minus 7-degrees C)
    Air screw... 1-1/2
    Slow jet... 30
    Needle clip position.. 3
    Main jet... 440
  19 to 40-degrees F (minus 6 to 4-degrees C)
    Air screw... 1-3/4
    Slow jet... 30
    Needle clip position.. 3
    Main jet... 430
  39 to 60-degrees F (3 to 15-degrees C)
    Air screw... 2
    Slow jet... 30
    Needle clip position.. 3
    Main jet... 420
  59 to 80-degrees F (14 to 26-degrees C)
    Air screw... 2-1/4
    Slow jet... 30
    Needle clip position.. 2
    Main jet... 410
  79 to 100-degrees F (25 to 38-degrees C)
    Air screw... 2-1/2
    Slow jet... 30
    Needle clip position.. 2
    Main jet... 400
  99 to 120-degrees F (37 to 49-degrees C)
    Air screw... 2
    Slow jet... 27.5
    Needle clip position.. 2
    Main jet... 390
5000 to 7499 feet (1500 to 2299 meters)
  Minus 21 to 0-degrees F (minus 35 to minus 18-degrees C)
    Air screw... 1-1/2
    Slow jet... 30
    Needle clip position.. 3
    Main jet... 440
  Minus 1 to 20-degrees F (minus 17 to minus 7-degrees C)
    Air screw... 1-3/4
    Slow jet... 30
    Needle clip position.. 3
    Main jet... 430

19 to 40-degrees F (minus 6 to 4-degrees C)
- Air screw 2
- Slow jet 30
- Needle clip position 3
- Main jet 420

39 to 60-degrees F (3 to 15-degrees C)
- Air screw 2-1/4
- Slow jet 30
- Needle clip position 2
- Main jet 410

59 to 80-degrees F (14 to 26-degrees C)
- Air screw 2-1/2
- Slow jet 30
- Needle clip position 2
- Main jet 400

79 to 100-degrees F (25 to 38-degrees C)
- Air screw 2
- Slow jet 27.5
- Needle clip position 2
- Main jet 390

99 to 120-degrees F (37 to 49-degrees C)
- Air screw 2-1/4
- Slow jet 27.5
- Needle clip position 2
- Main jet 380

7500 to 10,000 feet (2300 to 3050 meters)

Minus 21 to 0-degrees F (minus 35 to minus 18-degrees C)
- Air screw 1-3/4
- Slow jet 30
- Needle clip position 3
- Main jet 430

Minus 1 to 20-degrees F (minus 17 to minus 7-degrees C)
- Air screw 2
- Slow jet 30
- Needle clip position 3
- Main jet 420

19 to 40-degrees F (minus 6 to 4-degrees C)
- Air screw 2-1/4
- Slow jet 30
- Needle clip position 2
- Main jet 410

39 to 60-degrees F (3 to 15-degrees C)
- Air screw 2-1/2
- Slow jet 30
- Needle clip position 2
- Main jet 400

59 to 80-degrees F (14 to 26-degrees C)
- Air screw 2
- Slow jet 27.5
- Needle clip position 2
- Main jet 390

79 to 100-degrees F (25 to 38-degrees C)
- Air screw 2-1/4
- Slow jet 27.5
- Needle clip position 2
- Main jet 380

99 to 120-degrees F (37 to 49-degrees C)
- Air screw 2-1/2
- Slow jet 27.5
- Needle clip position 1
- Main jet 370

2004 CR125R

Sea level to 999 feet (299 meters)

Minus 21 to 0-degrees F (minus 35 to minus 18-degrees C)
- Air screw 1-3/4
- Slow jet 45
- Needle clip position 4
- Main jet 460

Carburetor settings (continued)

2004 CR125R (continued)

Sea level to 999 feet (299 meters)

Minus 1 to 20-degrees F (minus 17 to minus 7-degrees C)

Air screw	1-1/4
Slow jet	45
Needle clip position	4
Main jet	450

19 to 40-degrees F (minus 6 to 4-degrees C)

Air screw	1-1/2
Slow jet	40
Needle clip position	3
Main jet	440

39 to 60-degrees F (3 to 15-degrees C)

Air screw	1-3/4
Slow jet	40
Needle clip position	3
Main jet	430

59 to 80-degrees F (14 to 26-degrees C)

Air screw	2
Slow jet	40
Needle clip position	3
Main jet	420

79 to 100-degrees F (25 to 38-degrees C)

Air screw	2-1/4
Slow jet	40
Needle clip position	3
Main jet	410

99 to 120-degrees F (37 to 49-degrees C)

Air screw	2-1/2
Slow jet	40
Needle clip position	2
Main jet	400

1000 to 2499 feet (300 to 749 meters)

Minus 21 to 0-degrees F (minus 35 to minus 18-degrees C)

Air screw	1-1/4
Slow jet	45
Needle clip position	4
Main jet	450

Minus 1 to 20-degrees F (minus 17 to minus 7-degrees C)

Air screw	1-1/2
Slow jet	40
Needle clip position	3
Main jet	440

19 to 40-degrees F (minus 6 to 4-degrees C)

Air screw	1-3/4
Slow jet	40
Needle clip position	3
Main jet	430

39 to 60-degrees F (3 to 15-degrees C)

Air screw	2
Slow jet	40
Needle clip position	3
Main jet	420

59 to 80-degrees F (14 to 26-degrees C)

Air screw	2-1/4
Slow jet	40
Needle clip position	3
Main jet	410

79 to 100-degrees F (25 to 38-degrees C)

Air screw	2-1/2
Slow jet	40
Needle clip position	2
Main jet	400

99 to 120-degrees F (37 to 49-degrees C)

Air screw	2
Slow jet	40
Needle clip position	2
Main jet	390

2500 to 4999 feet (750 to 1499 meters)
  Minus 21 to 0-degrees F (minus 35 to minus 18-degrees C)
    Air screw 1-1/2
    Slow jet 40
    Needle clip position 3
    Main jet 440
  Minus 1 to 20-degrees F (minus 17 to minus 7-degrees C)
    Air screw 1-3/4
    Slow jet 40
    Needle clip position 3
    Main jet 430
  19 to 40-degrees F (minus 6 to 4-degrees C)
    Air screw 2
    Slow jet 40
    Needle clip position 3
    Main jet 420
  39 to 60-degrees F (3 to 15-degrees C)
    Air screw 2-1/4
    Slow jet 40
    Needle clip position 3
    Main jet 410
  59 to 80-degrees F (14 to 26-degrees C)
    Air screw 2-1/2
    Slow jet 40
    Needle clip position 2
    Main jet 400
  79 to 100-degrees F (25 to 38-degrees C)
    Air screw 2
    Slow jet 40
    Needle clip position 2
    Main jet 390
  99 to 120-degrees F (37 to 49-degrees C)
    Air screw 2-1/4
    Slow jet 37.5
    Needle clip position 2
    Main jet 380
5000 to 7499 feet (1500 to 2299 meters)
  Minus 21 to 0-degrees F (minus 35 to minus 18-degrees C)
    Air screw 1-3/4
    Slow jet 40
    Needle clip position 3
    Main jet 430
  Minus 1 to 20-degrees F (minus 17 to minus 7-degrees C)
    Air screw 2
    Slow jet 40
    Needle clip position 3
    Main jet 420
  19 to 40-degrees F (minus 6 to 4-degrees C)
    Air screw 2-1/4
    Slow jet 30
    Needle clip position 3
    Main jet 410
  39 to 60-degrees F (3 to 15-degrees C)
    Air screw 2-1/2
    Slow jet 40
    Needle clip position 2
    Main jet 400
  59 to 80-degrees F (14 to 26-degrees C)
    Air screw 2
    Slow jet 40
    Needle clip position 2
    Main jet 390
  79 to 100-degrees F (25 to 38-degrees C)
    Air screw 2-1/4
    Slow jet 37.5
    Needle clip position 2
    Main jet 380

Carburetor settings (continued)

2004 CR125R (continued)
5000 to 7499 feet (1500 to 2299 meters)
  99 to 120-degrees F (37 to 49-degrees C)
    Air screw... 2-1/2
    Slow jet... 37.5
    Needle clip position.. 2
    Main jet... 370
7500 to 10,000 feet (2300 to 3050 meters)
  Minus 21 to 0-degrees F (minus 35 to minus 18-degrees C)
    Air screw... 2
    Slow jet... 40
    Needle clip position.. 3
    Main jet... 420
  Minus 1 to 20-degrees F (minus 17 to minus 7-degrees C)
    Air screw... 2-1/4
    Slow jet... 40
    Needle clip position.. 3
    Main jet... 410
  19 to 40-degrees F (minus 6 to 4-degrees C)
    Air screw... 2-1/2
    Slow jet... 40
    Needle clip position.. 2
    Main jet... 400
  39 to 60-degrees F (3 to 15-degrees C)
    Air screw... 2
    Slow jet... 40
    Needle clip position.. 2
    Main jet... 390
  59 to 80-degrees F (14 to 26-degrees C)
    Air screw... 2-1/4
    Slow jet... 37.5
    Needle clip position.. 2
    Main jet... 380
  79 to 100-degrees F (25 to 38-degrees C)
    Air screw... 2-1/2
    Slow jet... 37.5
    Needle clip position.. 2
    Main jet... 370
  99 to 120-degrees F (37 to 49-degrees C)
    Air screw... 2-3/4
    Slow jet... 37.5
    Needle clip position.. 1
    Main jet... 360

2005 and later CR125R
Sea level to 999 feet (299 meters)
  Minus 21 to 0-degrees F (minus 35 to minus 18-degrees C)
    Air screw... 1-3/4
    Slow jet... 60
    Needle clip position.. 4
    Main jet... 470
  Minus 1 to 20-degrees F (minus 17 to minus 7-degrees C)
    Air screw... 1-1/4
    Slow jet... 60
    Needle clip position.. 4
    Main jet... 460
  19 to 40-degrees F (minus 6 to 4-degrees C)
    Air screw... 1-1/2
    Slow jet... 55
    Needle clip position.. 3
    Main jet... 450
  39 to 60-degrees F (3 to 15-degrees C)
    Air screw... 1-3/4
    Slow jet... 55
    Needle clip position.. 3
    Main jet... 440
  59 to 80-degrees F (14 to 26-degrees C)
    Air screw... 1-3/4
    Slow jet... 55

Needle clip position	3
Main jet	430
79 to 100-degrees F (25 to 38-degrees C)	
Air screw	2-1/4
Slow jet	55
Needle clip position	3
Main jet	420
99 to 120-degrees F (37 to 49-degrees C)	
Air screw	2-1/2
Slow jet	55
Needle clip position	2
Main jet	410
1000 to 2499 feet (300 to 749 meters)	
Minus 21 to 0-degrees F (minus 35 to minus 18-degrees C)	
Air screw	1-1/4
Slow jet	60
Needle clip position	4
Main jet	460
Minus 1 to 20-degrees F (minus 17 to minus 7-degrees C)	
Air screw	1-1/2
Slow jet	55
Needle clip position	3
Main jet	450
19 to 40-degrees F (minus 6 to 4-degrees C)	
Air screw	1-3/4
Slow jet	55
Needle clip position	3
Main jet	440
39 to 60-degrees F (3 to 15-degrees C)	
Air screw	2
Slow jet	55
Needle clip position	3
Main jet	430
59 to 80-degrees F (14 to 26-degrees C)	
Air screw	2-1/4
Slow jet	55
Needle clip position	3
Main jet	420
79 to 100-degrees F (25 to 38-degrees C)	
Air screw	2-1/2
Slow jet	55
Needle clip position	2
Main jet	410
99 to 120-degrees F (37 to 49-degrees C)	
Air screw	2
Slow jet	55
Needle clip position	2
Main jet	400
2500 to 4999 feet (750 to 1499 meters)	
Minus 21 to 0-degrees F (minus 35 to minus 18-degrees C)	
Air screw	1-1/2
Slow jet	55
Needle clip position	3
Main jet	450
Minus 1 to 20-degrees F (minus 17 to minus 7-degrees C)	
Air screw	1-3/4
Slow jet	55
Needle clip position	3
Main jet	440
10 to 40 degrees F (minus 6 to 4 degrees C)	
Air screw	2
Slow jet	55
Needle clip position	3
Main jet	430
39 to 60-degrees F (3 to 15-degrees C)	
Air screw	2-1/4
Slow jet	55
Needle clip position	3
Main jet	420

Carburetor settings (continued)

2005 and later CR125R (continued)
2500 to 4999 feet (750 to 1499 meters)
    59 to 80-degrees F (14 to 26-degrees C)

Air screw	2-1/2
Slow jet	55
Needle clip position	2
Main jet	410

    79 to 100-degrees F (25 to 38-degrees C)

Air screw	2
Slow jet	55
Needle clip position	2
Main jet	400

    99 to 120-degrees F (37 to 49-degrees C)

Air screw	2-1/4
Slow jet	50
Needle clip position	2
Main jet	390

5000 to 7499 feet (1500 to 2299 meters)
    Minus 21 to 0-degrees F (minus 35 to minus 18-degrees C)

Air screw	1-3/4
Slow jet	55
Needle clip position	3
Main jet	440

    Minus 1 to 20-degrees F (minus 17 to minus 7-degrees C)

Air screw	2
Slow jet	55
Needle clip position	3
Main jet	430

    19 to 40-degrees F (minus 6 to 4-degrees C)

Air screw	2-1/4
Slow jet	55
Needle clip position	3
Main jet	420

    39 to 60-degrees F (3 to 15-degrees C)

Air screw	2-1/2
Slow jet	55
Needle clip position	2
Main jet	410

    59 to 80-degrees F (14 to 26-degrees C)

Air screw	2
Slow jet	55
Needle clip position	2
Main jet	400

    79 to 100-degrees F (25 to 38-degrees C)

Air screw	2-1/4
Slow jet	50
Needle clip position	2
Main jet	390

    99 to 120-degrees F (37 to 49-degrees C)

Air screw	2-1/2
Slow jet	50
Needle clip position	2
Main jet	380

7500 to 10,000 feet (2300 to 3050 meters)
    Minus 21 to 0-degrees F (minus 35 to minus 18-degrees C)

Air screw	2
Slow jet	55
Needle clip position	3
Main jet	430

    Minus 1 to 20-degrees F (minus 17 to minus 7-degrees C)

Air screw	2-1/4
Slow jet	55
Needle clip position	3
Main jet	420

    19 to 40-degrees F (minus 6 to 4-degrees C)

Air screw	2-1/2
Slow jet	55
Needle clip position	2
Main jet	410

39 to 60-degrees F (3 to 15-degrees C)
    Air screw... 2
    Slow jet.. 55
    Needle clip position.. 2
    Main jet.. 400
59 to 80-degrees F (14 to 26-degrees C)
    Air screw... 2-1/4
    Slow jet.. 50
    Needle clip position.. 2
    Main jet.. 390
79 to 100-degrees F (25 to 38-degrees C)
    Air screw... 2-1/2
    Slow jet.. 50
    Needle clip position.. 2
    Main jet.. 380
99 to 120-degrees F (37 to 49-degrees C)
    Air screw... 2-3/4
    Slow jet.. 50
    Needle clip position.. 1
    Main jet.. 390

ATAC governor spring length limit... 58 mm (2.3 inches)

Honda Power Port (HPP)
    Spring gap .... 0.5 to 2.0 mm (0.020 to 0.079 inch)

Torque settings
    Drain screw... 10 Nm (84 inch-lbs)
    Right and left side cover bolts................................ 10 to 14 Nm (84 to 120 inch-lbs)
    Right side cover screw .... 2.5 Nm (22 inch-lbs)
    Cylinder top cover bolts .... 12 Nm (108 inch-lbs)
    Pinion holder Allen bolts... 5.5 Nm (48 inch-lbs)
    Valve guide lockplate hex bolts............................... 9 Nm (78 inch-lbs)
    Drive shaft nut .... 10 Nm (84 inch-lbs)

2.2 Squeeze the ends of the clamp together, slide it down the hose, then disconnect the fuel line from the tap

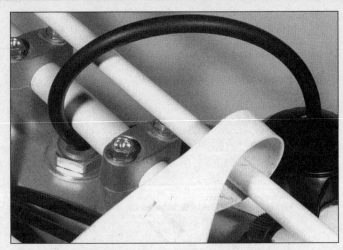

2.3a Pull the vent hose out of the steering stem nut

1 General information

All models use the slide carburetor design, in which the slide acts as the throttle valve. Basic design is the same for all CR80R/85R models and CR125R models through 1999. The 2000 and later CR125R uses a flat slide, rather than an oval slide, and the carburetor body is oval in cross section rather than cylindrical. For cold starting on all models, a choke plunger is actuated by a knob.

The exhaust system consists of an expansion chamber and muffler with a replaceable core. All CR125R models have a means of varying the effective exhaust port timing, to provide the ideal amount of exhaust flow at each end of the powerband. 1986 bikes have a butterfly valve mounted in the exhaust headpipe. 1987 through 1989 models use a rotary valve mounted in an integral cast housing at the front of the cylinder. 1990 through 1999 models use the Honda Power Port (HPP) system, in which a pair of sliding gates in the exhaust port actually increase the size (and thus the effective height) of the port as engine speed increases. 2000 and later models use the Radical Combustion (RC) system. This is similar to the HPP system, but the gates rotate upward out of the exhaust port, rather than sliding sideways. This simplified design is easier to work on and doesn't require adjustment.

2 Fuel tank - removal and installation

Warning: *Gasoline is extremely flammable, so take extra precautions when you work on any part of the fuel system. Don't smoke or allow open flames or bare light bulbs near the work area, and don't work in a garage where a gas-type appliance (such as a water heater or clothes dryer) is present. Since gasoline is carcinogenic, wear latex gloves when there's a possibility of being exposed to fuel, and, if you spill any fuel on your skin, rinse it off immediately with soap and water. Mop up any spills immediately and do not store fuel-soaked rags where they could ignite. When you perform any kind of work on the fuel system, wear safety glasses and have an extinguisher suitable for a class B type fire (flammable liquids) on hand.*

Removal

Refer to illustrations 2.2, 2.3a, 2.3b, 2.3c and 2.4
1   Remove the seat (see Chapter 8).
2   Turn the fuel tap to Off and disconnect the fuel line **(see illustration)**.
3   Pull the fuel tank vent hose out of the steering stem nut **(see illustration)**. Unhook the strap from the rear of the tank **(see illustrations)**.
4   If you're working on a 1998 or 1999 model, remove the side cov-

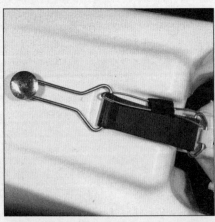

2.3b Note how the ends of the tank strap are shaped (one is designed for the button on the tank and the other for the hook on the frame), then unhook the strap . . .

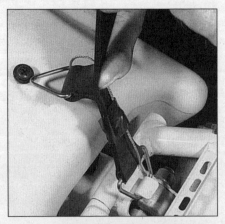

2.3c . . . some models have a pull tab to make this easier

2.4 Most models have a fuel tank mounting bolt on each side (shown); later CR125R models have a single bolt at the front of the tank

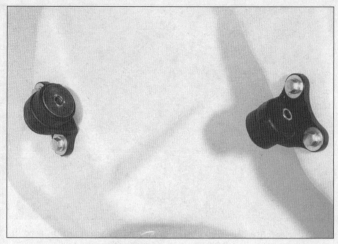

2.6a Check for deteriorated or damaged tank bushings . . .

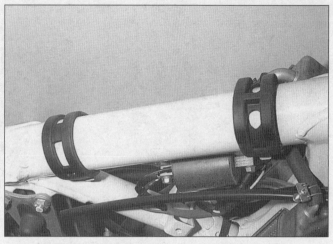

2.6b . . . and inspect the isolators on the frame

ers (see Chapter 8). If you're working on a 1998 or later model, remove the radiator shrouds (see Chapter 3).
5   Unbolt the front end of the fuel tank. All CR80R/85R and CR125R models through 1997 have two front mounting bolts, one on each side **(see illustration).** 1998 and later CR125R models have a single mounting bolt at the front of the tank. Lift the fuel tank off the bike together with the fuel tap.

Installation
Refer to illustrations 2.6a and 2.6b
6   Before installing the tank, check the condition of the rubber mounting bushings at the front, the isolators on the frame and the rubber strap at the rear - if they're hardened, cracked, or show any other signs of deterioration, replace them **(see illustration 2.3b and the accompanying illustrations)**.
7   When installing the tank, reverse the removal procedure. Make sure the tank does not pinch any wires. Tighten the tank mounting bolts securely, but don't overtighten them and strip the threads.

3   Fuel tank - cleaning and repair

1   All repairs to the fuel tank should be carried out by a professional who has experience in this critical and potentially dangerous work. Even after cleaning and flushing of the fuel system, explosive fumes can remain and ignite during repair of the tank.
2   If the fuel tank is removed from the vehicle, it should not be placed in an area where sparks or open flames could ignite the fumes coming out of the tank. Be especially careful inside garages where a gas-type appliance is located, because it could cause an explosion.

4   Carburetor adjustment

Fuel/air mixture adjustment
1   Fuel/air mixture and idle speed on these bikes are adjusted for best performance. There's no specified idle rpm setting.

CR80R/85R models
Refer to illustration 4.2
2   Mixture and idle speed are controlled by an air screw and throttle stop screw mounted in the side of the carburetor **(see illustration)**.
3   The standard settings are intended for a bike operated with the

specified premix (see Chapter 1), at sea level and an air temperature of 68-degrees F (20-degrees C).
4   Turn the air screw in until it bottoms lightly. Don't bottom the screw hard or its tip will be damaged, causing erratic settings. Back the screw out to the standard setting listed in this Chapter's Specifications.
5   Warm up the engine until it will run smoothly with the choke knob all the way in.
6   Ride the bike and check that it revs up smoothly as you accelerate out of turns. If it bogs down, the mixture is too rich; if it surges, the mixture is too lean. Shut off the bike and change the air screw setting in small amounts to correct the problem. Turn the screw in to enrich the mixture or out to make it leaner. **Note:** *If you have to go beyond the maximum air screw range listed in the Specifications, you'll need to change the slow jet size. If you're under the range, use the next larger slow jet. If you're over the range, use the next smaller slow jet.*
7   Set the idle speed to your preference by turning the throttle stop screw **(see illustration 4.2)**.

1986 through 1999 CR125R models
Refer to illustration 4.8
8   Mixture is controlled by an air screw. Idle speed is controlled by turning the knob on the choke valve **(see illustration)**.

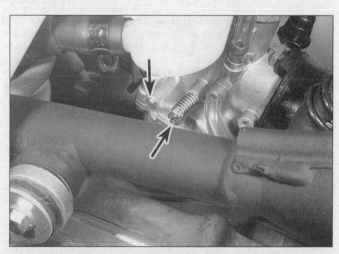

4.2 CR80R/85R idle mixture and speed are adjusted with an air screw (left arrow) and an idle speed screw (right arrow)

4.8 On 1986 through 1999 CR125R models, mixture is adjusted with an air screw and idle speed with a knob on the choke plunger

A	Air screw	C	Carburetor top
B	Idle speed knob	D	Clamping bands

9   The standard settings are intended for a bike operated with the specified premix (see Chapter 1), at sea level and an air temperature of 68-degrees F (20-degrees C).
10   Turn the air screw in until it bottoms lightly. Don't bottom the screw hard or its tip will be damaged, causing erratic settings. Back the screw out to the standard setting listed in this Chapter's Specifications.
11   Bottom the idle speed knob lightly, then back it out to the minimum amount listed in this Chapter's Specifications.
12   Warm up the engine until it will run smoothly with the choke knob all the way in.
13   Ride the bike and check that it revs up smoothly as you accelerate out of turns. If it bogs down, the mixture is too rich; if it surges, the mixture is too lean. Shut off the bike and change the air screw setting 1/4-turn at a time to correct the problem. Turn the screw in to enrich the mixture or out to make it leaner. **Note:** *If you have to go beyond the maximum air screw range listed in the Specifications, you'll need to change slow jet size. If you're under the range, use the next larger slow jet. If you're over the range, use the next smaller slow jet.*
14   Set the idle speed to your preference by turning the throttle stop screw **(see illustration 4.8)**.

2000 and later CR125R models
Refer to illustration 4.15
15   Mixture is controlled by an air screw. Idle speed is controlled by the throttle stop screw, which is secured by a locknut **(see illustration)**.
16   The standard settings are intended for a bike operated with the specified premix (see Chapter 1), at sea level and an air temperature of 68-degrees F (20-degrees C).
17   Turn the air screw in until it bottoms lightly. Don't bottom the screw hard or its tip will be damaged, causing erratic settings. Back the screw out to the standard setting listed in this Chapter's Specifications.
18   Warm up the engine until it will run smoothly with the choke knob all the way in.
19   Loosen the locknut on the throttle stop screw, then turn the screw to set idle speed (to rider's preference; there's no specified idle speed). Secure the throttle stop screw with the locknut.
20   Ride the bike and check that it revs up smoothly as you accelerate out of turns. If it blubbers, the mixture is too rich; if it surges, the mixture is too lean. Shut off the bike and change the air screw setting 1/4 turn at a time to correct the problem. Turn the screw in to enrich the mixture or out to make it leaner. **Note:** *If you have to go beyond the maximum air screw range listed in the Specifications, you'll need to change slow jet size. If you're under the range, use the next larger slow jet. If you're over the range, use the next smaller slow jet.*

4.15 Here are the 2000 and later CR125 air screw (right arrow) and throttle stop screw (left arrow)

Altitude and temperature adjustment
1986 through 1994 CR80R; 1986 through 1989 CR125R
Refer to illustration 4.21
21   These models should be rejetted to compensate for changes in temperature as well as altitude. This means you'll need a thermometer to determine the air temperature. To figure out whether you need to make any changes, find your altitude and the local air temperature on the accompanying chart **(see illustration)**. Draw a line up from the temperature setting to the altitude line. From where the two lines meet, read across to the correction factor.
22   Multiply the standard main jet number by the correction factor to determine the proper size of main jet. For example, if your main jet is a no. 165 and the correction factor is 0.92, multiply 165 X 0.92 to get 151.8. Rounded off, the correct size main jet is 152.
23   Look up the correction factor in this Chapter's Specifications to find out whether changes are needed in the needle clip position and air screw setting.

1995-on CR80R/85R; 1990-on CR125R
24   Jet sizes and needle clip positions for different altitude and temperature conditions are listed in this Chapter's Specifications.

All models
25   Refer to Section 7 for procedures to change the jet(s) and needle clip position.

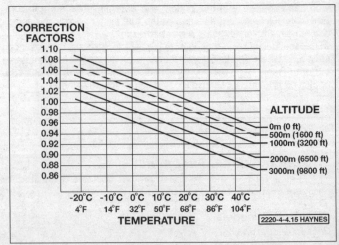

4.21 Correction factor chart – 1986 through 1994 CR80R and 1986 through 1989 CR125R

5 Carburetor overhaul - general information

1 Poor engine performance, hesitation, hard starting, stalling, flooding and backfiring are all signs that major carburetor maintenance may be required.

2 Keep in mind that many so-called carburetor problems are really not carburetor problems at all, but mechanical problems within the engine or ignition system malfunctions. Try to establish for certain that the carburetor is in need of maintenance before beginning a major overhaul.

3 Check the fuel tap and its strainer screen, the fuel lines, the intake manifold clamps, the O-ring between the intake manifold and cylinder head, the vacuum hoses, the air filter element, the cylinder compression, crankcase vacuum and compression, the spark plug and the ignition timing before assuming that a carburetor overhaul is required. If the bike has been unused for more than 24 hours, drain the float chamber and refill the tank with fresh fuel.

4 Most carburetor problems are caused by dirt particles, varnish and other deposits which build up in and block the fuel and air passages. Also, in time, gaskets and O-rings shrink or deteriorate and cause fuel and air leaks which lead to poor performance.

5 When the carburetor is overhauled, it is generally disassembled completely and the parts are cleaned thoroughly with a carburetor cleaning solvent and dried with filtered, unlubricated compressed air. The fuel and air passages are also blown through with compressed air to force out any dirt that may have been loosened but not removed by the solvent. Once the cleaning process is complete, the carburetor is reassembled using a new top gasket, O-rings and, generally, a new inlet needle valve and seat.

6 Before disassembling the carburetor, make sure you have the necessary gasket, O-rings and other parts, some carburetor cleaner, a supply of rags, some means of blowing out the carburetor passages and a clean place to work.

6 Carburetor - removal and installation

Warning: *Gasoline is extremely flammable, so take extra precautions when you work on any part of the fuel system. See the* **Warning** *in Section 2.*

Removal

1 Remove the seat and both side covers (see Chapter 8).
2 Remove the fuel tank (see Section 2). Remove the air cleaner case (see Section 9).

6.3 Unscrew the top cap and lift the throttle valve and jet needle out of the carburetor

All except 2000-on CR125R models
Refer to illustration 6.3

3 Unscrew the top cap from the carburetor **(see illustration)**. Lift out the spring, throttle valve and jet needle. Remove the air cleaner case (see Section 9).
4 Loosen the clamping bands on the air cleaner duct and intake manifold **(see illustration 4.8)**. Work the carburetor free of the duct and manifold and lift it off.

2000-on CR125R models
Refer to illustrations 6.7, 6.8a, 6.8b and 6.9

5 Disconnect the clutch cable from the lever inside the left crankcase cover (see Chapter 2A). This is necessary to provide removal access for the carburetor.
6 Disconnect the tap end of the fuel line that runs from the fuel tap to the carburetor (Section 2).
7 Loosen the clamping band screw on each side of the carburetor **(see illustration)**. Work the carburetor free of the intake manifold and air cleaner intake tube, then rotate it so you can get at the top of the carburetor.
8 Remove the top cap screws **(see illustration)**. Lift off the top cap and slide the throttle valve out of the carburetor body **(see illustration)**.

6.7 Loosen the clamping band screws (arrows)

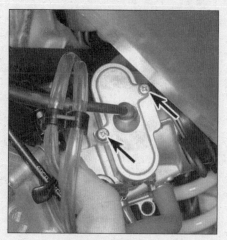

6.8a Remove the top cap screws (arrows) . . .

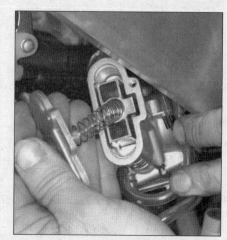

6.8b . . . take off the cap and slide the throttle valve out

6.9 Turn the carburetor to this position and remove it between the engine and frame

9   Rotate the carburetor and take it out between the left frame downtube and the engine **(see illustration)**. There's just enough room to do this.

All models

10   Check the intake tube for cracks, deterioration or other damage. If it has visible defects, or if there's reason to suspect its O-ring is leaking, remove it from the engine and inspect the O-ring.
11   After the carburetor has been removed, stuff clean rags into the intake (or the intake port in the cylinder head, if the reed valve has been removed) to prevent the entry of dirt or other objects.

Installation

12   Installation is the reverse of the removal steps, with the following additions:

a) *Adjust the throttle freeplay (see Chapter 1).*
b) *Adjust the idle speed and fuel/air mixture (see Section 4).*

---

7   Carburetor - disassembly, cleaning and inspection

Warning: *Gasoline is extremely flammable, so take extra precautions when you work on any part of the fuel system. See the* **Warning** *in Section 2.*

7.3a The CR80R/85R throttle cable fits through the spring seat like this

7.3b Compress the spring, pull the spring seat up and slip the cable through the slot in the throttle valve . . .

7.3c . . . then take the spring seat and spring off the cable

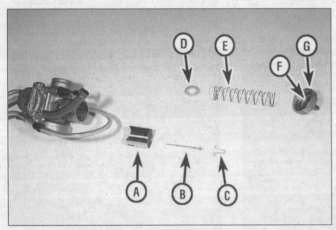

7.3d Pull the retaining clip out of the throttle valve and remove the jet needle

A	Throttle valve	E	Spring
B	Jet needle	F	O-ring
C	Retaining clip	G	Carburetor top
D	Spring seat		

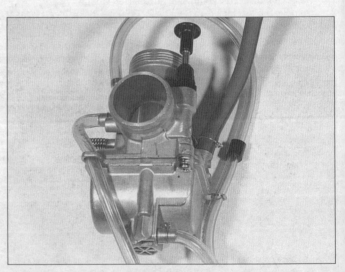

7.3e Before you disconnect the hoses from the carburetor, note how they're routed

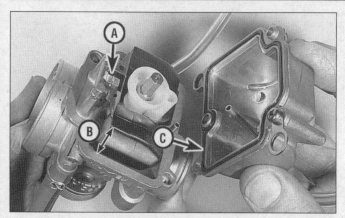

7.3f Remove the screws, lift the float chamber off and note how the needle valve clip fits over the float tang (A); on installation, check float height (B) and make sure the O-ring is in place (C)

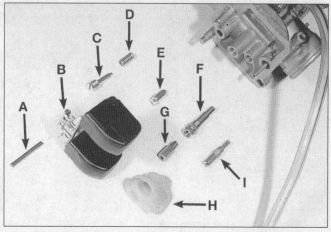

7.3g Carburetor bottom end components - CR80R/85R

A	Float pivot pin		F	Main jet holder
B	Float		G	Main jet
C	Air screw		H	Baffle
D	Spring		I	Slow jet
E	Needle valve			

Disassembly

1   Remove the carburetor from the machine as described in Section 6.

2   Set the carburetor on a clean working surface. Take note of how the vent hoses are routed, including locations of hose retainers.

CR80R/RB and CR85R/RB

Refer to illustrations 7.3a through 7.3i

3   To disassemble the carburetor on a 2004 or earlier CR80/85 model, refer to **illustrations 7.3a through 7.3h**. To disassemble the carburetor on a 2005 or earlier CR85 model, refer to **illustration 7.3i**.

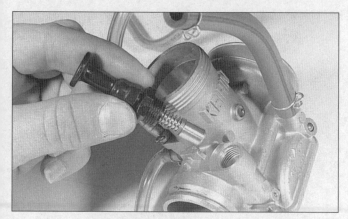

7.3h Unscrew the choke plunger

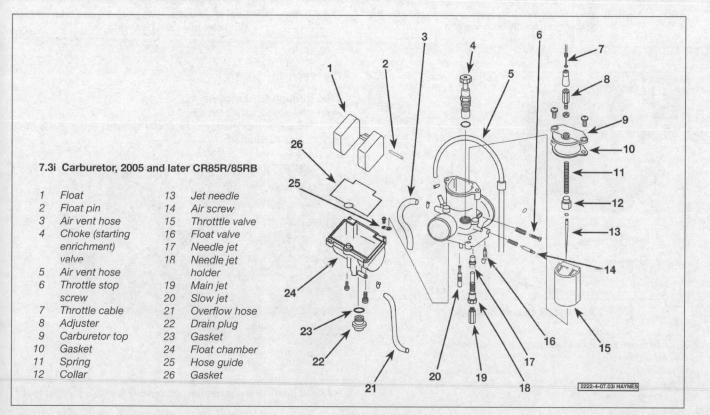

7.3i Carburetor, 2005 and later CR85R/85RB

1	Float	13	Jet needle
2	Float pin	14	Air screw
3	Air vent hose	15	Throtttle valve
4	Choke (starting enrichment) valve	16	Float valve
		17	Needle jet
		18	Needle jet holder
5	Air vent hose	19	Main jet
6	Throttle stop screw	20	Slow jet
7	Throttle cable	21	Overflow hose
8	Adjuster	22	Drain plug
9	Carburetor top	23	Gasket
10	Gasket	24	Float chamber
11	Spring	25	Hose guide
12	Collar	26	Gasket

2222-4-07.03i HAYNES

7.4a Compress the spring into the carburetor top . . .

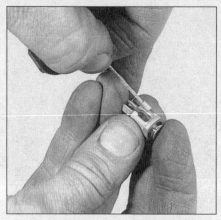

7.4b . . . and slip the cable out of the holder (holder removed for clarity) . . .

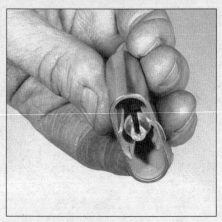

7.4c . . . the holder fits in the throttle valve like this . . .

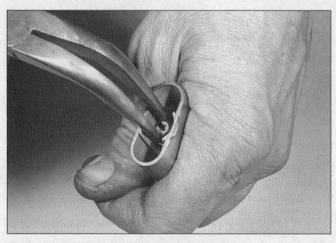

7.4d . . . rotate it one-quarter turn and press down to remove the holder from the throttle valve

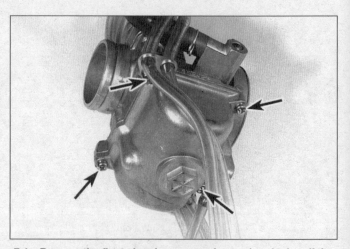

7.4e Remove the float chamber screws (arrows) and take off the float chamber and its O-ring

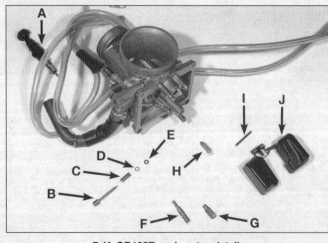

7.4f CR125R carburetor details

A	Idle speed knob/choke valve	F	Slow jet
B	Air screw	G	Main jet
C	Spring	H	Needle valve
D	Washer	I	Float pivot pin
E	O-ring	J	Float

CR125R

1986 through 1999 models

Refer to illustrations 7.4a through 7.4g

4   To disassemble the carburetor, refer to the accompanying illustrations **(see illustrations)**.

7.4g If the O-ring doesn't fall out, remove it with a pointed tool

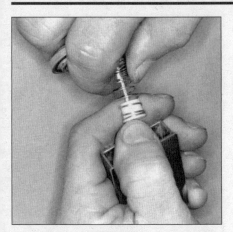

7.5a Push up on the collar to compress the spring . . .

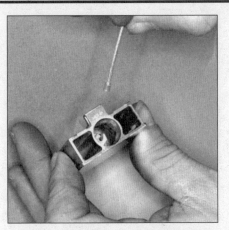

7.5b . . . slip the cable end out of the holder inside the throttle valve . . .

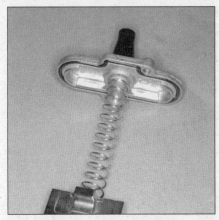

7.5c . . . and pull the spring off the base on the underside of the cap

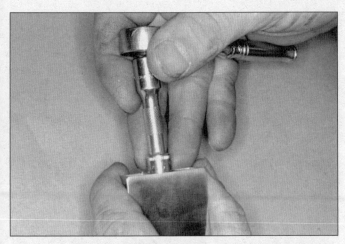

7.5d Unscrew the throttle cable holder with a thin wall socket . . .

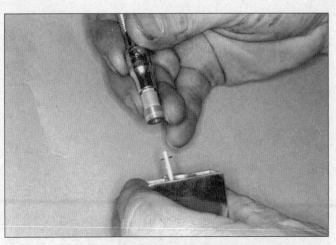

7.5e . . . then pull it out of the throttle valve and remove the jet needle and clip

2000 and 2001 models

Refer to illustrations 7.5a through 7.5u

5   To disassemble the carburetor, refer to the accompanying illustrations **(see illustrations)**.

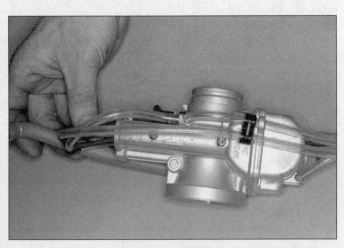

7.5f Note how the hoses are installed on the right side of the carburetor . . .

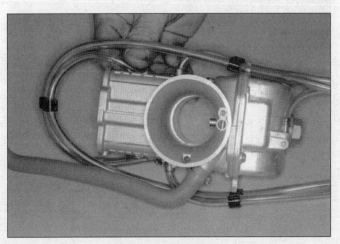

7.5g . . . at the rear . . .

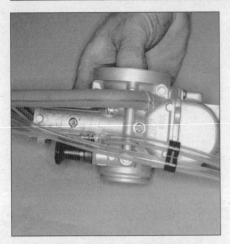

7.5h ... and on the left side

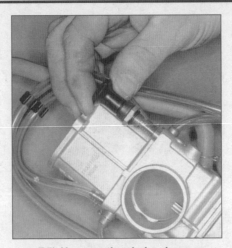

7.5i Unscrew the choke plunger

7.5j Unscrew the float chamber drain plug and remove its O-ring

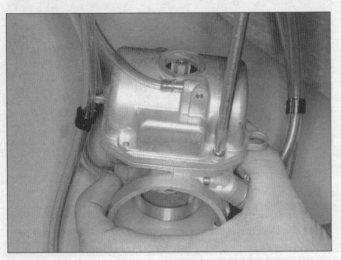

7.5k Remove the single float chamber screw ...

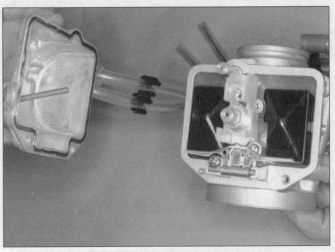

7.5l ... and take off the float chamber and its O-ring

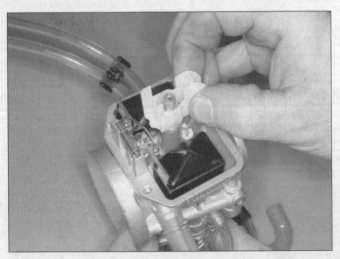

7.5m Lift off the float chamber baffle

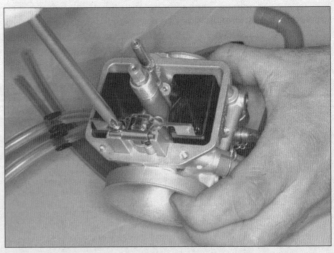

7.5n Remove the screw that secures the float pivot pin ...

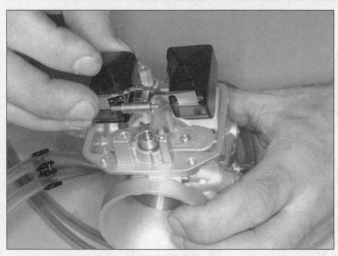

7.5o . . . and remove the pin, floats and needle valve

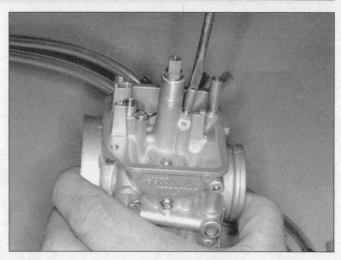

7.5p Unscrew the slow jet

7.5q Unscrew the main jet . . .

7.5r . . . the needle jet holder . . .

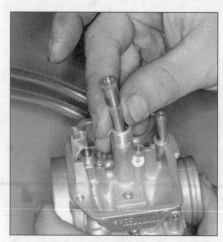

7.5s . . . and pull out the needle jet

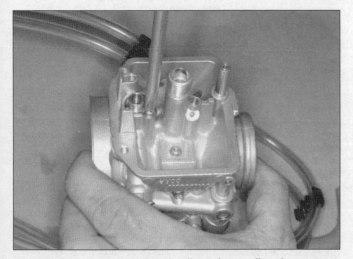

7.5t Remove the screw and pull out the needle valve seat

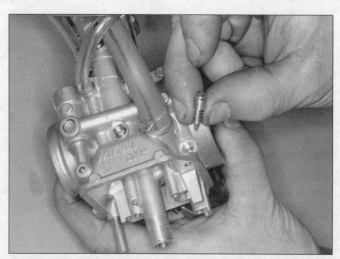

7.5u Remove the air screw and spring

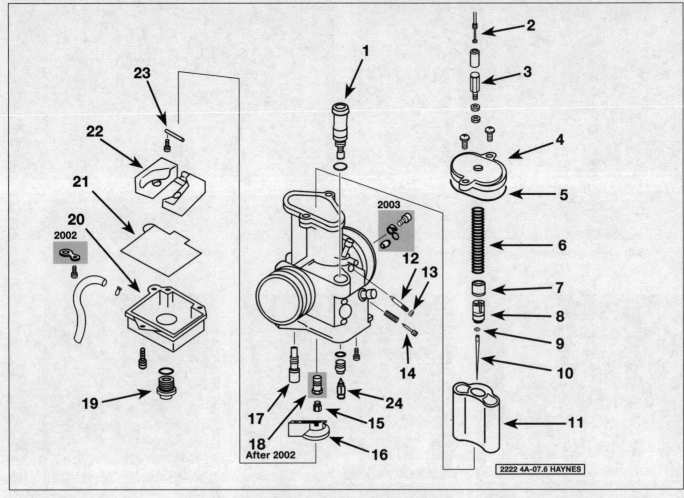

7.6 Carburetor, 2002 and 2003 CR125R

1	Choke knob	9	Jet needle clip	17	Slow jet
2	Throttle cable	10	Jet needle	18	Needle holder (after 2002)
3	Adjuster	11	Throttle valve	19	Drain plug
4	Carburetor top	12	Throttle stop screw	20	Float chamber
5	Gasket	13	Lock nut	21	Gasket
6	Spring	14	Air screw	22	Float
7	Collar	15	Main jet	23	Float pin
8	Cable holder	16	Baffle plate	24	Float valve

2003 and 2004 models

Refer to illustration 7.6

6   To disassemble the carburetor, refer to the accompanying illustration **(see illustration)**.

2005 and later models

Refer to illustration 7.7

7   To disassemble the carburetor, refer to the accompanying illustration **(see illustration)**.

Cleaning

Caution: *Use only a carburetor cleaning solution that is safe for use with plastic parts (be sure to read the label on the container).*

8   Submerge the metal components in the carburetor cleaner for approximately thirty minutes (or longer, if the directions recommend it).

9   After the carburetor has soaked long enough for the cleaner to loosen and dissolve most of the varnish and other deposits, use a brush to remove the stubborn deposits. Rinse it again, then dry it with

compressed air. Blow out all of the fuel and air passages in the carburetor body. **Caution:** *Never clean the jets or passages with a piece of wire or a drill bit, as they will be enlarged, causing the fuel and air metering rates to be upset.*

Inspection

10   Check the operation of the choke plunger. If it doesn't move smoothly, replace it.

11   Check the tapered portion of the air screw for wear or damage. Replace the screw if necessary.

12   Check the carburetor body, float chamber and carburetor top for cracks, distorted sealing surfaces and other damage. If any defects are found, replace the faulty component, although replacement of the entire carburetor will probably be necessary (check with your parts supplier for the availability of separate components).

13   Check the jet needle for straightness by rolling it on a flat surface (such as a piece of glass). Replace it if it's bent or if the tip is worn.

14   Check the tip of the fuel inlet valve needle. If it has grooves or

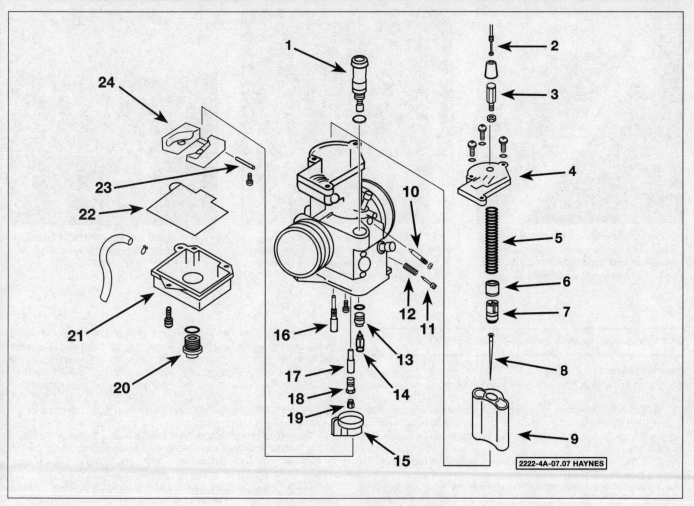

7.7 Carburetor, 2004 and later CR125R

1	Choke knob	9	Throttle valve	17	Needle jet
2	Throttle cable	10	Throttle stop screw	18	Needle jet holder
3	Adjuster	11	Air screw	19	Main jet
4	Carburetor top	12	Spring	20	Drain plug
5	Spring	13	Valve seat	21	Float chamber
6	Collar	14	Float valve	22	Gasket
7	Cable holder	15	Baffle plate	23	Float pin
8	Jet needle	16	Slow jet	24	Float

scratches in it, it must be replaced. Push in on the rod in the other end of the needle, then release it - if it doesn't spring back, replace the valve needle.

15   Check the O-rings on the float chamber and the main jet access plug (in the float chamber). Replace them if they're damaged.

16   Check the floats for damage. This will usually be apparent by the presence of fuel inside one of the floats. If the floats are damaged, they must be replaced.

17   Insert the throttle valve in the carburetor body and see that it moves up-and-down smoothly. Check the surface of the throttle valve for wear. If it's worn excessively or doesn't move smoothly in the bore, replace the carburetor.

---

8   Carburetor - reassembly and float height check

Caution: *When installing the jets, be careful not to over-tighten them - they're made of soft material and can strip or shear easily.*

Note: *When reassembling the carburetor, be sure to use new O-rings.*

1   Install the clip on the jet needle if it was removed. Place it in the needle groove listed in this Chapter's Specifications. Install the needle and clip in the throttle valve.

2   Install the air screw along with its spring, washer and O-ring, turning it in until it seats lightly. Now, turn the screw out the number of turns listed in this Chapter's Specifications.

3   Reverse the disassembly steps to install the jets.

4   Invert the carburetor. Attach the fuel inlet valve needle to the float. Set the float into position in the carburetor, making sure the valve needle seats correctly. Install the float pivot pin. To check the float height, hold the carburetor so the float hangs down, then tilt it back until the valve needle is just seated **(see illustration 7.3f)**. Measure the distance from the float chamber gasket surface to the top of the float and compare your measurement to the float height listed in this Chapter's Specifications. Bend the float tang as necessary to change the adjustment.

5   Install the O-ring into the groove in the float chamber. Place the float chamber on the carburetor and install the screws, tightening them securely.

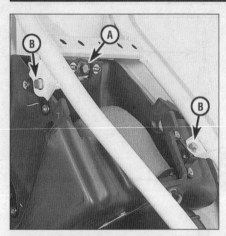

9.2 On 1996 and later CR80R/85R models, hold the clip nut for the center bolt (A) with pliers and remove this bolt first, then remove the smaller bolts (B)

9.3 If you separate the carburetor connecting tube from the housing, apply a ring of silicone sealant to its mating surface on installation

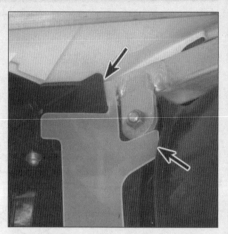

9.4 On 2000 and later CR125R models, position the air regulator tabs like this (arrows)

9   Air cleaner housing - removal and installation

Refer to illustrations 9.2, 9.3 and 9.4

1   Remove the seat, both side covers and the sub-frame (see Chapter 8).
2   Remove the air cleaner housing bolts. If you're working on a 1995 or later CR80R/85R, hold the clip nut on the center bolt with pliers and remove the center bolt first, then remove the remaining two bolts **(see illustration)**.
3   If necessary, detach the carburetor connecting tube from the housing **(see illustration)**.
4   Installation is the reverse of the removal steps. If you removed the connecting tube, apply a ring of silicone sealant to the mating surface of the connecting tube and air cleaner housing. If you're working on a 2000 or later CR125R, engage the tabs of the air regulator plate with the air cleaner housing and rear fender **(see illustration)**.

10   Throttle cable - removal and installation

Refer to illustration 10.4

1   Remove the fuel tank (see Section 2).
2   At the handlebar, loosen the throttle cable adjuster all the way (see Chapter 1).
3   Look for a punch mark on the handlebar next to the split in the throttle housing. If you don't see a mark, make one so the throttle housing can be installed in the correct position.
4   Later CR125R models are equipped with a throttle roller **(see illustration)**. If the roller has a removable cover, undo its screws and lift off the cover and gasket.
5   Remove the throttle housing screws. If the bike has a throttle roller, lift the cable out of the roller groove. Rotate the cable to align it with the slot in the throttle pulley, then slide the cable end out of the pulley.
6   To detach the cable from the carburetor, refer to Sections 6 and 7.
7   Route the cable into place. Make sure it doesn't interfere with any other components and isn't kinked or bent sharply.
8   Lubricate the throttle pulley end of the cable with multi-purpose grease. Reverse the disconnection steps to connect the throttle cable to the throttle grip pulley. If the bike has a throttle roller, install it, then install its gasket and cover (if equipped).
9   Coat the handlebar with silicone grease and slide the throttle

housing and grip on. On 1986 through 1994 models, align the punch marks on the throttle housing and handlebar. On 1995 and later models, align the triangular indicator mark on the throttle housing with the punch mark on the handlebar. If you're working on a 2001 CR125R model, align the index mark on the twistgrip with the edge of the throttle drum.
10   Reverse the removal steps in Sections 6 and 7 to connect the cable to the carburetor.
11   Operate the throttle and make sure it returns to the idle position by itself under spring pressure. **Warning:** *If the throttle doesn't return by itself, find and solve the problem before continuing with installation. A stuck throttle can lead to loss of control of the motorcycle.*
12   Follow the procedure outlined in Chapter 1, *Throttle and choke operation/grip freeplay - check and adjustment*, to adjust the cable.
13   Turn the handlebars back and forth to make sure the cable does not cause the steering to bind.
14   Once you're sure the cable operates properly, install the fuel tank.
15   With the engine idling, turn the handlebars through their full travel (full left lock to full right lock) and note whether idle speed increases. If it does, the cable is routed incorrectly. Correct this dangerous condition before riding the bike.

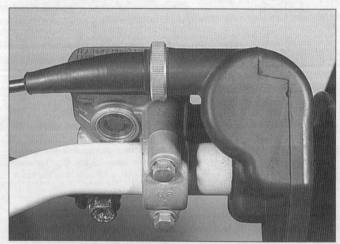

10.4 Later CR125R models use a throttle roller (1996 model shown)

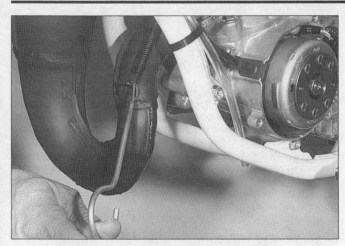

11.1 A tool like this one makes it easy to unhook the expansion chamber springs

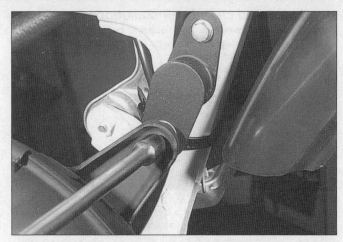

11.2a Note the direction of the offset brackets before removing them; leaving them bolted to the frame will help you remember how they go

11 Exhaust system - removal and installation

Refer to illustrations 11.1, 11.2a, 11.2b, 11.2c and 11.5

1   Unhook the springs that secure the expansion chamber to the cylinder head or head pipe **(see illustration)**. If you're working on a 1986 CR125R, also unhook the spring that secures the rear end of the expansion chamber to the muffler inlet pipe.

2   Remove the expansion chamber and muffler mounting bolts **(see illustrations)**.

3   Pull the exhaust system forward, separate the expansion chamber from the head pipe and remove the system from the machine.

4   To replace the muffler core, refer to Chapter 1. To remove the exhaust head pipe (models so equipped), see Chapter 2.

5   Installation is the reverse of removal. On 2001 models, position the exhaust spacer with the alignment mark upward and toward the left side of the bike **(see illustration)**.

12 Automatic Torque Amplification Chamber (ATAC) - removal, inspection and installation

1   This system varies exhaust backpressure according to engine speed for maximum efficiency. 1986 models use a butterfly valve mounted in the exhaust head pipe. 1987 through 1989 models use a rotary valve (similar to a fireplace damper) mounted in a chamber attached to the cylinder head.

2   Opening and closing of the ATAC valve is controlled by a governor mounted inside the right crankcase cover next to the water pump.

Head pipe and chamber removal

3   Remove the seat and the right side cover (see Chapter 8).

4   Refer to Section 11 and remove the expansion chamber.

5   Loosen the bolts that secure the ATAC chamber to the head pipe, then unbolt the head pipe from the cylinder and remove it with its ring.

6   Remove the ATAC chamber bolts and take the chamber off the head pipe.

Head pipe and chamber inspection

7   Take the ring off the head pipe and clean all gasket material from the head pipe and ATAC chamber mating surfaces.

8   Thoroughly clean all carbon deposits from inside the ATAC chamber and head pipe. Clean the butterfly valve inside the head pipe, making sure all deposits are removed from the valve shaft and the edges of the valve where it seats in the head pipe.

9   If you're working on a 1986 model, operate the butterfly valve by hand to make sure it moves smoothly and closes completely. If it doesn't, try cleaning it some more; if that doesn't help, replace the head pipe and butterfly valve as an assembly.

10   Check the ATAC chamber for cracks and a damaged gasket surface and replace it if any problems are found.

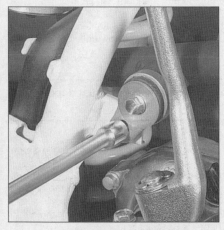

11.2b Some offset brackets include bushings

11.2c Bushings are used on all muffler-to-frame mounts

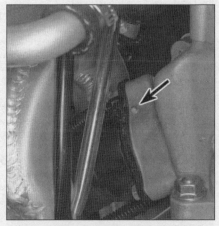

11.5 On 2001 CR125R models, position the spacer mark (arrow) up and to the left side of the bike

Head pipe and chamber installation

Note: *If you've removed the right crankcase cover on a 1986 model, install it before you install the head pipe and chamber. Otherwise, the butterfly valve won't stay in position.*

11   Place a new gasket on the ATAC chamber and bolt it to the head pipe.

12   Place a new gasket on the cylinder end of the head pipe and a new ring on the other end.

1986 models

13   Open the butterfly valve all the way and hold it open while you install the head pipe on the cylinder. The spring loop on the head pipe gasket goes next to the lower right bolt hole in the cylinder. The spring brackets go next to the top and lower left bolt holes. Engage the pinion of the butterfly valve with the rack in the cylinder.

14   Check the operation of the butterfly valve after the head pipe is installed. If it doesn't open all the way, refer to Section 13 and adjust it. If it's 45-degrees or more away from the fully open position, remove the head pipe and reinstall it.

All models

15   The remainder of installation is the reverse of the removal steps.

Governor removal

16   Remove the right crankcase cover (see Chapter 2).

17   Push the governor arm down against its spring and remove the two Phillips screws. Take off the rocker arm and the spring (there's a spring seat on each end of the spring).

18   Lift the governor off the water pump drive gear and remove the four steel balls from their pockets in the gear.

Governor inspection

19   Measure the free length of the governor spring. If it's sagged to less than the value listed in this Chapter's Specifications, or if it's broken or distorted, replace it.

20   Check all of the other governor parts for wear or damage and replace them if any problems are found.

Governor installation

21   Installation is the reverse of the removal steps, with the following addition: There are two bosses in the side of the governor that faces away from the water pump drive gear. Place the ends of the rocker arm over these.

Rack and cam removal (1986 models)

22   Refer to Section 11 and remove the expansion chamber. Unbolt the head pipe from the cylinder.

23   Unscrew the rack hole plug from the left front of the cylinder and remove its sealing washer.

24   Pull the spring out of the hole, then pull out the rack.

25   To remove the cam, remove the cylinder (see Chapter 2). Take the hairpin clip off the end of the spindle, then slide off the cam and spring. Pull the spindle out of the crankcase and remove the bushing.

Rack and cam inspection (1986 models)

26   Clean away all carbon deposits, check the parts for wear or damage and replace any parts that have problems.

Rack and cam installation (1986 models)

27   Installation is the reverse of the removal steps, with the following addition: Once the rack is installed, insert a screwdriver in the slot in the end of the rack. Turn the slot so it is parallel to the centerline of the head pipe bore (that is, angled slightly downward toward the front of the engine).

Linkage and valve removal (1987 through 1989 models)

28   Remove the valve linkage cover from the linkage case on the right front of the cylinder. It's secured by three screws (1987) or four screws (1988 and 1989).

29   Inside the linkage cavity in the cylinder, locate the two cast protrusions near the top and the two corresponding protrusions on the lockplate that the linkage bolt passes through. Pass a screw (6 mm shaft diameter) between the lockplate protrusions and between the cast protrusions to hold the linkage in position.

30   Note how the linkage spring is installed, then remove the bolt, washer, spring and bushing. To disconnect the link, remove the 6 mm screw, pull off the link and remove the lockplate.

31   Pull the linkage case off the cylinder and remove its O-ring. Pull the valve out of the cylinder.

Linkage and valve inspection (1987 through 1989 models)

32   Clean away all carbon deposits, check the parts for wear or damage and replace any parts that have problems.

33   Place the valve in its bore and rotate it by hand to make sure it moves smoothly.

Linkage and valve installation (1987 through 1989 models)

34   Installation is the reverse of the removal steps, with the following additions:

   a) *Use a new O-ring on the linkage case.*
   b) *The linkage bolt should line up exactly with its hole. If it doesn't, remove the right crankcase cover and turn the governor pinion gear slightly.*

---

13 ATAC valve (1986 models) - adjustment

1   The ATAC valve position is adjustable on 1986 models.

2   Remove the expansion chamber (Section 11) and the right crankcase cover (see Chapter 2).

3   Look into the head pipe and note the position of the butterfly valve. It should be closed all the way.

4   If the butterfly valve is part way open, make sure it isn't blocked by exhaust deposits. Clean the valve and surrounding area as necessary.

5   To adjust the valve, loosen the adjusting screw locknut on the right side of the cylinder below the head pipe. Turn the adjusting screw in just until it touches the upper cam, then turn it in another 1/8 to 1/4 turn.

6   Look at the valve. If it's closed all the way, tighten the locknut. If it's still slightly open, back out the adjusting screw until it closes, then tighten the locknut.

---

14 Honda Power Port (HPP) system - exhaust deposit draining

Refer to illustration 14.2

1   Exhaust deposits should be drained at the interval listed in Chapter 1.

2   To drain the deposits, remove the drain bolt **(see illustration)**.

Note: *Don't confuse the exhaust deposit drain bolt with the cooling system drain bolt, which is located lower on the water pump.*

3   Allow the deposits to drain, then reinstall the bolt and tighten it to the torque listed in this Chapter's Specifications.

14.2 Remove the drain screw (arrow) to drain exhaust deposits from the HPP system

15.1 The HPP exhaust valves are located in the top of the exhaust port (arrows)

15 Honda Power Port (HPP) system - removal, inspection and installation

Refer to illustrations 15.1 and 15.2

1   This system is used on 1990 through 1999 CR125R models. Its key components are a pair of moveable gates, mounted one in each side of the exhaust port **(see illustration)**. Honda refers to these as exhaust valves, but they aren't the same in design or function as the exhaust valves used in four-stroke engines. At low engine speeds, the exhaust valves are close together, effectively reducing the size of the exhaust port. As engine speed increases, the valves slide apart, expanding the port opening.

2   Movement of the valves is done by a pair of levers which fit into notches in the valves **(see illustration)**. The levers are mounted on pivot shafts, which are turned by a drive shaft mounted in the front of the cylinder. The drive shaft is operated by a link, which in turn is operated by a governor mounted in the right crankcase cover near the water pump.

Exhaust valve removal

Refer to illustrations 15.3a, 15.3b, 15.3c, 15.4, 15.5, 15.6a, 15.6b, 15.7, 15.8a, 15.8b, 15.9, 15.11, 15.12a, 15.12b and 15.12c

3   Remove the exhaust valve cover from each side of the cylinder **(see illustrations)**. On the right side, remove the cover grommet **(see illustration)**.

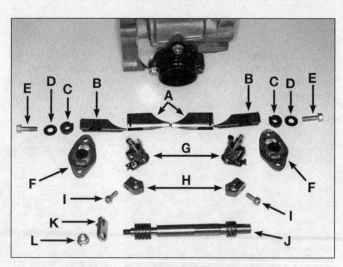

15.2 Honda Power Port (HPP) system details

A	Exhaust valve guides	G	Pinion shaft assemblies
B	Exhaust valves	H	Pinion holders
C	Lockplates	I	Allen bolts
D	Washers	J	Drive shaft
E	Hex bolts	K	Drive shaft lever
F	Cylinder upper covers and gaskets	L	Nut

15.3a Left side HPP cover bolt locations (arrows)

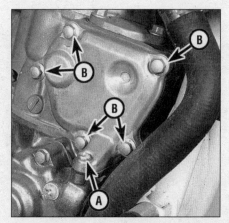

15.3b The right side cover has a screw (A) as well as bolts (B)

15.3c Remove the grommet (A), loosen the Allen bolt (B) and remove the hex bolt (C), its washer and the lockplate

15.4 Loosen the Allen bolt on the left side (arrow)

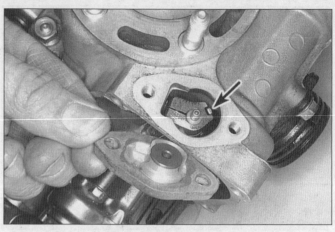

15.5 Remove the cylinder top covers and gaskets; note how the tang on the pinion lever fits into the notch on the pinion holder (arrow)

4   Loosen the pinion holder Allen bolts (one on each side of the cylinder) **(see illustration 15.3c and the accompanying illustration)**. On the right side, remove the hex bolt and the lockplate that secures the valve guide.

5   Remove the top cover and gasket from each side of the cylinder **(see illustration)**.

6   Pull the clip out of the pivot pin on the drive shaft lever, then separate the governor link and grommet from the pin **(see illustrations)**.

7   Slide the left exhaust valve out of its guide **(see illustration)**.

8   On the right side, remove the nut and lever from the drive shaft **(see illustration)**. This will allow the pinion shaft to rotate far enough so the valve and guide can be pulled out of the engine **(see illustration)**.

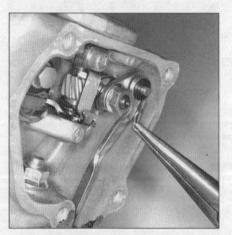

15.6a Pull out the clip . . .

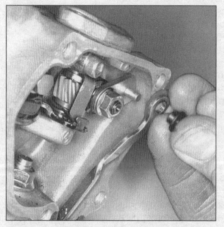

15.6b . . . and detach the link and bushing from the drive shaft lever

15.7 Pull out the left exhaust valve

15.8a Take the nut and lever (arrow) off the drive shaft . . .

15.8b . . . and pull the exhaust valve and its guide out

15.9 Remove the bolt, washer and lockplate; on installation, the flat on the lockplate fits into the slot in the exhaust valve guide

15.11 Slide the gear off the right end of the drive shaft and pull the drive shaft out of the bore (drive shaft removed for clarity)

15.12a Slip the pinion holder off the pinion shaft . . .

9   On the left side, remove the hex bolt and the lockplate, then pull the valve guide out of the engine **(see illustration)**.

10   If you're just removing the valves for periodic cleaning, further disassembly may be unnecessary. If inspection shows that more disassembly is needed, refer to the following steps.

11   Separate the gear from the right side of the drive shaft and pull the drive shaft out of the cylinder **(see illustration)**.

12   Lift the pinion holder off each pinion shaft assembly, then lift the assembly out of its bushing **(see illustrations)**. Note that the pinion levers are marked L and R (left and right) and that the teeth of the left pinion gear have notches **(see illustration)**.

Inspection and exhaust valve decarbonizing

Refer to illustrations 15.14 and 15.15

13   Start by cleaning all carbon deposits from the exhaust valves and guides. These deposits occur during normal operation of the motorcycle and must be removed periodically to maintain good performance.

14   Check the pinion shaft assemblies for wear, damage or broken springs. Pay special attention to the upper and lower pivot points and to the end of the lever where it rides in the exhaust valve. If individual parts need to be replaced, note how the assembly is put together **(see illustration)**, then take it apart.

15.12b . . . and lift the pinion shaft out of its bushing

15.12c The valve levers are marked R for right side (A) and L for left side (B); the left pinion gear has notches in its outer circumference (C)

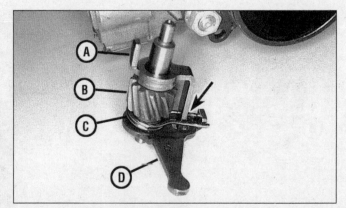

15.14 The long end of the pinion lever passes between the ends of the spring and into the square hole in the valve lever (arrow); the ends of the spring fit over the tab on the valve lever

A	Pinion lever	C	Spring
B	Pinion gear and shaft	D	Valve lever

15.15 Check the pinion shaft bushing (lower arrow) and drive shaft bearing (upper arrow)

15.16 Align the lever cutouts with the flats on the drive shaft

15   Check the pinion shaft bushings and drive shaft bearings for wear or damage **(see illustration)**. The bushings can't be replaced separately. If the bearings are rough, loose or noisy, remove them with a bearing puller, then drive in a new one with a bearing driver that applies pressure to the bearing's outer race (pressure on the inner race will damage the bearing).

Exhaust valve installation

Refer to illustration 15.16

16   Installation is the reverse of the removal steps, with the following additions:

a) *Be sure the valve levers and pinion gears are installed on the correct sides of the cylinder* **(see illustration 15.12c).**

b) *Align the cutout in the drive shaft lever with the flats on the shaft* **(see illustration).**

c) *Coat the exhaust valves and the tips of the pinion shafts with oil containing molybdenum disulfide.*

d) *Use new gaskets on the cylinder top covers and side covers.*

e) *Refer to Section 16 and adjust the exhaust valves.*

Governor and linkage removal

Refer to illustrations 15.19a, 15.19b and 15.20

17   Remove the right side cover and disconnect the link **(see illustrations 15.3a, 15.6a and 15.6b).**

18   Remove the right crankcase cover (see Chapter 2).

19   Pull out the grommet, remove the retaining screw and take the pinion gear and link out **(see illustrations)**.

20   Lift the governor out of the right crankcase cover **(see illustration)**.

Governor and linkage inspection

21   Check all parts for wear and damage and replace any that have problems. Don't try to disassemble the governor; replace it as a unit if problems are found. The grommet should be replaced if it's brittle or deteriorated.

22   Spin the bearing in the crankcase cover with a finger; if it's rough, loose or noisy, remove it with a slide hammer and blind hole puller. Put the new bearing in a freezer for several hours so it will contract. Heat the bearing bore area of the crankcase cover with a heat gun or in an oven (don't use a torch), then drive in the new bearing with a socket or bearing driver that applies pressure to the bearing's outer race.

Governor and linkage installation

Refer to illustration 15.25

23   Coat the teeth of the pinion gear with the transmission oil recommended in the Chapter 1 Specifications. Install the pinion gear in the right crankcase cover, then install the retaining screw and washer.

24   Lubricate the governor bearing and the joint in the link with oil containing molybdenum disulfide.

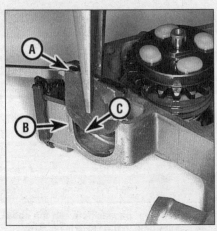

15.19a Pull out the grommet; after installation, the center of the link joint (A) should align with the edge of the grommet cutout (B); the tab on the grommet (C) faces outward

15.19b Remove the pinion gear retaining screw and its washer

15.20 Lift the governor out of the cover and remove the upper grommet (arrow)

15.25 Align the center of the link joint (upper arrow) with the mating surface of the cover (lower arrow)

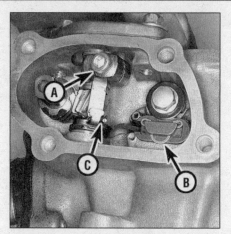

16.2 Loosen the Allen bolt (A) and push the valve in until its E-clip (B) touches the guide; after adjustment, there should be a gap between the pinion lever and rear spring end (C)

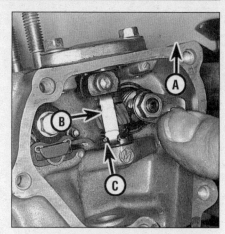

16.3 With the right side Allen bolt loose, push up on the drive shaft lever (A) or rearward on the pinion lever (B); after adjustment, there should be a gap between the pinion lever and rear spring end (C)

25 Align the center of the link joint with the gasket surface of the right crankcase cover (see illustration), then install the governor. After installation, the center of the joint should be aligned with the edge of the grommet cutout in the right crankcase cover (see illustration 15.19a).

26 Install the U-shaped grommet in the cutout of the right crankcase cover. The tab molded in the edge of the grommet goes to the outer side of the right crankcase cover.

27 The remainder of installation is the reverse of the removal steps.

16 Honda Power Port (HPP) system - adjustment

Refer to illustrations 16.2, 16.3 and 16.4

1 Remove the left and right side covers (see illustrations 15.3a and 15.3b).

2 Loosen the Allen bolt on each side's pinion holder, then push the exhaust valve all the way into the guide so the E-clip is positioned firmly against the guide (see illustration). Note: *If either side's E-clip won't push against the guide, remove and decarbonize the exhaust valves* (see Section 15).

3 On the right side, either lift up on the drive shaft lever or push the pinion lever rearward to take up slack in the linkage (see illustration).

Temporarily tighten the Allen bolt.

4 On the left side, push the pinion lever rearward and tighten the Allen bolt (see illustration).

5 Go back to the right side. Loosen the Allen bolt, then repeat Step 3.

6 Check for a gap between the pinion spring and valve lever tab on each side of the cylinder (see illustration 16.2 and 16.3). Measure the gap and compare it to the value listed in this Chapter's Specifications.

7 Install the left and right side covers.

17 Radical Combustion (RC) system – exhaust deposit draining

Refer to illustration 17.2

1 Exhaust deposits should be drained at the interval listed in Chapter 1.

2 Remove the drain screw to empty any built-up exhaust deposits (see illustration). Note: *Don't confuse the RC system drain screw with the water pump drain screw, which is located in the water pump cover.*

3 Allow the deposits to drain, reinstall the screw and tighten it securely.

16.4 Push rearward on the pinion lever (arrow) and tighten the Allen bolt

17.2 Remove the drain screw (arrow) to drain RC system exhaust deposits

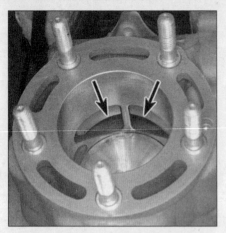

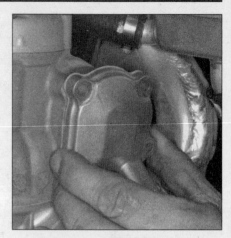

18.1 The RC valves (arrows) rotate upward out of the exhaust port

18.3a Remove the screw and four bolts . . .

18.3b . . . and take off the cover and gasket

18 Radical Combustion (RC) system – removal, inspection and installation

Shaft and valves

Removal

Refer to illustrations 18.1, 18.3a, 18.3b, 18.4a, 18.4b, 18.5a, 18.5b, 18.6a and 18.6b

Note: *Honda specifies removing the cylinder to remove the RC system shaft and valves, but we were able to remove them without removing the cylinder from the engine.*

1   This system is used on 2000 and later CR125R models. It is similar in function to the HPP system described in Section 15, but the moveable gates rotate up out of the exhaust port, rather than sliding sideways **(see illustration)**. This has the same effect (raising the effective height of the exhaust port), but the system is easier to maintain. 2004 CR125R models use an electric servo motor to control the operation of the valves. All other years use a mechanical governor.

2   Remove the exhaust system expansion chamber (Section 11) and the cylinder head (see Chapter 2A).

3   Remove the screw and four bolts that secure the RC cover to the cylinder, then take off the cover and gasket **(see illustrations)**.

4   Remove the clip and bushing, then separate the link from the shaft **(see illustrations)**.

5   If you're planning to disassemble the shaft, unscrew the nut and

18.4a Pull out the clip . . .

remove the washer **(see illustrations)**. This can be done later, but it's easier now while the shaft is mounted in the engine.

6   Reach into the cylinder opening with your left hand and grasp the valves so they won't fall, then pull out the shaft with your right hand **(see illustration)**. Put down the shaft and pass the valves through the exhaust port into your right hand **(see illustration)**.

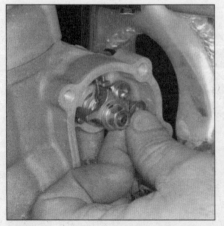

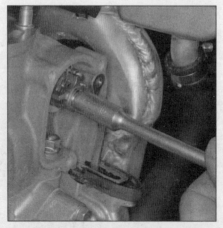

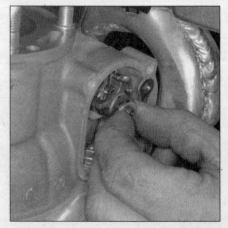

18.4b . . . and remove the bushing (its wide side faces out), then disconnect the link

18.5a It's easier to remove the nut while the shaft is in the engine . . .

18.5b . . . slide the washer off the shaft . . .

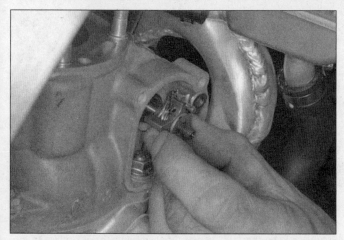

18.6a . . . hold the valves while you slide the shaft out . . .

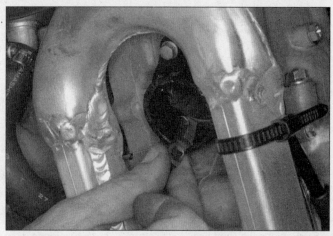

18.6b . . . then pass the valves out through the exhaust port

18.7 Note how the shaft ends of the valves are offset and how the spring ends fit over the levers

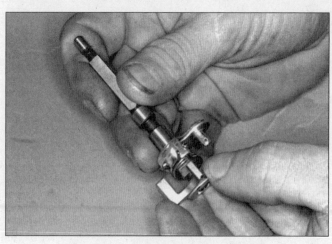

18.8a Take the spring lever off the shaft . . .

Inspection

Refer to illustrations 18.7, 18.8a, 18.8b, 18.8c, 18.8d and 18.9

7   Lay the parts on a workbench for inspection **(see illustration)**. Clean them thoroughly in solvent and blow them dry.

8   Check the shaft components for wear and damage. If necessary, disassemble the shaft so individual components can be inspected and replaced **(see illustrations)**. If any of the parts are worn or damaged, replace them. The shaft and valves must be replaced as a set.

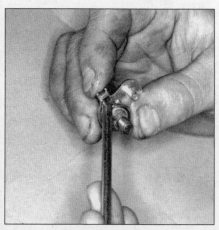

18.8b . . . spread the spring ends and take the spring off the link lever and shaft . . .

18.8c . . . remove the thrust washer from the other side (later models don't have this) . . .

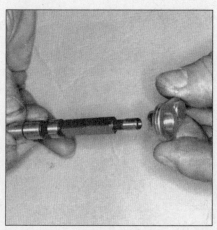

18.8d . . . and take the link lever off the shaft

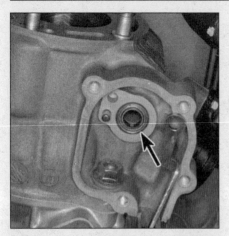

18.9 Replace the shaft bearing (arrow) if it's worn or damaged

18.10a Place a pin in the hole to keep the lever arm from turning while you tighten the nut

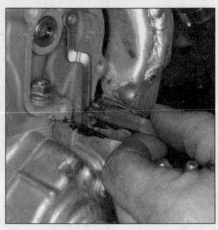

18.10b Apply a thin coat of sealant to the ridges the grommet seats on

9   Inspect the shaft bearing in the cylinder **(see illustration)**. If it's worn or damaged, replace it. You can either pull it out with a slide-hammer type puller **(see illustration 17.3c in Chapter 2A)** or drive it in with a bearing driver. If you drive it in, you'll need to remove the cylinder from the engine first (see Chapter 2A). In either case, heat the area around the bearing with a heat gun to expand it before removing the bearing. **Caution:** *Don't heat the area with a torch or you may warp the cylinder.*

Installation

Refer to illustrations 18.10a and 18.10b

10   Installation is the reverse of the removal steps, with the following additions:.

  a) *Insert a pin into the 5.5 mm hole in the cylinder casting, so the tab on the shaft lever can rest against it while you tighten the nut* **(see illustration)**. *A 4 mm Allen wrench or a 5.5 mm or smaller punch can be used for this.*

  b) *Measure the distance from the cylinder top surface to the lower edge of the flap valves. It should be 37.75 +/-0.4 mm (1.486 +/-0.020 inches). If it's not within this range, the flap valves are not installed correctly.*

  c) *Apply a thin coat of sealant to the ridges that the cover grommet seats on, then seat the grommet securely on the ridges* **(see illustration)**. *Use a new cover gasket.*

Governor and link (except 2004)

Removal

Refer to illustration 18.13

11   Remove the right crankcase cover (see Chapter 2A).

12   Remove the cover and disconnect the link as described in Steps 3 and 4 above.

13   Lift the governor out of the right crankcase cover **(see illustration)**.

Inspection

Refer to illustrations 18.14a, 18.14b, 18.15 and 18.16

14   Check the link and pinion gear for wear and damage **(see illustration)**. If problems are found, remove the retaining screw and washer **(see illustration)**. Pull the pinion gear and link out of the crankcase cover and install a new assembly. Secure it with the retaining screw.

15   Rotate the governor bearings in the crankcase cover and in the crankcase **(see illustration 18.14a and the accompanying illustration)**. If their rotation is rough or if the inner race wobbles, replace the bearing. Heat the surrounding area with a heat gun to expand it (don't use a torch) and pull the bearing out the a blind hole puller **(see illustration 17.3c in Chapter 2A)**. Drive in a new bearing with a bearing driver or socket the same diameter as the bearing outer race.

16   Check the governor for worn gear teeth and loose or damaged components **(see illustration)**. Replace the governor as a complete unit if problems are found.

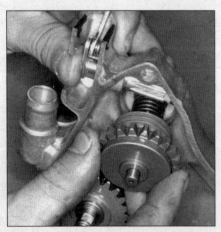

18.13 Pull the governor out of the crankcase cover

18.14a Check the pinion gear teeth and governor bearing (arrows) for wear or damage

18.14b This screw and washer (arrow) retain the governor in the crankcase cover

18.15 The other governor bearing is mounted in the crankcase (arrow)

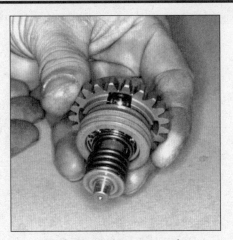

18.16 Check the governor for wear or damage

18.17a Raise the link lever to this position (arrow) . . .

Installation

Refer to illustrations 18.17a through 18.17e

17   Installation is the reverse of the removal steps, with the following additions:

a) *After installing the link and pinion gear, rotate the link lever upward from its installed position* **(see illustration)**. *Installing the governor will rotate the pinion gear and pull the link lever down to its* installed position **(see illustration)**. *The link lever should then be between the index lines on the crankcase cover. If you can't see the index lines, lay a straightedge across the governor gear in the direction shown* **(see illustration)**. *The link lever should align with it.*

b) *Install the crankcase cover grommet with its larger tab toward the outside of the cover* **(see illustrations)**.

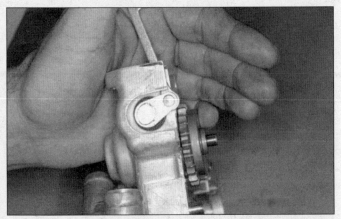

18.17b . . . it will rotate down to its installed position when the governor is installed

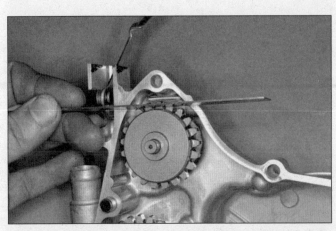

18.17c If the index lines aren't visible, check alignment of the link lever with a straightedge in this position

18.17d Install the grommet with its larger tab outward (arrow) . . .

18.17e . . . when installed, it overlaps the crankcase like this

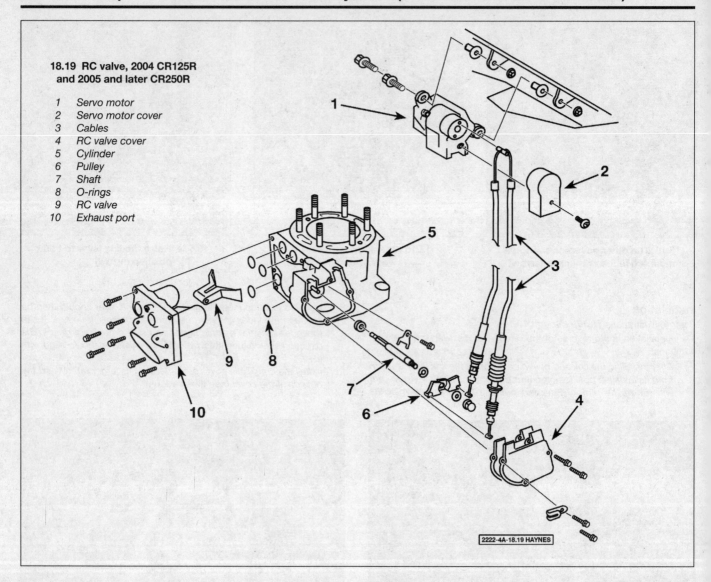

18.19 RC valve, 2004 CR125R and 2005 and later CR250R

1   Servo motor
2   Servo motor cover
3   Cables
4   RC valve cover
5   Cylinder
6   Pulley
7   Shaft
8   O-rings
9   RC valve
10   Exhaust port

Servo motor (2004 only)

Motor check

Refer to illustration 18.19

18   Remove the fuel tank (see Section 2).

19   Remove the RC valve cover from the left side of the cylinder **(see illustration)**. Loosen the cable locknuts, slip the cable end fittings out of their grooves and disengage the cable ends from the pulley.

20   Remove the screw that secures the servo motor cover, then take the cover off (it's located next to the left radiator). Disengage the cable ends from the servo motor pulley, free the wiring harness from any retainers and disconnect the motor wiring connector.

21   Unbolt the servo motor and take it out. The bolts are accessible from above, inside the left frame member.

22   Using a pair of jumper wires, connect a 12-volt battery to the terminals in the motor side of the wiring connector (battery positive to white/black; battery negative to white/green). The motor should turn clockwise.

23   Reverse the connections. The motor should now turn counterclockwise.

24   If the motor doesn't perform as described, replace it.

25   Installation is the reverse of the removal steps. Connect the cables to the motor pulley and valve pulley. Place the threaded portions of the cables in their grooves in the cylinder casting.

Cable adjustment

26   Back off the upper locknut on the rear cable until it seats against the adjuster (above it on the cable). Connect the cable to the lower pulley (the one on the valve, not the one on the motor).

27   Turn the lower pulley all the way counterclockwise. Holding it like this, turn the cable adjuster downward until it pulls the lower locknut up against the cylinder casting. Tighten the upper locknut securely.

28   Turn the lower pulley all the way clockwise, so the forward side of the pulley stops against the pin above it.

29   Loosen the locknut (if you haven't already done so) and connect the upper end of the cable to the motor pulley.

30   Compress the cable spring (inside the rubber boot) and install the spring seat over it.

31   Pull up on the cable while rocking it toward the front and rear of the motorcycle (to take up the slack). While pulling up on the cable, turn the adjuster down until the lower locknut seats against the cylinder casting. Tighten the upper locknut securely.

32   With the cover not yet installed, start the engine. The RC valve should be in the Off position. Rev the engine to 11,500 rpm and note the valve's movement. It should move all the way to the On position. If it doesn't, recheck the cable adjustment.

33   Once the cable adjustment is correct, install the cover.

Chapter 4 Part B
Fuel and exhaust systems (CR250R and CR500R models)

Contents

Specifications

General
Fuel type... See Chapter 1

Carburetor (CR250R)
Standard air screw setting

1986	1-1/2 turns out
1987 through 1992	2 turns out
1993	1-3/4 turns out
1994 through 1999	2 turns out
2000	1-1/2 turns out
2001	1-3/4 turns out
2002 through 2004	1-1/2 turns out
2005 and later	2 turns out

Carburetor (CR250R) (continued)

Identification mark

1986	PJ23A
1987	PJ26A
1988	PJ26B
1989	PJ26C
1990	PJ28A
1991	PJ28C
1992	PJ28E
1993	PJ28G
1994	PJ28H
1995 and 1996	PJ28J
1997 and 1998	PJ28L
1999	PWK00A
2000	PWK00B
2001	TMX 11A
2002	TMX 11B
2003	TMX 11C
2004	TMX 10A
2005 and later	TMX 11A

Jet sizes

Standard main jet

1986 and 1987	175
1988	185
1989	178
1990 through 1998	175
1999	190
2000	180
2001	420
2002	380
2003 and later	420

Slow jet

1986	60
1987	58
1988	62
1989	58
1990 through 1998	55
1999	42
2000	48
2001	35
2002	32.5
2003	30
2004	32.5
2005 and later	40

Jet needle clip position

1986	3rd groove from top
1987 through 1989	4th groove from top
1991 through 2001	3rd groove from top
2002 through 2004	2nd groove from top
2005 and later	3rd groove from top

Float level

1986 through 2000	16.0 mm (5/8 inch)
2001 through 2003	15.0 mm (19/32 inch)
2004 and later	7.5 mm (19/64 inch)

Correction factor, needle clip position and air screw setting

0.94 or below

Needle clip position	One groove above standard
Air screw setting	1 turn out from standard

0.94 to 0.98

Needle clip position	Standard
Air screw setting	1/2 turn out from standard

0.98 to 1.02

Needle clip position	Standard
Air screw setting	Standard

1.02 to 1.06

Needle clip position	Standard
Air screw setting	1/2 turn in from standard

1.06 or above

Needle clip position	One groove below standard
Air screw opening	1 turn in from standard

Carburetor (CR500R)

Standard air screw setting	
1986 through 1988	1-1/2 turns out
1989 through 1991	2 turns out
1992 on	1-1/2 turns out
Idle speed knob minimum setting	6 turns out (24 clicks) from seated position
Identification mark	
1986	PJ24A
1987	PJ27A
1988	PJ27B
1989	PJ27C
1990	PJ27E
1991	PJ27H
1992	PJ27J
1993	PJ27L
1994	PJ27M
1995	PJ27N
1996 on	7P
Jet sizes	
Standard main jet	
1986	172
1987	167
1988	175
1989 on	170
Slow jet	
1986	60
1987 on	55
Jet needle clip position	
1986 through 1988	4th groove from top
1989 and 1990	3rd groove from top
1991 on	4th groove from top
Float level	16.0 mm (5/8 inch)

Carburetor settings

1992 and 1994 through 1997 CR250R

Sea level to 999 feet (299 meters)	
Minus 21 to 0-degrees F (minus 35 to minus 18-degrees C)	
Air screw	1 turn out
Slow jet	60
Needle clip position	4th groove
Main jet	192
Minus 1 to 20-degrees F (minus 17 to minus 7-degrees C)	
Air screw	1 turn out
Slow jet	60
Needle clip position	4th groove
Main jet	185
19 to 40-degrees F (minus 6 to 4-degrees C)	
Air screw	1-1/2 turns out
Slow jet	58
Needle clip position	4th groove
Main jet	182
39 to 60-degrees F (3 to 15-degrees C)	
Air screw	1-3/4 turns out
Slow jet	55
Needle clip position	3rd groove
Main jet	178
59 to 80-degrees F (14 to 26-degrees C)*	
Air screw	2 turns out
Slow jet	55
Needle clip position	3rd groove
Main jet	175
79 to 100-degrees F (25 to 38-degrees C)	
Air screw	2-1/2 turns out
Slow jet	55
Needle clip position	3rd groove
Main jet	170

* Standard jetting

Carburetor settings (continued)

1992 and 1994 through 1997 CR250R (continued)

Sea level to 999 feet (299 meters)

   99 to 120-degrees F (37 to 49-degrees C)

Air screw	2-3/4 turns out
Slow jet	52
Needle clip position	2nd or 3rd groove
Main jet	168

1000 to 2499 feet (300 to 749 meters)

   Minus 21 to 0-degrees F (minus 35 to minus 18-degrees C)

Air screw	1 turn out
Slow jet	60
Needle clip position	4th groove
Main jet	190

   Minus 1 to 20-degrees F (minus 17 to minus 7-degrees C)

Air screw	1-1/4 turn out
Slow jet	58
Needle clip position	4th groove
Main jet	185

   19 to 40-degrees F (minus 6 to 4-degrees C)

Air screw	1-1/2 turns out
Slow jet	58
Needle clip position	4th groove
Main jet	180

   39 to 60-degrees F (3 to 15-degrees C)

Air screw	2 turns out
Slow jet	55
Needle clip position	3rd groove
Main jet	178

   59 to 80-degrees F (14 to 26-degrees C)

Air screw	2 turns out
Slow jet	55
Needle clip position	3rd groove
Main jet	172

   79 to 100-degrees F (25 to 38-degrees C)

Air screw	2-1/2 turns out
Slow jet	55
Needle clip position	3rd groove
Main jet	168

   99 to 120-degrees F (37 to 49-degrees C)

Air screw	3 turns out
Slow jet	52
Needle clip position	2nd or 3rd groove
Main jet	165

2500 to 4999 feet (750 to 1499 meters)

   Minus 21 to 0-degrees F (minus 35 to minus 18-degrees C)

Air screw	1 turn out
Slow jet	60
Needle clip position	4th groove
Main jet	185

   Minus 1 to 20-degrees F (minus 17 to minus 7-degrees C)

Air screw	1-1/2 turn out
Slow jet	58
Needle clip position	4th groove
Main jet	182

   19 to 40-degrees F (minus 6 to 4-degrees C)

Air screw	2 turns out
Slow jet	58
Needle clip position	4th groove
Main jet	180

   39 to 60-degrees F (3 to 15-degrees C)

Air screw	2-1/4 turns out
Slow jet	55
Needle clip position	3rd groove
Main jet	175

   59 to 80-degrees F (14 to 26-degrees C)

Air screw	2-1/2 turns out
Slow jet	55
Needle clip position	3rd groove
Main jet	170

79 to 100-degrees F (25 to 38-degrees C)
Air screw	2-3/4 turns out
Slow jet..	52
Needle clip position...	2nd or 3rd groove
Main jet...	168

99 to 120-degrees F (37 to 49-degrees C)
Air screw	3 turns out
Slow jet..	52
Needle clip position...	2nd or 3rd groove
Main jet...	162

5000 to 7499 feet (1500 to 2299 meters)

Minus 21 to 0-degrees F (minus 35 to minus 18-degrees C)
Air screw	1-1/2 turns out
Slow jet..	58
Needle clip position...	4th groove
Main jet...	182

Minus 1 to 20-degrees F (minus 17 to minus 7-degrees C)
Air screw	2 turns out
Slow jet..	55
Needle clip position...	4th groove
Main jet...	178

19 to 40-degrees F (minus 6 to 4-degrees C)
Air screw	2-1/4 turns out
Slow jet..	55
Needle clip position...	3rd groove
Main jet...	175

39 to 60-degrees F (3 to 15-degrees C)
Air screw	2-1/2 turns out
Slow jet..	52
Needle clip position...	3rd groove
Main jet...	170

59 to 80-degrees F (14 to 26-degrees C)
Air screw	3 turns out
Slow jet..	52
Needle clip position...	2nd or 3rd groove
Main jet...	165

79 to 100-degrees F (25 to 38-degrees C)
Air screw	3-1/4 turns out
Slow jet..	50
Needle clip position...	2nd or 3rd groove
Main jet...	162

99 to 120-degrees F (37 to 49-degrees C)
Air screw	3-1/2 turns out
Slow jet..	50
Needle clip position...	2nd groove
Main jet...	158

7500 to 10,000 feet (2300 to 3000 meters)

Minus 21 to 0-degrees F (minus 35 to minus 18-degrees C)
Air screw	2 turns out
Slow jet..	58
Needle clip position...	4th groove
Main jet...	180

Minus 1 to 20-degrees F (minus 17 to minus 7-degrees C)
Air screw	2-1/4 turns out
Slow jet..	55
Needle clip position...	4th groove
Main jet...	175

19 to 40-degrees F (minus 6 to 4-degrees C)
Air screw	2-1/2 turns out
Slow jet..	52
Needle clip position...	3rd groove
Main jet...	170

39 to 60-degrees F (3 to 15-degrees C)
Air screw	3 turns out
Slow jet..	52
Needle clip position...	2nd or 3rd groove
Main jet...	168

59 to 80-degrees F (14 to 26-degrees C)
Air screw	3-1/4 turns out
Slow jet..	52

Carburetor settings (continued)

1992 and 1994 through 1997 CR250R (continued)
7500 to 10,000 feet (2300 to 3000 meters)

59 to 80-degrees F (14 to 26-degrees C)

Needle clip position..	2nd groove
Main jet..	162

79 to 100-degrees F (25 to 38-degrees C)

Air screw	3-1/2 turns out
Slow jet..	52
Needle clip position..	2nd groove
Main jet..	162

99 to 120-degrees F (37 to 49-degrees C)

Air screw	3-3/4 turns out
Slow jet..	50
Needle clip position..	2nd groove
Main jet..	155

1993 CR250R
Sea level to 999 feet (299 meters)

Minus 21 to 0-degrees F (minus 35 to minus 18-degrees C)

Air screw	3/4 turn out
Slow jet..	60
Needle clip position..	4th groove
Main jet..	192

Minus 1 to 20-degrees F (minus 17 to minus 7-degrees C)

Air screw	3/4 turn out
Slow jet..	60
Needle clip position..	4th groove
Main jet..	185

19 to 40-degrees F (minus 6 to 4-degrees C)

Air screw	1-1/4 turns out
Slow jet..	58
Needle clip position..	4th groove
Main jet..	182

39 to 60-degrees F (3 to 15-degrees C)

Air screw	1-1/2 turns out
Slow jet..	55
Needle clip position..	3rd groove
Main jet..	178

59 to 80-degrees F (14 to 26-degrees C)*

Air screw	1-3/4 turns out
Slow jet..	55
Needle clip position..	3rd groove
Main jet..	175

79 to 100-degrees F (25 to 38-degrees C)

Air screw	2-1/4 turns out
Slow jet..	55
Needle clip position..	3rd groove
Main jet..	170

99 to 120-degrees F (37 to 49-degrees C)

Air screw	2-1/2 turns out
Slow jet..	52
Needle clip position..	2nd or 3rd groove
Main jet..	168

1000 to 2499 feet (300 to 749 meters)

Minus 21 to 0-degrees F (minus 35 to minus 18-degrees C)

Air screw	3/4 turn out
Slow jet..	60
Needle clip position..	4th groove
Main jet..	190

Minus 1 to 20-degrees F (minus 17 to minus 7-degrees C)

Air screw	1 turn out
Slow jet..	58
Needle clip position..	4th groove
Main jet..	185

19 to 40-degrees F (minus 6 to 4-degrees C)

Air screw	1-1/4 turns out
Slow jet..	58
Needle clip position..	4th groove
Main jet..	180

* Standard jetting

39 to 60-degrees F (3 to 15-degrees C)
    Air screw .... 1-3/4 turns out
    Slow jet... 55
    Needle clip position.. 3rd groove
    Main jet... 178
59 to 80-degrees F (14 to 26-degrees C)
    Air screw .... 1-3/4 turns out
    Slow jet... 55
    Needle clip position.. 3rd groove
    Main jet... 172
79 to 100-degrees F (25 to 38-degrees C)
    Air screw .... 2-1/4 turns out
    Slow jet... 55
    Needle clip position.. 3rd groove
    Main jet... 168
99 to 120-degrees F (37 to 49-degrees C)
    Air screw .... 2-3/4 turns out
    Slow jet... 52
    Needle clip position.. 2nd or 3rd groove
    Main jet... 165
2500 to 4999 feet (750 to 1499 meters)
  Minus 21 to 0-degrees F (minus 35 to minus 18-degrees C)
    Air screw .... 3/4 turn out
    Slow jet... 60
    Needle clip position.. 4th groove
    Main jet... 185
  Minus 1 to 20-degrees F (minus 17 to minus 7-degrees C)
    Air screw .... 1-1/4 turn out
    Slow jet... 58
    Needle clip position.. 4th groove
    Main jet... 182
19 to 40-degrees F (minus 6 to 4-degrees C)
    Air screw .... 1-3/4 turns out
    Slow jet... 58
    Needle clip position.. 4th groove
    Main jet... 180
39 to 60-degrees F (3 to 15-degrees C)
    Air screw .... 2 turns out
    Slow jet... 55
    Needle clip position.. 3rd groove
    Main jet... 175
59 to 80-degrees F (14 to 26-degrees C)
    Air screw .... 2-1/4 turns out
    Slow jet... 55
    Needle clip position.. 3rd groove
    Main jet... 170
79 to 100-degrees F (25 to 38-degrees C)
    Air screw .... 2-1/2 turns out
    Slow jet... 52
    Needle clip position.. 2nd or 3rd groove
    Main jet... 168
99 to 120-degrees F (37 to 49-degrees C)
    Air screw .... 2-3/4 turns out
    Slow jet... 52
    Needle clip position.. 2nd or 3rd groove
    Main jet... 162
5000 to 7499 feet (1500 to 2299 meters)
  Minus 21 to 0-degrees F (minus 35 to minus 18-degrees C)
    Air screw .... 1-1/4 turns out
    Slow jet... 58
    Needle clip position.. 4th groove
    Main jet... 182
  Minus 1 to 20-degrees F (minus 17 to minus 7-degrees C)
    Air screw .... 1-3/4 turns out
    Slow jet... 55
    Needle clip position.. 4th groove
    Main jet... 178
19 to 40-degrees F (minus 6 to 4-degrees C)
    Air screw .... 2 turns out
    Slow jet... 55

Carburetor settings (continued)

1993 CR250R (continued)

5000 to 7499 feet (1500 to 2299 meters)

   19 to 40-degrees F (minus 6 to 4-degrees C)

Needle clip position	3rd groove
Main jet	175

   39 to 60-degrees F (3 to 15-degrees C)

Air screw	2-1/4 turns out
Slow jet	52
Needle clip position	3rd groove
Main jet	170

   59 to 80-degrees F (14 to 26-degrees C)

Air screw	2-3/4 turns out
Slow jet	52
Needle clip position	2nd or 3rd groove
Main jet	165

   79 to 100-degrees F (25 to 38-degrees C)

Air screw	3 turns out
Slow jet	50
Needle clip position	2nd or 3rd groove
Main jet	162

   99 to 120-degrees F (37 to 49-degrees C)

Air screw	3-1/4 turns out
Slow jet	50
Needle clip position	2nd groove
Main jet	158

7500 to 10,000 feet (2300 to 3000 meters)

   Minus 21 to 0-degrees F (minus 35 to minus 18-degrees C)

Air screw	1-3/4 turns out
Slow jet	58
Needle clip position	4th groove
Main jet	180

   Minus 1 to 20-degrees F (minus 17 to minus 7-degrees C)

Air screw	2 turns out
Slow jet	55
Needle clip position	4th groove
Main jet	175

   19 to 40-degrees F (minus 6 to 4-degrees C)

Air screw	2-1/4 turns out
Slow jet	52
Needle clip position	3rd groove
Main jet	170

   39 to 60-degrees F (3 to 15-degrees C)

Air screw	2-3/4 turns out
Slow jet	52
Needle clip position	2nd or 3rd groove
Main jet	168

   59 to 80-degrees F (14 to 26-degrees C)

Air screw	3 turns out
Slow jet	52
Needle clip position	2nd groove
Main jet	162

   79 to 100-degrees F (25 to 38-degrees C)

Air screw	3-1/4 turns out
Slow jet	52
Needle clip position	2nd groove
Main jet	162

   99 to 120-degrees F (37 to 49-degrees C)

Air screw	3-1/2 turns out
Slow jet	50
Needle clip position	2nd groove
Main jet	155

1998 CR250R

Sea level to 999 feet (299 meters)

   Minus 21 to 0-degrees F (minus 35 to minus 18-degrees C)

Air screw	1 turn out
Slow jet	60
Needle clip position	4th groove
Main jet	192

Minus 1 to 20-degrees F (minus 17 to minus 7-degrees C)
   Air screw .... 1 turn out
   Slow jet.. 60
   Needle clip position.. 4th groove
   Main jet.. 185
19 to 40-degrees F (minus 6 to 4-degrees C)
   Air screw .... 1-1/2 turns out
   Slow jet.. 58
   Needle clip position.. 4th groove
   Main jet.. 182
39 to 60-degrees F (3 to 15-degrees C)
   Air screw .... 1-3/4 turns out
   Slow jet.. 55
   Needle clip position.. 3rd groove
   Main jet.. 178
59 to 80-degrees F (14 to 26-degrees C)*
   Air screw .... 2 turns out
   Slow jet.. 55
   Needle clip position.. 3rd groove
   Main jet.. 175
79 to 100-degrees F (25 to 38-degrees C)
   Air screw .... 2-1/2 turns out
   Slow jet.. 55
   Needle clip position.. 3rd groove
   Main jet.. 170
99 to 120-degrees F (37 to 49-degrees C)
   Air screw .... 2-1/2 turns out
   Slow jet.. 52
   Needle clip position.. 2nd or 3rd groove
   Main jet.. 168
1000 to 2499 feet (300 to 749 meters)
  Minus 21 to 0-degrees F (minus 35 to minus 18-degrees C)
   Air screw .... turn out
   Slow jet.. 60
   Needle clip position.. 4th groove
   Main jet.. 190
  Minus 1 to 20-degrees F (minus 17 to minus 7-degrees C)
   Air screw .... 1-1/4 turn out
   Slow jet.. 58
   Needle clip position.. 4th groove
   Main jet.. 185
  19 to 40-degrees F (minus 6 to 4-degrees C)
   Air screw .... 1-1/2 turns out
   Slow jet.. 58
   Needle clip position.. 4th groove
   Main jet.. 180
  39 to 60-degrees F (3 to 15-degrees C)
   Air screw .... 2 turns out
   Slow jet.. 55
   Needle clip position.. 3rd groove
   Main jet.. 178
  59 to 80-degrees F (14 to 26-degrees C)
   Air screw .... 2 turns out
   Slow jet.. 55
   Needle clip position.. 3rd groove
   Main jet.. 172
  79 to 100-degrees F (25 to 38-degrees C)
   Air screw .... 2-1/2 turns out
   Slow jet.. 55
   Needle clip position.. 3rd groove
   Main jet.. 168
  99 to 120-degrees F (37 to 49-degrees C)
   Air screw .... 3 turns out
   Slow jet.. 52
   Needle clip position.. 2nd or 3rd groove
   Main jet.. 165

Standard jetting

Carburetor settings (continued)

1998 CR250R (continued)

2500 to 4999 feet (750 to 1499 meters)

Minus 21 to 0-degrees F (minus 35 to minus 18-degrees C)

Air screw	1 turn out
Slow jet	60
Needle clip position	4th groove
Main jet	185

Minus 1 to 20-degrees F (minus 17 to minus 7-degrees C)

Air screw	1-1/2 turn out
Slow jet	58
Needle clip position	4th groove
Main jet	182

19 to 40-degrees F (minus 6 to 4-degrees C)

Air screw	2 turns out
Slow jet	58
Needle clip position	4th groove
Main jet	180

39 to 60-degrees F (3 to 15-degrees C)

Air screw	2-1/4 turns out
Slow jet	55
Needle clip position	3rd groove
Main jet	175

59 to 80-degrees F (14 to 26-degrees C)

Air screw	3-1/2 turns out
Slow jet	55
Needle clip position	3rd groove
Main jet	170

79 to 100-degrees F (25 to 38-degrees C)

Air screw	2-3/4 turns out
Slow jet	52
Needle clip position	2nd or 3rd groove
Main jet	168

99 to 120-degrees F (37 to 49-degrees C)

Air screw	3 turns out
Slow jet	52
Needle clip position	2nd or 3rd groove
Main jet	162

5000 to 7499 feet (1500 to 2299 meters)

Minus 21 to 0-degrees F (minus 35 to minus 18-degrees C)

Air screw	1-1/2 turns out
Slow jet	58
Needle clip position	4th groove
Main jet	182

Minus 1 to 20-degrees F (minus 17 to minus 7-degrees C)

Air screw	2 turns out
Slow jet	55
Needle clip position	4th groove
Main jet	178

19 to 40-degrees F (minus 6 to 4-degrees C)

Air screw	2-1/4 turns out
Slow jet	55
Needle clip position	3rd groove
Main jet	175

39 to 60-degrees F (3 to 15-degrees C)

Air screw	2-1/2 turns out
Slow jet	52
Needle clip position	3rd groove
Main jet	170

59 to 80-degrees F (14 to 26-degrees C)

Air screw	3 turns out
Slow jet	52
Needle clip position	2nd or 3rd groove
Main jet	165

79 to 100-degrees F (25 to 38-degrees C)

Air screw	3-1/4 turns out
Slow jet	50
Needle clip position	2nd or 3rd groove
Main jet	162

99 to 120-degrees F (37 to 49-degrees C)
Air screw .... 3-1/2 turns out
Slow jet.. 50
Needle clip position.. 2nd groove
Main jet.. 158
7500 to 10,000 feet (2300 to 3000 meters)
Minus 21 to 0-degrees F (minus 35 to minus 18-degrees C)
Air screw .... 2 turns out
Slow jet.. 58
Needle clip position.. 4th groove
Main jet.. 180
Minus 1 to 20-degrees F (minus 17 to minus 7-degrees C)
Air screw .... 2-1/4 turns out
Slow jet.. 55
Needle clip position.. 4th groove
Main jet.. 175
19 to 40-degrees F (minus 6 to 4-degrees C)
Air screw .... 2-1/2 turns out
Slow jet.. 52
Needle clip position.. 3rd groove
Main jet.. 170
39 to 60-degrees F (3 to 15-degrees C)
Air screw .... 3 turns out
Slow jet.. 52
Needle clip position.. 2nd or 3rd groove
Main jet.. 168
59 to 80-degrees F (14 to 26-degrees C)
Air screw .... 3-1/4 turns out
Slow jet.. 52
Needle clip position.. 2nd groove
Main jet.. 162
79 to 100-degrees F (25 to 38-degrees C)
Air screw .... 3-1/2 turns out
Slow jet.. 52
Needle clip position.. 2nd groove
Main jet.. 162
99 to 120-degrees F (37 to 49-degrees C)
Air screw .... 3-3/4 turns out
Slow jet.. 50
Needle clip position.. 2nd groove
Main jet.. 155

1999 CR250R
Sea level to 999 feet (299 meters)
Minus 21 to 0-degrees F (minus 35 to minus 18-degrees C)
Air screw .... 1 turn out
Slow jet.. 42
Needle clip position.. 4th groove
Main jet.. 205
Minus 1 to 20-degrees F (minus 17 to minus 7-degrees C)
Air screw .... 1 turn out
Slow jet.. 42
Needle clip position.. 4th groove
Main jet.. 202
19 to 40-degrees F (minus 6 to 4-degrees C)
Air screw .... 1-1/2 turns out
Slow jet.. 42
Needle clip position.. 4th groove
Main jet.. 198
39 to 60-degrees F (3 to 15-degrees C)
Air screw .... 1-3/4 turns out
Slow jet.. 42
Needle clip position.. 3rd groove
Main jet.. 195
59 to 80-degrees F (14 to 26-degrees C)*
Air screw .... 2 turns out
Slow jet.. 42
Needle clip position.. 3rd groove
Main jet.. 190

* Standard jetting

Carburetor settings (continued)

1999 CR250R (continued)

Sea level to 999 feet (299 meters)

79 to 100-degrees F (25 to 38-degrees C)

Air screw	2-1/2 turns out
Slow jet	42
Needle clip position	3rd groove
Main jet	185

99 to 120-degrees F (37 to 49-degrees C)

Air screw	2-3/4 turns out
Slow jet	52
Needle clip position	2nd or 3rd groove
Main jet	182

1000 to 2499 feet (300 to 749 meters)

Minus 21 to 0-degrees F (minus 35 to minus 18-degrees C)

Air screw	1 turn out
Slow jet	42
Needle clip position	4th groove
Main jet	202

Minus 1 to 20-degrees F (minus 17 to minus 7-degrees C)

Air screw	1-1/4 turn out
Slow jet	42
Needle clip position	4th groove
Main jet	200

19 to 40-degrees F (minus 6 to 4-degrees C)

Air screw	1-1/2 turns out
Slow jet	42
Needle clip position	4th groove
Main jet	195

39 to 60-degrees F (3 to 15-degrees C)

Air screw	2 turns out
Slow jet	42
Needle clip position	3rd groove
Main jet	190

59 to 80-degrees F (14 to 26-degrees C)

Air screw	2 turns out
Slow jet	42
Needle clip position	3rd groove
Main jet	188

79 to 100-degrees F (25 to 38-degrees C)

Air screw	2-1/2 turns out
Slow jet	42
Needle clip position	3rd groove
Main jet	182

99 to 120-degrees F (37 to 49-degrees C)

Air screw	3 turns out
Slow jet	42
Needle clip position	2nd or 3rd groove
Main jet	178

2500 to 4999 feet (750 to 1499 meters)

Minus 21 to 0-degrees F (minus 35 to minus 18-degrees C)

Air screw	1 turn out
Slow jet	42
Needle clip position	4th groove
Main jet	200

Minus 1 to 20-degrees F (minus 17 to minus 7-degrees C)

Air screw	1-1/2 turn out
Slow jet	42
Needle clip position	4th groove
Main jet	195

19 to 40-degrees F (minus 6 to 4-degrees C)

Air screw	2 turns out
Slow jet	42
Needle clip position	4th groove
Main jet	192

39 to 60-degrees F (3 to 15-degrees C)

Air screw	2-1/4 turns out
Slow jet	42
Needle clip position	3rd groove
Main jet	188

59 to 80-degrees F (14 to 26-degrees C)
 Air screw .... 3-1/2 turns out
 Slow jet.. 42
 Needle clip position... 3rd groove
 Main jet... 185

79 to 100-degrees F (25 to 38-degrees C)
 Air screw .... 2-3/4 turns out
 Slow jet.. 42
 Needle clip position... 2nd or 3rd groove
 Main jet... 180

99 to 120-degrees F (37 to 49-degrees C)
 Air screw .... 3 turns out
 Slow jet.. 42
 Needle clip position... 2nd or 3rd groove
 Main jet... 175

5000 to 7499 feet (1500 to 2299 meters)
 Minus 21 to 0-degrees F (minus 35 to minus 18-degrees C)
  Air screw .... 1-1/2 turns out
  Slow jet... 42
  Needle clip position.. 4th groove
  Main jet.. 198

 Minus 1 to 20-degrees F (minus 17 to minus 7-degrees C)
  Air screw .... 2 turns out
  Slow jet... 42
  Needle clip position.. 4th groove
  Main jet.. 192

 19 to 40-degrees F (minus 6 to 4-degrees C)
  Air screw .... 2-1/4 turns out
  Slow jet... 42
  Needle clip position.. 3rd groove
  Main jet.. 188

 39 to 60-degrees F (3 to 15-degrees C)
  Air screw .... 2-1/2 turns out
  Slow jet... 42
  Needle clip position.. 3rd groove
  Main jet.. 185

 59 to 80-degrees F (14 to 26-degrees C)
  Air screw .... 3 turns out
  Slow jet... 42
  Needle clip position.. 2nd or 3rd groove
  Main jet.. 180

 79 to 100-degrees F (25 to 38-degrees C)
  Air screw .... 3-1/4 turns out
  Slow jet... 42
  Needle clip position.. 2nd or 3rd groove
  Main jet.. 175

 99 to 120-degrees F (37 to 49-degrees C)
  Air screw .... 3-1/2 turns out
  Slow jet... 42
  Needle clip position.. 2nd groove
  Main jet.. 172

7500 to 10,000 feet (2300 to 3000 meters)
 Minus 21 to 0-degrees F (minus 35 to minus 18-degrees C)
  Air screw .... 2 turns out
  Slow jet... 42
  Needle clip position.. 4th groove
  Main jet.. 195

 Minus 1 to 20-degrees F (minus 17 to minus 7-degrees C)
  Air screw .... 2-1/4 turns out
  Slow jet... 42
  Needle clip position.. 4th groove
  Main jet.. 190

 19 to 40-degrees F (minus 6 to 4-degrees C)
  Air screw .... 2-1/2 turns out
  Slow jet... 42
  Needle clip position.. 3rd groove
  Main jet.. 185

 39 to 60-degrees F (3 to 15-degrees C)
  Air screw .... 3 turns out
  Slow jet... 42

Carburetor settings (continued)

1999 CR250R (continued)

7500 to 10,000 feet (2300 to 3000 meters)

    39 to 60-degrees F (3 to 15-degrees C)

Needle clip position	2nd or 3rd groove
Main jet	180

    59 to 80-degrees F (14 to 26-degrees C)

Air screw	3-1/4 turns out
Slow jet	42
Needle clip position	2nd groove
Main jet	178

    79 to 100-degrees F (25 to 38-degrees C)

Air screw	3-1/2 turns out
Slow jet	42
Needle clip position	2nd groove
Main jet	172

    99 to 120-degrees F (37 to 49-degrees C)

Air screw	3-3/4 turns out
Slow jet	42
Needle clip position	2nd groove
Main jet	170

2000 CR250R

Sea level to 999 feet (299 meters)

    Minus 21 to 0-degrees F (minus 35 to minus 18-degrees C)

Air screw	1-1/4 turns out
Slow jet	50
Needle clip position	4th groove
Main jet	195

    Minus 1 to 20-degrees F (minus 17 to minus 7-degrees C)

Air screw	1-1/2 turns out
Slow jet	50
Needle clip position	4th groove
Main jet	187

    19 to 40-degrees F (minus 6 to 4-degrees C)

Air screw	1 turn out
Slow jet	48
Needle clip position	4th groove
Main jet	188

    39 to 60-degrees F (3 to 15-degrees C)

Air screw	1-1/4 turns out
Slow jet	48
Needle clip position	3rd groove
Main jet	185

    59 to 80-degrees F (14 to 26-degrees C)*

Air screw	1-1/2 turns out
Slow jet	48
Needle clip position	3rd groove
Main jet	180

    79 to 100-degrees F (25 to 38-degrees C)

Air screw	2 turns out
Slow jet	48
Needle clip position	3rd groove
Main jet	175

    99 to 120-degrees F (37 to 49-degrees C)

Air screw	2-1/4 turns out
Slow jet	48
Needle clip position	2nd or 3rd groove
Main jet	172

1000 to 2499 feet (300 to 749 meters)

    Minus 21 to 0-degrees F (minus 35 to minus 18-degrees C)

Air screw	1-1/4 turns out
Slow jet	50
Needle clip position	4th groove
Main jet	187

    Minus 1 to 20-degrees F (minus 17 to minus 7-degrees C)

Air screw	1-1/2 turns out
Slow jet	50
Needle clip position	4th groove
Main jet	190

* Standard jetting

19 to 40-degrees F (minus 6 to 4-degrees C)

Air screw	1 turn out
Slow jet	48
Needle clip position	4th groove
Main jet	185

39 to 60-degrees F (3 to 15-degrees C)

Air screw	1-1/2 turns out
Slow jet	48
Needle clip position	3rd groove
Main jet	180

59 to 80-degrees F (14 to 26-degrees C)

Air screw	1-1/2 turns out
Slow jet	48
Needle clip position	3rd groove
Main jet	178

79 to 100-degrees F (25 to 38-degrees C)

Air screw	2 turns out
Slow jet	48
Needle clip position	3rd groove
Main jet	172

99 to 120-degrees F (37 to 49-degrees C)

Air screw	2-1/2 turns out
Slow jet	48
Needle clip position	2nd or 3rd groove
Main jet	168

2500 to 4999 feet (750 to 1499 meters)

Minus 21 to 0-degrees F (minus 35 to minus 18-degrees C)

Air screw	1-1/2 turns out
Slow jet	50
Needle clip position	4th groove
Main jet	190

Minus 1 to 20-degrees F (minus 17 to minus 7-degrees C)

Air screw	1 turn out
Slow jet	48
Needle clip position	4th groove
Main jet	185

19 to 40-degrees F (minus 6 to 4-degrees C)

Air screw	1-1/2 turns out
Slow jet	48
Needle clip position	4th groove
Main jet	182

39 to 60-degrees F (3 to 15-degrees C)

Air screw	1-3/4 turns out
Slow jet	48
Needle clip position	3rd groove
Main jet	178

59 to 80-degrees F (14 to 26-degrees C)

Air screw	2 turns out
Slow jet	48
Needle clip position	3rd groove
Main jet	175

79 to 100-degrees F (25 to 38-degrees C)

Air screw	2-1/4 turns out
Slow jet	48
Needle clip position	2nd or 3rd groove
Main jet	170

99 to 120-degrees F (37 to 49-degrees C)

Air screw	2-1/2 turns out
Slow jet	48
Needle clip position	2nd or 3rd groove
Main jet	162

5000 to 7499 feet (1500 to 2299 meters)

Minus 21 to 0-degrees F (minus 35 to minus 18-degrees C)

Air screw	1 turn out
Slow jet	48
Needle clip position	4th groove
Main jet	188

Minus 1 to 20-degrees F (minus 17 to minus 7-degrees C)

Air screw	1-1/2 turns out

Carburetor settings (continued)

2000 CR250R (continued)

5000 to 7499 feet (1500 to 2299 meters)

Minus 1 to 20-degrees F (minus 17 to minus 7-degrees C)
- Slow jet 48
- Needle clip position.. 4th groove
- Main jet.. 182

19 to 40-degrees F (minus 6 to 4-degrees C)
- Air screw .... 1-3/4 turns out
- Slow jet 48
- Needle clip position.. 3rd groove
- Main jet.. 175

39 to 60-degrees F (3 to 15-degrees C)
- Air screw .... 2 turns out
- Slow jet 48
- Needle clip position.. 3rd groove
- Main jet.. 175

59 to 80-degrees F (14 to 26-degrees C)
- Air screw .... 2-1/2 turns out
- Slow jet 48
- Needle clip position.. 2nd or 3rd groove
- Main jet.. 170

79 to 100-degrees F (25 to 38-degrees C)
- Air screw .... 2-3/4 turns out
- Slow jet 48
- Needle clip position.. 2nd or 3rd groove
- Main jet.. 165

99 to 120-degrees F (37 to 49-degrees C)
- Air screw .... 3 turns out
- Slow jet 48
- Needle clip position.. 2nd groove
- Main jet.. 162

7500 to 10,000 feet (2300 to 3000 meters)

Minus 21 to 0-degrees F (minus 35 to minus 18-degrees C)
- Air screw .... 1-1/2 turns out
- Slow jet 48
- Needle clip position.. 4th groove
- Main jet.. 185

Minus 1 to 20-degrees F (minus 17 to minus 7-degrees C)
- Air screw .... 1-3/4 turns out
- Slow jet 48
- Needle clip position.. 4th groove
- Main jet.. 180

19 to 40-degrees F (minus 6 to 4-degrees C)
- Air screw .... 2 turns out
- Slow jet 48
- Needle clip position.. 3rd groove
- Main jet.. 175

39 to 60-degrees F (3 to 15-degrees C)
- Air screw .... 2-1/2 turns out
- Slow jet 48
- Needle clip position.. 2nd or 3rd groove
- Main jet.. 170

59 to 80-degrees F (14 to 26-degrees C)
- Air screw .... 2-3/4 turns out
- Slow jet 48
- Needle clip position.. 2nd groove
- Main jet.. 168

79 to 100-degrees F (25 to 38-degrees C)
- Air screw .... 3 turns out
- Slow jet 48
- Needle clip position.. 2nd groove
- Main jet.. 162

99 to 120-degrees F (37 to 49-degrees C)
- Air screw .... 3-1/2 turns out
- Slow jet 45
- Needle clip position.. 2nd groove
- Main jet.. 160

2001 CR250R

Sea level to 999 feet (299 meters)

Minus 21 to 0-degrees F (minus 35 to minus 18-degrees C)

Air screw	1-1/4 turns out
Slow jet	37.5
Jet needle	6BEH1-73
Needle clip position	4th groove
Main jet	460

Minus 1 to 20-degrees F (minus 17 to minus 7-degrees C)

Air screw	1-1/2 turns out
Slow jet	37.5
Jet needle	6BEH1-73
Needle clip position	4th groove
Main jet	450

19 to 40-degrees F (minus 6 to 4-degrees C)

Air screw	1-1/4 turns out
Slow jet	35
Jet needle	6BEH2-73
Needle clip position	3rd groove
Main jet	440

39 to 60-degrees F (3 to 15-degrees C)

Air screw	1-1/2 turns out
Slow jet	35
Jet needle	6BEH1-73
Needle clip position	3rd groove
Main jet	430

59 to 80-degrees F (14 to 26-degrees C)*

Air screw	1-3/4 turns out
Slow jet	35
Jet needle	6BEH1-73
Needle clip position	3rd groove
Main jet	420

79 to 100-degrees F (25 to 38-degrees C)

Air screw	2 turns out
Slow jet	35
Jet needle	6BEH2-73
Needle clip position	2nd groove
Main jet	410

99 to 120-degrees F (37 to 49-degrees C)

Air screw	2-1/4 turns out
Slow jet	35
Jet needle	6BEH1-73
Needle clip position	2nd groove
Main jet	400

1000 to 2499 feet (300 to 749 meters)

Minus 21 to 0-degrees F (minus 35 to minus 18-degrees C)

Air screw	1 turn out
Slow jet	35
Jet needle	6BEH1-73
Needle clip position	4th groove
Main jet	450

Minus 1 to 20-degrees F (minus 17 to minus 7-degrees C)

Air screw	1-1/2 turns out
Slow jet	35
Jet needle	6BEH2-73
Needle clip position	3rd groove
Main jet	440

19 to 40-degrees F (minus 6 to 4-degrees C)

Air screw	1-1/2 turns out
Slow jet	35
Jet needle	6BEH1-73
Needle clip position	3rd groove
Main jet	430

39 to 60-degrees F (3 to 15-degrees C)

Air screw	1-3/4 turns out
Slow jet	35
Jet needle	6BEH1-73
Needle clip position	3rd groove
Main jet	420

Standard jetting

Carburetor settings (continued)

2001 CR250R (continued)

1000 to 2499 feet (300 to 749 meters)

59 to 80-degrees F (14 to 26-degrees C)

Air screw	2 turns out
Slow jet	35
Jet needle	6BEH2-73
Needle clip position	2nd groove
Main jet	410

79 to 100-degrees F (25 to 38-degrees C)

Air screw	2-1/4 turns out
Slow jet	35
Jet needle	6BEH2-73
Needle clip position	2nd groove
Main jet	400

99 to 120-degrees F (37 to 49-degrees C)

Air screw	2-1/2 turns out
Slow jet	35
Jet needle	6BEH1-73
Needle clip position	2nd groove
Main jet	390

2500 to 4999 feet (750 to 1499 meters)

Minus 21 to 0-degrees F (minus 35 to minus 18-degrees C)

Air screw	1-1/4 turns out
Slow jet	35
Jet needle	6BEH2-73
Needle clip position	3rd groove
Main jet	440

Minus 1 to 20-degrees F (minus 17 to minus 7-degrees C)

Air screw	1-1/2 turns out
Slow jet	35
Jet needle	6BE1-73
Needle clip position	3rd groove
Main jet	430

19 to 40-degrees F (minus 6 to 4-degrees C)

Air screw	1-3/4 turns out
Slow jet	35
Jet needle	6BEH1-73
Needle clip position	3rd groove
Main jet	420

39 to 60-degrees F (3 to 15-degrees C)

Air screw	2 turns out
Slow jet	35
Jet needle	6BEH22-73
Needle clip position	2nd groove
Main jet	410

59 to 80-degrees F (14 to 26-degrees C)

Air screw	2-1/4 turns out
Slow jet	35
Jet needle	6BEH2-73
Needle clip position	2nd groove
Main jet	400

79 to 100-degrees F (25 to 38-degrees C)

Air screw	2-1/2 turns out
Slow jet	35
Jet needle	6BEH1-73
Needle clip position	2nd groove
Main jet	390

99 to 120-degrees F (37 to 49-degrees C)

Air screw	2-3/4 turns out
Slow jet	35
Jet needle	6BEH1-73
Needle clip position	2nd groove
Main jet	380

5000 to 7499 feet (1500 to 2299 meters)

Minus 21 to 0-degrees F (minus 35 to minus 18-degrees C)

Air screw	1-1/2 turns out
Slow jet	35
Jet needle	6BEH1-73
Needle clip position	3rd groove
Main jet	430

Minus 1 to 20-degrees F (minus 17 to minus 7-degrees C)
    Air screw .... 1-3/4 turns out
    Slow jet... 35
    Jet needle... 6BEH1-73
    Needle clip position... 3rd groove
    Main jet.. 420
19 to 40-degrees F (minus 6 to 4-degrees C)
    Air screw .... 2 turns out
    Slow jet... 35
    Jet needle... 6BEH2-73
    Needle clip position... 2nd groove
    Main jet.. 410
39 to 60-degrees F (3 to 15-degrees C)
    Air screw .... 2-1/4 turns out
    Slow jet... 35
    Jet needle... 6BEH2-73
    Needle clip position... 2nd groove
    Main jet.. 400
59 to 80-degrees F (14 to 26-degrees C)
    Air screw .... 2-1/2 turns out
    Slow jet... 35
    Jet needle... 6BEH1-73
    Needle clip position... 2nd groove
    Main jet.. 390
79 to 100-degrees F (25 to 38-degrees C)
    Air screw .... 2-3/4 turns out
    Slow jet... 35
    Jet needle... 6BEH1-73
    Needle clip position... 2nd groove
    Main jet.. 380
99 to 120-degrees F (37 to 49-degrees C)
    Air screw .... 3 turns out
    Slow jet... 35
    Jet needle... 6BEH2-73
    Needle clip position... 1st groove
    Main jet.. 370
7500 to 10,000 feet (2300 to 3000 meters)
  Minus 21 to 0-degrees F (minus 35 to minus 18-degrees C)
    Air screw .... 1-3/4 turns out
    Slow jet... 35
    Jet needle... 6BEH1-73
    Needle clip position... 3rd groove
    Main jet.. 420
  Minus 1 to 20-degrees F (minus 17 to minus 7-degrees C)
    Air screw .... 2 turns out
    Slow jet... 35
    Jet needle... 6BEH2-73
    Needle clip position... 2nd groove
    Main jet.. 410
  19 to 40-degrees F (minus 6 to 4-degrees C)
    Air screw .... 2-1/4 turns out
    Slow jet... 35
    Jet needle... 6BEH2-73
    Needle clip position... 2nd groove
    Main jet.. 400
  39 to 60-degrees F (3 to 15-degrees C)
    Air screw .... 2-1/2 turns out
    Slow jet... 35
    Jet needle... 6BEH1-73
    Needle clip position... 2nd groove
    Main jet.. 390
  59 to 80-degrees F (14 to 26-degrees C)
    Air screw .... 2-3/4 turns out
    Slow jet... 35
    Jet needle... 6BEH1-73
    Needle clip position... 2nd groove
    Main jet.. 380
  79 to 100-degrees F (25 to 38-degrees C)
    Air screw .... 2-1/2 turns out
    Slow jet... 32.5

Carburetor settings (continued)

2001 CR250R (continued)

7500 to 10,000 feet (2300 to 3000 meters)

79 to 100-degrees F (25 to 38-degrees C)

Jet needle	6BEH2-73
Needle clip position	1st groove
Main jet	370

99 to 120-degrees F (37 to 49-degrees C)

Air screw	2-3/4 turns out
Slow jet	32.5
Jet needle	6BEH2-73
Needle clip position	1st groove
Main jet	360

2002 CR250R

Sea level to 999 feet (299 meters)

Minus 21 to 0-degrees F (minus 35 to minus 18-degrees C)

Air screw	1
Slow jet	35
Needle clip position	3
Jet needle	6BEY30-72
Main jet	420

Minus 1 to 20-degrees F (minus 17 to minus 7-degrees C)

Air screw	1-1/4
Slow jet	35
Needle clip position	3
Jet needle	6BEY30-73
Main jet	410

19 to 40-degrees F (minus 6 to 4-degrees C)

Air screw	1-1/2
Slow jet	35
Needle clip position	2
Jet needle	6BEY31-73
Main jet	400

39 to 60-degrees F (3 to 15-degrees C)

Air screw	1-1/4
Slow jet	32.5
Needle clip position	2
Jet needle	6BEY31-73
Main jet	390

59 to 80-degrees F (14 to 26-degrees C)

Air screw	1-1/2
Slow jet	32.5
Needle clip position	2
Jet needle	6BEY30-74
Main jet	380

79 to 100-degrees F (25 to 38-degrees C)

Air screw	1-3/4
Slow jet	32.5
Needle clip position	2
Jet needle	6BEY31-74
Main jet	370

99 to 120-degrees F (37 to 49-degrees C)

Air screw	2
Slow jet	32.5
Needle clip position	2
Jet needle	6BEY31-75
Main jet	360

1000 to 2499 feet (300 to 749 meters)

Minus 21 to 0-degrees F (minus 35 to minus 18-degrees C)

Air screw	1-1/4
Slow jet	35
Needle clip position	3
Jet needle	6BEY30-73
Main jet	410

Minus 1 to 20-degrees F (minus 17 to minus 7-degrees C)

Air screw	1-1/2
Slow jet	35
Needle clip position	3
Jet needle	6BEY31-73
Main jet	400

19 to 40-degrees F (minus 6 to 4-degrees C)
  Air screw 1-1/4
  Slow jet 32.5
  Needle clip position 2
  Jet needle 6BEY30-74
  Main jet 390
39 to 60-degrees F (3 to 15-degrees C)
  Air screw 1-1/2
  Slow jet 32.5
  Needle clip position 2
  Jet needle 6BEY30-74
  Main jet 380
59 to 80-degrees F (14 to 26-degrees C)
  Air screw 1-3/4
  Slow jet 32.5
  Needle clip position 2
  Jet needle 6BEY31-74
  Main jet 370
79 to 100-degrees F (25 to 38-degrees C)
  Air screw 2
  Slow jet 32.5
  Needle clip position 2
  Jet needle 6BEY31-75
  Main jet 360
99 to 120-degrees F (37 to 49-degrees C)
  Air screw 2-1/4
  Slow jet 32.5
  Needle clip position 1
  Jet needle 6BEY30-75
  Main jet 350
2500 to 4999 feet (750 to 1499 meters)
  Minus 21 to 0-degrees F (minus 35 to minus 18-degrees C)
    Air screw 1-1/2
    Slow jet 35
    Needle clip position 3
    Jet needle 6BEY31-73
    Main jet 400
  Minus 1 to 20-degrees F (minus 17 to minus 7-degrees C)
    Air screw 1-1/4
    Slow jet 32.5
    Needle clip position 2
    Jet needle 6BEY30-74
    Main jet 390
  19 to 40-degrees F (minus 6 to 4-degrees C)
    Air screw 1-1/2
    Slow jet 32.5
    Needle clip position 2
    Jet needle 6BEY30-74
    Main jet 380
  39 to 60-degrees F (3 to 15-degrees C)
    Air screw 1-3/4
    Slow jet 32.5
    Needle clip position 2
    Jet needle 6BEY31-74
    Main jet 370
  59 to 80-degrees F (14 to 26-degrees C)
    Air screw 2
    Slow jet 32.5
    Needle clip position 2
    Jet needle 6BEY31-75
    Main jet 360
  79 to 100-degrees F (25 to 38-degrees C)
    Air screw 2-1/4
    Slow jet 32.5
    Needle clip position 1
    Jet needle 6BEY30-75
    Main jet 350
  99 to 120-degrees F (37 to 49-degrees C)
    Air screw 2-1/2
    Slow jet 32.5

Carburetor settings (continued)

2002 CR250R (continued)

2500 to 4999 feet (750 to 1499 meters)

  99 to 120-degrees F (37 to 49-degrees C)

Needle clip position	1
Jet needle	6BEY30-75
Main jet	340

5000 to 7499 feet (1500 to 2299 meters)

  Minus 21 to 0-degrees F (minus 35 to minus 18-degrees C)

Air screw	1-1/4
Slow jet	32.5
Needle clip position	2
Jet needle	6BEY30-74
Main jet	390

  Minus 1 to 20-degrees F (minus 17 to minus 7-degrees C)

Air screw	1-1/2
Slow jet	32.5
Needle clip position	2
Jet needle	6BEY30-74
Main jet	380

  19 to 40-degrees F (minus 6 to 4-degrees C)

Air screw	1-3/4
Slow jet	32.5
Needle clip position	2
Jet needle	6BEY31-74
Main jet	370

  39 to 60-degrees F (3 to 15-degrees C)

Air screw	2
Slow jet	32.5
Needle clip position	2
Jet needle	6BEY31-75
Main jet	360

  59 to 80-degrees F (14 to 26-degrees C)

Air screw	2-1/4
Slow jet	32.5
Needle clip position	1
Jet needle	6BEY30-75
Main jet	350

  79 to 100-degrees F (25 to 38-degrees C)

Air screw	2-1/2
Slow jet	32.5
Needle clip position	1
Jet needle	6BEY30-75
Main jet	340

  99 to 120-degrees F (37 to 49-degrees C)

Air screw	2-1/4
Slow jet	50
Needle clip position	1
Jet needle	6BEY31-76
Main jet	330

7500 to 10,000 feet (2300 to 3050 meters)

  Minus 21 to 0-degrees F (minus 35 to minus 18-degrees C)

Air screw	1-1/2
Slow jet	32.5
Needle clip position	2
Jet needle	6BEY30-74
Main jet	380

  Minus 1 to 20-degrees F (minus 17 to minus 7-degrees C)

Air screw	1-3/4
Slow jet	32.5
Needle clip position	2
Jet needle	6BEY31-74
Main jet	370

  19 to 40-degrees F (minus 6 to 4-degrees C)

Air screw	2
Slow jet	32.5
Needle clip position	2
Jet needle	6BEY31-75
Main jet	360

39 to 60-degrees F (3 to 15-degrees C)
- Air screw 2-1/4
- Slow jet 32.5
- Needle clip position 1
- Jet needle 6BEY30-75
- Main jet 350

59 to 80-degrees F (14 to 26-degrees C)
- Air screw 2-1/2
- Slow jet 32.5
- Needle clip position 1
- Jet needle 6BEY30-75
- Main jet 340

79 to 100-degrees F (25 to 38-degrees C)
- Air screw 2-1/4
- Slow jet 30
- Needle clip position 1
- Jet needle 6BEY31-76
- Main jet 330

99 to 120-degrees F (37 to 49-degrees C)
- Air screw 2-1/2
- Slow jet 30
- Needle clip position 1
- Jet needle 6BEY31-76
- Main jet 320

2003 CR250R

Sea level to 999 feet (299 meters)

Minus 21 to 0-degrees F (minus 35 to minus 18-degrees C)
- Air screw 1
- Slow jet 35
- Needle clip position 3
- Jet needle 6BHY38-71
- Main jet 460

Minus 1 to 20-degrees F (minus 17 to minus 7-degrees C)
- Air screw 1-1/4
- Slow jet 35
- Needle clip position 3
- Jet needle 6BHY38-72
- Main jet 450

19 to 40-degrees F (minus 6 to 4-degrees C)
- Air screw 1-1/2
- Slow jet 35
- Needle clip position 3
- Jet needle 6BHY39-72
- Main jet 440

39 to 60-degrees F (3 to 15-degrees C)
- Air screw 1-1/2
- Slow jet 32.5
- Needle clip position 2
- Jet needle 6BHY38-73
- Main jet 430

59 to 80-degrees F (14 to 26-degrees C)
- Air screw 1-1/2
- Slow jet 30
- Needle clip position 2
- Jet needle 6BHY38-73
- Main jet 420

79 to 100-degrees F (25 to 38-degrees C)
- Air screw 1-3/4
- Slow jet 30
- Needle clip position 2
- Jet needle 6BHY38-73
- Main jet 410

99 to 120-degrees F (37 to 49-degrees C)
- Air screw 2
- Slow jet 30
- Needle clip position 2
- Jet needle 6BHY38-74
- Main jet 400

Carburetor settings (continued)

2003 CR250R (continued)

1000 to 2499 feet (300 to 749 meters)

Minus 21 to 0-degrees F (minus 35 to minus 18-degrees C)

Air screw	1-1/4
Slow jet	35
Needle clip position	3
Jet needle	6BHY38-72
Main jet	450

Minus 1 to 20-degrees F (minus 17 to minus 7-degrees C)

Air screw	1-1/2
Slow jet	35
Needle clip position	3
Jet needle	6BHY39-72
Main jet	440

19 to 40-degrees F (minus 6 to 4-degrees C)

Air screw	1-1/4
Slow jet	32.5
Needle clip position	2
Jet needle	6BHY38-73
Main jet	430

39 to 60-degrees F (3 to 15-degrees C)

Air screw	1-1/2
Slow jet	30
Needle clip position	2
Jet needle	6BHY38-73
Main jet	420

59 to 80-degrees F (14 to 26-degrees C)

Air screw	1-3/4
Slow jet	30
Needle clip position	2
Jet needle	6BHY38-73
Main jet	410

79 to 100-degrees F (25 to 38-degrees C)

Air screw	2
Slow jet	30
Needle clip position	2
Jet needle	6BHY38-74
Main jet	400

99 to 120-degrees F (37 to 49-degrees C)

Air screw	2-1/4
Slow jet	30
Needle clip position	1
Jet needle	6BHY38-74
Main jet	390

2500 to 4999 feet (750 to 1499 meters)

Minus 21 to 0-degrees F (minus 35 to minus 18-degrees C)

Air screw	1-1/2
Slow jet	35
Needle clip position	3
Jet needle	6BHY39-72
Main jet	440

Minus 1 to 20-degrees F (minus 17 to minus 7-degrees C)

Air screw	1-1/2
Slow jet	32.5
Needle clip position	2
Jet needle	6BHY38-73
Main jet	430

19 to 40-degrees F (minus 6 to 4-degrees C)

Air screw	1-1/2
Slow jet	30
Needle clip position	2
Jet needle	6BHY38-73
Main jet	420

39 to 60-degrees F (3 to 15-degrees C)

Air screw	1-3/4
Slow jet	30
Needle clip position	2

Jet needle	6BHY38-73
Main jet	410
59 to 80-degrees F (14 to 26-degrees C)	
Air screw	2
Slow jet	30
Needle clip position	2
Jet needle	6BHY38-74
Main jet	400
79 to 100-degrees F (25 to 38-degrees C)	
Air screw	2-1/4
Slow jet	30
Needle clip position	1
Jet needle	6BHY38-74
Main jet	390
99 to 120-degrees F (37 to 49-degrees C)	
Air screw	2-1/2
Slow jet	30
Needle clip position	1
Jet needle	6BHY38-74
Main jet	380
5000 to 7499 feet (1500 to 2299 meters)	
Minus 21 to 0-degrees F (minus 35 to minus 18-degrees C)	
Air screw	1-1/2
Slow jet	32.5
Needle clip position	2
Jet needle	6BHY38-73
Main jet	430
Minus 1 to 20-degrees F (minus 17 to minus 7-degrees C)	
Air screw	1-1/2
Slow jet	30
Needle clip position	2
Jet needle	6BHY38-73
Main jet	420
19 to 40-degrees F (minus 6 to 4-degrees C)	
Air screw	1-3/4
Slow jet	30
Needle clip position	2
Jet needle	6BHY38-73
Main jet	410
39 to 60-degrees F (3 to 15-degrees C)	
Air screw	2
Slow jet	30
Needle clip position	2
Jet needle	6BHY38-74
Main jet	400
59 to 80-degrees F (14 to 26-degrees C)	
Air screw	2-1/4
Slow jet	30
Needle clip position	1
Jet needle	6BHY38-74
Main jet	390
79 to 100-degrees F (25 to 38-degrees C)	
Air screw	2-1/2
Slow jet	30
Needle clip position	1
Jet needle	6BHY38-74
Main jet	380
99 to 120-degrees F (37 to 49-degrees C)	
Air screw	2-1/4
Slow jet	27.5
Needle clip position	1
Jet needle	6BHY39-75
Main jet	370
7500 to 10,000 feet (2300 to 3000 meters)	
Minus 21 to 0-degrees F (minus 35 to minus 18-degrees C)	
Air screw	1-1/2
Slow jet	30
Needle clip position	2
Jet needle	6BHY38-73
Main jet	420

Carburetor settings (continued)

2003 CR250R (continued)

7500 to 10,000 feet (2300 to 3000 meters)

Minus 1 to 20-degrees F (minus 17 to minus 7-degrees C)

Air screw	1-3/4
Slow jet	30
Needle clip position	2
Jet needle	6BHY38-73
Main jet	410

19 to 40-degrees F (minus 6 to 4-degrees C)

Air screw	2
Slow jet	30
Needle clip position	2
Jet needle	6BHY38-74
Main jet	400

39 to 60-degrees F (3 to 15-degrees C)

Air screw	2-1/4
Slow jet	30
Needle clip position	1
Jet needle	6BHY38-74
Main jet	390

59 to 80-degrees F (14 to 26-degrees C)

Air screw	2-1/2
Slow jet	30
Needle clip position	1
Jet needle	6BHY38-74
Main jet	380

79 to 100-degrees F (25 to 38-degrees C)

Air screw	2-1/4
Slow jet	27.5
Needle clip position	1
Jet needle	6BHY39-75
Main jet	370

99 to 120-degrees F (37 to 49-degrees C)

Air screw	2-1/2
Slow jet	27.5
Needle clip position	1
Jet needle	6BHY39-75
Main jet	360

2004 CR250R

Sea level to 999 feet (299 meters)

Minus 21 to 0-degrees F (minus 35 to minus 18-degrees C)

Air screw	1
Slow jet	35
Needle clip position	3
Jet needle	6CHY12-81
Main jet	460

Minus 1 to 20-degrees F (minus 17 to minus 7-degrees C)

Air screw	1-1/4
Slow jet	35
Needle clip position	3
Jet needle	6CHY12-82
Main jet	450

19 to 40-degrees F (minus 6 to 4-degrees C)

Air screw	1-1/2
Slow jet	35
Needle clip position	2
Jet needle	6CHY13-82
Main jet	440

39 to 60-degrees F (3 to 15-degrees C)

Air screw	1-1/4
Slow jet	32.5
Needle clip position	2
Jet needle	6CHY12-82
Main jet	430

59 to 80-degrees F (14 to 26-degrees C)

Air screw	1-1/2
Slow jet	32.5
Needle clip position	2

Jet needle	6CHY12-82
Main jet	420

79 to 100-degrees F (25 to 38-degrees C)

Air screw	1-1/2
Slow jet	30
Needle clip position	2
Jet needle	6CHY12-82
Main jet	420

99 to 120-degrees F (37 to 49-degrees C)

Air screw	1-3/4
Slow jet	30
Needle clip position	2
Jet needle	6CHY12-83
Main jet	410

1000 to 2499 feet (300 to 749 meters)

Minus 21 to 0-degrees F (minus 35 to minus 18-degrees C)

Air screw	1-1/4
Slow jet	35
Needle clip position	3
Jet needle	6CHY12-82
Main jet	450

Minus 1 to 20-degrees F (minus 17 to minus 7-degrees C)

Air screw	1-1/2
Slow jet	35
Needle clip position	2
Jet needle	6CHY13-82
Main jet	440

19 to 40-degrees F (minus 6 to 4-degrees C)

Air screw	1-1/4
Slow jet	32.5
Needle clip position	2
Jet needle	6CHY12-92
Main jet	430

39 to 60-degrees F (3 to 15-degrees C)

Air screw	1-1/2
Slow jet	32.5
Needle clip position	2
Jet needle	6CHY12-82
Main jet	420

59 to 80-degrees F (14 to 26-degrees C)

Air screw	1-1/2
Slow jet	30
Needle clip position	2
Jet needle	6CHY12-82
Main jet	420

79 to 100-degrees F (25 to 38-degrees C)

Air screw	1-3/4
Slow jet	30
Needle clip position	2
Jet needle	6CHY12-83
Main jet	410

99 to 120-degrees F (37 to 49-degrees C)

Air screw	2
Slow jet	30
Needle clip position	1
Jet needle	6CHY13-82
Main jet	400

2500 to 4999 feet (750 to 1499 meters)

Minus 21 to 0-degrees F (minus 35 to minus 18-degrees C)

Air screw	1-1/2
Slow jet	35
Needle clip position	2
Jet needle	6CHY113-82
Main jet	440

Minus 1 to 20-degrees F (minus 17 to minus 7-degrees C)

Air screw	1-1/4
Slow jet	32.5
Needle clip position	2
Jet needle	6CHY12-82
Main jet	430

Carburetor settings (continued)

2004 CR250R (continued)
2500 to 4999 feet (750 to 1499 meters)

19 to 40-degrees F (minus 6 to 4-degrees C)
- Air screw.. 1-1/2
- Slow jet... 32.5
- Needle clip position 2
- Jet needle.. 6CHY12-82
- Main jet... 420

39 to 60-degrees F (3 to 15-degrees C)
- Air screw.. 1-1/2
- Slow jet... 30
- Needle clip position 2
- Jet needle.. 6CHY12-82
- Main jet... 420

59 to 80-degrees F (14 to 26-degrees C)
- Air screw.. 1-3/4
- Slow jet... 30
- Needle clip position 2
- Jet needle.. 6CHY12-83
- Main jet... 410

79 to 100-degrees F (25 to 38-degrees C)
- Air screw.. 2
- Slow jet... 30
- Needle clip position 1
- Jet needle.. 6CHY13-82
- Main jet... 400

99 to 120-degrees F (37 to 49-degrees C)
- Air screw.. 2-1/4
- Slow jet... 30
- Needle clip position 1
- Jet needle.. 6CHY13-83
- Main jet... 390

5000 to 7499 feet (1500 to 2299 meters)

Minus 21 to 0-degrees F (minus 35 to minus 18-degrees C)
- Air screw.. 1-1/4
- Slow jet... 32.5
- Needle clip position 2
- Jet needle.. 6CHY12-82
- Main jet... 430

Minus 1 to 20-degrees F (minus 17 to minus 7-degrees C)
- Air screw.. 1-1/2
- Slow jet... 32.5
- Needle clip position 2
- Jet needle.. 6CHY12-82
- Main jet... 420

19 to 40-degrees F (minus 6 to 4-degrees C)
- Air screw.. 1-1/2
- Slow jet... 30
- Needle clip position 2
- Jet needle.. 6CHY12-82
- Main jet... 420

39 to 60-degrees F (3 to 15-degrees C)
- Air screw.. 1-3/4
- Slow jet... 30
- Needle clip position 2
- Jet needle.. 6CHY12-83
- Main jet... 410

59 to 80-degrees F (14 to 26-degrees C)
- Air screw.. 2
- Slow jet... 30
- Needle clip position 1
- Jet needle.. 6CHY13-82
- Main jet... 400

79 to 100-degrees F (25 to 38-degrees C)
- Air screw.. 2-1/4
- Slow jet... 30
- Needle clip position 1
- Jet needle.. 6CHY13-83
- Main jet... 390

99 to 120-degrees F (37 to 49-degrees C)
Air screw.. 2
Slow jet... 27.5
Needle clip position.. 1
Jet needle.. 6CHY12-82
Main jet... 370

7500 to 10,000 feet (2300 to 3050 meters)
Minus 21 to 0-degrees F (minus 35 to minus 18-degrees C)
Air screw.. 1-1/2
Slow jet... 32.5
Needle clip position.. 2
Jet needle.. 6CHY12-82
Main jet... 420
Minus 1 to 20-degrees F (minus 17 to minus 7-degrees C)
Air screw.. 1-3/4
Slow jet... 30
Needle clip position.. 2
Jet needle.. 6CHY12-82
Main jet... 420
19 to 40-degrees F (minus 6 to 4-degrees C)
Air screw.. 1-3/4
Slow jet... 30
Needle clip position.. 2
Jet needle.. 6CHY12-83
Main jet... 410
39 to 60-degrees F (3 to 15-degrees C)
Air screw.. 2
Slow jet... 30
Needle clip position.. 1
Jet needle.. 6CHY13-82
Main jet... 400
59 to 80-degrees F (14 to 26-degrees C)
Air screw.. 2-1/4
Slow jet... 30
Needle clip position.. 1
Jet needle.. 6CHY13-83
Main jet... 390
79 to 100-degrees F (25 to 38-degrees C)
Air screw.. 2
Slow jet... 27.5
Needle clip position.. 1
Jet needle.. 6CHY12-82
Main jet... 380
99 to 120-degrees F (37 to 49-degrees C)
Air screw.. 2-1/4
Slow jet... 27.5
Needle clip position.. 1
Jet needle.. 6CHY12-83
Main jet... 370

2005 and later CR250R

Sea level to 999 feet (299 meters)
Minus 21 to 0-degrees F (minus 35 to minus 18-degrees C)
Air screw.. 2
Slow jet... 45
Needle clip position.. 4
Jet needle.. 6DGY26-64
Main jet... 460
Minus 1 to 20-degrees F (minus 17 to minus 7-degrees C)
Air screw.. 1-3/4
Slow jet... 42.5
Needle clip position.. 4
Jet needle.. 6DGY26-65
Main jet... 450
19 to 40-degrees F (minus 6 to 4-degrees C)
Air screw.. 2
Slow jet... 42.5
Needle clip position.. 3
Jet needle.. 6DGY27-65
Main jet... 440

Carburetor settings (continued)

2005 and later CR250R (continued)

Sea level to 999 feet (299 meters)

  39 to 60-degrees F (3 to 15-degrees C)

Air screw	2
Slow jet	42.5
Needle clip position	3
Jet needle	6DGY27-65
Main jet	440

  59 to 80-degrees F (14 to 26-degrees C)

Air screw	2
Slow jet	40
Needle clip position	3
Jet needle	6DGY26-65
Main jet	420

  79 to 100-degrees F (25 to 38-degrees C)

Air screw	2
Slow jet	40
Needle clip position	3
Jet needle	6DGY26-65
Main jet	410

  99 to 120-degrees F (37 to 49-degrees C)

Air screw	2
Slow jet	37.5
Needle clip position	3
Jet needle	6DGY26-66
Main jet	400

1000 to 2499 feet (300 to 749 meters)

  Minus 21 to 0-degrees F (minus 35 to minus 18-degrees C)

Air screw	1-3/4
Slow jet	42.5
Needle clip position	4
Jet needle	6DGY26-65
Main jet	450

  Minus 1 to 20-degrees F (minus 17 to minus 7-degrees C)

Air screw	2
Slow jet	42.5
Needle clip position	3
Jet needle	6DGY27-65
Main jet	440

  19 to 40-degrees F (minus 6 to 4-degrees C)

Air screw	1-3/4
Slow jet	40
Needle clip position	3
Jet needle	6DGY26-65
Main jet	430

  39 to 60-degrees F (3 to 15-degrees C)

Air screw	2
Slow jet	40
Needle clip position	3
Jet needle	6DGY26-65
Main jet	420

  59 to 80-degrees F (14 to 26-degrees C)

Air screw	2
Slow jet	40
Needle clip position	3
Jet needle	6DGY26-65
Main jet	410

  79 to 100-degrees F (25 to 38-degrees C)

Air screw	2
Slow jet	37.5
Needle clip position	3
Jet needle	6DGY26-66
Main jet	400

  99 to 120-degrees F (37 to 49-degrees C)

Air screw	2-1/4
Slow jet	37.5
Needle clip position	2
Jet needle	6DGY27-66
Main jet	390

2500 to 4999 feet (750 to 1499 meters)

Minus 21 to 0-degrees F (minus 35 to minus 18-degrees C)

Air screw	2
Slow jet	42.5
Needle clip position	3
Jet needle	6DGY27-65
Main jet	440

Minus 1 to 20-degrees F (minus 17 to minus 7-degrees C)

Air screw	1-3/4
Slow jet	40
Needle clip position	3
Jet needle	6DGY26-5
Main jet	430

19 to 40-degrees F (minus 6 to 4-degrees C)

Air screw	2
Slow jet	40
Needle clip position	3
Jet needle	6DGY26-65
Main jet	420

39 to 60-degrees F (3 to 15-degrees C)

Air screw	2
Slow jet	40
Needle clip position	3
Jet needle	6DGY26-65
Main jet	410

59 to 80-degrees F (14 to 26-degrees C)

Air screw	2
Slow jet	37.5
Needle clip position	3
Jet needle	6DGY26-66
Main jet	400

79 to 100-degrees F (25 to 38-degrees C)

Air screw	2-1/4
Slow jet	37.5
Needle clip position	2
Jet needle	6DGY27-66
Main jet	390

99 to 120-degrees F (37 to 49-degrees C)

Air screw	2-1/2
Slow jet	37.5
Needle clip position	2
Jet needle	6DGY26-67
Main jet	390

5000 to 7499 feet (1500 to 2299 meters)

Minus 21 to 0-degrees F (minus 35 to minus 18-degrees C)

Air screw	1-3/4
Slow jet	40
Needle clip position	3
Jet needle	6DGY26-65
Main jet	430

Minus 1 to 20-degrees F (minus 17 to minus 7-degrees C)

Air screw	2
Slow jet	40
Needle clip position	3
Jet needle	6DGY26-65
Main jet	420

19 to 40-degrees F (minus 6 to 4-degrees C)

Air screw	2
Slow jet	40
Needle clip position	3
Jet needle	6DGY26-65
Main jet	410

39 to 60-degrees F (3 to 15-degrees C)

Air screw	2
Slow jet	37.5
Needle clip position	3
Jet needle	6DGY26-66
Main jet	400

59 to 80-degrees F (14 to 26-degrees C)

Air screw	2-1/4

Carburetor settings (continued)

2005 and later CR250R (continued)

5000 to 7499 feet (1500 to 2299 meters)

  59 to 80-degrees F (14 to 26-degrees C)

Slow jet	37.5
Needle clip position	2
Jet needle	6DGY27-66
Main jet	390

  79 to 100-degrees F (25 to 38-degrees C)

Air screw	2-1/2
Slow jet	37.5
Needle clip position	2
Jet needle	6DGY27-67
Main jet	390

  99 to 120-degrees F (37 to 49-degrees C)

Air screw	2-1/2
Slow jet	35
Needle clip position	2
Jet needle	6DGY26-67
Main jet	380

7500 to 10,000 feet (2300 to 3050 meters)

  Minus 21 to 0-degrees F (minus 35 to minus 18-degrees C)

Air screw	2
Slow jet	40
Needle clip position	3
Jet needle	6DYG26-65
Main jet	420

  Minus 1 to 20-degrees F (minus 17 to minus 7-degrees C)

Air screw	2
Slow jet	40
Needle clip position	3
Jet needle	6 DYG26-65
Main jet	410

  19 to 40-degrees F (minus 6 to 4-degrees C)

Air screw	2
Slow jet	37.5
Needle clip position	3
Jet needle	6DYG26-66
Main jet	400

  39 to 60-degrees F (3 to 15-degrees C)

Air screw	2-1/4
Slow jet	37.5
Needle clip position	2
Jet needle	6DYG27-66
Main jet	390

  59 to 80-degrees F (14 to 26-degrees C)

Air screw	2-1/2
Slow jet	37.5
Needle clip position	2
Jet needle	6DYG27-67
Main jet	390

  79 to 100-degrees F (25 to 38-degrees C)

Air screw	2-1/2
Slow jet	35
Needle clip position	2
Jet needle	6DYG26-67
Main jet	380

  99 to 120-degrees F (37 to 49-degrees C)

Air screw	2-1/2
Slow jet	35
Needle clip position	2
Jet needle	6DYG26-68
Main jet	370

1990 CR500R

  Sea level to 999 feet (299 meters)

    Minus 21 to 0-degrees F (minus 35 to minus 18-degrees C)

Air screw	1 turn out
Slow jet	60

Needle clip position.. 4th groove
Main jet... 185

Minus 1 to 20-degrees F (minus 17 to minus 7-degrees C)
  Air screw .... 1 turn out
  Slow jet... 58
  Needle clip position.. 4th groove
  Main jet... 180

19 to 40-degrees F (minus 6 to 4-degrees C)
  Air screw .... 1-1/2 turns out
  Slow jet... 58
  Needle clip position.. 4th groove
  Main jet... 178

Sea level to 999 feet (299 meters)
39 to 60-degrees F (3 to 15-degrees C)
  Air screw .... 1-3/4 turns out
  Slow jet... 55
  Needle clip position.. 3rd groove
  Main jet... 175

59 to 80-degrees F (14 to 26-degrees C)*
  Air screw .... 2 turns out
  Slow jet... 55
  Needle clip position.. 3rd groove
  Main jet... 170

79 to 100-degrees F (25 to 38-degrees C)
  Air screw .... 2-1/2 turns out
  Slow jet... 55
  Needle clip position.. 3rd groove
  Main jet... 165

99 to 120-degrees F (37 to 49-degrees C)
  Air screw .... 2-3/4 turns out
  Slow jet... 52
  Needle clip position.. 3rd groove
  Main jet... 162

1000 to 2499 feet (300 to 749 meters)
Minus 21 to 0-degrees F (minus 35 to minus 18-degrees C)
  Air screw .... 1 turn out
  Slow jet... 60
  Needle clip position.. 4th groove
  Main jet... 182

Minus 1 to 20-degrees F (minus 17 to minus 7-degrees C)
  Air screw .... 1-1/2 turn out
  Slow jet... 58
  Needle clip position.. 4th groove
  Main jet... 178

19 to 40-degrees F (minus 6 to 4-degrees C)
  Air screw .... 1-1/2 turns out
  Slow jet... 58
  Needle clip position.. 4th groove
  Main jet... 175

39 to 60-degrees F (3 to 15-degrees C)
  Air screw.. 2 turns out
  Slow jet... 55
  Needle clip position .... 3rd groove
  Main jet... 172

59 to 80-degrees F (14 to 26-degrees C)
  Air screw.. 2-1/4 turns out
  Slow jet... 55
  Needle clip position.. 3rd groove
  Main jet... 168

79 to 100-degrees F (25 to 38-degrees C)
  Air screw.. 2-1/2 turns out
  Slow jet... 52
  Needle clip position.. 3rd groove
  Main jet... 165

99 to 120-degrees F (37 to 49-degrees C)
  Air screw.. 2-3/4 turns out
  Slow jet... 52
  Needle clip position.. 3rd groove
  Main jet... 162

* Standard jetting

Carburetor settings (continued)

1990 CR500R (continued)

2500 to 4999 feet (750 to 1499 meters)

    Minus 21 to 0-degrees F (minus 35 to minus 18-degrees C)

Air screw	1 turn out
Slow jet	58
Needle clip position	4th groove
Main jet	180

    Minus 1 to 20-degrees F (minus 17 to minus 7-degrees C)

Air screw	1-1/2 turn out
Slow jet	58
Needle clip position	4th groove
Main jet	178

    19 to 40-degrees F (minus 6 to 4-degrees C)

Air screw	1-3/4 turns out
Slow jet	55
Needle clip position	3rd groove
Main jet	175

    39 to 60-degrees F (3 to 15-degrees C)

Air screw	2 turns out
Slow jet	55
Needle clip position	3rd groove
Main jet	170

    59 to 80-degrees F (14 to 26-degrees C)

Air screw	2 turns out
Slow jet	52
Needle clip position	3rd groove
Main jet	165

    79 to 100-degrees F (25 to 38-degrees C)

Air screw	2-1/2 turns out
Slow jet	52
Needle clip position	3rd groove
Main jet	162

    99 to 120-degrees F (37 to 49-degrees C)

Air screw	2-1/2 turns out
Slow jet	50
Needle clip position	2nd groove
Main jet	160

5000 to 7499 feet (1500 to 2299 meters)

    Minus 21 to 0-degrees F (minus 35 to minus 18-degrees C)

Air screw	1-1/2 turns out
Slow jet	58
Needle clip position	4th groove
Main jet	175

    Minus 1 to 20-degrees F (minus 17 to minus 7-degrees C)

Air screw	1-3/4 turns out
Slow jet	55
Needle clip position	4th groove
Main jet	172

    19 to 40-degrees F (minus 6 to 4-degrees C)

Air screw	2 turns out
Slow jet	55
Needle clip position	3rd groove
Main jet	168

    39 to 60-degrees F (3 to 15-degrees C)

Air screw	2-1/4 turns out
Slow jet	52
Needle clip position	3rd groove
Main jet	165

    59 to 80-degrees F (14 to 26-degrees C)

Air screw	2-1/2 turns out
Slow jet	52
Needle clip position	2nd groove
Main jet	160

    79 to 100-degrees F (25 to 38-degrees C)

Air screw	2-3/4 turns out
Slow jet	50
Needle clip position	2nd groove
Main jet	158

99 to 120-degrees F (37 to 49-degrees C)
- Air screw .... 3 turns out
- Slow jet 50
- Needle clip position .... 2nd groove
- Main jet 155

7500 to 10,000 feet (2300 to 3000 meters)

Minus 21 to 0-degrees F (minus 35 to minus 18-degrees C)
- Air screw .... 1-3/4 turns out
- Slow jet 55
- Needle clip position .... 3rd groove
- Main jet 172

Minus 1 to 20-degrees F (minus 17 to minus 7-degrees C)
- Air screw .... 2 turns out
- Slow jet 55
- Needle clip position .... 3rd groove
- Main jet 168

19 to 40-degrees F (minus 6 to 4-degrees C)
- Air screw .... 2-1/4 turns out
- Slow jet 52
- Needle clip position .... 3rd groove
- Main jet 165

39 to 60-degrees F (3 to 15-degrees C)
- Air screw .... 2-1/2 turns out
- Slow jet 52
- Needle clip position .... 3rd groove
- Main jet 162

59 to 80-degrees F (14 to 26-degrees C)
- Air screw .... 2-3/4 turns out
- Slow jet 50
- Needle clip position .... 2nd groove
- Main jet 155

79 to 100-degrees F (25 to 38-degrees C)
- Air screw .... 3 turns out
- Slow jet 50
- Needle clip position .... 2nd groove
- Main jet 152

99 to 120-degrees F (37 to 49-degrees C)
- Air screw .... 3-1/4 turns out
- Slow jet 50
- Needle clip position .... 2nd groove
- Main jet 150

1991 and later CR500R

Sea level to 999 feet (299 meters)

Minus 21 to 0-degrees F (minus 35 to minus 18-degrees C)
- Air screw .... 1/2 turn out
- Slow jet 60
- Needle clip position .... 5th groove
- Main jet 185

Minus 1 to 20-degrees F (minus 17 to minus 7-degrees C)
- Air screw .... 1/2 turn out
- Slow jet 58
- Needle clip position .... 5th groove
- Main jet 180

19 to 40-degrees F (minus 6 to 4-degrees C)
- Air screw .... 1 turn out
- Slow jet 58
- Needle clip position .... 5th groove
- Main jet 178

39 to 60-degrees F (3 to 15-degrees C)
- Air screw .... 1-1/4 turns out
- Slow jet 55
- Needle clip position .... 4th groove
- Main jet 175

59 to 80-degrees F (14 to 26-degrees C)*
- Air screw .... 1-1/2 turns out
- Slow jet 55
- Needle clip position .... 4th groove
- Main jet 170

Standard jetting

Carburetor settings (continued)

1991 and later CR500R (continued)

Sea level to 999 feet (299 meters)

79 to 100-degrees F (25 to 38-degrees C)

Air screw	2 turns out
Slow jet	55
Needle clip position	4th groove
Main jet	165

99 to 120-degrees F (37 to 49-degrees C)

Air screw	2-1/4 turns out
Slow jet	52
Needle clip position	4th groove
Main jet	162

1000 to 2499 feet (300 to 749 meters)

Minus 21 to 0-degrees F (minus 35 to minus 18-degrees C)

Air screw	1/2 turn out
Slow jet	60
Needle clip position	5th groove
Main jet	182

Minus 1 to 20-degrees F (minus 17 to minus 7-degrees C)

Air screw	1 turn out
Slow jet	58
Needle clip position	5th groove
Main jet	178

19 to 40-degrees F (minus 6 to 4-degrees C)

Air screw	1 turn out
Slow jet	58
Needle clip position	5th groove
Main jet	175

39 to 60-degrees F (3 to 15-degrees C)

Air screw	1-1/2 turn out
Slow jet	55
Needle clip position	4th groove
Main jet	172

59 to 80-degrees F (14 to 26-degrees C)

Air screw	1-3/4 turns out
Slow jet	55
Needle clip position	4th groove
Main jet	168

79 to 100-degrees F (25 to 38-degrees C)

Air screw	2 turns out
Slow jet	52
Needle clip position	4th groove
Main jet	165

99 to 120-degrees F (37 to 49-degrees C)

Air screw	2-1/4 turns out
Slow jet	52
Needle clip position	4th groove
Main jet	162

2500 to 4999 feet (750 to 1499 meters)

Minus 21 to 0-degrees F (minus 35 to minus 18-degrees C)

Air screw	1 turn out
Slow jet	58
Needle clip position	5th groove
Main jet	180

Minus 1 to 20-degrees F (minus 17 to minus 7-degrees C)

Air screw	1-1/2 turn out
Slow jet	58
Needle clip position	5th groove
Main jet	178

19 to 40-degrees F (minus 6 to 4-degrees C)

Air screw	1-3/4 turns out
Slow jet	55
Needle clip position	4th groove
Main jet	175

39 to 60-degrees F (3 to 15-degrees C)

Air screw	2 turns out
Slow jet	55

Needle clip position	4th groove
Main jet	170

59 to 80-degrees F (14 to 26-degrees C)

Air screw	2 turns out
Slow jet	52
Needle clip position	4th groove
Main jet	165

79 to 100-degrees F (25 to 38-degrees C)

Air screw	2-1/2 turns out
Slow jet	52
Needle clip position	4th groove
Main jet	162

99 to 120-degrees F (37 to 49-degrees C)

Air screw	2-3/4 turns out
Slow jet	50
Needle clip position	3rd groove
Main jet	160

5000 to 7999 feet (1500 to 2299 meters)

Minus 21 to 0-degrees F (minus 35 to minus 18-degrees C)

Air screw	1-1/2 turns out
Slow jet	58
Needle clip position	5th groove
Main jet	175

Minus 1 to 20-degrees F (minus 17 to minus 7-degrees C)

Air screw	1-3/4 turns out
Slow jet	55
Needle clip position	5th groove
Main jet	172

19 to 40-degrees F (minus 6 to 4-degrees C)

Air screw	2 turns out
Slow jet	55
Needle clip position	4th groove
Main jet	168

39 to 60-degrees F (3 to 15-degrees C)

Air screw	2-1/4 turns out
Slow jet	52
Needle clip position	4th groove
Main jet	165

59 to 80-degrees F (14 to 26-degrees C)

Air screw	2-1/2 turns out
Slow jet	52
Needle clip position	3rd groove
Main jet	160

79 to 100-degrees F (25 to 38-degrees C)

Air screw	2-3/4 turns out
Slow jet	50
Needle clip position	3rd groove
Main jet	158

99 to 120-degrees F (37 to 49-degrees C)

Air screw	3 turns out
Slow jet	50
Needle clip position	3rd groove
Main jet	155

7500 to 10,000 feet (2300 to 3000 meters)

Minus 21 to 0-degrees F (minus 35 to minus 18-degrees C)

Air screw	1-3/4 turns out
Slow jet	55
Needle clip position	4th groove
Main jet	172

Minus 1 to 20-degrees F (minus 17 to minus 7-degrees C)

Air screw	2 turns out
Slow jet	55
Needle clip position	4th groove
Main jet	168

19 to 40-degrees F (minus 6 to 4-degrees C)

Air screw	2-1/4 turns out
Slow jet	52
Needle clip position	4th groove
Main jet	165

Carburetor settings (continued)

1991 and later CR500R (continued)

7500 to 10,000 feet (2300 to 3000 meters)

39 to 60-degrees F (3 to 15-degrees C)

Air screw	2-1/2 turns out
Slow jet	52
Needle clip position	4th groove
Main jet	162

59 to 80-degrees F (14 to 26-degrees C)

Air screw	2-3/4 turns out
Slow jet	50
Needle clip position	3rd groove
Main jet	155

79 to 100-degrees F (25 to 38-degrees C)

Air screw	3 turns out
Slow jet	50
Needle clip position	3rd groove
Main jet	152

99 to 120-degrees F (37 to 49-degrees C)

Air screw	3-1/4 turns out
Slow jet	50
Needle clip position	3rd groove
Main jet	150

Honda Power Port (HPP)

Spring gap	0.5 to 2.0 mm (0.020 to 0.079 inch)
E-clip to valve guide distance (after adjustment)	
1986	Not applicable
1987	20.5 to 21.0 mm (0.81 to 0.83 inch)
1988 on	24.5 mm (0.96 inch)

Torque settings

Honda Power Port (HPP)

Side and top cover bolts	10 to 14 Nm (84 to 120 inch-lbs)
Rack hole plug	8 to 12 Nm (72 to 144 inch-lbs)
Adjusting screw locknuts (1987 and 1987)	6 to 8 Nm (48 to 72 inch-lbs)
Adjusting bolt locknuts (1988 through 1991)	5 to 7 Nm (48 to 60 inch-lbs)

Composite Racing Valve (CRV)

Right cylinder cover	10 Nm (84 inch-lbs)
Left cylinder plug	13 Nm (108 inch-lbs)
Exhaust valve lever Allen bolts	5.5 Nm (48 inch-lbs)
Exhaust valve stopper bolt	16 Nm (16 Nm (12 ft-lbs)

2.2 Disconnect the fuel line from the tap

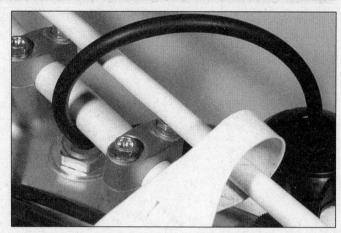

2.3a Pull the vent hose out of the steering stem nut

1 General information

The fuel system on all models consists of the fuel tank, fuel tap, filter screen, carburetor and connecting lines, hoses and control cable.

All models use the slide carburetor design, in which the slide acts as the throttle valve. Basic design is the same for all CR250 models through 2000 and all CR500R models. The 2001 CR250R uses a flat slide, rather than an oval slide, and the carburetor body is oval in cross section rather than cylindrical. This design is used on 2000 and later CR125R models, and is covered in detail in Part A of this Chapter. For cold starting on all models, a choke plunger is actuated by a knob. 1997 and 1998 CR250R models use an electrically operated power jet that supplies additional fuel to enrich the fuel/air mixture at low and medium engine speeds (below 8100 rpm).

The exhaust system consists of an expansion chamber and muffler with a replaceable core. All CR250R models have a means of varying the effective exhaust port size, to provide the ideal amount of exhaust flow at each end of the powerband. 1986 through 1991 models use the Honda Power Port system, in which a pair of moveable gates in the exhaust port increase the size of the port as engine speed increases. 1992 through 2004 models use the Composite Racing Valve, which controls both the effective size of the exhaust chamber and the timing of the exhaust. 2005 and later models use the Radical Combustion (RC) system, with the valve controlled by an electric servo motor. This is the same as for 2004 models (refer to Chapter 4A for service procedures).

Many of the fuel system service procedures are considered routine maintenance items and for that reason are included in Chapter 1.

2 Fuel tank - removal and installation

Warning: *Gasoline is extremely flammable, so take extra precautions when you work on any part of the fuel system. Don't smoke or allow open flames or bare light bulbs near the work area, and don't work in a garage where a gas-type appliance (such as a water heater or clothes dryer) is present. If you spill any fuel on your skin, rinse it off immediately with soap and water. When you perform any kind of work on the fuel system, wear safety glasses and have an extinguisher suitable for a class B type fire (flammable liquids) on hand.*

Removal
Refer to illustrations 2.2, 2.3a, 2.3b and 2.4
1   Remove the seat (see Chapter 8).
2   Turn the fuel tap to Off and disconnect the fuel line **(see illustration)**.
3   Pull the fuel tank vent hose out of the steering stem nut **(see illustration)**. Unhook the strap from the rear of the tank **(see illustration)**.
4   Remove the fuel tank mounting bolt (1997 and later CR250R) or bolts (all others) **(see illustration 2.3b and the accompanying illustration)**.
5   Lift the fuel tank off the bike together with the fuel tap.

2.3b Note how the ends of the tank strap are shaped (one's designed for the button on the tank and the other for the hook on the frame), then unhook the strap (left arrow); the 1997-on CR250R's tank mounting bolt is on top (right arrow) ...

2.4 ... on other models, they're beneath the tank

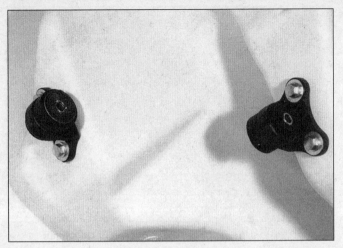

2.6a Check for deteriorated or damaged tank bushings . . .

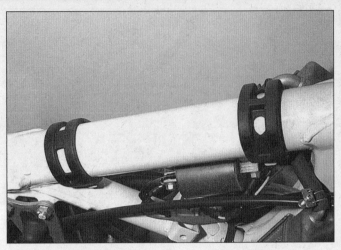

2.6b . . . and inspect the isolators on the frame

Installation

Refer to illustrations 2.6a and 2.6b

6   Before installing the tank, check the condition of the rubber mounting bushings at the front, the isolators on the frame and the rubber strap at the rear - if they're hardened, cracked, or show any other signs of deterioration, replace them **(see illustration 2.3b and the accompanying illustrations)**.

7   When installing the tank, reverse the removal procedure. Make sure the tank does not pinch any wires. Tighten the tank mounting bolts securely, but don't overtighten them and strip the threads.

3   Fuel tank - cleaning and repair

1   All repairs to the fuel tank should be carried out by a professional who has experience in this critical and potentially dangerous work. Even after cleaning and flushing of the fuel system, explosive fumes can remain and ignite during repair of the tank.

2   If the fuel tank is removed from the vehicle, it should not be placed in an area where sparks or open flames could ignite the fumes coming out of the tank. Be especially careful inside garages where a natural gas-type appliance is located, because the pilot light could cause an explosion.

4   Carburetor adjustment

Fuel/air mixture adjustment

All except 1999 and later CR250R models

Refer to illustration 4.2

1   Fuel/air mixture and idle speed on these bikes are adjusted for best performance. There's no specified idle rpm setting.

2   Mixture is controlled by an air screw. Idle speed is controlled by turning the knob on the choke valve **(see illustration)**.

3   The standard settings are intended for a bike operated with the specified premix (see Chapter 1), at sea level and an air temperature of 68-degrees F (20-degrees C).

4   Turn the air screw in until it bottoms lightly. Don't bottom the screw hard or its tip will be damaged, causing erratic settings. Back the screw out to the standard setting listed in this Chapter's Specifications.

5   Bottom the idle speed knob lightly, then back it out to the minimum amount listed in this Chapter's Specifications.

6   Warm up the engine until it will run smoothly with the choke knob all the way in.

7   Ride the bike and check that it revs up smoothly as you accelerate out of turns. If it blubbers, the mixture is too rich; if it surges, the mixture is too lean. Shut off the bike and change the air screw setting 1/4 turn at a time to correct the problem. Turn the screw in to enrich the mixture or out to make it leaner. **Note:** *If you have to go beyond the maximum air screw range listed in the Specifications, you'll need to change slow jet size. If you're under the range, use the next larger slow jet. If you're over the range, use the next smaller slow jet.*

8   Set the idle speed to your preference by turning the knob **(see illustration 4.2)**.

1999 and later CR250R models

9   Adjustment is the same as for the 2000 and later CR125R, described in Chapter 4A.

Altitude and temperature adjustment

1986 through 1991 CR250R; 1986 through 1989 CR500R

Refer to illustration 4.10

10   These models should be rejetted to compensate for changes in temperature as well as altitude. This means you'll need a thermometer to determine the air temperature. To figure out whether you need to make any changes, find your altitude and the local air temperature on

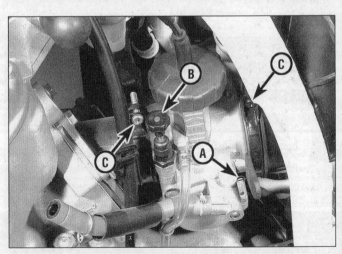

4.2 Idle mixture is adjusted with an air screw; idle speed is adjusted with a knob on the choke plunger

A   Air screw   C   Clamping bands
B   Idle speed knob

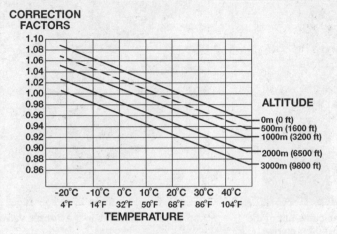

4.10 Correction factor chart - 1986 through 1991 CR250R and 1986 through 1989 CR500R

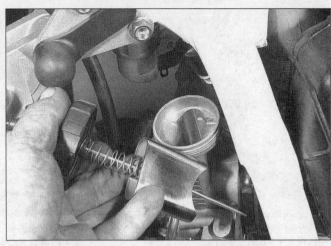

6.3 Unscrew the top cap and lift the throttle valve and jet needle out of the carburetor

the accompanying chart **(see illustration)**. Draw a line up from the temperature setting to the altitude line. From where the two lines meet, read across to the correction factor.

11   Multiply the standard main jet number by the correction factor to determine the proper size of main jet. For example, if your main jet is a no. 165 and the correction factor is 0.92, multiply 165 X 0.92 to get 151.8. Rounded off, the correct size main jet is 152.

12   Look up the correction factor in this Chapter's Specifications to find out whether changes are needed in the needle clip position and air screw setting.

1992 and later CR250R; 1990 and later CR500R

13   Jet sizes and needle clip positions for different altitude and temperature conditions are listed in this Chapter's Specifications.

All models

14   Refer to Section 7 for procedures to change the jet(s) and needle clip position.

5   Carburetor overhaul - general information

1   Poor engine performance, hesitation, hard starting, stalling, flooding and backfiring are all signs that major carburetor maintenance may be required.

2   Keep in mind that many so-called carburetor problems are really not carburetor problems at all, but mechanical problems within the engine or ignition system malfunctions. Try to establish for certain that the carburetor is in need of maintenance before beginning a major overhaul.

3   Check the fuel tap and its strainer screen, the fuel lines, the intake manifold clamps, the O-ring between the intake manifold and cylinder head, the reed valve, the air filter element, the cylinder compression, crankcase vacuum and compression, the spark plug and the ignition timing before assuming that a carburetor overhaul is required. If the bike has been unused for more than 24 hours, drain the float chamber and refill the tank with fresh fuel.

4   Most carburetor problems are caused by dirt particles, varnish and other deposits which build up in and block the fuel and air passages. Also, in time, gaskets and O-rings shrink or deteriorate and cause fuel and air leaks which lead to poor performance.

5   When the carburetor is overhauled, it is generally disassembled completely and the parts are cleaned thoroughly with a carburetor cleaning solvent and dried with filtered, unlubricated compressed air. The fuel and air passages are also blown through with compressed air to force out any dirt that may have been loosened but not removed by the solvent. Once the cleaning process is complete, the carburetor is

reassembled using a new top gasket, O-rings and, generally, a new inlet needle valve and seat.

6   Before disassembling the carburetor, make sure you have the necessary gasket, O-rings and other parts, some carburetor cleaner, a supply of rags, some means of blowing out the carburetor passages and a clean place to work.

6   Carburetor - removal and installation

Warning: *Gasoline is extremely flammable, so take extra precautions when you work on any part of the fuel system. Don't smoke or allow open flames or bare light bulbs near the work area, and don't work in a garage where a gas-type appliance (such as a water heater or clothes dryer) is present. If you spill any fuel on your skin, rinse it off immediately with soap and water. When you perform any kind of work on the fuel system, wear safety glasses and have a fire extinguisher suitable for a class B type fire (flammable liquids) on hand.*

Removal

Note: *This procedure applies to all except 2001 CR250R models. The procedure for 2001 CR250R models is the same as for the 2000 and later CR125R, described in Chapter 4A.*

Refer to illustration 6.3

1   Remove the seat and both side covers (see Chapter 8).

2   Remove the fuel tank (see Section 2).

3   Unscrew the top cap from the carburetor **(see illustration)**. Lift out the spring, throttle valve and jet needle. Remove the air cleaner case (see Section 10).

4   Loosen the clamping bands on the air cleaner duct and intake manifold **(see illustration 4.2)**. Work the carburetor free of the duct and manifold and lift it off.

5   Check the intake tube for cracks, deterioration or other damage. If it has visible defects, or if there's reason to suspect its O-ring is leaking, remove it from the engine and inspect the O-ring.

6   After the carburetor has been removed, stuff clean rags into the intake to prevent the entry of dirt or other objects.

Installation

7   Installation is the reverse of the removal steps, with the following additions:

a) *If you're working on a 1998 through 2000 CR250R, align the tab on the inside of the throttle cable collar with the groove in the throttle cable holder inside the throttle valve.*

b) *Adjust the throttle freeplay (see Chapter 1).*

c) *Adjust the idle speed and fuel mixture (Section 4).*

7.3a Compress the spring into the carburetor top . . .

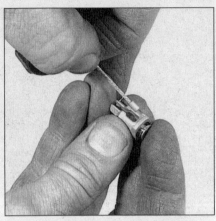

7.3b . . . and slip the cable out of the holder (holder removed for clarity) . . .

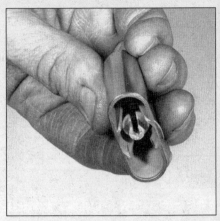

7.3c . . . the holder fits in the throttle valve like this . . .

7   Carburetor - disassembly, cleaning and inspection

Warning: *Gasoline is extremely flammable, so take extra precautions when you work on any part of the fuel system. Don't smoke or allow open flames or bare light bulbs near the work area, and don't work in a garage where a gas-type appliance (such as a water heater or clothes dryer) is present. If you spill any fuel on your skin, rinse it off immediately with soap and water. When you perform any kind of work on the fuel system, wear safety glasses and have a fire extinguisher suitable for class B fires (flammable liquids) on hand.*

Disassembly

Refer to illustrations 7.3a through 7.3i

Note: *On 2005 and later CR250R models, the carburetor is the same as for 2004 CR125R models. Refer to Chapter 2A for disassembly procedures.*

1   Remove the carburetor from the machine as described in Section 6.

2   Set the carburetor on a clean working surface. Take note of how the vent hoses are routed, including locations of hose retainers.

3   On all except 2001 CR250R models, refer to the accompanying illustrations to disassemble the carburetor **(see illustrations)**. On 2001

CR250R models, refer to the procedure for 2000 and later CR125R models in Chapter 4A.

Cleaning

Caution: *Use only a carburetor cleaning solution that is safe for use with plastic parts (be sure to read the label on the container).*

4   Submerge the metal components in the carburetor cleaner for approximately thirty minutes (or longer, if the directions recommend it).

5   After the carburetor has soaked long enough for the cleaner to loosen and dissolve most of the varnish and other deposits, use a brush to remove the stubborn deposits. Rinse it again, then dry it with compressed air. Blow out all of the fuel and air passages in the carburetor body. **Caution:** *Never clean the jets or passages with a piece of wire or a drill bit, as they will be enlarged, causing the fuel and air metering rates to be upset.*

Inspection

6   Check the operation of the choke plunger. If it doesn't move smoothly, replace it.

7   Check the tapered portion of the air screw for wear or damage. Replace the screw if necessary.

8   Check the carburetor body, float chamber and carburetor top for

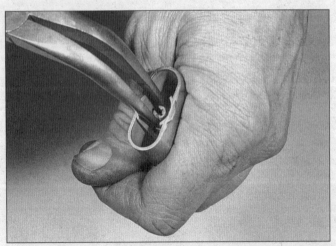

7.3d . . . rotate it one-quarter turn and press down to remove the holder from the throttle valve (all except 1999 and 2000 CR250R models)

7.3e Note the locations of the hose retainers

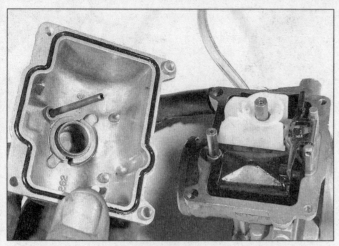

7.3f Remove the float chamber screws and take off the float chamber and its O-ring

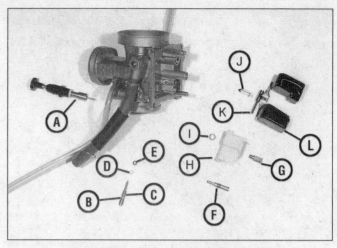

7.3g Carburetor details (except 2001 CR250R)

A	Idle speed knob/choke valve	G	Main jet
B	Air screw	H	Baffle (1997 and 1998 only)
C	Spring	I	Washer
D	Washer	J	Needle valve
E	O-ring	K	Float pivot pin
F	Slow jet	L	Float

cracks, distorted sealing surfaces and other damage. If any defects are found, replace the faulty component, although replacement of the entire carburetor will probably be necessary (check with your parts supplier for the availability of separate components).

9   Check the jet needle for straightness by rolling it on a flat surface (such as a piece of glass). Replace it if it's bent or if the tip is worn.

10   Check the tip of the fuel inlet valve needle. If it has grooves or scratches in it, it must be replaced. Push in on the rod in the other end of the needle, then release it - if it doesn't spring back, replace the valve needle.

11   Check the O-rings on the float chamber and the main jet access plug (in the float chamber). Replace them if they're damaged.

12   Check the floats for damage. This will usually be apparent by the presence of fuel inside one of the floats. If the floats are damaged, they must be replaced.

13   Insert the throttle valve in the carburetor body and see that it moves up-and-down smoothly. Check the surface of the throttle valve for wear. If it's worn excessively or doesn't move smoothly in the bore, replace the carburetor.

14   If you're working on a 1997 CR250R, check the shaft on the power jet solenoid for wear or damage **(see illustration 7.3i)**. Replace the solenoid if problems are found.

8   Carburetor - reassembly and float height check

Refer to illustration 8.4

Caution: *When installing the jets, be careful not to over-tighten them - they're made of soft material and can strip or shear easily.*

Note: *When reassembling the carburetor, be sure to use new O-rings.*

1   Install the clip on the jet needle if it was removed. Place it in the needle groove listed in this Chapter's Specifications. Install the needle and clip in the throttle valve. Install the throttle cable holder on top of the jet needle. On all except 1999 and 2000 CR250R models, turn it 1/4-turn to lock it in place.

2   Install the air screw along with its spring, washer and O-ring, turning it in until it seats lightly. Now, turn the screw out the number of turns listed in this Chapter's Specifications.

3   Reverse the disassembly steps to install the jets.

7.3h If the O-ring doesn't fall out, remove it with a pointed tool

7.3i On 1997 and 1998 models, remove the screws and detach the power jet solenoid from the carburetor body

8.4 Measure float height; this Honda tool is convenient, but you can also use a ruler

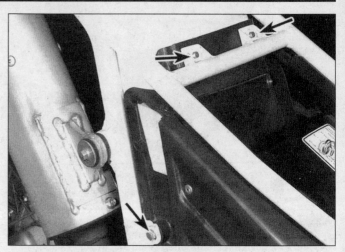

10.2 Unbolt the air cleaner housing from the sub-frame (later CR500R shown; others similar)

4   Invert the carburetor. Attach the fuel inlet valve needle to the float. Set the float into position in the carburetor, making sure the valve needle seats correctly. Install the float pivot pin. To check the float height, hold the carburetor so the float hangs down, then tilt it back until the valve needle is just seated **(see illustration)**. Measure the distance from the float chamber gasket surface to the top of the float and compare your measurement to the float height listed in this Chapter's Specifications. Bend the float tang as necessary to change the adjustment.

5   Install the O-ring into the groove in the float chamber. Place the float chamber on the carburetor and install the screws, tightening them securely.

9   Power jet (1997 and 1998 CR250R) - testing and replacement

1   Support the bike firmly with the rear wheel off the ground. The support must be stable enough that the bike can be run without danger of falling over.

2   Unplug the solenoid electrical connector (it's a two-pin gray connector located to the rear of the fuel tank tap).

3   Loosen the clamp screws on the carburetor connecting bands **(see illustration 4.2)**.

10.3 If you separate the carburetor connecting tube from the housing, apply a ring of silicone sealant to its mating surface on installation

4   Rotate the carburetor to the left so the solenoid screws are exposed, then unscrew them and take the power jet out of the carburetor **(see illustration 7.3i)**.

5   Reconnect the power jet connector. Place the solenoid where you can see its plunger and start the engine.

6   At engine speeds above 8100 rpm, the solenoid shaft should extend. At lower engine speeds, it should retract. The solenoid should extend and retract each time the engine is revved, then slowed down.

7   If the solenoid doesn't react properly in Step 6, disconnect the gray two-pin connector. Connect a 12-volt battery to the terminals in the solenoid side of the connector (positive to black/red and negative to black/brown). The solenoid should extend when the battery is connected, and retract when the battery is disconnected.

8   If the solenoid still doesn't work properly, replace it. If it does work properly, check the wiring harness for a break or bad connection. The problem may also be in the alternator, ignition control module or regulator/rectifier.

10   Air cleaner housing - removal and installation

Refer to illustrations 10.2 and 10.3

1   Remove the seat, both side covers and the sub-frame (see Chapter 8).

2   Remove the bolts that secure the rear and sides of the air cleaner housing to the sub-frame **(see illustration)**.

3   If necessary, detach the carburetor connecting tube from the housing **(see illustration)**.

4   Installation is the reverse of the removal steps. If you removed the connecting tube, apply a ring of silicone sealant to the mating surface of the connecting tube and air cleaner housing.

11   Throttle cables - removal and installation

Refer to illustration 11.4

1   Remove the fuel tank (see Section 2).

2   At the handlebar, loosen the throttle cable adjuster all the way (see Chapter 1).

3   Look for a punch mark on the handlebar next to the split in the throttle housing. If you don't see a mark, make one so the throttle housing can be installed in the correct position.

4   Later models are equipped with a throttle roller **(see illustration)**. If the roller has a removable cover, remove its screws and lift off the cover and gasket.

5   Remove the throttle housing screws. If the bike has a throttle

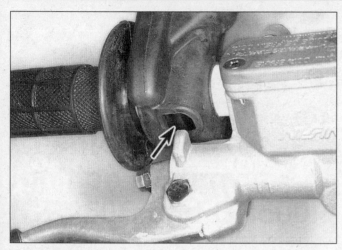

11.4 Later models use a throttle roller (1997 model shown)

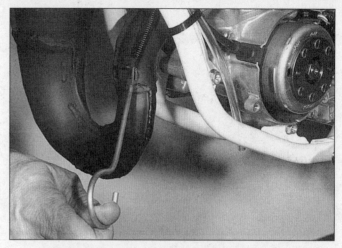

12.1 A hook like this one makes it easy to unhook the expansion chamber springs

roller, lift the cable out of the roller groove. Rotate the cable to align it with the slot in the throttle pulley, then slide the cable end out of the pulley.

6   To detach the cable from the carburetor, refer to Sections 6 and 7.

7   Route the cable into place. Make sure it doesn't interfere with any other components and isn't kinked or bent sharply.

8   Lubricate the throttle pulley end of the cable with multi-purpose grease. Reverse the disconnection steps to connect the throttle cable to the throttle grip pulley. If the bike has a throttle roller, install it, then install its gasket and cover (if equipped).

9   Coat the handlebar with silicone grease and slide the throttle housing and throttle grip on. Position the throttle housing so the parting line of the throttle housing and clamp is aligned with the punch mark on the handlebar, then install the clamp. Tighten the upper clamp screw, then the lower one.

10   Reverse the removal steps in Sections 6 and 7 to connect the cable to the carburetor.

11   Operate the throttle and make sure it returns to the idle position by itself under spring pressure. **Warning:** *If the throttle doesn't return by itself, find and solve the problem before continuing with installation. A stuck throttle can lead to loss of control of the motorcycle.*

12   Follow the procedure outlined in Chapter 1, *Throttle operation/*

grip freeplay - check and adjustment, to adjust the cable.

13   Turn the handlebars back and forth to make sure the cable doesn't cause the steering to bind.

14   Once you're sure the cable operates properly, install the fuel tank.

15   With the engine idling, turn the handlebars through their full travel (full left lock to full right lock) and note whether idle speed increases. If it does, the cable is routed incorrectly. Correct this dangerous condition before riding the bike.

12   Exhaust system - removal and installation

Refer to illustrations 12.1, 12.2a and 12.2b

1   Unhook the springs that secure the expansion chamber to the cylinder head or head pipe **(see illustration)**.

2   Remove the expansion chamber and muffler mounting bolts **(see illustrations)**.

3   Pull the exhaust system forward, separate the expansion chamber from the head pipe and remove the system from the machine.

4   To replace the muffler core, refer to Chapter 1. To remove the exhaust head pipe (models so equipped), see Chapter 2.

5   Installation is the reverse of removal.

12.2a Note the direction of offset brackets before removing them; leaving them bolted to the frame will help you remember how they go

12.2b The muffler is bolted to the right side of the sub-frame

13.1 The HPP exhaust valves are located in the top of the exhaust port

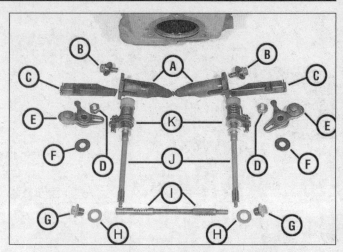

13.2 Honda Power Port (HPP) system details (1988 and later models shown; earlier models similar)

A	Exhaust valve guides	F	Washers
B	Valve guide bolts and washers	G	Rack hole plugs
C	Exhaust valves	H	Sealing washers
D	Locknuts	I	Rack
E	Assembled valve levers, adjuster levers and adjusting bolts	J	Pinion shaft assemblies
		K	Washers

13 Honda Power Port (HPP) system (1986 through 1991 CR250R) - removal, inspection and installation

Refer to illustrations 13.1 and 13.2

1   This system's key components are a pair of moveable gates, mounted one in each side of the exhaust port **(see illustration)**. Honda refers to these as exhaust valves, but they aren't the same in design or function as the exhaust valves used in four-stroke engines. At low engine speeds, the exhaust valves are close together, effectively reducing the size of the exhaust port. As engine speed increases, the valves slide apart, expanding the port opening.

2   Movement of the valves is done by a pair of levers which fit into notches in the valves **(see illustration)**. The levers are mounted on pivot shafts, which are turned by a rack (similar to an automotive steering rack) mounted in the front of the cylinder. The rack is operated by a link, which in turn is operated by a governor mounted in the right crankcase cover near the water pump.

3   The governor contains four steel balls mounted in a cone-shaped housing. As engine speed increases, centrifugal force moves the balls outward, away from the governor shaft. Since the housing they're mounted in is cone-shaped, the balls also move along the length of the shaft until they press against the governor linkage, causing the rack to rotate and spread the exhaust valves outward.

Exhaust valve, pinion shaft and rack removal

Refer to illustrations 13.4, 13.6a, 13.6b, 13.6c, 13.7, 13.8, 13.9a, 13.9b, 13.10a and 13.10b

Note: *It's a good idea to work on one side of the system at a time so the other side can be used for reference on reassembly.*

4   Remove the covers from the top and sides of the cylinder **(see illustration)**.

5   If you're working on a 1986 model, remove the nuts that secure the springs on top of the valve levers, then lift the springs off.

6   Lift the pinion shafts out of their bores **(see illustrations)**.

7   If you're working on a 1987 or later model, remove the locknut

13.4 Left side HPP top and side covers

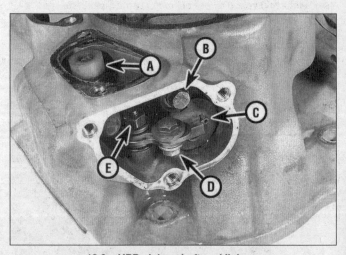

13.6a HPP pinion shaft and linkage (1988 and later models shown; 1987 and earlier similar)

A	Pinion shaft bushing	D	Adjusting bolt locknut
B	Eccentric adjusting bolt	E	Pivot locknut
C	Valve E-clip		

13.6b Lift the pinion shaft out of the cylinder . . .

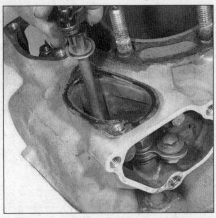

13.6c . . . and take the washer off the shaft

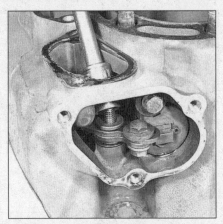

13.7 Remove the pivot locknut . . .

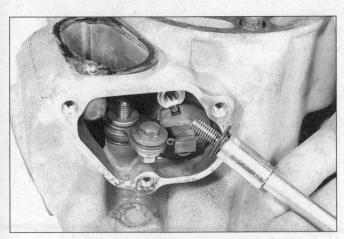

13.8 . . . and the valve guide bolt and washer

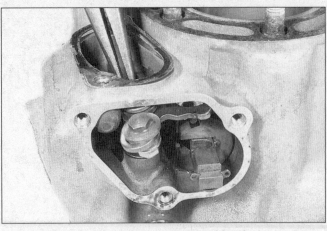

13.9a Take the adjusting lever and valve lever assembly off the pivot stud . . .

that secures the adjuster lever and valve lever to its pivot **(see illustration)**. Repeat the step on the other side of the cylinder.

8   Remove the valve guide retaining bolts **(see illustration)**.

9   Lift the valve lever and adjusting lever out of each exhaust valve, then lift the washer off the pivot **(see illustrations)**.

10   Pull the exhaust valves and guides out of the engine **(see illustrations)**.

11   If you're just removing the valves for periodic cleaning, further dis-

assembly may be unnecessary. If inspection shows that more disassembly is needed, refer to the following removal and inspection steps.

12   Unscrew the rack hole plug from the left side of the cylinder and pull the rack out of its bore. If you're working on a 1986 or 1987 model, loosen the locknut and remove the rack adjusting screw from the right side of the cylinder. If you're working on a 1988 or later model, remove the rack hole plug and sealing washer from the right side of the cylinder.

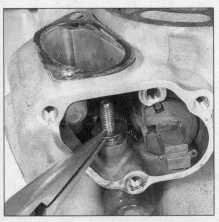

13.9b . . . then take the washer off the pivot stud

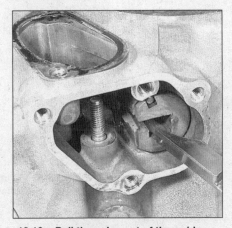

13.10a Pull the valve out of the guide . . .

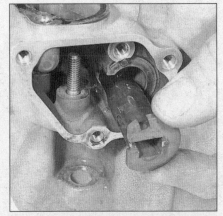

13.10b . . . then pull the guide out of its bore

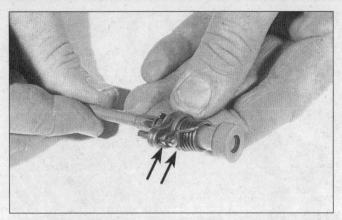

13.14a After adjusting the valves on 1988 and later models, check the gap between the spring ends and the post on the lever (left arrow); the ends of the spring also fit over the tabs on the upper pinion shaft lever (right arrow)

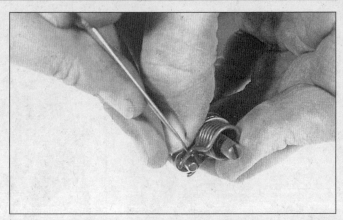

13.14b To remove or install the spring, spread it with a hooked tool so it will fit over the tabs of the upper pinion shaft lever

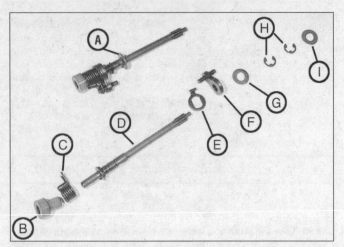

13.14c Pinion shaft details (1988 and later models shown; 1986 and 1987 similar)

A	Pinion shaft assembly	F	Lower pinion shaft lever
B	Upper bushing	G	Washer
C	Spring	H	E-clips
D	Pinion shaft	I	Washer
E	Upper pinion shaft lever		

Inspection and exhaust valve decarbonizing

Refer to illustrations 13.14a, 13.14b, 13.14c, 13.15a and 13.15b

13   Start by cleaning all carbon deposits from the exhaust valves and guides. These deposits occur during normal operation of the motorcycle and must be removed periodically to maintain good performance.

14   Check the pinion shaft assemblies for wear, damage or broken springs. Pay special attention to the upper and lower pivot points and to the end of the lever where it rides in the exhaust valve lever. If individual parts need to be replaced, note how the assembly is put together, then take it apart **(see illustrations)**.

15   Check the assembled valve and adjuster levers for wear, especially at the tip that engages the exhaust valve and the slot that engages the post on the pinion shaft lever **(see illustrations)**. If necessary, take the assembly apart so individual parts can be replaced.

Exhaust valve, pinion shaft and rack installation
1986 and 1987 models

16   Take the rack hole plug and sealing washer that normally go in the left side of the cylinder and temporarily install them in the hole at the lower right front of the cylinder (where the adjusting screw normally goes).

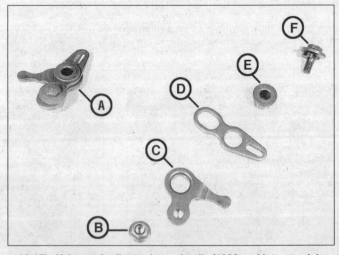

13.15b Valve and adjuster lever details (1988 and later models shown; 1986 and 1987 similar)

A	Lever assembly	D	Adjuster lever
B	Adjuster bolt locknut	E	Pivot collar
C	Valve lever	F	Eccentric adjusting bolt

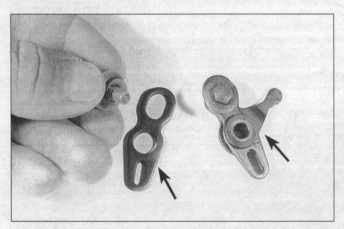

13.15a The eccentric adjuster bolt fits into the large slot in the adjuster lever; when the adjuster and valve levers are assembled, the pivot bushing fits through the round hole in each lever - the levers are labeled L and R for left and right (arrows)

13.30 Install the rack hole plug and sealing washer; the end of the rack with the cutout goes on the right side of the cylinder casting

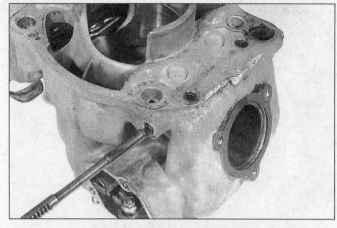

13.31a Pull the rack out of its bore

17   Coat the rack with moly-based grease and install it in its bore. The right side rack teeth face the rear of the cylinder and the left side rack teeth face the front.
18   Coat the friction surfaces of the exhaust valves and guides with clean two-stroke oil. Install the guides in the cylinder, then install their retaining bolts and washers and tighten the bolts to the torque listed in this Chapter's Specifications.
19   Make sure the E-clips are installed on the valves, then slide them into the guides.
20   Install each valve lever, then each adjusting lever, on the pivot stud in the cylinder casting. Fit the adjuster lever pins into the holes on the valve levers. **Note:** *Refer to the R and L marks stamped into the levers to make sure they're installed on the correct sides of the cylinder.*
21   Install the lever springs (1986 only) and pivot collars. The right spring on 1986 models has a longer end than the left spring. Install the locknuts on the pivot studs, but don't tighten them yet. If you're working on a 1986 model, don't hook the springs over the levers yet.
22   Coat the teeth on the bottom of each pinion shaft with moly-based grease.
23   Place a screwdriver in the slot on the end of the rack and push the rack into its bore with a to make sure it's all the way in and touching the plug in the right side hole. While you hold the rack in this position, install the left pinion shaft and engage its pin with the slot in the adjuster lever. If the teeth on the bottom of the pinion shaft won't engage the teeth on the rack, turn the rack slightly with the screwdriver until they do. Keep pushing the rack in while you turn it.
24   Install the right pinion shaft, engaging its gear teeth with the rack

and its pin with the adjuster lever slot.
25   Identify the right and left valve springs (the ones that fit over the pinion shafts). The right spring's lower end is longer than that of the left spring. Install the lower collars, springs and upper collars on the upper ends of the pinion shafts.
26   If you're working on a 1986 model, engage the valve springs with the levers.
27   Unscrew the rack hole plug from the right side, then install the plug and sealing washer in the left side.
28   Install the socket bolt with its sealing washer in the right rack hole and tighten them to the torque listed in this Chapter's Specifications. Install the adjusting screw and its locknut in the socket bolt.
29   Operate the linkage by hand to make sure the valves open and close freely. Install the cylinder on the engine (if it was removed), then refer to Section 14 and adjust the exhaust valves.

1988 and later models
Refer to illustrations 13.30, 13.31a, 13.31b, 13.31c and 13.32
30   Install the rack hole plug with its sealing washer in the hole on the right side of the cylinder, then tighten it to the torque listed in this Chapter's Specifications **(see illustration)**.
31   Coat the rack with moly-based grease and install it in its bore. The right side rack teeth face the rear of the cylinder and the left side rack teeth face the front **(see illustrations)**. The cutout in the right side of the rack faces the hole in the bottom of the cylinder casting so it can engage the follower cam when the cylinder is installed **(see illustration)**.

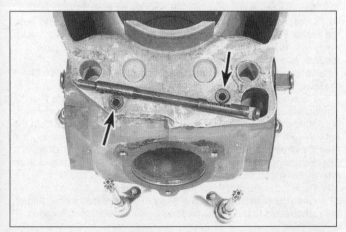

13.31b The rack is installed at an angle, so it pulls one pinion shaft and pushes the other; the lower ends of the pinion shafts fit in bushings (arrows) (rack and pinion shafts removed for clarity)

13.31c Be sure the cutout in the end of the rack faces downward (toward the bottom of the cylinder)

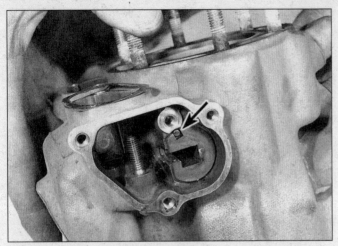

13.32 On installation, align the guide notch with the pin in the cylinder casting (arrow)

32   Install the valve guides, aligning the notch in each guide with the pin in the cylinder casting **(see illustration)**.
33   Coat the exhaust valves with clean two-stroke oil and install them in the guides with their E-clips facing down (toward the bottom of the cylinder) **(see illustration 13.10a)**.
34   Install the washer on the pivot stud **(see illustration 13.9b)**.
35   Install the valve lever over each pivot stud, making sure its R or L mark faces downward.
36   Install the adjuster lever on the valve lever with its R or L mark up. Align the pin on the valve lever with the hole in the exhaust lever. Slip the pivot collar through the levers and install the locknut, but don't tighten it yet.
37   Align the holes in the valve and adjuster levers that the eccentric adjuster bolt passes through (but don't install the eccentric adjuster bolts yet).
38   Coat the tips of the pinion shafts with clean two-stroke oil.
39   **Note:** *Honda specifies that this step be done with the exhaust valves fully closed (toward each other). However, we found that this restricted travel of the rack, preventing the valves from opening. When we did the step with the valves fully open, the system worked correctly.* Install the pinion shafts, aligning their pins with the slots in the adjuster levers. Install the eccentric adjusting bolts and locknuts, but don't tighten them yet **(see illustration 13.6a)**.
40   Install the left rack hole plug with its sealing washer and tighten it to the torque listed in this Chapter's Specifications.
41   Install the cylinder if it was removed (see Chapter 2).
42   Refer to Section 14 and adjust the exhaust valves.

Follower cam and governor removal

43   Remove the pinion shafts as described above.
44   If you're working on a 1986 or 1987 model, loosen the locknut and remove the adjusting screw from the pinion hole at the lower right corner of the cylinder. If you're working on a 1988 or later model, remove the rack hole plug. On all models, remove the rack hole plug from the left side of the cylinder and pull out the rack **(see illustrations 13.31a, 13.31b and 13.31c)**.
45   Remove the right crankcase cover (see Chapter 2).
46   Lay the crankcase cover on a workbench with its inner side upward. Press down on the governor (against its spring pressure), undo the two governor screws and release the spring pressure.
47   Lift the rocker arm off the governor. Take the spring and seats (1986 and 1987) or retainer shaft and spring (1988 and later) out of the bore in the crankcase cover.
48   Lift the governor off the water pump drive gear and inspect the steel balls. If they're worn or damaged, replace the governor.
49   Lift the water pump drive gear out of the crankcase cover.

50   If you need to remove the follower cam, which is mounted in the right front corner of the crankcase, remove the cylinder (see Chapter 2). Take the clip off the bottom of the cam spindle, then remove the follower cam from the spindle and lift the spindle out of the crankcase.

Governor and follower cam inspection

51   Check all parts for wear and damage and replace any that have problems. Replace the governor as a unit if problems are found.
52   Spin the bearing in the crankcase cover with a finger; if it's rough, loose or noisy, remove it with a slide hammer and blind hole puller. Put the new bearing in a freezer for several hours so it will contract. Heat the bearing bore area of the crankcase cover with a heat gun or in an oven (don't use a torch), then drive in the new bearing with a socket or bearing driver that applies pressure to the bearing's outer race.

Governor and follower cam installation

53   Installation is the reverse of the removal steps, with the following additions:

a) *Coat the teeth of the water pump drive gear with the transmission oil recommended in the Chapter 1 Specifications.*
b) *Coat the steel balls, follower cam, spindle and bushing, with grease that has a molybdenum disulfide content of at least 40 percent. Place the steel balls in the water pump drive gear and install the governor.*

---

14   Honda Power Port (HPP) system - adjustment

1   Remove the left and right side covers **(see illustration 13.4)**.
2   Remove the expansion chamber (see Section 12).
3   With the engine off, the exhaust valves should be all the way into the guides so the E-clip on each valve is positioned firmly against the guide **(see illustration 13.6a)**. **Note:** *If either side's E-clip won't push against the guide, remove and decarbonize the exhaust valves (see Section 13).*

1986 models

4   Loosen the locknuts that secure the valve lever to the adjusting lever. Let the valve springs push the valves into the closed position, then tighten the locknuts.

1987 models

Refer to illustration 14.9
5   Remove the cylinder top covers **(see illustration 13.4)**.
6   Loosen the locknuts on the valve and adjusting levers and push the exhaust valves all the way into the guides, until the E-clips touch the guides **(see illustration 13.6a)**. **Note:** *If the valves won't push in all the way, remove and decarbonize them* (see Section 13).
7   Loosen the locknut on the end of the rack where it protrudes from the lower right corner of the cylinder.
8   Place a screwdriver in the slot on top of the left pinion shaft. Turn the screwdriver counterclockwise until the exhaust valves open all the way.
9   Hold the exhaust valves open and measure the distance from the left valve guide to the E-clip surface that's farthest from the valve guide **(see illustration)**. If it's not within the range listed in this Chapter's Specifications, turn the adjusting screw on the end of the rack to change the measurement.
10   Repeat the procedure for the right valve guide.
11   Once the measured distance is within the specified range, tighten the rack locknut to the torque listed in this Chapter's Specifications.

1988 and later models

12   Remove the cylinder top covers **(see illustration 13.4)**.
13   Check the positions of the exhaust valves. They should be all the

14.9 Measure the distance from the outer surface of the E-clip to the outer surface of the valve guide

15.2 With the engine off, the groove should align with the line next to the L mark; at high engine speeds, it should turn to parallel the line next to the H mark

way into the guides, so the E-clips touch the guides **(see illustration 13.6a)**.

14   If the valves aren't all the way in, loosen the locknuts on the valve and adjusting levers **(see illustration 13.6a)**. Turn the eccentric adjusting bolts to close the valves completely, then tighten the locknuts. **Note:** *If the valves won't close all the way, remove and decarbonize them* (see Section 13).

15   Check the gap between the pinion shaft spring and the post that it fits over **(see illustration 13.13a)**. If it's not within the range listed in this Chapter's Specifications, disassemble the mechanism and check it for worn or damaged parts (see Section 13).

16   Place a screwdriver in the slot on top of the left pinion shaft. Turn the screwdriver counterclockwise until the left exhaust valve opens all the way.

17   Hold the exhaust valve open and measure the distance from the left valve guide to the E-clip surface that's farthest from the valve guide **(see illustration 14.9)**. If it's not within the range listed in this Chapter's Specifications, disassemble the mechanism and check it for worn or damaged parts (see Section 13).

18   Repeat the procedure for the right valve guide.

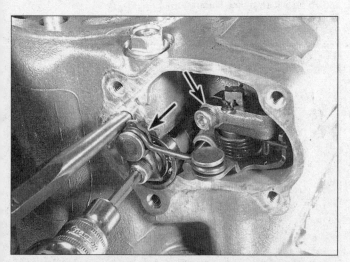

16.2 To adjust the CRV linkage, loosen the Allen bolt (right arrow) and rotate the link lever (left arrow) counterclockwise; to remove the right sub-exhaust valve, hold the lever with a punch and unscrew the Allen bolt, as shown here

All models
19   Install the left and right side covers.
20   Install the expansion chamber.

15   Composite racing valve (1992 through 2004 CR250R) - adjustment

Refer to illustration 15.2

1   Clean the engine so dirt won't get into the CRV mechanism. With the engine off, unscrew the cap from the left side of the cylinder. Start the engine, warm it up, then shut it off.

2   Look at the groove in the end of the left sub-exhaust valve **(see illustration)**. With the engine off, it should be straight up and down, aligning with the line next to the L mark on the cylinder.

3   Start the engine. Have an assistant operate the throttle, raising engine speed while you watch the groove. It should rotate to align with the H mark. If it doesn't, refer to the following Section and check for a loose Allen bolt on the pinion holder, exhaust deposits on the valves and linkage, and incorrect assembly of the valve linkage.

4   To adjust the linkage, remove the cover from the right side of the cylinder and loosen the drive pinion Allen bolt **(see illustration 16.2)**. Turn the valve link lever all the way counterclockwise, then tighten the bolt to the torque listed in this Chapter's Specifications.

5   Replace the cap O-ring if it's brittle, flattened or deteriorated. Coat the threads of the cap with molybdenum disulfide paste, then tighten it to the torque listed in this Chapter's Specifications.

16   Composite racing valve (1992 through 2004 CR250R) - removal, inspection and installation

Sub-exhaust valve and flap valve disassembly

Refer to illustrations 16.2, 16.3, 16.4a, 16.4b, 16.5a, 16.5b, 16.6a, 16.6b, 16.6c, 16.7a, 16.7b and 16.8

1   Refer to Section 15 and remove the cap from the left side of the cylinder. On the right side, remove four bolts and take off the cover.

2   Insert a punch or screwdriver blade through the notch of the exhaust valve lever into the hole in the cylinder **(see illustration)**. This will keep the lever from rotating while you unscrew the Allen bolt.

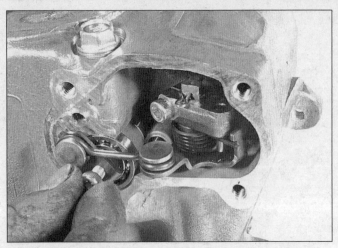

16.3 Pull out the Allen bolt and move the link aside

16.4a Back out the stopper bolt at least 5/16 inch . . .

3   Pull out the bolt **(see illustration)**. Pull the lever away from the cylinder and let it hang.
4   Unscrew the stopper bolt on top of the cylinder until there's a gap

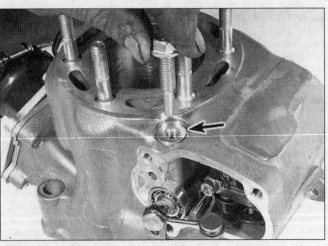

16.4b . . . if you remove it all the way, don't lose its washer

of at least 5/16 inch between the bolt head and the cylinder **(see illustration)**. You can remove the bolt all the way, but don't lose its washer if you do **(see illustration)**.
5   Pull out the bearing, the right sub-exhaust valve and the shaft **(see illustrations)**. **Note:** *The valve may stick on the shaft, especially if it's coated with deposits. Don't force it off and risk bending the shaft. Try removing the deposits with carburetor cleaner.*
6   On the left side of the cylinder, remove the snap-ring **(see illustration)**. Pull out the bearing collar, then pull out the bearing and the left sub-exhaust valve **(see illustrations)**.
7   Reach through the exhaust port with needle-nosed pliers and grasp the flap valve **(see illustration)**. Pull out the flap valve shaft **(see illustration)**, then withdraw the flap valve through the port.
8   Thoroughly clean all deposits from the flap valve and related parts **(see illustration)**. Be sure to clean the passages where the shafts pass though the flap valve. **Note:** *If you're just performing a routine cleaning, you can skip the following steps and reassemble the valve at this point.*

Valve linkage disassembly
Refer to illustrations 16.9, 16.10a, 16.10b, 16.10c and 16.11
9   Note how the spring fits over the pin in the drive pinion and the end of the link lever **(see illustration)**.

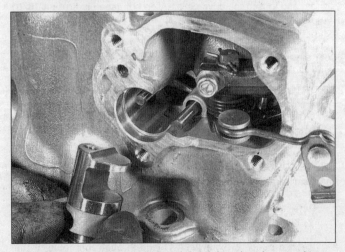

16.5a Remove the bearing and the right sub-exhaust valve

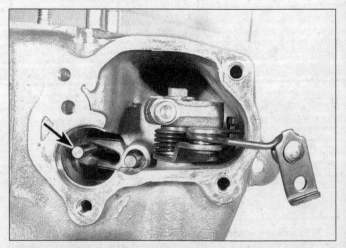

16.5b Pull the sub-exhaust valve shaft out of the slot; note how the slot angles upward from front to rear

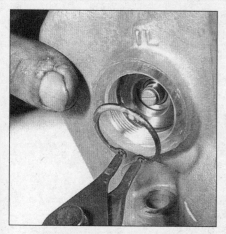

16.6a Remove the snap-ring from the bore . . .

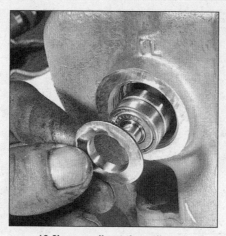

16.6b . . . pull out the collar . . .

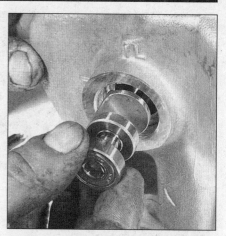

16.6c . . . and remove the bearing and left sub-exhaust valve

16.7a Grasp the flap valve with needle-nosed pliers . . .

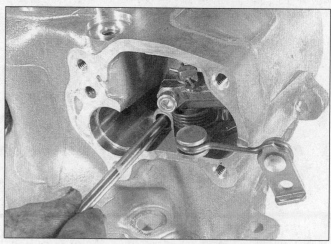

16.7b . . . pull out the shaft and remove the valve

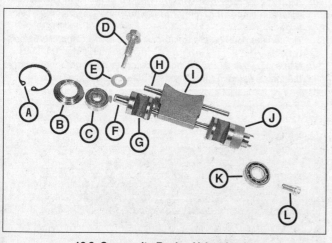

16.8 Composite Racing Valve details

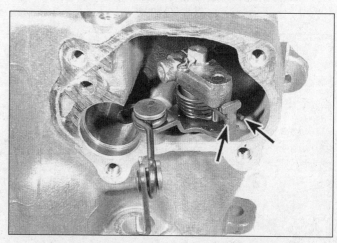

16.9 Note how the spring ends are installed (arrows)

A	Snap-ring	G	Left sub-exhaust valve
B	Collar	H	Flap valve shaft
C	Bearing	I	Flap valve
D	Stopper bolt	J	Right sub-exhaust valve
E	Washer	K	Bearing
F	Sub-exhaust valve shaft	L	Allen bolt

16.10a Pull out the clip . . .

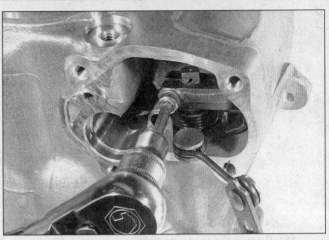

16.10b . . . and remove the drive pinion Allen bolt

10 Pull out the clip and remove the drive pinion Allen bolt **(see illustrations)**. Remove the shaft and bushing **(see illustration)**.

11 Thoroughly clean all deposits from the linkage and check its parts for wear and damage **(see illustration)**.

Assembly

Refer to illustration 16.12

12 Assembly is the reverse of the disassembly steps, with the following additions:

a) *Lubricate the pivot joints in the valve link with a 50/50 mixture of molybdenum disulfide grease and engine oil.*

b) *The linkage bushing fits inside the spring with its narrow end down* **(see illustration)**. *Install the spring with its ends upward, one end on each side of the drive pinion pin and the valve link lever.*

c) *Lubricate the linkage shaft and bushing with multi-purpose grease.*

d) *Lubricate the shaft holes in the flap valve with Honda Pro Moly 60 paste or equivalent.*

e) *If there's a projection on the rear (curved) edge of the flap valve, it faces upward when the valve is installed. The slot in the flap valve that the sub-exhaust valve shaft passes through angles upward from front to rear.*

f) *Lubricate the sub-exhaust valves with two-stroke engine oil.*

g) *Align the stopper bolt with the groove in the right sub-exhaust valve and tighten it to the torque listed in this Chapter's Specifications.*

h) *Tighten the Allen bolt to the torque listed in this Chapter's Specifications.*

i) *Use a new gasket on the right side cover and tighten its bolts to the torque listed in this Chapter's Specifications.*

16.10c Remove the shaft and bushing from the bottom of the cylinder

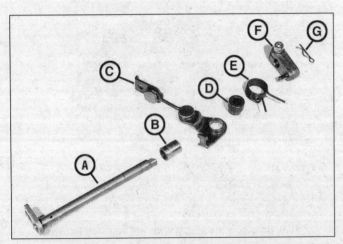

16.11 Composite Racing Valve linkage details

A   *Shaft*
B   *Bushing*
C   *Link lever*
D   *Collar*

E   *Spring*
F   *Drive pinion*
G   *Clip*

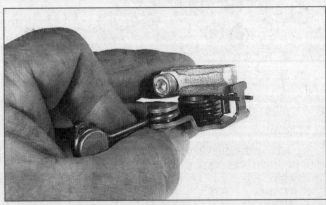

16.12 Install the spring with its ends up; cross the spring ends, then position them over the pin on the drive pinion and the end of the link lever

Chapter 5 Part A
Ignition system
(CR80R/85R and CR125R models)

Contents

Specifications

General

Ignition coil resistance

CR80R/85R

1986

Primary .... 0.2 to 0.04 ohms

Secondary .... 4600 to 7000 ohms

1987 through 1994

Primary .... 0.4 to 0.6 ohms

Secondary (without spark plug cap) .... 10,400 to 15,600 ohms

1995 on

Primary .... 0.4 to 0.6 ohms

Secondary (with spark plug cap) .... 14,000 to 23,000 ohms

Secondary (without spark plug cap) .... 10,000 to 16,000 ohms

CR125R

1986

Primary .... 0.2 to 0.04 ohms

Secondary (with spark plug cap .... 8300 to 14000 ohms

Secondary (without spark plug cap) .... 4600 to 7000 ohms

1987 through 1998

Primary .... 0.4 to 0.6 ohms

Secondary (with spark plug cap) .... 14,000 to 23,000 ohms

Secondary (without spark plug cap) .... 10,000 to 16,000 ohms

1999

Primary .... 0.2 to 0.4 ohms

Secondary (with spark plug cap) .... 9,000 to 16,000 ohms

Secondary (without spark plug cap) .... 4000 to 8000 ohms

2000 and 2001

Primary .... 0.1 to 0.3 ohms

Secondary (with spark plug cap) .... 9,000 to 16,000 ohms

Secondary (without spark plug cap) .... 4000 to 8000 ohms

2002

Primary .... 0.4 to 0.6 ohms

Secondary (with spark plug cap) .... 15,000 to 22,000 ohms

Secondary (without spark plug cap) .... 10,000 to 17,000 ohms

2003 and later

Primary .... 0.2 to 0.4 ohms

Secondary (with spark plug cap) .... 9000 to 16,000 ohms

Secondary (without spark plug cap) .... 4000 to 8000 ohms

Alternator exciter coil resistance

CR80R/85R

1986 through 1995 .... 290 to 350 ohms

1996 through 2004 .... 210 to 350 ohms

2005 and later

Yellow to blue .... 120 to 180 ohms

Blue to white .... 24 to 44 ohms

General (continued)

Alternator exciter coil resistance (continued)
CR125R
  1986 through 1989
    Brown-to-white .... 360 to 440 ohms
    Brown-to-blue .... 90 to 130 ohms
  1990 and 1991 .... 40 to 140 ohms
  1992 through 1997 .... 20 to 140 ohms
  1998 on .... 9 to 25 ohms
Pulse generator resistance
CR80/85R
  1985 through 2004 .... 150 to 240 ohms
  2005 and later .... 180 to 280 ohms
CR125R
  1986 through 1989 .... 90 to 110 ohms
  1990 on .... 180 to 280 ohms

Torque specification

Alternator rotor nut .... 55 Nm (40 ft-lbs)

1　General information

The only electrical circuit on these models is the ignition system. It consists of an alternator that generates the current, a capacitive discharge ignition (CDI) unit that receives and stores it, and a pulse generator that triggers the CDI unit to discharge its current into the ignition coil, where it is stepped up to a voltage high enough to jump the spark plug gap. To aid in locating a problem in the ignition circuit, complete wiring diagrams of each model are included at the end of this manual.

The CDI ignition system functions on the same principle as a breaker point ignition system, with the pulse generator and CDI unit performing the tasks previously associated with the breaker points and mechanical advance system. As a result, adjustment and maintenance of breakerless ignition components is eliminated (with the exception of spark plug replacement).

Because these models are intended for competition, they do not have a battery, ignition switch, fuses, turn signals or lights. The engine is started with a kickstarter and turned off with a kill button on the left handlebar.

Note: *Keep in mind that electrical parts, once purchased, can't be returned. To avoid unnecessary expense, make very sure the faulty component has been positively identified before buying a replacement part.*

2　Electrical troubleshooting

Electrical problems often stem from simple causes, such as loose or corroded connections. Prior to any electrical troubleshooting, always visually check the condition of the wires and connections in the circuit.

If testing instruments are going to be utilized, use the diagrams to plan where you will make the necessary connections in order to accurately pinpoint the trouble spot.

The basic tools needed for electrical troubleshooting include a test light or voltmeter, an ohmmeter or a continuity tester (which includes a bulb, battery and set of test leads) and a jumper wire, preferably with a circuit breaker incorporated, which can be used to bypass electrical components.

A continuity check is performed to see if a circuit, section of circuit or individual component is capable of passing electricity through it. Connect one lead of a self-powered test light or ohmmeter to one end of the circuit being tested and the other lead to the other end of the circuit. If the bulb lights (or the ohmmeter indicates little or no resistance), there is continuity, which means the circuit is passing electricity through it properly. The kill switch can be checked in the same way.

Remember that the electrical circuit on these motorcycles is designed to conduct electricity through the wires, kill switch, etc. to the electrical component (CDI unit, etc.). From there it is directed to the

frame (ground) where it is passed back to the alternator. Electrical problems are basically an interruption in the flow of electricity.

Because of their nature, the individual ignition system components can be checked but not repaired. If ignition system troubles occur, and the faulty component can be isolated, the only cure for the problem is to replace the part with a new one. Keep in mind that most electrical parts, once purchased, can't be returned. To avoid unnecessary expense, make very sure the faulty component has been positively identified before buying a replacement part.

3　Ignition system - check

Refer to illustrations 3.4 and 3.10

Warning: *Because of the very high voltage generated by the ignition system, extreme care should be taken when these checks are performed.*

1　If the ignition system is the suspected cause of poor engine performance or failure to start, a number of checks can be made to isolate the problem.

Engine will not start

2　Refer to Chapter 1 and disconnect the spark plug wire. Connect the wire to a spare spark plug and lay the plug on the engine with the threads contacting the engine. If necessary, hold the spark plug with an insulated tool. Crank the engine over and make sure a well-defined, blue spark occurs between the spark plug electrodes. **Warning:** *Don't remove the spark plug from the engine to perform this check - atomized fuel being pumped out of the open spark plug hole could ignite, causing severe injury!*

3　If no spark occurs, the following checks should be made:

4　Unscrew the spark plug cap from the plug wire and check the cap resistance with an ohmmeter **(see illustration)**. If the resistance is infinite, replace it with a new one.

5　Make sure all electrical connectors are clean and tight. Check all wires for shorts, opens and correct installation.

6　Check the pulse generator and exciter coil (see Section 6).

7　Refer to Section 4 and check the ignition coil primary and secondary resistance.

8　If the preceding checks produce positive results but there is still no spark at the plug, refer to Section 5 and check the CDI unit.

Engine starts but misfires

9　If the engine starts but misfires, make the following checks before deciding that the ignition system is at fault.

10　The ignition system must be able to produce a spark across a seven millimeter (1/4-inch) gap (minimum). A simple test fixture **(see illustration)** can be constructed to make sure the minimum spark gap can be jumped. Make sure the fixture electrodes are positioned seven millimeters apart.

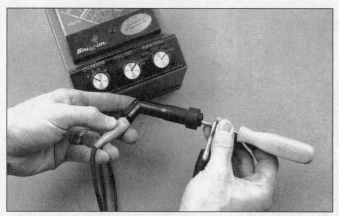

3.4 Unscrew the spark plug cap from the plug wire and measure its resistance with an ohmmeter

3.10 A simple spark gap testing fixture can be made from a block of wood, two nails, a large alligator clip, a screw and a piece of wire

11   Connect the spark plug wire to the protruding test fixture electrode, then attach the fixture's alligator clip to a good engine ground.
12   Crank the engine over with the kickstarter and see if well-defined, blue sparks occur between the test fixture electrodes. If the minimum spark gap test is positive, the ignition coil is functioning properly. If the spark will not jump the gap, or if it is weak (orange colored), refer to Steps 4 through 7 of this Section and perform the component checks described.

4   Ignition coil - check, removal and installation

Check

Refer to illustration 4.5
1   In order to determine conclusively that the ignition coil is defective, it should be tested by an authorized Honda dealer service department which is equipped with the special electrical tester required for this check.
2   However, the coil can be checked visually (for cracks and other damage) and the primary and secondary coil resistances can be measured with an ohmmeter. If the coil is undamaged, and if the resistances are as specified, it is probably capable of proper operation.
3   To check the coil for physical damage, it must be removed (see Steps 8 and 9). To check the resistance, remove the fuel tank (see Chapter 3), unplug the primary circuit electrical connector(s) from the coil and remove the spark plug wire from the spark plug. Mark the locations of all wires before disconnecting them.

4   Label the primary wires, then disconnect them.
5   Connect an ohmmeter between the primary terminals. Set the ohmmeter selector switch in the Rx1 position and compare the measured resistance to the primary resistance values listed in this Chapter's Specifications **(see illustration)**.
6   On models where coil secondary resistance is specified with the spark plug cap installed, connect the ohmmeter between the coil ground wire's primary terminal and the spark plug cap. Place the ohmmeter selector switch in the Rx100 position and compare the measured resistance to the secondary resistance values listed in this Chapter's Specifications.
7   If the resistances are not as specified, unscrew the spark plug cap from the plug wire and check the resistance between the ground wire's primary terminal and the end of the spark plug wire. If it's now within specifications, the spark plug cap is bad. If it's still not as specified, the coil is probably defective and should be replaced with a new one.

Removal and installation

Refer to illustration 4.8
8   To remove the coil, refer to Chapter 4 and remove the fuel tank, then disconnect the spark plug wire from the plug. Unplug the coil primary circuit electrical connector(s) **(see illustration)**. Some models have a single primary circuit connector and another wire that connects to one of the coil mounting bolts to provide ground.
9   Remove the coil mounting bolt(s), then lift the coil out.
10   Installation is the reverse of removal.

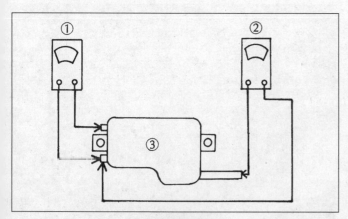

4.5 Ignition coil test
1   Measure primary winding resistance
2   Measure secondary winding resistance
3   Ignition coil

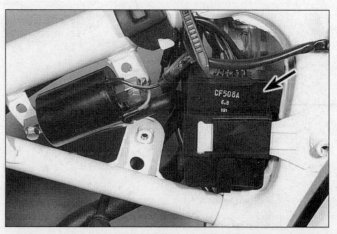

4.8 The ignition coil on all CR80Rs and CR125Rs through 1998 is mounted beneath the frame; the CDI unit on all CR80R/85R and early CR125R models is mounted near the coil (arrow) . . .

5.6a ... the CDI unit on later CR125Rs (through 1999) is mounted between the radiators (arrow) ...

5.6b ... while on 2000 and later CR125Rs the coil is mounted between the radiators ...

5.6c ... and the CDI unit is mounted on the front of the steering head

5   CDI unit - check, removal and installation

Check

1   The CDI unit is tested by process of elimination (when all other possible causes of ignition problems have been checked and eliminated, the CDI unit is at fault).
2   Check the ignition coil, alternator exciter coil, pulse generator and kill switch as described elsewhere in this Chapter.
3   Carefully check the wiring harnesses for breaks or bad connections.
4   If the harness and all other system components tested good, the CDI unit may be defective. Before buying a new one, it's a good idea to substitute a known good CDI unit.

Removal and installation

Refer to illustration 5.6

5   If you're working on a CR80R/85R, remove the fuel tank if you haven't already done so (see Chapter 4).
6   Locate the CDI unit **(see illustration 4.8 and the accompanying illustration)**. Unplug its connector and work the unit out of its mounting band.
7   Installation is the reverse of the removal steps.

6   Alternator and pulse generator - check and replacement

Check

1   Locate and disconnect the alternator coil connector on the left side of the vehicle frame.
2   To check the exciter coil, connect an ohmmeter between the specified terminals in the side of the connector that runs back to the exciter coil on the left side of the engine. Wire colors and connections are as follows:

a) *CR80R/85R - green-to-black/red*
b) *1986 through 1989 CR125R - brown-to-white and brown-to-blue*
c) *1990 and later CR125R - Blue-to-white*

If the readings are much outside the value listed in this Chapter's Specifications, replace the exciter coil as described below.
3   To check the pulse generator, connect the ohmmeter between the specified terminals in the side of the connector that runs back to the pulse generator (it's located next to the alternator on the left side of the engine). Wire colors and connections are as follows:

a) *CR80R/85R - blue-to-green/white*
b) *CR125R - blue/yellow-to-green/white*

If the readings are much outside the value listed in this Chapter's Specifications, replace the pulse generator as described below.

6.4a The CR80R/85R left engine cover includes the drive sprocket cover; remove its screws (arrows), then take off the cover and its O-ring

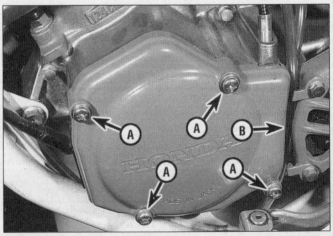

6.4b Remove the screws (A) to detach the CR125R left engine cover; note how the fuel system hoses (B) fit behind the cover

6.5a The CR80R/85R alternator rotor is secured by a hex nut and washer (left arrow); the pulse generator (right arrow) is mounted next to the rotor

6.5b The CR125R rotor is secured by a flange nut and a separate washer; the 1986 pulse generator is mounted above and to the right of the rotor; on later models (shown), it's mounted above and to the left (arrow)

Rotor replacement

Removal

Refer to illustrations 6.4a, 6.4b, 6.5a, 6.5b, 6.5c, 6.6 and 6.7

Note: *To remove the alternator rotor, the special Honda puller (part no. 07733-0010001) or an aftermarket equivalent will be required. Don't try to remove the rotor without the proper puller, as it's almost sure to be damaged. Pullers are readily available from motorcycle dealers and aftermarket tool suppliers.*

4   Remove the left engine cover **(see illustrations)**.

5   Hold the alternator rotor with a universal holder (Honda part no. 07725-003000 or equivalent). You can also use a strap wrench. If you don't have one of these tools and the engine is in the frame, the rotor can be locked by placing the transmission in gear and holding the rear brake on. Unscrew the rotor nut **(see illustrations)**.

6   Thread an alternator puller into the center of the rotor and use it to remove the rotor **(see illustration)**. If the rotor doesn't come off easily, tap sharply on the end of the puller to release the rotor's grip on the tapered crankshaft end. **Caution:** *Don't strike the rotor, as the magnets could be damaged.*

7   Pull the rotor off **(see illustration)**. Check the Woodruff key; if it's not secure in its slot, pull it out and set it aside for safekeeping. A convenient method is to stick the Woodruff key to the magnets inside the rotor, but be certain not to forget it's there, as serious damage to the rotor and stator coils will occur if the engine is run with anything stuck to the magnets.

6.5c Hold the rotor (universal holder shown) and remove the nut with a socket

Installation

Refer to illustration 6.8

8   Take a look to make sure there isn't anything stuck to the inside of the rotor **(see illustration)**.

6.6 Thread the puller into the rotor, hold the puller body with a wrench and tighten the puller screw to push the rotor off

6.7 Locate the Woodruff key (arrow); be sure it's in its slot on installation

6.8 Be sure there aren't any small metal objects stuck to the rotor magnets; an inconspicuous item like this Woodruff key (arrow) can ruin the rotor and stator if the engine is run

6.16a Remove the stator plate mounting bolts (arrows)

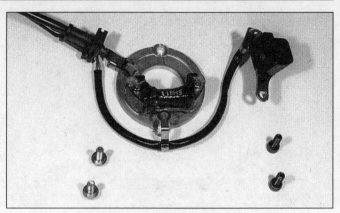

6.16b Take off the stator plate, together with the exciter coil, wiring harness and grommet; on 1992 and later CR80R/85R models (shown), the pulse generator is removed as a unit with the stator plate

9   Degrease the center of the rotor and the end of the crankshaft.
10   Make sure the Woodruff key is positioned securely in its slot **(see illustration 6.7)**.
11   Align the rotor slot with the Woodruff key. Place the rotor on the crankshaft.
12   Install the rotor washer and nut. Hold the rotor from turning with one of the methods described in Step 5 and tighten the nut to the torque listed in this Chapter's Specifications.
13   The remainder of installation is the reverse of the removal steps.

Stator coil and pulse generator replacement

Refer to illustrations 6.16a, 6.16b, 6.16c and 6.16d

14   The stator coil and pulse generator on 1986 through 1991 CR80R models can be replaced separately; on all others, the stator coil and pulse generator are replaced as a unit.
15   Remove the left engine cover and alternator rotor as described above.
16   Remove the stator coil and pulse generator bolts and take them off the engine **(see illustrations)**.
17   Installation is the reverse of the removal steps. Tighten the stator coil bolts securely, but don't overtighten them and strip the threads.

7   Kill switch - check, removal and installation

1   The kill switch, mounted on the left handlebar, shorts the ignition circuit to ground when its button is pressed.

Check

2   Follow the wires from the switch to their connectors and unplug them.
3   Connect an ohmmeter between the wire terminals in the switch side of the connectors (not the side that leads back to the wiring harness). With the switch in the released position, the ohmmeter should show no continuity (infinite resistance); with the button pushed, the ohmmeter should show continuity (little or no resistance).
4   Repeat the test several times. The ohmmeter should move from continuity to no continuity each time the button is released. If it continues to show continuity after it's released, the ignition system is being shorted out constantly and won't produce a spark.

Removal and installation

5   To remove the switch, undo its mounting screw, separate the clamp and take it off the handlebar. Remove the wiring harness retainers and unplug the switch electrical connector.
6   Installation is the reverse of removal. Note that the clamp screw secures the switch ground wire.

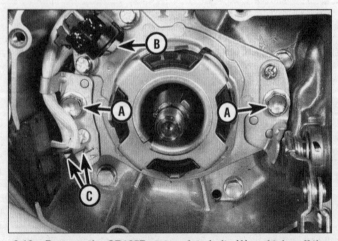

6.16c Remove the CR125R stator plate bolts (A) and take off the plate, together with the pulse generator (B); on installation, the stator plate line should align with the arrowhead mark on the crankcase (C) (1990 and later models shown; earlier models similar)

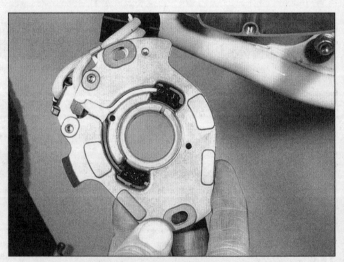

6.16d The wires on some models run through channels in the back of the stator plate; make sure they're routed correctly

Chapter 5 Part B
Ignition system
(CR250R and CR500R models)

Contents

Specifications

General

Ignition coil resistance
CR250R
  1986
    Primary .... 0.2 to 0.4 ohms
    Secondary (with spark plug cap).. 8300 to 14,000 ohms
    Secondary (without spark plug cap)................................... 4600 to 7000 ohms
  1987 through 1991
    Primary .... 0.4 to 0.6 ohms
    Secondary (with spark plug cap).. 14,000 to 23,000 ohms
    Secondary (without spark plug cap)................................... 10,400 to 15,600 ohms
  1992
    Primary .... 0.4 to 0.6 ohms
    Secondary (with spark plug cap).. 16,000 to 23,000 ohms
    Secondary (without spark plug cap)................................... 10,000 to 16,000 ohms
  1993 on
    Primary (1993 through 1999) .... 0.4 to 0.6 ohms
    Primary (2000 on)... 0.1 to 0.3 ohms
Secondary (with spark plug cap)... 9000 to 16,000 ohms
Secondary (without spark plug cap)... 4000 to 8000 ohms
CR500R
  1986
    Primary .... 0.2 to 0.4 ohms
    Secondary (with spark plug cap).. 8300 to 14,000 ohms
    Secondary (without spark plug cap)................................... 4600 to 7000 ohms
  1987 through 1989
    Primary .... 0.4 to 0.6 ohms
    Secondary (with spark plug cap).. 13,000 to 23,000 ohms
    Secondary (without spark plug cap)................................... 10,000 to 16,000 ohms
  1989 through 1991
    Primary .... 0.4 to 0.6 ohms
    Secondary (with spark plug cap).. 14,000 to 23,000 ohms
    Secondary (without spark plug cap)................................... 10,000 to 16,000 ohms
  1992 on
    Primary .... 0.4 to 0.6 ohms
    Secondary (with spark plug cap).. 13,000 to 23,000 ohms
    Secondary (without spark plug cap)................................... 10,000 to 16,000 ohms

Alternator exciter coil resistance

CR250R

1986 through 1988

Brown to white.. 360 to 440 ohms

Brown to blue .... 90 to 130 ohms

1989 through 1992... 40 to 140 ohms

1993 through 1996... 120 to 220 ohms

1997 and 1998... 2 to 20 ohms

1999 through 2001... 9 to 25 ohms

2002 and later.. 0.5 to 4 ohms

CR500R

1986

Brown to white.. 360 to 440 ohms

Brown to blue .... 90 to 130 ohms

1987 on .... 1 to 40 ohms

Alternator charging coil resistance (1997 and 1998 CR250R) .... 1 to 5 ohms

Pulse generator resistance

CR250R

1986 through 1988... 94 to 120 ohms

1989 .... 50 to 180 ohms

1990 on .... 180 to 280 ohms

CR500R

1986 .... 90 to 110 ohms

1987 through 1989... 50 to 180 ohms

1990 on .... 180 to 280 ohms

Torque specifications

Alternator rotor nut .... 55 Nm (40 ft-lbs)

1   General information

The only electrical circuit on these models is the ignition system. It consists of an alternator that generates the current, a capacitive discharge ignition (CDI) unit that receives and stores it, and a pulse generator that triggers the CDI unit to discharge its current into the ignition coil, where it is stepped up to a voltage high enough to jump the spark plug gap. To aid in locating a problem in the ignition circuit, wiring diagrams are included at the end of this manual.

The CDI ignition system functions on the same principle as a breaker point ignition system with the pulse generator and CDI unit performing the tasks previously associated with the breaker points and mechanical advance system. As a result, adjustment and maintenance of breakerless ignition components is eliminated (with the exception of spark plug replacement).

Because these models are intended for motocross competition, they do not have a battery, ignition switch, fuses, turn signals or lights. The engine is started with a kickstarter and turned off with a kill button on the left handlebar. **Note:** *Keep in mind that electrical parts, once purchased, can't be returned. To avoid unnecessary expense, make very sure the faulty component has been positively identified before buying a replacement part.*

2   Electrical troubleshooting

Electrical problems often stem from simple causes, such as loose or corroded connections. Prior to any electrical troubleshooting, always visually check the condition of the wires and connections in the circuit.

If testing instruments are going to be utilized, use the diagrams to plan where you will make the necessary connections in order to accurately pinpoint the trouble spot.

The basic tools needed for electrical troubleshooting include a test light or voltmeter, an ohmmeter or a continuity tester (which includes a bulb, battery and set of test leads) and a jumper wire, preferably with a circuit breaker incorporated, which can be used to bypass electrical components.

A continuity check is performed to see if a circuit, section of circuit or individual component is capable of passing electricity through it. Connect one lead of a self-powered test light or ohmmeter to one end of the circuit being tested and the other lead to the other end of the circuit. If the bulb lights (or the ohmmeter indicates little or no resistance), there is continuity, which means the circuit is passing electricity through it properly. The kill switch can be checked in the same way.

Remember that the electrical circuit on these motorcycles is designed to conduct electricity through the wires, kill switch, etc. to the electrical component (CDI unit, etc.). From there it is directed to the frame (ground) where it is passed back to the alternator. Electrical problems are basically an interruption in the flow of electricity.

Because of their nature, the individual ignition system components can be checked but not repaired. If ignition system troubles occur, and the faulty component can be isolated, the only cure for the problem is to replace the part with a new one. Keep in mind that most electrical parts, once purchased, can't be returned. To avoid unnecessary expense, make very sure the faulty component has been positively identified before buying a replacement part.

3   Ignition system - check

Refer to illustrations 3.4 and 3.10

Warning: *Because of the very high voltage generated by the ignition system, extreme care should be taken when these checks are performed.*

1   If the ignition system is the suspected cause of poor engine performance or failure to start, a number of checks can be made to isolate the problem.

Engine will not start

2   Refer to Chapter 1 and disconnect the spark plug wire. Connect the wire to a spare spark plug and lay the plug on the engine with the threads contacting the engine. If necessary, hold the spark plug with an insulated tool. Crank the engine over and make sure a well-defined, blue spark occurs between the spark plug electrodes. **Warning:** *Don't remove the spark plug from the engine to perform this check - atom-*

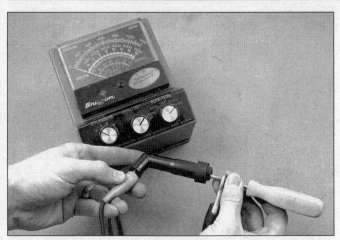

3.4 Unscrew the spark plug cap from the plug wire and measure its resistance with an ohmmeter

3.10 A simple spark gap testing fixture can be made from a block of wood, two nails, a large alligator clip, a screw and a piece of wire

ized fuel being pumped out of the open spark plug hole could ignite, causing severe injury!

3   If no spark occurs, the following checks should be made:

4   Unscrew the spark plug cap from the plug wire and check the cap resistance with an ohmmeter **(see illustration)**. If the resistance is infinite, replace it with a new one.

5   Make sure all electrical connectors are clean and tight. Check all wires for shorts, opens and correct installation.

6   Check the pulse generator and exciter coil (see Section 6).

7   Refer to Section 4 and check the ignition coil primary and secondary resistance.

8   If the preceding checks produce positive results but there is still no spark at the plug, refer to Section 5 and check the CDI unit.

Engine starts but misfires

9   If the engine starts but misfires, make the following checks before deciding that the ignition system is at fault.

10   The ignition system must be able to produce a spark across a seven millimeter (9/32-inch) gap (minimum). A simple test fixture **(see illustration)** can be constructed to make sure the minimum spark gap can be jumped. Make sure the fixture electrodes are positioned seven millimeters apart.

11   Connect the spark plug wire to the protruding test fixture electrode, then attach the fixture's alligator clip to a good engine ground.

12   Crank the engine over with the kickstarter and see if well-defined, blue sparks occur between the test fixture electrodes. If the minimum spark gap test is positive, the ignition coil is functioning properly. If the spark will not jump the gap, or if it is weak (orange colored), refer to Steps 4 through 7 of this Section and perform the component checks described.

---

4   Ignition coil - check, removal and installation

Check

Refer to illustration 4.5

1   In order to determine conclusively that the ignition coil is defective, it should be tested by an authorized Honda dealer service department which is equipped with the special electrical tester required for this check.

2   However, the coil can be checked visually (for cracks and other damage) and the primary and secondary coil resistances can be measured with an ohmmeter. If the coil is undamaged, and if the resistances are as specified, it is probably capable of proper operation.

3   To check the coil for physical damage, it must be removed (see

Steps 8 and 9). To check the resistance, remove the fuel tank (see Chapter 4), unplug the primary circuit electrical connector(s) from the coil and remove the spark plug wire from the spark plug. Mark the locations of all wires before disconnecting them.

4   Label the primary wires, then disconnect them.

5   Connect an ohmmeter between the primary terminals. Set the ohmmeter selector switch in the Rx1 position and compare the measured resistance to the primary resistance values listed in this Chapter's Specifications **(see illustration)**.

6   On models where coil secondary resistance is specified with the spark plug cap installed, connect the ohmmeter between the coil ground wire's primary terminal and the spark plug cap. Place the ohmmeter selector switch in the Rx100 position and compare the measured resistance to the secondary resistance values listed in this Chapter's Specifications.

7   If the resistances are not as specified, unscrew the spark plug cap from the plug wire and check the resistance between the ground wire's primary terminal and the end of the spark plug wire. If it's now within specifications, the spark plug cap is bad. If it's still not as specified, the coil is probably defective and should be replaced with a new one.

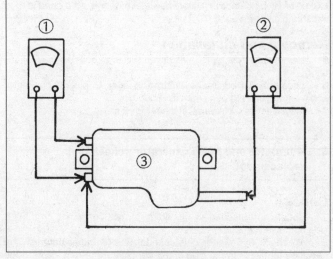

4.5 Ignition coil test

1   *Measure primary winding resistance*
2   *Measure secondary winding resistance*
3   *Ignition coil*

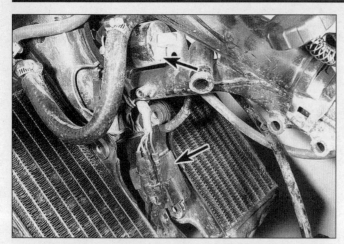

4.8a The ignition coil and CDI unit on all CR500Rs and CR250Rs through 1996 are mounted beneath the frame . . .

4.8b . . . the coil on 1997 and later CR250Rs is between the radiators, and the CDI unit on 2000 and later CR250Rs is in front of the steering head

Removal and installation

Refer to illustrations 4.8a and 4.8b

8   To remove the coil, refer to Chapter 4 and remove the fuel tank, then disconnect the spark plug wire from the plug. Unplug the coil primary circuit electrical connector(s) **(see illustration)**. Some models have a single primary circuit connector and another wire that connects to one of the coil mounting bolts to provide ground **(see illustration)**.
9   Remove the coil mounting bolt(s), then lift the coil out.
10   Installation is the reverse of removal.

5   CDI unit - check, removal and installation

Check

1   The CDI unit is tested by process of elimination (when all other possible causes of ignition problems have been checked and eliminated, the CDI unit is at fault).
2   Check the ignition coil, alternator exciter coil, pulse generator and kill switch as described elsewhere in this Chapter.
3   Carefully check the wiring harnesses for breaks or bad connections.
4   If the harness and all other system components tested good, the CDI unit may be defective. Before buying a new one, it's a good idea to substitute a known good CDI unit.

Removal and installation

5   Remove the fuel tank if you haven't already done so (see Chapter 4).
6   Locate the CDI unit **(see illustration 4.8a)**. Unplug its connector and work the unit out of its mounting band.
7   Installation is the reverse of the removal steps.

6   Alternator and pulse generator - check and replacement

Check

1   Locate and disconnect the alternator coil connector on the left side of the vehicle frame.
2   To check the exciter coil, connect an ohmmeter between the specified terminals in the side of the connector that runs back to the exciter coil on the left side of the engine. Wire colors and connections are as follows:

a) *1986 through 1988 CR250R and 1986 CR500R - brown to white and brown to blue*

b) *1989 through 1996 CR250R and 1987 and later CR500R - blue to white*
c) *1997 and later CR250R - yellow/white to yellow and blue to white*

If the readings are much outside the value listed in this Chapter's Specifications, replace the exciter coil as described below.
3   To check the pulse generator, connect the ohmmeter between the blue/yellow and green/white terminals in the side of the connector that runs back to the pulse generator (it's located next to the alternator on the left side of the engine). If the readings are much outside the value listed in this Chapter's Specifications, replace the pulse generator as described below.

Rotor replacement

Removal

Refer to illustrations 6.4, 6.5a, 6.5b, 6.6 and 6.7
Note: *To remove the alternator rotor, the special Honda puller (part no. 07733-0010001) or an aftermarket equivalent will be required. Don't try to remove the rotor without the proper puller, as it's almost sure to be damaged. Pullers are readily available from motorcycle dealers and aftermarket tool suppliers.*
4   Remove the left engine cover **(see illustration)**.
5   Hold the alternator rotor with a universal holder (Honda part no. 07725-003000 or equivalent. You can also use a strap wrench. If you don't have one of these tools and the engine is in the frame, the rotor can be locked by placing the transmission in gear and holding the rear brake on. Unscrew the rotor nut **(see illustrations)**.

6.4 The left engine cover is secured by screws (arrows)

6.5a The alternator rotor is secured by a nut and washer (lower arrow); the pulse generator is mounted above and behind the rotor (upper arrow)

6.5b Hold the rotor (universal holder shown) and remove the nut with a socket

6   Thread an alternator puller into the center of the rotor and use it to remove the rotor **(see illustration)**. If the rotor doesn't come off easily, tap sharply on the end of the puller to release the rotor's grip on the tapered crankshaft end.

7   Pull the rotor off **(see illustration)**. Check the Woodruff key; if it's not secure in its slot, pull it out and set it aside for safekeeping. A convenient method is to stick the Woodruff key to the magnets inside the rotor, but be certain not to forget it's there, as serious damage to the rotor and stator coils will occur if the engine is run with anything stuck to the magnets.

Installation

Refer to illustration 6.8

8   Take a look to make sure there isn't anything stuck to the inside of the rotor **(see illustration)**.

9   Degrease the center of the rotor and the end of the crankshaft.

10   Make sure the Woodruff key is positioned securely in its slot **(see illustration 6.7)**.

11   Align the rotor slot with the Woodruff key. Place the rotor on the crankshaft.

12   Install the rotor washer and nut. Hold the rotor from turning with one of the methods described in Step 5 and tighten the nut to the torque listed in this Chapter's Specifications.

13   The remainder of installation is the reverse of the removal steps.

Stator coil and pulse generator replacement

Refer to illustration 6.16

14   The stator coil and pulse generator are replaced as a unit.

15   Remove the left engine cover and alternator rotor as described above.

6.6 Thread the puller into the rotor, hold the puller body with a wrench and tighten the puller screw to push the rotor off

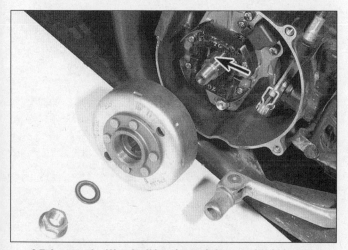

6.7 Locate the Woodruff key (arrow); be sure it's in its slot on installation

6.8 Be sure there aren't any small metal objects stuck to the rotor magnets; an inconspicuous item like this Woodruff key (arrow) can ruin the rotor and stator if the engine is run

6.16 Remove the stator plate mounting bolts (arrow)

16   Remove the stator coil and pulse generator bolts and take them off the engine **(see illustration)**.
17   Installation is the reverse of the removal steps. Tighten the stator coil bolts securely, but don't overtighten them and strip the threads.

7   Kill switch - check, removal and installation

1   The kill switch, mounted on the left handlebar, shorts the ignition circuit to ground when its button is pressed.

Check
2   Follow the wires from the switch to their connectors and unplug them.
3   Connect an ohmmeter between the wire terminals in the switch side of the connectors (not the side that leads back to the wiring harness). With the switch in the released position, the ohmmeter should show no continuity (infinite resistance); with the button pushed, the ohmmeter should show continuity (little or no resistance).
4   Repeat the test several times. The ohmmeter should move from continuity to no continuity each time the button is released. If it continues to show continuity after it's released, the ignition system is being shorted out constantly and won't produce a spark.

Removal and installation
5   To remove the switch, remove its mounting screw, separate the clamp and take it off the handlebar. Remove the wiring harness retainers and unplug the switch electrical connector.
6   Installation is the reverse of removal. Note that the clamp screw secures the switch ground wire.

Chapter 6 Part A
Steering, suspension and final drive (CR80R/85R and CR125R models)

Contents

Specifications

Front forks

Oil type
CR80R/85R
- 1986 through 1995 — Pro-Honda SS-8 suspension fluid or equivalent 10W fork oil
- 1996 on — Pro Honda HP 5W fork oil or equivalent

CR125R
- 1986 through 1991 — Pro-Honda SS7 suspension fluid or equivalent 5W fork oil
- 1992 on — Pro Honda HP 5W fork oil or equivalent

Oil capacity (CR80R)
- 1986 — 287 cc (9.7 fl oz)
- 1987 — 308 cc (10.4 fl oz)
- 1988 through 1991 — 305 cc (10.3 fl oz)
- 1992 through 1994 — 309 cc (10.4 fl oz)
- 1995
  - Standard — 309 cc (10.4 fl oz)
  - Maximum — 330 cc (11.2 fl oz)
  - Minimum — 297 cc (10.0 fl oz)
- 1996 through 1998
  - Standard — 359 cc (12.1 fl oz)
  - Maximum — 361.5 cc (12.2 fl oz)
  - Minimum — 356.5 cc (12.1 fl oz)
- 1999 through 2002
  - Standard — 357 cc (12.1 fl oz)
  - Maximum — 362.5 cc (12.3 fl oz)
  - Minimum — 354.5 cc (12.0 fl oz)

Front forks (continued)

Oil capacity (CR80RB Expert)

  1996 through 1998

    Standard and maximum .... 359 cc (12.1 fl oz)

    Minimum .... 354 cc (12.0 fl oz)

  1999 on

    Standard .... 359 cc (12.1 fl oz)

    Maximum .... 361.4 cc (12.2 fl oz)

    Minimum .... 356.5 cc (12.1 fl oz)

Oil capacity (CR85R)

  2003 and 2004

    Standard .... 357 cc (12.1 fl oz)

    Maximum .... 362.5 cc (12.3 fl oz)

    Minimum .... 354.5 cc (12.0 fl oz)

  2005 and later

    Standard .... 357 cc (12.1 fl oz)

    Maximum .... 361 cc (12.2 fl oz)

    Minimum .... 354 cc (12.0 fl oz)

Oil capacity (CR85RB Expert)

  2003 and 2004

    Standard .... 356 cc (12.0 fl oz)

    Maximum .... 361.4 cc (12.2 fl oz)

    Minimum .... 353.5 cc (12.0 fl oz)

  2005 and later

    Standard .... 356 cc (12.0 fl oz)

    Maximum .... 361.4 cc (12.2 fl oz)

    Minimum .... 353.5 cc (12.0 fl oz)

Oil capacity (CR125R)

  1986

    Standard .... 592 cc (20.0 fl oz)

    Maximum .... 612 cc (20.7 fl oz)

    Minimum .... 572 cc (19.3 fl oz)

  1987

    Standard .... 585 cc (19.8 fl oz)

    Maximum .... 605 cc (20.5 fl oz)

    Minimum .... 549 cc (18.6 fl oz)

  1988

    Standard .... 573 cc (19.4 fl oz)

    Maximum .... 597 cc (20.2 fl oz)

    Minimum .... 540 cc (18.3 fl oz)

  1989

    Standard .... 574 cc (19.4 fl oz)

    Maximum .... 583 cc (19.7 fl oz)

    Minimum .... 526 cc (17.8 fl oz)

  1990

    Standard .... 633 cc (21.4 fl oz)

    Maximum .... 642 cc (21.7 fl oz)

    Minimum .... 608 cc (20.6 fl oz)

  1991

    Standard .... 664 cc (22.5 fl oz)

    Maximum .... 674 cc (22.8 fl oz)

    Minimum .... 641 cc (21.7 fl oz)

  1992

    Standard .... 571 cc (19.31 fl oz)

    Maximum .... 585 cc (19.78 fl oz)

    Minimum .... 553 cc (18.70 fl oz)

  1993

    Standard .... 559 cc (18.91 fl oz)

    Maximum .... 584 cc (19.75 fl oz)

    Minimum .... 541 cc (18.30 fl oz)

  1994

    Standard .... 530 cc (17.92 fl oz)

    Maximum .... 545 cc (18.43 fl oz)

    Minimum .... 505 cc (17.08 fl oz)

  1995

    Standard .... 522 cc (17.65 fl oz)

    Maximum .... 537 cc (18.16 fl oz)

    Minimum .... 497 cc (16.81 fl oz)

1996
    Standard... 518 cc (17.52 fl oz)
    Maximum... 529 cc (17.89 fl oz)
    Minimum.. 489 cc (16.54 fl oz)
1997
    Standard... 620 cc (20.97 fl oz)
    Maximum... 647 cc (21.88 fl oz)
    Minimum.. 601 cc (20.33 fl oz)
1998
    Standard... 585 cc (19.8 fl oz)
    Maximum... 611 cc (20.7 fl oz)
    Minimum.. 566 cc (19.1 fl oz)
1999
    Standard... 590 cc (20.0 fl oz)
    Maximum... 621 cc (21.0 fl oz)
    Minimum.. 576 cc (19.5 fl oz)
2000
    Standard... 518 cc (17.5 fl oz)
    Maximum... 548 cc (18.5 fl oz)
    Minimum.. 484 cc (16.4 fl oz)
2001
    Standard... 502 cc (17.0 fl oz)
    Maximum... 537cc (18.2 fl oz)
    Minimum.. 473 cc (16.0 fl oz)
2002 and 2003
    Standard... 475 cc (16.1 fl oz)
    Maximum... 548 cc (18.5 fl oz)
    Minimum.. 445 cc (15.0 fl oz)
2004 and later
    Standard... 462 +/- 4 cc (15.6 +/- 0.14 fl oz)
    Maximum... 499 cc (16.9 fl oz)
    Minimum.. 420 cc (14.2 fl oz)
Oil level (CR80R) (fork fully compressed and spring removed)
1986
    Standard... 135 mm (5.31 inches)
    Maximum... 135 mm (5.31 inches)
    Minimum.. 160 mm (6.30 inches)
1987
    Standard... 142 mm (5.59 inches)
    Maximum... 142 mm (5.59 inches)
    Minimum.. 167 mm (6.57 inches)
1988 through 1991
    Standard... 146 mm (5.75 inches)
    Maximum... 111 mm (4.37 inches)
    Minimum.. 158 mm (6.22 inches)
1992 through 1995
    Standard... 132 mm (5.2 inches)
    Maximum... 103 mm (4.06 inches)
    Minimum.. 150 mm (5.91 inches)
1996 through 1998
    Standard... 96 mm (3.8 inches)
    Maximum... 92 mm (3.6 inches)
    Minimum.. 100 mm (3.9 inches)
1999 on
    Standard... 101 mm (4.0 inches)
    Maximum... 92 mm (3.6 inches)
    Minimum.. 105 mm (4.1 inches)
Oil level (CR80RB Expert) (fork fully compressed and spring removed)
1996 through 1998
    Standard... 96 mm (3.8 inches)
    Maximum... 96 mm (3.8 inches)
    Minimum.. 104 mm (4.09 inches)
1999 on
    Standard... 98 mm (3.9 inches)
    Maximum... 95 mm (3.7 inches)
    Minimum.. 102 mm (4.01 inches)

Front forks (continued)

Oil level (CR85R) (fork fully compressed and spring removed)

2003 and 2004
Standard .... 101 mm (4.0 inches)
Maximum .... 92 mm (3.6 inches)
Minimum .... 105 mm (4.1 inches)

2005 and later
Standard .... 101 mm (4.0 inches)
Maximum .... 95 mm (3.7 inches)
Minimum .... 106 mm (4.2 inches)

Oil level (CR85RB expert) (fork fully compressed and spring removed)
Standard .... 101 mm (4.0 inches)
Maximum .... 92 mm (3.6 inches)
Minimum .... 105 mm (4.1 inches)

Oil level (CR125R) (fork fully compressed and spring removed)

1986
Standard .... 131 mm (5.2 inches)
Maximum .... 113 mm (4.4 inches)
Minimum .... 149 mm (5.9 inches)

1987
Standard .... 119 mm (4.7 inches)
Maximum .... 100 mm (3.9 inches)
Minimum .... 152 mm (6.0 inches)

1988
Standard .... 125 mm (4.9 inches)
Maximum .... 102 mm (4.0 inches)
Minimum .... 157 mm (6.2 inches)

1989
Standard .... 124 mm (4.9 inches)
Maximum .... 115 mm (4.5 inches)
Minimum .... 170 mm (6.7 inches)

1990
Standard .... 130 mm (5.1 inches)
Maximum .... 121 mm (4.8 inches)
Minimum .... 152 mm (6.0 inches)

1991
Standard .... 96 mm (3.8 inches)
Maximum .... 87 mm (3.4 inches)
Minimum .... 115 mm (4.5 inches)

1992
Standard .... 106 mm (4.2 inches)
Maximum .... 92 mm (3.6 inches)
Minimum .... 123 mm (4.8 inches)

1993
Standard .... 118 mm (4.6 inches)
Maximum .... 93 mm (3.7 inches)
Minimum .... 136 mm (5.4 inches)

1994
Standard .... 95 mm (3.7 inches)
Maximum .... 80 mm (3.1 inches)
Minimum .... 120 mm (4.7 inches)

Oil level (CR125R) (fork fully compressed and spring removed)

1995
Standard .... 101 mm (4.0 inches)
Maximum .... 86 mm (3.4 inches)
Minimum .... 126 mm (5.0 inches)

1996
Standard .... 97 mm (3.8 inches)
Maximum .... 86 mm (3.4 inches)
Minimum .... 126 mm (5.0 inches)

1997
Standard .... 104 mm (4.1 inches)
Maximum .... 81 mm (3.2 inches)
Minimum .... 120 mm (4.7 inches)

1998
Standard .... 139 mm (5.5 inches)
Maximum .... 117 mm (4.6 inches)
Minimum .... 155 mm (6.1 inches)

1999
    Standard.. 135 mm (5.3 inches)
    Maximum... 108 mm (4.3 inches)
    Minimum.. 149 mm (5.9 inches)
2000
    Standard.. 60 mm (2.4 inches)
    Maximum... 35 mm (1.4 inches)
    Minimum.. 88 mm (3.5 inches)
2001
    Standard.. 59 mm (2.3 inches)
    Maximum... 30 mm (1.2 inches)
    Minimum.. 83 mm (3.3 inches)
2002 and 2003
    Standard.. 98 mm (3.9 inches)
    Maximum... 37 mm (1.5 inches)
    Minimum.. 123 mm (4.8 inches)
2004 and later
    Standard.. 71 mm (2.8 inches)
    Maximum... 37 mm (1.5 inches)
    Minimum.. 113 mm (4.4 inches)

Fork spring free length limit
CR80R/RB and CR85R/RB
    1986 .... 557.1 mm (21.93 inches)
    1987 .... 533.1 mm (29.99 inches)
    1988 through 1995.. 476.7 mm (18.77 inches)
    1996 through 2004.. 444.1 mm (17.48 inches)
    2005 and later
        CR85R .... 436.6 mm (17.19 inches)
        CR85RB .... 444.1 mm (17.48 inches)
CR125R
    1986 .... 501.3 mm (19.74 inches)
    1987 .... 570.7 mm (22.47 inches)
    1988 and 1989 .... 557.2 mm (21.94 inches)
    1990 .... 504.9 mm (19.88 inches)
    1991 .... 500.9 mm (19.72 inches)
    1992 .... 504.5 mm (19.86 inches)
    1993 .... 504.4 mm (19.86 inches)
    1994 through 1996.. 487.0 mm (19.17 inches)
    1997 through 2000.. 467.0 mm (18.39 inches)
    2001 through 2003.. 480 mm (18.9 inches)
    2004 and later .... 473 mm (18.6 inches)
Fork tube bend limit .... 0.2 mm (0.008 inch)

Rear suspension
Drive chain length
    CR80R/85R (21 pins) .... 259 mm (10.2 inches)
    CR125R
        1986 through 1997 .... Not specified. Relace the chain when it is visible in the wear window (see Chapter 1).
        1998 on (17 pins) .... 258.0 mm (10.16 inch)

Torque specifications
Handlebar bracket bolts... 22 Nm (16 ft-lbs)
Handlebar lower bracket-to-triple clamp nuts
    CR80R/85R, 2003 and earlier CR125R................................. Not specified
    2004 and later CR125R.. 44 Nm (33 ft-lbs)
Front axle nut or bolt .... See Chapter 7
Upper triple clamp bolts
    CR80R/85R .... 22 Nm (16 ft-lbs)
    CR125R
        1986 through 1989 .... 18 to 25 Nm (13 to 18 ft-lbs)
        1990 and 1991... 30 to 34 Nm (22 to 25 ft-lbs)
        1992 through 1997 .... 22 Nm (16 ft-lbs)
        1998 on .... 23 Nm (17 ft-lbs)

Torque specifications (continued)

Lower triple clamp bolts
    CR80R/85R .... 22 Nm (16 ft-lbs)
    CR125R
        1986 through 1989 .... 30 to 34 Nm (22 to 25 ft-lbs)
        1990 and 1991 .... 30 to 34 Nm (22 to 25 ft-lbs)
        1992 through 1997 .... 22 Nm (16 ft-lbs)
        1998 on .... 21 Nm (15 ft-lbs)
Fork center bolt *
    CR80R/85R
        1986 through 1995 .... 20 Nm (14 ft-lbs)
        1996 on .... 55 Nm (40 ft-lbs)
    CR125R
        1986 .... 60 to 84 Nm (43 to 61 ft-lbs)
        1987 through 1989 .... 30 to 40 Nm (22 to 29 ft-lbs)
        1990 .... 50 to 55 Nm (36 to 40 ft-lbs)
        1991 .... 40 to 50 Nm (29 to 36 ft-lbs)
        1992 through 1994 .... 80 Nm (58 ft-lbs)
        1995 on .... 78 Nm (56 ft-lbs)
Fork cap
    CR80R/85R
        1986 through 1995 .... 23 Nm (17 ft-lbs)
        1996 on .... 35 Nm (25 ft-lbs)
    CR125R
        1986 and 1987 .... 25 to 35 Nm (18 to 25 ft-lbs)
        1988 and 1989 .... 15 to 30 Nm (11 to 22 ft-lbs)
        1990 and 1991 .... 30 to 40 Nm (22 to 29 ft-lbs)
        1992 through 1994 .... 35 Nm (25 ft-lbs)
        1995 on .... 30 Nm (22 ft-lbs)
Fork cap locknut
    1996 and later CR80R/85R .... 20 Nm (14 ft-lbs)
    CR125R
        1987 through 1990 .... 17.5 to 22.5 Nm (13 to 16 ft-lbs)
        1991 .... 20 to 24 Nm (14 to 17 ft-lbs)
        1992 through 1994 .... 22 Nm (16 ft-lbs)
        1995 on .... 29 Nm (21 ft-lbs)
Steering stem bearing adjusting nut .... See Chapter 1
Steering stem nut
    CR80R/85R
        1986 through 1991 .... 90 to 120 Nm (65 to 90 ft-lbs)
        1992 .... 80 to 120 Nm (60 to 90 ft-lbs)
        1995 .... 100 Nm (72 ft-lbs)
        1996 on .... 130 Nm (94 ft-lbs)
    CR125R
        1986 through 1991 .... 95 to 140 Nm (69 to 101 ft-lbs)
        1992 .... 118 Nm (85 ft-lbs)
        1993 through 2000 .... 147 Nm (108 ft-lbs)
        2001 .... 108 Nm (80 ft-lbs)
Rear shock absorber upper mounting bolt .... 45 Nm (33 ft-lbs)
Rear shock absorber lower mounting bolt
    CR80/85R
        2002 and earlier .... 42 Nm (31 ft-lbs)
        2003 and later .... 44 Nm (33 ft-lbs)
    CR125R
        1986 through 1992 .... 43 Nm (31 ft-lbs)
        1993 on .... 45 Nm (33 ft-lbs)
Shock arm to swingarm
    CR80R/85R
        1986 through 1995 .... 45 Nm (33 ft-lbs)
        1996 on .... 60 Nm (43 ft-lbs)
    CR125R
        1986 through 1991 .... 55 to 70 Nm (40 to 51 ft-lbs)
        1992 .... 63 Nm (46 ft-lbs)
        1993 through 1999 .... 88 Nm (65 ft-lbs)
        2000 on .... 78 Nm (58 ft-lbs)
Shock arm to shock link
    CR80R/85R
        1986 through 1995 .... 45 Nm (33 ft-lbs)
        1996 on .... 60 Nm (43 ft-lbs)

Shock arm to shock link
  CR125R
    1986 through 1988 .... 40 to 50 Nm (29 to 36 ft-lbs)
    1989 through 1991 .... 50 to 70 Nm (40 to 51 ft-lbs)
    1992.. 63 Nm (46 ft-lbs)
    1993 through 1999 .... 88 Nm (65 ft-lbs)
    2000 on.. 78 Nm (58 ft-lbs)
Shock link to frame
  CR80R (1986 through 1995) .... 45 Nm (33 ft-lbs)
  CR125R
    1986 through 1988 .... 40 to 50 Nm (29 to 36 ft-lbs)
    1989 through 1991 .... 55 to 70 Nm (40 to 51 ft-lbs)
    1992.. 63 Nm (46 ft-lbs)
    1993 through 1997 .... 88 Nm (65 ft-lbs)
    1998 on.. 78 Nm (58 ft-lbs)
Shock arm to frame (1995 and later CR80R/85R)................. 60 Nm (43 ft-lbs)
Swingarm pivot bolt nut
  CR80R/85R... 80 Nm (58 ft-lbs)
  CR125R... 90 Nm (65 ft-lbs)
Engine sprocket bolts... Not specified
Rear sprocket bolts/nuts
  CR80R/85R
    1986 through 1995 .... 31 Nm (22 ft-lbs)
    1996 on.. 33 Nm (24 ft-lbs)
  CR125R
    1986 through 1989 .... 32 to 37 Nm (23 to 27 ft-lbs)
    1990 and 1991.. 25 to 31 Nm (18 to 21 ft-lbs)
    1992 on.. 33 Nm (24 ft-lbs)

* *Apply non-permanent thread locking agent to the threads.*

1 General information

The steering system on these models consists of a one-piece braced handlebar and a steering head attached to the front portion of the frame. The handlebars on all CR80R/85R models, as well as 1986 through 1999 CR125R models, rest in brackets integral with the upper triple clamp. On 2000 and later CR125R models, the handlebar brackets are secured to the upper triple clamp by studs and nuts. In their normal installed position, the brackets are offset 3 mm (0.12 inch) rearward from their studs. They can be turned 180-degrees, which locates the handlebars 6 mm (0.24 inch) forward of the normal installed position. An optional set of brackets with zero offset allows the handlebars to be placed 3 mm (0.12 inch) forward of the normal position. 1986 CR80R models use a ball bearing at the top of the steering head; all other models use a tapered roller bearing. All the motorcycles covered in this book use a tapered roller bearing at the bottom of the steering head.

The front suspension consists of damper rod forks (1986 through 1995 CR80R and 1986 CR125R models), or cartridge forks (all other models). Inverted cartridge forks are used on 1996 and later CR80R/85R and 1992 and later CR125R models.

The rear suspension consists of a single shock absorber with concentric coil spring, a swingarm and Honda's Pro-Link suspension linkage. The suspension linkage produces a progressive rising rate effect, where the suspension stiffens as its travel increases. This allows a softer ride over small bumps in the terrain, together with firmer suspension control over large irregularities.

2 Handlebars - removal, inspection and installation

Refer to illustrations 2.3a, 2.3b and 2.3c
1   If the handlebars must be removed for access to other components, such as the steering head bearings, simply remove the bolts and take the handlebars off the bracket. It's not necessary to disconnect the throttle or clutch cables, brake hose or the kill switch wires, but it is a good idea to support the assembly with a piece of wire or rope to avoid unnecessary strain on the cables.
2   If the handlebars are to be removed completely, refer to Chapter 2 for the clutch lever removal procedure, Chapter 4 for the throttle housing removal procedure, Chapter 5 for the kill switch removal procedure and Chapter 7 for the brake master cylinder removal procedure.

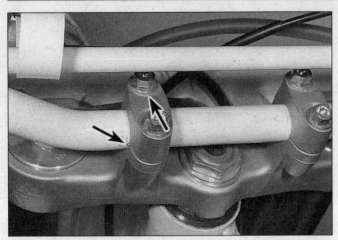

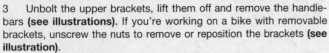

2.3a On all models, the bracket punch marks face forward (upper arrow) and the handlebar punch mark (lower arrow) aligns with the edge of the lower bracket (integral brackets shown)

2.3b On models with removable brackets, unscrew the bracket bolts (arrows) to remove the handlebar . . .

3   Unbolt the upper brackets, lift them off and remove the handle-bars (see illustrations). If you're working on a bike with removable brackets, unscrew the nuts to remove or reposition the brackets (see illustration).

4   Check the handlebars and brackets for cracks and distortion and replace them if any problems are found.

5   Place the handlebars in the lower brackets. Line up the punch mark on the handlebar with the parting line of the upper and lower brackets (see illustration 2.3).

6   Install the upper brackets with their punch marks facing forward (see illustration 2.3). Tighten the front bolts, then the rear bolts, to the torque listed in this Chapter's Specifications. Caution: *If there's a gap between the upper and lower brackets at the rear after tightening the bolts, don't try to close it by tightening beyond the recommended torque. You'll only crack the brackets.*

3   Forks - removal and installation

Removal

Refer to illustrations 3.3 and 3.4

1   Support the bike securely upright with its front wheel off the ground so it can't fall over during this procedure. If you're working on a bike with fork air valve caps, depress the valve cores to relieve any air pressure in the forks.

2   Remove the front wheel, unbolt the brake caliper and detach the brake hose retainer from the left fork leg (see Chapter 7).

3   If you plan to disassemble the forks, loosen the fork caps now (see illustration). This can be done later, but it will be easier while the forks are securely held in the triple clamps. Also, set the damping adjuster (if equipped) to its softest setting to prevent damage to the adjuster when the fork is reassembled.

4   Loosen the upper and lower triple clamp bolts (see illustration 3.3 and the accompanying illustration).

5   Lower the fork leg out of the triple clamps, twisting it if necessary.

Installation

6   Slide each fork leg into the lower triple clamp. Note: *If the fork cap had been loosened, slide the fork leg through the lower triple clamp, positioning it about half-way between the upper and lower triple clamps, then tighten the lower triple clamp bolts to the torque listed in this Chapter's Specifications. Now tighten the fork cap bolt to the torque listed in this Chapter's Specifications, loosen the lower triple clamp bolts and proceed to install the fork tube.*

7   Slide the fork legs up, installing the tops of the tubes into the upper triple clamp. If you're working on a 1987 through 1995 CR80R (or a 1996 or 1997 CR80RB with a 19-inch front wheel), or a 1988, 1989 or 1995 and later CR125R, the upper end of each fork tube should be even with the surface of the upper triple clamp. On all other models, align the groove near the top of the fork tube with the top of

2.3c . . . and unscrew the brackets nuts (arrow) to reposition or remove the brackets

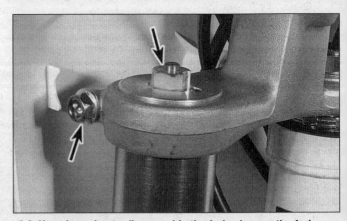

3.3 If you're going to disassemble the forks, loosen the fork cap (right arrow). Note the position of the fork in the upper triple clamp, then loosen the pinch bolt (left arrow); some models have two upper pinch bolts on each fork leg

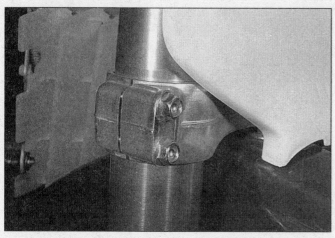

3.4 Loosen the lower triple clamp bolts and remove the fork

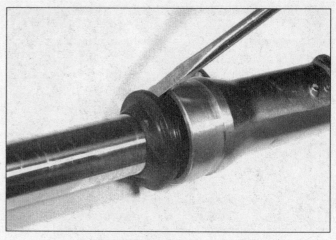

4.2a Pry the dust seal out of the outer fork tube

the upper triple clamp.

8   Tighten the upper and lower triple clamp bolts to the torque listed in this Chapter's Specifications.

9   Make sure the damping adjusters (if equipped) are at the same setting for both forks.

10   The remainder of installation is the reverse of the removal steps.

4   Forks (CR80R/85R) - disassembly, inspection and assembly

1   Remove the forks following the procedure in Section 3. Work on one fork at a time to prevent mixing up the parts.

1986 through 1995 CR80R
Disassembly
Refer to illustrations 4.2a through 4.2k

2   To disassemble the forks, refer to the accompanying illustrations (see illustrations).

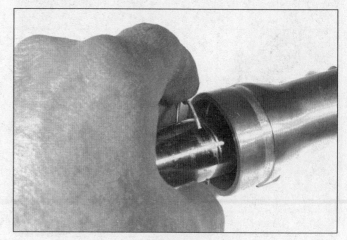

4.2b Pry the retaining ring out of its groove and slide it off the inner fork tube

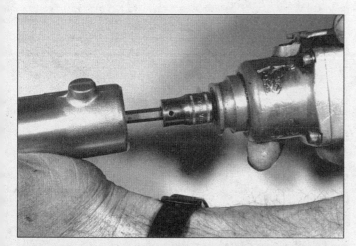

4.2c Loosen the Allen bolt in the bottom of the outer fork tube - an air wrench is the easiest way to do this if you have one, but if not, unscrew the bolt with an Allen wrench while the fork cap is still installed; the spring pressure will keep the damper rod from turning inside the fork

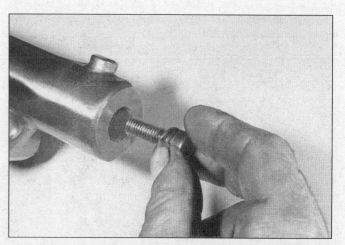

4.2d Remove the Allen bolt and its copper sealing washer; use a new washer on reassembly

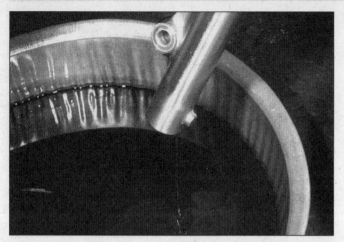

4.2e Let the oil drain from the bottom of the fork; pump the inner fork tube up and down to expel the oil

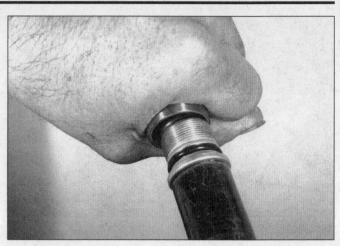

4.2f Unscrew the fork cap - be careful of spring tension!

4.2g Pull the spring out of the fork; on 1988 through 1995 models, pull out the TSV rod and its spring; the long end of the TSV rod faces down on assembly

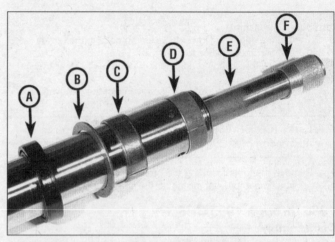

4.2h Pull the fork tubes sharply apart until they separate; the seal, back-up ring and bushings will come off with the inner tube

A	Oil seal	D	Fork tube bushing
B	Back-up ring	E	Damper rod
C	Fork slider bushing	F	Oil lock piece

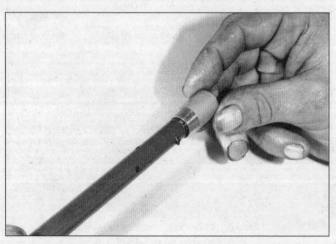

4.2i Take the oil lock piece off the end of the damper rod . . .

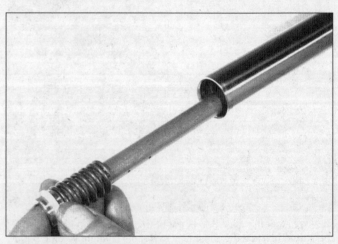

4.2j . . . and remove the damper rod from the inner fork tube

4.2k Pry the oil seal out of its bore; be careful not to scratch the seal's seating area in the fork tube

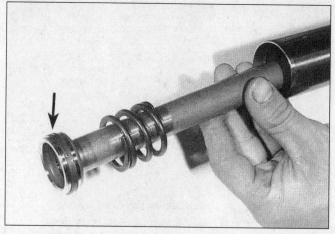

4.6 Replace the Teflon ring on the damper rod if it's worn or damaged

Inspection

Refer to illustration 4.6

3   Clean all parts in solvent and blow them dry with compressed air, if available. Check the inner and outer fork tubes and the damper rod for score marks, scratches, flaking of the chrome and excessive or abnormal wear. Look for dents in the tubes and replace them if any are found. Check the fork seal seat for nicks, gouges and scratches. If damage is evident, leaks will occur around the seal-to-outer tube junction. Replace worn or defective parts with new ones.

4   Have the inner fork tube checked for runout at a dealer service department or other repair shop. **Warning:** *If the tube is bent, it should be replaced with a new one. Don't try to straighten it.*

5   Measure the overall length of the fork spring and check it for cracks or other damage. Compare the length to the minimum length listed in this Chapter's Specifications. If it's defective or sagged, replace both fork springs with new ones. Never replace only one spring.

6   Check the Teflon ring on the damper rod for wear or damage and replace it if problems are found **(see illustration)**. **Note:** *Don't remove the ring from the damper rod unless you plan to replace it.*

7   Check the fork tube bushing and fork slider bushing for wear **(see illustration 4.2h)** and replace them if their condition is in doubt.

Assembly

Refer to illustrations 4.12a, 4.12b, 4.13, 4.14, 4.15a and 4.15b

8   Place the rebound spring over the damper rod and slide the rod assembly into the inner fork tube until it protrudes from the lower end **(see illustrations 4.2j and 4.2h)**.

9   Place the oil lock piece on the base of the damper rod **(see illustration 4.2h)**.

10   Insert the inner fork tube/damper rod assembly into the outer fork tube until the Allen-head bolt (with copper washer) can be threaded into the damper rod from the lower end of the outer tube **(see illustration 4.2d)**. **Note:** *Apply a non-permanent thread locking agent to the threads of the bolt. Keep the two tubes fairly horizontal so the oil lock piece doesn't fall off the damper rod inside the outer fork tube. Temporarily install the fork spring and cap to place tension on the damper rod so it won't spin inside the fork tube while you tighten the Allen bolt.*

11   Tighten the Allen bolt securely, then remove the fork cap and spring.

12   Lubricate the lips and outer diameter of the fork seal with the recommended fork oil (see this Chapter's Specifications). Slide the seal down the inner tube with the lips facing down. Drive the seal into position with a fork seal driver (Honda part no. 07747-0010100 and 07447-0010300 or 07947-1180001) **(see illustration)**. If you don't have access to one of these, it is recommended that you take the fork to a Honda dealer or other repair shop for seal installation. You can also make a substitute tool **(see illustration)**. If you're very careful, the seal can be driven in with a hammer and drift punch. Work around the circumference of the seal, tapping gently on the outer edge of the seal until it's seated **(see illustration 4.2k)**. Be careful - if you distort the seal, you'll

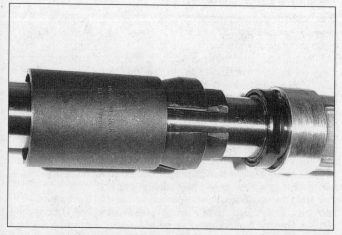

4.12a A seal driver like this one is the ideal way to seat outer tube bushings and install fork seals

4.12b If you don't have a seal driver, a section of pipe can be used the same way the seal driver would be used - as a slide hammer (be sure to tape the ends of the pipe so it doesn't scratch the fork tube)

4.13 Make sure the retaining ring seats in its groove

4.14 Push the dust seal down until it seats in the outer fork tube

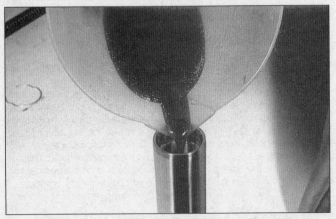

4.15a Pour the specified amount of oil into the fork

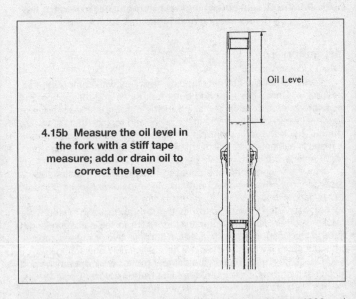

4.15b Measure the oil level in the fork with a stiff tape measure; add or drain oil to correct the level

Oil Level

have to disassemble the fork and end up taking it to a dealer anyway!

13   Install the retaining ring, making sure it's completely seated in its groove **(see illustration)**.

14   Install the dust seal, making sure it seats completely **(see illustration)**. Pull the fork boot down into its groove on the outer fork tube and secure the upper end to the inner fork tube with the clamping band.

15   Compress the fork fully and add the recommended type and quantity of fork oil listed in this Chapter's Specifications **(see illustration)**. Measure the fork oil level from the top of the fork tube **(see illustration)**. If necessary, add or remove oil to bring it to the proper level.

16   Fit the TSV valve spring over the long end of the valve, then install

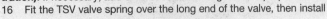

4.18 Turn the compression damper screw to its softest setting

the valve in the fork, long end first. Install the fork spring; on 1986 and 1987 models, install the narrow end first. Install the O-ring and fork cap.

17   Install the fork, following the procedure outlined in Section 3. Be sure to tighten the cap bolt to the torque listed in this Chapter's Specifications.

1996 and later CR80R/85R
Disassembly
Refer to illustrations 4.18, 4.19, 4.20, 4.21a, 4.21b, 4.24, 4.25, 4.26a, 4.26b and 4.27

18   Before you start, set the rebound and compression damping adjusters to their softest settings to prevent damage to the adjuster needle **(see illustration)**. **Note:** *The rebound damping adjuster is located in the fork cap; the compression damping adjuster is located in the center bolt at the bottom of the fork.* Thoroughly clean the outside of the fork, especially the sliding surface on the lower (inner) fork tube.

19   Remove three Allen bolts at the bottom of the fork and take off the plastic protector **(see illustration)**.

20   Hold the upper (outer) fork tube so it won't turn and unscrew the fork cap bolt. Carefully slide the outer tube down to the bottom of the fork to expose the fork spring **(see illustration)**.

21   Hold the cap bolt with one wrench and loosen the locknut away from the cap bolt with another wrench **(see illustration)**. Unscrew the cap bolt from the damper rod, then carefully pull the damping adjuster needle (which is attached to the cap bolt) out of the damper rod **(see illustration)**.

22   Remove the fork spring.

23   Place the open (upper) end of the fork over a drain pan, then com-

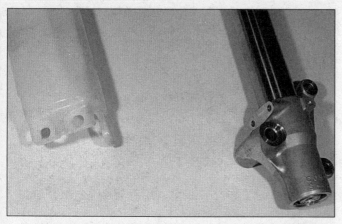

4.19 Remove the Allen bolts and take off the fork protector

4.20 Slide the outer fork tube down to expose the spring

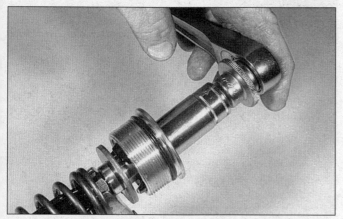

4.21a Hold the fork cap with one wrench and loosen the locknut with another

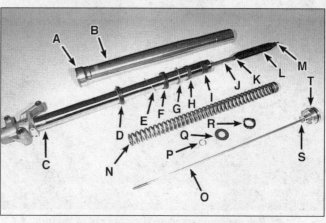

4.21b Fork details - 1996 and later CR80R/85R

press and extend the damper rod and fork tubes several times to pump out the oil.

24 Pry the dust seal out of its bore, taking care not to scratch the fork tube **(see illustration)**.

25 Pry the oil seal retainer out of its groove, again taking care not to scratch the fork tube **(see illustration)**.

26 Unscrew the center bolt and remove the bolt with its sealing washer **(see illustration 4.18)**. The bolt is threaded into the damper rod inside the lower fork tube. To keep the damper rod from spinning while you loosen the bolt, hold it with a holding tool such as Honda tool

A	Wear ring	K	Circlip
B	Outer fork tube	L	Spring guide
C	Inner fork tube	M	Locknut
D	Dust seal	N	Spring
E	Retainer	O	Damping adjuster rod
F	Oil seal	P	Circlip
G	Back-up ring	Q	Spring seat
H	Outer tube bushing	R	Stopper
I	Inner tube bushing	S	Fork cap
J	Damper rod	T	O-ring

4.24 Pry the dust seal out of its bore

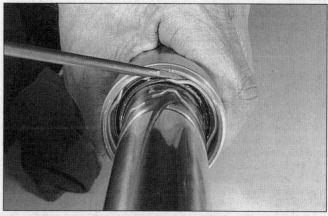

4.25 Pry the retaining ring out with a pointed tool; be careful not to scratch the seal bore

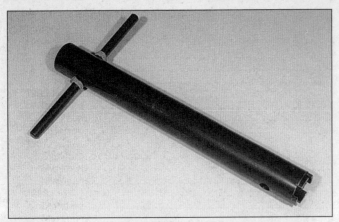

4.26a This tool is used to hold the damper rod from turning . . .

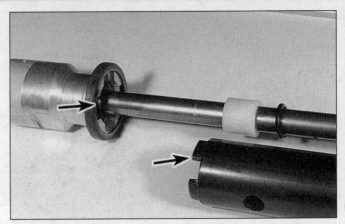

4.26b . . . its tabs engage the damper rod slots (arrows)

4.27 Pull the damper rod and damper out of the fork

4.34 Tape the end of the fork tube so the sharp edges won't cut the seals

07TMB-GBF010A **(see illustrations)**. The tool diameter is 24.5 mm (0.965 inch). If you don't have the Honda tool and you can locate a piece of steel tubing of the correct diameter, you can notch the end of the tubing to fit the damper rod slots.

27 Pull the damper rod out of the inner fork tube **(see illustration)**.

28 Hold the fork tubes over a drain pan and pump the fork several times to drain the fork oil from the damper.

29 Hold one fork tube in each hand and pull the tubes apart sharply several times (like a slide hammer) to separate them.

Inspection

30 Refer to Steps 3 through 7 to inspect the forks.

31 Check the wear ring on the outer fork tube. If it's worn, replace it.

32 Check the center bolt for wear or damage. Replace its O-rings and sealing washer whenever the fork is disassembled.

33 Check the inner circumference of the back-up ring for bending and replace it if any problems are found.

Assembly

Refer to illustrations 4.34 and 4.36

34 Wrap the end of the inner (lower) fork tube with electrical tape, covering the sharp edges so they don't cut the seals when they're installed **(see illustration)**.

35 Smear a coat of the fork oil listed in this Chapter's Specifications onto the inner circumference of the dust seal, the oil seal and both bushings.

36 Install the dust seal onto the inner fork tube, outer side first **(see illustration)**. Install the oil seal retaining ring, oil seal (marked side first) and the back-up ring. Remove the tape, then slip the guide (outer fork tube) bushing over the inner fork tube. Install the slider (inner fork tube) bushing in its groove, expanding it just enough to fit over the inner fork tube.

37 Install the inner fork tube in the outer tube. Position the outer tube bushing at the edge of its bore with the back-up ring on top of it. Tap on the back-up ring with a 38 mm fork seal driver or equivalent to drive the bushing into its bore **(see illustrations 4.12a and 4.12b)**.

38 Drive the oil seal, using the same seal driver, just past the retaining ring groove. If you're very careful, the seal can be driven in with a hammer and drift punch. Work around the circumference of the seal, tapping gently on the outer edge of the seal until it's seated. Be careful - if you distort the seal, you'll have to disassemble the fork and end up taking it to a dealer anyway! Compress the seal retaining ring into the groove, making sure it seats securely.

4.36 Seal and bushing details

A Dust seal	D Back-up ring
B Retainer	E Outer tube bushing
C Oil seal	F Inner tube bushing

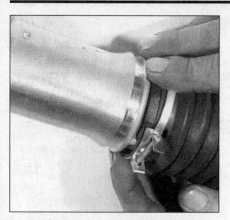

5.1 Loosen the clamps and detach the fork boots

5.5 Remove the bottom cover from the fork leg

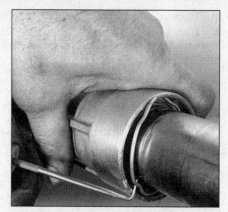

5.6 Pry the oil seal retainer out with a pointed tool; be careful not to scratch the seal bore or fork tube

39   Install the dust seal, making sure it seats completely.

40   Install the damper assembly in the fork. Place new O-rings and a new sealing washer on the center bolt. Coat the threads of the center bolt with non-permanent thread locking agent. Hold the damper rod with the special tool **(see illustrations 4.26a and 4.26b)**. Install the center bolt and tighten it to the torque listed in this Chapter's Specifications **(see illustration 4.18)**.

41   Compress the fork all the way. Pour fork oil of the type listed in this Chapter's Specifications into the fork tube until it covers the end of the damper rod.

42   Extend the fork all the way, then cover the top of the outer fork tube completely with one hand. Compress the fork all the way, keeping the top covered with your hand. Remove your hand from the top of the fork and slowly extend it all the way. Repeat this process two or three more times, ending with the fork fully extended.

43   Slowly pump the damper rod up and down eight to ten times, ending with the damper rod down.

44   Compress the outer fork tube all the way and leave the fork sitting upright for five minutes so the oil level can stabilize. Then measure the oil level and compare it to the values listed in this Chapter's Specifications. Add or drain oil as needed. **Note:** *Minimum oil level will make the suspension slightly softer near full compression; maximum oil level will make the suspension slightly stiffer near full compression.* **Warning:** *To prevent unstable handling, make sure the oil level is exactly the same in both forks.*

45   Coat new O-rings with fork oil and install them on the adjuster rod and fork cap.

46   Wind the end of a two-foot length of mechanic's wire around the damper rod just below the locknut. Slip the fork spring over the wire, then use the wire to hold the damper rod extended while you install the fork spring in the fork tube. Undo the wire from the damper rod and pull it out through the fork spring, in the meantime holding the damper rod in its extended position.

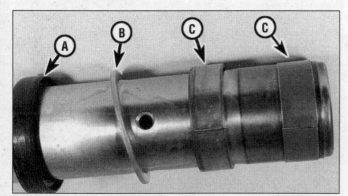

5.8 Don't remove the bushings unless they're worn

| A | Oil seal | B | Back-up ring | C | Bushings |

47   Thread the fork cap onto the damper rod against the locknut, then tighten the cap and nut against each other to the torque listed in this Chapter's Specifications. Thread the fork cap into the fork tube (tighten it to the specified torque during installation, when the fork is held in the triple clamp).

48   Apply non-permanent thread locking agent to the fork protector bolts, then install the protector and tighten the bolts to the torque listed in this Chapter's Specifications. **Note:** *Don't wait until the forks are installed to install the protector; there won't be access to install the protector bolts.*

5   Forks (CR125R) - disassembly, inspection and assembly

1986 CR125R

Disassembly

Refer to illustrations 5.1, 5.5, 5.6 and 5.8

1   Loosen the clamps and take the boot off the fork **(see illustration)**.

2   Unscrew the fork cap from the top of the fork. **Warning:** *The fork cap is under spring pressure. Wear safety glasses to protect yourself from the fork cap and flying oil.*

3   Remove the dished washer, spacer, spring seat, spring and a second spring seat. Lift out the TCV rod and its spring.

4   Hold the fork upside down over a drain pan and pump it several times to drain the oil.

5   If you haven't already done so, pry the rubber plug from the bottom of the fork **(see illustration)**. Unscrew the center bolt from the bottom of the fork, then take the damper rod and rebound spring out of the fork tube. If the center bolt wasn't loosened during the removal procedure, you'll need to keep the damper rod from rotating while you loosen it. A damper rod holder such as Honda tool 07930-KA40101 or equivalent is ideal. The tool consists of a hex head at the end of a long rod, with a T-handle at the other end. The hex fits into the hexagonal opening at the top of the damper rod. Insert the tool through the top of the fork into the top end of the damper rod, then hold the tool handle to keep the damper rod from rotating while you loosen the center bolt. Another method is to spin the center bolt loose with an air wrench. If you don't have the tool, an equivalent tool or an air wrench, take the fork to a dealer or motorcycle repair shop and have the center bolt removed.

6   Pry the seal retainer out of its groove **(see illustration)**.

7   Grasp one fork tube in each hand, compress them together, then yank them apart sharply as far as they'll go. Do this several times until the tubes separate; the slide hammer-like motion is necessary to pull the slider bushing out of its bore in the outer fork tube.

8   Remove the dust seal, oil seal and back-up ring from the inner fork tube **(see illustration)**. Don't remove the bushings unless you find excessive wear while inspecting them.

Inspection

9   Refer to Steps 3 through 7 of Section 4 to inspect the fork. Also check the TCV rod for bending or other damage and replace it if problems are found.

Assembly

10   Install a new bushing on the inner fork tube if the old one was removed. Expand the bushing just enough to fit over the tube and seat it in its groove.
11   Install the oil lock piece inside the bottom end of the inner fork tube.
12   Coat the lower portion of the inner fork tube with the recommended fork oil.
13   Install the inner fork tube in the outer fork tube.
14   Coat the lips and outer circumference of a new oil seal with the recommended fork oil, then slip the seal over the inner fork tube with its marked side upward. Drive the seal into its bore until it seats against the back-up ring, using the same tool used to install the bushing.
15   Coat the lips and outer circumference of a new dust seal with the recommended fork oil, then slip the seal over the inner fork tube with its retainer groove upward. Drive the seal into its bore just past the retainer groove in the outer fork tube, using the same tool used to install the oil seal.
16   Compress the retaining ring into its groove and make sure it seats securely.
17   Install the damper rod in the fork with its hexagonal opening upward. Place a new sealing washer on the center bolt. Coat the threads of the center bolt with non-permanent thread locking agent. Hold the damper rod with the special tool, install the center bolt and tighten it to the torque listed in this Chapter's Specifications.
18   Install the rubber plug in the bottom of the fork. Install the drain screw, using a new sealing washer.
19   Install the TCV rod in the fork, with its hat-shaped end upward.
20   Pour the amount and type of fork oil listed in this Chapter's Specifications into the fork (see illustration 4.15a). Compress the fork all the way, then measure the oil level in the fork (see illustration 4.15b). If necessary, add or remove oil to bring it to the proper level.
21   Install the lower spring seat, spring, upper spring seat and spacer. Install the dished washer on top of the spacer with its dished (extended) side facing down into the spring.
22   Coat a new O-ring with the recommended fork oil and install it on the fork cap. Install the fork cap and tighten it slightly (tighten it to the specified torque during installation, when the fork is held in the triple clamp).
23   Install the boot on the fork, facing its breather holes to the rear of the motorcycle. Position the upper clamp toward the inner side of the fork with its screw head forward. Position the lower clamp to the rear of the fork with its screw head facing away from the motorcycle.

1987 through 1989 CR125R

Disassembly

Refer to illustration 5.28

24   Loosen the clamps and take the boot off the fork leg (see illustration 5.1).
25   Hold the upper (outer) fork tube so it won't turn and unscrew the fork cap bolt.
26   Place the open (upper) end of the fork over a drain pan, then compress and extend the damper rod and fork tubes several times to pump out the oil.
27   Carefully slide the outer tube down to the bottom of the fork to expose the fork spring.
28   Hold the cap bolt with one wrench and loosen the locknut away from the cap bolt with another wrench (see illustration 4.21a). Unscrew the cap bolt from the damper rod, then remove the spacer (1988 models only), spring seat and spring (see illustration).
29   Unscrew the center bolt and remove the bolt with its sealing washer. Remove the damper rod from the fork tube.
30   Pry the dust seal out of its bore, taking care not to scratch the fork tube.

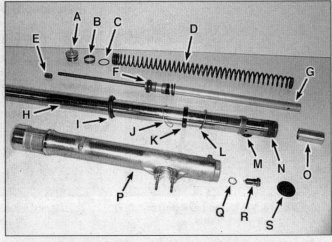

5.28 Fork details - 1987 through 1989 CR125R

A	Fork cap and O-ring	K	Oil seal
B	Spacer (1988 only)	L	Back-up ring
C	Spring seat	M	Outer tube bushing
D	Spring	N	Inner tube bushing
E	Locknut	O	Oil lock piece
F	Bushing	P	Outer fork tube
G	Damper assembly	Q	Sealing washer
H	Inner fork tube	R	Center bolt
I	Dust seal	S	Rubber plug
J	Retainer		

31   Pry the oil seal retainer out of its groove, again taking care not to scratch the fork tube.
32   Hold one fork tube in each hand and pull the tubes apart sharply several times (like a slide hammer) to separate them.
33   Remove the oil lock piece from the bottom of the inner fork tube. Slide the oil seal and back-up ring off the outside of the inner fork tube. Don't remove the bushings unless they need to be replaced.

Inspection

Refer to illustrations 5.36a and 5.36b

34   Refer to Steps 3 through 7 of Section 4 to inspect the forks.
35   Check the center bolt for wear or damage. Replace its O-rings and sealing washer whenever the fork is disassembled.
36   Check the bushing on the damper rod for wear or damage and replace it if any problems are found (see illustrations).
37   Check the inner circumference of the back-up ring for distortion and replace it if any problems are found.

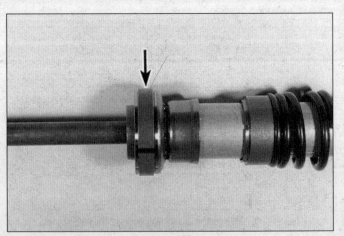

5.36a There's a bushing on the piston (arrow) . . .

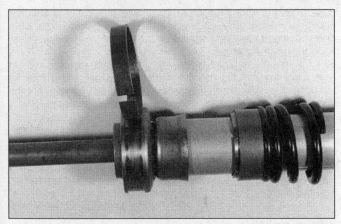

5.36b . . . to remove it, expand it at the slit and slip it off the fork

5.48 Measure oil level with the fork fully compressed and the spring removed

Assembly

Refer to illustration 5.48

38   If the damper rod was removed from the damper, install it, then thread the locknut onto the damper rod. If you're working on a 1988 or 1989 model, note that the inside of the locknut is only partially threaded. The threaded portion goes upward (away from the cartridge).

39   Install the damper rod and damper in the inner fork tube. Install the oil lock piece on the end of the damper, then install the inner fork tube in the outer fork tube.

40   Place a new sealing washer on the damping adjuster bolt. Coat the bolt threads with non-permanent thread locking agent, then install the bolt in the bottom of the fork and tighten it to the torque listed in this Chapter's Specifications.

41   Smear a coat of the fork oil listed in this Chapter's Specifications onto the inner circumference of the dust seal, the oil seal and the outer fork tube's bushing.

42   Slide the outer tube bushing onto the inner tube. Position the bushing at the edge of its bore, then use a fork seal driver or equivalent to drive the bushing into its bore **(see illustrations 4.12a and 4.12b)**. Install the back-up ring on top of the bushing.

43   Slide the oil seal onto the inner fork tube with its marked side facing up. Drive the oil seal, using the same seal driver, just past the retaining ring groove. If you're very careful, the seal can be driven in with a hammer and drift punch. Work around the circumference of the seal, tapping gently on the outer edge of the seal until it's seated. Be careful - if you distort the seal, you'll have to disassemble the fork and end up taking it to a dealer anyway! Compress the seal retaining ring into the groove, making sure it seats securely.

44   Install the dust seal, making sure it seats completely.

45   Compress the fork all the way.

46   If you're working on a 1987 model, pour fork oil of the type and amount listed in this Chapter's Specifications into the fork tube.

47   If you're working on a 1988 or 1989 model, measure the specified amount of fork oil into a container with a small pour spout. Pour fork oil into the top of the damper rod (not into the fork tube) until it begins to flow out the air relief holes. Then pour the remaining oil into the fork tube.

48   With the fork compressed, measure oil level to the top of the fork **(see illustration)**. Add or remove oil as needed. **Note:** *Minimum oil level will make the suspension slightly softer near full compression; maximum oil level will make the suspension slightly stiffer near full compression.* **Warning:** *To prevent unstable handling, make sure the oil level is exactly the same in both forks.*

49   Coat a new O-ring with fork oil and install on the fork cap.

50   Wind the end of a two-foot length of mechanic's wire around the damper rod just below the locknut. Slip the fork spring over the wire, then use the wire to hold the damper rod extended while you install the fork spring in the fork tube. Remove the wire from the damper rod and pull it out through the fork spring, in the meantime holding the damper rod in its extended position. Install the spring seat (and spacer on 1988

models) on the spring.

51   Thread the locknut all the way onto the damper rod, chamfered side first.

52   Thread the fork cap onto the damper rod against the locknut, then tighten the cap and nut against each other to the torque listed in this Chapter's Specifications. Thread the fork cap into the fork tube (tighten it to the specified torque during installation, when the fork is held in the triple clamp).

53   Install the fork boot with its breather holes toward the rear of the motorcycle.

1990 CR125R

Disassembly

Note: *Overhaul of the forks on these models requires special tools for which there are no good substitutes. The tools can be ordered from your local Honda dealer, or you may be able to buy equivalent tools from aftermarket suppliers. Read through the procedure and arrange to get the special tools or substitutes before starting. If you don't disassemble the forks on a regular basis, it may be more practical to have the job done by a Honda dealer or motorcycle repair shop.*

54   Slide fork slider spacer 07KMZ-KZ30101 onto the bottom of the inner fork tube so it rests on the axle bracket. This is necessary to keep the outer tube from sliding down against the axle bracket, which could damage the bushings and dust seal. It will also be needed later to adjust the fork oil level.

55   Wear safety glasses and undo the fork cap. The outer fork tube is now free to slide; lower it carefully against the tool.

56   Slide the spring collar down far enough to expose the locknut below the fork cap. Hold the lock nut with an open-end wrench and unscrew the fork cap from the damper rod.

57   Remove the locknut, spring collar, spring seat and fork spring from the fork.

58   Remove the spacer from the fork tube. **Caution:** *Don't let the outer fork tube slide against the axle bracket.*

59   Hold the fork upside down over a drain pan and pump the damper rod eight to ten times to pump out the fork oil.

60   Pry the rubber plug from the bottom of the fork. Hold the damper rod from turning with Honda tool 07KMB-KZ3010A or equivalent and unscrew the center bolt from the bottom of the fork. If you don't have the special tool, you can spin the center bolt loose with an air wrench. However, you'll still need a way to hold the damper rod during assembly so you can tighten the center bolt to the correct torque.

61   Pull the damper rod and damper out of the fork, then separate the damper rod from the damper. **Caution:** *Don't scratch the bushing with the damper rod threads during removal.*

62   Pry the dust seal out of its bore and remove the oil seal retainer ring **(see illustration 5.6)**.

63   Grasp one fork tube in each hand, compress them together, then yank them apart sharply as far as they'll go. Do this several times until

the tubes separate; the slide hammer-like motion is necessary to pull the slider bushing out of its bore in the outer fork tube.

64 Remove the dust seal, retaining ring, oil seal and back-up ring from the inner fork tube **(see illustration 4.36)**.

Inspection

65 Refer to Steps 3 through 7 of Section 4 to inspect the fork.

66 Check the oil seal case (on the bottom end of the outer fork tube) for wear or damage. Leave it in place if no problems are found. If you need to replace the oil seal case or the fork tube, remove the stop ring and slider from the oil seal case. Slide the oil seal case partway up the fork tube to expose the stop ring on the fork tube, then remove the stop ring. Slide the oil case off the fork tube, tapping it gently with a soft-faced hammer if necessary. Remove the O-ring from inside the oil seal case.

67 Check the wear rings on the damper rod and on the spring collar for wear or damage and replace them if problems are found.

Assembly

68 If the oil seal case was removed, install a new O-ring inside it and coat the O-ring with the type of fork oil listed in this Chapter's Specifications. Slide the oil seal case onto the fork tube past the stop ring groove, install the stop ring in the fork tube groove and pull the case back against the stop ring. Install the slider and the other stop ring on the oil seal case.

69 Wrap the end of the inner fork tube with electrical tape to protect the new oil seal on installation. Coat the lip of the new oil seal with the recommended fork oil. Install the bushings (if removed), back-up ring and oil seal on the inner fork tube **(see illustration 4.36)**.

70 Install the inner tube in the outer tube. Slide the outer tube's bushing all the way down the inner fork tube until it rests against its bore in the outer fork tube. Install the back-up ring on top of the bushing. With a seal driver or equivalent tool **(see illustrations 4.12a and 4.12b)**, tap against the back-up ring to drive the new bushing into its bore. Once the bushing is seated, use the same tool to seat the oil seal in the case just below the retainer ring groove.

71 Install the retainer ring and make sure it seats securely in its groove, then install the dust seal. **Caution:** *From this point on, be careful not to let the outer fork tube slide down the inner tube far enough that the dust seal hits the axle bracket.*

72 Install the damper rod in the fork damper, taking care not to scratch the bushing inside the damper. Install the damper and rod in the fork tube.

73 Place a new sealing washer and O-ring on the center bolt. Coat the threads of the center bolt with a non-permanent thread locking agent. Hold the damper rod with the tool mentioned in Step 60, then tighten the center bolt to the torque listed in this Chapter's Specifications.

74 Thread the locknut all the way onto the damper rod with its flat facing upward. Tighten it with your fingers only; you'll need to remove it later.

75 Slip the spacer onto the bottom end of the inner fork tube against the axle bracket, then lower the outer fork tube down onto the spacer.

76 Look up the amount of fork oil recommended in this Chapter's Specifications. Pour half that amount into the fork.

77 Compress the damper rod all the way, then slowly pour fork oil into the damper rod until it starts to flow out the breather hole in the side of the damper rod.

78 Slowly pump the damper rod and fork tube up and down eight to ten times. Compress the fork all the way and leave it sitting upright for five minutes so the oil level can stabilize. Then measure the oil level and compare it to the values listed in this Chapter's Specifications. Add or drain oil as needed. **Note:** *Minimum oil level will make the suspension slightly softer near full compression; maximum oil level will make the suspension slightly stiffer near full compression.* **Warning:** *To prevent unstable handling, make sure the oil level is exactly the same in both forks.*

79 Install the spring in the fork.

80 Attach a two-foot length of mechanic's wire to the damper rod locknut.

81 Make sure the white plastic sealing ring is in position on the spring

collar. Pass the collar over the length of wire, then carefully work the collar into the fork tube with a side-to-side rocking motion. **Caution:** *Don't damage the sealing ring. Use the wire to hold the damper rod up while you position the collar in the fork tube.*

82 Remove the wire and the damper rod locknut. Install the spring seat, push down on the spring collar to expose the locknut threads, then thread the locknut all the way onto the damper rod. Measure the distance from the top of the locknut to the end of the damper rod; it should be 14 mm (0.55, or 35/64-inch).

83 Thread the fork cap onto the damper rod until it reaches the locknut, then tighten them against each other to the torque listed in this Chapter's Specifications.

84 Extend the outer fork tube and thread the fork cap into it (tighten it to the specified torque during installation, when the fork leg is held in the triple clamp).

1991 CR125R

Disassembly

85 Before you disassemble the fork, loosen the center bolt in the bottom of the fork leg **(see illustration 4.18)**.

86 Slide fork slider spacer 07KMZ-KZ30101 onto the bottom of the inner fork tube so it rests on the axle bracket. This is necessary to keep the outer tube from sliding down against the axle bracket, which could damage the bushings and dust seal. It's also necessary to adjust the fork oil level.

87 Wear safety glasses and unscrew the fork cap. The outer fork tube is now free to slide; lower it carefully against the tool.

88 Hold the locknut with an open-end wrench and unscrew the fork cap from the damper rod **(see illustration 4.21a)**. Remove the spring seat from inside the fork cap.

89 Remove the locknut and spring guide from the damper rod.

90 Remove the slider from the fork tube. **Caution:** *Don't let the outer fork tube slide against the axle bracket.*

91 Hold the fork upside down over a drain pan and pump the damper rod eight to ten times to pump out the fork oil.

92 Unscrew the center bolt from the bottom of the fork.

93 Pull the damper rod and damper out of the fork. Hold the bottom end of the damper over a drain pan and pump the damper rod eight to ten times to drain the remaining oil.

94 Pry the dust seal out of its bore and remove the oil seal retainer ring **(see illustrations 4.24 and 4.25)**.

95 Grasp one fork tube in each hand, compress them together, then yank them apart sharply as far as they'll go. Do this several times until the tubes separate; the slide hammer-like motion is necessary to pull the slider bushing out of its bore in the outer fork tube.

96 Remove the dust seal, retaining ring, oil seal and back-up ring from the inner fork tube **(see illustration 4.36)**.

Inspection

97 Refer to Steps 3 through 7 of Section 4 to inspect the fork.

98 Check the oil seal case (on the bottom end of the outer fork tube) for wear or damage. Leave it in place if no problems are found. If you need to replace the oil seal case or the fork tube, remove the stop ring and slider from the oil seal case. Slide the oil seal case partway up the fork tube to expose the stop ring on the fork tube, then remove the stop ring. Slide the oil case off the fork tube, tapping it gently with a soft-faced hammer if necessary. Remove the O-ring from inside the oil seal case.

99 Check the needle on the center bolt for wear or bending and replace the center bolt if problems are found.

100 Check the oil lock valve (ring) on the damper rod for wear or damage and replace the damper assembly if any problems are found.

Assembly

101 If the oil seal case was removed, install a new O-ring inside it and coat the O-ring with the type of fork oil listed in this Chapter's Specifications. Slide the oil seal case onto the fork tube past the stop ring groove, install the stop ring in the fork tube groove and pull the case back against the stop ring. **Note:** *You may need a press to push the*

5.118 Hold the fork over a drain pan and dump the oil; only part of it will come out at this point

5.119 Hold the fork cap with a socket and loosen the locknut with an open-end wrench

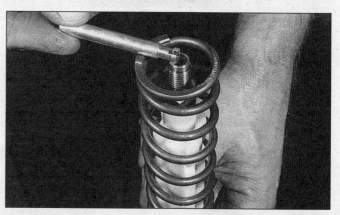

5.120 The adjuster rod is installed with its oil holes or cutout down (1997 shown)

fork tube into the oil seal case. If so, take the fork tube to a Honda dealer or motorcycle repair shop. Install the slider and the other stop ring on the oil seal case.

102 Wrap the end of the inner fork tube with electrical tape to protect the new oil seal on installation. Coat the lip of the new oil seal with the recommended fork oil. Install the bushings (if removed), back-up ring and oil seal on the inner fork tube **(see illustration 4.36)**.

103 Install the inner tube in the outer tube. Slide the outer tube's bushing all the way down the inner fork tube until it rests against its bore in the outer fork tube. Install the back-up ring on top of the bushing. With a seal driver or equivalent tool **(see illustrations 4.12a and 4.12b)**, tap against the back-up ring to drive the new bushing into its bore. Once the bushing is seated, use the same tool to seat the oil seal in the case just below the retainer ring groove.

104 Install the retainer ring and make sure it seats securely in its groove, then install the dust seal. **Caution:** *From this point on, be careful not to let the outer fork tube slide down the inner tube far enough that the dust seal hits the axle bracket.*

105 Install the damper and rod in the fork tube.

106 Place a new sealing washer and O-ring on the center bolt. Coat the threads of the center bolt with a non-permanent thread locking agent. Tighten the center bolt to the torque listed in this Chapter's Specifications. **Note:** *If the damper spins inside the fork tube when you try to tighten the center bolt, temporarily install the spring and fork cap. The spring pressure will keep the damper from turning.*

107 Install the spring guide on the damper rod; the end with holes goes upward. Thread the locknut all the way onto the damper rod with its flange facing downward.

108 Slip the spacer onto the bottom end of the inner fork tube against the axle bracket, then lower the outer fork tube down onto the spacer.

109 Look up the amount of fork oil recommended in this Chapter's Specifications. Pour half that amount into the fork.

110 Extend the fork, but don't expose any more than 250 mm (10 inches) of the lower fork tube. Cover the top of the fork tube with your hand so air can't escape, then slowly compress the fork. Repeat this two or three times.

111 Compress the damper rod all the way, then slowly pour fork oil into the damper rod until it starts to flow out the end of the damper rod.

112 Slowly pump the damper rod and fork tube up and down eight to ten times. Add the remainder of the specified amount of fork oil. Compress the fork all the way and leave it sitting upright for five minutes so the oil level can stabilize. Then measure the oil level and compare it to the values listed in this Chapter's Specifications. Add or drain oil as needed. **Note:** *Minimum oil level will make the suspension slightly softer near full compression; maximum oil level will make the suspension slightly stiffer near full compression.* **Warning:** *To prevent unstable handling, make sure the oil level is exactly the same in both forks.*

113 Attach a two-foot length of mechanic's wire to the damper rod locknut. Pass the fork spring (with its tapered end upward) over the length of wire into the fork tube.

114 Remove the wire. Install the spring seat, push down on the spring to expose the locknut threads, then thread the fork cap onto the damper rod until it reaches the locknut. Tighten them against each other to the torque listed in this Chapter's Specifications.

115 Install a new O-ring on the fork cap. Extend the outer fork tube and thread the fork cap into it (tighten it to the specified torque during installation, when the fork leg is held in the triple clamp).

1992 and later CR125R

Disassembly

Refer to illustrations 5.118, 5.119, 5.120 and 5.122

116 If you're working on a 1992 or 1993 model, slide fork slider spacer 07KMZ-KZ30101B onto the bottom of the inner fork tube so it rests on the axle bracket. This is necessary to keep the outer tube from sliding down against the axle bracket, which could damage the bushings and dust seal. It's also necessary for adjusting the fork oil level.

117 If you're working on a 1992 model, loosen the center bolt in the bottom of the fork now, before the fork cap and spring are removed. The spring tension will keep the damper rod inside the fork from turning while the center bolt is loosened.

118 Wear safety glasses and unscrew the fork cap. The outer fork tube is now free to slide; lower it carefully to the bottom. Turn the fork upside down over a drain pan and dump the oil **(see illustration)**.

119 Hold the locknut with an open-end wrench and unscrew the fork cap from the damper rod **(see illustration)**.

120 If you're working on a 1994 or later model, remove the adjuster from the top of the damper rod, then pull the spacer rod out of the damper rod **(see illustration)**.

121 If you're working on a 1992 or 1993 model, remove the spring seat from the fork cap.

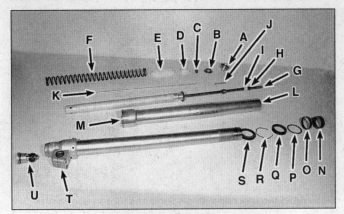

5.122 Fork details - 1995 and later CR125R

A	Fork cap and O-ring	L	Outer fork tube
B	Spring seat	M	Wear ring
C	Locknut	N	Outer tube bushing
D	Collar	O	Inner tube bushing
E	Spring guide	P	Back-up ring
F	Spring	Q	Oil seal
G	Damper rod	R	Retainer
H	O-ring	S	Dust seal
I	Spring collar (1997 only)	T	Inner fork tube and axle bracket
J	Adjuster rod (through 1997)	U	Center bolt
K	Spacer rod		

122 Remove the locknut from the damper rod, then remove the spring collar, spring guide and O-ring. Remove the second spring collar (1997 only) **(see illustration)**.

123 Turn the fork upside down over the drain pan and pump the damper rod eight to ten times to drain more oil.

124 Unscrew the center bolt from the bottom of the fork. If you're working on a 1992 model, simply unscrew (it was loosened earlier). If you're working on a 1993 or later model, you'll need to hold the damper rod from turning inside the fork with a special tool **(see illustrations 4.26a and 4.26b)**. If you can find a piece of metal tubing the same diameter as the damper, you can cut notches in it to fit the damper rod slots. Drill holes through the other end of the tubing and pass a rod through the holes to act as a handle.

125 Remove the center bolt and take the damper out of the fork. If you're working on a 1992 or 1993 model, pull the spacer rod out of the damper rod, then dump the rebound needle and spring out of the damper rod.

126 Hold the damper upside down over the drain pan and pump the damper rod eight to ten times to drain the remaining oil.

127 Pry the dust seal out of its bore, then pry the oil seal retainer out of its groove **(see illustrations 4.24 and 4.25)**.

128 If you're working on a 1994 model, unbolt the halves of the plastic protector guide from each other (they're installed on the bottom end of the outer fork tube). Take the guide halves off the fork tube. Don't remove the wear ring from the groove in the outer fork tube unless inspection shows that you need a new one.

129 Grasp one fork tube in each hand, compress them together, then yank them apart sharply as far as they'll go. Do this several times until the tubes separate; the slide hammer-like motion is necessary to pull the slider bushing out of its bore in the outer fork tube.

130 Remove the dust seal, oil seal and back-up ring from the inner fork tube **(see illustration 4.36)**. Don't remove the bushings unless you find excessive wear while inspecting them.

Inspection

131 Refer to Steps 3 through 7 of Section 4 to inspect the fork. Also inspect the wear ring in the groove on the bottom end of the outer fork tube **(see illustration 5.122)**. If the ring protrudes less than 1.5 mm (0.060 inch) from the fork, replace it.

5.138 Use new O-rings and a new sealing washer (arrows) on the center bolt

Assembly

Refer to illustration 5.138

132 Wrap the end of the inner (lower) fork tube with electrical tape, covering the sharp edges so they don't cut the seals when they're installed **(see illustration 4.34)**.

133 Smear a coat of the fork oil listed in this Chapter's Specifications onto the inner circumference of the dust seal, the oil seal and both bushings.

134 Install the dust seal onto the inner fork tube, outer side first **(see illustration 4.36)**. Install the oil seal retaining ring, oil seal (marked side first) and the back-up ring. Remove the tape, then slip the guide (outer fork tube) bushing over the inner fork tube. Install the slider (inner fork tube) bushing in its groove, expanding it just enough to fit over the inner fork tube.

135 Install the inner fork tube in the outer tube. Position the outer tube bushing at the edge of its bore with the back-up ring on top of it. Tap on the back-up ring with a fork seal driver or equivalent to drive the bushing into its bore **(see illustrations 4.12a and 4.12b)**.

136 Drive the oil seal, using the same seal driver, just past the retaining ring groove. If you're very careful, the seal can be driven in with a hammer and drift punch. Work around the circumference of the seal, tapping gently on the outer edge of the seal until it's seated **(see illustration 4.2k)**. Be careful - if you distort the seal, you'll have to disassemble the fork and end up taking it to a dealer anyway! Compress the seal retaining ring into the groove, making sure it seats securely.

137 Install the dust seal, making sure it seats completely.

138 Install the damper in the inner fork tube. Place a new sealing washer and O-rings on the center bolt **(see illustration)**. Apply fork oil to the O-rings and a coat of non-permanent thread locking agent to the center bolt threads, then install the center bolt in the fork. If you're working on a 1992 model, temporarily install the spring and fork cap to hold the damper rod from turning, then tighten the center bolt to the torque listed in this Chapter's Specifications. On all other models, hold the damper rod from turning with the tool described in Step 124, then tighten the center bolt to the specified torque.

139 If you're working on a 1997 model, install the bottom spring collar on the damper rod.

140 Install the O-ring, spring guide and upper spring collar on the damper rod **(see illustration 5.122)**. If you're working on a 1992 or 1993 model, the oil holes in the spring guide go upward.

141 Thread the locknut onto the damper rod with its flange downward (1992 and 1993) or with its cutout downward (1994 on).

142 If you're working on a 1992 or 1993 model, place the spring on the long end of the rebound needle, then install the rebound needle in the damper rod, long end first. Install the spacer rod in the damper rod on top of the rebound needle.

143 If you're working on a 1994 or later model, install the spacer rod in the damper rod. Install the adjuster rod on top of the spacer rod. On 1994 through 1996 models, the oil hole faces down; on 1997 and later models, the cutout faces down **(see illustration 5.120)**.

6.3a Loosen the steering stem nut with a socket . . .

6.3b . . . and unscrew it from the steering stem

6.3c Lift off the washer and the upper triple clamp

144 If you're working on a 1994 model, install the protector guide on the bottom of the outer fork tube.

145 Compress the fork all the way (against the spacer tool on 1992 and 1993 models); against the protector guide on 1994 models).

146 Look up the amount and type of fork oil listed in this Chapter's Specifications. Pour half the amount into a container and set it aside.

147 Pour specified fork oil (from the main container, not the container you set aside) into the damper rod until it overflows. Then pour the oil you set aside into the fork leg.

148 Extend the fork (but don't expose more than 250 mm (10 inches) of the inner fork tube).

149 Push down on the damper rod to make sure it's fully compressed, then pour fork into the damper rod until it overflows.

150 Slowly extend and compress the damper rod and fork tube eight to ten times.

151 Add the remainder of the specified amount of fork oil, then once more extend and compress the fork tube and damper rod eight to ten times.

152 Measure oil level inside the fork (see illustration 5.48). Add or drain oil as needed. Note: *Minimum oil level will make the suspension slightly softer near full compression; maximum oil level will make the suspension slightly stiffer near full compression.*

Warning: *To prevent unstable handling, make sure the oil level is exactly the same in both forks.*

153 Install the fork spring in the fork tube.

154 Dip a new fork cap O-ring in fork oil and place it on the fork cap.

155 Thread the locknut all the way onto the piston rod, then attach a two-foot length of mechanic's wire to the locknut.

156 Pass the fork spring over the length of wire, then use the wire to hold the piston rod up while you position the spring in the fork tube.

Position the spring seat on the spring.

157 Hold onto the locknut so the damper rod won't drop and remove the wire. Thread the cap bolt onto the rod, then tighten the cap bolt and locknut against each other to the torque listed in this Chapter's Specifications.

158 Thread the cap bolt into the fork tube, tightening it securely (tighten it to the specified torque during installation, when the fork leg is held in the triple clamp).

6 Steering head bearings - replacement

Refer to illustrations 6.3a, 6.3b, 6.3c, 6.4a, 6.4b, 6.5, 6.6a, 6.6b, 6.7, 6.9a, 6.9b, 6.9c, 6.11, 6.14 and 6.15

1 If the steering head bearing check/adjustment (see Chapter 1) does not remedy excessive play or roughness in the steering head bearings, the entire front end must be disassembled and the bearings and races replaced with new ones.

2 Remove the handlebars (see Section 2), the front wheel and brake caliper (see Chapter 7), the front fender (see Chapter 8) and the forks (see Section 3).

3 Loosen the steering stem nut with a socket (see illustration). Remove the nut, washer and upper triple clamp (see illustrations).

4 Using a spanner wrench of the type described in Chapter 1, Section 23, remove the stem locknut and bearing cover (see illustrations) while supporting the steering head from the bottom.

5 Remove the steering stem and lower triple clamp assembly (see illustration). If it's stuck, gently tap on the top of the steering stem with a plastic mallet or a hammer and a wood block.

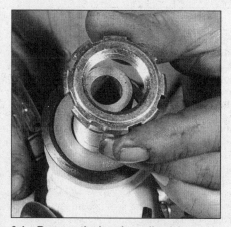

6.4a Remove the bearing adjusting nut . . .

6.4b . . . and lift off the bearing cover

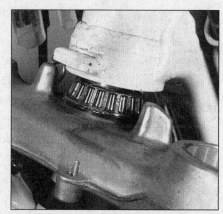

6.5 Lower the steering stem out of the steering head

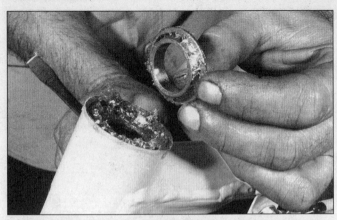

6.6a If the bike has upper ball bearings (1986 CR80R), lift out the top race and the ball cage

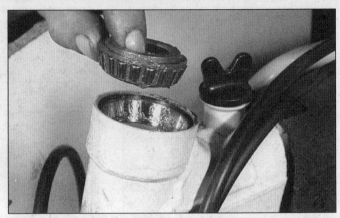

6.6b If the bike has upper roller bearings (all except 1986 CR80R), lift the upper bearing out of the steering head

6.7 Steering stem and bearing details (tapered roller bearings)

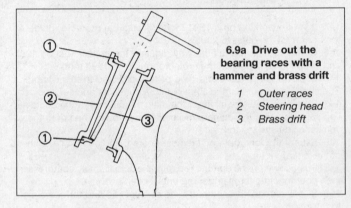

6.9a Drive out the bearing races with a hammer and brass drift

1   *Outer races*
2   *Steering head*
3   *Brass drift*

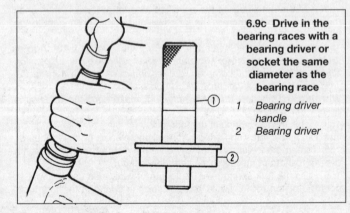

6.9c Drive in the bearing races with a bearing driver or socket the same diameter as the bearing race

1   *Bearing driver handle*
2   *Bearing driver*

6.9b Place the drift against the edge of the lower bearing race (arrow) and tap evenly around it to drive the bearing out

6   Remove the upper bearing **(see illustrations)**.
7   Clean all the parts with solvent and dry them thoroughly, using compressed air, if available **(see illustration)**. If you do use compressed air, don't let the bearings spin as they're dried - it could ruin them. Wipe the old grease out of the frame steering head and bearing races.
8   Examine the races in the steering head for cracks, dents, and pits. If even the slightest amount of wear or damage is evident, the races should be replaced with new ones.
9   To remove the races, drive them out of the steering head with Honda tool no. 07953-MJ10000 or a hammer and drift punch **(see illustrations)**. A slide hammer with the proper internal-jaw puller will also work. Since the races are an interference fit in the frame, installa-

tion will be easier if the new races are left overnight in a refrigerator. This will cause them to contract and slip into place in the frame with very little effort. When installing the races, use a bearing driver the same diameter as the outer race **(see illustration)**, or tap them gently into place with a hammer and punch or a large socket. Do not strike the bearing surface or the race will be damaged.
10   Check the bearings for wear. Look for cracks, dents, and pits in the races and flat spots on the bearings. Replace any defective parts with new ones. If a new bearing is required, replace both of them as a set.
11   Check the grease seal under the lower bearing and replace it with a new one if necessary **(see illustration)**.
12   To remove the lower bearing and grease seal from the steering stem, you may need to use a bearing puller, which can be rented. Don't remove this bearing unless it, or the grease seal underneath, must be replaced. Removal will damage the grease seal, so replace it whenever the bearing is removed.
13   Inspect the steering stem/lower triple clamp for cracks and other

6.11 Leave the lower bearing and grease seal (arrow) on the steering stem unless you plan to replace them

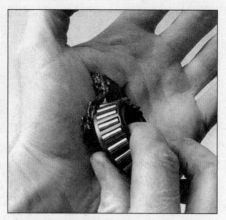

6.14 Work the grease completely into the rollers or balls

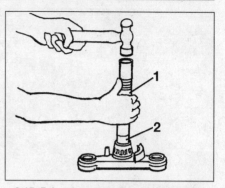

6.15 Drive the grease seal and bearing lower race on with a hollow driver (or an equivalent piece of pipe)

1 Driver
2 Bearing and grease seal

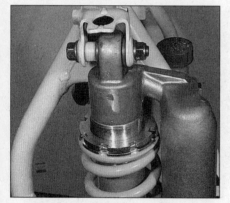

7.4a Remove the bolt and nut from the upper end of the shock absorber (CR80R/85R shown)

7.4b The lower bolt head on later CR125R models (arrow) fits against a stop, so you don't have to hold it with a wrench

7.8 Check the spherical bearing in the shock absorber for wear or damage

damage. Do not attempt to repair any steering components. Replace them with new parts if defects are found.

14 Pack the bearings with high-quality grease (preferably a moly-based grease) (see illustration). Coat the outer races with grease also.

15 Install the grease seal and lower bearing onto the steering stem. Drive the lower bearing onto the steering stem using a pipe the same diameter as the bearing inner race (see illustration). Drive the bearing on until it's fully seated.

16 Insert the steering stem/lower triple clamp into the frame head. Install the upper bearing, bearing cover and adjusting nut. Refer to the adjustment procedure in Chapter 1 and tighten the adjusting nut to the torque listed in the Chapter 1 Specifications.

17 Make sure the steering head turns smoothly and that there's no play in the bearings.

18 Install the fork tubes and tighten the lower triple clamp bolts to the torque listed in this Chapter's Specifications.

19 Tighten the steering stem nut to the torque listed in this Chapter's Specifications.

20 Check the alignment of the fork tubes with the upper triple clamp; the tops of the fork tubes should be even with the upper surface of the triple clamp. If necessary, loosen the lower triple clamp bolts and adjust the position of the fork tubes.

21 Tighten the triple clamp bolts to the torque listed in this Chapter's Specifications.

22 The remainder of installation is the reverse of removal.

23 Check the alignment of the handlebars with the front wheel. If necessary, loosen the upper triple clamp bolts and align the handle-bars with the front wheel, then tighten the upper triple clamp bolts to the torque listed in this Chapter's Specifications.

7 Rear shock absorber - removal, inspection and installation

Removal

Refer to illustrations 7.4a and 7.4b

1 Support the bike securely so it can't be knocked over during this procedure. Support the swingarm with a jack so the suspension can be raised or lowered as needed for access.

2 Remove the seat and sub-frame (see Chapter 8). If you're working on a 1992 through 1995 CR80R, remove the fuel tank (see Chapter 4). Cover the carburetor inlet with a rag to keep out dirt.

3 If you're working on a 1986 through 1995 CR80R or a 1986 CR125R, remove the shock reservoir's retaining bands and detach the reservoir from the bike.

4 Remove the upper and lower mounting bolts (see illustrations).

5 Remove the shock from the bike. If it has a separate reservoir, lift the reservoir out without placing strain on the hose.

Inspection

Refer to illustration 7.8

6 The shock absorber can be overhauled, but it's a complicated procedure that requires special tools not readily available to the typical owner. If inspection reveals problems, have the shock rebuilt by a dealer or motorcycle repair shop.

7 Check the shock absorber for damage and oil leaks. If these can be seen, have the shock overhauled.

8 Check the spherical bearing at the upper end of the shock for leaking grease, looseness or signs of damage (see illustration). If any

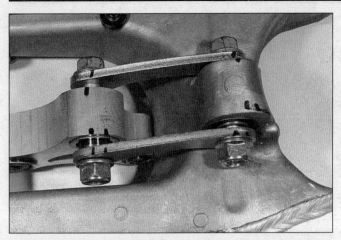

8.5a Labeling the shock linkage connections will make it easier to reassemble the linkage

8.5b Later CR80R/85R models use a two-piece shock link

of these problems can be seen, have the bearing pressed out and a new one pressed in by a dealer or motorcycle repair shop.
9 Clean all parts thoroughly with solvent and dry them with compressed air, if available. Check all parts for scoring, damage or heavy corrosion and replace them as necessary.

Installation

10 Installation is the reverse of the removal steps. Tighten the bolts to the torque values listed in this Chapter's Specifications.

8 Shock absorber linkage - removal, inspection and installation

Removal

1 Support the bike securely so it can't be knocked over during this procedure. Support the swingarm with a jack so the suspension can be raised or lowered as needed for access.

1986 through 1995 CR80R

2 Remove the shock absorber lower bolt.
3 Unbolt the shock arm from the swingarm, then remove the shock arm together with the shock link. Separate the shock arm from the link after removal.

1995 and later CR80R/85R

Refer to illustrations 8.5a, 8.5b and 8.6
4 Remove the shock absorber lower bolt.
5 Unbolt the shock link from the shock arm and swingarm and take

8.6 The arrow on the later CR80R/85R shock arm points to the front of the bike

it off the bike **(see illustrations)**.
6 Unbolt the shock arm from the frame and take it off **(see illustration)**.

CR125R

Refer to illustrations 8.8, 8.9a, 8.9b and 8.9c
7 On all except 1988 models, remove the lower drive chain roller.
8 If you're working on a 1989 or later model, pry the bolt caps out of

8.8 Pry the caps out of the swingarm . . .

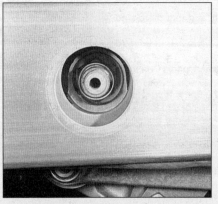

8.9a . . . to expose the nut . . .

8.9b . . . remove the nut and pull out the bolt

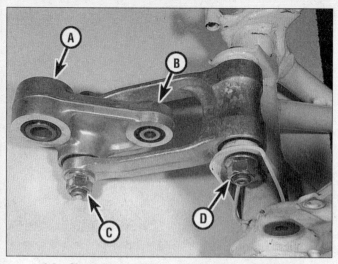

8.9c Shock linkage details (1989 and later CR125R)

A   *Swingarm fitting*
B   *Lower shock absorber fitting*
C   *Arm-to-link nut and bolt*
D   *Link-to-frame nut and bolt*

the swingarm to expose the shock arm-to-swingarm bolt and nut **(see illustration)**.

9   Remove the shock absorber lower mounting bolt. Unbolt the shock arm from the swingarm and the shock link from the frame **(see illustrations)**. Take the linkage out of the bike, then separate the arm from the link.

Inspection

Refer to illustrations 8.10a, 8.10b, 8.10c and 8.10d

10   Slip the collars out of the needle bearings **(see illustrations)**. Check the bearings for wear or damage. If the bearings are okay, pack them with molybdenum disulfide grease and reinstall the collars.

11   If the dust seals are worn or appear to have been leaking, pry them out and press in new ones with a seal driver or socket the same diameter as the seals.

12   If the bearings need to be replaced, press them out and press new ones in. To prevent damage to the new bearings, you'll need a shouldered drift with a narrow diameter the same size as the inside diameter of the bearings. If you don't have the proper tool, have the bearings replaced by a Honda dealer or motorcycle repair shop. A well-equipped automotive machine shop should also be able to do the job.

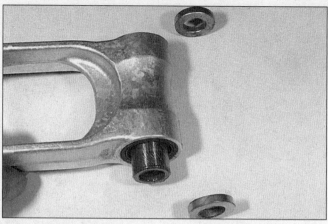

8.10a Pull the covers off the shock link pivots

Installation

13   Installation is the reverse of the removal steps. Tighten the nuts and bolts to the torque listed in this Chapter's Specifications.

9   Swingarm bearings - check

1   Refer to Chapter 7 and remove the rear wheel, then refer to Section 7 and remove the rear shock absorber.

2   Grasp the rear of the swingarm with one hand and place your other hand at the junction of the swingarm and frame. Try to move the rear of the swingarm from side-to-side. Any wear (play) in the bushings should be felt as movement between the swingarm and the frame at the front. The swingarm will actually be felt to move forward and backward at the front (not from side-to-side). If any play is noted, the bearings should be replaced with new ones (see Section 11).

3   Next, move the swingarm up and down through its full travel. It should move freely, without any binding or rough spots. If it doesn't move freely, refer to Section 11 for servicing procedures.

10   Swingarm - removal and installation

Refer to illustrations 10.2, 10.5a and 10.5b

1   Refer to Section 12 and disconnect the drive chain.

2   Remove the rear wheel and the brake pedal (see Chapter 7). If you're working on a bike with a rear disc brake, remove the caliper, and (without disconnecting the hose) detach the brake hose from the

8.10b Withdraw the pivot collars . . .

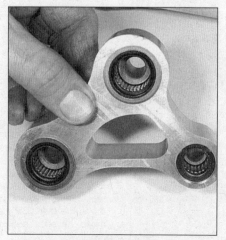

8.10c . . . and inspect the seals and needle bearings

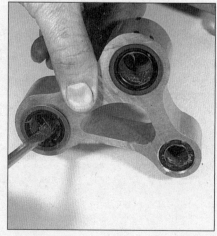

8.10d Pry the seals out if they're worn

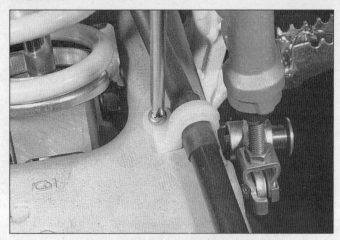

10.2 Unscrew the brake hose retainer

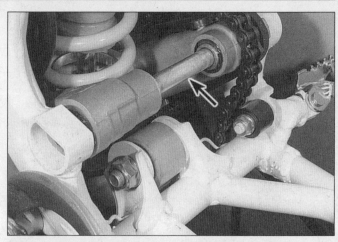

10.5a The swingarm pivot bolt passes through the engine case at the point shown (engine removed for clarity)

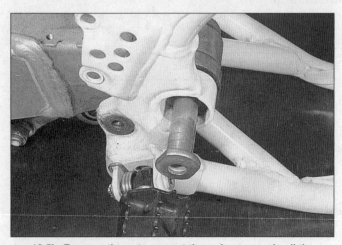

10.5b Remove the nut, support the swingarm and pull the pivot bolt out

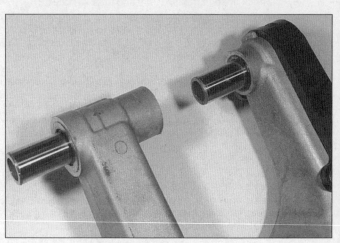

11.2a Slide the pivot collars out

retainer on the swingarm. Support the caliper so it doesn't hang by the hose **(see illustration)**.

3   Unbolt the shock absorber and shock linkage from the swingarm (Sections 7 and 8).

4   Check the chain guards on the swingarm for wear or damage and replace them if necessary (see Chapter 1).

5   Support the swingarm from below, then unscrew its pivot bolt nut and pull the bolt out **(see illustrations)**.

11.2b Have the needle bearings pressed out and new ones pressed in if they're worn . . .

6   Check the chain slider, chain adjuster plates and brake disc guard for wear or damage. Replace them as necessary.

7   Installation is the reverse of the removal steps, with the following additions:

a) Lubricate the swingarm bearings (see Section 11).

b) Tighten the swingarm pivot bolt and nut to the torque listed in this Chapter's Specifications.

c) Refer to Chapter 1 and adjust the drive chain and rear brake pedal (drum brake models).

11 Swingarm bearings - replacement

Refer to illustrations 11.2a, 11.2b and 11.2c

1   Refer to Section 10 and remove the swingarm.

2   Pull the pivot collars out of the swingarm bearings, then inspect the bearings and seals **(see illustrations)**.

3   If the dust seals are worn or appear to have been leaking, pry them out and press in new ones with a seal driver or socket the same diameter as the seals.

4   Check the needle bearings for wear or damage. Needle bearing replacement requires a special puller, a press and a shouldered drift the same diameter as the inside of the bearings. If you don't have these, have the bearings replaced by a Honda dealer or motorcycle repair shop.

5   Coat the bearings and pivot collars with moly-based grease and slip the collar into the swingarm. Install the dust covers.

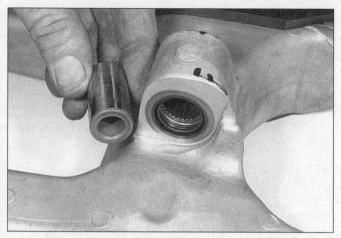

11.2c ... don't forget to check the shock link bearing

12.1 Remove the clip from the master link; its open end (arrow) faces rearward when the chain is on the top run

12 Drive chain - removal, cleaning, inspection and installation

Removal

Refer to illustrations 12.1, 12.2 and 12.3

1 Turn the rear wheel to place the drive chain master link where it's easily accessible **(see illustration)**.
2 Remove the clip and plate and pull the master link out of the chain **(see illustration)**.
3 If you're working on a CR80R/85R, remove the left engine cover (see Chapter 5). If you're working on a CR125R, remove the engine sprocket cover **(see illustration)**.
4 Lift the chain off the sprockets and remove it from the bike.
5 Check the chain guards and rollers on the swingarm and frame for wear or damage and replace them as necessary.

Cleaning and inspection

6 Soak the chain in a high flash point solvent for approximately five or six minutes. Use a brush to work the solvent into the spaces between the links and plates.
7 Wipe the chain dry, then check it carefully for worn or damaged links. Replace the chain if wear or damage is found at any point.
8 Stretch the chain taut and measure its length between the num-

ber of pins listed in this Chapter's Specifications. Compare the measured length to the specified value replace the chain if it's beyond the limit. If the chain needs to be replaced, refer to Section 13 and check the sprockets. If they're worn, replace them also. If a new chain is installed on worn sprockets, it will wear out quickly.
9 Lubricate the chain with spray chain lube compatible with O-ring chains.

Installation

10 Installation is the reverse of the removal steps, with the following additions:

a) *Install the master link clip so its opening faces the back of the motorcycle when the master link is in the upper chain run* **(see illustration 12.1)**. *Be sure to reinstall the O-rings in the master link.*
b) *Refer to Chapter 1 and adjust the chain.*

13 Sprockets - check and replacement

Refer to illustrations 13.3, 13.5, 13.6a, 13.6b and 13.7

1 Support the bike securely so it can't be knocked over during this procedure.
2 Whenever the sprockets are inspected, the chain should be inspected also and replaced if it's worn. Installing a worn chain on new

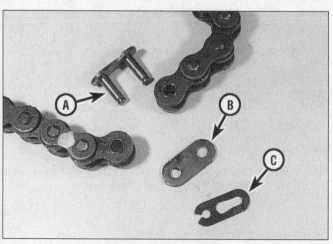

12.2 Master link details

A Link   B Plate   C Clip

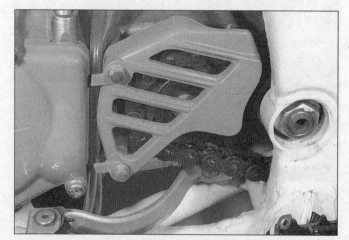

12.3 The CR80R/85R engine sprocket cover is part of the engine cover; the CR125R cover (shown) is a separate unit; note how the tubes fit between the sprocket cover and left engine cover

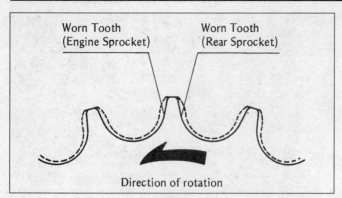

13.3 **Check the sprockets in the areas indicated to see if they're worn excessively**

13.5 **The driven sprocket is attached to the wheel hub with Allen bolts and nuts**

sprockets will cause them to wear quickly.

3   Check the teeth on the engine sprocket and rear sprocket for wear **(see illustration)**. The engine sprocket is visible through the cover slots.

13.6a **The CR80R/85R engine sprocket is secured by a plate and two bolts**

4   If the sprockets are worn, remove the chain (see Section 12) and the rear wheel (see Chapter 7).

5   Remove the sprocket from the rear wheel hub **(see illustration)**.

6   To remove a CR80R/85R engine sprocket, remove two bolts and lift off the retainer plate **(see illustration)**. To remove a CR125R engine sprocket, remove the bolt and washer **(see illustration)**. Lift the sprocket off the transmission shaft.

7   Inspect the seal behind the engine sprocket **(see illustration)**. If it has been leaking, pry it out (taking care not to scratch the seal bore) and tap in a new seal with a socket the same diameter as the seal.

8   Installation is the reverse of the removal steps, with the following additions:

a) *Tighten the driven sprocket bolts to the torque values listed in this Chapter's Specifications. Tighten the engine sprocket bolt(s) securely, but don't overtighten them and strip the threads*

b) *Install the master link clip so its opening faces the back of the motorcycle when the master link is in the upper chain run* **(see illustration 12.1)**.

c) *Refer to Chapter 1 and adjust the chain.*

13.6b **The CR125R engine sprocket is secured by a single bolt and washer**

13.7 **If the seal has been leaking, replace it; on CR125R models (shown) pull the collar out of the seal first**

Chapter 6 Part B
Steering, suspension and final drive (CR250R and CR500R models)

Contents

Specifications

Front forks

Oil type
  CR250R
    1986 through 1991 .... Pro-Honda SS-7 suspension fluid or equivalent 5W fork oil
    1995 on .... Pro Honda HP 5W fork oil or equivalent
  CR500R
    1986 through 1991 .... Pro-Honda SS-7M suspension fluid or equivalent 5W fork oil
    1992 on .... Pro Honda SS-7 5W fork oil or equivalent

Fork oil capacity

CR250R
  1986
    Standard .... 564 cc (19.1 fl oz)
    Maximum .... 584 cc (19.8 fl oz)
    Minimum .... 528 cc (17.9 fl oz)
  1987
    Standard .... 564 cc (19.1 fl oz)
    Maximum .... 584 cc (19.8 fl oz)
    Minimum .... 528 cc (19.7 fl oz)
  1988
    Standard .... Not specified (see text)
    Maximum .... 573 cc (19.4 fl oz)
    Minimum .... 516 cc (17.5 fl oz)
  1992
    Standard .... 572 cc (19.35 fl oz)
    Maximum .... 584 cc (19.75 fl oz)
    Minimum .... 552 cc (18.67 fl oz)
  1993
    Standard .... 559 cc (18.91 fl oz)
    Maximum .... 584 cc (19.75 fl oz)
    Minimum .... 541 cc (18.3 fl oz)

Fork oil capacity (continued)

CR250R

1994

Standard	549 cc (18.56 fl oz)
Maximum	567 cc (19.18 fl oz)
Minimum	524 cc (17.72 fl oz)

1995 and 1996

Standard	525 cc (17.76 fl oz)
Maximum	539 cc (18.23 fl oz)
Minimum	499 cc (16.88 fl oz)

1997

Standard	369 cc (12.5 fl oz)
Maximum	430 cc (14.5 fl oz)
Minimum	335 cc (11.3 fl oz)

1998

Standard	375 cc (12.5 fl oz)
Maximum	422 cc (14.3 fl oz)
Minimum	326 cc (11.0 fl oz)

1999

Standard	373 cc (12.6 fl oz)
Maximum	414 cc (14.0 fl oz)
Minimum	318 cc (10.8 fl oz)

2000

Standard	386 cc (13.6 fl oz)
Maximum	424 cc (14.3 fl oz)
Minimum	328 cc (11.1 fl oz)

2001

Standard	383 cc (13.0 fl oz)
Maximum	433 cc (14.6 fl oz)
Minimum	337 cc (11.4 fl oz)

2002	409 cc (13.8 fl oz)
2003	405 cc (13.7 fl oz)
2004	387 cc (13.1 fl oz)
2005 and later	394 ± 4 cc (13.3 ± 0.14 fl oz)

CR500R

1986 and 1987

Standard	557 cc (18.8 fl oz)
Maximum	584 cc (19.8 fl oz)
Minimum	520 cc (18.3 fl oz)

1988

Standard	575 cc (19.4 fl oz)
Maximum	584 cc (19.8 fl oz)
Minimum	527 cc (17.8 fl oz)

1989

Standard	641 cc (21.7 fl oz)
Maximum	655 cc (22.1 fl oz)
Minimum	620 cc (21.0 fl oz)

1990 and 1991

Standard	612 cc (20.7 fl oz)
Maximum	639 cc (21.6 fl oz)
Minimum	605 cc (20.5 fl oz)

1992

Standard	582 cc (19.7 fl oz)
Maximum	584 cc (19.8 fl oz)
Minimum	552 cc (18.7 fl oz)

1993

Standard	572 cc (19.8 fl oz)
Maximum	584 cc (19.75 fl oz)
Minimum	541 cc (18.3 fl oz)

1994

Standard	567 cc (19.2 fl oz)
Maximum	576 cc (19.5 fl oz)
Minimum	534 cc (18.1 fl oz)

1995

Standard	525 cc (17.8 fl oz)
Maximum	539 cc (18.2 fl oz)
Minimum	499 cc (16.9 fl oz)

1996 on

Standard	636 cc (21.5 fl oz)
Maximum	658 cc (22.3 fl oz)
Minimum	613 cc (20.7 fl oz)

Fork oil level (1986 through 1996 CR250R) (fork fully compressed and spring removed)

1986
Standard	136 mm (5.35 inches)
Maximum	117 mm (4.61 inches)
Minimum	169 mm (6.65 inches)

1987
Standard	136 mm (5.35 inches)
Maximum	142 mm (4.57 inches)
Minimum	169 mm (6.65 inches)

1988
Standard	124 mm (4.88 inches)
Maximum	115 mm (4.53 inches)
Minimum	170 mm (6.69 inches)

1989
Standard	115 mm (4.53 inches)
Maximum	105 mm (4.13 inches)
Minimum	132 mm (5.2 inches)

1990
Standard	124 mm (4.88 inches)
Maximum	114 mm (4.49 inches)
Minimum	144 mm (5.67 inches)

1991
Standard	107 mm (4.21 inches)
Maximum	95 mm (3.74 inches)
Minimum	124 mm (4.88 inches)

1992
Standard	105 mm (4.1 inches)
Maximum	93 mm (3.7 inches)
Minimum	124 mm (4.9 inches)

1993
Standard	118 mm (4.6 inches)
Maximum	93 mm (3.7 inches)
Minimum	126 mm (5.4 inches)

1994
Standard	114 mm (4.5 inches)
Maximum	96 mm (3.8 inches)
Minimum	139 mm (5.9 inches)

1995 and 1996
Standard	98 mm (3.9 inches)
Maximum	84 mm (3.3 inches)
Minimum	124 mm (4.9 inches)

Damper oil level (1997 and later CR250R)

2002 and earlier..	5 to 10 mm (0.2 to 0.4 inch)
2003 and later	42 to 47 mm (1.65 to 1.85 inch)

Fork oil level (CR500R) (fork fully compressed and spring removed)

1986 and 1987
Standard	142.0 mm (5.59 inches)
Maximum	124.0 mm (4.88 inches)
Minimum	176.0 mm (6.93 inches)

1988
Standard	123.0 mm (4.84 inches)
Maximum	114.0 mm (4.49 inches)
Minimum	169.0 mm (6.65 inches)

1989
Standard	127 mm (4.99 inches)
Maximum	116 mm (4.6 inches)
Minimum	146 mm (5.8 inches)

1990 and 1991
Standard	158.0 mm (6.22 inches)
Maximum	133 mm (5.2 inches)
Minimum	164 mm (6.5 inches)

1992
Standard	95 mm (3.74 inches)
Maximum	93 mm (3.66 inches)
Minimum	124 mm (4.88 inches)

1993
Standard	105 mm (4.13 inches)
Maximum	93 mm (3.66 inches)
Minimum	136 mm (5.35 inches)

Fork oil level (CR500R) (fork fully compressed and spring removed) (continued)
1994
    Standard .... 110 mm (4.33 inches)
    Maximum .... 101 mm (3.98 inches)
    Minimum .... 143 mm (5.63 inches)
1995
    Standard .... 98 mm (3.86 inches)
    Maximum .... 84 mm (3.3 inches)
    Minimum .... 124 mm (4.9 inches)
1996 on
    Standard .... 92 mm (3.62 inches)
    Maximum .... 73 mm (2.87 inches)
    Minimum .... 112 mm (4.41 inches)

Fork spring free length limit
1986 and 1987 .... 548.8 mm (21.61 inches)
1988 .... 557.2 mm (21.94 inches)
1989 and 1990 .... 504.9 mm (19.88 inches)
1991 .... 503.9 mm (19.84 inches)
1992 through 1994 .... 504.5 mm (19.86 inches)
1995 and 1996 .... 487.0 mm (19.17 inches)
1997 and 1998
    CR250R .... 483.6 mm (19.04 inches)
    CR500R .... 487.0 mm (19.17 inches)
1999 on
    2001 and earlier CR250R .... 486.0 mm (19.1 inches)
    2002 and later CR250R, all CR500R .... 487.0 mm (19.17 inches)
Fork tube bend limit .... 0.2 mm (0.008 inch)

Fork installed position in upper triple clamp (standard)
CR250R
    1986 and 1987 .... Fork groove flush with triple clamp
    1988 .... Top of fork flush with triple clamp
    1989 through 1993 .... Fork groove flush with triple clamp
    1994 through 1996 .... Top of fork flush with triple clamp
    1997 through 1999 .... Fork groove flush with triple clamp
    2000 and 2001 .... Top of fork flush with triple clamp
    2002 and later .... Fork groove flush with triple clamp
CR500R
    1986 and 1987 .... Fork groove flush with triple clamp
    1988 .... Top of fork flush with triple clamp
    1989 on .... Fork groove flush with triple clamp

Drive chain
Drive chain length
    All except 1997 CR250R .... Not specified (1)
    1997 CR250R (17 pins) .... 259 mm (10.20 inches)

Torque specifications
Handlebar bracket bolts .... 22 Nm (16 ft-lbs)
Handlebar bracket nuts
    CR250R
        1986 through 1988 .... 30 to 40 Nm (22 to 29 ft-lbs)
        1999 on .... 44 Nm (33 ft-lbs)
    CR500R .... 35 Nm (25 ft-lbs)
Front axle nut or bolt .... See Chapter 7
Triple clamp bolts
    CR250R
        1986 through 1988 .... 18 to 25 Nm (13 to 18 ft-lbs)
        1989 through 1991
            Upper .... 30 to 34 Nm (22 to 25 ft-lbs)
            Lower .... 24 to 30 Nm (17 to 22 ft-lbs)
        1992 through 1996 .... 22 Nm (16 ft-lbs)
        1997
            Upper .... 22 Nm (16 ft-lbs)
            Lower .... 21 Nm (15 ft-lbs)
        1998 on
            Upper .... 22 Nm (16 ft-lbs)
            Lower .... 20 Nm (14 ft-lbs)
            Upper .... 22 Nm (16 ft-lbs)
            Lower .... 21 Nm (15 ft-lbs)

CR500R
  1986 through 1988 .... 18 to 25 Nm (13 to 18 ft-lbs)
  1989
    Upper .... 30 to 40 Nm (22 to 29 ft-lbs)
    Lower .... 18 to 25 Nm (13 to 18 ft-lbs)
  1990 and 1991
    Upper .... 30 to 40 Nm (22 to 29 ft-lbs)
    Lower .... 24 to 30 Nm (17 to 22 ft-lbs)
  1992 on... 22 Nm (16 ft-lbs)
Fork center bolt (2)
  CR250R
    1986 through 1988 .... 30 to 40 Nm (22 to 29 ft-lbs)
    1989.. 40 to 45 Nm (29 to 33 ft-lbs)
    1990.. 50 to 55 Nm (36 to 40 ft-lbs)
    1991.. 40 to 50 Nm (29 to 36 ft-lbs)
    1992 through 1994 .... 80 Nm (58 ft-lbs)
    1995 and 1996.. 78 Nm (56 ft-lbs)
    1997 on... 69 Nm (51 ft-lbs)
  CR500R
    1986 through 1988 .... 30 to 40 Nm (22 to 29 ft-lbs)
    1989 and 1990.. 40 to 45 Nm (29 to 33 ft-lbs)
    1991.. 40 to 50 Nm (29 to 36 ft-lbs)
    1992 through 1994 .... 80 Nm (58 ft-lbs)
    1995 on... 55 Nm (40 ft-lbs)
Fork cap to fork
  CR250R
    1986 through 1988 .... 15 to 30 Nm (11 to 22 ft-lbs)
    1989 through 1994 .... 35 Nm (25 ft-lbs)
    1995 and 1996.. 30 Nm (22 ft-lbs)
    1997 and 1998.. 54 Nm (40 ft-lbs)
    1999 on... 29 Nm (22 ft-lbs)
  CR500R
    1986 through 1988 .... 15 to 30 Nm (11 to 22 ft-lbs)
    1989 through 1994 .... 35 Nm (25 ft-lbs)
    1995 on... 30 Nm (22 ft-lbs)
Fork cap locknut
  CR250R
    1986.. 12 to 15 Nm (108 to 132 in-lbs)
    1987 through 1990 .... 17.5 to 22.5 Nm (13 to 16 ft-lbs)
    1991 through 1997 .... 22 Nm (16 ft-lbs)
  CR500R
    1986.. 12 to 15 Nm (108 to 132 in-lbs)
    1987 through 1990 .... 17.5 to 22.5 Nm (13 to 16 ft-lbs)
    1991 through 1994 .... 22 Nm (16 ft-lbs)
    1995 on... 28 Nm (20 ft-lbs)
Fork cap to damper (1997 and later CR250R)
  1997... 118 Nm (87 ft-lbs)
  1998 on.. 54 Nm (40 ft-lbs)
Fork cap lockscrew (1997 CR250R)... 0.7 Nm (6 inch-lbs)
Steering stem bearing adjusting nut .... See Chapter 1
Steering stem nut
  CR250R
    1986 through 1991 .... 95 to 140 Nm (69 to 101 ft-lbs)
    1992 and 1993.. 118 ft-lbs (85 Nm)
    1994 through 2000 .... 147 Nm (108 ft-lbs)
    2001.. 108 Nm (80 ft-lbs)
  CR500R
    1986 through 1991 .... 95 to 140 Nm (69 to 101 ft-lbs)
    1992.. 118 Nm (85 Nm)
    1993 on... 130 Nm (94 ft-lbs)
Rear shock absorber upper mounting bolt .... 45 Nm (33 ft-lbs)
Rear shock absorber lower mounting bolt
  CR250R
    1986 through 1992 .... 43 Nm (31 ft-lbs)
    1993 on... 45 Nm (33 ft-lbs)
  CR500R
    1986 through 1992 .... 43 Nm (31 ft-lbs)
    1993.. 45 Nm (33 ft-lbs)
    1994 on... 43 Nm (31 ft-lbs)

Torque specifications (continued)

Shock arm to swingarm
  CR250R
    1986 through 1991 .... 55 to 70 Nm (40 to 51 ft-lbs)
    1992 through 1996 .... 90 Nm (65 ft-lbs)
    1997 on.. 79 Nm (59 ft-lbs)
  CR500R
    1986 through 1991 .... 55 to 70 Nm (40 to 51 ft-lbs)
    1992 .... 63 Nm (46 ft-lbs)
    1993 on.. 90 Nm (65 ft-lbs)
Shock arm to shock link
  CR250R
    1986 through 1988 .... 40 to 50 Nm (29 to 36 ft-lbs)
    1989 through 1991 .... 55 to 70 Nm (40 to 51 ft-lbs)
    1992 through 1996 .... 90 Nm (65 ft-lbs)
    1997 on.. 79 Nm (59 ft-lbs)
  CR500R
    1986 through 1988 .... 40 to 50 Nm (29 to 36 ft-lbs)
    1989 through 1991 .... 55 to 70 Nm (40 to 51 ft-lbs)
    1992 on.. 63 Nm (46 ft-lbs)
Shock link to frame
  CR250R
    1986 through 1988 .... 40 to 50 Nm (29 to 36 ft-lbs)
    1989 through 1991 .... 55 to 70 Nm (40 to 51 ft-lbs)
    1992 through 1996 .... 90 Nm (65 ft-lbs)
    1997 on.. 79 Nm (59 ft-lbs)
  CR500R
    1986 through 1988 .... 40 to 50 Nm (29 to 36 ft-lbs)
    1989 through 1991 .... 55 to 70 Nm (40 to 51 ft-lbs)
    1992 on.. 63 Nm (46 ft-lbs)
Swingarm pivot bolt nut .... 90 Nm (65 ft-lbs)
Engine sprocket bolts.. 27 Nm (20 ft-lbs)
Rear sprocket bolts/nuts
    1986 through 1989.. 32 to 37 Nm (23 to 27 ft-lbs)
    1990 and 1991 .... 25 to 31 Nm (23 to 27 ft-lbs) (3)
    1992 on.. 33 Nm (24 ft-lbs)

1. Replace the chain when it is visible in the wear window (see Chapter 1).
2. Apply non-permanent thread locking agent to the threads.
3. Lubricate the threads with oil.

1   General information

The steering system on these models consists of a one-piece braced handlebar and a steering head attached to the front portion of the frame. The steering stem rides in tapered roller bearings. The handlebars on all CR500R models, as well as 1986 through 1998 CR250R models, rest in brackets integral with the upper triple clamp. On 1999 and later CR250R models, the handlebar brackets are secured to the upper triple clamp by studs and nuts. In their normal installed position, the brackets are centered over their studs. An optional set of brackets with 3 mm offset allows the handlebars to be placed 3 mm (0.12 inch) forward or rearward of the normal position, depending on which way the brackets are turned when they are installed.

The front suspension uses cartridge forks. Inverted cartridge forks are used on 1989 and later models.

The rear suspension consists of a single shock absorber with concentric coil spring, a swingarm and Honda's Pro-Link suspension linkage. The suspension linkage produces a progressive rising rate effect, where the suspension stiffens as its travel increases. This allows a softer ride over small bumps in the terrain, together with firmer suspension control over large irregularities.

2   Handlebars - removal, inspection and installation

Refer to illustration 2.3

1   If the handlebars must be removed for access to other components, such as the steering head bearings, simply remove the bolts and take the handlebars off the bracket. It's not necessary to disconnect the throttle or clutch cables, brake hose or the kill switch wires, but it is a good idea to support the assembly with a piece of wire or rope, to avoid unnecessary strain on the cables.

2   If the handlebars are to be removed completely, refer to Chapter 2 for the clutch lever removal procedure, Chapter 4 for the throttle housing removal procedure, Chapter 5 for the kill switch removal procedure and Chapter 7 for the brake master cylinder removal procedure.

3   Remove the upper bracket bolts, lift off the brackets and remove the handlebars **(see illustration)**.

4   Check the handlebars and brackets for cracks and distortion and replace them if any problems are found.

5   Place the handlebars in the lower brackets. Line up the punch mark on the handlebar with the parting line of the upper and lower brackets **(see illustration 2.3)**.

6   Install the upper brackets with their punch marks facing forward **(see illustration 2.3)**. Tighten the front bolts, then the rear bolts, to the torque listed in this Chapter's Specifications. **Caution:** *If there's a gap*

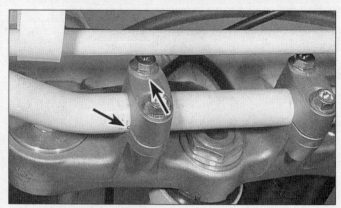

2.3 Remove the bolts and lift off the upper brackets; on installation, the bracket punch marks face forward (upper arrow) and the punch mark in the handlebar (lower arrow) aligns with the edge of the lower bracket (integral brackets shown)

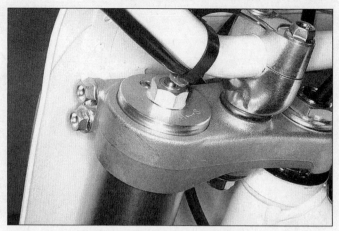

3.3 Note the position of the fork in the upper triple clamp, then loosen the pinch bolts

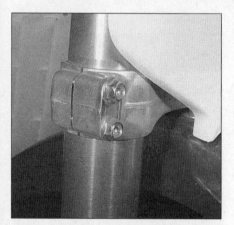

3.4 Loosen the lower triple clamp bolts and remove the fork

4.4 Empty the fork oil into a drain pan

4.5a Hold the cap bolt (upper arrow) with one wrench and the locknut (lower arrow) with another, then unscrew them from each other

between the upper and lower brackets at the rear after tightening the bolts, don't try to close it by tightening beyond the recommended torque. You'll only crack the brackets.

3 Front forks - removal and installation

Removal
Refer to illustrations 3.3 and 3.4

1   Support the bike securely upright with its front wheel off the ground so it can't fall over during this procedure. If you're working on a bike with fork air valve caps, use the valves to relieve any accumulated fork air pressure.
2   Remove the front wheel, unbolt the brake caliper and detach the brake hose retainer from the left fork leg (see Chapter 7).
3   If you plan to disassemble the forks, loosen the fork cap bolts now **(see illustration)**. This can be done later, but it will be easier while the forks are securely held in the triple clamps. Also, set the damping adjuster (if equipped) to its softest setting to prevent damage to the adjuster when the fork is reassembled. **Note:** *On 1998 and later CR250R models, loosening the fork cap bolt requires a 50 mm hex wrench (Honda part no. 07WMA-KZ30100 or equivalent). You can order the tool from a Honda dealer, or you may be able to buy one from an aftermarket tool supplier. Don't use an adjustable wrench or open end wrench, since they may damage the nut.*
4   Loosen the upper and lower triple clamp bolts **(see illustration 3.3 and the accompanying illustration)**.
5   Lower the fork leg out of the triple clamps, twisting it if necessary.

Installation
6   Slide each fork leg into the lower triple clamp.
7   Slide the fork legs up, installing the tops of the tubes into the upper triple clamp. Position the upper end of each fork tube at the distance from the upper triple clamp listed in this Chapter's Specifications. Make sure the forks protrude an equal amount above each triple clamp.
8   Tighten the triple clamp bolts to the torque listed in this Chapter's Specifications.
9   Make sure the damping adjusters (if equipped) are at the same setting for both forks.
10   The remainder of installation is the reverse of the removal steps.

4 Front forks (1986 through 1988) - disassembly, inspection and reassembly

1   Remove the forks following the procedure in Section 3. Work on one fork at a time to prevent mixing up the parts.

Disassembly
Refer to illustrations 4.4, 4.5a, 4.5b, 4.5c, 4.5d, 4.6a, 4.6b, 4.7, 4.8, 4.10a, 4.10b, 4.10c and 4.10d

2   Loosen the clamps and take the boot off the fork leg.
3   Hold the upper fork tube so it won't turn and unscrew the fork cap bolt. Release the spring tension.
4   Place the open end of the fork over a drain pan, then compress and extend the damper rod and fork tubes several times to pump out the oil **(see illustration)**.
5   Carefully slide the outer tube down to the bottom of the fork to

4.5b Some models have a spacer, as shown here; some have the dual springs shown here while others have a single fork spring

4.5c Remove the upper spring (if equipped), the upper spring seat and spring guide

4.5d Remove the lower spring seat (if equipped) and lower spring

4.6a Pry the rubber plug from the bottom of the fork and turn the damping adjuster to its softest setting

4.6b Unscrew the center bolt; use a new sealing washer on installation

4.7 Pry the dust seal out of its bore

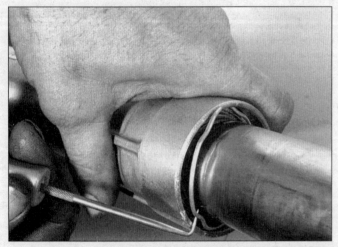

4.8 Pry the retaining ring out with a pointed tool; be careful not to scratch the seal bore

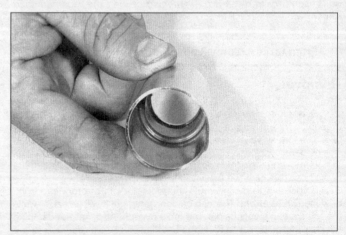

4.10a Remove the oil lock piece; note which way it fits

expose the fork spring. Hold the cap bolt with one wrench and loosen the locknut away from the cap bolt with another wrench **(see illustration)**. Unscrew the cap bolt from the damper rod, then remove the spacer (if equipped). Remove the spring seat(s) and spring(s) **(see illustrations)**.

6   Pry the rubber plug from the bottom of the fork **(see illustration)**. Unscrew the center bolt and remove the bolt with its sealing washer **(see illustration)**.

7   Pry the dust seal out of its bore, taking care not to scratch the fork tube **(see illustration)**.

8   Pry the oil seal retainer out of its groove, again taking care not to scratch the fork tube **(see illustration)**.

4.10b Pull the damper and rod out of the fork tube

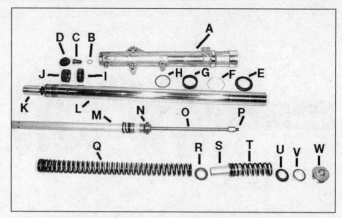

4.10c Fork details (1986 through 1988 models with dual springs)

A	Outer fork tube	M	Damper
B	Sealing washer	N	Bushing
C	Center bolt	O	Damper rod
D	Rubber plug	P	Locknut
E	Dust seal	Q	Lower spring
F	Retaining ring	R	Spring seat
G	Oil seal	S	Spring guide
H	Backup ring	T	Upper spring
I	Bushing	U	Spring seat
J	Bushing	V	Spacer
K	Oil lock piece	W	Fork cap
L	Inner fork tube		

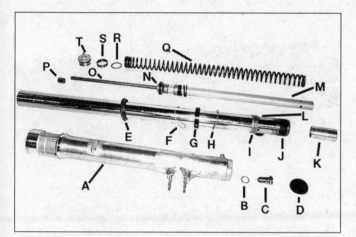

4.10d Fork details (1986 through 1988 models with single springs)

A	Outer fork tube	K	Oil lock piece
B	Sealing washer	L	Inner fork tube
C	Center bolt	M	Damper
D	Rubber plug	N	Bushing
E	Dust seal	O	Damper rod
F	Retaining ring	P	Locknut
G	Oil seal	Q	Spring
H	Backup ring	R	Spring seat
I	Bushing	S	Spacer
J	Bushing	T	Fork cap

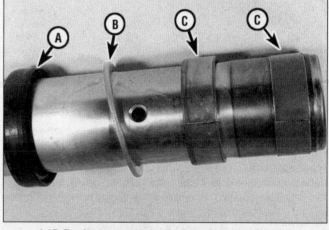

4.15 Don't remove the bushings unless they're worn

A	Oil seal	B	Back-up ring	C	Bushings

9   Hold one fork tube in each hand and pull the tubes apart sharply several times (like a slide hammer) to separate them.

10   Remove the oil lock piece from the bottom of the inner fork tube and the damper from the top **(see illustrations)**. Slide the oil seal and back-up ring off the outside of the inner fork tube. Don't remove the bushings unless they need to be replaced.

Inspection

Refer to illustrations 4.15, 4.17a and 4.17b

11   Clean all parts in solvent and blow them dry with compressed air, if available. Check the inner and outer fork tubes and the damper rod for score marks, scratches, flaking of the chrome and excessive or abnormal wear. Look for dents in the tubes and replace them if any are found. Check the fork seal seat for nicks, gouges and scratches. If damage is evident, leaks will occur around the seal-to-outer tube junction. Replace worn or defective parts with new ones.

12   Have the inner fork tube checked for runout at a dealer service department or other repair shop. **Warning:** *If the tube is bent, it should be replaced with a new one. Don't try to straighten it.*

13   Measure the overall length of the fork spring and check it for cracks or other damage. Compare the length to the minimum length listed in this Chapter's Specifications. If it's defective or sagged, replace both fork springs with new ones. Never replace only one spring.

14   Check the Teflon ring on the damper rod for wear or damage and replace it if problems are found. **Note:** *Don't remove the ring from the damper rod unless you plan to replace it.*

15   Check the fork tube bushing and fork slider bushing for wear **(see illustration)** and replace them if their condition is in doubt.

16   Check the center bolt for wear or damage. Replace its O-rings and sealing washer whenever the fork is disassembled.

17   Check the bushing on the damper rod for wear or damage and

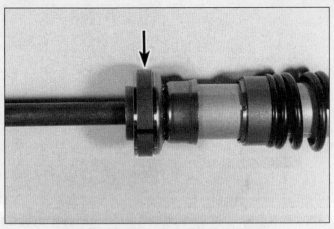

4.17a There's a bushing on the piston (arrow) . . .

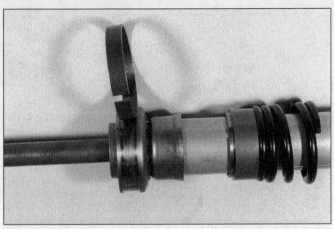

4.17b . . . to remove it, expand it at the slit and slip it off the fork

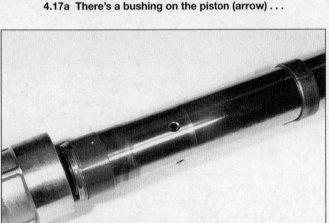

4.20 Slip the damper into the inner fork tube and install the oil lock piece on the damper

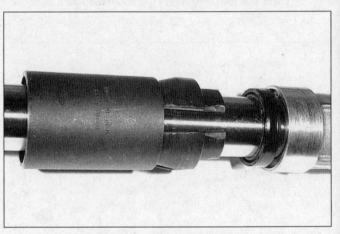

4.23a A seal driver like this one is the ideal way to seat outer tube bushings and install fork seals

replace it if any problems are found **(see illustrations)**.
18   Check the inner circumference of the back-up ring for distortion and replace it if any problems are found.

Reassembly

Refer to illustrations 4.20, 4.23a, 4.23b, 4.24, 4.25 and 4.29
19   If the damper rod was removed from the damper, install it, then

4.23b If you don't have a seal driver, a section of pipe can be used the same way the seal driver would be used - as a slide hammer (be sure to tape the ends of the pipe so it doesn't scratch the fork tube)

thread the locknut onto the damper rod. If there's a chamfer on the locknut, it faces downward (toward the damper).
20   Install the damper rod and damper in the inner fork tube. Install the oil lock piece on the end of the damper **(see illustration)**, then install the inner fork tube in the outer fork tube.
21   Place a new sealing washer on the damping adjuster bolt. Coat the bolt threads with non-permanent thread locking agent, then install the bolt in the bottom of the fork and tighten it to the torque listed in this Chapter's Specifications.
22   Smear a coat of the fork oil listed in this Chapter's Specifications onto the inner circumference of the dust seal, the oil seal and the outer fork tube's bushing.
23   Slide the outer tube bushing onto the inner tube. Position the bushing at the edge of its bore, then use a fork seal driver or equivalent to drive the bushing into its bore **(see illustrations)**. Install the backup ring on top of the bushing.
24   Slide the oil seal onto the inner fork tube with its marked side facing up. Drive the oil seal, using the same seal driver, just past the retaining ring groove **(see illustration)**. If you're very careful, the seal can be driven in with a hammer and drift punch. Work around the circumference of the seal, tapping gently on the outer edge of the seal until it's seated. Be careful - if you distort the seal, you'll have to disassemble the fork and end up taking it to a dealer anyway! Compress the seal retaining ring into the groove, making sure it seats securely.
25   Install the dust seal, making sure it seats completely **(see illustration)**.
26   Compress the fork all the way.
27   If you're working on a 1986 or 1987 model, pour fork oil of the type and amount listed in this Chapter's Specifications into the fork tube.

4.24 The seal driver is also the ideal way to install the oil seal

4.25 Tap the dust seal evenly into the fork tube

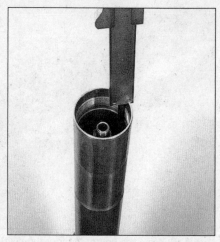

4.29 Measure the oil level from the top of the fork

28   If you're working on a 1988 model, measure the specified amount of fork oil into a container with a small pour spout. Pour fork oil into the top of the damper rod (not into the fork tube) until it begins to flow out the air relief holes. Then pour the remaining oil into the fork tube.

29   With the fork compressed, measure oil level to the top of the fork **(see illustration)**. Add or remove oil as needed. **Note:** *Minimum oil level will make the suspension slightly softer near full compression; maximum oil level will make the suspension slightly stiffer near full compression.* **Warning:** *To prevent unstable handling, make sure the oil level is exactly the same in both forks.*

30   Coat a new O-ring with fork oil and install it on the fork cap.

31   Wind the end of a two-foot length of mechanic's wire around the damper rod just below the locknut. Slip the fork spring(s) over the wire, then use the wire to hold the damper rod extended while you install the fork spring in the fork tube. Undo the wire from the damper rod and pull it out through the fork spring, in the meantime holding the damper rod in its extended position. Install the upper spring seat (and spacer if equipped) on the spring.

32   Thread the locknut all the way onto the damper rod, chamfered side first.

33   Thread the fork cap onto the damper rod against the locknut, then tighten the cap and nut against each other to the torque listed in this Chapter's Specifications. Thread the fork cap into the fork tube (tighten it to the specified torque after installation, when the fork is held in the triple clamps).

34   Install the fork boot with its breather holes toward the rear of the motorcycle.

---

5   Front forks (1989 and 1990) - disassembly, inspection and reassembly

---

Note: *Overhaul of the forks on these models requires special tools for which there are no good substitutes. The tools can be ordered from your local Honda dealer, or you may be able to buy equivalent tools from aftermarket suppliers. Read through the procedure and arrange to get the special tools or substitutes before starting. If you don't disassemble the forks on a regular basis, it may be more practical to have the job done by a Honda dealer or other motorcycle repair shop.*

1   Slide fork slider spacer 07KMZ-KZ30101 onto the bottom of the inner fork tube so it rests on the axle bracket. This is necessary to keep the outer tube from sliding down against the axle bracket, which could damage the bushings and dust seal. It will also be needed later to adjust the fork oil level.

2   Wear safety glasses and remove the fork cap. The outer fork tube is now free to slide; lower it carefully against the tool.

3   Slide the spring collar down far enough to expose the locknut

below the fork cap. Hold the lock nut with an open-end wrench and unscrew the fork cap from the damper rod.

4   Remove the locknut, spring collar, spring seat and fork spring from the fork.

5   Remove the spacer from the fork tube. **Caution:** *Don't let the outer fork tube slide against the axle bracket.*

6   Hold the fork upside down over a drain pan and pump the damper rod eight to ten times to pump out the fork oil.

7   Pry the rubber plug from the bottom of the fork. Hold the damper rod from turning with Honda tool 07KMB-KZ3010A or equivalent and unscrew the center bolt from the bottom of the fork. If you don't have the special tool, you can spin the center bolt loose with an air wrench. However, you'll still need a way to hold the damper rod during assembly so you can tighten the center bolt to the correct torque.

8   Pull the damper rod and damper out of the fork, then separate the damper rod from the damper. **Caution:** *Don't scratch the bushing with the damper rod threads during removal.*

9   Pry the dust seal out of its bore and remove the oil seal retainer ring **(see illustrations 4.7 and 4.8)**.

10   Grasp one fork tube in each hand, compress them together, then yank them apart sharply as far as they'll go. Do this several times until the tubes separate; the slide hammer-like motion is necessary to pull the slider bushing out of its bore in the outer fork tube.

11   Remove the dust seal, retaining ring, oil seal and backup ring from the inner fork tube **(see illustration 4.15)**.

Inspection

12   Refer to Steps 11 through 16 of Section 4 to inspect the fork.

13   Check the oil seal case (on the bottom end of the outer fork tube) for wear or damage. Leave it in place if no problems are found. If you need to replace the oil seal case or the fork tube, remove the stop ring and slider from the oil seal case. Slide the oil seal case partway up the fork tube to expose the stop ring on the fork tube, then remove the stop ring. Slide the oil case off the fork tube, tapping it gently with a soft-faced hammer if necessary. Remove the O-ring from inside the oil seal case.

14   Check the wear rings on the damper rod and on the spring collar for wear or damage and replace them if problems are found.

Assembly

Refer to illustration 5.16

15   If the oil seal case removed, install a new O-ring inside it and coat the O-ring with the type of fork oil listed in this Chapter's Specifications. Slide the oil seal case onto the fork tube past the stop ring groove, install the stop ring in the fork tube groove and pull the case back against the stop ring. Install the slider and the other stop ring on the oil seal case.

5.16 Wrap the end of the fork tube with electrical tape to protect the seals

16   Wrap the end of the inner fork tube with electrical tape to protect the new oil seal on installation **(see illustration)**. Coat the lip of the new oil seal with the recommended fork oil. Install the bushings (if removed), backup ring and oil seal on the inner fork tube **(see illustration 4.15)**.

17   Install the inner tube in the outer tube. Slide the outer tube's bushing all the way down the inner fork tube until it rests against its bore in the outer fork tube. Install the back-up ring on top of the bushing. With a seal driver or equivalent tool **(see illustrations 4.17a and 4.17b)**, tap against the backup ring to drive the new bushing into its bore. Once the bushing is seated, use the same tool to seat the oil seal in the case just below the retainer ring groove.

18   Install the retainer ring and make sure it seats securely in its groove, then install the dust seal. **Caution:** *From this point on, be careful not to let the outer fork tube slide down the inner tube far enough that the dust seal hits the axle bracket.*

19   Install the damper rod in the fork damper, taking care not to scratch the bushing inside the damper. Install the damper and rod in the fork tube.

20   Place a new sealing washer and O-ring on the center bolt. Coat the threads of the center bolt with a non-permanent thread locking agent. Hold the damper rod with the tool mentioned in Step 7, then tighten the center bolt to the torque listed in this Chapter's Specifications.

21   Thread the locknut all the way onto the damper rod with its flat upward. Tighten it with your fingers only; you'll need to remove it later.

22   Slip the spacer onto the bottom end of the inner fork tube against the axle bracket, then lower the outer fork tube down onto the spacer.

23   Pour fork oil of the type listed in this Chapter's Specifications into the damper rod (not into the fork tube) until a small amount flows from the air relief holes in the side of the damper rod.

24   Pump the damper rod slowly up-and-down eight to ten times, then push it all the way down.

25   With the fork vertical, measure the oil level in the fork **(see illustration 4.29)** and compare it to the value listed in this Chapter's Specifications. Add or drain oil as necessary to correct the level. **Note:** *Minimum oil level will make the suspension slightly softer near full compression; maximum oil level will make the suspension slightly stiffer near full compression.* **Warning:** *To prevent unstable handling, make sure the oil level is exactly the same in both forks.*

26   Install the spring in the fork with its tapered end upward. **Note:** *The tapered end of the spring will fit inside the fork cap, but the other end won't.*

27   Attach a two-foot length of mechanic's wire to the damper rod locknut.

28   Make sure the white plastic sealing ring is in position on the spring collar. Pass the collar over the length of wire, then carefully work the collar into the fork tube with a side-to-side rocking motion. **Caution:**

Don't damage the sealing ring. Use the wire to hold the damper rod up while you position the collar in the fork tube.

29   If you're working on a 1989 model, compress the spring by pushing down on the spring collar and install the spring seat on the damper rod under the locknut (the spring seat is slotted).

30   If you're working on a 1990 model, remove the wire and the damper rod locknut. Install the spring seat over the damper rod, push down on the spring collar to expose the locknut threads, then thread the locknut all the way onto the damper rod. Measure the distance from the top of the locknut to the end of the damper rod; it should be 14 mm (0.55 inch).

31   Thread the fork cap onto the damper rod until it reaches the locknut, then tighten them against each other to the torque listed in this Chapter's Specifications.

32   Extend the outer fork tube and thread the fork cap into it (tighten it to the specified torque later, when the fork leg is held in the triple clamps).

6   Front forks (1991) - disassembly, inspection and reassembly

Note: *Overhaul of the forks on these models requires special tools for which there are no good substitutes. The tools can be ordered from your local Honda dealer, or you may be able to buy equivalent tools from aftermarket suppliers. Read through the procedure and arrange to get the special tools or substitutes before starting. If you don't disassemble the forks on a regular basis, it may be more practical to have the job done by a Honda dealer or other motorcycle repair shop.*

1   Before you disassemble the fork, loosen the center bolt in the bottom of the fork leg **(see illustration 4.6a)**.

2   Slide fork slider spacer 07KMZ-KZ30101 onto the bottom of the inner fork tube so it rests on the axle bracket. This is necessary to keep the outer tube from sliding down against the axle bracket, which could damage the bushings and dust seal. It's also necessary to adjust the fork oil level.

3   Wear safety glasses and remove the fork cap. The outer fork tube is now free to slide; lower it carefully against the tool.

4   Hold the locknut with an open-end wrench and unscrew the fork cap from the damper rod **(see illustration 4.5a)**. Remove the spring seat from inside the fork cap.

5   Remove the locknut and spring guide from the damper rod.

6   Remove the slider from the fork tube. **Caution:** *Don't let the outer fork tube slide against the axle bracket.*

7   Hold the fork upside down over a drain pan and pump the damper rod eight to ten times to pump out the fork oil.

8   Unscrew the center bolt from the bottom of the fork.

9   Pull the damper rod and damper out of the fork. Hold the bottom end of the damper over a drain pan and pump the damper rod eight to ten times to drain the remaining oil.

10   Pry the dust seal out of its bore and remove the oil seal retainer ring **(see illustrations 4.7 and 4.8)**.

11   Grasp one fork tube in each hand, compress them together, then yank them apart sharply as far as they'll go. Do this several times until the tubes separate; the slide hammer-like motion is necessary to pull the slider bushing out of its bore in the outer fork tube.

12   Remove the dust seal, retaining ring, oil seal and backup ring from the inner fork tube **(see illustration 4.15)**.

Inspection

13   Refer to Steps 11 through 16 of Section 4 to inspect the fork.

14   Check the oil seal case (on the bottom end of the outer fork tube) for wear or damage. Leave it in place if no problems are found. If you need to replace the oil seal case or the fork tube, remove the stop ring and slider from the oil seal case. Slide the oil seal case partway up the fork tube to expose the stop ring on the fork tube, then remove the stop ring. Slide the oil case off the fork tube, tapping it gently with a soft-faced hammer if necessary. Remove the O-ring from inside the oil seal case.

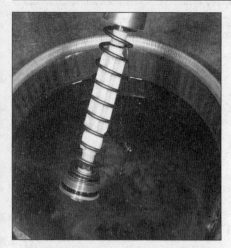

7.3 Empty the fork oil into a drain pan

7.4 Hold the cap bolt with one wrench and the locknut with another, then unscrew them from each other

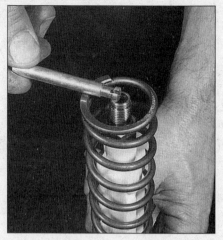

7.5 The adjuster rod is installed with its oil holes or cutout down

15   Check the needle on the center bolt for wear or bending and replace the center bolt if problems are found.
16   Check the oil lock valve (ring) on the damper rod for wear or damage and replace the damper assembly if any problems are found.

Reassembly

17   If the oil seal case was removed, install a new O-ring inside it and coat the O-ring with the type of fork oil listed in this Chapter's Specifications. Slide the oil seal case onto the fork tube past the stop ring groove, install the stop ring in the fork tube groove and pull the case back against the stop ring. **Note:** *You may need a press to push the fork tube into the oil seal case. If so, take the fork tube to a Honda dealer or motorcycle repair shop. Install the slider and the other stop ring on the oil seal case.*
18   Wrap the end of the inner fork tube with electrical tape to protect the new oil seal on installation. Coat the lip of the new oil seal with the recommended fork oil. Install the bushings (if removed), backup ring and oil seal on the inner fork tube **(see illustration 4.15)**.
19   Install the inner tube in the outer tube. Slide the outer tube's bushing all the way down the inner fork tube until it rests against its bore in the outer fork tube. Install the back-up ring on top of the bushing. With a seal driver or equivalent tool **(see illustrations 4.17a and 4.17b)**, tap against the backup ring to drive the new bushing into its bore. Once the bushing is seated, use the same tool to seat the oil seal in the case just below the retainer ring groove.
20   Install the retainer ring and make sure it seats securely in its groove, then install the dust seal. **Caution:** *From this point on, be careful not to let the outer fork tube slide down the inner tube far enough that the dust seal hits the axle bracket.*
21   Install the damper and rod in the fork tube.
22   Place a new sealing washer and O-ring on the center bolt. Coat the threads of the center bolt with a non-permanent thread locking agent. Tighten the center bolt to the torque listed in this Chapter's Specifications. **Note:** *If the damper spins inside the fork tube when you try to tighten the center bolt, temporarily install the spring and fork cap. The spring pressure will keep the damper from turning.*
23   Install the spring guide on the damper rod; the end with holes goes upward. Thread the locknut all the way onto the damper rod with its flange downward.
24   Slip the spacer onto the bottom end of the inner fork tube against the axle bracket, then lower the outer fork tube down onto the spacer.
25   Look up the amount of fork oil recommended in this Chapter's Specifications. Pour half that amount into the fork.
26   Extend the fork, but don't expose any more than 300 mm (11-3/4 inches) of the lower fork tube on CR250R models or 250 mm (10 inches) on CR500R models. Cover the top of the fork tube with your hand so air can't escape, then slowly compress the fork. Repeat this two or three times.

27   Compress the damper rod all the way, then slowly pour fork oil into the damper rod until it starts to flow out the end of the damper rod.
28   Slowly pump the damper rod and fork tube up and down eight to ten times. Add the remainder of the specified amount of fork oil. Compress the fork all the way and leave it sitting upright for five minutes so the oil level can stabilize. Then measure the oil level and compare it to the values listed in this Chapter's Specifications. Add or drain oil as needed. **Note:** *Minimum oil level will make the suspension slightly softer near full compression; maximum oil level will make the suspension slightly stiffer near full compression.* **Warning:** *To prevent unstable handling, make sure the oil level is exactly the same in both forks.*
29   Attach a two-foot length of mechanic's wire to the damper rod locknut. Pass the fork spring (with its tapered end upward) over the length of wire into the fork tube.
30   Remove the wire. Install the spring seat, push down on the spring to expose the locknut threads, then thread the fork cap onto the damper rod until it reaches the locknut. Tighten them against each other to the torque listed in this Chapter's Specifications.
31   Install a new O-ring on the fork cap. Extend the outer fork tube and thread the fork cap into it (tighten it to the specified torque later, when the fork leg is held in the triple clamps).

7   Front forks (1992 through 1996 CR250R, 1992 and later CR500R) - disassembly, inspection and reassembly

Disassembly

Refer to illustrations 7.3, 7.4, 7.5, 7.9a, 7.9b, 7.10 and 7.16
1   If you're working on a 1992 or 1993 model, slide fork slider spacer 07KMZ-KZ30101B onto the bottom of the inner fork tube so it rests on the axle bracket. This is necessary to keep the outer tube from sliding down against the axle bracket, which could damage the bushings and dust seal. It's also necessary to adjust the fork oil level.
2   If you're working on a 1992 model, loosen the center bolt in the bottom of the fork now, before the fork cap and spring are removed. The spring tension will keep the damper rod inside the fork from turning while the center bolt is loosened.
3   Wear safety glasses and undo the fork cap. The outer fork tube is now free to slide; lower it carefully to the bottom. Turn the fork upside down over a drain pan and dump the oil **(see illustration)**.
4   Hold the locknut with an open-end wrench and unscrew the fork cap from the damper rod **(see illustration)**.
5   If you're working on a 1995 or later model, remove the adjuster from the top of the damper rod, then pull the spacer rod out of the damper rod **(see illustration)**.
6   If you're working on a 1992 or 1993 model, remove the spring seat from the fork cap.

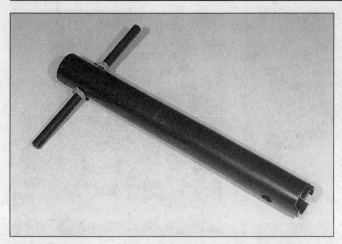

7.9a This tool is used to hold the damper rod from turning . . .

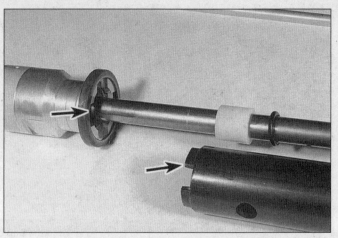

7.9b . . . its tabs engage the damper rod slots (arrows)

7.10 Use new O-rings and a new sealing washer (arrows) on the center bolt

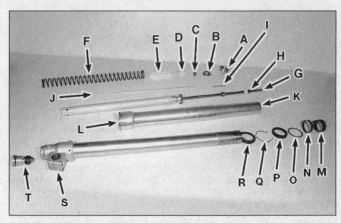

7.16 Fork details - 1995 and 1996 CR250R, 1995 and later CR500R

A	Fork cap and O-ring	L	Wear ring
B	Spring seat	M	Outer tube bushing
C	Locknut	N	Inner tube bushing
D	Collar	O	Backup ring
E	Spring guide	P	Oil seal
F	Spring	Q	Retainer
G	Damper rod	R	Dust seal
H	O-ring	S	Inner fork tube and axle
I	Adjuster rod		bracket
J	Spacer rod	T	Center bolt
K	Outer fork tube		

7   Remove the locknut from the damper rod, then remove the spring collar, spring guide and O-ring.

8   Turn the fork upside down over the drain pan and pump the damper rod eight to ten times to drain more oil.

9   Unscrew the center bolt from the bottom of the fork. If you're working on a 1992 model, simply unscrew it (it was loosened earlier). If you're working on a 1993 or later model, you'll need to hold the damper rod from turning inside the fork with a special tool **(see illustrations)**. If you can find a piece of metal tubing the same diameter as the damper, you can cut notches in it to fit the damper rod slots. Drill holes through the other end of the tubing and pass a rod through the holes to act as a handle.

10   Remove the center bolt **(see illustration)** and take the damper out of the fork. If you're working on a 1992 or 1993 model, pull the spacer rod out of the damper rod, then dump the rebound needle and spring out of the damper rod.

11   Hold the damper upside down over the drain pan and pump the damper rod eight to ten times to drain the remaining oil.

12   Pry the dust seal out of its bore, then pry the oil seal retainer out of its groove **(see illustrations 4.7 and 4.8)**.

13   If you're working on a 1992 through 1994 CR250R, unbolt the halves of the plastic protector guide from each other (they're installed on the bottom end of the outer fork tube). Take the guide halves off the fork tube. Don't remove the wear ring from the groove in the outer fork tube unless inspection shows that you need a new one.

14   Grasp one fork tube in each hand, compress them together, then yank them apart sharply as far as they'll go. Do this several times until the tubes separate; the slide hammer-like motion is necessary to pull the slider bushing out of its bore in the outer fork tube.

15   Remove the dust seal, oil seal and back-up ring from the inner

fork tube **(see illustration 4.15)**. Don't remove the bushings unless you find excessive wear while inspecting them.

Inspection
Refer to illustration 7.16

16   Refer to Steps 11 through 16 of Section 4 to inspect the fork. Also inspect the wear ring in the groove on the bottom end of the outer fork tube **(see illustration)**. The ring protects the fork tube from the plastic leg protector. If the ring protrudes less than 1.5 mm (0.060 inch) from the fork, replace it.

Reassembly

17   Wrap the end of the inner (lower) fork tube with electrical tape, covering the sharp edges so they don't cut the seals when they're installed **(see illustration 5.16)**.

18   Smear a coat of the fork oil listed in this Chapter's Specifications onto the inner circumference of the dust seal, the oil seal and both bushings.

19   Install the dust seal onto the inner fork tube, outer side first **(see illustration 4.15)**. Install the oil seal retaining ring, oil seal (marked side

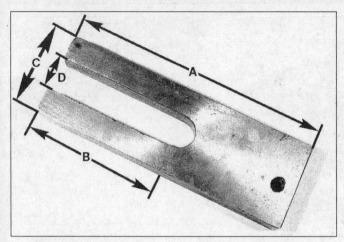

8.1 This support tool can be made from aluminum plate 1/8 to 1/2 inch thick

A   55 mm (2 inches)   C   30 mm (1-1/4 inch)
B   25 mm (1 inch)   D   15 mm (5/8 inch)

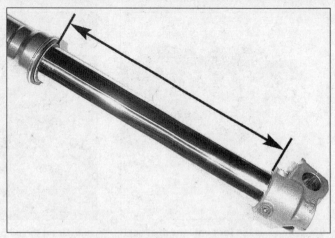

8.4 The distance from the dust seal to the axle holder should be the same when the fork is reassembled

first) and the backup ring. Remove the tape, then slip the guide (outer fork tube) bushing over the inner fork tube. Install the slider (inner fork tube) bushing in its groove, expanding it just enough to fit over the inner fork tube.

20   Install the inner fork tube in the outer tube. Position the outer tube bushing at the edge of its bore with the backup ring on top of it. Tap on the backup ring with a fork seal driver or equivalent to drive the bushing into its bore **(see illustrations 4.17a and 4.17b)**.

21   Drive the oil seal, using the same seal driver, just past the retaining ring groove **(see illustration 4.24)**. If you're very careful, the seal can be driven in with a hammer and drift punch. Work around the circumference of the seal, tapping gently on the outer edge of the seal until it's seated. Be careful - if you distort the seal, you'll have to disassemble the fork and end up taking it to a dealer anyway! Compress the seal retaining ring into the groove, making sure it seats securely.

22   Install the dust seal, making sure it seats completely.

23   Install the damper in the inner fork tube. Place a new sealing washer and O-rings on the center bolt **(see illustration 7.10)**. Apply fork oil to the O-rings and a coat of non-permanent thread locking agent to the center bolt threads, then install the center bolt in the fork. If you're working on a 1992 model, temporarily install the spring and fork cap to hold the damper rod from turning, then tighten the center bolt to the torque listed in this Chapter's Specifications. On all other models, hold the damper rod from turning with the tool described in Step 9, then tighten the center bolt to the specified torque.

24   Install the O-ring, spring guide and spring collar on the damper rod **(see illustration 7.16)**. If you're working on a 1992 or 1993 model, the oil holes in the spring guide go upward.

25   Thread the locknut onto the damper rod with its flange downward (1992 and 1993) or with its cutout downward (1994 on).

26   If you're working on a 1992 or 1993 model, place the spring on the long end of the rebound needle, then install the rebound needle in the damper rod, long end first. Install the spacer rod in the damper rod on top of the rebound needle.

27   If you're working on a 1994 or later model, install the spacer rod in the damper rod. Install the adjuster rod on top of the spacer rod with its oil hole facing down.

28   If you're working on a 1994 CR250R, install the protector guide on the bottom of the outer fork tube.

29   Compress the fork all the way (against the protector guide on 1994 CR250R models; against the spacer tool on all others).

30   Look up the amount and type of fork oil listed in this Chapter's Specifications. Pour half the amount into a container and set it aside.

31   Pour specified fork oil (from the main container, not the container you set aside) into the damper rod until it overflows. Then pour the oil you set aside into the fork leg.

32   Extend the fork (but don't expose more than 250 mm (10 inches) of the inner fork tube). Place your hand over the top of the fork to make an airtight seal, then press down with your hand to compress the fork.

33   Push down on the damper rod to make sure it's fully compressed, then pour fork into the damper rod until it overflows.

34   Slowly extend and compress the damper rod and fork tube eight to ten times.

35   Add the remainder of the specified amount of fork oil, then once more extend and compress the fork tube and damper rod eight to ten times.

36   Measure the oil level inside the fork **(see illustration 4.29)**. Add or drain oil as needed. **Note:** *Minimum oil level will make the suspension slightly softer near full compression; maximum oil level will make the suspension slightly stiffer near full compression.* **Warning:** *To prevent unstable handling, make sure the oil level is exactly the same in both forks.*

37   Install the fork spring in the fork tube.

38   Dip a new fork cap O-ring in fork oil and place it on the fork cap.

39   Thread the locknut all the way onto the piston rod, then attach a two-foot length of mechanic's wire to the locknut.

40   Pass the fork spring over the length of wire, then use the wire to hold the piston rod up while you position the spring in the fork tube. Position the spring seat on the spring.

41   Hold onto the locknut so the damper rod won't drop and remove the wire. Thread the cap bolt onto the rod, then tighten the cap bolt and locknut against each other to the torque listed in this Chapter's Specifications.

42   Thread the cap bolt into the fork tube. After installing the fork in the motorcycle, tighten it to the torque listed in this Chapter's Specifications.

8   Front forks (1997 and later CR250R) - disassembly, inspection and reassembly

Disassembly

Refer to illustrations 8.1, 8.4, 8.5, 8.6, 8.8, 8.9, 8.10, 8.11, 8.12a and 8.12b

1   Before you start, make a support tool out of aluminum plate **(see illustration)**. You can also use Honda tool 07958-2500001 if it's available.

2   Remove the plastic protectors from the fork legs if you haven't already done so.

3   Thoroughly clean the outside of the fork, paying special attention to the surface of the inner fork tube and the cavity around the center bolt on the bottom of the fork.

4   Before you take the fork apart, measure the distance from the dust seal to the axle holder and write it down **(see illustration)**.

8.5 Compress the fork until the dust seal touches the axle holder

8.6 Drain the oil from the fork tube and the small hole in the damper (arrow)

8.8 Place the fork in a vise and unscrew the center bolt

5   If you're working on a 1997 model, unscrew the fork cap from the outer fork tube (it's also screwed into the damper rod, but don't worry about this yet). If you're working on a 1998 or later model, unscrew the damper from the outer fork tube, using the 50 mm hex wrench described in Section 3.

6   Turn the fork upside down over a drain pan and drain the oil from the fork tube and the small hole in the damper (see illustration).

7   Thread the fork cap (1997) or damper (1998 on) back into the fork tube, tightening it with your fingers only.

8   Support the fork in a padded vise gripping the axle holder. **Caution:** *Don't tighten the vise enough to damage the axle holder.* Unscrew the center bolt until it disengages from the fork, but don't try to remove

8.9 Push the center bolt out and slide the support tool over the damper, then release the center bolt

it completely yet **(see illustration)**.

9   Push in on the fork cap so the center bolt and locknut protrude from the bottom of the fork, then slip the support tool in above the locknut **(see illustration)**.

10   **Caution:** *DO NOT remove the locknut from the damper during this step, or the damper rod will fall out of position, with no way to reinstall it.* Hold the locknut with one wrench and unscrew the center bolt with another **(see illustration)**.

11   Pull the pushrod out of the damper **(see illustration)**.

12   Unscrew the fork cap (1997) or damper (1998 on) from the fork, then pull the fork cap/damper out of the fork tube as a unit. On 1997 models only, remove the setscrew from the fork cap with an Allen wrench **(see illustration)**. **Note:** *This takes a good deal of effort and will be accompanied by a creaking sound.* **Caution:** *Don't squeeze the damper or place it in a vise, or it may be damaged.*

13   Take the fork out of the vise and dump out the spring.

14   Compress the fork tubes together, then yank them sharply apart, several times. The slide hammer-like motion is necessary to dislodge the guide bushing from the outer fork tube. Once this happens, separate the fork tubes.

Inspection

Refer to illustration 8.16

15   Refer to Steps 11 through 16 of Section 4 to inspect the fork.

16   Inspect the fork cap bushing **(see illustration)**. The bushing can't be replaced separately; you'll need a new fork cap assembly if the bushing is worn or damaged. Remove the fork cap O-ring and use a new one on reassembly.

17   Compress and extend the damper rod and check for smooth movement. If it doesn't move smoothly, check its movement again

8.10   Hold the locknut and unscrew the center bolt; DO NOT unscrew the locknut or the damper rod will fall out of place and the damper will be ruined

8.11 Remove the center bolt and pull the pushrod (arrow) out of the damper rod

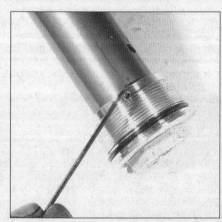

8.12a Remove the setscrew with an Allen wrench (1997 models only)

8.12b Secure the fork cap in a vise and unscrew the damper from it; it's tight, so be sure the wrench fits exactly

8.16 Replace the fork cap if the bushing is worn (right arrow); use a new O-ring on reassembly (left arrow)

8.19 Wrap the end of the fork tube with tape to protect the seals

after assembling the fork and bleeding the air from it. If there's visible wear or damage, replace the damper.

18   Clean all oil from the threads of the fork cap and damper.

Reassembly

Refer to illustrations 8.19, 8.20, 8.21, 8.26, 8.28, 8.31, 8.36, 8.41, 8.42 and 8.46

19   Wrap the end of the inner fork tube with tape so it won't cut the seals on installation **(see illustration)**.

20   Install the dust seal and retainer on the inner fork tube, then install the oil seal with its open end toward the dust seal. Install the backup ring next to the oil seal. If the bushings were removed, make sure there aren't any burrs in the bushing seating areas on the fork tubes. Coat the bushings with the recommended fork oil and install them **(see illustration)**.

21   Install the inner tube in the outer tube until the outer tube's bushing rests against its bore. Place the backup ring against the outer bushing, then tap on the backup ring with a seal driver (Honda tool 07VMD-KZ30100 or equivalent) to seat the bushing in its bore **(see illustration)**.

22   Use the same driver to tap the oil seal into the outer fork tube just past the retaining ring groove. Install the retaining ring in the groove, making sure it seats securely.

23   Slide the dust seal down the inner fork tube and seat it in the outer fork tube.

24   Hold the damper in its upright position (rod down). Extend the rod all the way.

25   Pour the amount and type of fork oil listed in this Chapter's Specifications into the top of the damper, then slowly pump the damper rod

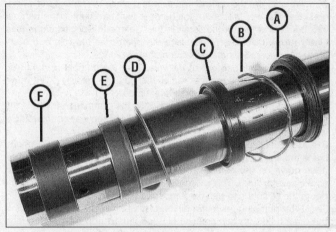

8.20 Don't remove the bushing from the inner fork tube unless it's worn

| A | Dust seal | C | Oil seal | E | Bushing |
| B | Retaining ring | D | Backup ring | F | Bushing |

up and down eight to ten times to bleed out air.

26   With the damper rod fully extended, measure the oil level in the damper **(see illustration)**. Add or remove oil as necessary to adjust the level. **Note:** *The fork cap will be difficult to install if the oil level is too high.*

27   Dip a new fork cap O-ring in fork oil and install it on the fork cap. Coat the fork cap bushing with fork oil.

8.21 Drive the bushing into its bore in the outer fork tube with a seal driver; use the same tool to install the oil seal

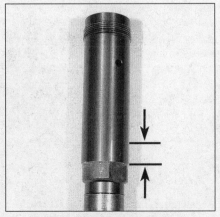

8.26 Measure the fork oil level in the damper

8.28 Tighten the fork cap onto the damper

8.31 Pad the surface so you don't damage the damper rod and push up and down on the damper to pump it

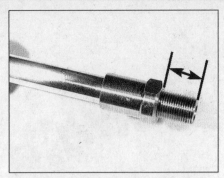

8.36 Be sure the threads protrude the specified distance past the locknut

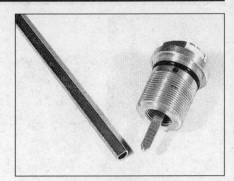

8.41 The adjusting rod in the center bolt fits inside the pushrod, which fits inside the damper rod

28   While holding the damper rod in its fully extended position, thread the fork cap onto the damper rod and tighten it as firmly as possible with fingers. Turn the damper rod over and place the fork cap in a padded vise. Place a wrench on the damper flats and tighten the damper into the cap to the torque listed in this Chapter's Specifications **(see illustration)**. **Caution:** *Don't place the damper in the vise and don't place a wrench anywhere but on the damper flats.*

29   Take the fork cap out of the vise. Turn the damper upright (rod down). Compress the damper rod all the way, then slowly pull it down 100 mm (3-7/8 inches). Do this several times.

30   Thread the locknut all the way onto the damper rod. Place the rebound and compression damping adjusters all the way counterclockwise (softest positions).

31   Coat the damper rod surface with fork oil. With the damper upright, place the end of the damper rod on a rag or similar soft surface, then push down on the damper to pump the damper rod through its full stroke several times. This will force any extra fork oil in the spring chamber to the oil hole so it can be dumped out **(see illustration)**.

32   After dumping any extra oil, blow the remaining oil residue out of the drain hole with compressed air **(see illustration 8.6)**. If you don't have a compressor, remove the air relief screw from the top of the fork cap **(see illustration 13.5b in Chapter 1)**, then prop the damper upside down for ten minutes (rod upward) so the oil can finish draining. Reinstall the air relief screw (if removed).

33   All the air should have been bled out of the damper at this point. As a final check of its operation, repeat Steps 29 and 30. If the damper rod doesn't move smoothly at this point, check the damper rod for bending or other damage. Replace the damper as an assembly if problems are found.

34   Hold the damper in a horizontal position and compress the damper rod all the way. It should extend fully by itself. If it doesn't, repeat Steps 28 to 30 to bleed any remaining air.

35   Thoroughly clean any oil off the outside of the damper and rod. Place the damper in its upright position (rod down) and compress the rod 200 to 250 mm (eight to ten inches) from its fully extended position. Hold the damper like this for 10 minutes and check for oil leaks from the spring chamber drain hole and the point where the damper rod enters the damper. If any oil leaks can be seen, replace the damper as an assembly.

36   Measure the length of the damper rod threads that protrude past the locknut **(see illustration)**. They should be within the range listed in this Chapter's Specifications.

37   Install the spring and damper assembly in the fork.

38   Place the fork in a vise, push in on the fork cap and install the support tool **(see illustration 8.9)**.

39   Recheck the thread protrusion from the damper rod locknut and make sure it's still within the Specifications.

40   Install the pushrod in the damper rod. Rotate it back and forth as you install it to make sure it goes in all the way.

41   Slip the adjusting rod on the center bolt into the pushrod, then tighten the center bolt as much as possible with your fingers **(see illustration)**.

42   Measure the gap between the locknut and center bolt **(see illustration)**. If it's not within the range listed in this Chapter's Specifications, make sure the locknut is installed the specified distance from the end of the damper rod.

43   Hold the center bolt with a wrench and tighten the locknut against it with fingers. Then hold the locknut with a wrench and tighten the center bolt to the torque listed in this Chapter's Specifications.

44   Coat the threads of the center bolt with non-permanent thread locking agent. Push in the on the fork and pull out the support tool. Thread the center bolt into the fork and tighten it to the torque listed in this Chapter's Specifications.

45   Measure the distance from the dust seal to the axle holder **(see illustration 8.4)**. It should be the same as it was before disassembly. If

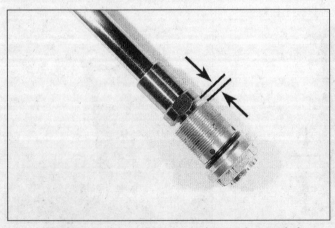

8.42 Measure the gap between locknut and center bolt

8.46 Flattening the tip of an aluminum funnel will make it easier to pour oil into the fork tube

9.3 Unscrew the steering stem nut, then lift off the washer and the upper triple clamp

9.4a Remove the bearing adjusting nut . . .

9.4b . . . and lift off the bearing cover

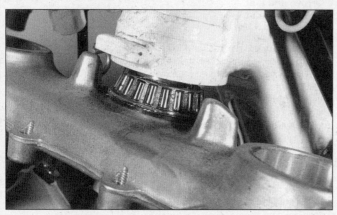

9.5 Lower the steering stem out of the head

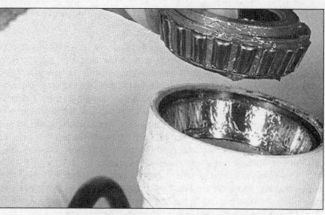

9.6 Lift the upper bearing out of the steering head

it isn't, recheck the installation of the locknut and center bolt.

46   Lower the upper fork tube away from the fork cap and pour the recommended amount of oil into the fork **(see illustration)**. **Note**: *Minimum oil level will make the suspension slightly softer near full compression; maximum oil level will make the suspension slightly stiffer near full compression.* **Warning:** *To prevent unstable handling, make sure the oil level is exactly the same in both forks.*

47   Pull the tube up to the fork cap or damper, then thread the fork cap or damper into the tube. Tighten the fork cap to the specified torque after installation, when it's held in the triple clamps. On 1998 and later models, use the special 50 mm hex wrench described in Section 3. The wrench has a square hole for a torque wrench, which changes the effective setting of the torque wrench (the torque reading on the wrench is different from the actual torque applied to the damper). The specified torque setting takes this into account.

9   Steering head bearings - replacement

Refer to illustrations 9.3, 9.4a, 9.4b, 9.5, 9.6, 9.7, 9.9a, 9.9b, 9.9c, 9.11, 9.14 and 9.15

1   If the steering head bearing check/adjustment (see Chapter 1) does not remedy excessive play or roughness in the steering head bearings, the entire front end must be disassembled and the bearings and races replaced with new ones.

2   Remove the handlebars (see Section 2), the front wheel and brake caliper (see Chapter 7), the front fender (see Chapter 8) and the forks (see Section 3).

3   Loosen the steering stem nut with a socket **(see illustration)**. Remove the nut, washer and upper triple clamp.

4   Using a spanner wrench of the type described in Chapter 1,

remove the stem locknut and bearing cover **(see illustrations)** while supporting the steering head from the bottom.

5   Remove the steering stem and lower triple clamp assembly **(see illustration)**. If it's stuck, gently tap on the top of the steering stem with a plastic mallet or a hammer and a wood block.

6   Remove the upper bearing **(see illustration)**.

7   Clean all the parts with solvent and dry them thoroughly, using compressed air, if available **(see illustration)**. If you do use compressed air, don't let the bearings spin as they're dried - it could ruin them. Wipe the old grease out of the frame steering head and bearing races.

8   Examine the races in the steering head for cracks, dents, and pits. If even the slightest amount of wear or damage is evident, the races should be replaced with new ones.

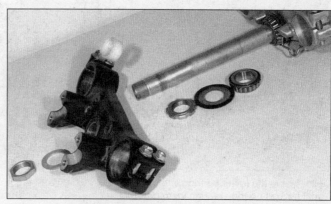

9.7 Steering stem and bearing details

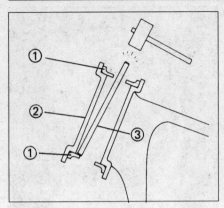

9.9a Drive out the bearing races with a hammer and brass drift

1   Outer races
2   Steering head
3   Brass drift

9.9b Place the drift against the edge of the lower bearing race (arrow) and tap evenly around it to drive the bearing out

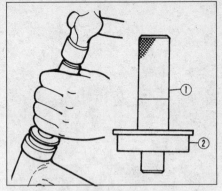

9.9c Drive in the bearing races with a bearing driver or socket the same diameter as the bearing race

1   Bearing driver handle
2   Bearing driver

9   To remove the races, drive them out of the steering head with Honda tool no. 07953-MJ10000 or a hammer and drift punch **(see illustrations)**. A slide hammer with the proper internal-jaw puller will also work. Since the races are an interference fit in the frame, installation will be easier if the new races are left overnight in a refrigerator. This will cause them to contract and slip into place in the frame with very little effort. When installing the races, use a bearing driver the same diameter as the outer race **(see illustration)**, or tap them gently into place with a hammer and punch or a large socket. Do not strike the bearing surface or the race will be damaged.

10   Check the bearings for wear. Look for cracks, dents, and pits in the races and flat spots on the bearings. Replace any defective parts with new ones. If a new bearing is required, replace both of them as a set.

11   Check the grease seal under the lower bearing and replace it with a new one if necessary **(see illustration)**.

12   To remove the lower bearing and grease seal from the steering stem, you may need to use a bearing puller, which can be rented. Don't remove this bearing unless it, or the grease seal underneath, must be replaced. Removal will damage the grease seal, so replace it whenever the bearing is removed.

13   Inspect the steering stem/lower triple clamp for cracks and other damage. Do not attempt to repair any steering components. Replace them with new parts if defects are found.

14   Pack the bearings with high-quality grease (preferably a moly-based grease) **(see illustration)**. Coat the outer races with grease also.

15   Install the grease seal and lower bearing onto the steering stem. Drive the lower bearing onto the steering stem using a pipe the same diameter as the bearing inner race **(see illustration)**. Drive the bearing on until it's fully seated.

16   Insert the steering stem/lower triple clamp into the frame head. Install the upper bearing, bearing cover and adjusting nut. Refer to the adjustment procedure in Chapter 1 and tighten the adjusting nut to the torque listed in the Chapter 1 Specifications.

17   Make sure the steering head turns smoothly and that there's no play in the bearings.

18   Install the fork tubes and tighten the lower triple clamp bolts to the torque listed in this Chapter's Specifications.

19   Tighten the steering stem nut to the torque listed in this Chapter's Specifications.

20   Check the alignment of the fork tubes with the upper triple clamp; the tops of the fork tubes should be even with the upper surface of the triple clamp. If necessary, loosen the lower triple clamp bolts and adjust the position of the fork tubes.

21   Tighten the triple clamp bolts to the torque listed in this Chapter's Specifications.

22   The remainder of installation is the reverse of removal.

23   Check the alignment of the handlebars with the front wheel. If necessary, loosen the upper triple clamp bolts and align the handlebars with the front wheel, then tighten the upper triple clamp bolts to the torque listed in this Chapter's Specifications.

9.11 Leave the lower bearing and grease seal (arrow) on the steering stem unless you plan to replace them

9.14 Work the grease completely into the bearing

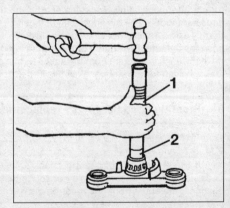

9.15 Drive the grease seal and bearing lower race on with a hollow driver (or an equivalent piece of pipe)

1   Driver
2   Bearing and grease seal

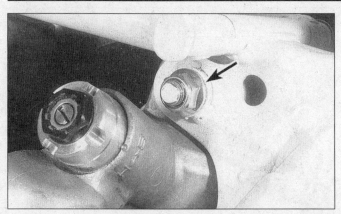

10.4a Remove the bolt and nut from the upper end of the shock absorber (1997 CR500R shown) . . .

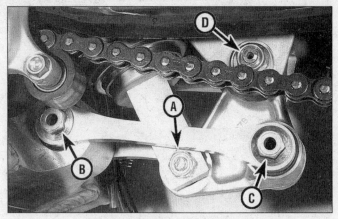

10.4b . . . and from the lower end

A   Shock absorber lower bolt and nut
B   Shock link-to-frame bolt and nut
C   Shock link-to-shock arm bolt and nut
D   Shock arm-to-swingarm bolt and nut

10 Rear shock absorber - removal, inspection and installation

Removal

Refer to illustrations 10.4a and 10.4b

1   Support the bike securely so it can't be knocked over during this procedure. Support the swingarm with a jack so the suspension can be raised or lowered as needed for access.
2   Remove the seat and sub-frame (see Chapter 8).
3   If you're working on a 1986 model, remove the shock reservoir's retaining bands and detach the reservoir from the bike.
4   Remove the upper and lower mounting bolts **(see illustrations)**.
5   Remove the shock from the bike. If it has a separate reservoir, lift the reservoir out without placing strain on the hose.

Inspection

Refer to illustration 10.8

6   The shock absorber can be overhauled, but it's a complicated procedure that requires special tools not readily available to the typical owner. If inspection reveals problems, have the shock rebuilt by a dealer or motorcycle repair shop.
7   Check the shock absorber for damage and oil leaks. If these can be seen, have the shock overhauled.
8   Check the spherical bearing at the upper end of the shock for leaking grease, looseness or signs of damage **(see illustration)**. If any of these problems can be seen, have the bearing pressed out and a new one pressed in by a dealer or motorcycle repair shop.

9   Clean all parts thoroughly with solvent and dry them with compressed air, if available. Check all parts for scoring, damage or heavy corrosion and replace them as necessary.

Installation

10   Installation is the reverse of the removal steps. Tighten the bolts to the torques listed in this Chapter's Specifications.

11 Shock linkage - removal, inspection and installation

Removal

Refer to illustrations 11.4, 11.5a, 11.5b and 11.5c

1   Support the bike securely so it can't be knocked over during this procedure. Support the swingarm with a jack so the suspension can be raised or lowered as needed for access.
2   On all except 1988 models, remove the lower drive chain roller.
3   If you're working on a 1997 CR250R, remove the brake pedal spring and both footpegs (see Chapters 7 and 8).
4   If you're working on a 1988 or later CR250R or a 1989 or later CR500R, pry the bolt caps out of the swingarm to expose the shock arm-to-swingarm bolt and nut **(see illustration)**.
5   Remove the shock absorber lower mounting bolt. Unbolt the shock arm from the swingarm and the shock link from the frame **(see illustrations)**. Take the linkage out of the bike, then separate the arm from the link.

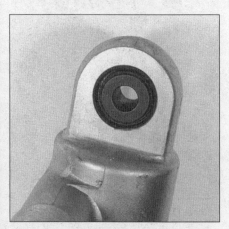

10.8 Check the spherical bearing in the shock absorber for wear or damage

11.4 Pry the caps out of the swingarm . . .

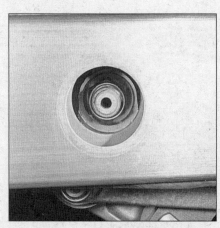

11.5a . . . to expose the nut . . .

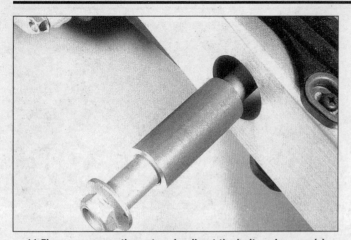

11.5b . . . unscrew the nut and pull out the bolt and spacer(s)

11.5c If the bike has a spacer on each side, as shown here, reinstall them on the pivot bolt so you won't forget how they go

Inspection

Refer to illustrations 11.6a and 11.6b

6   Slip the collars out of the needle bearings **(see illustrations)**. Check the bearings for wear or damage. If the bearings are okay, pack them with molybdenum disulfide grease and reinstall the collars.

7   If the dust seals are worn or appear to have been leaking, pry them out and press in new ones with a seal driver or socket the same diameter as the seals.

8   If the bearings need to be replaced, press them out and press new ones in. To prevent damage to the new bearings, you'll need a shouldered drift with a narrow diameter the same size as the inside diameter of the bearings. If you don't have the proper tool, have the bearings replaced by a Honda dealer or other motorcycle repair shop. A well-equipped automotive machine shop should also be able to do the job.

Installation

9   Installation is the reverse of the removal steps. Tighten the nuts and bolts to the torques listed in this Chapter's Specifications.

12 Swingarm bearings - check

1   Refer to Chapter 7 and remove the rear wheel, then refer to Section 10 and remove the rear shock absorber.

2   Grasp the rear of the swingarm with one hand and place your

other hand at the junction of the swingarm and frame. Try to move the rear of the swingarm from side-to-side. Any wear (play) in the bushings should be felt as movement between the swingarm and the frame at the front. The swingarm will actually be felt to move forward and backward at the front (not from side-to-side). If any play is noted, the bearings should be replaced with new ones (see Section 11).

3   Next, move the swingarm up and down through its full travel. It should move freely, without any binding or rough spots. If it doesn't move freely, refer to Section 11 for servicing procedures.

13 Swingarm - removal and installation

Refer to illustrations 13.5a and 13.5b

1   Refer to Section 15 and disconnect the drive chain.

2   Remove the rear wheel and unhook the brake pedal return spring from the swingarm (see Chapter 7). If you're working on a bike with a rear disc brake, detach the brake hose from the retainer on the swingarm and support the caliper so it doesn't hang by the hose.

3   Unbolt the shock absorber and shock linkage from the swingarm (Sections 10 and 11).

4   Check the chain guards on the swingarm for wear or damage and replace them if necessary (see Chapter 1).

5   Support the swingarm from below, then unscrew its pivot bolt nut and pull the bolt out **(see illustrations)**.

6   Check the chain slider, chain adjuster plates and brake disc guard

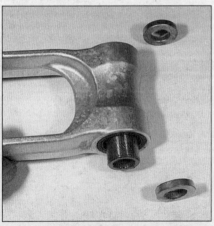

11.6a Pull the covers off the shock link pivots and inspect the seals and needle bearings

11.6b . . . Pull out the collar to inspect the needle roller bearings

13.5a On 1986 and 1987 CR250R and all CR500R models, the pivot bolt nut is on the right side . . .

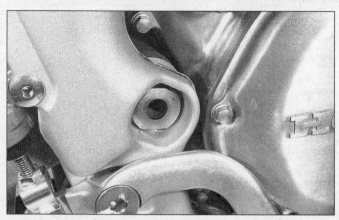

13.5b ... the 1988 and later CR250R pivot bolt head is on the right side; all models except the 1986 and 1987 CR250R have this type of bolt head, which fits into a shaped socket on the bike

14.2a Slide the pivot collars out

14.2b Have the needle bearings pressed out and new ones pressed in if they're worn ...

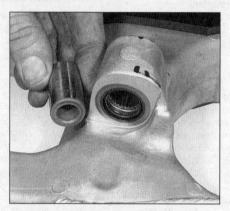

14.2c ... don't forget to check the shock link bearing

15.1 Remove the clip from the master link; its open end (arrow) faces rearward when the chain is on the top run

for wear or damage. Replace them as necessary.

7 Installation is the reverse of the removal steps, with the following additions:

a) Lubricate the swingarm bearings (see Section 14).
b) Tighten the swingarm pivot bolt and nut to the torque listed in this Chapter's Specifications.
c) Refer to Chapter 1 and adjust the drive chain and rear brake pedal (drum brake models).

14 Swingarm bearings - replacement

Refer to illustrations 14.2a, 14.2b and 14.2c

1 Refer to Section 13 and remove the swingarm.
2 Pull the pivot collars out of the swingarm bearings, then inspect the bearings and seals (see illustrations).
3 If the dust seals are worn or appear to have been leaking, pry them out and press in new ones with a seal driver or socket the same diameter as the seals.
4 Check the needle bearings for wear or damage. Needle bearing replacement requires a special puller, a press and a shouldered drift the same diameter as the inside of the bearings. If you don't have these, have the bearings replaced by a Honda dealer or other motorcycle repair shop.
5 Coat the bearings and pivot collars with moly-based grease and slip the collar into the swingarm. Install the dust covers.

15 Drive chain - removal, cleaning, inspection and installation

Removal

Refer to illustrations 15.1, 15.2 and 15.3

1 Turn the rear wheel to place the drive chain master link where it's easily accessible (see illustration).
2 Remove the clip and plate and pull the master link out of the chain (see illustration).

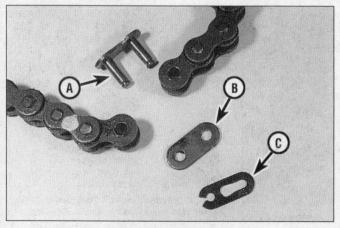

15.2 Master link details

A Link   B Plate   C Clip

15.3 Unbolt the sprocket cover (1997 CR250R shown)

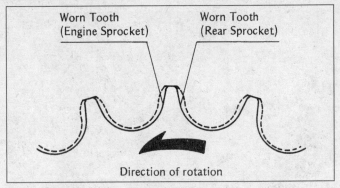

16.3 Check the sprockets in the areas indicated to see if they're worn excessively

3   Remove the engine sprocket cover **(see illustration)**.
4   Lift the chain off the sprockets and remove it from the bike.
5   Check the chain guards and rollers on the swingarm and frame for wear or damage and replace them as necessary.

Cleaning and inspection

6   Soak the chain in a high flash point solvent for approximately five or six minutes. Use a brush to work the solvent into the spaces between the links and plates.
7   Wipe the chain dry, then check it carefully for worn or damaged links. Replace the chain if wear or damage is found at any point.
8   Stretch the chain taut and measure its length between the number of pins listed in this Chapter's Specifications. Compare the measured length to the specified value replace the chain if it's beyond the limit. If the chain needs to be replaced, refer to Section 16 and check the sprockets. If they're worn, replace them also. If a new chain is installed on worn sprockets, it will wear out quickly.
9   Lubricate the chain with spray chain lube compatible with O-ring chains.

Installation

10   Installation is the reverse of the removal steps, with the following additions:
a) Install the master link clip so its opening faces the back of the motorcycle when the master link is in the upper chain run **(see illustration 15.1)**. Be sure to reinstall the O-rings in the master link.
b) Refer to Chapter 1 and adjust the chain.

16 Sprockets - check and replacement

Refer to illustrations 16.3, 16.5, 16.6 and 16.7
1   Support the bike securely so it can't be knocked over during this procedure.
2   Whenever the sprockets are inspected, the chain should be inspected also and replaced if it's worn. Installing a worn chain on new sprockets will cause them to wear quickly.
3   Check the teeth on the engine sprocket and rear sprocket for wear **(see illustration)**. The engine sprocket is visible through the cover slots.
4   If the sprockets are worn, remove the chain (Section 15) and the rear wheel (see Chapter 7).
5   Remove the sprocket from the rear wheel hub **(see illustration)**.
6   To remove the engine sprocket, remove the bolt and washer **(see illustration)**. Lift the sprocket off the transmission shaft.
7   Inspect the seal behind the engine sprocket **(see illustration)**. If it has been leaking, remove the collar and O-ring (see Chapter 2). Pry the seal out (taking care not to scratch the seal bore) and tap in a new seal with a socket the same diameter as the seal.
8   Installation is the reverse of the removal steps, with the following additions:
a) Tighten the driven sprocket bolts to the torques listed in this Chapter's Specifications. Tighten the engine sprocket bolts securely, but don't overtighten them and strip the threads
b) Install the master link clip so its opening faces the back of the motorcycle when the master link is in the upper chain run **(see illustration 15.1)**.
c) Refer to Chapter 1 and adjust the chain.

16.5 The driven sprocket is attached to the wheel hub with Allen bolts and nuts

16.6 The drive sprocket is secured by a single bolt and washer

16.7 If the countershaft seal (upper arrow) seal has been leaking, pull out the collar and O-ring and replace it; also replace the shift shaft seal (lower arrow) if it's been leaking

Chapter 7 Part A
Brakes, wheels and tires
(CR80R/85R and CR125R models)

Contents

Specifications

Disc brakes

Brake fluid type	See Chapter 1
Brake pad minimum thickness	See Chapter 1
Pad pin wear groove limit (CR80R/85R)	3.0 mm (0.12 inch)
Front disc thickness	
Standard	3.0 mm (0.12 inch)
Limit	2.5 mm (0.10 inch)*
Rear disc thickness	
CR80R/85R	
Standard	3.0 mm (0.12 inch)
Limit	2.5 mm (0.10 inch)*
CR125R	
1987 through 1997	
Standard	4.5 mm (0.18 inch)
Limit	4.0 mm (0.16 inch)*
1998 on	
Standard	4.0 mm (0.16 inch)
Limit	3.5 mm (0.14 inch)*
Disc runout limit (front or rear)	0.15 mm (0.006 inch)

* Refer to marks stamped into the disc (they supersede information printed here)

Drum brakes

Brake lining minimum thickness	See Chapter 1
Brake pedal height	See Chapter 1
Drum diameter	
1986 through 1990 CR80R	
Standard	85.0 mm (3.35 inches)
Wear limit	86.0 mm (3.39 inches)*
1986 CR125R	
Standard	130.0 mm (5.12 inches)
Wear limit	131.0 mm (5.16 inches)*

*Refer to marks cast into the drum (they supersede information printed here)

Wheels and tires

Tire pressures	See Chapter 1
Tire tread depth	See Chapter 1
Axle runout limit	
CR80R/85R front axle	
1986 through 1995	0.2 mm (0.008 inch)
1996 on	0.3 mm (0.012 inch)
CR80R/85R rear axle, CR125R front and rear axles	0.2 mm (0.008 inch)
Wheel out-of-round and lateral runout limit (front and rear)	2.0 mm (0.08 inch)

Torque specifications

Front axle
  CR80R/85R
    1986 through 1994 .... 55 to 70 Nm (40 to 50 ft-lbs)
    1995 on.. 63 Nm (46 ft-lbs)
  CR125R
    1986 through 1989 .... 55 to 70 Nm (40 to 50 ft-lbs)
    1990 and 1991... 80 to 93 Nm (58 to 68 ft-lbs)
    1992 on.. 90 Nm (65 ft-lbs)
Front axle holder nuts (1986 through 1991 CR125R)........... 10 to 12 Nm (54 to 108 in-lbs)
Front axle pinch bolts (1992 and later CR125R) .... 20 Nm (168 in-lbs)
Rear axle nut
  CR80R/85R
    1986 through 1994 .... 80 to 100 Nm (58 to 72 ft-lbs)
    1995 on.. 90 Nm (65 ft-lbs)
  CR125R
    1986 through 1991 .... 85 to 105 Nm (61 to 76 ft-lbs)
    1992 through 1997 .... 95 Nm (69 ft-lbs)
    1998 and 1999... 108 Nm (80 ft-lbs)
    2000 on.. 128 Nm (94 ft-lbs)
Front caliper
  CR80R/85R
    Caliper bracket bolts
      1986 through 1994.. 18 to 25 Nm (13 to 18 ft-lbs)
      1995 .... 27 Nm (20 ft-lbs)
      1996 on .... 31 Nm (22 ft-lbs)
    Caliper pad pins
      1986 through 1994.. 15 to 20 Nm (132 to 168 in-lbs)
      1995 on .... 18 Nm (156 in-lbs)
    Slider pin to bracket
      1986 through 1994.. Not specified
      1995 on .... 18 Nm (156 in-lbs) (1)
    Slider pin to caliper.. 23 Nm (17 ft-lbs) (1)
  CR125R
    Caliper bracket bolts
      1986 through 1991.. 32 to 36 Nm (23 to 26 ft-lbs)
      1992 on .... 31 Nm (22 ft-lbs)
    Pad pins
      1986 through 1991.. 15 to 20 Nm (84 to 168 in-lbs)
      1992 on .... 18 Nm (156 in-lbs)
    Pad pin plugs
      1986 through 1991.. Not specified
      1992 through 1997.. 2.5 Nm (22 inch-lbs)
      1998 on .... 3 Nm (26 inch-lbs)
    Upper slider pin .... Not specified (1)
    Lower slider pin to bracket................................... Not specified (1)
Rear caliper
  Allen head slider pin to caliper
    CR80R/85R.. 28 Nm (20 ft-lbs) (1)
    CR125R .... Not specified
  Slider pin to bracket
    CR80R/85R.. 13 Nm (108 inch-lbs) (1)
    CR125R .... Not specified
  Pad pins .... 18 Nm (156 in-lbs)
  Pad pin plugs
    1992 through 1997 .... 2.5 Nm (22 inch-lbs)
    1998 on.. 3 Nm (26 inch-lbs)
Brake line union bolts... 35 Nm (25 ft-lbs) (2)
Front brake disc-to-wheel bolts
  CR80R/85R
    1986 through 1991 .... 14 to 16 Nm (120 to 144 in-lbs) (1)
    1992 through 1994 .... 20 to 24 Nm (14 to 17 ft-lbs) (1)
    1995 .... 22 Nm (16 ft-lbs) (1)
    1996 on.. 20 Nm (168 in-lbs) (1)
  CR125R
    1986 through 1989 .... 14 to 16 Nm (120 to 144 in-lbs) (1)
    1990 and 1991... 40 to 45 Nm (29 to 33 ft-lbs) (1)
    1992 through 1994 .... 20 Nm (168 in-lbs) (1)
    1995 on.. 16 Nm (144 in-lbs) (1)
Front brake disc cover bolts (1995 and later CR125R)....... 13 Nm (108 in-lbs) (1)

Rear brake disc-to-wheel bolts
 CR80R/85R
  1991 through 1994 .... 18 to 22 Nm (13 to 16 ft-lbs) (1)
  1995 on.. 20 Nm (168 in-lbs) (1)
 CR125R
  1987 through 1989 .... 14 to 16 Nm (120 to 144 in-lbs) (1)
  1990 and 1991 .... 40 to 45 Nm (29 to 33 ft-lbs) (1)
  1992 on.. 43 Nm (31 ft-lbs) (1)
Rear drum brake arm pinch bolt .... Not specified
Front master cylinder
 Mounting bolts
  CR80R/85R
   1986 through 1994.. 8 to 12 Nm (72 to 108 inch-lbs)
   1995 on .... Not specified
  CR125R
   1986 .... Not specified
   1987 and 1988 .... 8 to 12 Nm (72 to 108 inch-lbs)
   1989 through 1991 .... Not specified
   1992 on .... 10 Nm (84 inch-lbs)
 Brake lever pivot bolt
  CR80R/85R
   1986 through 1994.. Not specified
   1995 .... 10 Nm (84 in-lbs)
   1996 on .... 6 Nm (52 inch-lbs)
  CR125R
   1986 .... Not specified
   1987 through 1991.. 8 to 12 Nm (72 to 108 inch-lbs)
   1992 through 1997 .... Not specified
   1998 on .... 6 Nm (52 inch-lbs)
 Brake lever pivot bolt locknut
  CR80R/85R
   1986 .... Not specified
   1987 through 1994.. 8 to 12 Nm (72 to 108 inch-lbs)
   1995 .... 10 Nm (84 inch-lbs)
   1996 on .... 6 Nm (52 inch-lbs)
  CR125R
   1986 through 1991.. Not specified
   1992 through 1997 .... 10 Nm (84 inch-lbs)
   1998 on .... 6 Nm (52 inch-lbs)
Rear master cylinder mounting bolts .... 15 Nm (132 in-lbs)
Pedal pivot bolt
 CR80R/85R
  1986 through 1994 .... Not specified
  1995 through 2002 .... 22 Nm (16 ft-lbs)
  2003 and later.. 32 Nm (24 ft-lbs)
 CR125R
  2004 and earlier... 26 Nm (17 ft-lbs)
  2005 and later.. 36 Nm (27 ft-lbs)

1. Apply non-permanent thread locking agent to the threads.
2. Use new sealing washers on each side of the bolt.

1 General information

The front wheel on all motorcycles covered by this manual is equipped with a hydraulic disc brake using a pin slider caliper. The CR80R/85R front caliper has a single piston; the CR125R front caliper has dual pistons. The rear wheel on 1986 through 1990 CR80R models and 1986 CR125R models is equipped with a drum brake. The rear wheel on all other models is equipped with a hydraulic disc brake using a single-piston pin slider caliper.

All models are equipped with spoked steel wheels. **Caution:** *Disc brake components rarely require disassembly. Do not disassemble components unless absolutely necessary. If any hydraulic brake line connection in the system is loosened, the entire system should be disassembled, drained, cleaned and then properly filled and bled upon reassembly. Do not use solvents on internal brake components. Solvents will cause seals to swell and distort. Use only clean brake fluid, brake system cleaner or alcohol for cleaning. Use care when working with brake fluid as it can injure your eyes and it will damage painted surfaces and plastic parts.*

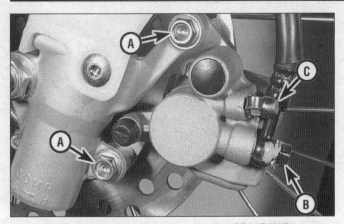

2.2 Front caliper mounting details - CR80R/85R

A   Mounting bolts   C   Bleeder valve
B   Union bolt

2   Brake pads - replacement

Warning: *The dust created by the brake system is harmful to your health. Honda hasn't used asbestos in brake parts for a number of years, but aftermarket parts may contain it. Never blow it out with compressed air and don't inhale any of it. An approved filtering mask should be worn when working on the brakes.*

1   Support the bike securely upright.

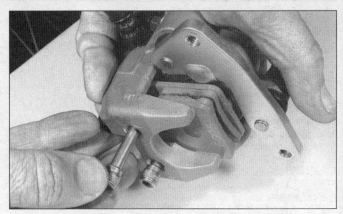

2.3 Unscrew the pad pins and pull out the pads

Removal

CR80R/85R front caliper

Refer to illustrations 2.2, 2.3 and 2.4

2   Remove the caliper mounting bolts **(see illustration)**. Pull the caliper off without disconnecting the fluid hose and support it so the hose won't be strained.

3   Unscrew the pad retaining pin(s) with an Allen wrench **(see illustration)**. Pull the pins out and remove the pads from the caliper.

4   Note the direction of the arrow on the shim that's installed on the piston-side pad **(see illustration)**. It points upward when the shim is installed.

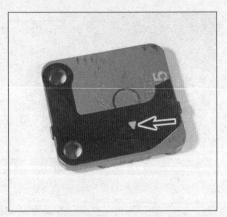

2.4 On CR80R/85R models there's a shim between the piston and pad; its arrowhead (arrow) points up when installed

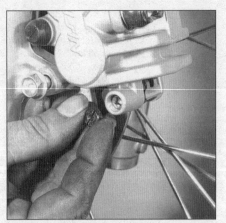

2.6a Unscrew the pad pin plug; it's at the bottom of the CR125R front caliper . . .

2.6b . . . and at the rear of the rear caliper on all models

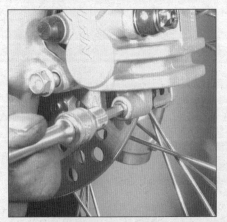

2.7a Unscrew the pad retaining pin; this is a CR125R front caliper . . .

2.7b . . . and this is a rear caliper

2.8a Pull out the pad retaining pin (arrow) and lift out the brake pad farthest from the piston . . .

2.8b . . . then pull the pin out the rest of the way and remove the remaining pad

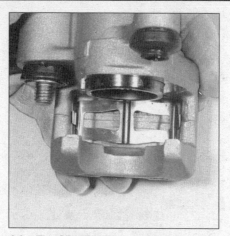

2.9a The CR80R/85R's pad spring fits into the pad cavity like this

2.9b The CR125R's front caliper pad spring fits under the pad pin like this . . .

CR125R front caliper and all rear calipers

Refer to illustrations 2.6a, 2.6b, 2.7a, 2.7b, 2.8a and 2.8b

5   The caliper doesn't need to be removed for pad replacement.
6   Unscrew the plug that covers the pad retaining pin **(see illustrations)**.
7   Unscrew the pad retaining pin with an Allen wrench **(see illustrations)**.
8   Pull the pads out of the caliper **(see illustrations)**.

Inspection

Refer to illustrations 2.9a through 2.9e

9   Inspect the pad spring **(see illustrations)**. If you're working on a CR125R front caliper or any rear caliper, inspect the steel shield that protects the caliper bracket **(see illustrations)**. Replace the spring or shield it if it's rusted or damaged.
10   If you're working on a CR80R/85R, check the pad pins for wear grooves where they contact the pads. If the grooves are worn to more than the depth listed in this Chapter's Specifications, replace the pins.
11   Refer to Chapter 1 and inspect the pads.
12   Check the condition of the brake disc (see Section 4). If it's in need of machining or replacement, follow the procedure in that Section to remove it. If it's okay, deglaze it with sandpaper or emery cloth, using a swirling motion.

Installation

13   Remove the cover from the master cylinder reservoir and siphon out some fluid. Push the piston(s) into the caliper as far as possible,

while checking the master cylinder reservoir to make sure it doesn't overflow. If you can't depress the pistons with thumb pressure, try using a C-clamp. If the pistons stick, remove the caliper and overhaul it as described in Section 3.
14   Install the spring, caliper shield (if equipped) and new pads. Coat the threads of the retaining pin(s) with non-permanent thread locking agent and install the retaining pins. Tighten the retaining pins to the torque listed in this Chapter's Specifications.
15   If you're working on a CR125R front caliper or any rear caliper, install the plug over the retaining pin and tighten it to the torque listed in this Chapter's Specifications.
16   Operate the brake lever or pedal several times to bring the pads into contact with the disc. Check the operation of the brake carefully before riding the motorcycle.

3   Brake caliper - removal, overhaul and installation

Warning: *If a caliper indicates the need for an overhaul (usually due to leaking fluid or sticky operation), all old brake fluid must be flushed from the system. Also, the dust created by the brake system is harmful to your health. Never blow it out with compressed air and don't inhale any of it. An approved filtering mask should be worn when working on the brakes. Do not, under any circumstances, use petroleum-based solvents to clean brake parts. Use brake system cleaner or denatured alcohol only!*
Note: *If you are removing the caliper only to remove the front forks or rear swingarm, don't disconnect the hose from the caliper.*

2.9c . . . and the rear caliper pad spring fits like this

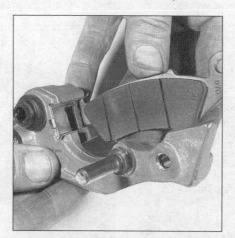

2.9d The CR125R front pads ride on the steel shield in the caliper bracket . . .

2.9e . . . there's a similar shield on all rear caliper brackets (arrow)

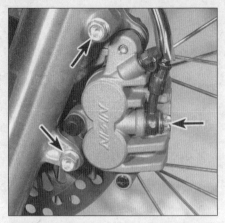

3.2 Unscrew the union bolt (right arrow) if you're planning to remove the caliper for overhaul; remove the mounting bolts to (left arrows) to detach the caliper from the fork leg

3.3 The hose can be left connected if you're removing the caliper for access to other components; on installation, be sure the brake hose fits in the notches (arrows)

3.4a These are the caliper shield bolts on all except late CR125R models . . .

Removal

1   Support the bike securely upright. **Note:** *If you're planning to disassemble the caliper, read through the overhaul procedure, paying particular attention to the steps involved in removing the pistons with compressed air.* If you don't have access to an air compressor, you can use the bike's hydraulic system to force the pistons out instead. To do this, remove the pads and pump the brake lever or pedal. If one front caliper piston comes out before the other, push it back into its bore and hold it in with a C-clamp while pumping the brake lever to remove the remaining piston. Be prepared for brake fluid spillage.

Front caliper

Refer to illustrations 3.2 and 3.3

2   **Note:** *Remember, if you're just removing the caliper to remove the forks, ignore this step.* Disconnect the brake hose from the caliper. Remove the brake hose banjo fitting bolt and separate the hose from the caliper **(see illustration 2.2 or the accompanying illustration)**. Discard the sealing washers. Plug the end of the hose or wrap a plastic bag tightly around it to prevent excessive fluid loss and contamination.

3   Unscrew the caliper mounting bolts and lift it off the fork leg, being careful not to strain or twist the brake hose if it's still connected **(see illustration)**.

Rear caliper

Refer to illustrations 3.4a, 3.4b and 3.5

4   If you're planning to overhaul the caliper, remove its protective bracket and loosen the brake hose union bolt (it's easier to loosen the

bolts while the caliper is mounted on the bike) **(see illustrations)**.
5   Refer to Section 11 and remove the rear wheel. Slide the caliper bracket backward off its rail **(see illustration)**. Support the caliper so it doesn't hang by the brake hose.
6   Disconnect the brake hose from the caliper. Remove the brake hose banjo fitting bolt and separate the hose from the caliper. Discard the sealing washers. Plug the end of the hose or wrap a plastic bag tightly around it to prevent excessive fluid loss and contamination.

Overhaul

Refer to illustrations 3.8a, 3.8b, 3.8c, 3.9, 3.10a, 3.10b, 3.14, 3.17a, 3.17b and 3.17c

7   Remove the brake pads and anti-rattle spring from the caliper (see Section 2, if necessary). Clean the exterior of the caliper with denatured alcohol or brake system cleaner.
8   If you're working on a CR80R/85R front caliper, remove the rubber plug and unscrew the bracket pin. Separate the caliper from the bracket and remove the washer **(see illustrations)**.
9   If you're working on a CR125R front caliper or any rear caliper, slide the caliper off the bracket **(see illustration)**. One pin will stay in the bracket and the other in the caliper.
10   Pack a shop rag into the space that holds the brake pads. Use compressed air, directed into the caliper fluid inlet, to remove the piston(s) **(see illustrations)**. Use only enough air pressure to ease the piston(s) out of the bore. If a piston is blown out forcefully, even with the rag in place, it may be damaged. **Warning:** *Never place your fingers in front of the piston in an attempt to catch or protect it when*

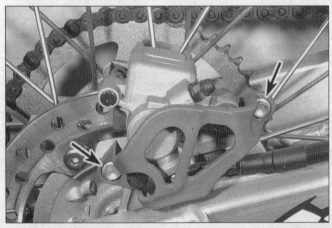

3.4b . . . these are the caliper shield bolts on late CR125R models

3.5 Slide the caliper backward off its rail on the swingarm

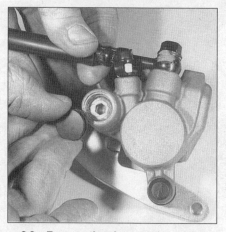

3.8a Remove the plug to unscrew the slider pin from the CR80R/85R caliper body

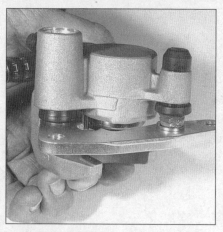

3.8b Slide the caliper off the bracket . . .

3.8c . . . and remove the washer

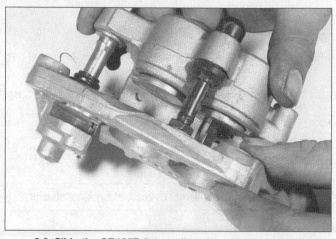

3.9 Slide the CR125R front caliper (or any rear caliper) off the bracket

3.10a Front caliper piston and seal details (one of two pistons shown); the metal cap on the end of the piston (arrow) faces out of the bore

applying compressed air, as serious injury could occur.

11   Using a wood or plastic tool, remove the piston seals. Metal tools may cause bore damage.

12   Clean the pistons and the bores with denatured alcohol, clean brake fluid or brake system cleaner and blow dry them with filtered, unlubricated compressed air. Inspect the surfaces of the pistons for nicks and burrs and loss of plating. Check the caliper bores, too. If surface defects are present, the caliper must be replaced. If the caliper is in bad shape, the master cylinder should also be checked.

13   If you have precision measuring equipment, measure the diameter of the piston(s) and bore(s) and compare the measurements to the values listed in this Chapter's Specifications.

14   Lubricate the piston seals with clean brake fluid and install them in their grooves in the caliper bore **(see illustration)**. Make sure they seat completely and aren't twisted.

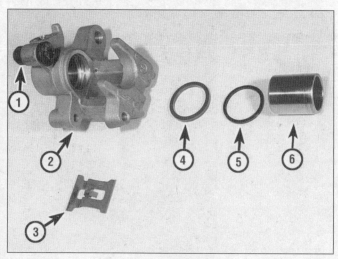

3.10b Rear caliper details

1	Pin boot	3	Pad spring	5	Piston seal
2	Caliper body	4	Dust seal	6	Piston

3.14 Install the seals all the way into their grooves

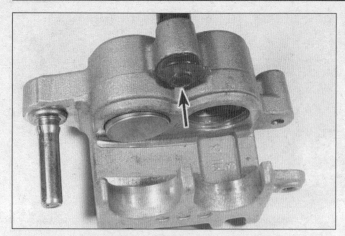

3.17a   Install the boot in the front caliper with its wide end facing the same direction as the pistons (arrow)

3.17b   Install the boot in the front caliper bracket with its wide end facing the same direction as the pin (right arrow) and install the spring (shield) in the bracket notch (left arrow)

15   Lubricate the dust seals with clean brake fluid and install them in their grooves, making sure they seat correctly.

16   Lubricate the piston (both pistons on CR125R front calipers) with clean brake fluid and install it into the caliper bore. Using your thumbs, push the piston all the way in, making sure it doesn't get cocked in the bore.

17   Pull the old pin boots out of the caliper and bracket. Coat new ones with silicone grease and install them, making sure they seat completely **(see illustration 3.8b and the accompanying illustrations)**.

18   If you're working on a CR125R front caliper or any rear caliper, make sure the shields are in position on the caliper brackets **(see illustrations 3.17b and 3.17c)**.

Installation

Refer to illustrations 3.19a and 3.19b

19   Installation is the reverse of the removal steps, with the following additions:

a)   *Apply silicone grease to the slider pins on the caliper bracket and caliper* **(see illustration)**.

b)   *If you're working on a CR80R/85R front caliper, tighten the slider pin to the torque listed in this Chapter's Specifications. Install the washer* **(see illustration 3.8c)**.

c)   *Space the pads apart so the disc will fit between them.*

d)   *Use new sealing washers on the brake hose fitting. If you're working on a CR125R front caliper, position the brake hose fitting in the caliper notches* **(see illustration 3.3)**. *If you're working on a*

rear caliper, position the brake hose against the stop on the swingarm **(see illustration)**.

e)   *Tighten the front caliper mounting bolts, rear caliper shield bolts and brake line union bolt to the torque listed in this Chapter's Specifications.*

f)   *If you're working on a rear caliper, adjust chain slack (see Chapter 1).*

20   Fill the master cylinder with the recommended brake fluid (see Chapter 1) and bleed the system (see Section 10). Check for leaks.

21   Check the operation of the brakes carefully before riding the motorcycle.

---

4   Brake disc(s) - inspection, removal and installation

Inspection

Refer to illustrations 4.3, 4.4a and 4.4b

1   Support the bike securely upright. Place a jack beneath the bike and raise the wheel being checked off the ground. Be sure the bike is securely supported so it can't be knocked over.

2   Visually inspect the surface of the disc(s) for score marks and other damage. Light scratches are normal after use and won't affect brake operation, but deep grooves and heavy score marks will reduce braking efficiency and accelerate pad wear. If the discs are badly grooved they must be machined or replaced.

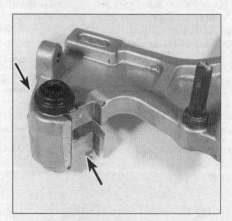

3.17c   Install the boot in the rear caliper bracket with its wide end facing the same direction as the pin (left arrow) and install the spring (shield) in the bracket notch (right arrow)

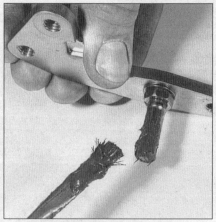

3.19a   Coat the slider pins with silicone grease

3.19b   Be sure the brake hose fits in the caliper bracket notch (arrow) when the union bolt is tightened

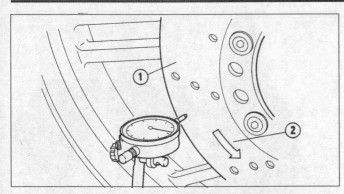

4.3 Set up a dial indicator against the brake disc (1) and turn the disc in its normal direction of rotation (2) to measure runout

3   To check disc runout, mount a dial indicator to a fork leg or the swingarm, with the plunger on the indicator touching the surface of the disc about 1/2-inch from the outer edge **(see illustration)**. Slowly turn the wheel and watch the indicator needle, comparing your reading with the limit listed in this Chapter's Specifications. If the runout is greater than allowed, check the hub bearings for play (see Chapter 1). If the bearings are worn, replace them and repeat this check. If the disc runout is still excessive, the disc will have to be replaced.
4   The disc must not be machined or allowed to wear down to a thickness less than the minimum allowable thickness listed in this Chapter's Specifications. The thickness of the disc can be checked with a micrometer. If the thickness of the disc is less than the minimum allowable, it must be replaced. The minimum thickness is also stamped into the disc **(see illustrations)**.

Removal
5   Remove the wheel (see Section 11). **Caution:** *Don't lay the wheel down and allow it to rest on the disc - the disc could become warped. Set the wheel on wood blocks so the disc doesn't support the weight of the wheel.*
6   Mark the relationship of the disc to the wheel, so it can be installed in the same position. Remove the hex head or Allen head bolts that retain the disc to the wheel **(see illustration 4.4a or 4.4b)**. Loosen the bolts a little at a time, in a criss-cross pattern, to avoid distorting the disc. **Note:** *Allen head bolts must be replaced with new ones on installation.*

Installation
7   Position the disc on the wheel, aligning the previously applied matchmarks (if you're reinstalling the original disc). On models so equipped, make sure the arrow (stamped on the disc) marking the

4.4a Marks on the disc indicate the minimum thickness and direction of rotation

A   *Brake disc mounting bolts*
B   *Wheel bearing collar*
C   *Wheel bearing cover (if equipped)*

direction of rotation is pointing in the proper direction.
8   If the brake disc is secured by Allen head bolts, use new ones. Apply a non-hardening thread locking compound to the threads of the nuts or bolts. Install the nuts or bolts, tightening them a little at a time in a criss-cross pattern, until the torque listed in this Chapter's Specifications is reached. Clean off all grease from the brake disc using acetone or brake system cleaner.
9   Install the wheel.
10   Operate the brake lever or pedal several times to bring the pads into contact with the disc. Check the operation of the brakes carefully before riding the motorcycle.

---

5   Brake drum and shoes - removal, inspection and installation

---

Warning: *The dust created by the brake system is harmful to your health. Never blow it out with compressed air and don't inhale any of it. An approved filtering mask should be worn when working on the brakes.*

Removal
Refer to illustration 5.2
1   Remove the wheel (see Section 11).
2   Lift the brake panel out of the wheel **(see illustration)**.

4.4b The rear brake disc is secured to the hub by Allen bolts (arrows)

5.2 Lift the brake panel out of the drum

5.3 The maximum diameter is cast inside the brake drum

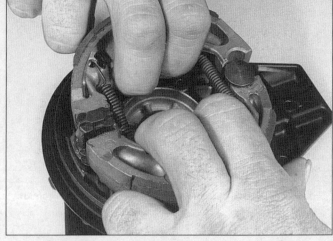

5.6 Spread the shoes and fold them into a V to release the
spring tension

Inspection

Refer to illustrations 5.3, 5.6, 5.9, 5.10, 5.11, 5.12a and 5.12b

3   Check the brake drum for wear or damage. Measure the diameter at several points with a drum micrometer (or have this done by a Honda dealer). If the measurements are uneven (indicating that the drum is out-of-round) or if there are scratches deep enough to snag a finger-nail, replace the drum. The drum must also be replaced if the diameter is greater than that cast inside the drum **(see illustration)**. Honda recommends against machining brake drums.

4   Check the linings for wear, damage and signs of contamination from dirt or water. If the linings are visibly defective, replace them.

5   Measure the thickness of the lining material (just the lining material, not the metal backing) and compare it with the value listed in the Chapter 1 Specifications. Replace the shoes if the material is worn to the minimum or less.

6   To remove the shoes, fold them toward each other to release the spring tension and lift them off the brake panel **(see illustration)**.

7   Check the ends of the shoes where they contact the brake cam and anchor pin. Replace the shoes if there's visible wear.

8   Check the brake cam and anchor pin for wear and damage. The brake cam can be replaced separately; the brake panel must be replaced if the anchor pin is unserviceable.

9   Look for alignment marks on the brake arm and cam **(see illustration)**. Make your own if they aren't visible.

10   Remove the pinch bolt and nut and pull the brake arm off the cam **(see illustration)**.

11   Lift off the wear indicator **(see illustration)**. Pull the brake cam out of the brake panel.

12   Check the brake cam dust seal for wear and damage **(see illustration)**. To replace it, pry it out of the brake panel and tap in a new one using a socket or seal driver the same diameter as the seal **(see illustration)**.

Installation

Refer to illustration 5.16

13   Apply high temperature brake grease to the brake cam, the anchor pin and the ends of the springs.

14   Install the cam through the dust seal. Install the wear indicator **(see illustration 5.11)**. Align its wide groove with the wide spline in the cam.

15   Install the brake arm on the cam, aligning the punch marks. Tighten the nut and bolt to the torque listed in this Chapter's Specifications.

16   Hook the ends of the springs to the shoes. Position the shoes in a V on the brake panel, then fold them down into position **(see illustration)**. Make sure the ends of the shoes fit correctly on the cam and the anchor pin.

17   The remainder of installation is the reverse of the removal steps.

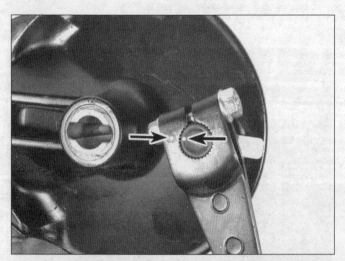

5.9 Look for alignment marks on the brake arm and cam (arrows);
make your own marks if you can't see any

5.10 Remove the pinch bolt and nut and take the brake arm off
the cam

5.11 Remove the wear indicator; the wide spline on the wear indicator fits into a wide groove in the brake cam

5.12a Replace the brake cam seal if it's worn or damaged

5.12b Pry out the old seal, then press a new one in with a socket the same diameter as the seal

6 Front brake master cylinder - removal, overhaul and installation

1   If the master cylinder is leaking fluid, or if the lever doesn't produce a firm feel when the brake is applied, and bleeding the brakes doesn't help, master cylinder overhaul is recommended. Before disassembling the master cylinder, read through the entire procedure and make sure that you have the correct rebuild kit. Also, you will need some new, clean brake fluid of the recommended type, some clean rags and internal snap-ring pliers. **Note:** *To prevent damage to the paint from spilled brake fluid, always cover the gas tank when working on the master cylinder.*

2   **Caution:** *Disassembly, overhaul and reassembly of the brake master cylinder must be done in a spotlessly clean work area to avoid contamination and possible failure of the brake hydraulic system components.*

Removal

Refer to illustration 6.5

3   Place rags beneath the master cylinder to protect the paint in case of brake fluid spills.

4   Brake fluid will run out of the upper brake hose during this step, so either have a container handy to place the end of the hose in, or have a plastic bag and rubber band handy to cover the end of the hose. The objective is to prevent excess loss of brake fluid, fluid spills and system contamination.

5   On all except 1992 and later CR125R models, disconnect the brake hose at the caliper, then unscrew the brake hose fitting from the

5.16 The assembled brakes should look like this

master cylinder **(see illustration)**.

6   On 1992 and later CR125R models, remove the banjo fitting bolt and sealing washers from the master cylinder.

7   Remove the master cylinder mounting bolts **(see illustration 6.5)**. Take the master cylinder off the handlebar.

Overhaul

Refer to illustrations 6.9a, 6.9b, 6.10a, 6.10b, 6.11a, 6.11b and 6.13

8   Remove the master cylinder cover, retainer (if equipped) and diaphragm (see Chapter 1).

9   Remove the locknut from the underside of the lever pivot bolt,

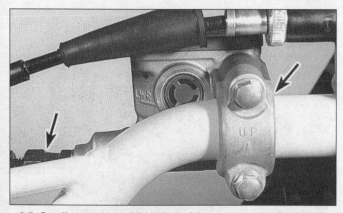

6.5 On all except late CR125R models, unscrew the fitting (left arrow) to disconnect the hose from the master cylinder; on installation, be sure the UP mark on the clamp is upright and align the split in the clamp with the handlebar punch mark (right arrow)

6.9a Remove the locknut (arrow) . . .

6.9b . . . and unscrew the pivot bolt to detach the lever

6.10a Remove the lever and spring from the master cylinder

6.10b . . . the spring fits in the lever like this

6.11a Remove the snap-ring from the master cylinder bore

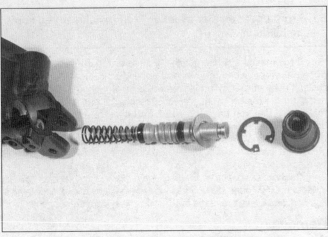

6.11b Remove the piston assembly from the bore

then unscrew the bolt **(see illustrations)**. Remove the lever pivot cover (it's held on by the pivot bolt).

10   The lever is equipped with a spring **(see illustrations)**. This doesn't have to be removed to remove the hydraulic components, but make sure it doesn't get lost.

11   Using snap-ring pliers, remove the snap-ring and slide out the piston assembly and the spring **(see illustrations)**. Lay the parts out in the proper order to prevent confusion during reassembly.

12   Clean all of the parts with brake system cleaner (available at auto parts stores), isopropyl alcohol or clean brake fluid. **Caution:** *Do not, under any circumstances, use a petroleum-based solvent to clean brake parts. If compressed air is available, use it to dry the parts thoroughly (make sure it's filtered and unlubricated).* Check the master cylinder bore and piston for corrosion, scratches, nicks and score marks. If damage or wear can be seen, the master cylinder must be replaced with a new one. If the master cylinder is in poor condition, then the caliper should be checked as well.

13   If there's a baffle plate in the bottom of the reservoir, make sure it's securely held by its retainer **(see illustration)**.

14   Honda supplies a new piston in its rebuild kits. If the cup seals are not installed on the new piston, install them, making sure the lips face away from the lever end of the piston **(see illustration 6.11b)**. Use the new piston regardless of the condition of the old one.

15   Before reassembling the master cylinder, soak the piston and the rubber cup seals in clean brake fluid for ten or fifteen minutes. Lubricate the master cylinder bore with clean brake fluid, then carefully insert the piston and related parts in the reverse order of disassembly. Make sure the lips on the cup seals do not turn inside out when they are slipped into the bore.

16   Depress the piston, then install the snap-ring (make sure the snap-ring is properly seated in the groove with the sharp edge facing out) **(see illustration 6.11a)**. Install the rubber dust boot (make sure the lip is seated properly in the piston groove).

17   Install the brake lever, pivot cover and pivot bolt. Tighten the pivot bolt locknut.

Installation
Refer to illustration 6.18

18   Installation is the reverse of the removal steps, with the following additions:

6.13 Make sure the baffle plate is securely retained in the bottom of the reservoir

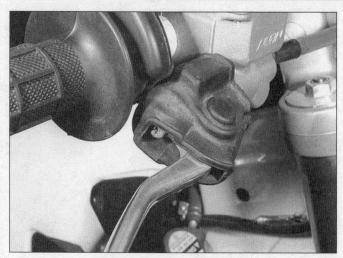

6.18 The pivot cover fits like this

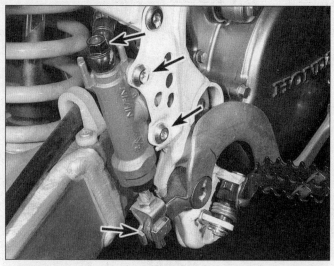

7.4 Remove the cotter pin and clevis pin (lower arrow) to detach the master cylinder from the pedal; remove the mounting bolts (center arrows) to detach the master cylinder from the frame; on installation, use new sealing washers on the union bolt and be sure the neck of the fluid hose fits between the stoppers (upper arrow, 2001 and earlier shown)

a) *Attach the master cylinder to the handlebar. Align the upper gap between the master cylinder and clamp with the punch mark on the handlebar* **(see illustration 6.5)**.

b) *Make sure the arrow and the word UP on the master cylinder clamp are pointing up, then tighten the bolts to the torque listed in this Chapter's Specifications* **(see illustration 6.5)**.

c) *Use new sealing washers at the brake hose banjo fitting. Tighten the union bolt to the torque listed in this Chapter's Specifications.*

d) *Install the pivot cover over the lever and pivot* **(see illustration)**.

19   Refer to Section 10 and bleed the air from the system.

7   Rear brake master cylinder - removal, overhaul and installation

1   If the master cylinder is leaking fluid, or if the pedal does not pro-duce a firm feel when the brake is applied, and bleeding the brake does not help, master cylinder overhaul is recommended. Before dis-assembling the master cylinder, read through the entire procedure and make sure that you have the correct rebuild kit. Also, you will need some new, clean brake fluid of the recommended type, some clean rags and internal snap-ring pliers.

2   **Caution:** *Disassembly, overhaul and reassembly of the brake master cylinder must be done in a spotlessly clean work area to avoid contamination and possible failure of the brake hydraulic system com-ponents.*

Removal

Refer to illustrations 7.4 and 7.6

3   Support the bike securely upright.

4   Remove the cotter pin from the clevis pin on the master cylinder pushrod **(see illustration)**. Remove the clevis pin.

5   Have a container and some rags ready to catch spilling brake fluid. Using a six-point box-end wrench, unscrew the banjo fitting bolt from the top of the master cylinder. Discard the sealing washers on either side of the fitting.

6   Remove the two master cylinder mounting bolts and detach the cylinder from the bracket. Pull the master cylinder out from behind the bracket, squeeze the fluid feed hose clamp with pliers and slide the clamp up the hose. Disconnect the hose from the fitting and take the master cylinder out. If necessary, remove the reservoir mounting bolt and detach it from the frame **(see illustration)**.

Overhaul

Refer to illustrations 7.7a, 7.7b, 7.8, 7.9, 7.10a, 7.10b and 7.14

7   Using a pair of snap-ring pliers, remove the snap-ring from the fluid inlet fitting and detach the fitting from the master cylinder. Remove the O-ring from the bore **(see illustrations)**.

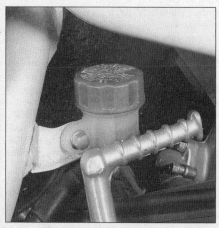

7.6 The fluid reservoir is secured by a single bolt

7.7a Remove the snap-ring . . .

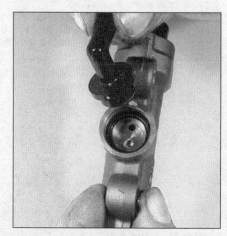

7.7b . . . then work the fluid feed fitting free of its bore and remove the O-ring

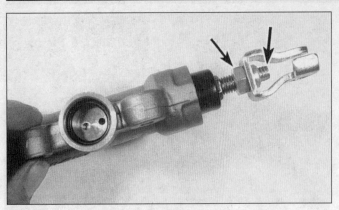

7.8 Write down the number of exposed threads in the clevis (right arrow), then loosen the locknut (left arrow) and unscrew the locknut and clevis from the pushrod

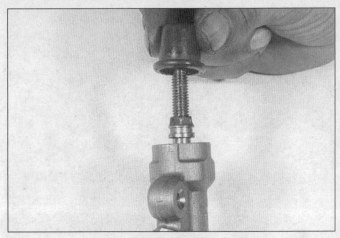

7.9 Take the dust boot off the pushrod

7.10a Remove the snap-ring from the master cylinder bore and withdraw the piston assembly and spring

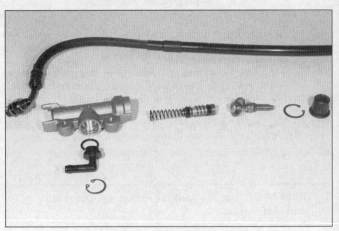

7.10b Rear master cylinder details

8   Count the number of exposed threads on the end of the pushrod inside the clevis **(see illustration)**. Write this number down for use on assembly. Hold the clevis with a pair of pliers and loosen the locknut, then unscrew the clevis and locknut from the pushrod.

9   Carefully remove the rubber dust boot from the pushrod **(see illustration)**.

10   Depress the pushrod and, using snap-ring pliers, remove the snap-ring **(see illustration)**. Slide out the piston, the cup seal and spring. Lay the parts out in the proper order to prevent confusion during reassembly **(see illustration)**.

11   Clean all of the parts with brake system cleaner (available at motorcycle dealerships and auto parts stores), isopropyl alcohol or clean brake fluid. **Caution:** *Do not, under any circumstances, use a*

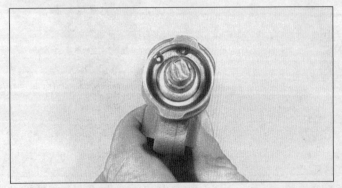

7.14 Make sure the snap-ring is securely seated in its groove

petroleum-based solvent to clean brake parts. If compressed air is available, use it to dry the parts thoroughly (make sure it's filtered and unlubricated). Check the master cylinder bore for corrosion, scratches, nicks and score marks. If damage is evident, the master cylinder must be replaced with a new one. If the master cylinder is in poor condition, then the caliper should be checked as well.

12   Honda supplies a new piston in its rebuild kits. If the cup seals are not installed on the new piston, install them, making sure the lips face away from the lever end of the piston **(see illustration 7.10b)**. Use the new piston regardless of the condition of the old one.

13   Before reassembling the master cylinder, soak the piston and the rubber cup seals in clean brake fluid for ten or fifteen minutes. Lubricate the master cylinder bore with clean brake fluid, then carefully insert the parts in the reverse order of disassembly. Make sure the lips on the cup seals do not turn inside out when they are slipped into the bore.

14   Lubricate the end of the pushrod with PBC (poly butyl cuprysil) grease, or silicone grease designed for brake applications, and install the pushrod and stop washer into the cylinder bore. Depress the pushrod, then install the snap-ring (make sure the snap-ring is properly seated in the groove with the sharp edge facing out) **(see illustration)**. Install the rubber dust boot (make sure the lip is seated properly in the groove in the piston stop nut).

15   Install the locknut and clevis to the end of the pushrod, leaving the same number of exposed threads inside the clevis as was written down during removal. Tighten the locknut. This will ensure the brake pedal will be positioned correctly.

16   Install the feed hose fitting, using a new O-ring. Install the snap-ring, making sure it seats properly in its groove.

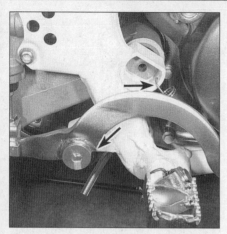

8.2 Unhook the brake pedal spring from the frame (upper arrow); unscrew the pivot to remove the pedal (lower arrow)

9.4a The front brake hose is secured to the fork leg by a clamp

9.4b The rear brake hose is secured to the swingarm by one or more clips; use non-permanent thread locking agent on the threads of the clip screws

Installation

17   Install the fluid reservoir if it was removed. Connect the fluid feed hose to the fitting on the master cylinder and secure it with the clamp.
18   Position the master cylinder on the frame and install the bolts, tightening them securely.
19   Connect the banjo fitting to the top of the master cylinder, using new sealing washers on each side of the fitting. Tighten the banjo fitting bolt to the torque listed in this Chapter's Specifications.
20   Connect the clevis to the brake pedal and secure the clevis pin with a new cotter pin.
21   Fill the fluid reservoir with the specified fluid (see Chapter 1) and bleed the system following the procedure in Section 10.
22   Check the position of the brake pedal (see Chapter 1) and adjust it if necessary. Check the operation of the brakes carefully before riding the motorcycle.

8   Brake pedal - removal and installation

Refer to illustration 8.2
1   Support the bike securely upright so it can't be knocked over during this procedure.
2   Unhook the pedal return spring from the frame **(see illustration)**.
3   Remove the cotter pin and clevis pin to detach the master cylinder pushrod from the pedal.
4   Unscrew the brake pedal pivot shaft and slide the brake pedal out of the frame.
5   Inspect the pedal pivot shaft seals. If they're worn, damaged or appear to have been leaking, pry them out and press in new ones.
6   Installation is the reverse of the removal steps, with the following additions:
a)   *Lubricate the pedal shaft or pivot arm seal lips and the pivot hole with multi-purpose grease.*
b)   *Tighten the pedal pivot shaft to the torque listed in this Chapter's Specifications.*
c)   *Use a new cotter pin.*
d)   *Refer to Chapter 1 and adjust brake pedal height (all models).*

9   Brake hoses and lines - inspection and replacement

Inspection

1   Once every 2.5 operating hours or before every race, check the condition of the brake hoses.

2   Twist and flex the rubber hoses while looking for cracks, bulges and seeping fluid. Check extra carefully around the areas where the hoses connect with the metal fittings, as these are common areas for hose failure.

Replacement

Refer to illustrations 9.4a and 9.4b
3   The pressurized brake hoses have banjo fittings on each end of the hose. The fluid feed hose that connects the rear master cylinder reservoir to the master cylinder is secured by spring clamps.
4   Cover the surrounding area with plenty of rags and unscrew the banjo bolt on either end of the hose. Detach the hose or line from any clips that may be present and remove the hose **(see illustrations)**.
5   Position the new hose or line, making sure it isn't twisted or otherwise strained. On hoses equipped with banjo fittings, make sure the metal tube portion of the banjo fitting is located against the stop on the component it's connected to, if equipped. Install the banjo bolts, using new sealing washers on both sides of the fittings, and tighten them to the torque listed in this Chapter's Specifications.
6   Flush the old brake fluid from the system, refill the system with the recommended fluid (see Chapter 1) and bleed the air from the system (see Section 10). Check the operation of the brakes carefully before riding the motorcycle.

10   Brake system bleeding

Refer to illustrations 10.5a and 10.5b
1   Bleeding the brakes is simply the process of removing all the air bubbles from the brake fluid reservoir, the lines and the brake caliper. Bleeding is necessary whenever a brake system hydraulic connection is loosened, when a component or hose is replaced, or when the master cylinder or caliper is overhauled. Leaks in the system may also allow air to enter, but leaking brake fluid will reveal their presence and warn you of the need for repair.
2   To bleed the brakes, you will need some new, clean brake fluid of the recommended type (see Chapter 1), a length of clear vinyl or plastic tubing, a small container partially filled with clean brake fluid, some rags and a wrench to fit the brake caliper bleeder valve.
3   Cover the fuel tank and other painted components to prevent damage in the event that brake fluid is spilled.
4   Remove the reservoir cover or cap and slowly pump the brake lever or pedal a few times, until no air bubbles can be seen floating up from the holes at the bottom of the reservoir. Doing this bleeds the air from the master cylinder end of the line. Reinstall the reservoir cover or cap.

10.5a Pull the rubber cap off the bleed valve (CR125R front caliper shown) . . .

10.5b . . . and connect a clear plastic hose to the valve (rear caliper shown)

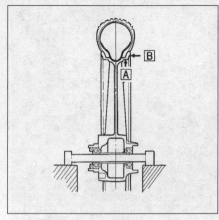

11.2 Check the wheel for out-of-round (A) and lateral movement (B)

5   Attach one end of the clear vinyl or plastic tubing to the brake caliper bleeder valve and submerge the other end in the brake fluid in the container **(see illustrations)**.

6   Check the fluid level in the reservoir. Do not allow the fluid level to drop below the lower mark during the bleeding process.

7   Carefully pump the brake lever or pedal three or four times and hold it while opening the caliper bleeder valve. When the valve is opened, brake fluid will flow out of the caliper into the clear tubing and the lever will move toward the handlebar or the pedal will move down.

8   Retighten the bleeder valve, then release the brake lever or pedal gradually. Repeat the process until no air bubbles are visible in the brake fluid leaving the caliper and the lever or pedal is firm when applied. Remember to add fluid to the reservoir as the level drops. Use only new, clean brake fluid of the recommended type. Never reuse the fluid lost during bleeding.

9   Be sure to check the fluid level in the master cylinder reservoir frequently.

10   Replace the reservoir cover or cap, wipe up any spilled brake fluid and check the entire system for leaks. **Note:** *If bleeding is difficult, it may be necessary to let the brake fluid in the system stabilize for a few hours (it may be aerated).* Repeat the bleeding procedure when the tiny bubbles in the system have settled out.

---

11   Wheels - inspection, removal and installation

Inspection
Refer to illustrations 11.2 and 11.5

1   Clean the wheels thoroughly to remove mud and dirt that may interfere with the inspection procedure or mask defects. Make a general check of the wheels and tires as described in Chapter 1.

2   Support the motorcycle securely upright with the wheel to be checked in the air, then attach a dial indicator to the fork slider or the swingarm and position the stem against the side of the rim **(see illustration)**. Spin the wheel slowly and check the side-to-side (axial) runout of the rim, then compare your readings with the value listed in this Chapter's Specifications. In order to accurately check radial runout with the dial indicator, the wheel would have to be removed from the machine and the tire removed from the wheel. With the axle clamped in a vise, the wheel can be rotated to check the runout.

3   An easier, though slightly less accurate, method is to attach a stiff wire pointer to the outer fork tube or the swingarm and position the end a fraction of an inch from the wheel (where the wheel and tire join). If the wheel is true, the distance from the pointer to the rim will be constant as the wheel is rotated. Repeat the procedure to check the runout of the rear wheel. **Note:** *If wheel runout is excessive, refer to the appropriate Section in this Chapter and check the wheel bearings very carefully before replacing the wheel.*

4   The wheels should also be visually inspected for cracks, flat spots

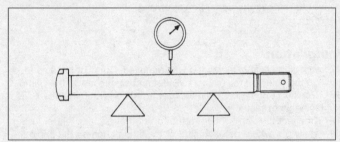

11.5 Check the axle for runout using a dial indicator and V-blocks (divide the reading by two to obtain the actual runout)

on the rim and other damage. Individual spokes can be replaced. If other damage is evident, the wheel will have to be replaced with a new one. Never attempt to repair a damaged wheel.

5   Before installing the wheel, check the axle for straightness. If the axle is corroded, first remove the corrosion with fine emery cloth. Set the axle on V-blocks and check it for runout with a dial indicator **(see illustration)**. If the axle exceeds the maximum allowable runout limit listed in this Chapter's Specifications, it must be replaced.

Removal
Front wheel
Refer to illustrations 11.7a, 11.7b, 11.8, 11.9 and 11.10

6   Support the bike from below with a jack beneath the engine. Securely prop the bike upright so it can't fall over when the wheel is removed.

7   If you're working on an early CR125R, remove the axle holder

11.7a 1986 through 1991 CR125R models have an axle holder on the right fork leg; the UP mark must be upright when it's installed . . .

11.7b 1990 and 1991 CR125R models also have an axle holder on the left fork leg

11.8 Loosen the axle pinch bolts

11.9 Hold the axle so it won't turn and remove the nut from the left side

11.10 Remove the wheel bearing collars, noting which end faces the hub (CR80R shown)

11.14a Remove the axle nut . . .

11.14b . . . pull the axle out . . .

from the right fork leg (1986 through 1989) or both fork legs (1990 and 1991) **(see illustrations)**.

8   On all CR80R/85R and 1992 and later CR125R models, unscrew the axle pinch bolts **(see illustration)**.

9   If you're working on a 1986 through 1989 CR125R, unscrew the axle from the left fork leg. On all others, hold the axle from turning by placing a socket on the hex, then remove the axle nut from the left side **(see illustration)**.

10   Remove the axle from the right fork leg. Support the wheel and pull the axle out. Lower the wheel away from the motorcycle, sliding the brake disc out from between the pads. Collect the wheel bearing spacers **(see illustration)**.

Rear wheel

Refer to illustrations 11.14a, 11.14b and 11.14c

11   Support the bike from below with a jack beneath the swingarm. Securely prop the bike upright so it can't fall over when the wheel is removed.

12   If you're working on a drum brake model, remove the rear brake adjuster wingnut from the brake rod (see Chapter 1). Pull the rod out of its pivot and remove the pivot from the brake drum arm. Unbolt the torque link from the brake panel.

13   Loosen the rear axle nut and back off the chain adjusters all the way (see Chapter 1). Disengage the drive chain from the rear sprocket.

14   Hold the axle with a wrench or socket and remove the axle nut, then support the wheel, pull the axle out and remove the chain adjusters **(see illustrations)**.

15   Lower the wheel away from the motorcycle.

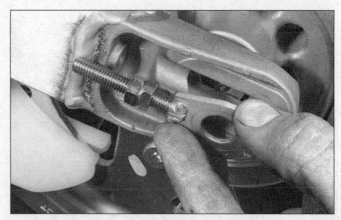

11.14c . . . and slide off the chain adjusters

Installation

16   Installation is the reverse of the removal steps, with the following additions:

a)   *If you're installing a rear wheel on a drum brake model, connect the brake rod to the arm and the torque rod to the brake panel.*

b)   *If you're working on a front wheel, tighten the axle nut to the torque listed in this Chapter's Specifications, then tighten the holder nuts or pinch bolts to the torque listed in this Chapter's Specifications.*

c) *If you're working on a rear wheel, tighten the axle nut to the torque listed in this Chapter's Specifications.*

d) *Refer to Chapter 1 and adjust the rear brake (drum brake models) and drive chain slack.*

12 Wheels - alignment check

1   Misalignment of the wheels, which may be due to a cocked rear wheel or a bent frame or triple clamps, can cause strange and possibly serious handling problems. If the frame or triple clamps are at fault, repair by a frame specialist or replacement with new parts are the only alternatives.

2   To check the alignment you will need an assistant, a length of string or a perfectly straight piece of wood and a ruler graduated in 1/64-inch increments. A plumb bob or other suitable weight will also be required.

3   Support the motorcycle securely upright, then measure the width of both tires at their widest points. Subtract the smaller measurement from the larger measurement, then divide the difference by two. The result is the amount of offset that should exist between the front and rear tires on both sides.

4   If a string is used, have your assistant hold one end of it about half way between the floor and the rear axle, touching the rear sidewall of the tire.

5   Run the other end of the string forward and pull it tight so that it is

roughly parallel to the floor. Slowly bring the string into contact with the front sidewall of the rear tire, then turn the front wheel until it is parallel with the string. Measure the distance from the front tire sidewall to the string.

6   Repeat the procedure on the other side of the motorcycle. The distance from the front tire sidewall to the string should be equal on both sides.

7   As was previously pointed out, a perfectly straight length of wood may be substituted for the string. The procedure is the same.

8   If the distance between the string and tire is greater on one side, or if the rear wheel appears to be cocked, refer to Chapter 6, *Swingarm bearings - check*, and make sure the swingarm is tight.

9   If the front-to-back alignment is correct, the wheels still may be out of alignment vertically.

10   Using the plumb bob, or other suitable weight, and a length of string, check the rear wheel to make sure it is vertical. To do this, hold the string against the tire upper sidewall and allow the weight to settle just off the floor. When the string touches both the upper and lower tire sidewalls and is perfectly straight, the wheel is vertical. If it is not, place thin spacers under one leg of the centerstand.

11   Once the rear wheel is vertical, check the front wheel in the same manner. If both wheels are not perfectly vertical, the frame and/or major suspension components are bent.

13 Wheel bearings - inspection and maintenance

Front wheel bearings
Refer to illustrations 13.6a, 13.6b, 13.6c and 13.6d

1   Support the bike securely and remove the front wheel (see Section 11).

2   Set the wheel on blocks so as not to allow the weight of the wheel rest on the brake disc.

3   Remove the spacers (if you haven't already done so) and the left-side bearing cover from the wheel **(see illustration 4.4a)**.

4   Remove the seal or dust cover from the right side of the wheel.

5   Turn the wheel over. Remove the cover and pry the grease seal out of the left side.

6   A common method of removing front wheel bearings is to insert a metal rod (preferably a brass drift punch) through the center of one hub bearing and tap evenly around the inner race of the opposite bearing to drive it from the hub **(see illustration)**. The bearing spacer will also come out. On these motorcycles, it's generally not possible to tilt the rod enough to catch the edge of the opposite bearing's inner race. In this case, use a bearing remover tool consisting of a shaft and remover head

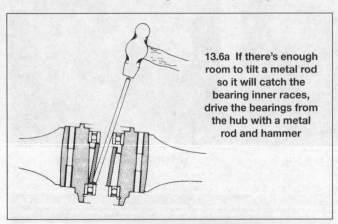

13.6a If there's enough room to tilt a metal rod so it will catch the bearing inner races, drive the bearings from the hub with a metal rod and hammer

13.6b If you can't position a metal rod against the bearings, this tool can be used instead - place the split portion inside the bearing and pass the wedged rod through the hub into the split; tapping on the end of the rod will spread the split portion, locking it to the bearing, so the split portion and bearing can be driven out together

13.6c The split portion fits into the bearing like this - if it keeps slipping out when you tap on it, coat it with valve grinding compound

13.6d The tool can be used for front or rear wheel bearings - the wedged rod fits through the hub like this

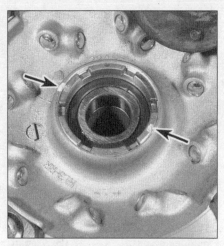

13.14 The bearing retainer is staked in place (arrows); this makes it impractical to remove it with makeshift tools

13.16a Remove the collar from the sprocket side of the wheel

(see illustration). The head fits inside the bearing **(see illustration)**, then the wedge end of the shaft is tapped into the groove in the head to expand the head and lock it inside the bearing. Tapping on the shaft from this point will force the bearing out of the hub **(see illustration)**.

7   Lay the wheel on its other side and remove the remaining bearing using the same technique. **Note:** *The bearings must be replaced with new ones whenever they're removed, as they're almost certain to be damaged during removal.*

8   If you're installing bearings that aren't sealed on both sides, pack the new bearings with grease from the open side. Rotate the bearing to work the grease in between the bearing balls.

9   Thoroughly clean the hub area of the wheel. Install the bearing into the recess in the right side of the hub, with the sealed side facing out. Using a bearing driver or a socket large enough to contact the outer race of the bearing, drive it in until it seats.

10   Turn the wheel over and install the bearing spacer and bearing, driving the bearing into place as described in Step 9.

11   Coat the lip of a new grease seal with grease.

12   Install the grease seal on the right side of the wheel; it should go in with thumb pressure but if not, use a seal driver, large socket or a flat piece of wood to drive it into place.

13   Clean off all grease from the brake disc using acetone or brake system cleaner. Install the wheel.

Rear wheel bearings

Refer to illustrations 13.14, 13.16a, 13.16b, 13.18, 13.19a, 13.19b, 13.19c and 13.27

14   The right rear wheel bearing on early CR80R and all CR125R models is held in place by a threaded retainer that's staked in position **(see illustration)**. Removal requires special tools for which there are no good substitutes. Before you try to replace the bearings, read through the procedure. If you race the bike and work on it regularly, you might want to buy the tools (you should be able to order them from a Honda dealer). Otherwise, it may be more practical to take the wheel to a Honda dealer and have the bearings replaced.

15   Refer to Section 11 and remove the rear wheel.

16   Remove the collar and pry the grease seal from the sprocket side of the wheel **(see illustrations)**. If you're working on a 1986 through 1988 CR125R, remove the three-toothed washer from under the grease seal.

17   If you're working on a 1988 through 1991 CR80R, remove the snap-ring from the right side of the wheel.

18   On the right side of the wheel, remove the collar from the grease seal **(see illustration)**. You may need to pry it out with a pair of screwdrivers. If it's really stuck, use a bearing remover tool. Pry the grease seal out. If you're working on a 1987 or 1988 CR125R, remove the

13.16b This seal removal tool is convenient, but a screwdriver will also work

three-toothed washer from under the grease seal.

19   If the bike has a bearing retainer, insert the shaft of the retainer wrench into the hub from the retainer side. Engage the pins of the wrench with the holes in the retainer, then thread the retainer wingnut

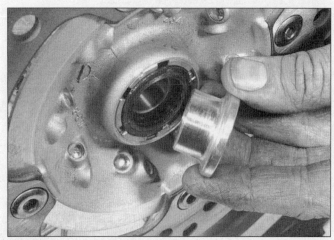

13.18 Turn the wheel over and remove the collar from the disc side, then pry out the seal

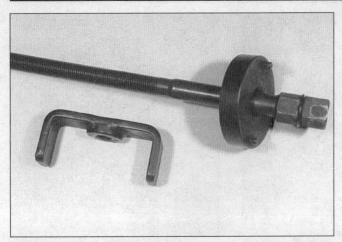

13.19a These tools are used to remove the bearing retainer; pass the shaft through the hub and fit the pins on the disc into the holes in the bearing retainer

13.19b Thread the nut portion of the tool onto the shaft and tighten it to lock the pins on the disc securely into the holes in the bearing retainer

13.19c Turn the shaft (arrow) with a socket or wrench to unscrew the retainer from the hub

13.27 Drive in the bearing on the sprocket side, using a bearing driver that contacts the outer race (the sealed side of the bearing faces out)

onto the shaft **(see illustrations)**. Turn the retainer wrench with a socket to unscrew the retainer.

20 Remove the bearings with the special tools used for front wheel bearings (see Step 6). **Note:** *1992 and later CR125R models have two bearings on the left side of the hub and one on the right side. All other models have one bearing on each side of the hub.*

21 If you're working on a 1986 through 1988 CR125R, remove the spacer cap, bearing spacer, and another bearing spacer cap. On all other models, remove the bearing spacer.

22 Thoroughly clean the hub area of the wheel.

23 If you're working on a 1986 or 1987 CR125R, install the spacer cap in the right side of the hub with its dished side facing into the hub.

24 Install the right bearing into the recess in the hub, with the sealed side facing out. Using a bearing driver or a socket large enough to contact the outer race of the bearing, drive it in until it seats.

25 Turn the wheel over. Apply a coat of multi-purpose grease to the inside of the spacer and install it in the hub.

26 If you're working on a 1986 through 1988 CR125R, install the left spacer cap on the spacer.

27 Pack the remaining bearing from the open side with grease, then install it in the hub, driving the bearing in with a socket or bearing driver large enough to contact the outer race of the bearing **(see illustration)**. Drive the bearing in until it seats.

28 Thread the retainer partway into the hub, then install it with the same tools used for removal **(see illustrations 13.19a through 13.19c)**. Stake the retainer in place.

29 If you're working on a 1986 through 1988 CR125R, install the

three-pointed washer on each bearing.

30 Install a new grease seal in each side of the hub **(see illustration 13.18)**. It may go in with thumb pressure, but if not, use a seal driver, large socket or a flat piece of wood to drive it into place.

31 Install the collars in the grease seals.

32 Clean off all grease from the brake discs using acetone or brake system cleaner. Install the wheel.

14 Tires - removal and installation

1 To properly remove and install tires, you will need at least two motorcycle tire irons, some water and a tire pressure gauge.

2 Begin by removing the wheel from the motorcycle. If the tire is going to be re-used, mark it next to the valve stem, wheel balance weight or rim lock.

3 Deflate the tire by removing the valve stem core. When it is fully deflated, push the bead of the tire away from the rim on both sides. In some extreme cases, this can only be accomplished with a bead breaking tool, but most often it can be carried out with tire irons. Riding on a deflated tire to break the bead is not recommended, as damage to the rim and tire will occur.

4 Dismounting a tire is easier when the tire is warm, so an indoor tire change is recommended in cold climates. The rubber gets very stiff and is difficult to manipulate when cold.

TIRE CHANGING SEQUENCE - TUBED TIRES

1 Deflate tire. After pushing tire beads away from rim flanges push tire bead into well of rim at point opposite valve. Insert tire lever adjacent to valve and work bead over edge of rim.

2 Use two levers to work bead over edge of rim. Note use of rim protectors.

3 Remove inner tube from tire.

4 When first bead is clear, remove tire as shown.

5 When fitting, partially inflate inner tube and insert in tire.

6 Work first bead over rim and feed valve through hole in rim. Partially screw on retaining nut to hold valve in place.

7 Check that inner tube is positioned correctly and work second bead over rim using tire levers. Start at a point opposite valve.

8 Work final area of bead over rim while pushing valve inwards to ensure that inner tube is not trapped.

5   Place the wheel on a thick pad or old blanket. This will help keep the wheel and tire from slipping around.

6   Once the bead is completely free of the rim, lubricate the inside edge of the rim and the tire bead with water only. Honda recommends against the use of soap or other tire mounting lubricants, as the tire may shift on the rim. Remove the locknut and push the tire valve through the rim.

7   Insert one of the tire irons under the bead of the tire at the valve stem and lift the bead up over the rim. This should be fairly easy. Take care not to pinch the tube as this is done. If it is difficult to pry the bead up, make sure that the rest of the bead opposite the valve stem is in the dropped center section of the rim.

8   Hold the tire iron down with the bead over the rim, then move about 1 or 2 inches to either side and insert the second tire iron. Be careful not to cut or slice the bead or the tire may split when inflated. Also, take care not to catch or pinch the inner tube as the second tire iron is levered over. For this reason, tire irons are recommended over screwdrivers or other implements.

9   With a small section of the bead up over the rim, one of the levers can be removed and reinserted 1 or 2 inches farther around the rim until about 1/4 of the tire bead is above the rim edge. Make sure that the rest of the bead is in the dropped center of the rim. At this point, the bead can usually be pulled up over the rim by hand.

10   Once all of the first bead is over the rim, the inner tube can be withdrawn from the tire and rim. Push in on the valve stem, lift up on the tire next to the stem, reach inside the tire and carefully pull out the tube. It is usually not necessary to completely remove the tire from the rim to repair the inner tube. It is sometimes recommended though, because checking for foreign objects in the tire is difficult while it is still mounted on the rim.

11   To remove the tire completely, make sure the bead is broken all the way around on the remaining edge, then stand the tire and wheel up on the tread and grab the wheel with one hand. Push the tire down over the same edge of the rim while pulling the rim away from the tire. If the bead is correctly positioned in the dropped center of the rim, the tire should roll off and separate from the rim very easily. If tire irons are used to work this last bead over the rim, the outer edge of the rim may be marred. If a tire iron is necessary, be sure to pad the rim as described earlier.

12   Refer to Section 15 for inner tube repair procedures.

13   Mounting a tire is basically the reverse of removal. Some tires have a balance mark and/or directional arrows molded into the tire sidewall. Look for these marks so that the tire can be installed properly. The dot should be aligned with the valve stem.

14   If the tire was not removed completely to repair or replace the inner tube, the tube should be inflated just enough to make it round. Sprinkle it with talcum powder, which acts as a dry lubricant, then carefully lift up the tire edge and install the tube with the valve stem next to the hole in the rim. Once the tube is in place, push the valve stem through the rim and start the locknut on the stem.

15   Lubricate the tire bead, then push it over the rim edge and into the dropped center section opposite the inner tube valve stem. Work around each side of the rim, carefully pushing the bead over the rim. The last section may have to be levered on with tire irons. If so, take care not to pinch the inner tube as this is done.

16   Once the bead is over the rim edge, check to see that the inner tube valve stem and the rim lock are pointing to the center of the hub. If they're angled slightly in either direction, rotate the tire on the rim to straighten it out. Run the locknut the rest of the way onto the stem and rim lock but don't tighten them completely.

17   Inflate the tube to approximately 1-1/2 times the pressure listed in the Chapter 1 Specifications and check to make sure the guidelines on the tire sidewalls are the same distance from the rim around the circumference of the tire. **Warning:** *Do not overinflate the tube or the tire may burst, causing serious injury.*

18   After the tire bead is correctly seated on the rim, allow the tire to deflate. Replace the valve core and inflate the tube to the recommended pressure, then tighten the valve stem locknut securely and tighten the cap. Tighten the locknut on the rim locknut to the torque listed in the Chapter 1 Specifications.

15   Tubes - repair

1   Tire tube repair requires a patching kit that's usually available from motorcycle dealers, accessory stores or auto parts stores. Be sure to follow the directions supplied with the kit to ensure a safe repair. Patching should be done only when a new tube is unavailable. Replace the tube as soon as possible. Sudden deflation can cause loss of control and an accident.

2   To repair a tube, remove it from the tire, inflate and immerse it in a sink or tub full of water to pinpoint the leak. Mark the position of the leak, then deflate the tube. Dry it off and thoroughly clean the area around the puncture.

3   Most tire patching kits have a buffer to rough up the area around the hole for proper adhesion of the patch. Roughen an area slightly larger than the patch, then apply a thin coat of the patching cement to the roughened area. Allow the cement to dry until tacky, then apply the patch.

4   It may be necessary to remove a protective covering from the top surface of the patch after it has been attached to the tube. Keep in mind that tubes made from synthetic rubber may require a special patch and adhesive if a satisfactory bond is to be achieved.

5   Before replacing the tube, check the inside of the tire to make sure the object that caused the puncture is not still inside. Also check the outside of the tire, particularly the tread area, to make sure nothing is projecting through the tire that may cause another puncture. Check the rim for sharp edges or damage. Make sure the rubber trim band is in good condition and properly installed before inserting the tube.

Chapter 7 Part B
Brakes, wheels and tires
(CR250R and CR500R models)

Contents

Specifications

Disc brakes

Brake fluid type	See Chapter 1
Brake pad minimum thickness	See Chapter 1
Front disc thickness	
Standard	3.0 mm (0.12 inch)
Limit*	2.5 mm (0.10 inch)
Rear disc thickness	
All except 1997 CR250R	
Standard	4.5 mm (0.18 inch)
Limit	4.0 mm (0.16 inch)*
1997 and later CR250R	
Standard	4.0 mm (0.16 inch)
Limit	3.5 mm (0.14 inch)
Disc runout limit	0.15 mm (0.006 inch)

* Refer to marks stamped into the disc (they supersede information printed here)

Drum brakes

Brake lining minimum thickness	See Chapter 1
Brake pedal height	See Chapter 1
Drum diameter	
Standard	130.0 mm (5.12 inches)
Wear limit	131.0 mm (5.16 inches)*

* Refer to marks cast into the drum (they supersede information printed here)

Wheels and tires

Tire pressures	See Chapter 1
Tire tread depth	see Chapter 1
Axle runout limit (front and rear)	0.2 mm (0.008 inch)
Wheel out-of-round and lateral runout limit (front and rear)	2.0 mm (0.08 inch)

Torque specifications

Front axle	
1986 through 1989	55 to 70 Nm (40 to 50 ft-lbs)
1000 and 1001	80 to 93 Nm (58 to 67 ft-lbs)
1992 through 1994	87 Nm (63 ft-lbs)
1995 on	90 Nm (65 ft-lbs)
Front axle holder nuts (1986 through 1991)	10 to 12 Nm (84 to 108 in-lbs)
Front axle pinch bolts (1992 on)	20 Nm (168 in-lbs)
Rear axle nut	95 Nm (69 ft-lbs)
Front caliper	
Caliper bracket bolts	
1986 through 1988	20 to 30 Nm (14 to 22 ft-lbs)
1989	32 to 36 Nm (23 to 26 ft-lbs)

Torque specifications (continued)

Front caliper (continued)
    1990
        CR250R .... 24 to 30 Nm (17 to 22 ft-lbs) (1)
        CR500R .... 32 to 36 Nm (23 to 26 ft-lbs) (1)
    1991 .... 28 to 34 Nm 20 to 25 ft-lbs) (1)
    1992 on .... 31 Nm (22 ft-lbs) (1)
  Pad retaining pins
    1986 through 1991 .... 15 to 20 Nm (132 to 168 in-lbs)
    1992 on .... 18 Nm (13 ft-lbs)
  Slider pin(s) to bracket
    1986 (upper pin) .... 20 to 25 Nm (14 to 18 ft-lbs)
    1986 (lower pin) .... 15 to 20 Nm (132 to 168 in-lbs)
    1987 through 1994 .... 13 Nm (108 in-lbs) (1)
    1995 and 1996 .... 23 Nm (17 ft-lbs) (1)
    1997 and later CR250R .... Not specified
    1997 and later CR500R .... 23 Nm (17 ft-lbs)
  Slider pin to caliper .... 23 Nm (17 ft-lbs) (1)
Rear caliper
  Pad retaining pins .... 18 Nm (156 in-lbs)
  Pad pin plugs (2001 and earlier) .... 2.5 Nm (22 inch-lbs)
Brake hose master cylinder fitting (1986 through 1991)
  To master cylinder .... 30 to 40 Nm (22 to 29 ft-lbs)
  To brake hose .... 12 to 15 Nm (108 to 132 in-lbs)
Brake hose union bolts
  1986 .... 30 to 40 Nm (22 to 29 ft-lbs) (2)
  1987 and 1988 .... 25 to 35 Nm (18 to 25 ft-lbs) (2)
  1989 on .... 35 Nm (25 ft-lbs) (2)
Front brake disc-to-wheel bolts
  CR250R
    1986 through 1989 .... 14 to 16 Nm (10 to 12 ft-lbs) (1)
    1990 and 1991 .... 40 to 45 Nm (29 to 33 ft-lbs)
    1992 through 1994 .... 20 Nm (168 in-lbs) (1)
    1995 on .... 16 Nm (144 in-lbs) (1)
  CR500R
    1986 through 1989 .... 14 to 16 Nm (120 to 144 in-lbs) (1)
    1990 and 1991 .... 40 to 45 Nm (29 to 33 ft-lbs) (1)
    1992 through 1994 .... 20 Nm (168 in-lbs) (1)
    1995 on .... 16 Nm (144 in-lbs) (1)
Front brake disc cover bolts (1995 on) .... 13 Nm (108 in-lbs) (1)
Rear brake disc-to-wheel bolts/nuts
  1987 through 1989 .... 14 to 16 Nm (120 to 144 in-lbs) (1)
  1990 through 2001 .... 43 Nm (31 ft-lbs) (1)
  2002 and later .... 16 Nm (144 inch-lbs)
Rear drum brake arm pinch bolt .... Not specified
Front master cylinder
  Mounting bolts .... 10 Nm (84 in-lbs)
  Brake lever pivot bolt
    CR250R
      1986 through 1996 .... Not specified
      1997 through 2001 .... 6 Nm (52 inch-lbs)
    CR500R
      2002 through 2004 .... Not specified
      2005 and later .... 6 Nm (52 inch-lbs)
  Brake lever pivot bolt locknut
    CR250R
      1986 .... Not specified
      1987 through 1991 .... 8 to 12 Nm (72 to 108 in-lbs)
      1992 through 1996 .... Not specified
      1997 through 2001 .... 6 Nm (52 inch-lbs)
      2002 through 2004 .... Not specified
      2005 and later .... 1 Nm (8.4 inch-lbs)
    CR500R
      1986 through 1996 .... Not specified
      1992 on .... 10 Nm (84 in-lbs)
Rear master cylinder mounting bolts .... 15 Nm (132 in-lbs)
Pedal pivot bolt
  2003 and earlier .... 26 Nm (20 ft-lbs)
  2004 .... 25 Nm (19 ft-lbs)
  2005 and later .... 36 Nm (27 ft-lbs)

1. Apply non-permanent thread locking agent to the threads.
2. Use new sealing washers on each side of the bolt.

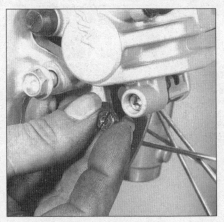

2.3a Unscrew the pad pin plug; it's at the bottom of the front caliper . . .

2.3b . . . and at the rear of the rear caliper

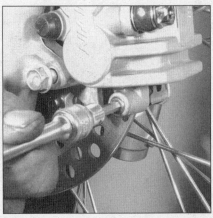

2.4a Unscrew the pad retaining pin; this is a front caliper . . .

1 General information

The front wheel on all motorcycles covered by this manual is equipped with a hydraulic disc brake using a pin slider caliper. The front caliper has dual pistons. The rear wheel on 1986 models is equipped with a drum brake. The rear wheel on all other models is equipped with a hydraulic disc brake using a single-piston pin slider caliper. **Caution:** *Disc brake components rarely require disassembly. Do not disassemble components unless absolutely necessary. If any hydraulic brake line connection in the system is loosened, the entire system should be disassembled, drained, cleaned and then properly filled and bled upon reassembly. Do not use solvents on internal brake components. Solvents will cause seals to swell and distort. Use only clean brake fluid or alcohol for cleaning. Use care when working with brake fluid as it can injure your eyes and it will damage painted surfaces and plastic parts.*

2.4b . . . and this is a rear caliper

2 Brake pads - replacement

Warning: *The dust created by the brake system is harmful to your health. Never blow it out with compressed air and don't inhale any of it. An approved filtering mask should be worn when working on the brakes.*

Removal
Refer to illustrations 2.3a, 2.3b, 2.4a, 2.4b, 2.5a and 2.5b
1   Support the bike securely upright.

2   The caliper doesn't need to be removed for pad replacement.
3   Unscrew the plug that covers the pad retaining pin **(see illustrations)**.
4   Unscrew the pad retaining pin with an Allen wrench **(see illustrations)**.
5   Pull the pads out of the caliper **(see illustrations)**.

Inspection
Refer to illustrations 2.6a, 2.6b, 2.6c and 2.6d
6   Inspect the pad spring and the steel shield that protects the cali-

2.5a Pull out the pad retaining pin (arrow) and lift out the brake pad farthest from the piston . . .

2.5b . . . then pull the pin out the rest of the way and remove the remaining pad

2.6a The front caliper's pad spring fits under the pad pin like this . . .

2.6b . . . and the rear caliper's pad spring fits like this

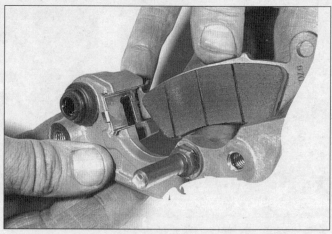

2.6c The front pads ride on the steel shield in the caliper bracket . . .

2.6d . . . there's a similar shield on the rear caliper bracket

3.2 Unscrew the union bolt (right arrow) if you're planning to remove the caliper for overhaul; remove the mounting bolts to (left arrows) to detach the caliper from the fork leg

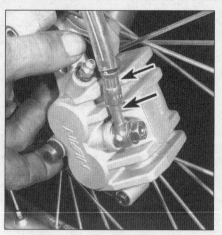

3.3 The hose can be left connected if you're removing the caliper for access to other components; on installation, be sure the brake hose fits in the notches (arrows)

per bracket **(see illustrations)**. Replace the spring or shield it if it's rusted or damaged.

7   Refer to Chapter 1 and inspect the pads.

8   Check the condition of the brake disc (see Section 4). If it's in need of machining or replacement, follow the procedure in that Section to remove it. If it's okay, deglaze it with sandpaper or emery cloth, using a swirling motion.

Installation

9   Remove the cover from the master cylinder reservoir and siphon out some fluid. Push the piston(s) into the caliper as far as possible, while checking the master cylinder reservoir to make sure it doesn't overflow. If you can't depress the pistons with thumb pressure, try using a C-clamp. If the pistons stick, remove the caliper and overhaul it as described in Section 3.

10   Install the spring, caliper shield and new pads. Coat the threads of the retaining pin(s) with non-permanent thread locking agent and install the retaining pins. Tighten the retaining pins to the torque listed in this Chapter's Specifications.

11   Install the plug over the retaining pin and tighten it to the torque listed in this Chapter's Specifications.

12   Operate the brake lever or pedal several times to bring the pads into contact with the disc. Check the operation of the brake carefully before riding the motorcycle.

3   Brake caliper - removal, overhaul and installation

Warning: *If a caliper indicates the need for an overhaul (usually due to leaking fluid or sticky operation), all old brake fluid must be flushed from the system. Also, the dust created by the brake system is harmful to your health. Never blow it out with compressed air and don't inhale any of it. An approved filtering mask should be worn when working on the brakes. Do not, under any circumstances, use petroleum-based solvents to clean brake parts. Use clean brake fluid or denatured alcohol only!*

Note: *If you are removing the caliper only to remove the front forks or rear swingarm, don't disconnect the hose from the caliper.*

Removal

1   Support the bike securely upright. **Note:** *If you're planning to disassemble the caliper, read through the overhaul procedure, paying particular attention to the steps involved in removing the pistons with compressed air. If you don't have access to an air compressor, you can use the bike's hydraulic system to force the pistons out instead. To do this, remove the pads and pump the brake lever or pedal. If one front caliper piston comes out before the other, push it back into its bore and hold it in with a C-clamp while pumping the brake lever to remove the remaining piston.*

3.4a These are the caliper shield bolts on early models . . .

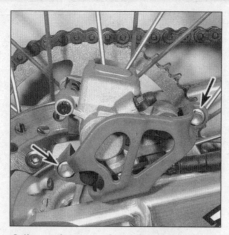

3.4b . . . these are the caliper shield bolts on late models

3.5 Slide the caliper backward off its rail on the swingarm

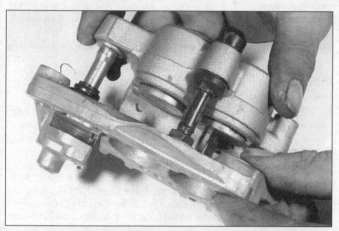

3.8 Slide the caliper off the bracket

3.9a Front caliper piston and seal details (one of two pistons shown); the metal cap on the end of the piston (arrow) faces out of the bore

Front caliper

Refer to illustrations 3.2 and 3.3

2 **Note:** *Remember, if you're just removing the caliper to remove the forks, ignore this step.* Disconnect the brake hose from the caliper. Remove the brake hose banjo fitting bolt and separate the hose from the caliper **(see illustration)**. Discard the sealing washers. Plug the end of the hose or wrap a plastic bag tightly around it to prevent excessive fluid loss and contamination.

3 Unscrew the caliper mounting bolts and lift it off the fork leg, being careful not to strain or twist the brake hose if it's still connected **(see illustration)**.

Rear caliper

Refer to illustrations 3.4a, 3.4b and 3.5

4 If you're planning to overhaul the caliper, remove its protective bracket and loosen the brake hose union bolt (it's easier to loosen the bolts while the caliper is mounted on the bike) **(see illustrations)**.

5 Refer to Section 11 and remove the rear wheel. Slide the caliper bracket backward off its rail **(see illustration)**. Support the caliper so it doesn't hang by the brake hose.

6 Disconnect the brake hose from the caliper. Remove the brake hose banjo fitting bolt and separate the hose from the caliper. Discard the sealing washers. Plug the end of the hose or wrap a plastic bag tightly around it to prevent excessive fluid loss and contamination.

Overhaul

Refer to illustrations 3.8, 3.9a, 3.9b, 3.13, 3.16a, 3.16b and 3.16c

7 Remove the brake pads and anti-rattle spring from the caliper (see Section 2, if necessary). Clean the exterior of the caliper with

denatured alcohol or brake system cleaner.

8 Slide the caliper off the bracket **(see illustration)**. One pin will stay in the bracket and the other in the caliper.

9 Pack a shop rag into the space that holds the brake pads. Use compressed air, directed into the caliper fluid inlet, to remove the piston(s) **(see illustrations)**. Use only enough air pressure to ease the

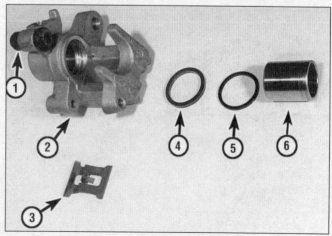

3.9b Rear caliper details

1	Pin boot	3	Pad spring	5 Piston seal
2	Caliper body	4	Dust seal	6 Piston

3.13 Fit the seals all the way into their grooves

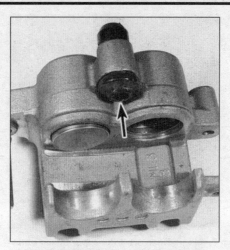

3.16a Install the boot in the front caliper with its wide end facing the same direction as the pistons (arrow)

3.16b Install the boot in the front caliper bracket with its wide end facing the same direction as the pin (right arrow) and install the spring in the bracket notch (left arrow)

piston(s) out of the bore. If a piston is blown out forcefully, even with the rag in place, it may be damaged. **Warning:** *Never place your fingers in front of the piston in an attempt to catch or protect it when applying compressed air, as serious injury could occur.*

10   Using a wood or plastic tool, remove the piston seals. Metal tools may cause bore damage.

11   Clean the pistons and the bores with denatured alcohol, clean brake fluid or brake system cleaner and blow dry them with filtered, unlubricated compressed air. Inspect the surfaces of the pistons for nicks and burrs and loss of plating. Check the caliper bores, too. If surface defects are present, the caliper must be replaced.

12   If the caliper is in bad shape, the master cylinder should also be checked.

13   Lubricate the piston seals with clean brake fluid and install them in their grooves in the caliper bore **(see illustration)**. Make sure they seat completely and aren't twisted.

14   Lubricate the dust seals with clean brake fluid and install them in their grooves, making sure they seat correctly.

15   Lubricate the piston (both pistons on front calipers) with clean brake fluid and install it into the caliper bore. Using your thumbs, push the piston all the way in, making sure it doesn't get cocked in the bore.

16   Pull the old pin boots out of the caliper and bracket. Coat new ones with silicone grease and install them, making sure they seat completely **(see illustrations)**.

17   Make sure the shields are in position on the caliper brackets **(see illustrations 3.16b and 3.16c)**.

Installation

Refer to illustration 3.18

18   Installation is the reverse of the removal steps, with the following additions:

a) *Apply silicone grease to the slider pins on the caliper bracket and caliper.*

b) *Space the pads apart so the disc will fit between them.*

c) *Use new sealing washers on the brake hose fitting. If you're working on a front caliper, position the brake hose fitting in the caliper notches **(see illustration 3.3)**. If you're working on a rear caliper, position the brake hose against the stop on the swingarm **(see illustration)**.*

d) *Tighten the front caliper mounting bolts, rear caliper shield bolts and brake line union bolt to the torque listed in this Chapter's Specifications.*

e) *If you're working on a rear caliper, adjust chain slack (see Chapter 1).*

19   Fill the master cylinder with the recommended brake fluid (see Chapter 1) and bleed the system (see Section 10). Check for leaks.

20   Check the operation of the brakes carefully before riding the motorcycle.

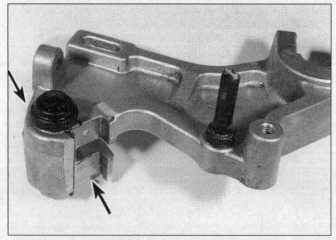

3.16c Install the boot in the rear caliper bracket with its wide end facing the same direction as the pin (left arrow) and install the spring in the bracket notch (right arrow)

3.18 Be sure the brake hose fits in the caliper bracket notch (arrow) when the union bolt is tightened

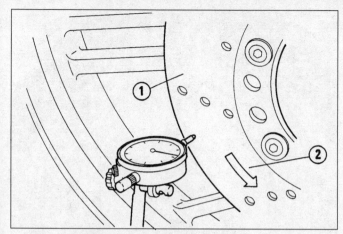

4.3 Set up a dial indicator against the brake disc (1) and turn the disc in its normal direction of rotation (2) to measure runout

4.4 Marks on the disc indicate the minimum thickness and direction of rotation

A *Brake disc mounting bolts*
B *Wheel bearing collar*
C *Wheel bearing cover (some models)*
D *Minimum thickness marks*

4   Brake disc(s) - inspection, removal and installation

Inspection

Refer to illustrations 4.3 and 4.4

1   Support the bike securely upright. Place a jack beneath the bike and raise the wheel being checked off the ground. Be sure the bike is securely supported so it can't be knocked over.

2   Visually inspect the surface of the disc(s) for score marks and other damage. Light scratches are normal after use and won't affect brake operation, but deep grooves and heavy score marks will reduce braking efficiency and accelerate pad wear. If the discs are badly grooved they must be machined or replaced.

3   To check disc runout, mount a dial indicator to a fork leg or the swingarm, with the plunger on the indicator touching the surface of the disc about 1/2-inch from the outer edge **(see illustration)**. Slowly turn the wheel and watch the indicator needle, comparing your reading with the limit listed in this Chapter's Specifications. If the runout is greater than allowed, check the hub bearings for play (see Chapter 1). If the bearings are worn, replace them and repeat this check. If the disc runout is still excessive, the disc will have to be replaced.

4   The disc must not be machined or allowed to wear down to a thickness less than the minimum allowable thickness, listed in this Chapter's Specifications. The thickness of the disc can be checked with a micrometer. If the thickness of the disc is less than the minimum allowable, it must be replaced. The minimum thickness is also stamped into the disc **(see illustrations)**.

Removal

Refer to illustration 4.6

5   Remove the wheel (see Section 11). **Caution**: *Don't lay the wheel down and allow it to rest on the disc - the disc could become warped.* Set the wheel on wood blocks so the disc doesn't support the weight of the wheel.

6   Mark the relationship of the disc to the wheel, so it can be installed in the same position. Remove the hex head or Allen head bolts that retain the disc to the wheel **(see illustration 4.4 and the accompanying illustration)**. Loosen the bolts a little at a time, in a criss-cross pattern, to avoid distorting the disc. **Note**: *Allen head bolts must be replaced with new ones on installation.*

Installation

7   Position the disc on the wheel, aligning the previously applied matchmarks (if you're reinstalling the original disc). On models so equipped, make sure the arrow (stamped on the disc) marking the direction of rotation is pointing in the proper direction **(see illustration 4.4)**.

8   If the brake disc is secured by Allen head bolts, use new ones. Apply a non-hardening thread locking compound to the threads of the nuts or bolts. Install the nuts or bolts, tightening them a little at a time in a criss-cross pattern, until the torque listed in this Chapter's Specifications is reached. Clean off all grease from the brake disc using acetone or brake system cleaner.

9   Install the wheel.

10   Operate the brake lever or pedal several times to bring the pads into contact with the disc. Check the operation of the brakes carefully before riding the motorcycle.

5   Brake drum and shoes - removal, inspection and installation

Warning: *The dust created by the brake system is harmful to your health. Never blow it out with compressed air and don't inhale any of it. An approved filtering mask should be worn when working on the brakes.*

4.6 The rear brake disc is secured to the hub by Allen bolts (arrows)

5.2 Lift the brake panel out of the drum

5.3 The maximum diameter is cast inside the brake drum

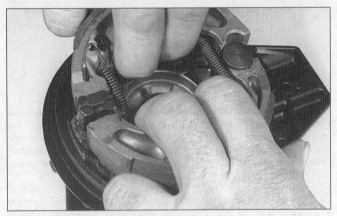

5.6 Spread the shoes and fold them into a V to release the spring tension

Removal

Refer to illustration 5.2

1   Remove the wheel (see Section 11).
2   Lift the brake panel out of the wheel **(see illustration)**.

Inspection

Refer to illustrations 5.3, 5.6, 5.9, 5.10, 5.11a and 5.11b

3   Check the brake drum for wear or damage. Measure the diameter at several points with a drum micrometer (or have this done by a Honda dealer or other qualified repair shop). If the measurements are uneven (indicating that the drum is out-of-round) or if there are scratches deep enough to snag a fingernail, replace the drum. The drum must also be replaced if the diameter is greater than that cast inside the drum **(see illustration)**. Honda recommends against machining the brake drums.
4   Check the linings for wear, damage and signs of contamination from road dirt or water. If the linings are visibly defective, replace them.
5   Measure the thickness of the lining material (just the lining material, not the metal backing) and compare with the value listed in the Chapter 1 Specifications. Replace the shoes if the material is worn to the minimum or less.
6   To remove the shoes, fold them toward each other to release the spring tension and lift them off the brake panel **(see illustration)**.
7   Check the ends of the shoes where they contact the brake cam and anchor pin. Replace the shoes if there's visible wear.
8   Check the brake cam and anchor pin for wear and damage. The brake cam can be replaced separately; the brake panel must be replaced if the anchor pin is unserviceable.
9   Look for alignment marks on the brake arm and anchor pin **(see illustration)**. Make your own if they aren't visible.
10   Remove the pinch bolt and nut and pull the brake arm off the cam **(see illustration)**.
11   Check the brake cam dust seal for wear and damage **(see illustration)**. To replace it, pry it out of the brake panel and tap in a new one using a socket or seal driver the same diameter as the seal **(see illustration)**.

5.9 Look for alignment marks on the brake arm and cam (arrows); make your own marks if you can't see any

5.10 Remove the pinch bolt and nut and take the brake arm off the cam

5.11a Replace the brake cam seal if it's worn or damaged

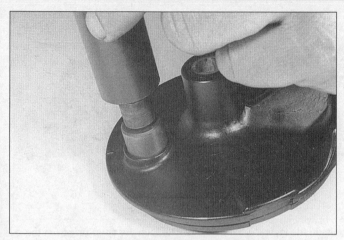

5.11b Pry out the old seal, then press a new one in with a socket the same diameter as the seal

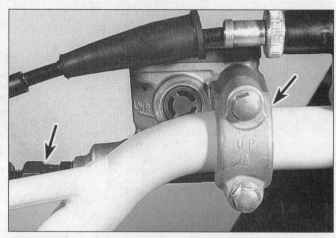

6.5 On 1986 through 1991 models, unscrew the fitting (left arrow) to disconnect the hose from the master cylinder; on installation, be sure the UP mark on the clamp is upright and align the split in the clamp with the handlebar punch mark (right arrow)

Installation

12 Apply high temperature brake grease to the brake cam, the anchor pin and the ends of the springs.
13 Install the cam through the dust seal.
14 Install the brake arm on the cam, aligning the punch marks. Tighten the nut and bolt to the torque listed in this Chapter's Specifications.
15 Hook the ends of the springs to the shoes. Position the shoes in a V on the brake panel, then fold them down into position. Make sure the ends of the shoes fit correctly on the cam and the anchor pin.
16 The remainder of installation is the reverse of the removal steps.

6 Front brake master cylinder - removal, overhaul and installation

1 If the master cylinder is leaking fluid, or if the lever doesn't produce a firm feel when the brake is applied, and bleeding the brakes doesn't help, master cylinder overhaul is recommended. Before disassembling the master cylinder, read through the entire procedure and make sure that you have the correct rebuild kit. Also, you will need some new, clean brake fluid of the recommended type, some clean rags and internal snap-ring pliers. **Note:** *To prevent damage to the paint from spilled brake fluid, always cover the gas tank when working on the master cylinder.*
2 **Caution:** *Disassembly, overhaul and reassembly of the brake master cylinder must be done in a spotlessly clean work area to avoid contamination and possible failure of the brake hydraulic system components.*

Removal

Refer to illustrations 6.5 and 6.6
3 Place rags beneath the master cylinder to protect the paint in case of brake fluid spills.
4 Brake fluid will run out of the upper brake hose during this step, so either have a container handy to place the end of the hose in, or have a plastic bag and rubber band handy to cover the end of the hose. The objective is to prevent excess loss of brake fluid, fluid spills and system contamination.
5 On 1986 through 1991 models, disconnect the brake hose at the caliper, then unscrew the brake hose fitting from the master cylinder **(see illustration)**.
6 On 1992 and later models, remove the banjo fitting bolt and sealing washers from the master cylinder **(see illustration)**.
7 Remove the master cylinder mounting bolts **(see illustration 6.5)**. Take the master cylinder off the handlebar.

Overhaul

Refer to illustrations 6.9a, 6.9b, 6.10a, 6.10b, 6.11a, 6.11b and 6.13
8 Remove the master cylinder cover, retainer (if equipped) and diaphragm (see Chapter 1).
9 Remove the locknut from the underside of the lever pivot bolt, then unscrew the bolt **(see illustrations)**. Remove the lever pivot cover (it's held on by the pivot bolt).

6.6 On 1992 and later models, remove the union bolt and sealing washers from the banjo fitting; use new sealing washers on installation

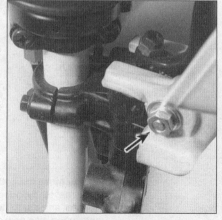

6.9a Remove the locknut (arrow) . . .

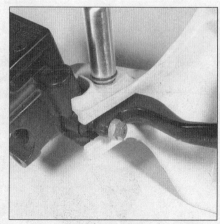

6.9b . . . and unscrew the pivot bolt to detach the lever

6.10a Remove the lever and spring from the master cylinder

6.10b . . . the spring fits in the lever like this

6.11a Remove the snap-ring from the master cylinder bore

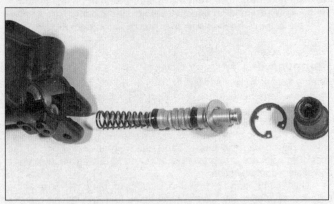

6.11b Remove the piston assembly from the bore

6.13 Make sure the baffle plate is securely retained in the bottom of the reservoir

10   The lever is equipped with a spring **(see illustrations)**. This doesn't have to be removed to remove the hydraulic components, but make sure it doesn't get lost.

11   Using snap-ring pliers, remove the snap-ring and slide out the piston assembly and the spring **(see illustrations)**. Lay the parts out in the proper order to prevent confusion during reassembly.

12   Clean all of the parts with brake system cleaner (available at auto parts stores), isopropyl alcohol or clean brake fluid. **Caution:** *Do not, under any circumstances, use a petroleum-based solvent to clean brake parts. If compressed air is available, use it to dry the parts thoroughly (make sure it's filtered and unlubricated).* Check the master cyl-

inder bore and piston for corrosion, scratches, nicks and score marks. If damage or wear can be seen, the master cylinder must be replaced with a new one. If the master cylinder is in poor condition, then the caliper should be checked as well.

13   If there's a baffle plate in the bottom of the reservoir, make sure it's securely held by its retainer **(see illustration)**.

14   Honda supplies a new piston in its rebuild kits. If the cup seals are

6.18 The pivot cover fits like this

7.4 Remove the cotter pin and clevis pin (lower arrow) to detach the master cylinder from the pedal; remove the mounting bolts (center arrows) to detach the master cylinder from the frame; on installation, use new sealing washers on the union bolt and be sure the neck of the fluid hose fits between the stoppers (upper arrow, 2001 and earlier shown)

7.6 The fluid reservoir is secured by a single bolt

7.7a Remove the snap-ring . . .

7.7b . . . then work the fluid feed fitting free of its bore and remove the O-ring

not installed on the new piston, install them, making sure the lips face away from the lever end of the piston **(see illustration 6.11b)**. Use the new piston regardless of the condition of the old one.

15   Before reassembling the master cylinder, soak the piston and the rubber cup seals in clean brake fluid for ten or fifteen minutes. Lubricate the master cylinder bore with clean brake fluid, then carefully insert the piston and related parts in the reverse order of disassembly. Make sure the lips on the cup seals do not turn inside out when they are slipped into the bore.

16   Depress the piston, then install the snap-ring (make sure the snap-ring is properly seated in the groove with the sharp edge facing out) **(see illustration 6.11a)**. Install the rubber dust boot (make sure the lip is seated properly in the piston groove).

17   Install the brake lever, pivot cover and pivot bolt. Tighten the pivot bolt locknut.

Installation

Refer to illustration 6.18

18   Installation is the reverse of the removal steps, with the following additions:

a) *Attach the master cylinder to the handlebar. Align the upper gap between the master cylinder and clamp with the punch mark on the handlebar* **(see illustration 6.5)**.

b) *Make sure the arrow and the word UP on the master cylinder clamp are pointing up, then tighten the bolts to the torque listed in this Chapter's Specifications (see illustration 6.5).*

c) *Use new sealing washers at the brake hose banjo fitting. Tighten the union bolt to the torque listed in this Chapter's Specifications.*

d) *Install the pivot cover over the lever and pivot* **(see illustration)**.

19   Refer to Section 10 and bleed the air from the system.

7   Rear brake master cylinder - removal, overhaul and installation

1   If the master cylinder is leaking fluid, or if the pedal does not produce a firm feel when the brake is applied, and bleeding the brake does not help, master cylinder overhaul is recommended. Before disassembling the master cylinder, read through the entire procedure and make sure that you have the correct rebuild kit. Also, you will need some new, clean brake fluid of the recommended type, some clean rags and internal snap-ring pliers.

2   **Caution:** *Disassembly, overhaul and reassembly of the brake master cylinder must be done in a spotlessly clean work area to avoid contamination and possible failure of the brake hydraulic system components.*

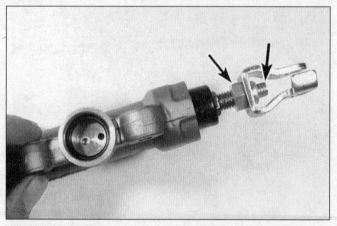

7.8 Write down the number of exposed threads in the clevis (right arrow), then loosen the locknut (left arrow) and unscrew the locknut and clevis from the pushrod

Removal

Refer to illustrations 7.4 and 7.6

3   Support the bike securely upright.

4   Remove the cotter pin from the clevis pin on the master cylinder pushrod **(see illustration)**. Remove the clevis pin.

5   Have a container and some rags ready to catch spilling brake fluid. Using a six-point box wrench, unscrew the banjo fitting bolt from the top of the master cylinder. Discard the sealing washers on either side of the fitting.

6   Remove the two master cylinder mounting bolts and detach the cylinder from the bracket. Pull the master cylinder out from behind the bracket, squeeze the fluid feed hose clamp with pliers and slide the clamp up the hose. Disconnect the hose from the fitting and take the master cylinder out. If necessary, remove the reservoir mounting bolt and detach it from the frame **(see illustration)**.

Overhaul

Refer to illustrations 7.7a, 7.7b, 7.8, 7.9, 7.10a, 7.10b and 7.14

7   Using a pair of snap-ring pliers, remove the snap-ring from the fluid inlet fitting and detach the fitting from the master cylinder. Remove the O-ring from the bore **(see illustrations)**.

8   Count the number of exposed threads on the end of the pushrod inside the clevis **(see illustration)**. Write this number down for use on assembly. Hold the clevis with a pair of pliers and loosen the locknut, then unscrew the clevis and locknut from the pushrod.

7.9 Take the dust boot off the pushrod

7.10a Remove the snap-ring from the master cylinder bore and withdraw the piston assembly and spring

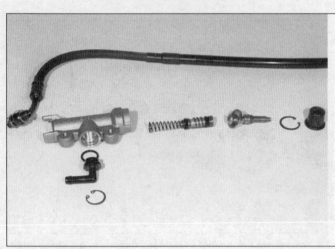

7.10b Rear master cylinder details (2001 and earlier shown; later models similar)

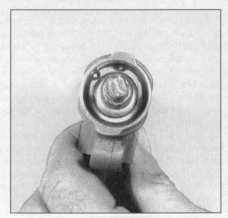

7.14 Make sure the snap-ring is securely seated in its groove

9   Carefully remove the rubber dust boot from the pushrod **(see illustration)**.
10   Depress the pushrod and, using snap-ring pliers, remove the snap-ring **(see illustration)**. Slide out the piston, the cup seal and spring. Lay the parts out in the proper order to prevent confusion during reassembly **(see illustration)**.
11   Clean all of the parts with isopropyl alcohol or clean brake fluid. **Caution:** *Do not, under any circumstances, use a petroleum-based solvent to clean brake parts. If compressed air is available, use it to dry the parts thoroughly (make sure it's filtered and unlubricated).* Check the master cylinder bore for corrosion, scratches, nicks and score marks. If damage is evident, the master cylinder must be replaced with a new one. If the master cylinder is in poor condition, then the caliper should be checked as well.
12   Honda supplies a new piston in its rebuild kits. If the cup seals are not installed on the new piston, install them, making sure the lips face away from the lever end of the piston **(see illustration 7.10b)**. Use the new piston regardless of the condition of the old one.
13   Before reassembling the master cylinder, soak the piston and the rubber cup seals in clean brake fluid for ten or fifteen minutes. Lubricate the master cylinder bore with clean brake fluid, then carefully insert the parts in the reverse order of disassembly. Make sure the lips on the cup seals do not turn inside out when they are slipped into the bore.
14   Lubricate the end of the pushrod with PBC (poly butyl cuprysil) grease, or silicone grease designed for brake applications, and install the pushrod and stop washer into the cylinder bore. Depress the pushrod, then install the snap-ring (make sure the snap-ring is properly seated in the groove with the sharp edge facing out) **(see illustration)**. Install the rubber dust boot (make sure the lip is seated properly in the

groove in the piston stop nut).
15   Install the locknut and clevis to the end of the pushrod, leaving the same number of exposed threads inside the clevis as was written down during removal. Tighten the locknut. This will ensure the brake pedal will be positioned correctly.
16   Install the feed hose fitting, using a new O-ring. Install the snap-ring, making sure it seats properly in its groove.

Installation
17   Install the fluid reservoir if it was removed. Connect the fluid feed hose to the fitting on the master cylinder and secure it with the clamp.
18   Position the master cylinder on the frame and install the bolts, tightening them securely.
19   Connect the banjo fitting to the top of the master cylinder, using new sealing washers on each side of the fitting. Tighten the banjo fitting bolt to the torque listed in this Chapter's Specifications.
20   Connect the clevis to the brake pedal and secure the clevis pin with a new cotter pin.
21   Fill the fluid reservoir with the specified fluid (see Chapter 1) and bleed the system following the procedure in Section 10.
22   Check the position of the brake pedal (see Chapter 1) and adjust it if necessary. Check the operation of the brakes carefully before riding the motorcycle.

8   Brake pedal - removal and installation

Refer to illustrations 8.2 and 8.4
1   Support the bike securely upright so it can't be knocked over dur-

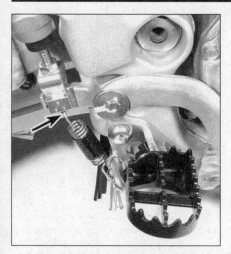

8.2 Unhook the brake pedal spring from the pedal (arrow) . . .

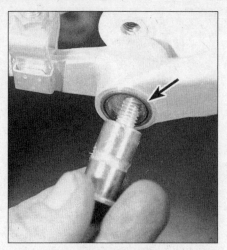

8.4 . . . and unscrew the pivot to remove the pedal (arrow)

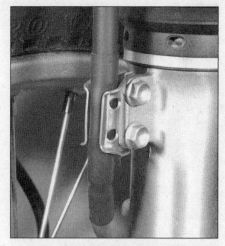

9.4a The front brake hose is secured to the fork leg by a clamp

ing this procedure.

2   Unhook the pedal return spring from the frame **(see illustration)**.

3   Remove the cotter pin and clevis pin to detach the master cylinder pushrod from the pedal.

4   Unscrew the brake pedal pivot shaft and remove the pedal **(see illustration)**.

5   Inspect the pedal pivot shaft seals. If they're worn, damaged or appear to have been leaking, pry them out and press in new ones.

6   Installation is the reverse of the removal steps, with the following additions:

a) *Lubricate the pedal shaft or pivot arm seal lips and the pivot hole with multi-purpose grease.*

b) *Tighten the pedal pivot shaft to the torque listed in this Chapter's Specifications.*

c) *Use a new cotter pin.*

d) *Refer to Chapter 1 and adjust brake pedal height (all models).*

9   Brake hoses and lines - inspection and replacement

Inspection

1   Once every 2.5 operating hours or before every race, check the condition of the brake hoses.

2   Twist and flex the rubber hoses while looking for cracks, bulges and seeping fluid. Check extra carefully around the areas where the hoses connect with the metal fittings, as these are common areas for hose failure.

Replacement

Refer to illustrations 9.4a and 9.4b

3   The pressurized brake hoses have banjo fittings on each end of the hose. The fluid feed hose that connects the rear master cylinder reservoir to the master cylinder is secured by spring clamps.

4   Cover the surrounding area with plenty of rags and unscrew the banjo bolt on either end of the hose. Detach the hose or line from any clips that may be present and remove the hose **(see illustrations)**.

5   Position the new hose or line, making sure it isn't twisted or otherwise strained. On hoses equipped with banjo fittings, make sure the metal tube portion of the banjo fitting is located against the stop on the component it's connected to, if equipped. Install the banjo bolts, using new sealing washers on both sides of the fittings, and tighten them to the torque listed in this Chapter's Specifications.

6   Flush the old brake fluid from the system, refill the system with the recommended fluid (see Chapter 1) and bleed the air from the system (see Section 10). Check the operation of the brakes carefully before riding the motorcycle.

9.4b The rear brake hose is secured to the swingarm by one or more clips; use non-permanent thread locking agent on the threads of the clip screws

10   Brake system bleeding

Refer to illustrations 10.5a and 10.5b

1   Bleeding the brake is simply the process of removing all the air bubbles from the brake fluid reservoir, the lines and the brake caliper. Bleeding is necessary whenever a brake system hydraulic connection is loosened, when a component or hose is replaced, or when the master cylinder or caliper is overhauled. Leaks in the system may also allow air to enter, but leaking brake fluid will reveal their presence and warn you of the need for repair.

2   To bleed the brake, you will need some new, clean brake fluid of the recommended type (see Chapter 1), a length of clear vinyl or plastic tubing, a small container partially filled with clean brake fluid, some rags and a wrench to fit the brake caliper bleeder valve.

3   Cover the fuel tank and other painted components to prevent damage in the event that brake fluid is spilled.

4   Remove the reservoir cover or cap and slowly pump the brake lever or pedal a few times, until no air bubbles can be seen floating up from the holes at the bottom of the reservoir. Doing this bleeds the air from the master cylinder end of the line. Reinstall the reservoir cover or cap.

5   Attach one end of the clear vinyl or plastic tubing to the brake caliper bleeder valve and submerge the other end in the brake fluid in

10.5a Pull the rubber cap off the bleed valve (front caliper shown) . . .

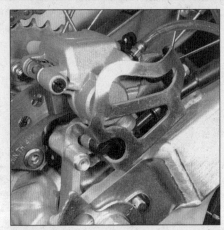

10.5b . . . and connect a clear plastic hose to the valve (rear caliper shown)

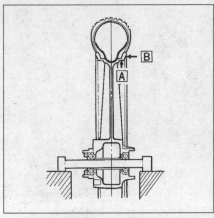

11.2 Check the wheel for out-of-round (A) and lateral movement (B)

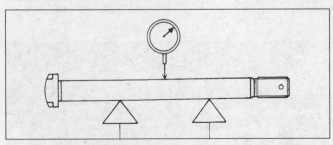

11.5 Check the axle for runout using a dial indicator and V-blocks

11.7a 1986 through 1989 models have an axle holder on the right fork leg; the UP mark must be upright when it's installed . . .

the container **(see illustrations)**.

6   Check the fluid level in the reservoir. Do not allow the fluid level to drop below the lower mark during the bleeding process.

7   Carefully pump the brake lever or pedal three or four times and hold it while opening the caliper bleeder valve. When the valve is opened, brake fluid will flow out of the caliper into the clear tubing and the lever will move toward the handlebar or the pedal will move down.

8   Retighten the bleeder valve, then release the brake lever or pedal gradually. Repeat the process until no air bubbles are visible in the brake fluid leaving the caliper and the lever or pedal is firm when applied. Remember to add fluid to the reservoir as the level drops. Use only new, clean brake fluid of the recommended type. Never reuse the fluid lost during bleeding.

9   Be sure to check the fluid level in the master cylinder reservoir frequently.

10   Replace the reservoir cover or cap, wipe up any spilled brake fluid and check the entire system for leaks. **Note:** *If bleeding is difficult, it may be necessary to let the brake fluid in the system stabilize for a few hours (it may be aerated). Repeat the bleeding procedure when the tiny bubbles in the system have settled out.*

---

11   Wheels - inspection, removal and installation

Inspection

Refer to illustrations 11.2 and 11.5

1   Clean the wheels thoroughly to remove mud and dirt that may interfere with the inspection procedure or mask defects. Make a general check of the wheels and tires as described in Chapter 1.

2   Support the motorcycle securely upright with the wheel to be checked in the air, then attach a dial indicator to the fork slider or the swingarm and position the stem against the side of the rim **(see illustration)**. Spin the wheel slowly and check the side-to-side (axial) runout of the rim, then compare your readings with the value listed in this Chapter's Specifications. In order to accurately check radial runout

with the dial indicator, the wheel would have to be removed from the machine and the tire removed from the wheel. With the axle clamped in a vise, the wheel can be rotated to check the runout.

3   An easier, though slightly less accurate, method is to attach a stiff wire pointer to the outer fork tube or the swingarm and position the end a fraction of an inch from the wheel (where the wheel and tire join). If the wheel is true, the distance from the pointer to the rim will be constant as the wheel is rotated. Repeat the procedure to check the runout of the rear wheel. **Note:** *If wheel runout is excessive, refer to the appropriate Section in this Chapter and check the wheel bearings very carefully before replacing the wheel.*

4   The wheels should also be visually inspected for cracks, flat spots on the rim and other damage. Individual spokes can be replaced. If other damage is evident, the wheel will have to be replaced with a new one. Never attempt to repair a damaged wheel.

5   Before installing the wheel, check the axle for straightness. If the axle is corroded, first remove the corrosion with fine emery cloth. Set the axle on V-blocks and check it for runout with a dial indicator **(see illustration)**. If the axle exceeds the maximum allowable runout limit listed in this Chapter's Specifications, it must be replaced.

Removal

Front wheel

Refer to illustrations 11.7a, 11.7b, 11.8, 11.9, 11.10a and 11.10b

6   Support the bike from below with a jack beneath the engine. Securely prop the bike upright so it can't fall over when the wheel is removed.

7   If you're working on a 1986 through 1991 model, remove the axle holder from the right fork leg (1986 through 1989) or both fork legs (1990 and 1991) **(see illustrations)**.

11.7b 1990 and later models also have an axle holder on the left fork leg

11.8 On 1992 and later models, loosen the axle pinch bolts . . .

11.9 . . . then hold the axle so it won't turn and remove the nut from the left side

11.10a Remove the cap (if equipped)

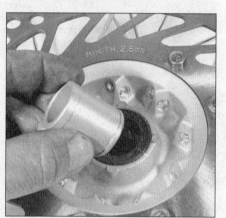

11.10b Remove the wheel bearing collars, noting which end faces the hub

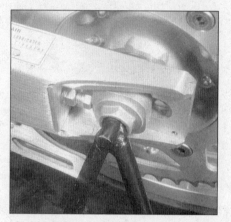

11.14a If the axle has a hex head, hold it with a wrench or socket . . .

8   On 1992 and later models, unscrew the axle pinch bolts **(see illustration)**.
9   If you're working on a 1986 through 1989 model, unscrew the axle from the left fork leg. On all others, hold the axle from turning by placing a socket on the hex, then remove the axle nut from the left side **(see illustration)**.
10   Remove the axle from the right fork leg. Support the wheel and pull the axle out. Lower the wheel away from the motorcycle, sliding the brake disc out from between the pads. Collect the wheel bearing spacers **(see illustrations)**.

Rear wheel

Refer to illustrations 11.14a, 11.14b and 11.14c
11   Support the bike from below with a jack beneath the swingarm. Securely prop the bike upright so it can't fall over when the wheel is removed.
12   If you're working on a drum brake model, remove the rear brake adjuster wingnut from the brake cable (see Chapter 1). Pull the cable out of its pivot and remove the pivot from the brake drum arm. Unbolt the torque link from the brake panel.
13   Loosen the rear axle nut and back off the chain adjusters all the way (see Chapter 1). Disengage the drive chain from the rear sprocket.
14   Hold the axle with a wrench or socket and remove the axle nut and chain adjusters **(see illustrations)**.

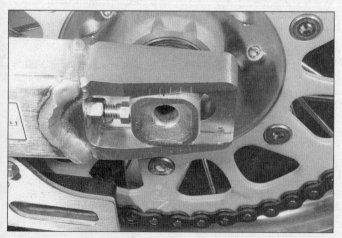

11.14b . . . the axle head on some models fits into a shaped recess on the swingarm, so you don't need to hold the axle

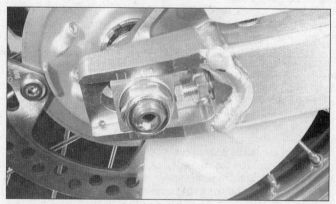

11.14c Remove the axle nut and washer

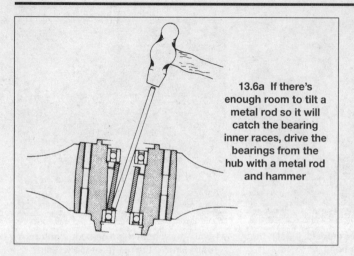

13.6a If there's enough room to tilt a metal rod so it will catch the bearing inner races, drive the bearings from the hub with a metal rod and hammer

13.6b If you can't position a metal rod against the bearings, this tool can be used instead - place the split portion inside the bearing and pass the wedged rod through the hub into the split; tapping on the end of the rod will spread the split portion, locking it to the bearing, so the split portion and bearing can be driven out together

15   Support the wheel and slide it back until the axle clears the swingarm, then lower the wheel away from the motorcycle. Pull the axle out.

Installation

16   Installation is the reverse of the removal steps, with the following additions:

   a) *If you're installing a rear wheel on a drum brake model, connect the brake rod to the arm and the torque rod to the brake panel.*

   b) *If you're working on a front wheel, tighten the axle nut to the torque listed in this Chapter's Specifications, then tighten the holder nuts or pinch bolts to the torque listed in this Chapter's Specifications.*

   c) *If you're working on a rear wheel, tighten the axle nut to the torque listed in this Chapter's Specifications.*

   d) *Refer to Chapter 1 and adjust the rear brake (drum brake models) and drive chain slack.*

12   Wheels - alignment check

1   Misalignment of the wheels, which may be due to a cocked rear wheel or a bent frame or triple clamps, can cause strange and possibly serious handling problems. If the frame or triple clamps are at fault, repair by a frame specialist or replacement with new parts are the only alternatives.

2   To check the alignment you will need an assistant, a length of string or a perfectly straight piece of wood and a ruler graduated in 1/64 inch increments. A plumb bob or other suitable weight will also be required.

3   Support the motorcycle securely upright, then measure the width of both tires at their widest points. Subtract the smaller measurement from the larger measurement, then divide the difference by two. The result is the amount of offset that should exist between the front and rear tires on both sides.

4   If a string is used, have your assistant hold one end of it about half way between the floor and the rear axle, touching the rear sidewall of the tire.

5   Run the other end of the string forward and pull it tight so that it is roughly parallel to the floor. Slowly bring the string into contact with the front sidewall of the rear tire, then turn the front wheel until it is parallel with the string. Measure the distance from the front tire sidewall to the string.

6   Repeat the procedure on the other side of the motorcycle. The distance from the front tire sidewall to the string should be equal on both sides.

7   As was previously pointed out, a perfectly straight length of wood may be substituted for the string. The procedure is the same.

8   If the distance between the string and tire is greater on one side, or if the rear wheel appears to be cocked, refer to Swingarm bearings - check, Chapter 6, and make sure the swingarm is tight.

9   If the front-to-back alignment is correct, the wheels still may be

out of alignment vertically.

10   Using the plumb bob, or other suitable weight, and a length of string, check the rear wheel to make sure it is vertical. To do this, hold the string against the tire upper sidewall and allow the weight to settle just off the floor. When the string touches both the upper and lower tire sidewalls and is perfectly straight, the wheel is vertical. If it is not, place thin spacers under one leg of the centerstand.

11   Once the rear wheel is vertical, check the front wheel in the same manner. If both wheels are not perfectly vertical, the frame and/or major suspension components are bent.

13   Wheel bearings - inspection and maintenance

Front wheel bearings

Refer to illustrations 13.6a, 13.6b, 13.6c and 13.6d

1   Support the bike securely and remove the front wheel (see Section 11).

2   Set the wheel on blocks so as not to allow the weight of the wheel rest on the brake disc.

3   Remove the spacers (if you haven't already done so) from the wheel **(see illustration 4.4a)**. If you're working on a 1989 or a 1992 through 1994 model, remove the left-side bearing cover.

4   Remove the seal or dust cover from the right side of the wheel **(see illustration 11.8)**.

5   Turn the wheel over. Remove the cover and pry the grease seal out of the left side.

6   A common method of removing front wheel bearings is to insert a metal rod (preferably a brass drift punch) through the center of one hub bearing and tap evenly around the inner race of the opposite bearing to drive it from the hub **(see illustration)**. The bearing spacer will also come out. On these motorcycles, it's generally not possible to tilt the rod enough to catch the edge of the opposite bearing's inner race. In this case, use a bearing remover tool consisting of a shaft and remover head **(see illustration)**. The head fits inside the bearing **(see illustration)**, then the wedge end of the shaft is tapped into the groove in the head to expand the head and lock it inside the bearing. Tapping on the shaft from this point will force the bearing out of the hub **(see illustration)**.

7   Lay the wheel on its other side and remove the remaining bearing using the same technique. **Note:** *The bearings must be replaced with new ones whenever they're removed, as they're almost certain to be damaged during removal.*

13.6c The split portion fits into the bearing like this - if it keeps slipping out when you tap on it, coat it with valve grinding compound

13.6d The tool can be used for front or rear wheel bearings - the wedged rod fits through the hub like this

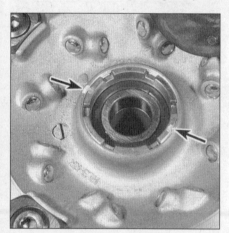

13.14 The bearing retainer is staked in place (arrows); this makes it impractical to remove it with makeshift tools

13.16a Remove the collar from the sprocket side of the wheel

13.16b This seal removal tool is convenient, but a screwdriver will also work

8   If you're installing bearings that aren't sealed on both sides, pack the new bearings with grease from the open side. Rotate the bearing to work the grease in between the bearing balls.

9   Thoroughly clean the hub area of the wheel. Install the bearing into the recess in the right side of the hub, with the sealed side facing out. Using a bearing driver or a socket large enough to contact the outer race of the bearing, drive it in until it seats.

10   Turn the wheel over and install the bearing spacer and bearing, driving the bearing into place as described in Step 9.

11   Coat the lip of a new grease seal with grease.

12   Install the grease seal on the right side of the wheel; it should go in with thumb pressure but if not, use a seal driver, large socket or a flat piece of wood to drive it into place.

13   Clean off all grease from the brake disc using acetone or brake system cleaner. Install the wheel.

Rear wheel bearings

Refer to illustrations 13.14, 13.16a, 13.16b, 13.17, 13.18a through 13.18e and 13.23

14   One rear wheel bearing is held in place by a threaded retainer that's staked in position **(see illustration)**. On most models, the retainer is on the right side; on 1987 and 1988 CR250R models it's on the left side. Removal requires special tools for which there are no good substitutes. Before you try to replace the bearings, read through the procedure. If you race the bike and work on it regularly, you might want to buy the tools (you should be able to order them from a Honda dealer). Otherwise, it may be more practical to take the wheel to a

Honda dealer and have the bearings replaced.

15   Refer to Section 11 and remove the rear wheel.

16   Remove the collar and pry the grease seal from the sprocket side of the wheel **(see illustrations)**. If you're working on a 1987 model, remove the three-toothed washer from under the grease seal.

17   On the right side of the wheel, remove the collar from the grease seal **(see illustration)**. You may need to pry it out with a pair of screw-

13.17 Turn the wheel over and remove the collar from the disc side, then pry out the seal

13.18a Drill out the staked portions of the bearing retainer

13.18b These tools are used to remove the bearing retainer; pass the shaft through the hub and fit the pins on the disc into the holes in the bearing retainer

13.18c Thread the nut portion of the tool onto the shaft and tighten it to lock the pins on the disc securely into the holes in the bearing retainer

13.18d Turn the shaft (arrow) with a socket or wrench to unscrew the retainer from the hub

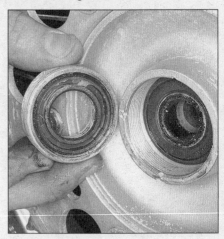

13.18e Remove the retainer and inspect its seal

drivers. If it's really stuck, use a bearing remover tool. Pry the grease seal out. If you're working on a 1987 model, remove the three-toothed washer from under the grease seal.

18   Insert the shaft of the retainer wrench into the hub from the retainer side. Engage the pins of the wrench with the holes in the retainer, then thread the retainer wingnut onto the shaft **(see illustrations)**. Turn the retainer wrench with a socket to unscrew the retainer.

19   Remove the bearings with the special tools used for front wheel bearings (see Step 6). **Note:** *1986 and 1990 and later models have two bearings on the left side of the hub and one on the right side. Earlier models have one bearing on each side of the hub.*

20   If you're working on a 1986 or 1987 model, remove the spacer cap, bearing spacer, and another bearing spacer cap. On all other models, remove the bearing spacer.

21   Thoroughly clean the hub area of the wheel.

22   If you're working on a 1986 or 1987 model, install the spacer cap in the right side of the hub with its dished side facing into the hub.

23   Install the right bearing into the recess in the hub, with the sealed side facing out. Using a bearing driver or a socket large enough to contact the outer race of the bearing, drive it in until it seats **(see illustration)**.

24   Turn the wheel over. Apply a coat of multi-purpose grease to the inside of the spacer and install it in the hub.

25   If you're working on a 1986 or 1987 model, install the left spacer cap on the spacer.

26   Install the left inner bearing on models so equipped. On 1986 models, the sealed side faces into the hub; on all others, it faces out.

27   Pack the remaining bearing from the open side with grease, then install it in the hub, driving the bearing in with a socket or bearing driver large enough to contact the outer race of the bearing. Drive the bearing in until it seats.

13.23 Drive in the bearing on the sprocket side, using a bearing driver that contacts the outer race (the sealed side of the bearing faces out)

TIRE CHANGING SEQUENCE - TUBED TIRES

1 Deflate tire. After pushing tire beads away from rim flanges push tire bead into well of rim at point opposite valve. Insert tire lever adjacent to valve and work bead over edge of rim.

2 Use two levers to work bead over edge of rim. Note use of rim protectors.

3 Remove inner tube from tire.

4 When first bead is clear, remove tire as shown.

5 When fitting, partially inflate inner tube and insert in tire.

6 Work first bead over rim and feed valve through hole in rim. Partially screw on retaining nut to hold valve in place.

7 Check that inner tube is positioned correctly and work second bead over rim using tire levers. Start at a point opposite valve.

8 Work final area of bead over rim while pushing valve inwards to ensure that inner tube is not trapped.

28   Thread the retainer partway into the hub, then install it with the same tools used for removal **(see illustrations 13.18a through 13.18c)**. Stake the retainer in place.

29   If you're working on a 1986 or 1987 model, install the three-pointed washer on each bearing.

30   Install a new grease seal in each side of the hub **(see illustration 13.17)**. It may go in with thumb pressure, but if not, use a seal driver, large socket or a flat piece of wood to drive it into place.

31   Install the collars in the grease seals.

32   Clean off all grease from the brake discs using acetone or brake system cleaner. Install the wheel.

14   Tires - removal and installation

1   To properly remove and install tires, you will need at least two motorcycle tire irons, some water and a tire pressure gauge.

2   Begin by removing the wheel from the motorcycle. If the tire is going to be re-used, mark it next to the valve stem, wheel balance weight or rim lock.

3   Deflate the tire by removing the valve stem core. When it is fully deflated, push the bead of the tire away from the rim on both sides. In some extreme cases, this can only be accomplished with a bead breaking tool, but most often it can be carried out with tire irons. Riding on a deflated tire to break the bead is not recommended, as damage to the rim and tire will occur.

4   Dismounting a tire is easier when the tire is warm, so an indoor tire change is recommended in cold climates. The rubber gets very stiff and is difficult to manipulate when cold.

5   Place the wheel on a thick pad or old blanket. This will help keep the wheel and tire from slipping around.

6   Once the bead is completely free of the rim, lubricate the inside edge of the rim and the tire bead with water only. Honda recommends against the use of soap or other tire mounting lubricants, as the tire may shift on the rim. Remove the locknut and push the tire valve through the rim.

7   Insert one of the tire irons under the bead of the tire at the valve stem and lift the bead up over the rim. This should be fairly easy. Take care not to pinch the tube as this is done. If it is difficult to pry the bead up, make sure that the rest of the bead opposite the valve stem is in the dropped center section of the rim.

8   Hold the tire iron down with the bead over the rim, then move about 1 or 2 inches to either side and insert the second tire iron. Be careful not to cut or slice the bead or the tire may split when inflated. Also, take care not to catch or pinch the inner tube as the second tire iron is levered over. For this reason, tire irons are recommended over screwdrivers or other implements.

9   With a small section of the bead up over the rim, one of the levers can be removed and reinserted 1 or 2 inches farther around the rim until about 1/4 of the tire bead is above the rim edge. Make sure that the rest of the bead is in the dropped center of the rim. At this point, the bead can usually be pulled up over the rim by hand.

10   Once all of the first bead is over the rim, the inner tube can be withdrawn from the tire and rim. Push in on the valve stem, lift up on the tire next to the stem, reach inside the tire and carefully pull out the tube. It is usually not necessary to completely remove the tire from the rim to repair the inner tube. It is sometimes recommended though, because checking for foreign objects in the tire is difficult while it is still mounted on the rim.

11   To remove the tire completely, make sure the bead is broken all the way around on the remaining edge, then stand the tire and wheel up on the tread and grab the wheel with one hand. Push the tire down over the same edge of the rim while pulling the rim away from the tire. If the bead is correctly positioned in the dropped center of the rim, the tire should roll off and separate from the rim very easily. If tire irons are used to work this last bead over the rim, the outer edge of the rim may be marred. If a tire iron is necessary, be sure to pad the rim as described earlier.

12   Refer to Section 15 for inner tube repair procedures.

13   Mounting a tire is basically the reverse of removal. Some tires have a balance mark and/or directional arrows molded into the tire sidewall. Look for these marks so that the tire can be installed properly. The dot should be aligned with the valve stem.

14   If the tire was not removed completely to repair or replace the inner tube, the tube should be inflated just enough to make it round. Sprinkle it with talcum powder, which acts as a dry lubricant, then carefully lift up the tire edge and install the tube with the valve stem next to the hole in the rim. Once the tube is in place, push the valve stem through the rim and start the locknut on the stem.

15   Lubricate the tire bead, then push it over the rim edge and into the dropped center section opposite the inner tube valve stem. Work around each side of the rim, carefully pushing the bead over the rim. The last section may have to be levered on with tire irons. If so, take care not to pinch the inner tube as this is done.

16   Once the bead is over the rim edge, check to see that the inner tube valve stem and the rim lock are pointing to the center of the hub. If they're angled slightly in either direction, rotate the tire on the rim to straighten it out. Run the locknut the rest of the way onto the stem and rim lock but don't tighten them completely.

17   Inflate the tube to approximately 1-1/2 times the pressure listed in the Chapter 1 Specifications and check to make sure the guidelines on the tire sidewalls are the same distance from the rim around the circumference of the tire. **Warning:** *Do not overinflate the tube or the tire may burst, causing serious injury.*

18   After the tire bead is correctly seated on the rim, allow the tire to deflate. Replace the valve core and inflate the tube to the recommended pressure, then tighten the valve stem locknut securely and tighten the cap. Tighten the locknut on the rim locknut to the torque listed in the Chapter 1 Specifications.

15   Tubes - repair

1   Tire tube repair requires a patching kit that's usually available from motorcycle dealers, accessory stores or auto parts stores. Be sure to follow the directions supplied with the kit to ensure a safe repair. Patching should be done only when a new tube is unavailable. Replace the tube as soon as possible. Sudden deflation can cause loss of control and an accident.

2   To repair a tube, remove it from the tire, inflate and immerse it in a sink or tub full of water to pinpoint the leak. Mark the position of the leak, then deflate the tube. Dry it off and thoroughly clean the area around the puncture.

3   Most tire patching kits have a buffer to rough up the area around the hole for proper adhesion of the patch. Roughen an area slightly larger than the patch, then apply a thin coat of the patching cement to the roughened area. Allow the cement to dry until tacky, then apply the patch.

4   It may be necessary to remove a protective covering from the top surface of the patch after it has been attached to the tube. Keep in mind that tubes made from synthetic rubber may require a special patch and adhesive if a satisfactory bond is to be achieved.

5   Before replacing the tube, check the inside of the tire to make sure the object that caused the puncture is not still inside. Also check the outside of the tire, particularly the tread area, to make sure nothing is projecting through the tire that may cause another puncture. Check the rim for sharp edges or damage. Make sure the rubber trim band is in good condition and properly installed before inserting the tube.

Chapter 8 Part A
Frame and bodywork
(CR80R/85R and CR125R models)

Contents

Specifications

Torque specifications
Seat mounting bolts
  CR80R/85R
    1986 through 1995 .... 10 Nm (84 inch-lbs)
    1996 on.. Not specified
  CR125R
    1986 through 1991 .... 18 to 25 Nm (13 to 18 ft-lbs)
    1992 through 1995 .... 22 Nm (16 ft-lbs)
    1996 on.. 27 Nm (20 ft-lbs)
Sub-frame mounting bolts
  CR80R/85R .... 22 Nm (16 ft-lbs)
  CR125R
    1986 through 1990 .... 18 to 25 Nm (13 to 18 ft-lbs)
    1991 and 1992.. 27 Nm (20 ft-lbs)
    1993 through 1997
      Upper .... 33 Nm (24 ft-lbs)
      Lower .... 43 Nm (31 ft-lbs)
    1998 and 1999
      Upper .... 29 Nm (22 ft-lbs)
      Lower .... 39 Nm (29 ft-lbs)
    2000 through 2003
      Upper .... 29 Nm (22 ft-lbs)
      Lower .... Not specified
    2004 and later.. 29 Nm (22 ft-lbs)

1 General information

This Chapter covers the procedures necessary to remove and install the fenders and other body parts. Since many service and repair operations on these motorcycles require removal of the fenders and/or other body parts, the procedures are grouped here and referred to from other Chapters.

In the case of damage to plastic body parts, it is usually necessary to remove the broken component and replace it with a new (or used) one. The material that the fenders and other plastic body parts are composed of doesn't lend itself to conventional repair techniques. There are, however, some shops that specialize in "plastic welding", so it would be advantageous to check around before throwing the damaged part away.

Note: *When attempting to remove any body panel, first study the panel closely, noting any fasteners and associated fittings, to be sure of returning everything to its correct place on installation. In some cases, the aid of an assistant may be required when removing panels, to help avoid damaging the paint. Once the visible fasteners have been removed, try to lift off the panel as described but DO NOT FORCE the panel - if it will not release, check that all fasteners have been removed and try again. Where a panel engages another by means of lugs and grommets, be careful not to break the lugs or damage the bodywork. Remember that a few moments of patience at this stage will save you a lot of money in replacing broken panels!*

2.2 Remove the seat bolts from under the rear fender or from each side (shown) . . .

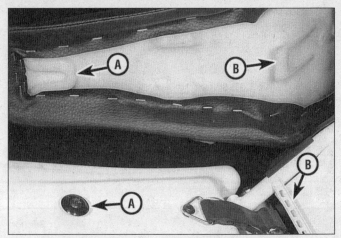

2.3 . . . detach the hook under the front of the seat from the button on the tank (A) and the center tab (some models have two center tabs) from the frame (B)

2   Seat - removal and installation

Refer to illustrations 2.2 and 2.3

1   If you're working on a 1986 through 1995 CR80R, remove the three seat bolts (they're accessible from under the rear fender.
2   If you're working on a 1996 or later CR80R/85R or any CR125R, remove one bolt from each side of the seat **(see illustration)**.
3   Pull the seat back and down to detach its front hook and center tab(s) **(see illustration)**. Lift the seat off.
4   Installation is the reverse of removal. Be sure to engage the center tab(s); it's possible to engage the front hook but miss the center tab(s). If the bike is ridden like this, the center tab(s) will be damaged by the rider's weight. Tighten the seat bolts to the torque listed in this Chapter's Specifications.

3   Side covers - removal and installation

1   Remove the seat (see Section 2).
2   Remove the side cover bolt and take the cover off **(see illustration 2.2)**.
3   Installation is the reverse of the removal steps.

4   Footpegs - removal and installation

Refer to illustration 4.2

1   Support the bike securely so it can't be knocked over during this procedure.
2   To detach the footpeg from the pivot pin, note how the spring is installed, then remove the cotter pin, washer and pivot pin **(see illustration)**. Separate the footpeg from the motorcycle.
3   Installation is the reverse of removal, with the following addition: Use a new cotter pin and wrap its ends around the pivot pin.

5   Number plate - removal and installation

Refer to illustrations 5.1 and 5.3

1   On all CR80R/85R models and 1986 through 1997 CR125R models, unscrew the number plate bolt **(see illustration)**.
2   On all models, unhook the number plate's integral strap.
3   Installation is the reverse of the removal steps. On 1988 and 1999 CR125R models, insert the pin on the number plate into the hole in the lower triple clamp. On 2000 and later CR125R models, place the hole in the number plate over the pin on the upper triple clamp **(see illustration)**.

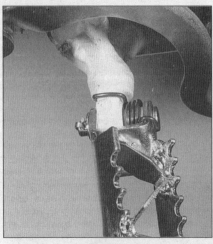

4.2 Remove the cotter pin, washer and pivot pin to detach the footpeg from the bracket

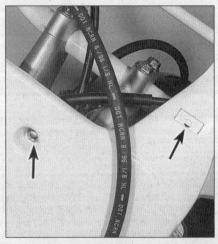

5.1 Remove the bolt and unhook the strap (arrows) to detach the number plate

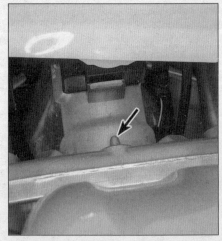

5.3 The number plate on later CR125R models fits over this pin on the upper triple clamp (arrow)

6.1 Remove the bolts (arrows), then remove the shroud and grommets

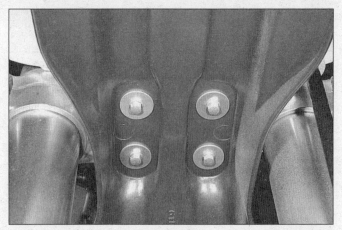

7.1 The front fender bolts and washers are accessible from below; the grommets are accessible once the fender has been removed

6   Radiator shrouds - removal and installation

Refer to illustration 6.1

1   To remove the shrouds, unscrew their bolts and remove them from the motorcycle **(see illustration)**.
2   Installation is the reverse of the removal steps.

7   Front fender - removal and installation

Refer to illustration 7.1

1   Remove the fender bolts **(see illustration)**. Lower the fender clear of the lower triple clamp and remove the washers.
2   Installation is the reverse of removal. Be sure to reinstall the grommets in their correct locations. Tighten the bolts securely, but don't overtighten them and strip the threads.

8   Rear fender - removal and installation

Refer to illustrations 8.2a and 8.2b

1   Remove the seat and both side covers (see Sections 2 and 3).
2   Remove the fender mounting bolts (and grommets if equipped) and take the fender off **(see illustrations)**.
3   If necessary, unbolt the inner fender from the air cleaner housing and lift it off.
4   Installation is the reverse of removal. Tighten the bolts securely, but don't overtighten them and strip the threads.

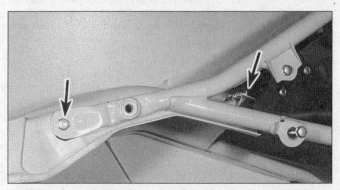

8.2a If you're working on a later CR80R/85R with a clip on the fender center bolt (right arrow) support the clip with a wrench and remove the center bolt first, then remove the two side bolts (left arrow)

9   Sub-frame - removal and installation

Refer to illustrations 9.3a and 9.3b

1   Remove the seat (Section 2).
2   Loosen the clamping band that secures the carburetor to the air cleaner housing (see Chapter 4).
3   Unbolt the sub-frame from the main frame and lift it off, together with the air cleaner housing and rear fender **(see illustrations)**.

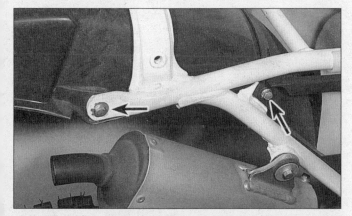

8.2b Where the side fender bolts are secured by clip nuts, as on the late CR125R shown here, support the clip nut with a wrench as you unscrew the bolt

9.3a The sub-frame is secured by a lower bolt on each side of the bike and two upper bolts or a single through-bolt (arrows)

4   Installation is the reverse of the removal steps. Tighten the sub-frame bolts to the torques listed in this Chapter's Specifications.

10 Frame - general information, inspection and repair

1   All CR80R/85R models, and 1986 through 1997 CR125R models, use a semi-double cradle frame made of round-section steel tubing. The 1998 and later CR125R uses a twin-spar aluminum frame similar to that used on the CR250R. All models have a detachable sub-frame.

2   The frame shouldn't require attention unless accident damage has occurred. In most cases, frame replacement is the only satisfactory remedy for such damage. A few frame specialists have the jigs and other equipment necessary for straightening the frame to the required standard of accuracy, but even then there is no simple way of assessing to what extent the frame may have been overstressed.

3   After the motorcycle has accumulated a lot of running time, the frame should be examined closely for signs of cracking or splitting at the welded joints. Corrosion can also cause weakness at these joints. Loose engine mount bolts can cause ovaling or fracturing to the mounting bolt holes. Minor damage can often be repaired by welding, depending on the nature and extent of the damage.

4   Remember that a frame that is out of alignment will cause han-

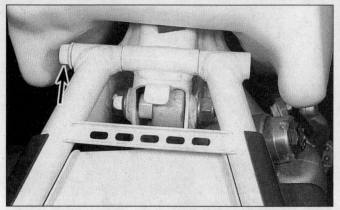

9.3b The through-bolt on later models (CR80R shown) threads directly into the frame; other models use nuts - note the direction of the bolt head(s) before removing the bolt(s)

dling problems. If misalignment is suspected as the result of an accident, it will be necessary to strip the machine completely so the frame can be thoroughly checked.

Chapter 8 Part B
Frame and bodywork
(CR250R and CR500R models)

Contents

Specifications

Torque specifications

Seat mounting bolts
 CR250R
  1986 through 1996 .... 22 Nm (16 inch-lbs)
  1997 on .... 26 Nm (20 ft-lbs)
 CR500R .... 22 Nm (16 ft-lbs)
Sub-frame mounting bolts
 CR250R
  1986 through 1989 .... 18 to 25 Nm (13 to 18 ft-lbs)
  1990 through 1992 .... 22 Nm (16 ft-lbs)
  1993 through 1996
   Upper .... 33 Nm (24 ft-lbs)
   Lower .... 43 Nm (31 ft-lbs)
  1997 through 1999
   Upper .... 29 Nm (22 ft-lbs)
   Lower .... 41 Nm (30 ft-lbs)
  2000 through 2003
   Upper .... 29 Nm (22 ft-lbs)
   Lower .... Not specified
  2004 and later .... 29 Nm (22 ft-lbs)
 CR500R
  1986 through 1990 .... 18 to 25 Nm (13 to 18 ft-lbs)
  1991-on .... 27 Nm (20 ft-lbs)

1 General information

This Chapter covers the procedures necessary to remove and install the fenders and other body parts. Since many service and repair operations on these motorcycles require removal of the fenders and/or other body parts, the procedures are grouped here and referred to from other Chapters.

In the case of damage to plastic body parts, it is usually neces-sary to remove the broken component and replace it with a new (or used) one. The material that the fenders and other plastic body parts are composed of doesn't lend itself to conventional repair techniques. There are, however, some shops that specialize in "plastic welding", so it would be advantageous to check around before throwing the damaged part away.

Note: *When attempting to remove any body panel, first study the panel closely, noting any fasteners and associated fittings, to be sure of returning everything to its correct place on installation. In some cases,*

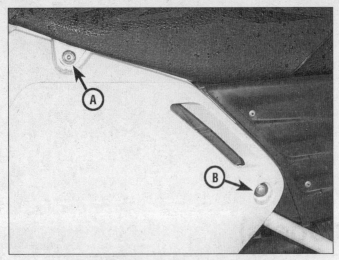

2.1a Seat and side cover mounting bolts (except 1997 and later CR250R, typical)

A   *Seat mounting bolt*   B   *Side cover mounting bolt*

the aid of an assistant will be required when removing panels, to help avoid damaging the paint. Once the visible fasteners have been removed, try to lift off the panel as described but DO NOT FORCE the panel - if it will not release, check that all fasteners have been removed and try again. Where a panel engages another by means of lugs and grommets, be careful not to break the lugs or damage the bodywork. Remember that a few moments of patience at this stage will save you a lot of money in replacing broken panels!

2   Seat - removal and installation

Refer to illustrations 2.1a, 2.1b and 2.2

1   Remove one bolt from each side of the seat **(see illustrations)**.
2   Pull the seat back and down to detach its front hook and center tab(s) **(see illustration)**. Lift the seat off.
3   Installation is the reverse of removal. Be sure to engage the center tab(s); it's possible to engage the front hook but miss the center tab(s). If the bike is ridden like this, the center tab(s) will be damaged by the rider's weight. Tighten the seat bolts to the torque listed in this Chapter's Specifications.

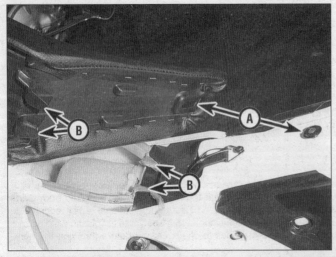

2.2 Detach the hook under the front of the seat from the button on the tank (A) and the center tabs (some models have two center tabs) from the frame (B)

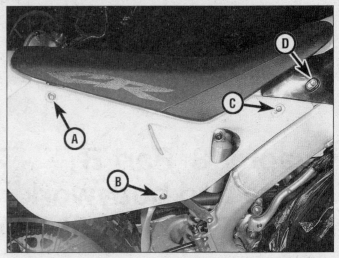

2.1b Seat and side cover fasteners (1997 and later CR250R)

A	*Seat mounting bolt*	D *Side cover screw (also*
B	*Side cover bolt*	*secures forward side*
C	*Side cover screw*	*cover)*

3   Side covers - removal and installation

1   Remove the seat (see Section 2).
2   Remove the side cover bolts and screws and take it off **(see illustrations 2.1a and 2.1b)**.
3   Installation is the reverse of the removal steps.

4   Footpegs - removal and installation

Refer to illustration 4.2

1   Support the bike securely so it can't be knocked over during this procedure.
2   To detach the footpeg from the pivot pin, note how the spring is installed, then remove the cotter pin, washer and pivot pin **(see illustration)**. Separate the footpeg from the motorcycle.
3   Installation is the reverse of removal, with the following addition: Use a new cotter pin and wrap its ends around the pivot pin.

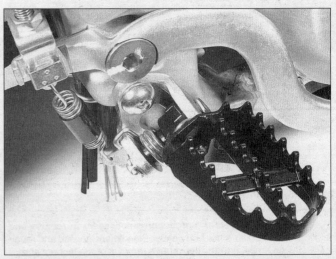

4.2 Remove the cotter pin, washer and pivot pin to detach the footpeg from the bracket; remove the Allen screw to detach the bracket from the frame

5.1 Remove the bolt and unhook the strap (arrows) to detach the number plate

6.1a Remove the bolts or screws and their collars (arrows), then remove the shroud and grommets . . .

6.1b . . . the rear shroud screw on 1997 CR250R-on models secures the front end of the side cover as well . . .

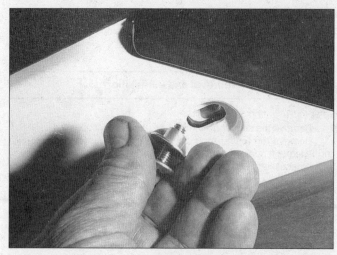

6.1c . . . a long aluminum collar fits through the two panels

5 Number plate - removal and installation

Refer to illustration 5.1

1   To remove the number plate, undo its bolt and unhook its integral strap **(see illustration)**.

2   Installation is the reverse of the removal steps. On all except 2000 and later CR250R models, insert the pin on the number plate into the hole in the lower triple clamp. On 2000 and later CR250R models, place the hole in the number plate over the pin on the upper triple clamp **(see illustration 5.3 in Chapter 8A)**.

6 Radiator shrouds - removal and installation

Refer to illustrations 6.1a, 6.1b and 6.1c

1   To remove the shrouds, undo their bolts and screws and remove them from the motorcycle **(see illustrations)**.

2   Installation is the reverse of the removal steps.

7 Front fender - removal and installation

Refer to illustration 7.1

1   Remove the fender bolts **(see illustration)**. Lower the fender clear of the lower triple clamp and remove the washers.

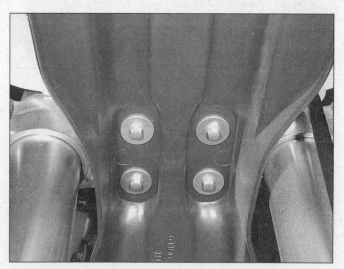

7.1 The front fender bolts and washers are accessible from below; the grommets are accessible once the fender has been removed

8.2 Remove the fender mounting bolts and washers (1997 CR500R shown); the forward bolts are accessible from below

9.3a The sub-frame on steel-frame bikes is secured by a lower bolt on each side of the bike and a single through-bolt at the top (arrows)

2   Installation is the reverse of removal. Be sure to reinstall the grommets in their correct locations. Tighten the bolts securely, but don't overtighten them and strip the threads.

8   Rear fender - removal and installation

Refer to illustration 8.2
1   Remove the seat and both side covers (see Sections 2 and 3).
2   Remove the fender mounting bolts (and grommets if equipped) and take the fender off **(see illustration)**.
3   If necessary, unbolt the inner fender from the air cleaner housing and lift it off.
4   Installation is the reverse of removal. Tighten the bolts securely, but don't overtighten them and strip the threads.

9   Sub-frame - removal and installation

Refer to illustrations 9.3a and 9.3b
1   Remove the seat (Section 2).
2   Loosen the clamping band that secures the carburetor to the air cleaner housing (see Chapter 4).
3   Unbolt the sub-frame from the main frame and lift it off, together with the air cleaner housing and rear fender **(see illustrations)**.
4   Installation is the reverse of the removal steps. Tighten the sub-frame bolts to the torques listed in this Chapter's Specifications.

10   Frame - general information, inspection and repair

1   All except 1997 and later CR250R models use a semi-double cradle frame made of round-section steel tubing, with a detachable sub-frame. The 1997 and later CR250R uses a twin-tube aluminum frame with a detachable sub-frame, similar to the type used on many high-performance street bikes.
2   The frame shouldn't require attention unless accident damage

9.3b The sub-frame on the 1997 CR250R is secured by two bolts at the top and two at the bottom (right side bolts shown)

has occurred. In most cases, frame replacement is the only satisfactory remedy for such damage. A few frame specialists have the jigs and other equipment necessary for straightening the frame to the required standard of accuracy, but even then there is no simple way of assessing to what extent the frame may have been overstressed.
3   After the motorcycle has accumulated a lot of running time, the frame should be examined closely for signs of cracking or splitting at the welded joints. Corrosion can also cause weakness at these joints. Loose engine mount bolts can cause ovaling or fracturing to the mounting bolt holes. Minor damage can often be repaired by welding, depending on the nature and extent of the damage.
4   Remember that a frame that is out of alignment will cause handling problems. If misalignment is suspected as the result of an accident, it will be necessary to strip the machine completely so the frame can be thoroughly checked.

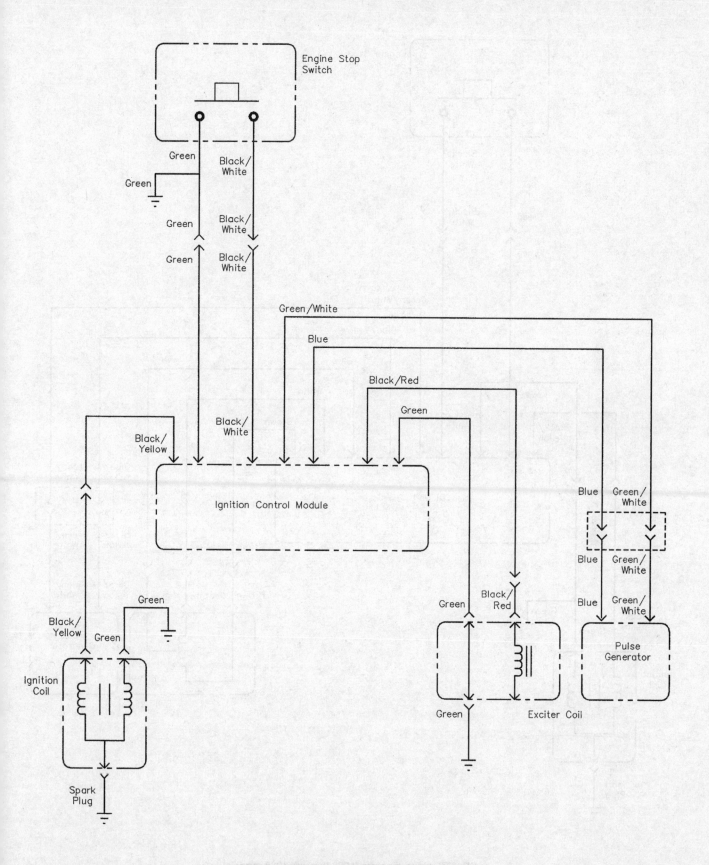

CR80R wiring diagram (1986 and later models)

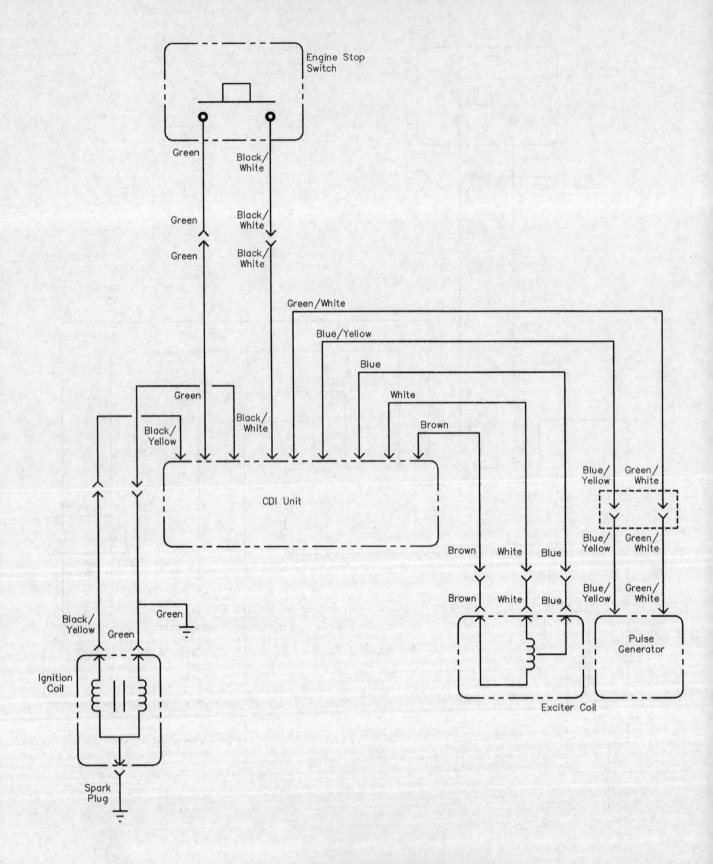

CR125R wiring diagram (1986 through 1988 models)

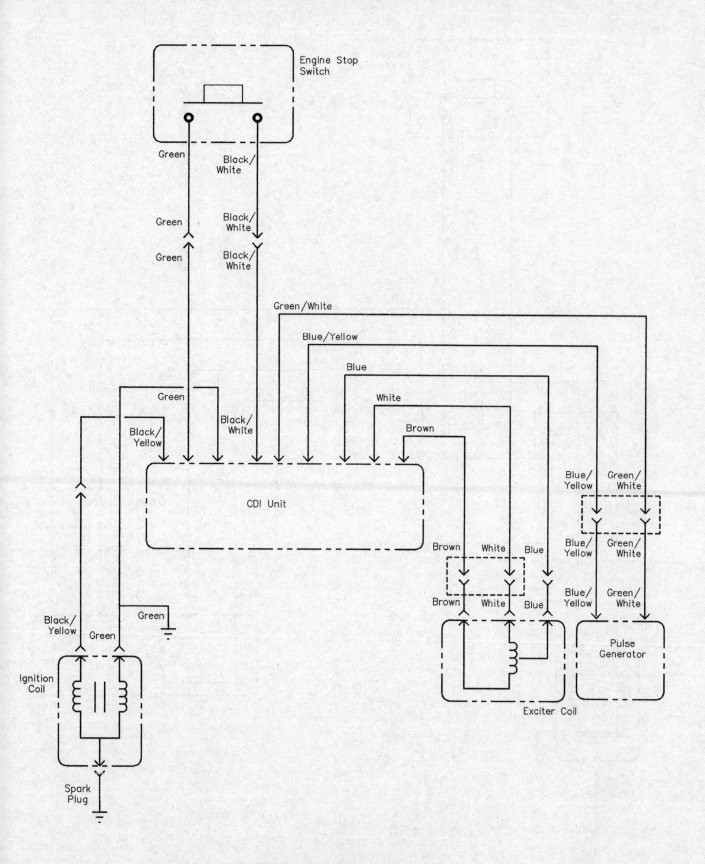

CR125R wiring diagram (1989 models)

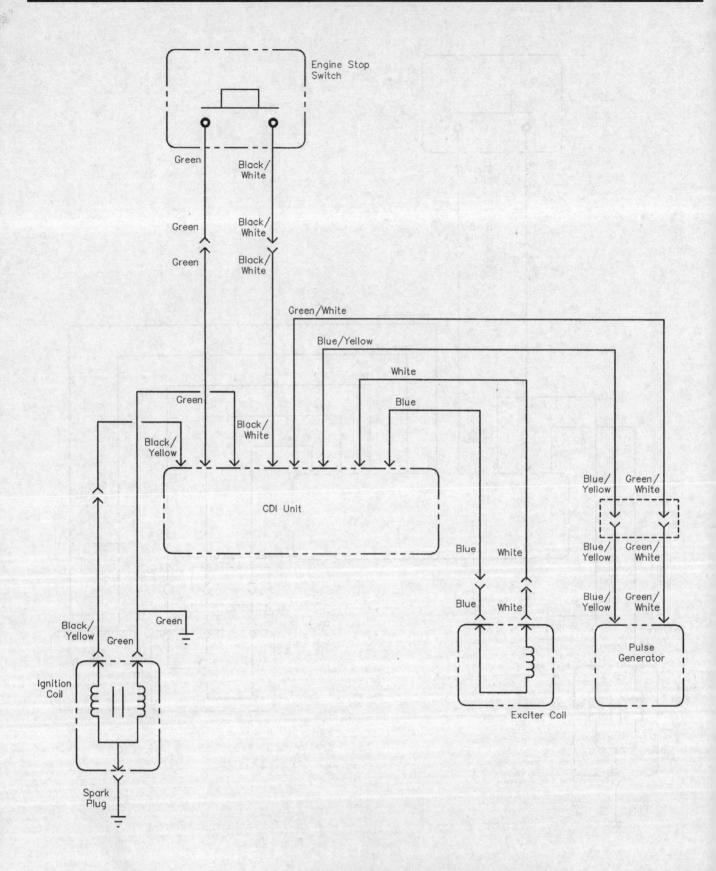

CR125R wiring diagram (1990 and later models)

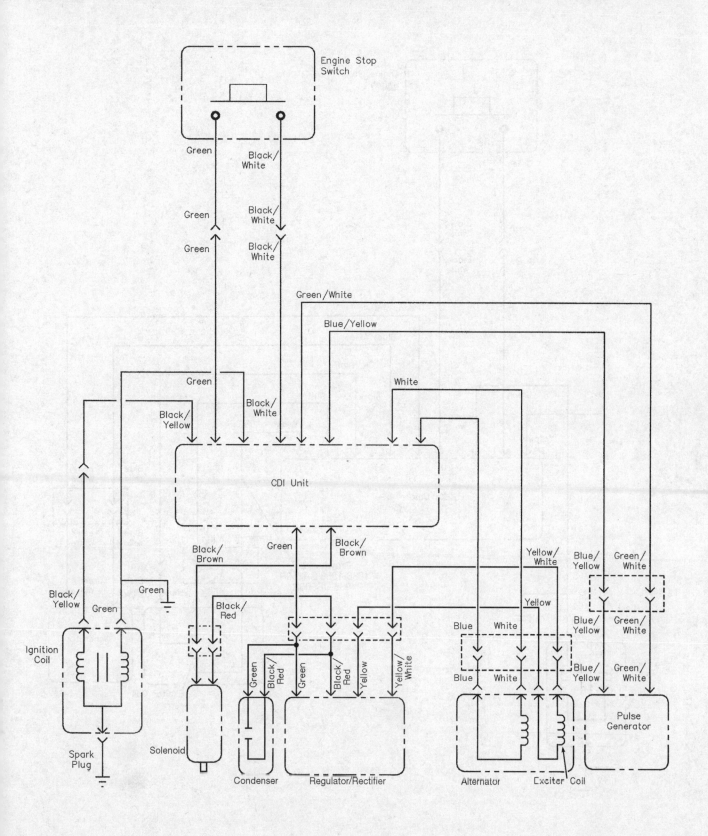

Wiring diagram - 1986 through 1996 CR250R; all CR500R

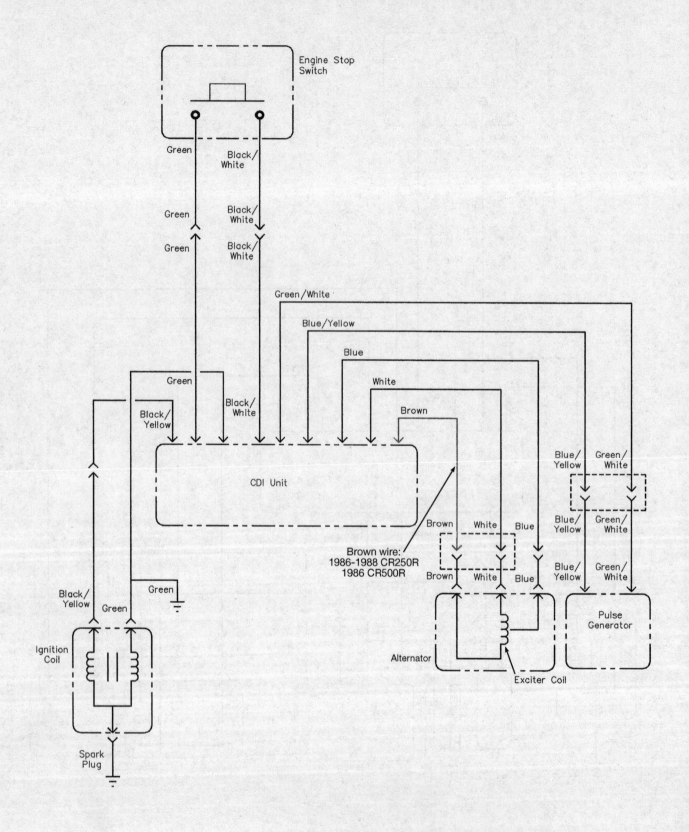

Wiring diagram - 1997 and 1998 CR250R (1999 through 2003 models similar)

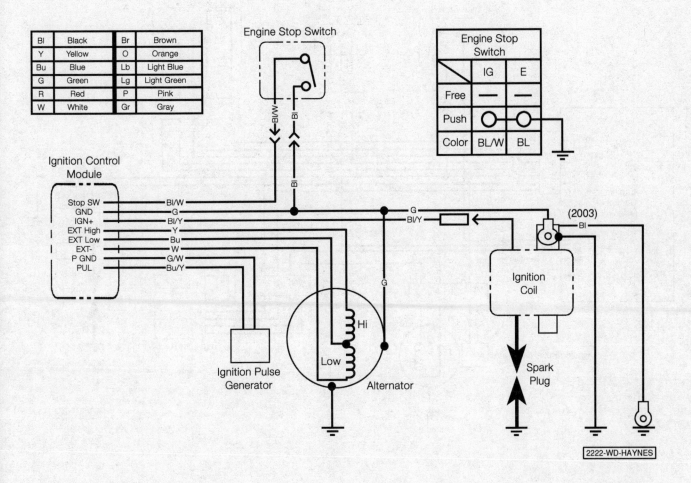

Bl	Black	Br	Brown
Y	Yellow	O	Orange
Bu	Blue	Lb	Light Blue
G	Green	Lg	Light Green
R	Red	P	Pink
W	White	Gr	Gray

Engine Stop Switch

Engine Stop Switch		
	IG	E
Free	—	—
Push	O	O
Color	BL/W	BL

Ignition Control Module

- Stop SW — Bl/W
- GND — G
- IGN+ — Bl/Y
- EXT High — Y
- EXT Low — Bu
- EXT- — W
- P GND — G/W
- PUL — Bu/Y

Ignition Pulse Generator

Alternator

Hi
Low

Ignition Coil

Spark Plug

(2003)

2222-WD-HAYNES

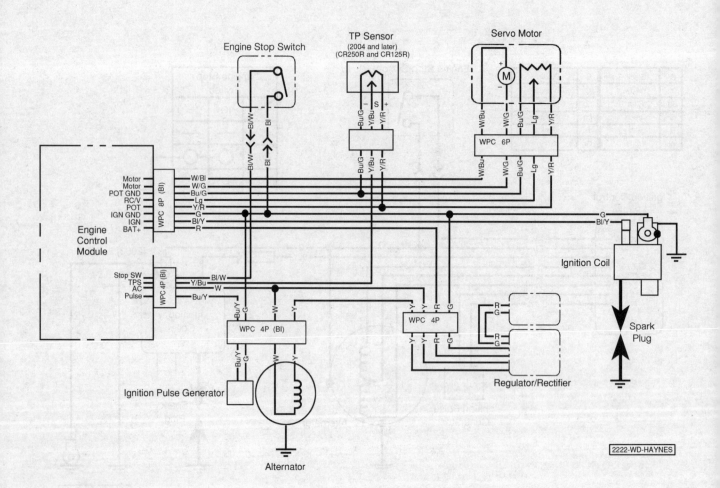

Wiring diagram - 2004-on CR125R and CR250R

Conversion factors

Length (distance)
Inches (in)	X	25.4	= Millimetres (mm)	X 0.0394	= Inches (in)
Feet (ft)	X	0.305	= Metres (m)	X 3.281	= Feet (ft)
Miles	X	1.609	= Kilometres (km)	X 0.621	= Miles

Volume (capacity)
Cubic inches (cu in; in^3)	X	16.387	= Cubic centimetres (cc; cm^3)	X 0.061	= Cubic inches (cu in; in^3)
Imperial pints (Imp pt)	X	0.568	= Litres (l)	X 1.76	= Imperial pints (Imp pt)
Imperial quarts (Imp qt)	X	1.137	= Litres (l)	X 0.88	= Imperial quarts (Imp qt)
Imperial quarts (Imp qt)	X	1.201	= US quarts (US qt)	X 0.833	= Imperial quarts (Imp qt)
US quarts (US qt)	X	0.946	= Litres (l)	X 1.057	= US quarts (US qt)
Imperial gallons (Imp gal)	X	4.546	= Litres (l)	X 0.22	= Imperial gallons (Imp gal)
Imperial gallons (Imp gal)	X	1.201	= US gallons (US gal)	X 0.833	= Imperial gallons (Imp gal)
US gallons (US gal)	X	3.785	= Litres (l)	X 0.264	= US gallons (US gal)

Mass (weight)
Ounces (oz)	X	28.35	= Grams (g)	X 0.035	= Ounces (oz)
Pounds (lb)	X	0.454	= Kilograms (kg)	X 2.205	= Pounds (lb)

Force
Ounces-force (ozf; oz)	X	0.278	= Newtons (N)	X 3.6	= Ounces-force (ozf; oz)
Pounds-force (lbf; lb)	X	4.448	= Newtons (N)	X 0.225	= Pounds-force (lbf; lb)
Newtons (N)	X	0.1	= Kilograms-force (kgf; kg)	X 9.81	= Newtons (N)

Pressure
Pounds-force per square inch (psi; lbf/in^2; lb/in^2)	X	0.070	= Kilograms-force per square centimetre (kgf/cm^2; kg/cm^2)	X 14.223	= Pounds-force per square inch (psi; lbf/in^2; lb/in^2)
Pounds-force per square inch (psi; lbf/in^2; lb/in^2)	X	0.068	= Atmospheres (atm)	X 14.696	= Pounds-force per square inch (psi; lbf/in^2; lb/in^2)
Pounds-force per square inch (psi; lbf/in^2; lb/in^2)	X	0.069	= Bars	X 14.5	= Pounds-force per square inch (psi; lbf/in^2; lb/in^2)
Pounds-force per square inch (psi; lbf/in^2; lb/in^2)	X	6.895	= Kilopascals (kPa)	X 0.145	= Pounds-force per square inch (psi; lbf/in^2; lb/in^2)
Kilopascals (kPa)	X	0.01	= Kilograms-force per square centimetre (kgf/cm^2; kg/cm^2)	X 98.1	= Kilopascals (kPa)

Torque (moment of force)
Pounds-force inches (lbf in; lb in)	X	1.152	= Kilograms-force centimetre (kgf cm; kg cm)	X 0.868	= Pounds-force inches (lbf in; lb in)
Pounds-force inches (lbf in; lb in)	X	0.113	= Newton metres (Nm)	X 8.85	= Pounds-force inches (lbf in; lb in)
Pounds-force inches (lbf in; lb in)	X	0.083	= Pounds-force feet (lbf ft; lb ft)	X 12	= Pounds-force inches (lbf in; lb in)
Pounds-force feet (lbf ft; lb ft)	X	0.138	= Kilograms-force metres (kgf m; kg m)	X 7.233	= Pounds-force feet (lbf ft; lb ft)
Pounds-force feet (lbf ft; lb ft)	X	1.356	= Newton metres (Nm)	X 0.738	= Pounds-force feet (lbf ft; lb ft)
Newton metres (Nm)	X	0.102	= Kilograms-force metres (kgf m; kg m)	X 9.804	= Newton metres (Nm)

Vacuum
Inches mercury (in. Hg)	X	3.377	= Kilopascals (kPa)	X 0.2961	= Inches mercury
Inches mercury (in. Hg)	X	25.4	= Millimeters mercury (mm Hg)	X 0.0394	= Inches mercury

Power
Horsepower (hp)	X	745.7	= Watts (W)	X 0.0013	= Horsepower (hp)

Velocity (speed)
Miles per hour (miles/hr; mph)	X	1.609	= Kilometres per hour (km/hr; kph)	X 0.621	= Miles per hour (miles/hr; mph)

Fuel consumption*
Miles per gallon, Imperial (mpg)	X	0.354	= Kilometres per litre (km/l)	X 2.825	= Miles per gallon, Imperial (mpg)
Miles per gallon, US (mpg)	X	0.425	= Kilometres per litre (km/l)	X 2.352	= Miles per gallon, US (mpg)

Temperature
Degrees Fahrenheit = (°C x 1.8) + 32   Degrees Celsius (Degrees Centigrade; °C) = (°F - 32) x 0.56

*It is common practice to convert from miles per gallon (mpg) to litres/100 kilometres (l/100km), where mpg (Imperial) x l/100 km = 282 and mpg (US) x l/100 km = 235

Fraction/Decimal/Millimeter Equivalents

DECIMALS TO MILLIMETERS				FRACTIONS TO DECIMALS TO MILLIMETERS					
Decimal	mm	Decimal	mm	Fraction	Decimal	mm	Fraction	Decimal	mm
0.001	0.0254	0.500	12.7000	1/64	0.0156	0.3969	33/64	0.5156	13.0969
0.002	0.0508	0.510	12.9540	1/32	0.0312	0.7938	17/32	0.5312	13.4938
0.003	0.0762	0.520	13.2080	3/64	0.0469	1.1906	35/64	0.5469	13.8906
0.004	0.1016	0.530	13.4620						
0.005	0.1270	0.540	13.7160						
0.006	0.1524	0.550	13.9700	1/16	0.0625	1.5875	9/16	0.5625	14.2875
0.007	0.1778	0.560	14.2240						
0.008	0.2032	0.570	14.4780						
0.009	0.2286	0.580	14.7320	5/64	0.0781	1.9844	37/64	0.5781	14.6844
		0.590	14.9860	3/32	0.0938	2.3812	19/32	0.5938	15.0812
0.010	0.2540			7/64	0.1094	2.7781	39/64	0.6094	15.4781
0.020	0.5080								
0.030	0.7620								
0.040	1.0160	0.600	15.2400	1/8	0.1250	3.1750	5/8	0.6250	15.8750
0.050	1.2700	0.610	15.4940						
0.060	1.5240	0.620	15.7480						
0.070	1.7780	0.630	16.0020	9/64	0.1406	3.5719	41/64	0.6406	16.2719
0.080	2.0320	0.640	16.2560	5/32	0.1562	3.9688	21/32	0.6562	16.6688
0.090	2.2860	0.650	16.5100	11/64	0.1719	4.3656	43/64	0.6719	17.0656
		0.660	16.7640						
0.100	2.5400	0.670	17.0180						
0.110	2.7940	0.680	17.2720	3/16	0.1875	4.7625	11/16	0.6875	17.4625
0.120	3.0480	0.690	17.5260						
0.130	3.3020								
0.140	3.5560								
0.150	3.8100			13/64	0.2031	5.1594	45/64	0.7031	17.8594
0.160	4.0640	0.700	17.7800	7/32	0.2188	5.5562	23/32	0.7188	18.2562
0.170	4.3180	0.710	18.0340	15/64	0.2344	5.9531	47/64	0.7344	18.6531
0.180	4.5720	0.720	18.2880						
0.190	4.8260	0.730	18.5420						
		0.740	18.7960	1/4	0.2500	6.3500	3/4	0.7500	19.0500
0.200	5.0800	0.750	19.0500						
0.210	5.3340	0.760	19.3040						
0.220	5.5880	0.770	19.5580	17/64	0.2656	6.7469	49/64	0.7656	19.4469
0.230	5.8420	0.780	19.8120	9/32	0.2812	7.1438	25/32	0.7812	19.8438
0.240	6.0960	0.790	20.0660	19/64	0.2969	7.5406	51/64	0.7969	20.2406
0.250	6.3500								
0.260	6.6040								
0.270	6.8580	0.800	20.3200	5/16	0.3125	7.9375	13/16	0.8125	20.6375
0.280	7.1120	0.810	20.5740						
0.290	7.3660	0.820	20.8280						
		0.830	21.0820	21/64	0.3281	8.3344	53/64	0.8281	21.0344
0.300	7.6200	0.840	21.3360	11/32	0.3438	8.7312	27/32	0.8438	21.4312
0.310	7.8740	0.850	21.5900	23/64	0.3594	9.1281	55/64	0.8594	21.8281
0.320	8.1280	0.860	21.8440						
0.330	8.3820	0.870	22.0980						
0.340	8.6360	0.880	22.3520	3/8	0.3750	9.5250	7/8	0.8750	22.2250
0.350	8.8900	0.890	22.6060						
0.360	9.1440								
0.370	9.3980								
0.380	9.6520			25/64	0.3906	9.9219	57/64	0.8906	22.6219
0.390	9.9060			13/32	0.4062	10.3188	29/32	0.9062	23.0188
		0.900	22.8600	27/64	0.4219	10.7156	59/64	0.9219	23.4156
0.400	10.1600	0.910	23.1140						
0.410	10.4140	0.920	23.3680						
0.420	10.6680	0.930	23.6220	7/16	0.4375	11.1125	15/16	0.9375	23.8125
0.430	10.9220	0.940	23.8760						
0.440	11.1760	0.950	24.1300						
0.450	11.4300	0.960	24.3840	29/64	0.4531	11.5094	61/64	0.9531	24.2094
0.460	11.6840	0.970	24.6380	15/32	0.4688	11.9062	31/32	0.9688	24.6062
0.470	11.9380	0.980	24.8920	31/64	0.4844	12.3031	63/64	0.9844	25.0031
0.480	12.1920	0.990	25.1460						
0.490	12.4460	1.000	25.4000	1/2	0.5000	12.7000	1	1.0000	25.4000

Index